MEDICAL NEGLIGENCE:
NON-PATIENT AND THIRD PARTY CLAIMS

For Valda

Medical Negligence:
Non-Patient and Third Party Claims

RACHAEL MULHERON
Queen Mary University of London, UK

ASHGATE

Published by
Ashgate Publishing Limited
Wey Court East
Union Road
Farnham
Surrey, GU9 7PT
England

Ashgate Publishing Company
Suite 420
101 Cherry Street
Burlington
VT 05401-4405
USA

www.ashgate.com

British Library Cataloguing in Publication Data
Mulheron, Rachael P.
  Medical negligence : non-patient and third party claims.
  1. Medical personnel--Malpractice. 2. Medical laws and
  legislation--Interpretation and construction.
  3. Assistance in emergencies--Law and legislation.
  4. Third parties (Law)
  I. Title
  344'.0411-dc22

Library of Congress Cataloging-in-Publication Data
Mulheron, Rachael P.
  Medical negligence : non-patient and third party claims / by Rachael Mulheron.
     p. cm.
  Includes bibliographical references and index.
  ISBN 978-0-7546-4697-6 (hardback) -- ISBN 978-0-7546-9112-9 (ebook)
  1. Medical personnel--Malpractice--England. 2. Third parties (Law)--England. I. Title.
  KD2960.M55M85 2010
  344.4204'11--dc22

2010011720

ISBN: 978-0-7546-4697-6 (hbk)
ISBN: 978-0-7546-9112-9 (ebk)

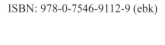

Mixed Sources
Product group from well-managed
forests and other controlled sources
www.fsc.org Cert no. SGS-COC-2482
© 1996 Forest Stewardship Council
FSC

Printed and bound in Great Britain by
TJ International Ltd, Padstow, Cornwall

Contents

Preface

My interest in non-patient claims in medical negligence developed from a confluence of circumstances. Firstly, while teaching the subject of Advanced Medical Negligence within the University of London Masters of Law and Queen Mary University of London's MA in Medical Law and Ethics degree programmes over the past several years, there have been ample opportunities to explore some of the non-patient conundrums discussed later in this book with a diverse complement of knowledgable and enthusiastic students. Additionally, third party claims in professional negligence was always an area of interest whilst I was a practising lawyer, given the lack of clarity in the legal principles governing liability of all professionals towards such parties. The abovementioned interests have been cobbled to my class actions reform work over the past decade, where prospects of third party suits in class actions jurisprudence involving groups of non-patients who share a common grievance are a real possibility.

Overall, then, the interweaving of medical negligence, third parties, non-patients, class actions, limited insurance funds, and so on, represent a fertile and thought-provoking field for academic analysis and practitioner relevance.

My approach to this book, focussed as it is solely upon non-patient and third party claims against healthcare professionals, is to present a unique monograph within the medico-legal literature. As such, it is written with both the legal and the medical professions squarely in mind. The lack of clarity and consistency in the area of professional liability towards third parties—particularly in determining when a duty of care is or is not owed—is especially apparent in the field of medical professional liability. The book seeks to elucidate, for a legal readership, the principles which go towards either establishing or debunking negligence liability, and which apply across a range of non-patient scenarios. The analysis adopts a comparative perspective as and where appropriate, drawing parallels and counterpoints from other jurisdictions which have also grappled with the complexities of non-patient claims.

One of the further key aims of the book is that it be useful to healthcare professionals, to enable them to recognise and increase their awareness of just what a 'non-patient' may present as. With greater recognition and awareness comes a better capacity to avoid liabilities by taking steps to achieve 'the reasonable standard' of conduct towards such parties. With that in mind, it is hoped that the Appendix to the book, *'Potential Liability to Non-Patients and Third Parties: A Synopsis for Healthcare Professionals'*, will assist a range of medically-qualified defendants in understanding their actual or potential liability towards some parties whom they may never even meet in their daily medical practice, yet who may pose a real threat of mounting a claim in negligence.

I am indebted to the Society of Legal Scholars of England and Wales for the award of a travel grant to enable a short study trip to be undertaken to Toronto and Harvard to collect and check North American materials which could not be accessed either in London or via online sources. I am also very grateful for the kind assistance and support offered by the law librarians at the Osgoode Hall Law Library in Toronto and at the Harvard Law Library during that excursion.

Particular thanks are also due to both Holly Abbott, whose meticulous attention to the compilation of case and legislation tables, bibliography, and index, provided a huge support at crucial times during the production of the book (it goes without saying, however, that any errors in these sections remain mine solely); to Ann Hoban, who expertly assisted with some key word-processing issues during finalisation of the manuscript; and to Blackson Osas Ogbeibor of BG Computer Medics Ltd, whose unflappable and knowledgeable assistance smoothed over some notable IT crises along the road. I am also grateful to Professor Mark Mildred, who kindly provided back issues of several journals which were difficult to acquire from other sources, and which were very helpful throughout the research for the book.

In addition, I would like to convey my thanks to Alison Kirk, my commissioning editor at Ashgate Publishing, for her endless support and patience during the project, together with all the team at Ashgate (in particular, Nikki Selmes, Sarah Horsley and Kathryn Ely) for the valuable editorial and other assistance rendered in order to bring this book to completion. Finally, the constant encouragement and assistance offered, and the belief in the project shown, by my parents was a key inspiration for the book coming to fruition, and for this, together with the ongoing pillars of support provided by many friends and colleagues throughout, I am very grateful.

The law is stated as at 30 September 2009 (except for some later legislative developments concerning class actions reform in England and Wales which occurred just prior to submission of the manuscript and to which brief reference has been possible).

Rachael Mulheron

Table of Cases

-D-

-E-

-F-

-G-

-H-

-M-

-R-

-S-

Table of Legislation

UNITED STATES

Statutes and Codes

Rules of Court

INTERNATIONAL CONVENTIONS

List of Abbreviations

GENERAL

[31]	paragraph 31
76	page 76
§ or s 12	section 12
r 3.4	rule 3.4
A&E	Accident and Emergency
aff'd	affirmed
A-G or AG	Attorney-General
AHA	Area Health Authority
Am	American
Ass	Assurance
Assn	Association
Aust or Aus	Australian
BC	Borough Council
BC	British Columbia
BMA	British Medical Association
Bull	Bulletin
CC	County Council
CJ	Chief Justice
cl, cll	clause/s
Co	Company or Corporation
Comm	Commission or Committee
Comp	Comparative
Commr	Commissioner
Corp	Corporation
CP	Consultation Paper
DC	District Council
Dept	Department
Dist	District
Div	Division
DP	Discussion Paper
edn	edition
Euro	European
EWLC	England and Wales Law Commission
GMC	General Medical Council of England and Wales
GP	General practitioner
HA	Health Authority
HCP	Healthcare professional

Hosp	Hospital or Hospitals
Ins	Insurance
Intl	International
J	Journal
J, JJ	Justice or Judge, Justices or Judges
JA, JJA	Judge of Appeal, Judges of Appeal
LBC	London Borough Council
Litig	Litigation
LJ	Law Journal
LJ	Lord Justice
LRC	Law Reform Commission
L Rev	Law Review
M	Million
MBC	Metropolitan Borough Council
Med	Medical
MOD	Ministry of Defence
MR	Master of the Rolls
NHS	National Health Service
P	President
Pt	Part
PD	Practice Direction
pp	pinpoint
Prod/s	Product/s
Q	Quarterly
QC	Queen's Counsel
reg/s	regulation/s
ref'd	refused
rev'd	reversed
s, ss	section/s
SC	Shire Council
SC	Senior Council
Soc	Society
Sys	System
U or Uni	University
UK	United Kingdom
US	United States
WP	Working Paper

COURTS

CA	Court of Appeal (of the jurisdiction referred to by the reporter series)
CCA	Court of Criminal Appeal (England and Wales)
Ch	Chancery Division of the High Court of England and Wales
DC	District Court (of the jurisdiction referred to by the reporter series)
Div Ct	Superior Court of Justice (Divisional Court of Ontario)
ECtHR	European Court of Human Rights
FCA	Federal Court of Australia

Full FCA	Full Bench of the Federal Court of Australia
Gen Div	Ontario Court of Justice (General Division)
HC	High Court (of the jurisdiction referred to)
HCA	High Court of Australia
HL	House of Lords
CSIH	Inner House of the Court of Session (Scotland)
QB	Queen's Bench Division
SC	Supreme Court (of the relevant jurisdiction)
SCC	Supreme Court of Canada
SCJ	Superior Court of Justice (Ontario)
Scot CS	Scotland Court of Session
SD NY	United States District Court Southern District New York (sample jurisdiction only)
2d Cir	United States Court of Appeals Second Circuit

LAW JOURNALS

ALJ	Australian Law Journal
BMJ	British Medical Journal
CFLQ	Child and Family Law Quarterly
CJQ	Civil Justice Quarterly
CLJ	Cambridge Law Journal
CLY	Current Law Year Book
ICLQ	International and Comparative Law Quarterly
JLM	Journal of Law and Medicine
JPIL	Journal of Personal Injury Law
LQR	Law Quarterly Review
Med L Rev	Medical Law Review
MLR	Modern Law Review
PN	Professional Negligence

LAW REPORTS

A 2d	Atlantic Reporter, Second Series
AC	Law Reports, Appeal Cases (Third Series)
ACWS (3d)	All Canada Weekly Summaries, Third Series
All ER	All England Law Reports
All ER (D)	All England Direct Law Reports (Digests)
ALR	Australian Law Reports
Alta LR (3d)	Alberta Law Reports, Third Series
Aust Torts Rep	Australian Torts Reports
BCJ	British Columbia Judgments
BCLR (3d)	British Columbia Law Reports, Third Series
BMLR	Butterworths Medico-Legal Reports
Cal 2d	California Reports, Second Series
CCLT (3d)	Canadian Cases on the Law of Torts, Third Series
Ch	Law Reports, Chancery Division (Third Series)

Ch D	Law Reports, Chancery Division (Second Series)
CLR	Commonwealth Law Reports
CPC (3d)	Carswell's Practice Cases, Third Series
DLR (4th)	Dominion Law Reports, Fourth Series
EHRR	European Human Rights Reports
ER	English Reports
F 2d	Federal Reporter, Second Series
F 3d	Federal Reporter, Third Series
FCR	Federal Court Reports (Australia)
FLR	Family Law Reports
FRD	Federal Rules Decisions
F Supp	Federal Supplement
F Supp (2d)	Federal Supplement, Second Series
Ga	Georgia Reports
Kan	Kansas Reports
KB	Law Reports, King's Bench
LGR	Knight's Local Government Reports
Lloyd's Rep	Lloyd's Law Reports
Lloyd's Rep Med	Lloyd's Law Reports Medical
LRC	Law Reports of the Commonwealth
Med LR	Medical Law Reports
NSWLR	New South Wales Law Reports
NZLR	New Zealand Law Reports
OAC	Ontario Appeal Cases
OH	Outer House
OJ	Ontario Judgments
OR (2d)	Ontario Reports, Second Series
OR (3d)	Ontario Reports, Third Series
PIQR	Personal Injuries and Quantum Reports
PNLR	Professional Negligence and Liability Reports
P 3d	Pacific Reporter, Third Series
QB	Law Reports, Queen's Bench
SA	South African Law Reports
SC	Session Cases, Scotland
SCLR	Scottish Civil Law Reports
SCR	Supreme Court Reports, Canada
SLR	Singapore Law Reports
SLT	Scots Law Times
So 2d	Southern Reporter, Second Series
Sol Jo	Solicitors' Journal
SW 2d	South Western Reporter, Second Series
US	United States Supreme Court Reports
WLR	Weekly Law Reports
WN	Weekly Notes of Cases, England and Wales
WWR	Western Weekly Reports

List of Tables

List of Figures

Notes on Mode of Citation and Style

Throughout this book, the following protocols are adopted:

1. In the endnotes, the order of preference of case law citations is as follows:

   a. where the case has been designated a neutral citation by the adjudicating court, the neutral citation is used;
   b. where the case has been reported in an authorised series of reports, the authorised citation is used in addition to the neutral citation;
   c. in the absence of (b), where the case has been reported in an unauthorised series of reports, the unauthorised citation is used in addition to the neutral citation;
   d. in the absence of (a)–(c), the case is cited in the following manner: (court, date of decision).

2. Paragraph numbers are used in preference to page numbers, where pinpoints from primary or secondary sources are required.

3. For each case, the court is referred to in parentheses in all instances where it is not obvious from the report series or mode of citation which court made the decision.

4. The scholarship and opinion of many entities and persons are referenced throughout this book, and have been cited and pinpointed in accordance with British citation conventions. All reasonable efforts have been made to pinpoint as accurately and fulsomely as possible.

5. Wherever quotations appear from primary or secondary sources, in the interests of brevity, footnotes within those quotations have not been reproduced, and the conventional usage of 'footnotes omitted' should be assumed throughout.

6. In the text and endnotes, references to the masculine gender should be taken to import the feminine gender, unless expressly indicated otherwise.

7. For the purposes of accuracy and succinctness, the factual summaries of the cases which appear as indented passages throughout the book are frequently reproduced substantially from either the judgment or the headnote of the relevant cases.

8. Where the facts of cases are described, the healthcare professional is denoted as 'Dr [name]', regardless of whether or not the title is customarily used by the healthcare professional. This protocol is adopted in order to signify more conveniently for readers which parties in a fact scenario were non-patient, patient, and healthcare professional, respectively.

9.   Occasionally, where a primary or secondary source was accessed online and could not be located in hard copy feasibly, or at all, so as to locate a pinpoint for a quotation, the following is noted: (accessed online, no pp available).

10.   Some medical terms referred to in the text are explained briefly by endnote. Where this occurs, readers are referred to a fuller explanation of the term appearing either in the relevant case (if cited) or in, e.g., *The Oxford Concise Colour Medical Dictionary* (4th edn, OUP, Oxford, 2007).

PART I
Setting the Context

Chapter 1

The Book: An Overview

A INTRODUCTION

Lord Atkin asked, back in 1932, 'who then in law is my neighbour?'.[1] Almost eight decades later, the healthcare professional (HCP) must increasingly ask himself the more specific, 'Who is my "non-patient", one whom I've never medically treated, either as a formal patient, or at all? To whom, of the indeterminate mass of people at large with whom I have no HCP–patient relationship, might I be potentially liable in negligence?'.

This book propounds the thesis that, insofar as doctors and other HCPs are concerned, their 'neighbours' in law are (or could be) a considerably wider group of people—non-patients, third parties, even total strangers—than they may have perceived! The issue is, presently, an under-litigated (and sparsely-written[2]) aspect of medical liability in English law, but developments elsewhere presage a 'creeping expansion' of such claims. Class (or group) actions against health professionals for culpable acts or omissions that affect a wide number of people are also a potential factor in the field of non-patient and third party claims, piquing the area with further interest and importance. Hence, it is projected that this book will be of relevance and utility to claimants (and their legal representatives), to health professional defendants (and their indemnity insurers and legal representatives), to healthcare professional associations, and to governing medical authorities such as the General Medical Council.

Of course, imposing liability for negligence, in *any* case where the claimant is a 'third party' to a defendant professional, remains 'exceptional'.[3] These will not be the run-of-the-mill cases of alleged negligence against medical defendants. To that end, it has been judicially said that negligent doctors rarely harm people who are not their patients,[4] and that there are very few cases involving doctors and third parties.[5] However, that so-called rarity is certainly becoming 'less rare'—and the issue of liability to those with whom the HCPs would not regard themselves as being in a 'normal', or indeed *any*, professional relationship, is being recognised as constantly evolving and, correspondingly, legally difficult.

With that lightly-sketched background in mind, the aims of this book are two-fold. Its first, and primary, purpose, is to critically analyse the challenging manifestations of non-patient and third party categories of claims which have arisen in English medico-legal jurisprudence, and from elsewhere around the common law world. Throughout the book, the terms 'non-patient' and 'third party' are used interchangeably. Via this analysis, the author seeks to identify the legal pointers towards the establishment (or denial) of a HCP's liability in negligence towards hitherto rather unfamiliar claimants. This matrix of pointers will be used to foreshadow future developments in this area of litigation. As and where appropriate, statutory developments or law reform proposals from other jurisdictions that directly impact upon the liabilities of HCPs towards non-patients and third parties will also be addressed. Suggestions will be proffered as to whether or not these reform proposals/legislative enactments appear to offer any advantages for the clarity and utility of English law.

The second aim of this book is to assist the medical profession, by highlighting just how its ambit of liability in negligence may potentially extend to an ever-widening group of claimants whose profiles are nothing at all like those of the traditional patient. To that end, the author has prepared an Appendix to the book[6] entitled, '*Potential Liability to Non-Patients and Third Parties: A Synopsis for Healthcare Professionals*', which is intended to abbreviate the legal analysis undertaken in the book by means of a succinct and legally useful reference for the benefit of the medical profession. In so doing, a proposed spin-off of the book is that it raise awareness among the medical profession (and medical insurers and governing bodies) of how liability towards non-patients is becoming increasingly litigated, and how that thread of litigation may be anticipated and protected against by the exercise of reasonable care towards, or in respect of, non-patients.

B THE COVERAGE OF THE BOOK

Most of the conundrums considered in this book arise out of an *already-existing relationship between a HCP and a patient*, where the third party or non-patient is a 'stranger' to that relationship, yet brings a grievance against the HCP. Hence, the arrangement is often tri-partite, as Figure 1.1 shows:

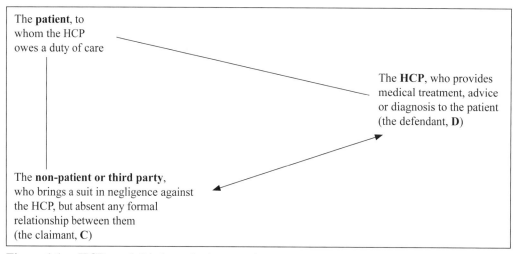

Figure 1.1   HCPs and third parties/non-patients

Insofar as non-patients are concerned, the analysis conveniently divides into two substantive Parts.

1. Claims arising out of physical injury to the non-patient

Part II of the book considers the various scenarios in which non-patients and third parties may seek to sue a HCP for physical injuries sustained. By way of illustration:

What if a *mentally*-disabled patient is negligently given leave from a psychiatric institution, and runs amok and kills a number of strangers? What if it is a *physically*-disabled patient who causes death or injury, say, by driving a vehicle or operating machinery, when he was in no physical condition to so do? The potential liability of a HCP towards the killed or injured 'strangers' is examined in Chapter 3.

Suppose that a doctor negligently fails to diagnose that a patient in hospital is suffering from a transmissible disease. The patient dies, and 1,500 visitors to the hospital contract the same transmissible disease. Or suppose that a family member claims that a doctor ought to have warned him that he was at risk of inheriting a genetically-transmitted disease from that doctor's patient, and that had the doctor done so, then the family member could have taken precautions—however, the doctor does not pass on the information, and the disease ultimately manifests for the family member. The complex issues associated with the liability of a HCP towards non-patients and third parties who either *contract or inherit a disease from the HCP's patient*, are considered in detail in Chapter 4.

Plainly, the abovementioned situations arise out of a tri-partite relationship—there is a patient whom the HCP examined or treated (allegedly negligently), and a stranger to that HCP–patient relationship brings suit against the HCP/health authority in negligence. In a departure from that tri-partite scenario, however, suppose that a person complains that he was in a medical emergency, that the defendant HCP could have intervened to assist him but held back or 'looked the other way', and that he suffered adverse consequences from the lack of medical treatment. That 'victim' who claims that emergency assistance should have been rendered is another non-patient scenario (but, this time, involving no formal patient). This scenario, one of so-called *'Bad Samaritan' liability*, is critiqued, from both common law and statutory angles, in Chapter 5.

By contrast, suppose that a HCP *does* intervene where he sees a medical emergency unfolding or where he is requested to do so—and then, allegedly, negligently makes the victim's situation worse. That victim has become the HCP's patient in a limited sense, dictated by circumstances (thus distinguishing this claimant, factually and legally, from the case of 'Bad Samaritan' liability, where the HCP does not intervene at all). The legal position of the *medical 'Good Samaritan'*, both at common law and under various statutory initiatives, is considered in Chapter 6.

2. Claims arising out of non-physical injury to the non-patient

Part III considers scenarios in which the non-patient has suffered psychiatric or economic injuries. By way of illustration:

Suppose that a HCP fails to carefully sterilise his patient, and a child is subsequently conceived and born. The other biological parent of the child claims that he sustained financial losses as a result of that unwanted pregnancy and birth. Or suppose a patient is negligently-treated by a doctor, and suffers personal injury—and a third party is put to financial expense in looking after that patient. These, and other, scenarios in which a *third party claims economic injury* as a result of a HCP's dealings with a patient, are the subject of consideration in Chapter 7.

What if the HCP's treatment of the patient causes, not economic injury, but *psychiatric injury* (e.g., depressive illness, post-traumatic-stress disorders) to family members of the patient? These claims which amount to pure psychiatric injury, i.e., not consequential upon any physical injury or property damage to the claimant third party, are legally difficult at the best of times, but in the context of medical negligence, some further conundrums are constantly thrown up by the factual scenarios. The difficulties posed by such claims, brought on the part of third parties against the allegedly-negligent HCP, are examined in Chapter 8.

What if a HCP allegedly causes the exposure of persons to the risk of contracting a disease, and while they 'wait and see' whether it develops, they *develop a fear of developing the disease, and that fear manifests as a recognised psychiatric illness*? The leading case in English law involving fear-of-the-future claims (as these cases are known) arose out of the fears of those involved in a clinical trial conducted in England in the 1970s. The participants were treated as a version of limited patients, as something 'akin to a doctor–patient relationship'. However, this scenario may equally occur in respect a HCP's non-patients (e.g., visitors to a hospital who are exposed to a patient's contagious disease which is negligently undiagnosed), as has occurred frequently in other jurisdictions. The difficult legal issues thrown up by fear-of-the-future claims arising out of medical negligence, whatever the type of claimant, are discussed in Chapter 9.

When investigations of alleged child abuse 'go wrong', such that the finger of blame is pointed at the wrong party, that wrongfully accused may suffer a number of injuries, both psychiatric and economic. The special policy and other legal issues that have invested the claims of the *wrongfully accused in negligently-diagnosed child abuse cases* with repeated judicial attention are considered in Chapter 10.

The Appendix draws together, as a supplementary document which is intended to have relevance and utility for the medical profession, a '*Potential Liability to Non-Patients and Third Parties: A Synopsis for Healthcare Professionals*'. This guideline summarises the relevant English legal principles which govern liability towards those who do not take on the appearance of the traditional patient.

Before embarking upon these chapters, however, and to put the detailed discussion of relevant non-patient and third party suits into context, a brief outline of the relevant legal framework follows in Chapter 2. To this framework (and particularly the duty of care component), detail is gradually and constantly being applied, as lawyers and those involved in the provision of medical services, around the common law world, encounter complex legal problems that sit apart from the traditional HCP–patient relationship.

As a note regarding presentation, and for the sake of convenience, the cases arising for discussion which involve claims by non-patients and third parties—whether emanating from England or from another jurisdiction—are 'showcased' by indentation. The facts/verdicts of these cases are briefly summarised at the indented passages, while the legal reasoning underpinning these verdicts (and a critique of that reasoning) is to be found in the text. Interestingly, there are over 120 such indented cases examined in this book, highlighting the topicality and importance which the topic of HCP liability in the wider context deserves.

C WHY THE TOPIC IS IMPORTANT

1. No 'neat and tidy' boundaries

In the well-known 1985 House of Lords' decision in *Sidaway v Board of Governors of the Bethlem Royal Hospital and the Maudsley Hospital*, Lord Diplock stated that:

> a doctor's duty of care, whether he be general practitioner or consulting surgeon or physician, is owed to that patient and none other, idiosyncrasies and all.[7]

This sentiment was endorsed, in the following decade, in *Powell v Boldaz*, where Stuart-Smith LJ said that whether doctors owe claimants any duty of care—

depends upon whether they are called upon, or undertake, to treat them as patients. There are many situations where a doctor will have close contact with another person, without the relationship of doctor–patient arising so as to involve the duty of care.[8]

Alas, whilst neat and tidy, these judicial statements (and others like them[9]) cannot be taken strictly at face value. A HCP *can* owe a duty of care to a person with whom he is not in a formal professional–patient relationship, i.e., to a person who is not, was not, and never will be, the HCP's patient. Further, and contrary to the suggestion that there needs to be some 'close contact with another person', a HCP *can* be found to have been negligent towards a third party, for the consequences of his negligent treatment towards *his patient*, in circumstances where he may have never known of the existence, much less the identity, of that third party.

Insofar as HCP liability is concerned, it is not a question of *whether or not* a duty of care can be owed (and, therefore, negligence liability incurred) to third parties—as several of the scenarios in this book demonstrate, it *can* be. The legally important question has shifted to whether, given all the facts and circumstances, a duty of care *is* owed, and *should* be owed, to the non-patient (and, in some scenarios, whether the remainder of the negligence action, particularly proof of a causal link, should be made out). Lord Clyde encapsulated the point in the following passage in *Phelps v Hillingdon LBC*:

> whether a duty *can* exist and whether a duty *does* exist are different kinds of questions, and it seems to me that the law gives different kinds of answers to them. The former may be resolved by considerations of policy, and in particular whether it is fair, just and reasonable to admit such a duty. The latter requires a consideration of the facts of the case and may be susceptible to different answers in different circumstances.[10]

That Lord Diplock's statement in *Sidaway* is too prescriptive a statement of modern authority is plain. What is much less clear, however, are the boundaries which circumscribe a HCPs' liability in negligence towards parties who are not their patients.

This is particularly so, given that HCPs' negligence can cause different types of injury to non-patients and third parties—from physical injuries, to psychiatric injuries which are not consequent upon any physical injury, to economic or financial damage. The law of negligence does not adopt a necessarily uniform set of principles to govern when claimants can recover for each type of injury. In addition, while the non-patient scenarios have been separated into chapters for the sake of convenience and detailed treatment, it is evident that there is a great deal of cross-fertilisation of ideas, factors and legal issues among categories. Although some non-patient litigation (say, concerning harm done to non-patient by a mentally-ill patient) is not directly on point in a case involving a different sort of non-patient (say, the type who suffers pure economic loss because of a HCP's treatment of his patient), the former judgment may well have some bearing on the issue of whether (and why) a duty of care is offered in the latter case. This cross-fertilisation is important to the entire rubric of the 'non-patient claim'. As Cullity J ironically noted in an important Canadian non-patient case (involving the spread of disease from a patient to non-patients at a hospital), '[h]ardening of the categories [of types of claimants] has been identified as an intellectual affliction of the legal profession'.[11] The variety of cases considered in this book aptly demonstrate that the parameters of legal liability are expanding, and overlapping, in this area of negligence law.

It should be noted, in passing, that the scenarios considered in Parts II and III of this book do *not* concern the question of *when* the claimant may become a formal patient of the defendant HCP.[12] The question of when a doctor–patient relationship legally forms is quite a separate issue, and is not relevant for present purposes, because there is no question of the claimant's ever becoming, or being, a formal patient of the HCP, in the legal situations described in later chapters.

2. An area of increasing appellate and extra-jurisdictional consideration

To achieve the overall aims of this book entails a comparative treatment of HCPs' potential liability, and draws upon relevant Commonwealth and United States (US) jurisprudence as and where appropriate, where interesting and innovative attempts have been made to expand the limits of a HCP's liability towards non-patients and third parties.

The utility of a comparative analysis of non-patient suits is underpinned by three features. First, the English common law of negligence broadly shares a common framework with that operative in these other jurisdictions, and the particular problems of establishing both a duty of care on the part of a HCP towards a non-patient, and a causal link between a HCP's wrongdoing and the damage suffered by the non-patient, are recurring themes of difficulty in the relevant case law emanating from all the jurisdictions. The answers reached by other courts in relation to these conundrums are of much interest to an English common lawyer, and where these may lend some insights for English jurists and lawyers, they are duly noted and explored.

Secondly, in some areas (e.g., the harm done to strangers by the mentally-ill) there has been extensive reference by English courts and academic literature to relevant US jurisprudence.[13] Interestingly, too, some courts in Commonwealth jurisdictions have sought to distinguish key English authorities on non-patient and third party claims, in finding for such a claimant (or, at least, in denying a strike-out application[14]). In so doing, the judges have deliberately re-interpreted, or refused to follow, their English counterparts' reasoning, thereby vesting in the Commonwealth jurisprudence persuasive authorities which litigants in England may be motivated to use to challenge the English decisions themselves in the future. All of this emphasises the important cross-fertilisation of relevant authorities across jurisdictions which often features in this area of negligence law.[15]

Finally, the problem which non-patient suits present for the healthcare profession (and for professional indemnity insurers) is a universal one across jurisdictions, which calls to mind the comments of leading comparative scholar Markesinis—that comparative studies are particularly apposite where similar problems are being confronted in many jurisdictions, which 'legitimately encourage[s] a search for help in the reasoning ... of other countries.'[16]

It should be stated at the outset that the instances in which these types of claims have been considered by English courts have been sporadic, and generally speaking, decided *against* the claimant. Establishing a duty of care has been notoriously difficult. In a notable recent third party claim against a negligent NHS Trust (which conceded a systemic failure of communication that had allowed a medical receptionist to inform a patient wrongly that she should not resume taking her medication), Buxton LJ frankly admitted that the case 'raised a number of difficult issues'.[17] The claimant third party (a local authority which was put to the cost of providing residential care for the stroke-disabled patient)—

> proposes a pioneering method of righting the injustice, ... [seeking] to use the law of negligence, to give it a direct claim against the tortfeasor. The action raises some novel questions, not only as being a claim for economic loss that falls outside the normal range of cases that arise from a direct relationship between claimant and defendant; but also more generally as taking the law of negligence into areas that it has not previously entered.[18]

The vexed legal conundrums at play in this field of HCPs' liability towards the other-than-usual-type-patient have variously been highlighted by occurrences of appellate overrule, cases in which courts have refused to follow previous decisions or have distinguished them away, and House of Lords' retreat from its own earlier views. For example, regarding HCPs who mis-diagnose child abuse and point the finger, wrongly and negligently, at the (third party) accused, the House of Lords changed its view in a remarkable manner as to whether the child has a claim in negligence open to him; but it has refused to shift its position in the case of the wrongfully-accused third party, denying that party a cause of action. Pioneering arguments that explicitly seek to 'get around' the House of Lords' reasoning have also generally failed for the wrongfully-accused non-patients. Yet the 'hardline' stance of the House of Lords in the context of negligently-diagnosed child abuse has not necessarily translated to other non-patient contexts easily, or, indeed, at all—in which case the lower courts have had to fashion a way forward, in what are often legally difficult and sensitive areas of dispute.

The area of non-patient and third party claims is also afflicted with some older decisions[19] in which a duty of care by the HCP towards the non-patient was either assumed by the court, or taken to be common ground, whereas nowadays, the issue would be worthy of more detailed analysis as to whether the elements of a duty are really, and realistically, established. Of course, as with any 'cutting-edge' area of negligence law, it is also significant that much of the jurisprudence is developing within the context of interlocutory applications for summary judgment[20] or strike out applications,[21] or the setting down for trial of a preliminary issue as to whether, say, a duty of care was owed by the HCP to the third party[22]—and hence, the issue has often been considered on a hypothetical set of facts and in the absence of a full factual analysis. Some of the cases discussed in this book must be read in that context. Undoubtedly, this has all contributed towards the difficulties which beset the wider category of third party claims (of which non-patients' claims against HCPs is but a subset), and which were highlighted by McIvor, in her work on third party liability, in the following pithy terms:

> Unfortunately, in third party actions, there has been a systematic failure to articulate with any degree of precision the actual grounds of decisions. Often the relevant issues are not properly isolated and individual decisions are typically arrived at without detailed reference to other related third party liability cases, and with little or no exploration of the inter-relationships between them. Consequently, the current law on third party liability is unstructured, unprincipled and incoherent.[23]

Recent Commonwealth developments have been particularly interesting too, where third parties have been seeking to push the boundaries of their claims against those in the medical profession. Several of these have been cases of first impression, and not surprisingly, therefore, the law has been described as 'unsettled' and 'uncertain'.[24] As the Ontario Court of Appeal recently admitted, with unreserved frankness, 'the nature of the doctor's duty of care to the third party and the legal basis for imposing a duty of care are not fully developed.'[25] In these other jurisdictions too, a lack of clear appellate authority has been noted,[26] and on occasions when a duty of care towards a non-patient has been (briefly) discussed at trial, the appellate court has later, and frustratingly, refused to deal with it.[27]

Of course, third party claims have arisen in English law, in other contexts which have proven equally as controversial as in the medical sector. To name just a few that have warranted appellate attention: suits against *police* authorities, where a criminal injures or kills a third party arising from alleged police negligence in their criminal investigations;[28] suits against *prison* authorities for negligently allowing escapees[29] or those awaiting trial[30] or deportation[31] to harm members of the public; suits against *social welfare* authorities, which have allegedly failed to take adequate precautions to protect children from being violently treated by those having custody and control of them;[32] and suits against *local authorities* who failed to protect one local authority housing tenant from a violent and fatal attack committed by a co-tenant.[33] HCPs and medical institutions are simply another category of defendant that has attracted the attention of third parties, this time in the guise of the non-patient claimant.

It is undoubtedly the case that the area of third party liability is a potential minefield for medical negligence suits, which non-patients are already seeking to test (or which, this book foreshadows, non-patients will increasingly seek to do), by reliance upon innovative argument, sympathetically receptive courts, and some rather *ad hoc*, even irreconcilable, outcomes, in the medico-legal jurisprudence. All of this renders the area an inviting one for legal research and analysis.

3. Legislative and human rights impacts

Another feature that fixes non-patient and third party claims against HCPs with legal interest is that, from time to time, both in England and elsewhere, law reform commissions have introduced proposals, or legislatures have enacted statutory instruments, which directly impact upon the legal issues governing such claims. This has occurred, for example, in the areas of 'Good Samaritan' and 'Bad Samaritan' liability, and recovery for pure psychiatric illness. These innovations will be examined, as and where appropriate, throughout the book.

Interestingly, in its review of the Australian law of negligence in 2002,[34] the Ipp Committee considered the scenario in which a duty had been cast upon a defendant to protect a third party claimant from suffering harm from the accidental or deliberate act of another, and where that harm could have been avoided by the defendant intervening to protect the claimant. By contrast to the large number of recommendations for legislative enactment curtailing or otherwise amending the common law, this complex area was one which the Committee thought best left to the judiciary to deal with on a case-by-case basis, and without any recommendations for legislation being made about the 'incidence of protective relationships'—'[d]uties of protection play a very important part in the law in safeguarding the interests of vulnerable members of society. We think that this area of the law is best left for development by the courts.'[35] Skene, one of Australia's leading medical law commentators, has since noted that the Ipp Committee's position on this indicates that the existence and scope of a HCP's duty to third parties is 'still a "grey area"', notwithstanding that some Australian authorities have recognised a duty on the part of a HCP in those circumstances.[36] Indeed, the law is equally, if not more, uncertain in England, given the latter's greater dearth of directly-relevant authorities.

Furthermore, the Human Rights Act 1998 (HRA), and the Convention rights to which it gives further effect,[37] exercise some considerable influence upon certain of the non-patient claims considered in this book. The Act has had, as Steele puts it, 'an indirect effect as the ordinary law of tort is developed by reference to Convention jurisprudence'.[38] The interplay between some of the non-patient suits canvassed in this book, and the impact of the Convention, has been evident in two particular respects.

First, as courts themselves are public authorities, pursuant to s 6(3) of the HRA,[39] they must ensure that English common law is compatible with the Convention, even when adjudicating on disputes between purely private parties (the so-called 'horizontal effect' of the HRA[40]). This has raised the question, at times, as to whether aspects of the English common law can survive the implementation of Convention rights, and whether the common law should be developed in order to ensure its compatibility with the Convention. Nowhere has this been more evident in the non-patient field, perhaps, than in the case of wrongful and negligent accusations of sexual abuse being levied against parents regarding their children. As has already been mentioned (and as will be explored more fully in Chapter 10), the development of the child's claim against negligent HCPs in this context has followed a markedly different path from that of the parental claim against those *same* HCPs. The no-duty-to-rescue rule has also attracted comment about whether or not such a rule is compatible with Convention rights, a subject which is considered further in the context of 'Bad Samaritan' HCPs who fail to assist non-patients (Chapter 5).

Secondly, and quite apart from alleging that the court should develop principles of tort law to be compatible with the Convention, some of the non-patient claims alleged against health authorities which are considered in this book have featured both as suits brought in negligence (which may be framed on the basis of either direct or vicarious liability on the part of the relevant health authority), *and* as suits brought against the relevant health authority pursuant to the HRA, where, as a public authority, it has allegedly acted in a way that was incompatible with the non-patient's Convention rights (again, the wrongfully-accused parent is one notable example). As and where appropriate, reference will be made in later chapters to non-patient HRA suits of this type.

Separately from the above, where a patient has died or has committed suicide, allegedly as a result of negligent diagnosis or treatment at the hands of an NHS-employed HCP, non-patient *relatives* have occasionally brought HRA claims against the relevant NHS Trust, claiming that the relatives were themselves 'victims' of the alleged wrongdoing, and seeking reparation for an alleged violation of art 2 of the Convention.[41] This is a different sort of non-patient claim, because (unlike the scenario in the previous paragraph) the non-patient is **not** alleging any direct duty of care owed by the HCP or health authority to himself. For this type of non-patient, two actions are already potentially possible under English law—an action by the estate of the deceased patient, in respect of the patient's pain and suffering and other damages which accrued between the date of the NHS's alleged negligence and the patient's death (which action is brought under the Law Reform (Miscellaneous Provisions) Act 1934[42]), and an action by any persons who were financial dependants of the patient at the time of the patient's death (pursuant to the Fatal Accidents Act 1976). Both statutory actions will be predicated upon proof of negligence by the NHS or by its employed staff towards the patients themselves.[43] Independently of these, the HRA claims by the relatives allege that the (mis)conduct of the NHS or of its employed staff towards the patient was in violation of art 2 of the Convention, entitling them to damages under s 8 of the HRA, or a further inquiry into the circumstances surrounding the death. As these HRA claims are not tortious actions *per se*, they fall strictly outside the purview of this book, although the controversies associated with them are discussed more fully by the author elsewhere.[44]

4. The potential to give rise to group/class actions

(a) The current position
The reality is that instances of third party and non-patient claims against HCPs may arise in the class actions context. Take scenarios arising out of, say, transmission of diseases by a patient to a group of strangers; psychiatric illnesses on the part of various close family members and friends if a HCP's negligence causes a patient or a series of patients to die; or those killed or injured by a mentally-ill or physically-disabled patient. All of these have the potential to involve large groups of similarly-affected claimants whose claims share common issues of fact or law, and who may

allege wrongdoing from the same negligent event—and who then collectively sue the allegedly negligent professional.

This type of collective action by non-patients against HCPs—via group action in England, class action in many other jurisdictions—is gradually losing its 'rarity' tag. Their incidence will be pointed out, as and where appropriate, throughout the book. Judges have been quick to recognise the fact that third party claims, brought as a class against a HCP, raise questions that '[have] obvious importance that extends beyond the specific facts of this case',[45] while commentators have pointed out that, where successfully instituted, such actions may involve 'very considerable amounts of money' for medical insurers.[46]

Were non-patients and third parties to band together as a group and sue a relevant HCP, in circumstances where their claims shared questions of law or fact in common, there are, theoretically, two ways in which such litigation could be conducted. It could be based on *opt-in* principles, whereby each group member must file individual proceedings, so as to take a proactive step to initiate their claim against the HCP, and then have those proceedings grouped under the one 'umbrella'. Typically, some of the group members' claims may be stayed while others are taken forward as lead or test cases in order to obtain a determination on common issues of fact or law which all the claims share.

 The other possible basis upon which such actions can be conducted is on *opt-out* principles, under which a representative claimant sues on his own behalf and on behalf of a number of other persons (the class members), such that *only* the representative claimant is a party to the action with the defendant HCP, and the class members are not usually identified at the outset but are merely described. Under this approach, class members have the choice to opt-out of the litigation, and if they do not, then they are bound by the outcome of the litigation on the common issues, whether that outcome is favourable or adverse to the class. Under an opt-out collective action (typically called a 'class action' in the United States,[47] a 'representative proceeding' in Australia,[48] and a 'class proceeding' in Canada[49]), class members do not take any active part in the litigation, unless and until it comes time to seek to prove the individual aspects of their claims.[50] Generally speaking, and for a variety of legal, economic, psychological and other reasons, the opt-out approach facilitates a greater range, and number, of collective actions than does the opt-in approach.[51]

As things stand presently, if (a group of) non-patients and third parties were intending to seek damages against a HCP for their separate and individual injuries, then the most suitable collective action regime in English civil procedure[52] would be the Group Litigation Order (GLO).[53] This regime operates on opt-in principles, the litigation conducted under it is closely case-managed, and the relevant rules can permit the taking forth of a test or lead action, as the case-managing court sees fit.[54] To date, three GLO's have been implemented against HCPs for alleged medical wrongdoing—two of which arose out the retention of tissue and organs of stillborn children without parental consent, allegedly causing the parents psychiatric injury,[55] and the other concerning a case of alleged negligent and inappropriate treatment of a group of patients by a psychiatrist.[56]

(b) The winds of reform?

English civil procedure does not *currently* embrace an opt-out collective action. The author has consistently challenged this state of affairs, contending that the law of England and Wales should facilitate the introduction, by primary legislation, of an opt-out class action, generic in type, that could handle a range of disputes, including those arising in the health sector.[57]

In this regard, significant legislative developments at the time of writing foreshadow that the collective redress landscape may change in the not-too-distant future. There have been a number of signs supporting the introduction of opt-out collective redress (including a landmark report by the Civil Justice Council of England and Wales[58] and a response from the Ministry of Justice[59]), culminating in a most important decision, that is, the introduction of a Bill[60] which facilitates an opt-out collective redress regime for England and Wales (albeit, in the financial services sector).

Any opt-out collective action in the field of health services is likely to lag, rather than lead, the implementation of such a regime in other sectors. However, should an opt-out action become accessible to the health sector, that, to some extent, will be a sea-change, not least for HCPs engaged in negligence suits.

In summary then, given the propensity for groups of non-patients and third parties to be affected by a single instance of alleged medical negligence, the possibility of group actions against a HCP on an opt-in basis remains a *presently*-available avenue in English law; and the *potential* advent of class actions-type litigation against a single HCP will be of intense interest to the medical profession, indemnity insurers such as the Medical Defence Union, the General Medical Council, and commentators/scholars in this country.

5. The contrast with other 'patient-centric' contexts

The fact that a HCP can feasibly be liable in negligence towards someone who is not his patient is an important concept, especially when that notion is contrasted with the patient-focussed practice that pervades medical law, both old and new.

The Hippocratic Oath itself refers to the obligations owed to 'patients' more than once— and refers to obligations to 'persons' or 'third parties' not at all.[61] According to the Oath, 'I will prescribe regimen for the good of my patients ... I will not cut for stone, even for patients in whom the disease is manifest ... In every house where I come I will enter only for the good of my patients ..'. The same is true of the General Medical Council's *Good Medical Practice* guidance to doctors.[62] The paragraphs of that guidance that define what being a 'good doctor' is,[63] and what amounts to 'good clinical care',[64] refer to 'patients' only. 'Good clinical care' is described by the GMC in the following terms:

a. adequately assessing the patient's conditions, taking account of the history (including the symptoms, and psychological and social factors), the patient's views, and where necessary examining the patient;
b. providing or arranging advice, investigations or treatment where necessary; and
c. referring a patient to another practitioner, when this is in the patient's best interests.

The legal landscape, however, is, and is becoming, far more complicated, and the boundaries of a HCP's actual and potential liability are being pushed out well beyond these literal texts.

Moreover, in the case of patients whose capacity to give consent to treatment is impaired, the 'best interests' mantra has been judicially suggested to be 'patient-centric'. Where an adult patient is mentally incapable of giving his consent, then treatment may lawfully be provided by a doctor where the treatment is in the best interests of the patient: Hence, in *Re F (Mental Patient: Sterilisation)*,[65] it was held to be lawful to sterilise a female mental patient who was incapable of giving consent to the procedure. The basis of the decision was that sterilisation would be in the patient's best interests because her life would be fuller and more agreeable if she were sterilised than if she were not. Similarly, in *Re B (A Minor) (Wardship: Medical Treatment)*,[66] the Court of Appeal held that, in the case of a child who was born with Down's Syndrome and who required an urgent operation to remove an intestinal blockage which would otherwise have proved fatal to the child, the relevant question was whether the operation was in the best interests of the child, and not whether the parents' wishes should be respected (the parents took the view that it would be kinder to allow the child to die).[67] Case points out[68] that in such cases, the courts have been 'generally adamant in refusing to recognise interests external to the instant patient as legitimate considerations',[69] and cites a number of cases in which the courts refused to have regard to, say, the interests of the wider community (in *Airedale NHS Trust v Bland*[70]), to the interests of those charged with the care of the long-term incompetent (in *Re F*[71]), and to the interests of any future child who may be born to the disabled patient (in *Re X (Adult Patient: Sterilisation)*[72]).

Extra-judicially, it is also of interest to note the 'patient-centric' nature of the notable Consultation Paper, *Making Amends*,[73] in which reference to patient redress and better solutions for *patient* compensation were regularly referred to, and the non-patient hardly at all.[74]

Hence, given the above, it is something of an oddity when the law expects HCPs to owe a duty of care to non-patients to avoid or minimise injury (be it personal, economic or psychiatric), and to conduct themselves in a reasonable and competent way toward that non-patient so as to discharge that duty of care. As another commentator has succinctly stated, '[m]odern medicine is afflicted by conflicts of loyalties threatening its traditional patient-centred orientation.'[75]

In summary, then, the increasing judicial acknowledgment that professional liability towards third parties can exist, the array of non-patient suits which have been the subject of important appellate and extra-jurisdictional consideration, the interplay between non-patient suits and Convention jurisprudence, the potential for non-patient suits to give rise to financially-onerous class and group action judgments, and the contrast which may be drawn between the literal text of the Hippocratic Oath and the GMC's *Good Medical Practice* and the reality at the coal-face of medical practice, all render the topic of non-patient and third party claims of great importance to the legal and medical professions alike.

D   SCENARIOS AND CLAIMS OUTSIDE THE AMBIT OF THE BOOK

For the sake of completeness, it is perhaps useful to delineate the boundaries of the non-patient and third party suits discussed in this book, and to expressly articulate what will **not** be covered herein.

1. General exclusions

Some varieties of non-patient, strictly so-called, fall outside the scope of the book:

- the book will exclude from consideration those non-patient cases whose connection with the medical context is coincidental only, and which are quite unrelated to the medical treatment rendered to any person—for example, where a person visiting a patient in hospital was assaulted by a trespasser within the hospital building,[76] or where a lift became jammed in a hospital, causing the trapped occupants to suffer psychiatric illnesses[77]—for such incidents may have occurred in any context;
- the book does not consider the sort of non-patient (e.g., an insurer or employer) who may suffer economic losses by reason of the non-disclosure by the HCP of a patient's disease, and with whom the HCP usually has a contractual relationship. The dilemmas associated with examinations of patients for the purposes of insurance, employment, forensic police

investigations, compulsory mental detention, or litigation—and the potential liability of the HCP who performs those examinations, both towards the examinees *and* towards those who request the medical services—are considered by the author elsewhere.[78] By contrast with the aforementioned employers, insurers, etc., the non-patients the focus of this book do not share any contractual relationship with the HCP, whatsoever;

- employee claims against health authorities, alleging negligence in the way in which violent or disturbed patients are managed within the system of work at the employer's facility, are a type of third party claim which is also excluded from consideration, given their employment-related focus;[79] and

- finally, the book excludes from consideration any claims for compensation by relatives of a person who dies as a result of medical negligence which may be issued under the Fatal Accidents Act 1976.

2. Tri-partite scenarios involving patients as claimants

In some evolving and complex scenarios, a traditional HCP–patient relationship exists, but has given rise to a tri-partite arrangement in which it is the *patient*, strictly so-called, who has brought the action:

- in some cases, a patient has sought to by-pass his treating doctor or the responsible health authority, and instead sue a third party—e.g., a regulatory body,[80] or an ancillary healthcare service provider with no direct contact with the patient[81]—for alleged wrongdoing and culpability. Given that these particular claimants are themselves patients who have been treated within an acknowledged HCP–patient setting but who are suing a third party instead, they fall outside the scope of this book;

- a different category of case arises where the patient alleges that a defendant health authority, with responsibility for the oversight of the way in which HCPs treat their patients, was inadequate and careless, thus providing the HCP with an opportunity to cause harm to the patient[82]—again, this is a patient, and not a non-patient, claim;

- psychiatric patients who have harmed (sometimes fatally) third parties, and who then claim that their treating HCPs were negligent in delivering their psychiatric care (their damage being a longer period of detention or incarceration than would otherwise have been the case), involve tri-partite relationships—among HCP, patient, and third party. It is another unusual and evolving type of medico-legal claim which has been raised for judicial consideration in England,[83] and elsewhere,[84] but as it again comprises a patient claim, it does not fall within the province of this book;

- where an action is brought against a HCP by a patient for harm done to him by a mentally-unbalanced or aggressive co-patient within the same hospital, due to breaches of security or failure of supervision,[85] a tri-partite relationship—between HCP, patient perpetrator and patient victim—arises on the facts, but again, such *patient* claims fall outside the scope of discussion in this book;

- a child who is damaged, negligently, either *in utero* or due to some treatment of his parents prior to the child's conception, can only recover compensation, in English law, if he is born alive (in legal-speak, it 'is an injury sustained before the child develops a legal personality'[86]). A HCP owes a duty of care to a child ultimately born alive, for injuries arising from negligence which occurred during the pre-natal and pre-conception stages of a pregnancy—a position that has been acknowledged, both at English common law,[87] and statutorily.[88] The position adopted, for the purposes of this book, is that both mother *and damaged child* are *patients* of the HCP. It has been opined by other commentators, too, that '[t]he analogy might be made that the foetus is in effect a "patient" of the physician',[89] and the position that a HCP has a doctor–patient relationship with the foetus has been supported by judicial statement too.[90] Hence, the book excludes from consideration those suits by children born alive who claim against the HCP that, 'but for your negligence, HCP, I would have been born a healthy child, and not as an injured and disabled child', where such injuries result from, say: a scanning procedure, or an invasive gynaeological procedure, performed on the mother, that injures a foetus in utero;[91] medical treatment of the mother's conditions, independent of her pregnancy (e.g., acne, epilepsy), which treatment adversely affects the foetus;[92] and negligent delivery of the foetus.[93] These types of claims are considered in detail in commentary elsewhere.[94] Similarly, a child's 'wrongful life' claim against a HCP— predicated upon the claim by the child that, in the absence of negligence, he or she would not have been conceived or that the pregnancy would have been terminated and the child would not have been born'[95]—falls outside the scope of this work. Such claims are barred in English law,[96] both statutorily[97] and at common law,[98] as being contrary to public policy, and are discussed in detail elsewhere.[99]

3. Non-patient claims for compensation for violation of a Convention right

A non-patient claimant may argue that a NHS Trust, which was responsible for the management and control of the health services at its hospital, acted (either directly, or via its employees) in a way which was incompatible with its obligations under the European Convention on Human Rights; and that this behaviour was accordingly unlawful within the meaning of s 6(1) of the Human Rights Act 1998 (HRA).

Where a patient is being treated in a NHS hospital, that hospital is a public authority.[100] The European Court of Human Rights has stated that '[w]here a hospital is a public institution, the acts and omissions of its medical staff are capable of engaging the responsibility of the respondent State under the Convention.'[101] Section 7 of the HRA provides that anyone who alleges that a public authority acted unlawfully under s 6(1) may bring proceedings against the relevant authority, if he is 'a victim of the unlawful act'.

In this way, the legal framework of ss 6 and 7 of the HRA provides a potential avenue for non-patient suits, whereby the non-patient may claim that he was a victim of unlawful conduct by the NHS Trust (or one of its employees). For example, a non-patient may allege that, due to the way in which *a patient* was treated (or not treated) by NHS-employed HCPs, he, the non-patient, has suffered distress, anxiety, vexation, bereavement, or other loss. Alternatively, a non-patient may allege that, due to an act or omission on the part of a health authority towards him *personally*, that authority has acted in a way that was incompatible with his Convention rights, thus entitling him to obtain a judicial remedy. Either way, if the claimant non-patient establishes 'victim status', if a violation of a Convention obligation is proven, and if the claimant has indeed suffered a legally-recognisable and compensable harm, then s 7 of the HRA provides a free-standing basis for damages.

For example, in the case of the non-patient *parent wrongfully accused* of sexually abusing or neglecting his child, a claim under the HRA, alleging a contravention of art 8 (the right to a private and family life) has been attempted, with mixed success.[102] Additionally, there are signs of an increasing willingness on the part of *close relatives of patients* to sue for compensation under the HRA for an alleged violation of art 2 (the right to life), where the patient has died as a result of treatment at a NHS hospital, causing loss and damage to close family members. Litigation of this type has arisen where the patient's condition was mis-diagnosed,[103] or the patient was inadequately supervised,[104] or the patient, undergoing treatment for depression, committed suicide as a result of the alleged negligence on the part of NHS-employed staff, or as a result of some systemic breach by the NHS Trust—the 'suicidal patient' scenario has received House of Lords' consideration in 2008 (in *Savage v South Essex NHS Trust*[105]) and again in the High Court in mid-2009 (in *Rabone v Pennine Care NHS Trust*[106]), and hence, clearly this is one emerging area of non-patient suits under the HRA. Furthermore, where a *physically-disabled or mentally-psychotic patient kills a non-patient* because the patient was not supervised or medically treated in an appropriate manner, and an opportunity was created for that patient to harm or kill a non-patient, then the estate of that non-patient, or the relatives of that dead non-patient, may seek to bring a HRA claim, again for a violation of art 2 (although, to the author's knowledge, no claim has been brought to date by an English litigant). In addition, if a HCP were to act as a '*Bad Samaritan*' and fail to assist a person in medical need, it has been mooted that the victim may have a claim for breach of his Convention rights (although, again, such a claim has yet to be brought).

The framework created by, and around, s 7 of the HRA has, in the words of Pannick and Lester, created 'a new cause of action against public authorities (widely defined) for a new public law tort of acting in breach of the victim's Convention rights'.[107] A s 7 claim may be particularly useful where it may be difficult for the non-patient to establish any duty of care owed by the hospital or by its employed medical staff towards that claimant himself, so as to substantiate a claim in negligence.[108]

As and where appropriate in later chapters, the interplay between the non-patient suit at issue, and Convention jurisprudence, will be flagged. However, a detailed discussion of the non-patient's action based upon an alleged violation of a Convention right, and the issues arising thereunder (e.g., the legal circumstances which trigger the state's obligations to, say, 'protect life' under art 2 or to respect family life under art 8; and whether the non-patient can establish that he was a 'victim' at all) falls outside the scope of this book,[109] given the book's emphasis upon the common law action in negligence.

E CONCLUSION

Liability of professionals (solicitors,[110] valuers,[111] financial advisers,[112] insurance advisers,[113] social workers[114]) towards third parties who are not their traditional 'client' is already a feature of the English legal landscape. Even so, third party liability is exceptional—the House of Lords has observed, in *JD v East Berkshire Community Health NHS Trust*, that '[f]or the most part, the settled policy of the law is opposed to granting remedies to third parties for the effects of injuries to other people.'[115]

As part of that coterie of exceptional cases, whether a legal duty of care is to a non-patient or third party, as a separate and additional duty to that which the HCP owes to his patient, is evolving into a difficult and significant issue. The scope and complexity of non-patient suits warrants their separate and detailed treatment herein.

Obviously, some of the non-patient claimants whose cases are examined in this book suffered grievously at the hands of impaired patients, or by reason of the HCP's negligence, and courts have not been slow to express sympathy for several of the claimants concerned. For example,

Stuart-Smith LJ's comments in *Palmer v Tees HA*[116] reflect common sentiment when he said, 'it is impossible not to have the deepest sympathy for Mrs Palmer for this truly appalling catastrophe' (she failed, however, in her non-patient claim against the medical defendants). Even where the non-patient or third party has 'only' suffered economic injury from the defendant's culpability, the claimant's case may attract 'a good deal of sympathy'.[117] In many of the cases, either a breach in the medical services offered, or (notwithstanding the lack of any determination of breach in strike-out and preliminary issue applications) some medical misjudgment, was clearly evident on the facts. Whether sympathy should be permitted to trump a fairly narrow application of legal principle in this particular nook of negligence law is where the battle-lines have been drawn.

As the wide variety of English and extra-jurisdictional case law analysed in later chapters of this book demonstrates, the innovative and imaginative arguments mounted by non-patients and third parties, are falling on some receptive judicial ears. No other aspect of HCP liability threatens to engulf medical insurance funds quite like this developing area of tort. Although successful English cases in this area remain something of a scarce commodity, case law from those other jurisdictions which share similar negligence principles with England demonstrate that the boundaries of liability are perceptibly shifting—partly because of the greater willingness of some courts to find a necessary nexus between defendant HCP and the claimant, to construe legal and public policy in favour of so finding, and so to uphold a duty of care.

Given the paucity of successful English case law to date in which a non-patient has successfully recovered against a HCP, it must be said that, as a general rule, HCPs do **not** owe a duty of care to non-patients/third parties. Some English commentators have downplayed the possibility of such suits in English law, with Khan *et al* remarking, for example, that any notion that a duty of care may be directly owed by a HCP to a third party by reason of a patient's acts or omissions 'is stated with the utmost caution, since the significant authorities to support it are almost exclusively foreign'.[118] However, by means of either directly precedential English authorities or cases of interest from jurisdictions which share the English common law's principles of negligence-based liability, numerous exceptions have been created to the general rule, and in this author's view, these exceptional circumstances are likely to be litigated further in English courts in the future.

In that sense, it is doubtful whether English law will ever steer the law back to a simpler age when Lord Diplock's statement in *Sidaway*[119] was a truer representation of HCP liability than it is today. The prospect of HCPs' liability towards claimants of whose identities, or even existence, they may have no direct knowledge, is surely an alarming and controversial one. Clearly, an increasingly-sophisticated analysis is now needed, in order to answer Lord Atkin's (paraphrased) question: 'Just who *is* the healthcare professional's neighbour in law these days?'.

ENDNOTES

[1]　*Donoghue v Stevenson* [1932] AC 562 (HL) 580.

[2]　Insofar as English literature is concerned, the topic is covered to some extent as part of excellent specialist medical monographs, e.g., M Jones, *Medical Negligence* (4th edn, Sweet & Maxwell, 2008), paras 2–071– 2–204; 'Duties in Contract and Tort', in A Grubb, J Laing and J McHale (eds), *Principles of Medical Law* (3rd edn, OUP, Oxford, 2010), ch 3, which chapter the author updated for the revised edition; M Stauch, K Wheat and J Tingle, *Text, Cases and Materials on Medical Law* (5th edn, Routledge Cavendish, London, 2006) 286–90; M Khan, M Robson and K Swift, *Clinical Negligence* (2nd edn, Cavendish Publishing, London, 2002); I Kennedy and A Grubb, *Medical Law* (3rd edn, Butterworths, London, 2000) 369–92. However, these treatments are a small part of a much larger canvas of coverage in those books, and cannot be, and do not purport to be, an exhaustive and comparative consideration of the issue. See, too, for earlier

and thoughtful academic treatment of the issue: K de Haan, 'My Patient's Keeper: Liability of Medical Practitioners for Negligent Injuries to Third Parties' (1986) 2 *PN* 86. In addition, the topic is considered as part of a wider context of third party claims generally, in the insightful work by: C McIvor, *Third Party Liability in Tort* (Hart Publishing, Oxford, 2006).

3   *K v Secretary of State for the Home Dept* [2002] EWCA Civ 775, (2002) 152 NLJ 917, [24].

4   *Phase Three Properties Ltd v 529952 Ontario Ltd* (1996), 63 ACWS (3d) 192 (Ont Gen Div) [57], contrasting the position of engineers.

5   *Islington LBC v University College London Hospital NHS Trust* [2004] EWHC 1754 (QB) [37].

6   Refer to pp 381–91.

7   [1985] AC 871 (HL) 890. In one of the non-patient cases considered later in this book, it was subsequently pointed out, by Lord Bingham in *JD v East Berkshire Community Health NHS Trust* [2005] UKHL 23, [2005] 2 AC 373, [46], that Lord Diplock's was an obiter statement, and that no other member of the House expressly agreed with it.

8   (1998) 39 BMLR 35 (CA) 45.

9   In Malaysia, e.g.: *Foo Fio Na v Dr Soo Fook Mun* [2007] 1 MLJ 593, [2006] MLJU 518 (Federal Court of Malaysia (Appeal Court)) [24] ('the duty of care owed by a doctor arises out of his relationship with his patient. Without the doctor and patient relationship, there is no duty on the part of the doctor to diagnose, advise and treat his patient'). In Singapore, e.g.: *Ju v See Tho Kai Yin* [2005] SGHC 140, [2005] 4 SLR 96, [87] ('It would place an onerous and unfair burden on medical practitioners and specialist alike, if the law was to decree that their duty of care to patients began even before the first consultation, and extended to cover telephone advice and/or opinions sought by callers who may not even become their patients later'). In Texas, e.g.: *Edinburg Hospital Authority v Trevino*, 941 SW 2d 76, 81 (Tex 1997) ('[a] physician's primary duty is to the patient, not to the patient's relatives').

10   [2001] 2 AC 619 (HL) 671 (emphasis added).

11   *Healey v Lakeridge Health Corp* (2006), 38 CPC (6th) 145 (Ont SCJ) [69].

12   The formal doctor–patient relationship was described in: *R v Bateman* [1925] All ER Rep 45 (CCA) 48 (Lord Hewart CJ) (if a doctor 'holds himself out as possessing special skill and knowledge, and he is consulted, as possessing such skill and knowledge, by or on behalf of a patient, he owes a duty to the patient to use due caution in undertaking the treatment. If he accepts the responsibility and undertakes the treatment and the patient submits to his direction and treatment accordingly, he owes a duty to the patient to use diligence, care, knowledge, skill and caution in administering the treatment'). Generally speaking, a GP's patients, and the GP's obligations thereto, are determined by the Terms of Service contained in the National Health Service (General Medical Services Contracts) Regulations 2004, SI 2004/291. See, further: 'Duties in Contract and Tort', in A Grubb, J Laing and J McHale (eds), *Principles of Medical Law* (3rd edn, OUP, Oxford, 2010) [3.28]–[3.34].

13   Particularly, to the decision in *Tarasoff v The Regents of the University of California*, 17 Cal 3d 425, 551 P 2d 334, 131 Cal Rptr 14 (Cal 1976).

14   Strike-out powers, contained in r 3.4(2)(a) of the Civil Procedure Rules, permit a claim to be struck out without a full trial, on the basis that even if the claimants were able to prove all of the facts which they allege (the truth of which is assumed at the strike-out hearing), those claimants could not establish a cause of action.

15   As evident, e.g., in: *Robertson v Adigbite* [2000] BCSC 1189, 2 CCLT (3d) 120 (SC) [67]–[71].

16   B Markesinis, *Foreign Law and Comparative Methodology* (Hart Publishing, Oxford, 1997) 204.

17   *Islington LBC v University College London Hospital NHS Trust* [2005] EWCA Civ 596, [1].

18   *ibid*, [5].

19   e.g.: *Partington v Wandsworth LBC* (QB, 3 Nov 1989) (autistic patient on an outing from hospital pushed over elderly stranger in street, breaking non-patient's wrist; duty of care by hospital to non-patient was common ground, *viz*, a duty 'to take reasonable care to prevent her from injuring her fellow citizens'); *Holgate v Lancashire Mental Hosp Board, Gill and Robertson* [1937] 4 All ER 19 (Liverpool Summer Assizes) (duty of care assumed; no breach made out). Both of these cases are among those considered in Chapter 3.

20   On the basis that no genuine issue for trial existed.

[21] On the basis that there was no reasonable cause of action disclosed on the face of the pleadings, a tactic that was successful, e.g., in: *Goodwill v British Pregnancy Advisory Service* [1996] 1 WLR 1397, (1996) 31 BMLR 83 (CA).

[22] As occurred, e.g., in: *Islington LBC v University College London Hospital NHS Trust* [2005] EWCA Civ 596.

[23] C McIvor, *Third Party Liability in Tort* (Hart Publishing, Oxford, 2006) 1.

[24] As in, e.g.: *Bakker v Van Santen* [2003] ABQB 804, [56], [60].

[25] *Paxton v Ramji* [2008] ONCA 697, (2008), 299 DLR (4th) 614, [58].

[26] In Australia: *Harvey v PD* [2004] NSWCA 97, (2004) 59 NSWLR 639, [22] ('This appeal therefore raises a number of difficult questions, not so far directly dealt with at appellate level in Australia'). In Canada: *Bakker v Van Santen* [2003] ABQB 804, [57].

[27] As occurred in: *Ahmed v Stefaniu* (2006), 275 DLR (4th) 101 (Ont CA). In *Healey v Lakeridge Health Corp* (2006), 38 CPC (6th) 145 (Ont SCJ) [71], Cullity J noted: 'In *Ahmed*, proximity must have been found at trial between the psychiatrist and the [non-patient] patient's sister but the Court of Appeal was careful to exclude that finding from the ambit of its decision').

[28] *Hill v Chief Constable of West Yorkshire* [1989] AC 53 (HL) (no duty); *Osman v Ferguson* [1993] 4 All ER 344 (CA), and later: *Osman v UK* (1998) 5 EHRR 293 (no duty); *Alexandrou v Oxford* [1993] 4 All ER 328 (CA) (no duty); *Brooks v Metropolitan Police Commr* [2005] UKHL 24, [2005] 1 WLR 1495 (HL) (no duty); *Smith v Chief Constable of Sussex Police; Van Colle v Chief Constable of Hertfordshire* [2008] UKHL 50 (no duty).

[29] *Home Office v Dorset Yacht Co Ltd* [1970] AC 1004 (HL) (duty).

[30] *Surrey CC v McManus* [2001] EWCA Civ 691 (no duty).

[31] *K v Secretary of State for the Home Dept* [2002] EWCA Civ 775 (no duty).

[32] *Barrett v Enfield LBC* [2001] 2 AC 550 (HL) (duty).

[33] *Mitchell v Glasgow CC* [2009] UKHL 11, [2009] 1 AC 874 (HL) (no duty).

[34] The Hon D Ipp (Chairman) *et al*, *Review of the Law of Negligence* (Sep 2002).

[35] *ibid*, [8.36].

[36] L Skene, *Law and Medical Practice: Rights, Duties, Claims and Defences* (2nd edn, Butterworths, Sydney, 2004) 219.

[37] European Convention for the Protection of Human Rights and Fundamental Freedoms 1950 (as set out in Sch 1 to the Human Rights Act 1998), in force Oct 2000.

[38] I Steele, 'Public Law Liability—A Common Law Solution?' (2005) 64 *CLJ* 543, 543.

[39] Section 6(3) provides: 'In this section, "public authority" includes—(a) a court or tribunal, and (b) any person certain of whose functions are functions of a public nature, but does not include either House of Parliament or a person exercising functions in connection with proceedings in Parliament.'

[40] e.g.: J Wright, *Tort Law and Human Rights* (Hart Publishing, Oxford, 2001) 21–33; D Beyleveld and S Pattinson, 'Horizontal Applicability and Horizontal Effect' (2002) 118 *LQR* 623; H Wade, 'Horizons of Horizontality' (2000) 116 *LQR* 217; M Hunt, 'The "Horizontal Effect" of the Human Rights Act' [1998] *Public Law* 423. Lord Rodger has described the so-called 'horizontal effect' of the Convention as 'controversial': *Wilson v First County Trust Ltd (No 2)* [2003] UKHL 40, [2003] 4 All ER 97, [174], and Lord Walker has called the whole issue of the HRA's 'horizontal effect' 'the subject of enormous academic interest when the HRA had been enacted ... Since then this topic has been overtaken by others, and the law may still have some way to go before it is fully developed': *Doherty v Birmingham CC* [2008] UKHL 57, [2009] AC 367, [99].

[41] As occurred in: *Rabone v Pennine Care NHS Trust* [2009] EWHC 1827 (QB); *Savage v South Essex Partnership NHS Foundation Trust* [2008] UKHL 74, [2009] 1 AC 681.

[42] But for this Act, the patient's claim against the NHS or its staff would be extinguished at common law.

[43] As discussed by Lord Scott in *Savage v South Essex Partnership NHS Foundation Trust* [2008] UKHL 74, [2009] 1 AC 681 (HL) [3].

[44] R Mulheron, 'Patient Deaths, Medical Negligence, and Article 2 of the Convention: Some Emerging Themes' [forthcoming, 2010, and co-authored with M Amos].

45 As quoted from, e.g., *Healey v Lakeridge Health Corp* (2006), 38 CPC (6th) 145 (Ont SCJ) [41]–[42] (Cullity J).

46 G Robertson, 'A View of the Future: Emerging Developments in Health Care Liability' in 'Visions' [2008] *Health LJ (Special Edn)* 11.

47 The United States' federal action is contained in r 23 of the Federal Rules of Civil Procedure (US). Although the US is often perceived as the home of the class action, class actions originated in England, in the 12th century, by virtue of the compulsory joinder rule: as discussed, e.g., in: Ontario LRC, *Report on Class Actions* (1982) 5–6, 8; W Weiner and D Szyndrowski, 'The Class Action from the English Bill of Peace to Federal Rule of Civil Procedure 23: Is There is a Common Thread?' (1987) 8 *Whittier L Rev* 935; S Yeazell, *From Medieval Group Litigation to the Modern Class Action* (Yale Uni Press, New Haven, 1098); Z Chafee, 'Bills of Peace with Multiple Parties' (1932) 45 *Harvard L Rev* 1297.

48 Australia's federal action is contained in Pt IVA of the Federal Court of Australia Act 1976 (Aus). Inserted by s 3 of the Federal Court of Australia Amendment Act 1991, and commenced operation on 4 Mar 1992.

49 Canadian provincial actions are typically termed as either 'class proceedings' or 'class actions'. The first of the common law provincial regimes to be introduced was Ontario's: Class Proceedings Act 1992, SO 1992, c 6.

50 For discussion of the North American and Australian class action regimes, see, e.g.: R Mulheron, *The Class Action in Common Law Legal Systems: A Comparative Perspective* (Hart Publishing, Oxford, 2004) ch 1.

51 A wide variety of reasons as to why class members do not opt in were elicited as part of the author's legal and empirical study: R Mulheron, *Reform of Collective Redress in England and Wales: A Perspective of Need* (A Research Paper for the Civil Justice Council of England and Wales, 2008) ch 7, available full-text at: <http://www.civiljusticecouncil.gov.uk/files/collective_redress.pdf>.

52 Reference to 'England' and 'English', in this context, encompasses reference to 'Wales' and 'Welsh' too, as the Civil Procedure Act 1997, and the rules promulgated thereunder, apply to both jurisdictions alike.

53 Contained in Pt 19.III, rr 19.10–19.15, of the Civil Procedure Rules (CPR), and implemented in May 2000. A list of the GLO's certified (permitted to go forth in the group context) to date are available at: <http://www.hmcourts-service.gov.uk/cms/150.htm>.

54 CPR 19.13(b), 19.15(1).

55 The Nationwide Organ Retention Group Litigation Order (GLO No 9); and the Royal Liverpool Children's Hospital Group Litigation Order (GLO No 2).

56 Kerr/North Yorkshire Group Litigation Order (GLO No 3).

57 See, for the author's publications in this area: *The Class Action in Common Law Legal Systems: A Comparative Perspective* (Hart Publishing, Oxford, 2004); 'The Case for an Opt-out Class Action for European Member States: A Legal and Empirical Analysis' (2009) 15 *Columbia J of European Law* 409; 'Building Blocks and Design Points for an Opt-out Class Action' [2008] *JPIL* 308; 'Antitrust Litigation: A White Paper Tinged with Green?' *Brussels Agenda*, May 2008 (the 'Viewpoint' contribution); 'Justice Enhanced: Framing an Opt-Out Class Action for England' (2007) 70 *MLR* 550; 'Some Difficulties with Group Litigation Orders—and Why a Class Action is Superior' (2005) 24 *CJQ* 40; and 'From Representative Rule to Class Action: Steps rather than Leaps' (2005) 24 *CJQ* 424; *Reform of Collective Redress in England and Wales: A Perspective of Need* (Research Paper for submission to the Civil Justice Council, Feb 2008).

58 *Improving Access to Justice Through Collective Actions: Developing a More Efficient Procedure for Collective Actions: Final Report* (Civil Justice Council, Dec 2008). The author was a contributing author to this report.

59 *The Government's Response to the Civil Justice Council's Report: 'Improving Access to Justice through Collective Actions'* (Ministry of Justice, Jul 2009). See, especially, the Executive Summary, p 3, second bullet point.

60 *Viz,* the Financial Services Bill, introduced into the House of Commons on 19 Nov 2009. For background information provided by HM Treasury, together with links to the Bill, see: <http://www.hm-treasury.gov.uk/fin_bill_index.htm>. The opt-out regime is contained in cll 18–25 of the Bill. For further updated

information about the Bill's progress, see the relevant Parliamentary website: <http://services.parliament.uk/bills/2009-10/financialservices.html>.

[61] See the text of the Hippocratic Oath, reproduced at: <http://users.hal-pc.org/~ollie/hippocratic.oath.html>.

[62] General Medical Council, *Good Medical Practice* (2006) (updated Mar 2009), available full-text at: <http://www.gmc-uk.org/guidance/good_medical_practice.asp>. According to the GMC, '*Good Medical Practice* sets out the principles and values on which good practice is founded; these principles together describe medical professionalism in action. The guidance is addressed to doctors, but it is also intended to let the public know what they can expect from doctors.'

[63] *ibid*, [1].

[64] *ibid*, [2]–[3].

[65] [1990] 2 AC 1 (HL) (also known as *F v West Berkshire HA*).

[66] [1981] 1 WLR 1421 (CA).

[67] See discussion of the patient focus in such cases in, e.g.: *Airedale NHS Trust v Bland* [1993] AC 789 (HL) 858.

[68] P Case, 'Confidence Matters: The Rise and Fall of Informational Autonomy in Medical Law' (2003) 11 *Med L Rev* 208, (accessed online, no pp available).

[69] Although Case notes that some cases do appear to leave open the question as to whether third party interests, such as those of the patient's sexual partner, or family members, could 'ever legitimately play a part in the best interests calculation', citing, e.g.: *Re A (Medical Treatment: Male Sterilisation)* [2000] Lloyd's Rep Med 87 (CA); *Re Y (Mental Incapacity: Bone Marrow Transplant)* (1997) 35 BMLR 111 (Fam).

[70] [1993] AC 789 (HL) 896 (Lord Mustill).

[71] [1990] 2 AC 1 (HL) 83 (Lord Jauncey).

[72] [1998] 2 FLR 1124 (Fam) (Holman J).

[73] Department of Health (Sir Liam Donaldson), *Making Amends: A Consultation Paper Setting Out Proposals for Reforming the Approach to Clinical Negligence in the NHS* (A Report by the Chief Medical Officer, Jun 2003).

[74] Families of neurologically-impaired babies were the subject of specific recommendations in the report, concerning entitlements under the prospective NHS Redress Scheme: *ibid*, 16, and Recommendation 2, 120–21.

[75] A Sutton, 'The New Genetics and Traditional Hippocratic Medicine' in P Doherty and A Sutton (eds), *Man Made Man* (Open Air Press, 1998) 61, cited in: P Case, 'Confidence Matters: The Rise and Fall of Informational Autonomy in Medical Law' (2003) 11 *Med L Rev* 208, fn 15.

[76] As in: *Prosko v Regina Qu'Appelle Regional HA* [2008] SKQB 144, (2008), 316 Sask R 164 (QB).

[77] As in: *Reilly v Merseyside HA* (1994) 23 BMLR 26 (CA).

[78] R Mulheron, 'Medical Examinations for Insurance, Employment and Litigation: An Evolving Liability of the Health Professionals towards Examinee and Client' [forthcoming, 2010], discussing English cases such as: *Re N* [1999] Lloyd's Rep Med 257 (CA); *Kapfunde v Abbey National plc* [1998] EWCA Civ 535, (1998) 45 BMLR 176 (CA); *Baker v Kaye* (1996) 39 BMLR 12 (QBD); *R v Croydon HA* (1997) 40 BMLR 40 (CA); *Multiple Claimants v MOD* [2003] EWHC 1134 (QB); *Rice v Secretary of State for Trade and Industry* [2006] EWHC 1257 (QB); and significant cases from elsewhere, which purport to rely upon, or to distinguish, English authorities in this area, e.g.: *Johnson v State Farm Mutual Automobile Ins Co* (1998), 81 ACWS (3d) 547 (Ont Gen Div); *Lowe v Guarantee Co of North America* (2005), 80 OR (3d) 222 (CA); *Lynch v Appell* (2001), 110 ACWS (3d) 204 (SCJ); *Ho Ying Wai v Keliston Marine (Far East) Ltd* [2002] HKCU 646, [2002] HKCFI 542 and 543.

[79] As in, e.g.: *Cook v Bradford Community Health NHS Trust* [2002] EWCA Civ 1616; *Buck v Nottinghamshire Healthcare NHS Trust* [2006] EWCA Civ 1576.

[80] As in: *Watson v British Boxing Board of Control Ltd* [2001] QB 1134 (CA) (professional boxer W suffered serious brain damage from injuries sustained during final round of professional fight; Board's rules required three doctors and ambulance in attendance; Board owed W a duty of care, despite the fact that the Board neither provided the medical care nor promoted the fight; duty was to take reasonable care to ensure

that personal injuries already sustained during fight were properly treated by provision of appropriate and immediate ringside medical assistance; and to make regulations imposing the duty to achieve these results). For discussion, see, e.g.: R Oppenheim, 'The "Mosaic" of Tort Law: The Duty of Care Question' [2003] *JPIL* 151, 155; H Opie, 'Negligence Liability of Rule-making Bodies in Sport' (2002) 2 *Intl Sports L Rev* 60, 60, contrasting *Watson* with the contrary result reached in: *Agar v Hyde* (2001) 201 CLR 552 (HCA) (re the rugby union governing authority, and the rules governing scrums, where two players suffered serious neck injuries); N Block, 'Case Comment' (2001) 1 *Intl Sports L Rev* 168; B Gardiner, 'Liability for Sporting Injuries' [2008] *JPIL* 16. Applied, in the context of a fatal accident at a motor-racing event, in: *Wattleworth v Goodwood* [2004] EWHC 140, [2004] PIQR P25 (QB).

[81] As in: *Farraj v King's Healthcare NHS Trust* [2006] EWHC 1228, (2006) 90 BMLR 21 (QB) (duty of care owed by laboratory CSL to Mr and Mrs F re mis-diagnosis that their son did not suffer from beta-thalassaemia major, a severe hereditary blood disease). For later proceedings determining apportionment between hospital and CSL, see: *Farraj v King's Healthcare NHS Trust* [2008] EWHC 2468 (QB). For comment, see, e.g.: S Lindsay, 'Wrongful Birth, Clinical Negligence, and Third Party Laboratory' [2006] *JPIL* C191, C193–C194.

[82] As in: *Godden v Kent and Medway Strategic HA* [2004] EWHC 1629, [2004] Lloyd's Rep Med 521 (QB) (G and other former patients of GP were indecently assaulted or negligently treated between 1993–2000; GP subsequently struck off, convicted of indecent assault and sentenced to four years' imprisonment; G argued that health authority owed patients a duty to monitor adequately all contracted GP's, or take reasonable steps to ensure that all contracted GP's within their area provided a safe and/or competent medical service for patients, or act upon any complaints made and/or concerns raised in respect of a contracted GP in its area; employees of the health authority *did* arguably owe the patients a duty of care to act on information received concerning the risk posed by the GP). For a Canadian equivalent, see: *McClelland v Stewart* [2004] BCCA 458, (2004), 245 DLR (4th) 162, leave to appeal denied: (2005), 220 BCAC 318 (SCC) (claimants, 19 women, sued College of Physicians and Surgeons of BC in negligence for failure to investigate allegations against a GP that he allegedly committed sexual assaults of patients during 1969–96 and to take appropriate action; strike-out application failed). Hence, since *McClelland*, Canadian regulators can no longer rest easy, thinking that they are immune from liability in negligence, and regulators *may* owe a duty of care to individual members of the public: L Mrozinksi, 'Monetary Remedies for Administrative Law Errors' (2009) 22 *Canadian J of Administrative Law and Practice* 133, 155–56.

[83] *Clunis v Camden and Islington HA* [1998] QB 978 (CA) (C knifed and killed another at Finsbury Park tube station; C pleaded guilty to manslaughter on the grounds of diminished responsibility and sued defendant health authority, claiming that psychiatrist should have realised that he was in urgent need of treatment/dangerous, and that, had he been given careful and proper treatment, he would not have committed manslaughter and would not have been subject to the prolonged detention which he faced; no duty of care owed to C; no duty owed). Cf: *K v Central and NorthWest London Mental Health NHS Trust* [2008] EWHC 1217, [2008] PIQR P19 (QB), in which King J held that *Clunis* could not be regarded as the 'final chapter' on this type of claim: at [55]–[58].

[84] See, e.g., in NZ: *Ellis v Counties Manukau District Health Board* [2006] NZHC 826, [2007] 1 NZLR 196 (HC) (psychiatric patient killed his father following release from in-patient psychiatric care; alleged that defendant Health Board owed him a common law duty of care to properly assess, treat and, if necessary, detain him against his wishes to prevent him from causing harm to himself and others; no such duty of care was owed). In Australia: *Hunter Area Health Service v Presland* [2005] NSWCA 33, (2005) 63 NSWLR 22 (Sheller & Santow JJA, Spigelman CJ dissenting) (psychiatric patient assessed and treated by defendant hospital staff, discharged into brother's custody, and six hours later, killed brother's fiancée; alleged that had he been detained and competently treated, he would not have committed the homicide and would have ultimately spent less time in involuntary detention; case succeeded at trial and awarded $369,300, but this was overturned on appeal, by majority). For discussion, see, e.g.: K Peterson, 'Where is the Line to be Drawn? Medical Negligence and Insanity in *Hunter Area Health Service v Presland*' (2006) 28 *Sydney L Rev* 181. As McIlwraith and Madden note, subsequent to *Hunter*, the Civil Liability Act 2002 (NSW) was amended, by the insertion of s 54A, which provision limited damages if a loss

resulted from a serious offence committed by a mentally ill person: J McIlwraith and B Madden, *Health Care and the Law* (4th edn, Thomson Law Book Co, Sydney, 2006) 182.

[85] On this point, see, e.g.: *Hatch v Central Sydney Area Health Service* [1999] NSWCA 168; *Steward v Extendicare Ltd* [1986] 4 WWR 559, (1986) 48 Sask R 86 (QB); *H(M) v Bederman* (1995), 27 CCLT (2d) 152 (Ont Gen Div); *C (CL) v Lions Gate Hospital* (2001), 95 BCLR (3d) 347 (SC); *McConnell v Lemky* [1992] BCJ No 596 (SC); *S v Midcentral District Health Board (No 2)* [2004] NZAR 342 (HC).

[86] *Yearworth v North Bristol NHS Trust* [2009] EWCA Civ 37, [14].

[87] *Burton v Islington HA; De Martell v Merton and Sutton HA* [1993] QB 204 (CA).

[88] Congenital Disabilities (Civil Liability) Act 1976, s 1(2), and s 4(2).

[89] S Pegalis, *The American Law of Medical Malpractice*, vol 1 (3rd edn, Thomson West, Eagan MN, 2005) 253.

[90] See, e.g.: *Nold v Binyon*, 272 Kan 87, 111 (Kan 2001); *Draper v Jasionowski*, 858 A 2d 1141, 1148 (NJ Super 2004), noting that it is recognised in legislation too that 'an infant *in utero* is as much a "patient" as the expectant mother'.

[91] As occurred, e.g., in: *Burton v Islington HA* [1993] QB 204 (CA) (Tina Burton injured by dilation and curettage procedure performed on her mother when mother was about 6 weeks pregnant; no pregnancy test carried out beforehand).

[92] For recent relevant Canadian authority, see: *Paxton v Ramji* [2008] ONCA 697, (2008), 299 DLR (4th) 614 (mother treated with acne drug Accutane, and foetal abnormalities, a risk of such medication, occurred to the claimant child, born alive; no duty of care owed).

[93] As occurred, e.g., in: *de Martell v Merton and Sutton HA* [1993] QB 204 (CA) (Christopher de Martell injured during his mother's labour, where mother underwent an attempted forceps delivery and a caesarean section).

[94] See, e.g.: M Jones, *Medical Negligence* (4th edn, Sweet & Maxwell, London, 2008) 145–49; S Rodgers, 'A Mother's Loss is the Price of Parenthood: The Failure of Tort Law to Recognize Birth as a Compensable Reproductive Injury' in Rodgers *et al* (eds), *Critical Torts* (Lexisnexis Canada Inc, Toronto, 2009) 161–79. For English law reform discussion: EWLC, *Report on Injuries to Unborn Children* (Rep 60, 1974).

[95] Rodgers, *ibid*, fn 23.

[96] In other jurisdictions, see, e.g., in South Africa: *Stewart v Botha* [2008] 1 LRC 370 ((HC (Cape of Good Hope Provincial Div)) (claim barred), *Friedman v Glicksman* 1996 (1) SA 1134 (W) (claim barred). In Australia: *Harriton v Stephens* [2006] HCA 15, (2006) 226 CLR 52 (HCA) (claim barred, by majority). In Canada: *Bovingdon v Hergott* (2008), 88 OR (3d) 641 (Ont CA) (action barred), *Mickle v Salvation Army Grace Hospital* (1998), 166 DLR (4th) 743 (action barred); *Arndt v Smith* (1995), 126 DLR (4th) 487 (BCCA), rev'd [1997] 2 SCR 539, (1997), 148 DLR (4th) 48 (SCC) (claim abandoned). In Scotland: *P's Curator Bonis v Criminal Injuries Compensation Board* 1997 SLT 1180 (OH). In Singapore: *Ju v See Tho Kai Yin* [2005] 4 SLR 96 (HC) (claim barred). In France: *Perruche* (Cass ass plén, 17 Nov 2000). America authorities have both allowed (e.g., *Procanik v Cillo*, 478 A 2d 755 (1984)) and disallowed (e.g., *Speck v Finegold*, 408 A 2d 496 (1979)) 'wrongful life' claims by disabled children.

[97] Congenital Disabilities (Civil Liability) Act 1976, s 1(2)(b). The Act only applies to children born on or after 22 July 1976. Prior to that, the common law applies.

[98] *McKay v Essex AHA* [1982] 1 QB 1166 (CA). The Congenital Disabilities (Civil Liability) Act 1976, *ibid*, did not apply to the child's claim in this case, as she was born on 15 August 1975.

[99] For relevant commentary, see, e.g.: P Beaumont, 'Wrongful Life and Wrongful Birth' in S McLean, *Contemporary Issues in Law, Medicine and Ethics* (Dartmouth, Aldershot, 1996) ch 6; A Morris and S Saintier, 'To Be or Not to Be: Is That the Question? Wrongful Life and Misconceptions' (2003) 11 *Med L Rev* 167; P Dimopoulos and M Bagaric, 'The Moral Status of Wrongful Life Claims' (2003) 32 *Common Law World Rev* 35; M Jones, *Medical Negligence* (4th edn, Sweet & Maxwell, London, 2008) 149–53; D Stretton, 'The Birth Torts: Damages for Wrongful Birth and Wrongful Life' (2005) 10 *Deakin L Rev* 319; S Todd, 'Wrongful Conception Wrongful Birth and Wrongful Life' (2005) 27 *Sydney L Rev* 525.

[100] Within the meaning of that term in s 6(3)(b) of the Human Rights Act 1998. On the other hand, a privately-run care home was not carrying on a function of a 'public nature' in *YL v Birmingham CC* [2007] UKHL 27, [2007] 3 WLR 112 (HL).

101 *Tarariyeva v Russia* (2009) 48 EHRR 26 (App No 4353/03, 14 Dec 2006).

102 As discussed later in Chapter 10.

103 e.g., *Powell v UK* (2000) 30 EHRR CD 362 (ECtHR) (mis-diagnosis of Addison's disease; art 2 claim failed).

104 e.g., *Dodov v Bulgaria* (2008) 47 EHRR 41 (ECtHR) (nursing home patient disappeared from home, never seen again; claim succeeded, in respect of art 2's investigative obligation).

105 [2008] UKHL 74, [2009] AC 681 (art 2 claim failed).

106 [2009] EWHC 1827 (QB), decided 23 July 2009 (art 2 claim failed).

107 D Pannick and A Lester, 'The Impact of the Human Rights Act on Private Law: The Knight's Move' (2000) 116 *LQR* 380, 382, and see too, by the same authors (eds): *Human Rights Law and Practice* (2nd edn, Butterworths, London, 2004) 26, 48–53. Also: C McIvor, 'The Positive Duty of the Police to Protect Life' (2008) 24 *PN* 27, 34; J Wright, *Tort Law and Human Rights* (Hart Publishing, Oxford, 2001) ch 3.

108 M Lyons, 'Human Rights, Mental Health, Negligence and Mental Patients' [2009] *JPIL* C1, C3.

109 See, further: R Mulheron, 'Patient Deaths, Medical Negligence, and Article 2 of the Convention: Some Emerging Themes' [forthcoming, 2010, and co-authored with M Amos].

110 e.g., *White v Jones* [1995] 2 AC 207 (HL).

111 e.g., *Smith v Eric S Bush (a firm)* [1990] 1 AC 831 (HL).

112 e.g., *Spring v Guardian Ass plc* [1995] 2 AC 296 (HL).

113 e.g., *Gorham v British Telecommunications Ltd plc* [2000] EWCA Civ 234, [2000] 1 WLR 2129.

114 *W v Essex CC* [2001] 2 AC 592 (HL); *A and B v Essex CC* [2003] EWCA Civ 1848.

115 [2005] UKHL 23, [2005] 2 AC 373, [105] (Lord Rodger), citing: *Best v Samuel Fox & Co Ltd* [1952] AC 716 (HL) 734 (Lord Morton) ('it has never been the law of England that an invitor, who has negligently but unintentionally injured an invitee, is liable to compensate other persons who have suffered, in one way or another, as a result of the injury to the invitee ... the invitor is under no liability to compensate such persons, for he owes them no duty and may not even know of their existence').

116 [1999] EWCA Civ 1533, (1998) 39 BMLR 35, [37].

117 As expressed by Buxton LJ in: *Islington LBC v University College London Hospital NHS Trust* [2005] EWCA Civ 596, [42].

118 M Khan, M Robson and K Swift, *Clinical Negligence* (2nd edn, Cavendish Publishing, London, 2002) 82.

119 Note 7 above.

Chapter 2
Establishing Negligence in Novel Non-Patient Scenarios

A INTRODUCTION

One of the challenges in a book of this type is to consider whether there are universal themes and principles of liability which determine whether a HCP owes a duty to a non-patient, or whether the examples of non-patient liability constitute nothing more than a 'laundry list'.[1]

It is suggested in this chapter that the case law, both in England and elsewhere, is producing a number of common themes across different categories of non-patients, which can usefully form a framework for analysing decided cases to date, and for predicting the likely future outcome of non-patient cases yet to be brought. The discussion which ensues seeks to set out those common themes, as a backdrop for the chapters which follow.

B THE NEGLIGENCE ACTION IN THE CONTEXT OF NON-PATIENT CLAIMS

Where a claimant with a grievance against the HCP defendant is a non-patient, and regardless of whether he is claiming compensation for physical injury, for psychiatric injury, or for economic injury, he must establish the four requirements of the action in negligence, *viz*:

- that the HCP owed him a duty of care to avoid causing him the type of injury of which he complains;
- that the HCP breached the duty of care by falling below the standard of reasonable care which the law demands of a HCP who professes to exercise that particular skill or profession;
- that the breach by the HCP (whether it be an act or an omission) caused the particular damage complained of by the non-patient; and
- that the damage complained of by the non-patient is not too remote (unforeseeable) at law to be recoverable.

Undoubtedly, of these elements, establishing a duty of care at all—or, alternatively, establishing a duty of care which has, within its scope, a duty to avoid the particular injury complained of—has been the most problematical aspect of the non-patient claims discussed throughout this book.

In general terms, where a novel scenario giving rise to a pleaded duty of care is being considered (and claims by non-patients definitely fall within the 'novel' category), then there are three broad approaches or tests which have been outlined by the House of Lords[2] as the 'conceptual basis' for deciding whether a duty of care exists in particular circumstances. Adapting these to the non-patient scenario, these are:

   a. whether the three-fold test of foreseeability, proximity and 'fairness, justice and reasonableness' has been met (per the so-called *Caparo* test[3]);

   b. whether there has been an assumption of responsibility by the HCP towards the non-patient (and consequential reliance by that non-patient upon the HCP's conducting himself with due care and skill); and

   c. whether any duty owed by HCP to non-patient would be 'incremental' to previously-decided cases.

Of these tests, the *Caparo* tri-partite test is said[4] to be currently the most-favoured test for imposing a duty of care in novel scenarios—partly because of the structure that it provides, so as to 'make the analysis more easily intelligible'.[5] In the context of difficult third party claims in medical negligence, the English Court of Appeal has reiterated, in *Islington LBC v University College London Hospital NHS Trust*, that *Caparo's* is the correct approach.[6] However, given that the House of Lords has approved all three tests,[7] some courts since have felt compelled to deal with the 'assumption of responsibility' and 'incremental' tests too, both generally,[8] and in suits against HCPs that raised novel duty of care questions.[9] Indeed, one judge has said that 'it is reaching for the moon—and not required by authority', to expect that one 'single short abstract formulation' of when a duty of care arises could be framed.[10] With this in mind, later chapters will focus upon the analysis dictated by *Caparo*, but will reference the other two tests, as and where appropriate.

Unsurprisingly, this multiplicity of approaches to the duty of care question has drawn mixed academic commentary. On the one hand, Clerk and Lindsell have remarked that the tests are 'mutually supportive rather than exclusive in their application. Each may be used to check the provisional conclusion reached by application of the other approaches'.[11] On the other hand, Oppenheim is more critical, stating that it all 'give[s] rise to an impression of judicial smoke and mirrors in the determination of whether a duty of care is owed. The effect is a marked degree of uncertainty as to the boundaries of when a duty of care is or is not recognised.'[12]

In reality, the tests provide convenient reference points, or 'high-level' principles, of what a court will search for, in order to fix a defendant with liability, but none of them is particularly helpful as it stands. Each of the three tests is said to 'operate at a high level of abstraction', and that '[w]hat matters is how and by reference to what lower-level factors they are interpreted in practice', in a given fact situation.[13] In truth, without such detail, the tests verge upon meaningless phraseology. To that end, the following sections in this chapter outline, in summary form, these 'lower-level factors' which have been particularly important in assessing whether a HCP has owed a duty of care to a non-patient or third party. These factors will be referenced in later chapters, as and where appropriate, but it may be convenient to gather the most significant of them together, at the outset.

C   THE LEGAL FRAMEWORK FOR ESTABLISHING A DUTY OF CARE: SOME PRELIMINARY COMMENTS

1. The relevant application of the *Caparo* test to non-patient suits

According to the classic test stipulated by Lord Bridge in *Caparo Industries plc v Dickman*:

it is necessary to consider the matter not only by inquiring about *foreseeability* but also by considering the *nature of the relationship* between the parties; and to be satisfied that in all the circumstances it is *fair, just and reasonable* to impose a duty of care. Of course ... these three matters overlap with each other ..[14]

(a) Reasonable foreseeability of harm

As a first requirement, the non-patient must prove that a reasonable person in the HCP's position would have foreseen that injury of some type would, or would be likely to, be suffered by the non-patient, if the HCP did not exercise due care and skill.

Reasonable foreseeability is a rather ill-defined concept. Buxton LJ remarked, in *Islington LBC v University College London Hospital NHS Trust*, that it was a matter of 'fluidity or flexibility', and that '[t]he level of certainty required for an outcome to be deemed, after the event, to have been foreseeable is to a large extent a matter of impression'.[15] The threshold of what is 'foreseeable' is not determined on strict percentage probabilities, or even on a balance of probabilities assessment. As the House of Lords recently reiterated in a difficult duty of care scenario involving a third party claimant (but outside of the healthcare context),

> the concept of reasonable foreseeability embraced a wide range of degrees of possibility, from the highly probable to the possible but highly improbable. As the possible adverse consequences of carelessness increase in seriousness, so will a lesser degree of likelihood of occurrence suffice to satisfy the test of reasonable foreseeability.[16]

At the very least, anything that the HCP would dismiss as a risk of injury that was 'far-fetched' or 'fanciful' will not meet the foreseeability threshold.[17]

Notably, it is the *particular defendant* whose breach brought about the injury to the non-patient to whom the test of reasonable foreseeability must be applied. Should *that* defendant have reasonably foreseen that his act or omission would, or would be likely to, give rise to injury to the claimant? In *Islington LBC*,[18] it was a cardiac surgeon's secretary who informed the patient, Mrs J, that her operation was cancelled and that she should not recommence her medication. The secretary could not have foreseen the ramifications of the care which Mrs J would require, should she suffer a stroke. But what the secretary could reasonably foresee was not the issue here, because *she* was not the breaching party—the NHS Trust was:

> The failure in this case was not that, or simply that, of the secretary. The failure was an institutional one, in that University College Hospital [operated by the defendant NHS Trust] did not make proper arrangements for advising persons whose drug regime had been varied in anticipation of an operation and whose operation was then cancelled. The question is therefore what was foreseeable by the Trust.[19]

It follows, then, that in suits against HCPs, the particular defendant whose notional foresight has to be assessed 'possesses a significant degree of medical knowledge'[20] as to how injury can manifest in medical scenarios, and that, inevitably, makes the foreseeability component of *Caparo's* test easier for the non-patient to satisfy.

In fact, proving that the injury or loss (whether it be physical, psychiatric or economic) was reasonably foreseeable has **not**, typically, been a problem for non-patients/third parties. There has been the odd failure to surmount the first requirement of the *Caparo* test—e.g., in *Powell v Boldaz*,[21] the parents who suffered psychiatric illnesses following the death of their son as a result of a mis-diagnosis of Addison's disease were unable to prove that their injuries were reasonably foreseeable—but such cases are unusual.

(b) The role of proximity and public policy

By contrast, proving the requisite legal proximity between non-patient and HCP, and establishing that a duty to the non-patient to avoid the harm that befell him ought to be upheld as a matter of policy (that it is 'fair, just and reasonable' to impose such a duty) has been fraught with problems for non-patients. The law has to impose limits or boundaries, and these are effectively set by an application of the proximity and policy tests, which act as the limiting factors. It all makes for what appears, at times, to be a fluid and pragmatic (but, some would say, uncertain) approach.

There is a fair degree of overlap between *Caparo's* elements. Indeed, it has been said that they are 'merely facets of the same thing.'[22] For this reason, some of the factors identified in the following section may be listed as going to proximity, whereas some may prefer the view that they are matters of legal and public policy. Regardless, it is worth noting Ouseley LJ's comment that 'it may matter little under which particular heading the particular factors are posted. There is after all only one question: is there a duty of care? The three stages or tests overlap to a greater or lesser extent'.[23]

In cases involving difficult and new duty of care scenarios, it is impossible to identify a formula, or a common denominator, or a 'one-size-fits-all' approach, to the questions of proximity and policy. This has been oft-reiterated by senior appellate tribunals, and these sentiments are worth setting out in full, because of the importance which they have for the focus of this book as a whole:

> It has been said almost too frequently to require repetition that foreseeability of likely harm is not in itself a sufficient test of liability in negligence. Some further ingredient is invariably needed to establish the requisite proximity of relationship between plaintiff and defendant ... The nature of the ingredient will be found to vary in a number of different categories of decided cases (per the House of Lords in *Hill v Chief Constable of West Yorkshire Police*[24]).

> [the law can only provide] a framework, a more or less methodical way of tackling a problem ... Ultimately the exercise can only be a balancing one and the important object is that all relevant factors be weighed. There is no escape from the truth that, whatever formula be used, the outcome in a grey area case has to be determined by judicial judgment. Formulae can help to organise thinking but they cannot provide answers (per the New Zealand Court of Appeal in *South Pacific Manufacturing Co Ltd v New Zealand Security Consultants & Investigations Ltd* [25]).

> the concepts of proximity and fairness ... are not susceptible of any such precise definition as would be necessary to give them utility as practical tests, but amount in effect to little more than convenient labels to attach to the features of different specific situations which, on a detailed examination of all the circumstances, the law recognises pragmatically as giving rise to a duty of care of a given scope' and '[the concept of] proximity is a convenient expression [but] no more than a label which embraces not a definable concept but merely a description of circumstances (per the House of Lords in *Caparo Industries plc v Dickman*[26]).

> The failure of the law in general to compensate for injuries sustained by persons unconnected with the event [non-patients], precipitated by the defendant's negligence [the injury to the

patient, in our context], cannot ... be attributable to some arbitrary but unenunciated rule of 'policy' which draws a line as the outer boundary of the duty. Nor can it rationally be made to rest upon such inquiry being within the area of reasonable foreseeability. It must, it seems to me to be attributable simply to the fact that such persons are not, in contemplation of law, in a relationship of sufficient proximity or directness with the tortfeasor as to give rise to a duty of care ... the impracticability or unreasonableness of entertaining claims to the ultimate consequences of human activity, necessarily plays a part in the court's perception of what is sufficiently proximate (per *Alcock v Chief Constable of South Yorkshire Police*[27]).

Hence, whether a non-patient will ultimately recover against a HCP can be viewed as the ultimate exercise in judicial pragmatism and policy-setting. A few words about the non-patient's task in establishing the requisite proximity and policy elements of a duty of care may be helpful to set the context for the chapters which follow.

(c) The 'proximity basket'[28]

Probably the most difficult aspect of the non-patient's suit is whether there is a sufficient proximity or nexus—a close or direct relationship—between the HCP and the non-patient to justify imposing a duty on the former. Although it has been judicially said that proximity has 'an uncertain status'[29] and is a 'slippery word',[30] it has certainly proven effective in circumscribing the number of non-patients/third parties who have scrambled through the duty of care door in English jurisprudence. To put the point another way, in all third party cases, 'the nexus is not given, but has to be found.'[31]

When seeking to prove the requisite nexus or closeness between non-patient and HCP, various factors or 'ingredients' have emerged from the relevant case law discussed in later chapters. These are summarised, for convenience, in Table 2.1. Albeit that different weighting may be given to these various factors across different jurisdictions and fact scenarios, and that none of them is being put forward here as an absolute pre-requisite or unifying characteristic, for legal proximity between HCP and non-patient to be found, they have all proven to be of *some* relevance, as ingredients of proximity under the *Caparo* test.

One factor that has been raised and discounted as a proximity factor, at least in England, is the gravity of harm to the non-patient resulting from the HCP's breach. Say that the non-patient dies as a result of the HCP's negligence—that fact, of itself, does **not** supply a nexus, or relationship, between non-patient and HCP, sufficient to create a duty of care. This point has been made, both generally,[32] and in the context of a non-patient suit against a HCP,[33] on the basis that it would render a HCP 'the world's insurer against grave danger'.[34]

As a final point, in all non-patient claims against the HCP which involve a tri-partite relationship with a patient, the court is looking for the requisite nexus, or proximity, *between HCP and non-patient*. Hence, having regard to Figure 1.1,[35] it is the hypotenuse relationship which is crucial. The court may well have regard to factors along the other sides of the triangular relationship—as between patient and HCP, and as between patient and third party victim—but they will only be relevant insofar as they are used to establish a duty of care owed by the HCP to that non-patient claimant. In that regard, English law adopts a stricter position than has been evident, at times, in other jurisdictions. For example, where the California Supreme Court stated that 'the common law has traditionally imposed liability only if the [HCP] bears some special relationship *to the dangerous person [patient]* or to the potential victim [non-patient]',[36] the former of these two alternatives would **not** be sufficient in English law. The necessary 'close and direct relations' (to adopt the words of Lord Atkin in *Donoghue v Stevenson*[37]) between HCP

Table 2.1   Relevant factors determining proximity between HCP and non-patient

- what **degree of control** could the HCP exercise over the patient's actions towards the non-patient? For example, does the HCP control the physical space surrounding the patient and the non-patient? The lower the extent of control (or the complete absence of it), the less likely the requisite proximity will be found;
- what **warnings** could the HCP have reasonably provided to the non-patient directly to guard him against the harm that befell him? The HCP's inability to take feasible or practicable precautions, or to instigate medical practices and measures, to protect the non-patient from harm, will tend against a finding of proximity. On the other hand, if the HCP could reasonably have taken such precautions, then failure to do so enhanced the non-patient's **vulnerability**;
- does the HCP have crucial information about the patient, about which the non-patient knows nothing and cannot ascertain for himself from any other source, and which the HCP was in a position to pass on to the non-patient (i.e., **an information monopoly**)? If so, then the non-patient is in a vulnerable position, and proximity is enhanced; but if the non-patient could have ascertained the information himself, proximity with the HCP is less likely;
- was there a considerable time-lag between the alleged wrongdoing of the HCP and the harm caused to the non-patient by a patient's actions? If so, then lack of any **temporal proximity** may count against a sufficient nexus between HCP and non-patient;
- did the harm that befell the non-patient take place **remotely in geographic terms** from the HCP's province of control? That may militate against any proximity between HCP and non-patient;
- along a spectrum: is the **actual identity** of the non-patient known to the HCP? Or, is the **existence** of the non-patient known to the HCP, but his precise identity is unknown? Or, is the non-patient one of an identifiable class of persons known to the HCP? Or, is the non-patient merely a member of a general public? The further along this spectrum, the less likely that the requisite proximity will be found;
- as a matter of '**causal proximity**', has the HCP's breach towards the patient precluded a step which, had it occurred, would have almost certainly protected the non-patient from the harm that eventuated? The availability of that **intervening step** (so that not taking it enhanced the non-patient's **vulnerability**) can enhance a finding of proximity between HCP and non-patient;
- was the non-patient at '**special risk**' as a result of the HCP's breach, over and above the risk faced by the general public? If not (i.e., if the same measure of risk was faced by all, or a large cross-section of, the public), then the requisite proximity between HCP and non-patient is unlikely.

and non-patient is the one which 'counts' in the proximity analysis. This distinction between the softer American position and the stricter position under English common law was remarked upon in *Palmer v Tees HA*.[38]

(d) Relevant policy factors

As Lord Clyde has put it, the third policy element of the *Caparo* test—

has the advantage of flexibility, enabling the court to define the boundaries of claims for negligence in the light of new situations and the recognition that incremental growth may require to be controlled, albeit at the risk of some uncertainty at least in the prediction of the directions in which the law may develop.[39]

In somewhat less complimentary terms, some academic commentary has eviscerated the notion of policy. Lunney and Oliphant remark that this stage of the duty of care test 'can be regarded as the general repository for a miscellaneous set of policy arguments, undefined in nature and unlimited in number, which are invoked haphazardly and in an *ad hoc* fashion by the courts'.[40] Harlow is even less positive, describing the policy limb as 'a euphemistic way of describing virtually unstructured judicial discretion'.[41] Markesinis and Fedtke dismiss its utility altogether, describing the 'fair, just and reasonable' formula as 'meaningless'.[42] This impression must surely be enhanced by Buxton LJ's elliptical comment, in *Islington LBC v University College London Hospital NHS Trust*, that '"fair just and reasonable" is not to be read literally, nor is it to be read solely in the context of the relationship between the instant claimant and defendant. It still assumes ... that wider issues of policy may have to intervene.'[43] In other words, while it may appear entirely fair, just and reasonable for *that particular non-patient* to recover for his injury, his entitlement may be forsaken because of what other types of damaged non-patients could seek to press through the doorway, over time.

Policy has a tendency to change over time too. No duty may be owed for public policy reasons by, say, the police, in a suit in 1989,[44] whereas in 2008, the House of Lords can admit that those reasons 'do not all stand up to critical examination today'.[45] Public policy can be something of a moving feast.

A long line of leading English cases, in which novel duty scenarios have arisen for consideration, have thrown up various policy factors favouring, or precluding, a duty of care.[46] In many respects, they serve as 'potent counter-considerations' to the rule that 'every wrong should have a remedy'.[47] Several of them have been adapted to the HCP–non-patient context. As the Supreme Court of Texas put it (when considering whether doctors were liable in negligence to a deceased driver killed by their epileptic patient who suffered an attack while driving), the various decisions concerning HCP liability towards non-patients conveniently 'illuminate the competing considerations' that arise in determining if a duty should be recognised under tort law.[48] As the Texas court hinted, the outcome will depend upon a balancing exercise, and may be unpredictable for that reason. It is also important to note that, just as with any other defendant, HCPs may owe separate duties of care to more than one person—that is legally acceptable, provided that the duties are not irreconcilable and conflicting.

A non-exhaustive sample of policy arguments which have been framed in third party suits in English law are summarised, for convenience, in Table 2.2.

These various policy factors will be considered, as and where appropriate, throughout later chapters. Obviously, the huge array of them gives an early indication as to why courts, in England and elsewhere, have had ample grounds upon which to say that any duty towards a non-patient would **not** be 'fair, just and reasonable'.

It is worth noting at the outset, too, that the prospect of indeterminate liability is very acute in non-patient suits. For example, in England, a 'free-standing duty of candour' on the part of HCPs to those who were not their patients was rejected in *Powell v Boldaz*, partly due to the potentially large number of persons to whom it might be owed;[49] and one of the reasons that a doctor owes no duty to the future sexual partners of his patient is that the non-patients comprise an 'indeterminately large class of females'.[50] The factor has also figured prominently across the range of 'dangerous patients'.

Table 2.2   Relevant factors determining public policy between HCP and non-patient

- would a HCP's duty to the non-patient require him to put those interests above those of his patient? Any **conflict of duties** (actual or potential) will preclude a duty to the non-patient. One possible conflict that could arise is a duty of confidentiality to the patient, versus a duty to minimise injury to the non-patient;
- would a HCP's duty to the non-patient **discourage his own patient** from undertaking full, frank and confidential disclosure of information that is in the best interests of the patient to disclose to the HCP? If so, then that will likely preclude a duty to the non-patient;
- if what is required of the HCP to discharge any duty to the non-patient would *also* discharge his duty to the patient, then the **duties are coincident**, and no conflict arises, and a duty may be upheld;
- if to hold that the instant non-patient was owed a duty of care would expose the HCP to potential liability from many persons in the same position as that particular claimant, then that may preclude a duty of care (the **'floodgates' argument**);
- if the losses sustained by the non-patient were very large, and if the losses of other claimants in like cases would also be very large, and the quantum of the damages could be very large to indeterminate, then that prospect of exposing the HCP to the **indeterminate liability** may preclude a duty of care;
- if the non-patient is claiming only for **economic loss**, and not for personal injury, the scope of the HCP's duty to avoid such economic loss is more likely to be precluded by policy (personal injury being considered more worthy of compensation);
- if to impose a duty on the HCP to the non-patient would promote overly cautious practices/assessments/ treatments, or would divert manpower, money and staff resources away from frontline medicine into reviews of old cases (i.e., **defensive medicine**), then no duty is likely;
- the **inability of a HCP to disclaim liability**, charge a fee for, or explain the risks associated with, his professional services, may count against a duty of care being owed to the non-patient;
- if the non-patient has available to him **other forms of redress**, or there are other ways for making the HCP accountable, that may militate against a duty—e.g., public law remedies in respect of exercise of statutory powers; health departments subject to ministerial oversight; health workers subject to departmental disciplinary regimes; compensation via a criminal injuries compensation scheme; or complaints to the Health and Disability Commissioner, Ombudsman, etc;
- if a HCP has harmed a non-patient by his conduct, and if there was no justification for causing that harm to the non-patient, then should the balance between them be restored by holding that a duty of care was owed? (i.e., **corrective justice**);
- how should the law justly distribute the burdens and losses and risks associated with the provision of medical services within a community (i.e., the principle of **distributive justice**)?
- should the HCP (or his insurer) bear the loss, or is it a form of loss against which the **non-patient ought to have insured himself**? If so, then the loss does (or should) fall upon the non-patient's insurer, and not on the HCP's insurer;
- if the law has 'advisedly' decreed that the patient would not have, himself, a cause of action in negligence against the HCP or against any other party, then it would **not** be fair, just and reasonable to fill a **'gap in compensation'** for the patient, by finding a duty of care in favour of the non-patient (who would be at liberty to spend the money as he wished to in any event, without necessarily passing it on to the patient).

2. The assumption of responsibility/reliance test

A second approach by which to establish a duty of care in novel and unusual scenarios is to prove that the defendant assumed responsibility to the claimant in respect of his conduct towards the claimant, and in turn, the claimant relied on the defendant to exercise due skill and care in so conducting himself.

The genesis of the test was the financial case of *Hedley Byrne & Co Ltd v Heller & Partners Ltd*,[51] where Lord Morris stated that 'if someone possessed of a special skill undertakes, quite irrespective of contract, to apply that skill for the assistance of another person who relies upon that skill, a duty of care will arise.'[52] *Hedley Byrne* was, of course, a world away from most of the suits brought against HCPs which are canvassed in this book, involving, as it did, negligent advice from a bank which caused a third party bank economic loss. Nevertheless, its test has come to have a much wider application than that (albeit that economic loss cases are where it is *still* most centrally significant[53]). The *Hedley Byrne* test is as equally applicable to the *negligent provision of services* as it is to cases of negligent misstatement,[54] and as equally relevant to cases of *personal injury* as it is to economic injury.[55] This, at least, fits it well with most cases of alleged medical negligence. The test has certainly featured in several of the non-patient and third party claims examined in later chapters.

A few preliminary comments about each of the components of the two-part test—derived, in the main, from Lord Bingham's analysis in *Customs and Excise v Barclays Bank plc*[56] (another case involving banking negligence)—may be apposite. The following principles are adapted to fit the HCP and non-patient context.

(a) Proving an assumption of responsibility by the healthcare professional

First, the 'paradigm situation' in which a defendant can be said to have assumed legal responsibility for what he does to the claimant is where the parties are in some relationship 'having all the indicia of contract, save consideration'.[57] In fact, this type of relationship is rarely applicable in the case of non-patient/third party claims against HCPs in medical negligence. The argument that a situation 'close to contract' existed between HCP and non-patient failed, e.g., in *West Bromwich Albion Football Club Ltd v El-Safty*[58]—but, notably, something akin to contract, justifying an assumption of responsibility, *has* occurred in the context of good Samaritans (in the case of *Kent v Griffiths*[59]).

Secondly, a HCP may give an express or implied undertaking to apply his special skill to assist another, and to use his best endeavours in a careful, competent and reasonable manner. The undertaking is **not**, however, to bring about a good result or outcome for the claimant. A promise or undertaking to achieve a particular result for a patient is rarely upheld, and if it is, only if the HCP has entered into a contract with the patient, a term of which has been to guarantee the outcome in clear and unequivocal terms.[60] Otherwise, in the law of negligence, an assumption of responsibility on the HCP's part is only to exercise reasonable care and skill in the medical treatment, diagnosis or advice which he gives to a patient;[61] and the same principle necessarily applies in respect of the HCP's duty towards a non-patient/third party.

Thirdly, any assumption of responsibility on the HCP's part is to be determined objectively, from all the surrounding circumstances, and **not** by reference to what the HCP thought or intended.[62] That is why it has been said that the phrase, 'assumed responsibility', can be misleading: 'it can suggest that the professional person must knowingly and deliberately accept responsibility ... [but] the phrase means simply that the law recognises that there is a duty of care. It is not so much that responsibility is assumed as that it is recognised or imposed by law'.[63] This seems counter-intuitive, because the test seems to imply that, subjectively speaking, the defendant chose to exercise some responsibility for the task undertaken for the claimant. That, however, is not the legal position.[64] Hence, HCPs may be taken to have assumed responsibility for the performance of a medical task that affects a non-patient/third party, even where they do not consciously intend to do so.

Fourthly, because the concept of whether the HCP assumed any responsibility is objective, then as Lord Bingham remarked in *Customs and Excise*, 'the further this test is removed from the actions and intentions of the actual defendant, and the more notional the assumption of responsibility becomes, the less difference there is between this test and the threefold [*Caparo*] test'.[65] It is for this reason that there will, inevitably, be some cross-over between the two tests. In the event that the non-patient cannot establish assumption of responsibility and reliance, the court will still have regard to proximity and policy factors (canvassed previously), in order to determine whether or not a duty can be made out. Essentially, notwithstanding that an express assumption of responsibility by the HCP cannot be found, a duty of care could still feasibly be imposed by operation of law, by reason of the *Caparo* test.

The case law repeatedly shows that it has been rather difficult to prove that the HCP assumed any responsibility towards someone whom he never regarded as his patient, or in respect of persons of whom, perhaps, he did not even know of their existence. To hold that the HCP objectively assumed responsibility towards that unknown party, for the medical tasks that he performed, is highly artificial. The sentiments expressed in *Kovacvich v Ortho Pharmaceutical (Canada) Ltd*[66] (where a GP negligently prescribed the wrong birth control pill to his female patient, and the non-patient partner thereafter sued for economic loss for the costs of raising the child subsequently conceived) are typical: the father of the child was owed no duty of care by the GP, because he 'neither sought information from Dr Henshaw, nor did Dr Henshaw know of his existence. It would not in my view be reasonable to infer that the doctor knew or should have known that reliance was being placed on his skill and judgment by the [father].'[67] Nevertheless, there *have* been some occasions when the relevant HCP has been taken to have assumed a responsibility for one with whom he had no formal HCP–patient relationship, as later chapters will show.

(b) Proving reliance by the non-patient

In general terms, there are three requirements to make out the requisite reliance on the claimant's part.

First, as Lord Bingham observed in *Customs and Excise*, 'reliance in the law is usually taken to mean that if A had not relied on B, he [A] would have acted differently'.[68] Hence, if a non-patient cannot show some adjustment in his position because of the care and skill which he expected the HCP to exercise, in doing or not doing X, then reliance will be absent. Conversely, if the non-patient did indeed adjust his position in the expectation that the HCP would do X, reliance will be proven.

For example, this issue is one of particular importance in the Good Samaritan law considered later: if a victim in urgent need of medical care had the chance to choose between doing Y, and relying upon the HCP to do X, and the victim in fact relied upon the defendant to do X carefully and competently, then that victim has changed his position in reliance upon the intervention of the HCP. In that type of case, a duty of care is more likely.[69]

A somewhat more difficult scenario occurs, however, if a non-patient realistically had no alternative course of action open to him (to do Y, or to protect himself in some other way), and placed his trust in the HCP to perform his medical task carefully and competently. Can this constitute legally-recognised 'reliance'? The Irish Law Reform Commission tackled this problem in its recent report on Good Samaritan law. Its acutely-observed comments have a wider application to all negligence contexts:

the law is reluctant to recognise non-detrimental reliance as a ground for holding the Good Samaritan [or any other type of HCP] liable for his or her intervention [or any medically-related activity], as such reliance implies that the stranger [or any claimant] has not succumbed to actual injury or damage because of the reliance itself ... However, the Commission observes that it is uncertain whether a Good Samaritan [or other defendant] could be held liable for speeding up the arrival of the inevitable consequence, i.e., illness, injury or death ... Detrimental reliance, on the other hand, suggests that the stranger [or other claimant] has changed his position for the worse, based on the intervention of the Good Samaritan [or other HCP's medical activity]. This is more likely to give rise to a duty of care, as the Good Samaritan's intervention [or HCP's medical activity] has caused the stranger [or other claimant] to be in a position of greater risk or to sacrifice a potentially more successful alternative option.[70]

The Commission thereafter noted that, if no detrimental reliance (based upon a change of position) could be proven, then a duty of care could possibly be fashioned from 'relationships of control and dependence'.[71]

Although relationships of control, based upon the HCP's greater skill, could well feature in the medical context, the Commission's approach would take the analysis out of the realms of the assumption of responsibility/reliance test, and would require an analysis of whether, under the *Caparo* test, there was sufficient proximity and policy reasons to warrant the imposition of a duty of care. Hence, if the non-patient cannot point to some change of position in reliance upon his expectation that the HCP would conduct himself with reasonable care and skill, then the *Caparo* test will be the better approach in analysing whether or not a duty of care was owed by the HCP.

Secondly, any reliance on the claimant's part must have been *reasonable*. In the present context, several non-patients have not been able to prove that they reasonably relied upon the skill and judgment of the HCP, in circumstances where the non-patients had feasible options to preserve their own interests.

As later chapters will demonstrate, courts in England and elsewhere have been dismissive that any reliance sufficient to base a duty could be found where, for example, it was not reasonable for the non-patient to act upon any information that the patient might pass on ('receiving [the GP's] advice at second hand'[72]) or where the non-patient should have made independent enquiry or sought independent medical treatment himself. Conversely, reliance is more reasonable where, say, a HCP has voluntarily entered the fray to assist someone in medical emergency—direct and physical intervention renders reliance by the victim reasonable (i.e., what other option would a reasonable victim have relied upon?).[73]

Thirdly, the non-patient must prove that the HCP knew, or should have known, that his undertaking would be relied upon by the non-patient.[74] The HCP's actual or constructive knowledge that another is relying upon him is essential (as the previously-cited case of *Kovacvich v Ortho Pharmaceutical (Canada) Ltd*[75] illustrates).

Finally, on its own, reliance by the non-patient, but without any corresponding assumption of responsibility on the part of the HCP, will cause the two-part test to fail. In that event, reliance may still constitute one of the proximity factors under the *Caparo* test, but it will be a hard case for the non-patient to prove a duty. This is precisely how the dispute in *West Bromwich Albion Football Club Ltd v El-Safty*[76] panned out, for example: the claimant third party, the football club, relied upon the defendant orthopaedic surgeon not to cause it economic injury when treating and advising one of its premiership players in respect of a serious injury picked up in training. However, the surgeon did not assume any responsibility to avoid the club's economic injury (said the Court of Appeal), and proximity was not made out.[77]

3. The incremental test in the context of non-patients

According to the third broad approach adopted for novel and unusual fact scenarios giving rise to duty of care conundrums—

> It is preferable ... that the law should develop novel categories of negligence incrementally and by analogy with established categories, rather than by a massive extension of a *prima facie* duty of care restrained only by indefinable considerations which ought to negative, or to reduce or limit the scope of the duty or the class of person to whom it is owed.[78]

As an analytical tool, this approach appears to give little direct help to non-patients who find themselves at the cutting-edge of negligence law. As Lord Bingham subsequently explained, the incremental test is 'of little value as a test in itself', and that all that it essentially means is that '[t]he closer the facts of the case in issue to those of a case in which a duty of care has been held to exist, the readier a court will be ... to find that there has been an assumption of responsibility or that the proximity and policy conditions of the threefold test are satisfied. The converse is also true.'[79] Buxton LJ has said, too, that the status of the test 'is not easy to discern',[80] but probably only means that if a claimant 'could demonstrate that his case did no more than incrementally extend an already recognised head of liability, that was a good indication that his claim met the *Caparo* requirements.'[81]

Academic commentary has, similarly, been rather lukewarm about the degree of significance the incremental test may hold in practice. As Spencer has aptly put it, the incremental test merely reflects the view that 'the common law should move by little steps, like centipedes and corgis, not leaps and bounds, like kangaroos.'[82] Oppenheim makes the further point that the leaps that the court is prepared to make may be larger and 'more expansive' in the personal injury context than in cases of pure economic loss,[83] while Stanton regards the test as opaque because its application by the House of Lords has been so frequent, but vague, that 'there is now considerable support for the use of incrementalism, but its status and meaning remain unclear'.[84]

Given that so many of the non-patient and third party claims discussed in this book were new and unusual, the incremental test has really been of little assistance to the claimants involved. The battle-lines are typically drawn, whereby the HCP argues that the absence of any analogous cases or direct precedent supports the argument that liability should not be made out against him in the instant circumstances either; while the non-patient contends that there 'has to be a first time', that the common law develops incrementally and so the fact that there is no similar reported case is not necessarily determinative, and that it is not as if third party claims against a defendant professional have never been recognised.[85]

The real difficulty with the incremental test, in an area of evolving jurisprudence and innovative argument which non-patient claims against HCPs entail, is that there could be a number of cases which are distinctly helpful, and some which are very unhelpful, to the claimant's case, and the result of the incremental test can therefore be considered as 'somewhat inconclusive'[86] at best, and akin to a lottery, at worst.

D SOME COMMON THEMES OF DIFFICULTY IN NON-PATIENT CLAIMS

Five particular conundrums commonly arise in the area of potential liability of a defendant HCP towards a non-patient, where some alleged medical culpability has been exercised by that HCP either towards the non-patient directly, or towards a patient which occasions loss or damage to the non-patient (the latter tri-partite scenario of which is depicted in Figure 1.1[87]).

First, is the HCP's liability towards the third party derivative from, or is it independent of, any duty which he may owe to the patient? Secondly, if a HCP is to owe a duty of care to a non-patient, then in several scenarios, the scope of that duty will conflict with a duty of confidentiality owed to the patient. How the law has resolved this has not been free of difficulty. Thirdly, how does the law treat the fact that the HCP's alleged wrongdoing towards a non-patient is frequently based upon an *omission* to act? Fourthly, the problem of just how many exist in the class of whom the third party is one is a constant theme, and on this point, English law has not always been entirely consistent. Fifthly, the tripartite scenarios involving a HCP inevitably throw up a key question: how is the duty to be cast? Is it a duty to take some step in relation to the patient (e.g., to control or to advise him) to protect the non-patient against harm, or is it a wider duty to take some direct step in relation to the third party (e.g., to give warnings)?

These conundrums will be considered in more detail as and where appropriate in the chapters themselves, but briefly dealing with each in turn:

1. Derivative liability versus independent liability

Where a HCP has diagnosed, treated or advised a patient, negligently, and some loss or damage is then occasioned to a non-patient, is the liability of the defendant HCP inextricably linked with his liability towards the patient? In other words, is the non-patient's claim derivative, in that it stands or falls upon how the law treats the *patient's claim* against the HCP?

Certainly, it will **not** assist the non-patient (the claimant) to argue that, just because the HCP was negligent towards the patient, then it would be 'fair, just and equitable' that he should be found to owe a duty to the non-patient too. It may well be incontrovertible that the HCP owed a duty to the patient, and will have to compensate him for his losses. But it does not follow that, as a matter of policy, the HCP ought to owe a duty to the non-patient too. That argument was specifically put, and rejected, in *West Bromwich Albion Football Club Ltd v El-Safty*[88] (and, indeed, it was ultimately held that to owe a duty to WBA, as the non-patient in this scenario, 'would be several steps too far',[89] a view upheld on appeal[90]).

Some courts have put the position that a non-patient's claim is, or should be, derivative upon the willingness and/or ability of the patient to sue the HCP. As Lord Rodger pointed out in *JD v East Berkshire Community Health NHS Trust*,[91] the legislature ensured that this position was maintained under ss 1(1) and 1A of the Fatal Accidents Act 1976, for example, which modify the common law by providing that a defendant is liable to certain dependants for the loss they suffer due to the death of the victim, and to certain relatives for their bereavement—but only if that defendant would have been liable to the victim if he had lived: '[t]he statute thus remains true to the common law position that the tortfeasor owed a duty of care to the victim but not to the dependants' (and, hence, that any claim by third parties is derivative, not independent). On the same note, it has been contended by one Canadian court[92] that a parental non-patient could only bring a derivative claim, i.e., one that stood, or fell, upon whatever happened to the claim of the other parent (the patient) in this latter's own direct action in negligence against the defendant HCP. Thus, if the latter did not even institute a claim, then there could be no successful claim brought by the non-patient parent. It was said that '[n]o authority has been brought to our attention which has extended the liability for the negligent act of a doctor to a third party who received neither treatment nor advice, and where the claim is not derivative to a claim by the patient herself.'[93]

Some courts, however, have been equally adamant that the patient's own position *vis-à-vis* that of the HCP has nothing to do with the success or otherwise of the non-patient's claim, and that the two claims (and the duties of care which the HCP may owe to each) are entirely independent. For example, in *McLelland v Greater Glasgow Health Board*,[94] Lord Prosser rejected the submission that Mr McLelland, the non-patient, had to be considered as a 'secondary' claimant, dependent upon proof of a wrong done to his wife (the patient). Instead, it was held that Mr McLelland was the victim of a 'direct wrong', and that the failure to carry out an amniocentesis test upon his wife during pregnancy was 'a wrong done to him directly'.[95] Moreover, it is clear that, in English law, non-patient claims brought for pure psychiatric illness do not have to be derivative upon a successful claim being instituted by the immediate victim who was put in the 'zone of physical danger' by the defendant's negligence—the House of Lords (per Lord Oliver) made this plain in *Alcock v Chief Constable of the South Yorkshire Police*.[96] Furthermore, for third parties who are harmed by the acts of a physically-disabled or mentally-ill patient, the HCP will not be liable in negligence towards that patient, for whilst undoubtedly a duty of care is owed to the patient, he may in fact suffer no damage—it is the third party who suffers at the hands of the patient. The patient himself could not successfully institute any action in negligence against the HCP. Hence, it may be that the HCP has not been negligent in the treatment of the patient at all, yet a third party claim against the HCP may still be brought. In that context, the duties owed to patient and to non-patient are entirely independent of each other.

The various diverse scenarios in this book emphasise that third party claims against HCPs (in the sense of *any* claim that is brought by someone who is not the HCP's patient) can arise, even if that third party is not seeking to 'hang onto the coat tails of the duty of care owed to the primary victim',[97] that primary victim being the patient. In fact, it is not a mandatory pre-requisite that the third party claim should be derivative upon a claim brought by the patient against the HCP concerned, or upon whether the patient is himself owed a duty of care by the HCP, or upon the ultimate success of the patient's claim. In many cases, that 'coat-tail' effect *is* present—but it does not need to be, in order for some third parties/non-patients to succeed. Rather, in third party cases, the position is as Hickinbottom J recently explained—the ultimate question for the court (per the classic *Caparo* analysis) is whether it was reasonably foreseeable that the third party would suffer damage if the defendant acted as he allegedly did, whether there was a relationship of sufficient proximity between the third party and the defendant, and whether it was fair, just and reasonable to impose a duty of care on the defendant to avoid the damage of which the third party complains, in all the circumstances.[98] Hence, in the context of medical negligence the focus of this book, whether there is a lack of proximity between HCP and non-patient, or whether policy factors should preclude a duty of care from being owed to the non-patient because it would not be 'fair, just and reasonable' to cast such a duty on the HCP, is an independent question, to be determined by a full consideration of the facts and circumstances which govern the relationship between the non-patient and the HCP.

2. The duty of confidentiality owed to a patient

Actual or potential conflicts of duties owed to patients and to non-patients have proven to be particularly acute in some of the contexts considered in later chapters. After all, the General Medical Council (GMC) instructs its members as to what being a 'good doctor' means—and that is to 'make the care of their patients their first concern'.[99]

Unfortunately, the law is somewhat more complicated than that, given that there are instances where the care of a non-patient must become an equal concern, or where non-patients have vehemently argued that it *should* have been.

The importance of the HCP's duty of confidentiality to his patient cannot be overstated. As Rose J stated in *X HA v Y* (a case which concerned doctors who were believed to be continuing to practise medicine, despite having contracted AIDS):

> In the long run, preservation of confidentiality is the only way of securing public health; otherwise doctors will be discredited as a source of education, for future individual patients will not come forward if doctors are going to squeal on them. Consequently, confidentiality is vital to secure public as well as private health, for unless those infected come forward they cannot be counselled and self-treatment does not provide the best care.[100]

However, the duty of confidentiality which the law imposes upon HCPs towards a patient is neither absolute nor perfectly delineated.

HCPs have various statutory duties or discretions to report about patient behaviour or capacity to relevant authorities. For example, according to the Public Health (Control of Diseases) Act 1984,[101] a HCP must notify the relevant health authority when he suspects that his patient suffers from a notifiable disease. Other information disclosure scenarios include the provision of information: to vehicle registration authorities about patients with dangerous conditions; to health authorities about patients with serious drug-dependent habits; to medical registration bodies about HCPs who are seriously impaired to practise; or to welfare authorities about suspected child abuse.[102]

Other (common law) contexts in which information may be shared are: among members of a medical team; and where disclosure of patient information is justified in the public interest, in those exceptional circumstances in which the patient poses a real risk of danger to the public. In regard to the latter of these, in *W v Egdell*,[103] Bingham LJ stated that '[t]he decided cases very clearly establish: (1) that the law recognises an important public interest in maintaining professional duties of confidence; but (2) that the law treats such duties not as absolute but as liable to be overridden where there is held to be a stronger public interest in disclosure.' Furthermore, Lord Goff confirmed in the *Spycatcher* case[104] that the public interest exception to the duty of confidence 'may apply ... to *all types* of confidential information', including medical information.

These authorities confirm that English law is certainly prepared to uphold an *ability* to directly warn a non-patient, should it be shown that the public interest favours disclosure to that non-patient (be it a family member, a close associate of the patient, or members of the general public), although as later chapters will canvas, transposing that ability into a *duty to directly warn* is quite a different issue.

Moreover, several of the professional guidelines regarding disclosure of information have, as their basis, the *protection of third parties*. HCPs who treat dangerous patients are instructed by the GMC's guidelines, under the heading, 'Disclosures to protect others', as follows:

> **Confidentiality (2009):**
> *Paras* 53–55. Disclosure of personal information about a patient without consent may be justified in the public interest if failure to disclose may expose others to a risk of death or serious harm. You should still seek the patient's consent to disclosure if practicable and consider any reasons given for refusal. Such a situation might arise, for example, when a disclosure would be likely to assist in the prevention, detection or prosecution of serious crime, especially crimes against the person. ... If a patient's refusal to consent to disclosure leaves others exposed to a risk so serious that it outweighs the patient's and the public interest in maintaining confidentiality, or if it is not practicable or safe to seek the patient's consent, you should disclose information promptly to an appropriate person or authority. You should inform the patient before disclosing the information, if practicable and safe, even if you intend to disclose without their consent.

Previous GMC guidance also counselled HCPs to breach confidentiality in exceptional cases where failing to disclose could 'expose others to risk of death or serious harm'.[105]

Under the headings, 'Disclosures in the public interest', the position of a HCP who is dealing with a 'dangerous patient' (say, one who is carrying a contagious or sexually-transmitted disease, or one who is mentally-disturbed, psychotic or physically-disabled, and thereby presents a danger to others in the community) is dealt with, in part, by the GMC as follows:[106]

> **Confidentiality (2009):**
> *Paras* 36–37. ... Confidential medical care is recognised in law as being in the public interest. However, there can also be a public interest in disclosing information: to protect individuals or society from risks of serious harm, such as serious communicable diseases or serious crime; ... Personal information may, therefore, be disclosed in the public interest, without patients' consent, and in exceptional cases where patients have withheld consent, if the benefits to an individual or to society of the disclosure outweigh both the public and the patient's interest in keeping the information confidential. You must weigh the harms that are likely to arise from non-disclosure of information against the possible harm both to the patient, and to the overall trust between doctors and patients, arising from the release of that information

Moreover, in the context of cases of suspected abuse or neglect, the following is the GMC's professional guidance to HCPs who suspect such abuse, under the heading, 'Disclosures where a patient may be a victim of neglect or abuse':

> **Confidentiality (2009):**
> *Para* 63. If you believe that a patient may be a victim of neglect or physical, sexual or emotional abuse, and that they lack capacity to consent to disclosure, you must give information promptly to an appropriate responsible person or authority, if you believe that the disclosure is in the patient's best interests or necessary to protect others from a risk of serious harm. If, for any reason, you believe that disclosure of information is not in the best interests of a neglected or abused patient, you should discuss the issues with an experienced colleague. If you decide not to disclose information, you should document in the patient's record your discussions and the reasons for deciding not to disclose. You should be prepared to justify your decision.

In the same 2009 guidance, the GMC also flags that disclosure of a patient's genetic information to persons with whom the patient shares that information may be in the public interest, where, say, '[t]he diagnosis of an illness in the patient might ... point to the certainty or likelihood of the same illness in a blood relative', albeit that if the patient refuses consent to disclose, then a balancing assessment of the patient's and the other person's interests will be required (at *paras* 67–69).

Interestingly, the GMC further recommends that a GP report to the Driver and Vehicle Licensing Agency (DVLA) if a patient is medically unfit to drive, and that the HCP should 'make every reasonable effort to persuade them to [stop driving]'.[107] In addition, the HCP is under certain further obligations, according to the DVLA guidelines:[108]

DVLA, *For Medical Practitioners: At a Glance Guide to the Current Medical Standards of Fitness to Drive* **(2008)**:

Para 17. If you do not manage to persuade patients to stop driving, or you are given or find evidence that a patient is continuing to drive contrary to advice, you should disclose relevant medical information immediately, in confidence, to the medical adviser at DVLA.

In legal terms, the fact that professional guidelines or statutory enactments may require a HCP to disclose information about a patient, or bestow the HCP with a discretion to do so, may be relevant to both the establishment of a duty of care, and the question of whether the HCP, in failing to disclose, met the standard of reasonable care in relation to the non-patient. As subsequent chapters will discuss, the duty of confidentiality, and its relationship with any duty of care that may be owed to a non-patient, will arise for consideration, particularly in instances of the transmission or inheritance of diseases, and the potential harm that physically-impaired or mentally-ill patients may do to non-patients.

3. Omissions to act

Whether it be a failure to attend to a victim in a medical emergency, or a failure to control or supervise a dangerous patient who then harms a non-patient, many of the allegations arising in non-patient suits concern omissions by HCPs. As McIvor notes, although not all third party liability cases will necessarily involve omissions on the defendant's part, most of them (and the most contentious of them) will do so.[109]

By contrast to its treatment of positive acts, the common law does not, generally speaking, impose liability for 'mere omissions', as they were referred to in diminutory terms in *Smith (or Maloco) v Littlewoods Organisation Ltd*.[110] This principle applies, regardless of whether some human agency or natural cause actuated the injury to, or illness of, the non-patient. Simply put, omissions are treated more leniently by the English common law, as Lord Hoffmann explained in *Stovin v Wise*:

> It is one thing for the law to say that a person who undertakes some activity shall take reasonable care not to cause damage to others. It is another thing for the law to require that a person who is doing nothing in particular shall take steps to prevent another from suffering harm from the acts of third parties ... or natural causes.[111]

The proposition is, of course, controversial, especially when the failure to do something to assist another can result in tragic and adverse consequences for that other. As one English judge has recently commented, '[t]he problem of fixing liability, whether in tort or in crime, on the basis of omission, has generated much, indeed prolonged, debate.'[112]

The numerous reasons for this judicially-made policy will be examined in the specific context of 'bad Samaritan' HCP liability (in Chapter 5[113]), for it is in that context that the arguments have been most clearly and vehemently stated. Hence, there is no general rule that HCPs owe a duty to take positive steps to protect the persons, lives and property of a non-patient. However, as this book describes, several cases have proven to be the exception to that rule—although the reasons underpinning these exceptions struggle to form any coherent framework.

One of the by-products of the English law's position on mere omissions is that the law does not, as a general rule, cast a duty on a defendant to prevent a claimant from being harmed by the criminal act of a third party—even where harm rendered to the claimant by the third party was reasonably foreseeable.[114] So, in the case of harm caused by a dangerous patient, before any duty of care can exceptionally be imposed upon the treating HCP, that defendant and the non-patient victim must have been in a sufficiently proximate relationship, and policy reasons must also not negate the existence of any such duty.

The distinction between positive acts and omissions to act was again drawn, very recently, in *Mitchell v Glasgow CC*,[115] where the suit in negligence against the defendant Council was based upon the allegation that its officers failed to warn a third party (Mr Mitchell, the victim) of the fact that his neighbouring council tenant, Mr Drummond, with whom the officers had had a torrid meeting about continuing anti-social conduct, was likely to be upset about the meeting. Mr Drummond was indeed upset, so much so that he went straight home and battered the victim with an iron bar, leaving him with horrific injuries from which he died 10 days later in hospital. Although the defendant here was a public housing authority and not a HCP, the tri-partite relationship with a person doing the harm to the claimant has parallels with many of the medical scenarios considered later. The Council was not liable in negligence (nor under a separate claim for violation of art 2's right to the protection of life). Lord Scott essentially categorised the failure-to-warn allegation as a 'mere omission',[116] and explained that, exceptionally, it could give rise to a duty of care, but only rarely. His Lordship's discussion of just when an omission to act converts from a benign form of behaviour to something that can give rise to legal culpability indicates just how uncertain and unpredictable the whole area has become:

> The requisite additional feature that transforms what would otherwise be a mere omission, a breach at most of a moral obligation, into a breach of a legal duty to take reasonable steps to safeguard, or to try to safeguard, the person in question from harm or injury may take a wide variety of forms. Sometimes the additional feature may be found in the manner in which the victim came to be at risk of harm or injury. If a defendant has played some causative part in the train of events that have led to the risk of injury, a duty to take reasonable steps to avert or lessen the risk may arise. Sometimes the additional feature may be found in the relationship between the victim and the defendant: (e.g., employee/employer or child/parent) or in the relationship between the defendant and the place where the risk arises ... Sometimes the additional feature may be found in the assumption by the defendant of responsibility for the person at risk of injury ... In each case where particular circumstances are relied on as constituting the requisite additional feature alleged to be sufficient to cast upon the defendant the duty to take steps that, if taken, would or might have avoided or lessened the injury to the victim, the question for the court will be whether the circumstances were indeed sufficient for that purpose or whether the case remains one of mere omission.[117]

As will be discussed later, while English law is notoriously hesitant to impose a positive duty to act where the essential rubric of the allegation is that the defendant failed to act to prevent harm befalling the claimant, some HCPs have found themselves embroiled in cases where the so-called 'additional feature' *has* been present, rendering a duty of care active.

4. The size of the non-patient class

In some of the non-patient scenarios considered in this book, the size of the non-patient class consists of one—say, the partner of the patient to whom a sexually-transmissible disease has been passed by the patient, and who was the patient's partner at the time of the alleged medical negligence perpetrated by the HCP (e.g., where, say, a GP failed to organise for the patient to be tested for the disease). In many others, however, the class ranges between small-and-defined to large-and-amorphous. The problem is particularly evident in the case of psychotic patients who injure or kill third parties, with the spectrum of possibilities in that scenario shown in Figure 2.1:

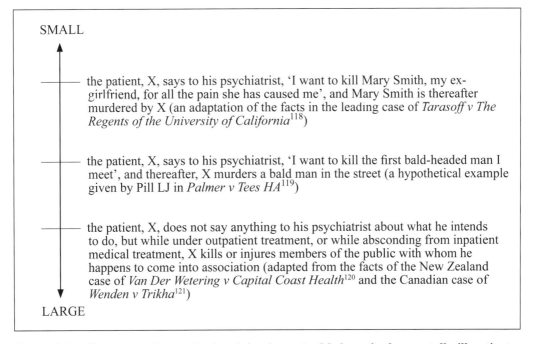

SMALL

the patient, X, says to his psychiatrist, 'I want to kill Mary Smith, my ex-girlfriend, for all the pain she has caused me', and Mary Smith is thereafter murdered by X (an adaptation of the facts in the leading case of *Tarasoff v The Regents of the University of California*[118])

the patient, X, says to his psychiatrist, 'I want to kill the first bald-headed man I meet', and thereafter, X murders a bald man in the street (a hypothetical example given by Pill LJ in *Palmer v Tees HA*[119])

the patient, X, does not say anything to his psychiatrist about what he intends to do, but while under outpatient treatment, or while absconding from inpatient medical treatment, X kills or injures members of the public with whom he happens to come into association (adapted from the facts of the New Zealand case of *Van Der Wetering v Capital Coast Health*[120] and the Canadian case of *Wenden v Trikha*[121])

LARGE

Figure 2.1   Spectrum of scenarios involving harm to third parties by mentally-ill patients

Hence, non-patient classes can vary from a class of one, to a class which constitutes a demographic section of the general public, to the general public itself.

The larger the class, the greater the need for the non-patient to prove that he was 'at special risk' of harm or injury as a result of the HCP's breach, in order to prove a sufficient proximity between himself and the HCP. No special risk over and above that of the general public, on the other hand, is likely to mean that the class of persons, of whom the unfortunate victim was one, was simply too large—calling to mind the oft-cited statement of Cardozo CJ, that courts will be reluctant to impose 'liability in an indeterminate amount for an indeterminate time to an indeterminate class'.[122]

In fact, the task faced by third party claimants to prove a 'special risk' to themselves from X's activities, over and above the risk faced by the general public from X, has particularly arisen in the case of suits against *police or correctional authorities* in English law. No duty was owed to Ms Jacqueline Hill, the 13[123] and last victim of the serial murderer dubbed the 'Yorkshire Ripper';[123] or to a prosecution witness at a theft trial who had been exposed to a constant and frightening campaign of intimidation by the accused,[124] because, in part, neither claimant had a particularly distinguishing characteristic that insulated them from the risks posed to the general public by the criminally-minded individual. On the other hand, a duty *was* owed to a police informant who was subject to threats and abuse, subsequent to her information being lost by the police and acquired by criminal interests;[125] to yacht owners whose property was in close physical proximity to Borstal Island from which a group of detained youths escaped on a boat;[126] and (in a notable Canadian case) to a female rape victim within the specific demographic that had been targeted by a serial rapist, but whom the police had failed to warn.[127]

Similarly, the notion of large classes, and the need for the claimant to prove 'special risk', has arisen frequently in non-patient claims against HCPs in English law. It has been particularly striking in cases involving: non-patients injured or killed by dangerous patients, and against whom there had been no specific threat before the deed was done; non-patients who sustained pure economic losses because of the medical treatment of the patient (say, the 'indeterminately large class of females' that could comprise the patient's future sexual partners[128]); and non-patients who contracted contagious diseases from other non-patients who were themselves negligently exposed to an ill patient.

From a combined reading of the abovementioned medical and non-medical cases, it appears that there are a number of factors that will render a non-patient claimant 'at special risk'—e.g., where the victim may have been specially identified to the defendant prior to the attack; or the victim and the third party shared a close relationship or were geographically proximate; or the claimant fell within a particular and narrowly-defined demographic that was at risk from the criminally-minded individual; or the defendant's loosening of control over X placed the claimants at particular risk, above the general public. However, as will be seen, a coherent and consistent framework of what makes a claimant 'at special risk' has been somewhat difficult to ascertain from non-patient suits against HCPs.

Nowhere is the problem more evident than in respect of the class of persons who are road users. In Canada, a possible duty of care by a HCP towards that (very large) class of persons, of whom the non-patient victim was one, has been countenanced. In *Wenden v Trikha*,[129] a schizophrenic student absconded from hospital where he was under regular observations, took off in his car which he imagined to be a time capsule, ran a red light, and collided with the claimant, severely injuring both her and her then-unborn child. Some aforementioned English jurisprudence would surely suggest that this class would be too large for any duty to be owed by the HCP to any member of that class (the duty would be owed by one driver to the other, but not by the HCP). Yet, in one English case—the 1955 House of Lords' decision of *Carmarthenshire CC v Lewis*[130]— a kindergarten was found liable to a third party road user (a lorry driver) who was killed when he took drastic evasive action to avoid a young child who had wandered out into the road adjacent to the kindergarten. This case was decided well prior to the tri-partite test of *Caparo*, and rested very forcibly upon the notion of reasonable foreseeability of injury to Mr Lewis, the third party victim of the kindergarten's negligence.[131] However, *Lewis* was from a different era—Lord Bridge's tri-partite test in *Caparo* provides much stronger control mechanisms upon third party claims in the modern age.

Apart from floodgates concerns, there is also the prospect of how other non-patients could align themselves with a claimant's success, should a duty of care be held to be owed by the HCP to non-patient in the instant case (i.e., the 'precedential effect' of any decision to permit recovery). As will be seen, this has also been adverted to in some non-patient cases as a reason for precluding any duty of care being owed by the HCP.[132]

5. How the duty of care is framed, and how the standard of care is set

Finally, whether a duty of care is to be recognised at all, on the part of the HCP, may depend very much upon how it is defined. There are a variety of different approaches which could be adopted to the duty question:

- it could be cast as a duty on the HCP to take some active conduct in relation to *the non-patient* (say, by giving that non-patient a warning or some advice about the patient—which raises breach-of-confidentiality issues); or
- it could take the form of treating *the patient* in such a way as to try to protect the non-patient indirectly (e.g., by advising the patient to pass on information to the non-patient, or by counselling the patient in some other way); or
- it could take the form of requiring the HCP to involve an external party (say, the police, or some professional regulator) who could take steps *vis-à-vis* the patient—which, again, would have the indirect effect of seeking to protect the non-patient; or
- it could entail a duty upon the HCP to take some onerous and draconian step in respect of the patient by which to safeguard the non-patient (e.g., involuntarily detaining him, which raises issues as to whether that is ultimately in the best interests of the patient himself); or
- the duty cast upon the HCP could combine aspects of all of these individual duties.

Courts have not necessarily been consistent in their treatment of this issue, which gives rise to legal unpredictability. Crucially, it is not sufficient, in this field of negligence law, to merely say, 'the HCP owed a duty of care to the non-patient to avoid the risk of harm or of injury [of a certain type, physical, economic, etc]'. The *scope* of the duty is all-important—and how courts cast the duty has been critical, in many cases, as to whether a duty should be found at all. Other academic commentary concurs that this constitutes more than mere terminological confusion; the challenge is to properly and specifically articulate the particular type of 'affirmative duty' which is said to be imposed on the defendant.[133]

Furthermore, the ease or difficulty with which the non-patient will be able to prove a *breach* by the HCP of the standard of reasonable care may highly depend on how the duty of care is framed. Essentially, if the duty is to control or otherwise affect the patient, so as prevent any creation of the opportunity on the part of the patient to do harm, then that is a narrower duty, and it may be easier to prove that the HCP did not discharge it. On the other hand, if the duty of care imposed upon the HCP requires that he reasonably act to protect the non-patient (e.g., warn him, pass on certain information to him, etc.), then it can be very difficult to perceive of what a *reasonable* HCP could have done, so as to prevent the harm that befell the non-patient victim. After all, the law is not interested (supposedly) with what a perfect HCP, resourced with an army of assistants and a practice that allows unlimited time to be spent on one particular patient, might have done. Perfection is not the touchstone of medical negligence liability, any more than it is for professional negligence liability generally. English courts have been keen to reiterate that '[t]he law does not require of a professional man that he be a paragon, combining the qualities of polymath and prophet',[134] that HCPs 'are not insurers',[135] and that a HCP's duty of care 'is not a warranty of a perfect result'.[136]

These sentiments have particular resonance wherever HCPs are charged with a duty of care to third parties who have been harmed by 'dangerous' patients. Once the law takes the step of requiring HCPs to deal with non-patients to counter the risk that their patients present to others, the boundaries of what amounts to reasonable conduct can become problematical.[137]

As a further point—suppose that a HCP does not report, disclose, or otherwise act in relation to a patient, per professional guidelines; and suppose that, as a result of a patient's conduct, a third party non-patient is injured or killed. As later chapters will canvass, the very existence of professional guidelines that speak of a HCP's conduct towards or in respect of non-patients can assist to find a legal duty of care to the same effect—although that result does not follow automatically, and the guidelines do not, of themselves, dictate that a duty of care should be owed. Additionally, if that non-patient (or his estate) should sue the HCP, alleging that a duty of care was owed to him, does non-compliance with the guidelines, of itself, constitute *proof of breach*? Again, professional guidelines do not have the force of law in that a failure to adhere to the guidelines' recommended procedures will not, of itself, establish that the relevant HCP breached the standard of care set by law. In this respect, Samanta *et al* have described the position as follows:

> Guidelines are consensus statements developed to assist clinicians in making decisions about treatment for specific conditions. They are systematically developed on the basis of evidence and aim to promote effectiveness and efficiency of healthcare delivery ... The precise role of guidelines in determining the legal standard of care is uncertain. A plethora of academic commentary exists in the legal and medical literature analysing the theoretical basis as to why guidelines should, or should not, set the legal standard of care in clinical negligence litigation ... As yet the higher courts have never been asked to make a definitive pronouncement on the role of guidelines as standards for liability in clinical negligence.[138]

Since then, there has been no judicial discussion of the issue in English law, so far as the author's searches can ascertain. However, the issue became very relevant in one Canadian non-patient case, *viz*, *Spillane v Wasserman*.[139] Mr Wasserman, who suffered nocturnal and daytime epileptic seizures regularly, suffered another episode while driving his truck. He drove through a red light, and struck and killed bicycle rider, Mr Spillane. Not only did the treating GP and neurologist both owe non-patient Mr Spillane a duty of care, but they also breached that duty, because they failed to run blood tests on Mr Wasserman routinely, in order to check control and compliance, and in that event, they 'neglected to follow the minium standards set out in the notices provided by the College of Physicians and the guides for physicians prepared on behalf of the Canadian Medical Association.'[140] *Spillane* was re-evaluated by the Saskatchewan Court of Queen's Bench in *Kock v Brydon*,[141] where the precise question for determination was 'whether the standard of care is breached by a physician's failure to conform to recommended procedures or guidelines of the governing professional body?'[142]. According to *Kock*, non-conformity to the guidelines and recommendations of the governing professional body is not, of itself, proof of breach on its own (it is one factor in the matrix of all the circumstances), but non-conformity does constitute strong evidence of breach.[143]

E CAUSATION CONUNDRUMS ARISING IN SOME NON-PATIENT SCENARIOS

1. Causation and omissions to act

In many non-patient scenarios, the essential allegation levied against the HCP is that he failed to act to protect the non-patient—either by failing to assist the non-patient directly (as in the case of HCPs who had a common law duty of care to go to the assistance of a stranger but who behaved as a 'Bad Samaritan') or where the third party was harmed by some action of the patient's, and the HCP, it is alleged, failed to control, treat, supervise, or advise the patient, so as to prevent the harm befalling the non-patient.

In any such cases, failing to act/warn/treat, etc., will constitute the breach. However, proving the causal link between that breach, and the non-patient's injury and damage, raises two potential causation problems for the non-patient victim. Dealing with each in turn:

(a) How can omissions 'cause' the non-patient's harm?

The dilemma can be demonstrated by means of an example—by failing to stop a blind man from walking over a cliff, has the bystander's omission to shout out a warning caused the blind man's injury or death?

Arguably, it has not. The harm to the blind man has arisen independently of the bystander—the more immediate causes being the blind man's own disability, and the natural features of the land. Essentially, 'if inaction is incapable of *causing* harm, then it cannot form the basis for a claim in negligence',[144] observed the Irish Law Reform Commission. Otherwise (said the Commission), if merely failing to act could give rise to liability, then 'this would be akin to creating a conduct offence under negligence, which would go against the basis of negligence, which seeks to redress those situations in which damage has been caused.'[145] Consistently with this, in the aforementioned decision of *Mitchell v Glasgow CC*, Lord Rodger remarked that, in the case of a person watching a child drown in a pool or a blind man walking out into traffic, that observer 'plays no part in the events'.[146]

On the other hand, however, were a HCP to be held to be under a legal duty to have assisted/attended to a stranger whom he declined to assist, or to act/intervene/rescue a third party non-patient, then there are, arguably, strong grounds for establishing the requisite causal link between his breach by omission and the non-patient's damage, by reference to three existing English lines of authority.

First, English tort law has already created a number of exceptions to the general rule that there is no duty to intervene/act/rescue—and, in these cases, the causal link *has* successfully been made out, thereby indicating that pure omissions or non-feasances can constitute a 'cause' of harm, based upon the more elliptical method of saying that the defendant *created the opportunity for harm to occur*. As others have termed it, this is 'causation of an indirect nature'.[147] For example, in *Haynes v Harwood*,[148] a carter left a horse-drawn van unattended in a crowded street, and the horses bolted when a boy threw a stone at them. The claimant police officer suffered injury in stopping the horses before they injured a woman and children in the path of the bolting animals. The police officer could recover damages from the carter's employer, even though it were the actions of the mischievous boy (and the inherent nature of the animals, susceptible to sudden noise and movement) which were most directly responsible for the danger. The carter merely created a source of danger by leaving his horses unattended in a busy street—and that was enough to establish causation between breach and the police officer's injury. Hence, instances involving an affirmative duty to act do not appear to have presented any particular difficulty in thereafter alleging that inaction may, in fact, 'cause' harm.

Secondly, in those instances in which a defendant has been liable for failing to prevent damage to a third party claimant that was brought about by reason of the deliberate acts of wrongdoing of a *third party who was under the control or supervision of the defendant*, then causation has also not been thwarted. Of course, no positive act of the defendant supervisor directly inflicted the claimant's injuries (the third party did that), yet the supervisor has been held capable of being liable in negligence to the victim. Also, rather than treating the acts of the third party as interrupting any causal link between the breach (i.e., the supervisor's failure to control third party) and the harm suffered by the claimant, leading authorities have, instead, accepted a weaker causal link in these circumstances. For example, in *Dorset Yacht Co Ltd v Home Office*,[149] Borstal officers owed a duty to take reasonable care to prevent seven boys under their control from escaping from custody on Brownsea Island and causing damage to the claimants' yacht moored nearby in Poole Harbour. Again, this link is best described as the defendant 'creating the opportunity for harm to occur'.

Thirdly, given recent House of Lords' general treatment of causation, the difficulties of proving causation in the case of a defendant who declines or fails to act/intervene/rescue/warn, etc, may be somewhat overstated. There are exceptional cases existing in English tort law in which courts have imposed liability in circumstances where, as a matter of policy, they have been prepared to jump 'evidential gaps', or turn their faces against the usual 'but-for' test ('would the claimant's harm have occurred, but for the omission to act?') and find for the claimant, despite the fact that that test could not be proven. As discussed in the two preceding points, not only have omissions to act themselves given rise to successful causal link, but *Fairchild v Glenhaven Funeral Services Ltd*,[150] *Barker v Corus UK Ltd*,[151] and *Chester v Afshar*[152] were policy-driven decisions in which the various claimants succeeded in their actions in negligence without proof of causation against the liable defendants on the classic 'but-for' test. In the context of HCPs, it is arguable that policy reasons (e.g., civil punishment should be visited upon those who were in a position to effect an 'easy rescue', but who did not) may be suitably invoked in rescue cases too, were an affirmative duty to rescue become more widely countenanced.

Hence, 'mere omissions' have been held to 'cause' a claimant's harm in English law, and there are clear indications that a weaker causal link would be countenanced, should some of the novel scenarios outlined against HCPs in this book be upheld or more seriously considered in the future. With the greatest respect to Lord Rodger's assertion in *Mitchell v Glasgow CC* that a bystander has 'played no part in the events', a successful causal link would nevertheless be strongly arguable in 'omissions' cases, whether they arose out of tri-partite scenarios or the 'bad Samaritan'-type scenario.

(b) Pure omissions require a hypothetical scenario to prove causation

Say that a HCP fails to attend a non-patient, or fails to warn a non-patient of the risk posed to him by a patient. At causation stage, the non-patient's argument will run along the lines, 'if the HCP had done X (i.e., warned/intervened/acted), then more probably than not, doing X would have prevented the harm from occurring to me'. Hence, the causal argument requires the court to hypothesise about what *would have happened*, and no absolute answer is possible, given that the HCP never warned, never attended, or never intervened. As one court put it, '[the] court is being asked to consider what might have been'.[153]

Again, the classic but-for test is also difficult to satisfy in such cases, for if the court asks, 'would the non-patient's harm have occurred, but for that omission to act?', the answer may well be: yes, that victim's harm would have occurred anyway, because hypothetically fixing the breach (by the HCP assisting or warning or intervening) would not have prevented the victim's damage. Had the HCP fixed the omission and acted, he may *still* not have prevented the harm befalling the non-patient. That gives rise to the conclusion that the breach—failing to attend/rescue/intervene—did not cause the non-patient's damage on the 'but-for' test.

However, it is submitted that neither of these matters would necessarily pose a problem for the victim in a negligence action against a HCP who failed to, say, warn a non-patient or who failed to assist in an emergency. Two analogous lines of authority support that view.

First of all, English law already countenances that, where a HCP's negligence is an omission to attend upon a patient, a hypothetical analysis *is* acceptable, and the 'but-for' test can be overcome by the analysis adopted in *Bolitho v City and Hackney HA*.[154] To do so, the non-patient must prove one of two scenarios. Hypothetically speaking, after fixing the breach (and attending to the emergency), either: (a) the HCP would have intervened to do an act (X) to prevent the victim's harm—he was not legally compelled to do X (i.e., it would not have been negligent if he had not done X), but on the balance of probabilities, he would have done X; or (b) the HCP would not have done X, and it would have been negligent for him not to have done X—the proper discharge of the HCP's duty towards the victim required that he do X. In other words, the HCP cannot escape liability by saying that the victim's damage would have occurred in any event, because he would have committed some other breach (breach #2, not doing X) after the original omission (breach #1, failing to attend).

Secondly, in leading medical cases in which a duty to assist/attend *was* held (and where the HCP did not attend promptly or at all), the courts were prepared to hypothesise what the HCP would have done. For example, in *Barnett v Chelsea and Kensington Hospital Management Committee*,[155] it was held that the deceased night watchman would have been admitted, a blood and urine specimen taken, and an antidote to arsenic poisoning administered. However, because that antidote would have been given too late to reverse the disturbance of the enzyme processes which arsenical poisoning causes, causation failed. Similarly, in the instructive Australian case of *Lowns v Woods*, the trial judge held[156] that if the HCP had attended, he would have administered diazepam to the claimant Patrick Woods either intravenously at about 9.08–9.10 a.m. or rectally by about 9.12 a.m. (should intravenous access have not been attained), which would have ended the status epilepticus; and if a first dose given in those circumstances had not proved effective, a second dose about 10 minutes later would have been successful, before 9.30 a.m., in which event, Patrick Woods would not have sustained the serious irreversible brain damage (conclusions which were approved on appeal[157]). Also, in *Kent v Griffiths*, where the ambulance took an unexplained 34 minutes to turn up, and that delay caused Mrs Kent's damage, the English Court of Appeal remarked: '[o]n the findings of the judge it was delay which caused the further injuries. If wrong information had not been given about the arrival of the ambulance, other means of transport could have been used', and the claimant's respiratory arrest would have been prevented.[158]

As Khoury rightly observes, the but-for test of causation does, by its very nature, involve questions of what would have happened, and on that, with '[d]irect evidence about hypothetical situations rarely being available, the matter must be decided on the basis of generalisations about how things and people normally behave or ought to behave in given circumstances. This is often an evident inference'.[159] In other words, the court is customarily used to dealing with this task of hypothesising about the unknown.

Hence, if an affirmative duty to act/intervene/warn, etc, is to be imposed on a HCP, as an exceptional scenario, then a causal link would be, legally-speaking, sustainable.

2. Long chains of causation/intervening acts

In some non-patient scenarios, the most direct agent of the non-patient's harm was the *patient* who was being treated by the defendant HCP, and the non-patient's claim for damages may ultimately depend upon whether the patient's own conduct broke the chain of causation between HCP's breach and the non-patient's damage. Moreover, the longer the period between the alleged breach and the harm to the non-patient, the more difficult an unbroken chain of events will be to sustain. As other commentators have put it, some cases involving a HCP's potential liability towards non-patients 'involv[e] more distant impacts of negligent treatment or advice to a patient affecting another ... [and] in such cases, a role may arise for [causation and remoteness] consideration[s]'.[160]

For example, in the sphere of a third party's pure economic loss, take the case of *McLelland v Greater Glasgow Health Board*,[161] where Mr McLelland sued on the basis that he suffered economic and other injuries as a non-patient, given that the HCPs failed to carry out an amniocentesis test upon his wife during pregnancy which would, if performed, have shown that the foetus was suffering from Down's Syndrome. Mr McLelland argued that this was 'a wrong done to him directly'.[162] Of course, to make out his case, Mr McLelland's claim depended upon what his wife would or would not have done, had she been advised of the results of the test accurately. In order to recover damages in that claim, Mr McLelland had to establish that his wife would have aborted the foetus. In that regard, the judge at first instance found that the requisite causal link was established, because he accepted that the wife's decision would have been to terminate the pregnancy. Mrs McLelland knew that she had a genetic abnormality which carried an increased risk that a child of hers would be affected by Down's Syndrome, she had discussed the matter with her husband before she became pregnant, and had 'made a definite decision to terminate if tests showed that the child would be affected'.[163] Hence, if the tests had been performed as they should have been, the trial judge held that Gary, the baby affected by Down's Syndrome, would not have been born.

In the context of dangerous mentally-ill patients who commit murder or do a third party some grievous injury, causally linking the non-patient's damage to the HCP can seem tricky, not just because of the omission-to-act point which has been canvassed previously, but also because of the fact that the dangerous patient *himself* will have committed some significant damage to the non-patient by reason of his own criminal behaviour. Intriguingly, in what is the leading and best-known case of harm done to a third party by a mentally-deranged patient, the California case of *Tarasoff v The Regents of the University of California*, the Supreme Court there did not address causation at all, when finding in favour of Tarasoff's estate—an omission which has rightly been academically criticised.[164] However, it should be noted that, in *Dorset Yacht*, the criminal behaviour of the Borstal boys did not sever the chain of causation (and, thus, did not constitute a *novus actus interveniens*[165]) between the Borstal officers' lack of supervision and the property damage which ultimately occurred to the claimants' yacht. Indeed, the concept of a *novus actus* operating here is implausible—for, as McIvor discusses:

> it would be nonsensical to decide that there is a duty to control the acts of a third party, but then to hold that the third party conduct breaks the chain of causation. Therefore, in third party liability claims involving a specific affirmative duty of control, it will not be open to the defendant to raise a *novus actus* argument.[166]

The causal conundrums that apply in the abovementioned non-patient scenarios—regarding the occurrence of pure economic loss, or physical harm inflicted by a 'dangerous patient'—are considered further in Chapters 7 and 3, respectively.

F CONCLUSION

Non-patient claims against HCPs are, generally speaking, novel, and at the 'cutting edge' of the law of negligence. Indeed, whether a non-patient can establish a successful suit against a HCP throws into sharp relief the limitations of the negligence action in the health care setting.[167] Hallmarks of an evolving area of the law abound in non-patient scenarios—e.g., strike-out applications, determinations of preliminary points of law, and distinguishing prior leading cases as being the product of another era of judicial thinking.

The main (but not the only) 'battle-grounds' for a non-patient minded to bring such a suit will be establishing a duty of care on the part of the HCP to avoid the harm which the non-patient suffered, and proving the requisite causal link.

In Parts II and III, attention will turn to those legally-fascinating lawsuits brought by those claimants who do **not** resemble the traditional visitor to a hospital or surgery or who otherwise defy the usual HCP–patient relationship.

ENDNOTES

[1] To adopt a phrase from: M Hall *et al, Health Care Law and Ethics* (7th edn, Aspen Publishers Wolsters Kluwer, New York NY, 2007) 192–96.

[2] For discussion of these three tests, see, e.g.: *Customs and Excise v Barclays Bank plc* [2006] UKHL 28, [2007] 1 AC 181, [4] (Lord Bingham), [82] (Lord Mance) (*Customs and Excise*).

[3] Derived from *Caparo Industries plc v Dickman* [1990] 2 AC 605 (HL) 617–18 (Lord Bridge) ('*Caparo*').

[4] *Van Colle v Chief Constable of the Hertfordshire Police* [2008] UKHL 50, [2009] 1 AC 225, [42] (Lord Bingham), and endorsed in *Mitchell v Glasgow CC* [2009] UKHL 11, [2009] 1 AC 874, [21] (Lord Hope).

[5] Remarked upon in: *Neil Martin Ltd v Revenue and Customs* [2006] EWHC 2425 (Ch) [86].

[6] [2005] EWCA Civ 596, [6].

[7] *Customs and Excise v Barclays Bank plc* [2006] UKHL 28, [2007] 1 AC 181, [4] (Lord Bingham).

[8] e.g.: *Rowley v Secretary of State for Dept of Work and Pensions* [2007] EWCA Civ 598, [2007] 1 WLR 2861, [26]; *Patchett v Swimming Pool & Allied Trades Assn Ltd* [2009] EWCA Civ 717, [18].

[9] e.g.: *Parkinson v St James & Seacroft University Hosp NHS Trust* [2001] EWCA Civ 530, [2002] QB 266, [17]–[18] (Brooke LJ). In *Groom v Selby* [2001] EWCA Civ 1522, (2002) 64 BMLR 47, [31], Hale LJ said that '[a]s I also made clear in *Parkinson*, insofar as we are required to apply the battery of tests laid down by the House of Lords in determining the ambit of liability in any novel type of case, I agreed with the careful analysis and application of those tests by Brooke LJ in that case'. See too, the comment by Rix LJ in *West Bromwich Albion Football Club Ltd v El-Safty* [2006] EWCA Civ 1299, [2007] PIQR P7, [56], that 'whether the focus of interest was foreseeability, the assumption of responsibility, reliance, proximity, an incremental approach, or what was fair, just and equitable, all these concepts were well capable of producing an answer in this case in favour of Mr El-Safty's liability to WBA' (ultimately, no duty of care was owed).

[10] *Merrett v Babb* [2001] EWCA Civ 214, [2001] QB 1174, [41] (May LJ).

11   A Dugdale and M Jones (eds), *Clerk and Lindsell on Torts* (19ᵗʰ edn, Sweet & Maxwell, London, 2006) [7.95], citing: *Bank of Credit and Commerce Intl (Overseas) Ltd v Price Waterhouse (No 2)* [1998] PNLR 564 (CA) 583–87 (Sir Brian Neill).

12   R Oppenheim, 'The "Mosaic" of Tort Law: The Duty of Care Question' [2003] *JPIL* 151, 152.

13   *Customs and Excise* [2006] UKHL 28, [2007] 1 AC 181, [83] (Lord Mance), citing: *Caparo* [1990] 2 AC 605 (HL) 617–18 (Lord Bridge), 633 (Lord Oliver).

14   [1990] 2 AC 605 (HL) 618. The quote is taken from Saville LJ's later judgment in *Marc Rich & Co AG v Bishop Rock Marine Co Ltd* [1994] 1 WLR 1071 (CA) 1077, which was cited on further appeal as being a convenient paraphrase of the *Caparo* principle governing novel scenarios: [1996] 1 AC 211 (HL) 235 (Lord Steyn).

15   [2005] EWCA Civ 596, [14].

16   *Mitchell v Glasgow CC* [2009] UKHL 11,[2009] 2 WLR 481, [18] (Lord Hope), citing: *A-G of the British Virgin Islands v Hartwell* [2004] UKPC 12, [2004] 1 WLR 1273, [21] (Lord Nicholls).

17   Both terms used in, e.g.: *Hartwell, ibid,* [21], [38].

18   [2005] EWCA Civ 596.

19   *ibid,* [15].

20   *ibid,* [16].

21   (1997) 39 BMLR 35 (CA).

22   *Caparo* [1990] 2 AC 605 (HL) 633 (Lord Oliver). See, too, *Stovin v Wise* [1996] AC 923 (HL) 932 (Lord Nicholls) ('[p]roximity is convenient shorthand for a relationship between two parties which makes it fair and reasonable one should owe the other a duty of care', suggesting a close overlap between the second and third limbs of *Caparo's* test); and *Sutradhar v Natural Environment Research Council* [2006] UKHL 33, [2006] 4 All ER 490, [49] (Lord Brown) ('the three pre-conditions to the imposition of a duty of care classically formulated in *Caparo* ... to a substantial degree overlap. There are copious statements throughout the case law and the academic commentaries to that effect').

23   *Islington LBC v University College London Hospital NHS Trust* [2005] EWCA Civ 596, [49].

24   [1989] AC 53 (HL) 60.

25   [1992] 2 NZLR 282 (NZCA) 294 (Cooke P).

26   [1990] 2 AC 606 (HL) 618 (Lord Bridge), 633 (Lord Oliver).

27   [1992] 1 AC 310 (HL) 410 (Lord Oliver).

28   To borrow a phrase from *Ellis v Counties Manukau District Health Board* [2006] NZHC 826, [2007] 1 NZLR 196 (HC) [131] (Potter J).

29   *Islington LBC v University College London Hospital NHS Trust* [2005] EWCA Civ 596, [20] (Buxton LJ).

30   *Stovin v Wise* [1996] AC 923 (HL) 932 (Lord Nicholls).

31   *K v Secretary of State for the Home Dept* [2002] EWCA Civ 775, [26].

32   *K, ibid,* [24]–[30] (re an escapee awaiting deportation who raped a member of the public while at large).

33   *Palmer v Tees HA* (1998) 45 BMLR 88 (QB) 101 (Gage J).

34   *K v Secretary of State for the Home Dept* [2002] EWCA Civ 775, [29], [35].

35   See p 4.

36   *Tarasoff v The Regents of the University of California,* 17 Cal 3d 425, 435, 551 P 2d 334, 343, 131 Cal Rptr 14, 23 (Cal 1976) (emphasis added).

37   [1932] AC 562 (HL) 581.

38   (1998) 39 BMLR 35 (CA) [29] (Stuart-Smith LJ).

39   *Phelps v Hillingdon LBC* [2001] 2 AC 619 (HL) 671–72.

40   M Lunney and K Oliphant, *Tort Law: Text and Materials* (3ʳᵈ edn, OUP, Oxford, 2007) 143.

41   C Harlow, *State Liability—Tort Law and Beyond* (OUP, Oxford, 2004) 30, as cited in: I Steele, 'Public Law Liability: A Common Law Solution?' (2005) 64 *CLJ* 543, 545.

42   B Markesinin and J Fedtke, 'Damages for the Negligence of Statutory Bodies: The Empirical and Comparative Dimension to an Unending Debate' [2007] *Public Law* 299, 325.

43 [2005] EWCA Civ 596, [34]; and also [53] (Ouseley LJ) ('Although I can see that recovery for Islington would be fair just and reasonable in ordinary terminology, that test is the point at which the factors of public policy ... are brought in. They make a duty of care owed to Islington ... a leap too far').

44 *Hill v Chief Constable of West Yorkshire* [1989] AC 53 (HL) 63–64 (Lord Keith).

45 *Smith v Chief Constable of Sussex Police; Van Colle v Chief Constable of Hertfordshire Police* [2008] UKHL 50, [2009] 1 AC 225, [73] (Lord Hope), referring to suits against the police for failing to prevent crime. For comments about changing policy in the context of barristers' immunity from prosecution in negligence, see too: *Arthur JS Hall & Co v Simons* [2002] 1 AC 615 (HL) 682–83, 688.

46 e.g.: *Hill v Chief Constable of West Yorkshire* [1989] AC 53 (HL) 63 (Lord Keith) 65 (Lord Templeman); *Phelps v Hillingdon LBC* [2001] 2 AC 619 (HL) 672–74 (Lord Clyde), and earlier: [1998] EWCA Civ 1686, [65] (Stuart-Smith LJ); *McFarlane v Tayside Health Board* [2000] 2 AC 59 (HL) 83 (Lord Steyn); *X (Minors) v Bedfordshire CC* [1995] 2 AC 633 (CA) 661–63 (Sir Thomas Bingham MR), and on appeal: [1995] 2 AC 633 (HL) 749–51 (Lord Browne-Wilkinson); *Alexandrou v Oxford* [1993] 4 All ER 328 (CA); *Osman v Ferguson* [1993] 4 All ER 344 (CA).

47 The phrase used in: *X (Minors) v Bedfordshire CC* (CA), *ibid*, 663 (Sir Thomas Bingham MR) and (HL) 749 (Lord Browne-Wilkinson). See too: *Capital & Counties plc v Hampshire CC* [1997] QB 1004 (CA) 1040.

48 *Praesel v Johnson*, 967 SW 2d 391, 397 (Tex 1998).

49 *Powell v Boldaz* (1997) 39 BMLR 35 (CA) 46.

50 *Goodwill v British Pregnancy Advisory Service* (1996) 31 BMLR 83 (CA) 92 (Thorpe LJ) 91 (Peter Gibson LJ).

51 [1964] AC 465 (HL).

52 *ibid*, 502–3.

53 *Hedley Byrne & Co Ltd v Heller & Partners Ltd* [1964] AC 465 (HL), and applied/cited several times since, in the context of pure economic loss, e.g.: *Smith v Eric S Bush (a firm)* [1990] 1 AC 831 (HL); *Caparo Industries plc v Dickman* [1990] 2 AC 605 (HL); *Williams v Natural Life Health Foods Ltd* [1998] 1 WLR 830 (HL); *Phelps v Hillingdon LBC* [2001] 2 AC 619 (HL).

54 *Spring v Guardian Ass plc* [1995] 2 AC 296 (HL) 318 (Lord Goff); *Henderson v Merrett Syndicates Ltd* [1995] 2 AC 145 (HL) 180 (Lord Goff); *White v Jones* [1995] 2 AC 207 (HL).

55 As occurred, e.g., in: *Watson v British Boxing Board of Control* [2001] QB 1134 (CA); *Kent v Griffiths* [2001] QB 36 (CA); *L (a minor) v Reading BC* [2001] EWCA Civ 346, [2001] 1 WLR 1575. See too: *Sutradhar v Natural Environment Research Council* [2006] UKHL 33, [2006] 4 All ER 490, [36]–[39] (no duty of care owed by the Natural Environment Research Council to persons in Bangladesh re contaminated drinking water, arising from allegedly misleading geological report, according to the *Hedley Byrne* test).

56 [2006] UKHL 28, [2007] 1 AC 18 (HL).

57 *ibid*, [4] (Lord Bingham).

58 [2006] EWCA Civ 1299, [2007] PIQR P7 (CA).

59 [2001] QB 36 (CA).

60 *Thake v Maurice* [1986] QB 644 (CA); and, more recently: *Dow v Tayside University Hosp NHS Trust* 2006 SCLR 865 (Sheriff Ct). In neither case was a guaranteed successful outcome upheld. Note too, *A v Ministry of Defence* [2003] EWHC 849 (QB) (the MOD had assumed responsibility to exercise reasonable care to select appropriate medical service providers in Germany for MOD employees and their families, but had not assumed responsibility to ensure that the German medical professionals acted non-negligently).

61 See, e.g., the discussion of this point in: Irish LRC, *Civil Liability of Good Samaritans and Volunteers* (Rep 93, 2009) [3.26]; and 'Duties in Contract and Tort', in A Grubb, J Laing and J McHale (eds), *Principles of Medical Law* (3rd edn, OUP, Oxford, 2010), ch 3, [3.17]–[3.23], [3.28].

62 *Henderson v Merrett Syndicates Ltd* [1995] 2 AC 145 (HL) 181.

63 *Phelps v Hillingdon LBC* [2001] 2 AC 619 (HL) 654 (Lord Slynn).

64 See, e.g., the discussion in: *Merrett v Babb* [2001] EWCA Civ 214, [2001] QB 1174, [41] (May LJ).

65 *Customs and Excise* [2006] UKHL 28, [5].

66 (1995), 57 ACWS (3d) 119 (BCSC).

67   *ibid*, [32], [35].
68   *Customs and Excise* [2006] UKHL 28, [14].
69   Irish LRC, *Civil Liability of Good Samaritans and Volunteers* (Rep 93, 2009) [3.28].
70   *ibid*, [3.29].
71   *ibid*, [3.31], citing: J Kortmann, *Altruism in Private Law* (OUP, Oxford, 2005) 64.
72   As occurred, e.g., in *Goodwill v British Pregnancy Advisory Service* [1996] 1 WLR 1397, (1996) 31
     BMLR 83 (CA) 92 (Thorpe LJ).
73   Irish LRC, *Civil Liability of Good Samaritans and Volunteers* (Rep 93, 2009) [3.30].
74   See references in *Hedley Byrne & Co Ltd v Heller & Partners Ltd* [1964] AC 465 (HL) 497, 503 (Lord
     Morris), 510 (Lord Hodson), 529 (Lord Devlin).
75   (1995), 57 ACWS (3d) 119 (BCSC).
76   [2007] PIQR P7 (CA).
77   *ibid*, [59]–[60] (Rix LJ).
78   This statement was Brennan J's in *Sutherland SC v Heyman* (1985) 157 CLR 424 (HCA) 481, and was
     expressly approved and adopted in *Caparo* [1990] 2 AC 605 (HL) 618 (Lord Bridge).
79   *Customs and Excise* [2006] UKHL 28, [2007] 1 AC 181, [7].
80   *Islington LBC v University College London Hospital NHS Trust* [2005] EWCA Civ 596, [25], who called
     it a reaction to the two-part test of duty of care—foreseeability and public policy—put forward by Lord
     Wilberforce in *Anns v Merton LBC* [1978] AC 728 (HL) 752.
81   *Islington LBC, ibid*, [27].
82   J Spencer, 'Liability for Purely Economic Loss Again: "Small Earthquake in Chile, Not Many Dead?" (2006)
     65 *CLJ* 13, 14.
83   R Oppenheim, 'The "Mosaic" of Tort Law: The Duty of Care Question' [2003] *JPIL* 151, 161, citing, as
     illustration: *Perrett v Collins* [1998] 2 Lloyd's Rep 255 (CA).
84   K Stanton, 'Professional Negligence: Duty of Care Methodology in the Twenty-First Century' (2006) 22
     PN 134, 141.
85   See, e.g., the positions noted at trial in: *West Bromwich Albion Football Club Ltd v El-Safty* [2005] EWHC
     2866, [2006] PNLR 18 (QB) [48] (Royce J); and see too the discussion of the respective positions in:
     Islington LBC v University College London Hospital NHS Trust [2005] EWCA Civ 596, [28]. Note, also,
     the comments in *Waters v Commr of Police* [2000] 1 WLR 1607 (HL) 1613 (Lord Steyn).
86   As noted in *Islington, ibid*, [32].
87   See p 4.
88   [2005] EWHC 2866, [2006] PNLR 18 (QB) [67] (Royce J).
89   *ibid*, [67].
90   [2007] PIQR P7 (CA).
91   [2005] UKHL 23, [2005] 2 AC 373, [102].
92   *Freeman v Sutter* (1996), 4 WWR 748, 110 Man R (2d) 23 (Man CA) [10]–[11].
93   *ibid*, [13].
94   2001 SLT 446 (CSIH).
95   *ibid*, [9], [11].
96   [1992] 1 AC 310 (HL) 412.
97   To borrow a phrase from: *Merthyr Tydfil County BC v C* [2010] EWHC 62 (QB) [32] (Hickinbottom J).
98   *ibid*, [30]–[36], with reference to *Caparo's* test at [12]. This was a third party case where a parent sued a
     local authority, allegedly for failing to act appropriately upon her information that her two children were
     being sexually abused by a neighbour's child.
99   GMC, *Good Medical Practice* (2006) [1]. See too, [21d], that doctors 'must respect patients' privacy and
     right to confidentiality'.
100 [1988] 2 All ER 648 (QB) 653.
101 c 22, s 10, 11 (in force 26 Sep 1984). The list of 'notifiable diseases' is contained in s 10, and includes
     cholera, small pox and typhus. See too, the Public Health (Infectious Diseases) Regulations 1988 (SI No
     1546).

[102] See, e.g.: J Herring, *Medical Law and Ethics* (2nd edn, OUP, Oxford, 2008) ch 2, 5; J Montgomery, *Health Care Law* (2nd edn, OUP, Oxford, 2003) ch 11; E Jackson, *Medical Law: Text, Cases and Materials* (OUP, Oxford, 2006) ch 6. See too: GMC, *Confidentiality* (2009) [17]–[23].

[103] [1989] EWCA Civ 13, [1990] 1 Ch 359 (CA) 419.

[104] *A-G v Guardian Newspapers Ltd (No 2)* [1990] 1 AC 109 (HL) 282.

[105] See GMC, *Confidentiality* (2009), and see, earlier: GMC, *Confidentiality: Protecting and Providing Information* (2004) [27]. See, too: *Good Medical Practice* (2006) [37], 'Confidentiality'. The GMC's guidance, *Consent: Patients and Doctors Making Decisions Together* (2008) expressly does not cover doctors' responsibilities to disclose information about patients (at 4).

[106] See also: GMC, *Confidentiality: Disclosing Information about Serious Communicable Diseases* (2009), and, previously: GMC, *Serious Communicable Diseases* (Oct 1997) [22].

[107] See the Frequently Asked Questions of real-life scenarios, quotations from FAQ 17, available at: <http://www.gmc-uk.org /guidance/current/library/ confidentiality_faq.asp#q17>. Since embodied in new guidance: GMC, *Confidentiality: Reporting Concerns About Patients to the DVLA or the DVA* (2009) [6].

[108] Drivers Medical Group DVLA (Feb 2008) 4, citing: *Confidentiality: Protecting and Providing Information*, *ibid*. See now, the GMC's new DVLA guidance, *ibid*, [7].

[109] C McIvor, *Third Party Liability in Tort* (Hart Publishing, Oxford, 2006) 16.

[110] [1987] AC 241 (HL) 261, 272 (Lord Goff), and reiterated in, e.g.: *Gorringe v Calderdale MBC* [2004] 1 WLR 1057 (HL) [17] (Lord Hoffmann); *Customs and Excise v Barclays Bank plc* [2006] UKHL 28, [2007] 1 AC 181, [39]; *Mitchell v Glasgow CC* [2009] UKHL 11, [2009] 1 AC 874, [15] (Lord Hope), [39] (Lord Scott).

[111] [1996] AC 923 (HL) 943–45 (Lord Hoffmann).

[112] *R v Evans* [2009] EWCA Crim 650, [17] (Lord Judge CJ).

[113] See pp 160–67.

[114] *Stovin v Wise* [1996] AC 923 (HL) 943–45.

[115] [2009] UKHL 11, [2009] 1 AC 874.

[116] *ibid*, [44]. Cf: Lord Rodger and Baroness Hale were not quite so prepared to dismiss this case as one of mere omission, given that the Council called the meeting with Mr Drummond and hence, 'played a part' in the tragedy which eventually unfolded that afternoon: at [55] and [76], respectively.

[117] *ibid*, [40].

[118] 17 Cal 3d 425, 551 P 2d 334 (Cal 1976).

[119] [1999] EWCA Civ 1533, [2000] PNLR 87 (CA) 108.

[120] NZHC, Master Thomson, 19 May 2000.

[121] (1991), 116 AR 81 (Alta QB).

[122] *Ultramares Corporation v Touche*, 174 NE 441, 444 (1931).

[123] *Hill v Chief Constable of West Yorkshire* [1989] AC 53 (HL). Followed in, e.g.: *Brooks v Metropolitan Police Commr* [2005] 1 WLR 1495 (HL); *Osman v Ferguson* [1993] 4 All ER 344 (CA) (where there *was* a special risk to the victim here, but the claim was struck out for the same policy reasons as articulated in *Hill*).

[124] *Smith v Chief Constable of Sussex Police; Van Colle v Chief Constable of Hertfordshire Police* [2008] UKHL 50, [2009] 1 AC 225 (HL).

[125] *Swinney v Chief Constable of Northumbria Police* [1997] QB 464 (CA).

[126] *Dorset Yacht Co Ltd v Home Office* [1970] AC 1004 (HL) 1070.

[127] *Doe v Metropolitan Toronto (Municipality) Commrs of Police* (1989), 39 OR (3d) 487 (Gen Div) (victim single, white female, living in the Church-Wellesley area of Toronto; victims all resided in 2nd or 3rd floor apartments; duty of care owed).

[128] *Goodwill v British Pregnancy Advisory Service* (1996) 31 BMLR 83 (CA) 92 (Thorpe LJ), 91 (Peter Gibson LJ).

[129] (1991), 116 AR 81 (Alta QB).

[130] [1955] UKHL 2, [1955] AC 549 (HL).

[131] *ibid*, 564 (Lord Tucker). Reinforced in, e.g., *Dorset Yacht Co Ltd v Home Office* [1970] AC 1004 (HL) 1039 ('there may be a duty of care which may be owed to any one of a class of persons: it could be owed to all persons who could reasonably be foreseen as being liable to be injured by a failure to exercise reasonable care. That was the position in *Carmarthenshire CC v Lewis*').

[132] As in, e.g.: *Islington LBC v University College London Hospital NHS Trust* [2005] EWCA Civ 596.

[133] C McIvor, *Third Party Liability in Tort* (Hart Publishing, Oxford, 2006) 11–12, 160–62.

[134] *Eckersley v Binnie & Partners* (1988) 18 Con LR 1 (CA) 80 (Bingham LJ).

[135] *Bull v Devon AHA* [1993] 4 Med LR 117, (1989) 22 BMLR 79 (CA) (Dillon LJ) (the judgment date in this case was 2 Feb 1989).

[136] *Wilsher v Essex AHA* [1987] QB 730 (CA) 747 (Mustill LJ). See too: *Cardin v La Cité de Montréal* [1961] SCR 655 (SCC), 29 DLR (2d) 492 (SCC) 494 (Taschereau J) ('Cases necessarily occur in which, in spite of exercising the greatest caution, accidents supervene and for which nobody can be held responsible. The doctor is not a guarantor of the operation which he performs or the attention he gives ... Perfection is a standard required by law no more for a doctor than for other professional men, lawyers, engineers, architects, etc.').

[137] A point also made in: M Thomas, 'Expanded Liability for Psychiatrists: *Tarasoff* Gone Crazy?' [2009] *J of Mental Health Law* 45, 54–55.

[138] A Samanta *et al*, 'The Role of Clinical Guidelines in Medical Negligence Litigation: A Shift from the *Bolam* Standard?' (2006) 14 *Med L Rev* 32 (accessed online, no pp available).

[139] (1992), 13 CCLT (2d) 267 (Ont Gen Div), additional reasons at: (Ont Gen Div, 1 Apr 1993), aff'd: (1998), 41 CCLT (2d) 292 (Ont CA).

[140] *ibid*, [31].

[141] [2008] SKQB 464, (2008), 327 Sask R 35 (QB).

[142] *ibid*, [20].

[143] *ibid*, [21]–[23], and citing, at [21]: J Campion and D Dimmer, *Professional Liability in Canada* (Carswell Publishing, Ontario, 1994, looseleaf) [9–33].

[144] *Civil Liability of Good Samaritans and Volunteers* (CP 47, 2007) [2.42]–[2.43] and fn 33, citing both J Kortmann, *Altruism in Private Law* (OUP, Oxford, 2005) 24–27 and E Weinrib, 'The Case for a Duty to Rescue' (1980) 90 *Yale LJ* 247, 249–51.

[145] *Civil Liability of Good Samaritans and Volunteers* (Rep 93, 2009) [2.75].

[146] *Mitchell v Glasgow CC* [2009] UKHL 11, [2009] 1 AC 874, [55] (Lord Scott).

[147] C McIvor, *Third Party Liability in Tort* (Hart Publishing, Oxford, 2006) 15; J Steele, *Tort Law: Text, Cases, and Materials* (OUP, Oxford, 2007) 164–65.

[148] [1935] 1 KB 146 (CA) (also known as *Hynes v Harwood*). See too: *Goldman v Hargrave* [1967] 1 AC 645 (PC) (occupier of West Australian station property failed to douse burning tree which had been struck by lightning; he felled preparatory to it being removed; fire spread to adjoining land when gusty hot winds blew up; natural windy conditions and tinder-dry land the most immediate causes of property damage suffered by adjoining landowner; yet the occupier was liable in damages).

[149] [1970] AC 1004 (HL). See too: *Carmarthenshire CC v Lewis* [1955] AC 549 (HL) 571 (kindergarten liable for failing to keep its premises secure, allowing toddler to escape onto main road into the path of Mr Lewis's lorry; Mr Lewis killed in trying to avoid toddler; negligence proven; kindergarten created opportunity for harm to occur to Mr Lewis).

[150] [2002] UKHL 22, [2003] 1 AC 32.

[151] [2006] UKHL 20, [2006] 2 AC 572.

[152] [2005] 1 AC 134 (HL).

[153] *Lowns v Woods* [1996] Aust Torts R ¶81-376 (NSWCA) 63,156 (Kirby P).

[154] [1998] AC 232 (HL), where Lord Browne-Wilkinson adopted the earlier analysis of Hobhouse LJ in *Joyce v Merton, Sutton and Wandsworth HA* (1995) 7 Med LR 1 (CA) 20.

[155] [1969] 1 QB 428.

[156] (1995) 36 NSWLR 344 (SC). However, this report does not contain Badgery-Parker J's discussion of causation. Instead, that is to be found at the unreported citation, Butterworths Cases (BC) 9504451, at 65, and 82–90.

[157] [1996] Aust Torts R ¶81-376 (NSWCA) 63,155–63,156 (Kirby P), 63,176 (Cole JA).

[158] [2001] QB 36 (CA) [49].

[159] L Khoury, *Uncertain Causation in Medical Liability* (Hart Publishing, Oxford, 2006) 19.

[160] B Madden and J McIllwraith, *Australian Medical Liability* (Lexisnexis Butterworths, Sydney, 2008) [4.22].

[161] [2001] Scot CS 53, 2001 SLT 446 (CSIH).

[162] *ibid*, [9], [11].

[163] *ibid*, [5].

[164] M Thomas, 'Expanded Liability for Psychiatrists: *Tarasoff* Gone Crazy?' [2009] *J of Mental Health Law* 45, 53–54.

[165] *ibid*, 1030 (Lord Reid).

[166] C McIvor, *Third Party Liability in Tort* (Hart Publishing, Oxford, 2006) 19.

[167] For a similar comment: J Devereux, *Australian Medical Law* (2nd edn, Cavendish Publishing, Sydney, 2002) 111.

PART II
Actual or Potential Negligence Liability for Physical Injuries to Non-Patients

Chapter 3

Injuries to Non-Patients Caused by Physically-impaired or Mentally-ill Patients

A INTRODUCTION

It is a sad reality of life that, due to their medical conditions, patients can do grievous physical harm to others. Where a mentally-ill patient is being treated by a psychiatrist, is released under medical approval, and mixes with friends or strangers whilst being mentally unhinged, it is unsurprising that tragedy may, and sometimes does, follow. Alternatively, where a GP is treating a patient for a medical condition or physical impairment, and the GP does not take steps to ensure that the patient does not drive while suffering from that condition or impairment, the patient may become involved in a car accident. Several cases have arisen, in England and elsewhere, whereby the afflicted patient has killed or harmed another—from a family member to a complete stranger—in these circumstances. Where such misfortune arises, a potential non-patient suit may be considered against the relevant HCP.

In fact, this scenario of the so-called 'dangerous patient' is a clear indicator of the uncertain development of a HCP's liability to non-patients under English law. In 1937, in *Holgate v Lancashire Mental Hospitals Board, Gill and Robertson*,[1] a woman was seriously assaulted and injured in her house by a mentally-ill patient who had been released on a month's extended leave from a psychiatric institution. The woman's case in negligence against the relevant psychiatrist was put to the jury on the basis that a duty of care was owed by the psychiatrist to the injured woman. Three decades later, the House of Lords said that it would reserve its opinion as to whether *Holgate* was correctly decided.[2] Other jurisdictions which form the basis for the comparative study undertaken in this book have not been nearly so loath to recognise the potential for negligence liability in this scenario, however. Hence, the area is intriguing and controversial.

Section B outlines the key scenarios, and the main cases, which illustrate the problem of non-patients' suits against HCPs for harm done by physically-impaired or mentally-ill patients. Section C then considers the time-tested conundrum that arises in all third party suits against HCPs—whether (and, if so, why) a duty of care was, or arguably should be, owed by the HCP to the non-patient. Any duty of care established therein involves a novel scenario, and hence, the analysis undertaken in this Section adheres to the broad tri-partite framework established by *Caparo Industries plc v Dickman*.[3] Section D then focuses upon the various ways in which the leading and best-known United States case on the issue—*Tarasoff v The Regents of the University of California*[4]—has been treated in that jurisdiction. A duty of care was, in that case, owed by the patient's psychotherapist to a pre-identified third party whom the patient murdered. The case has a certain significance for English jurists, given that:– it has been cited by the House of Lords as authority for the proposition that, '[i]n some American jurisdictions, it has been accepted that a doctor may owe a duty to a person who is not his patient';[5] it was referred to by the English Court of Appeal in England's closest *Tarasoff* equivalent, the tragic case of *Palmer v Tees HA*;[6] and it has been referred to in other English case law too.[7] However, the House of

Lords' brief statement does not, and cannot, do justice to the lack of universal regard in which *Tarasoff* has been held by many American jurists and commentators. The stark disparity of views about the decision in its source jurisdiction conveys some important lessons for English law, which are explored in Section D. Section E concludes.

Given the book's focus upon *non-patients*, this chapter does *not* address the separate issue of a claim in negligence being brought by the *mentally-ill patient himself* against a HCP, alleging that the patient ought to have been better detained or better treated.[8] Similarly, the chapter also excludes from consideration negligence actions brought by *patients* against a health authority, for harm done to them by mentally-unbalanced co-patients within the same hospital, due to breaches of security or failure of supervision.[9]

In respect of 'dangerous patients', whatever the empirical evidence may suggest as to what HCPs *actually* do when they believe a third party to be at risk of serious physical harm from a patient, and whatever the general public may *expect* HCPs to do in that scenario,[10] the question of whether a HCP is under an *affirmative legal duty* to warn, or otherwise protect, the third party in danger is a difficult legal question. Its answer is the specific focus of this chapter.

B   THE POTENTIAL SCENARIOS

1. Injuries to non-patients caused by mentally-ill patients

A range of scenarios have arisen which signify that non-patients increasingly have HCPs in their litigious sights, when mentally-ill patients wreak havoc upon others, and when the allegation is made that the patient was medically ill-supervised or mis-treated and should never have been left in a position to do harm.

These lawsuits have been heard with more frequency in other comparator jurisdictions than in England, where the relevant case law remains relatively sparse. In chronological order:

> In *Holgate v Lancashire Mental Hosp Board, Gill and Robertson*,[11] John Lawson (L), a mentally-ill patient, was given a short leave pass from a prison hospital facility, on the assumption that he would stay with his brother. During this period, L attacked and seriously injured Mrs Holgate (the non-patient) in her house nearby, while she was home alone **Held:** a duty of care was owed by the treating prison doctors, Dr G and Dr R, to Mrs Holgate. This was implicitly acknowledged by the trial judge in his address to the jury—only breach was ultimately decided by the jury, who ruled in favour of the victim, and awarded damages in her favour.

> In *Partington v Wandsworth LBC*,[12] a 17-year-old patient with autistic tendencies, Claudia (C), was on a supervised outing from hospital with a care-worker. C pushed over Mrs Partington (P), an elderly stranger, in the street, breaking P's wrist. P sued the local authority which operated the hospital where Claudia was residing. **Held:** it was said to be 'common ground' that the hospital operators owed a duty of care to P, *viz*, a duty 'to take reasonable care to prevent [Claudia] from injuring her fellow citizens'. However, there was no breach proven on the part of the hospital or its employees, and hence, no liability.

> In *Palmer v Tees HA*,[13] the patient, Shaun Armstrong (A), was released from a mental facility on an out-patient basis, having disclosed to a psychiatrist before his release that he harboured sexual feelings towards children. A was released as an in-patient on 21 June 1993, and on 30 June

1994, he abducted, assaulted, killed and mutilated a four-year old neighbour, Rosie Palmer (RP), who lived nearby in the same street. As a result, RP's mother succumbed to psychiatric illness (both mother and daughter were non-patients in this case). Both sued the health authorities which conducted the hospital at which A was treated. They claimed that the health authorities and their employed medical and nursing staff were responsible for failing to provide any or any adequate treatment for A to reduce the risk of his committing such a heinous offence, for failing to prevent his release, and for failing to diagnose that there was a real, substantial and foreseeable risk of his committing serious, sexual offences against children. **Held:** no duty of care was owed by the health authorities, to either Mrs Palmer[14] or to her daughter RP, and the claim was struck out as disclosing no cause of action.[15]

In *Palmer*, the previous decision of *Partington* was not referred to at all, and *Holgate* was referenced in lukewarm terms only.

Suits around the Commonwealth jurisdictions, in which actions in negligence against HCPs were either successful or not ruled out altogether, have involved a wide range of claimants, from close family members to total strangers encountered in the street. To give a sample only:[16]

In the Canadian case of *Ahmed v Stefaniu*,[17] William Johannes (J) was diagnosed with acute psychosis. His status was re-classified by the defendant psychiatrist Dr S from involuntary mental patient to voluntary mental patient, which enabled his release into the community, where he lived with his sister, Roslyn Knipe (K) and her family. J murdered his sister K (the non-patient), less than two months after his release. K's husband, Mr Ahmed, commenced an action in negligence, inter alia, on his own behalf against Dr S. At the time of the murder, J was described as 'in a floridly psychotic, acutely delusional rage in which he believed that his sister was possessed by the devil'.[18] **Held:** a duty of care was owed by Dr S to K, the sister (accepted at first instance and not raised on appeal).

In the Canadian case of *Wenden v Trikha*,[19] Anil Trikha (T), the patient, was treated as a voluntary patient in the mental ward of a hospital, for serious mental illness (depressive and psychotic conditons). He eloped from the ward between 15-minute observations, retrieved his vehicle from the hospital carpark, and drove it at high speed through a red traffic light while suffering delusions (*viz*, that the car was a time machine). T severely injured the pregnant non-patient, Johanna Wenden (W), travelling in another vehicle at the intersection. T subsequently claimed to have no memory of the episode. W was severely injured in the accident, and eventually lost custody of her children, being unable to care for them. **Held:** no liability was proven—the treating physicians were held to be 'not in breach of any duty they may have owed to Trikha or to anyone else',[20] but the existence of a duty by T's treating doctors to W was not ruled out. The Alberta Court of Queen's Bench (affirmed on appeal) expressly left the question of any duty to W as a non-patient open—'[h]ad I found either the hospital or Dr Yaltho to have been in breach of their duty of care, the question whether [Mrs Wenden] fell within that class of persons to whom the duty was owed is not readily answerable ... Having made the findings I have, this question need not be answered'.[21]

However, in respect of non-patient claims against HCPs in negligence for the devastation wreaked by their mentally-ill patients, there have been a number of non-successful suits, both in Canada and New Zealand. The following is a sample of such cases, in which **no** duty of care has been owed by the relevant HCPs to the victims/non-patients:[22]

In the New Zealand decision of *Maulolo v Hutt Valley Health Corp Ltd*,[23] a patient was released from a psychiatric treatment facility, by certification of the defendant psychiatrists. About a year later, he killed his girlfriend, Miss Maulolo (the non-patient, M).

In *Van Der Wetering v Capital Coast Health*,[24] another New Zealand decision, a voluntary psychiatric patient, who was being treated as an in-patient, was released from hospital, following a re-assessment by his treating psychiatrists. A celebratory barbeque was held for neighbours, friends and relatives at his property shortly afterwards. During the barbeque, the patient shot dead his father and three others (the non-patients).

In the British Columbia case of *Robertson v Adigbite*,[25] Mr Adigbite (A), a mentally disabled adult male aged 27, was on an outing at a Costco store, in the company of two careworkers and another resident from the group home at which he lived. Arden Robertson (R), 65, the non-patient, was also shopping at the store. A attacked R without warning or provocation.

In the Manitoban case of *Mustafic v Smith*,[26] Ramiz Mustafic (RM), a voluntary patient in a hospital psychiatric unit, was let out on day pass by psychiatrist Dr S. During that temporary release, RM shot both of his children in the head and then shot himself. A child survived, and both widow and child sued Dr S in negligence for failing to sufficiently investigate whether RM was suffering from a mental disorder which made him a risk to himself and others. RM had been examined three days prior to the day of the shooting, and exhibited no suicidal or homicidal tendencies, had never in the past threatened or attempted suicide, or exhibited any tendency to do so.

While some of the abovementioned appear to be difficult to reconcile, Section C teases out the leading grounds on which decisions have turned.

As mentioned in the introduction, *Tarasoff*, a Californian decision, was the first American case to hold that a HCP may be burdened with an affirmative duty to protect a person from the actions of a violent patient—although, to be contrasted with this outcome is another, and subsequent, Californian case, the facts and verdict of which have some eerie parallels with *Palmer*:

In *Tarasoff v The Regents of the University of California*,[27] Prosenjit Poddar (P), a graduate student at University of California (Berkeley campus) had formed a friendly relationship with a fellow student which he took to be a serious romance, but which the young woman, Tatiana Tarasoff (T, the non-patient), did not. As a result, upon learning of T's true feelings, P underwent a severe emotional crisis. He eventually became a voluntary outpatient at the defendant hospital, and confided to the defendant psychotherapist Dr Moore that he intended to kill a friend 'when she returns from Brazil' (T spent the summer in Brazil). From the conversation, T was an unnamed but identifiable person. The therapist and his superiors decided that P should be confined by police. Later, the campus police at Berkeley interviewed P and were satisfied that P was rational, could not be involuntarily detained, and released him, on his promise to stay away from T. Neither T nor her parents were informed of the threat made by P. Two months later, P went to T's house and shot and fatally stabbed her. T's parents brought an action against the hospital, doctors and police on behalf of their daughter's estate. **Held**: the action in negligence against the medical and other defendants was permitted to proceed.[28]

In *Thompson v County of Alameda*,[29] Mr and Mrs Thompson and their five-year-old son Jonathan lived in the City of Piedmont, California, a few doors from the home of the mother of James F

(F), a juvenile offender. F had previously been held in an offenders' institution, where HCPs knew that F had 'latent, extremely dangerous and violent propensities regarding young children', and that violent sexual assaults upon young children were a 'likely result' of his being released into the community. F had conversations with his treating doctors which indicated that, if released, he would 'take the life of a young child residing in the neighborhood', but F gave no indication of which, if any, young child he intended as his victim. F was released on temporary leave into his mother's custody at her home. The County officials did not advise or warn F' mother, or the police, or the parents of young children within the immediate vicinity of the mother's house, of F's known propensities. Within 24 hours of his release, F murdered Jonathan in the garage of F's mother's home. Jonathan's estate sued the County, alleging that its HCP employees had been negligent in releasing F into the community, and/or failing to advise or warn the relevant parties (mother, police, parents of Jonathan), and/or for failing to exercise reasonable care in selecting F's mother to serve as the County's agent in maintaining custody and control over F. **Held:** the action was struck out as disclosing no cause of action. There was no duty of care imposed upon the County's employed doctors to the murdered child.

Further American authorities will be considered in Section D, when the ramifications of the '*Tarasoff* principle' in US jurisprudence will be more fully explored.

2. Injuries to non-patients caused by physically-impaired patients

To date, there have been no English cases concerning injury or deaths to non-patients, arising from the acts of a physically-impaired patient who was under the care of a defendant HCP. However, relevant case law from North America indicates that such litigation may arise in one of two circumstances.

First, where a patient has a naturally-occurring physical impairment or disability, for which he is being treated by the HCP, and that patient causes injury or death to a non-patient by losing control of his car, then the non-patient may allege that the treating HCP had a duty to prevent the patient from being in a position to drive and hence cause the damage. It may be alleged that the HCP failed to warn the patient of the risks associated with his physical condition and that he should not drive with that condition; or more tangentially, that the HCP failed to notify the relevant car licensing authorities of a patient's lack of fitness to drive. The following selection of Canadian decisions provide some interesting examples of what can go wrong:

In *Spillane v Wasserman*,[30] Mr Wasserman (W), a patient of the GP and neurologist defendants, suffered an epileptic seizure whilst driving his truck. W had a long history of epilepsy. W drove through a red light, and struck and killed Mr Spillane, who was riding a bicycle. Mrs Spillane sued the defendants, alleging that they owed a duty of care to her husband as a non-patient. **Held:** a duty of care was owed by the HCPs to S; and they were negligent for failing to properly monitor W, and for failing to report W's epileptic condition to the Registrar of Motor Vehicles.

In *Bakker v Van Santen*,[31] Mrs Van Santen (VS), the patient, had visual problems and wore an eye patch. She was involved in an accident whereupon she collided with Mr Bakker (B) on his bicycle, and B was seriously injured. B sued VS's GP in negligence, for not taking reasonable precautions to ensure that VS did not drive while wearing an eye patch, and while she was suffering from vision problems. **Held:** this was a consolidation application only, and the possibility of a duty of care was left open, with the court observing that '[t]he issue of whether a duty of care is owed by physicians to third parties other than patients, and the extent of that duty, is an unsettled area of law in Canada'.[32]

In *Toms v Foster*,[33] John Foster (F), the patient, had cervical spondylosis, a degenerative spinal condition, which caused both residual weakness and a lack of agility. F was involved in a motor vehicle accident in which Mark and Donald Toms (T), the rider and passenger on a motorcycle, were seriously injured. An action was brought by T against two HCPs (a GP and neurologist) who attended F before the accident. It was alleged that they knew that F's medical condition made it inadvisable that he be driving and that they failed to take appropriate steps to prevent him from driving. **Held:** the HCPs owed T a duty of care; and that, knowing that F suffered from a condition that might make it dangerous for him to operate a motor vehicle, it was negligent not to report F to the Registrar of Motor Vehicles.

The second scenario of potential liability for a HCP is where the patient's physical disabilities arise, not from natural circumstances, but because of medical treatment or medication that has been prescribed for him by the defendant HCP. It may be alleged that the HCP prescribed inappropriate medication for the patient, or failed to monitor medication correctly prescribed, or inappropriately reduced or ceased altogether medication for the patient, or failed to warn the patient not to drive because of the risks of seizure, drowsiness, blackout, etc, associated with use of that medication. As the following few examples of American cases illustrate,[34] this type of patient is not necessarily suffering from a physical ailment which of itself renders the patient disabled—the medical treatment or medication does that:

In *Taylor v Smith*,[35] Glenda Ennis (E) was treated by Dr S for heroin addiction at a drug treatment centre, on an out-patient basis. The almost daily treatment at the centre (at which E received a dose of methadone) was not particularly successful—over a five-month period, 13/14 urine analyses for E revealed the presence of either marijuana, benzodiazepines, or both. Moreover, E was not attending group counseling sessions and 'reported having no desire to stop using'. After each treatment, E drove herself home, an approximately 90-minute trip. On one of these trips, and while under the influence of methadone, E collided with a car driven by Ms Taylor (T), causing T serious personal injury. **Held:** Dr S owed a duty of care to T. Considering the distance and frequency of E's travel, as well as her persistent substance abuse, a vehicle accident was reasonably foreseeable, and there were no 'strong countervailing public policy reasons' as to why a duty of care should not be owed.

In *Myers v Quesenberry*,[36] two doctors, Q and B, were treating a pregnant patient, Ms Hansen (H), for diabetes. During an examination at Dr Q's office, Dr Q concluded that H's foetus had died. When Dr Q told H to have the dead foetus removed within 18 hours, H became emotionally upset. She was directed by the doctors to drive straightaway to a local hospital for preliminary laboratory tests. On the way, H lost control of her car, due to a diabetic attack, and struck Mr Myers (M) as he was standing by the side of the road. M sued the two doctors in negligence. **Held:** a duty of care was owed by the two doctors to M, for negligently failing to warn H not to drive in an irrational and uncontrolled diabetic condition.

In *Cram v Howell*,[37] patient Rodney Weninger (W) visited Dr H's office, where he was given certain immunizations and/or vaccinations. This treatment caused W to experience episodes of loss of consciousness, two of which occurred in Dr H's office. Despite this, Dr H did not monitor W for a sufficient period of time thereafter nor warn W of the dangers of driving after receiving the immunizations and/or vaccinations. While driving away from Dr H's office, W lost consciousness, and his out-of-control vehicle collided with George Cram (C), causing C's death. **Held:** Dr H owed C a duty of care, to take reasonable precautions in monitoring, releasing, and warning his patient for the protection of unknown third persons potentially jeopardized by W's driving upon leaving his office.

As the abovementioned authorities show, Canadian and American courts have been reasonably robust in their preparedness to find that a HCP may owe a duty of care to a non-patient in circumstances where the non-patient is harmed by a physically-disabled or physically-ill patient. Inevitably, in such cases, the non-patients will be complete strangers to the HCP—persons who happened to 'be in the wrong place at the wrong time', so as to literally collide with the HCP's patient. Whether such a finding would be likely to be upheld in English law is the subject of discussion in Section C.

Before proceeding to that analysis, however, it should be reiterated that there have, equally, been cases in the US which have denied liability of a HCP to a non-patient, where, say, a doctor advised a patient who suffered from seizures that it was safe for her to drive,[38] or prescribed Quaalude pills to a known drug addict,[39] or where a patient suffered from an epileptic attack and killed the non-patient in a car accident.[40] One of the key reasons given by some American courts for refusing to cast any duty on a HCP towards a non-patient harmed by a physically-disabled patient was that the responsibility for the safe operation of the vehicle should remain, primarily, with the driver, who was capable of ascertaining whether it was reasonable to continue driving in light of his physical difficulties. It has been stressed that physical impairment (unlike mental impairment) does **not** deprive the patient of self-autonomy and self-determination. Hence, if a patient suffers two blackouts and consults a HCP about them, and then suffers another blackout while driving, and collides with the non-patient's vehicle, the non-patient cannot complain, as against the HCP, that he ought to have warned the patient not to drive—that such a patient ought not to be driving, with that medical history, may be taken to be a matter of 'common knowledge based on common sense', and any duty on the part of the HCP has been precluded for that very reason.[41]

3. Injuries to non-patients by reason of medically-caused physical injury to the patient

The previous section has considered scenarios whereby a HCP prescribes medication to a patient which causes him some physical impairment, and the patient, in turn, does some positive act of driving to injure or kill the non-patient.

By contrast, and unusually, a twist in the scenario occurs where the HCP visits some medical negligence upon the patient in the form of an operative procedure, and that, in turn, causes a non-patient to suffer physical (as well as economic) injury. Again, Canadian case law illustrates just how non-patient suits have arisen from this rather bizarre scenario:

In *Urbanski v Patel*,[42] patient Mrs Firman (F) underwent a tubal ligation and investigatory surgery for abdominal pain. The defendant surgeon mistakenly mistook a kidney which was out of place (ectopic) as an ovarian cyst, and removed it. Disastrously, this was F's *only* kidney, the result of a congenital accident hitherto unknown or even suspected. F's father, Mr Urbanski (U), the non-patient, donated one of his own kidneys ('as what father would not?', asked Wilson J), 'in a vain effort to ease the disaster', but the transplant was not successful, and it was removed five days later. F was, as at the date of trial, undergoing thrice-weekly dialysis sessions, and had a very shortened life expectancy. Liability was admitted towards F and her husband for their joint claim for damages. Separately, donor U claimed damages for the operation and for other expenses associated with that operation. **Held:** general damages and expenses were recoverable by U. The transplant was a foreseeable consequence of the surgeon's negligent act. U had intervened, as a 'rescuer', and on that basis, a duty of care was owed to him by the surgeon who placed U in peril.

Interestingly, in a remarkably similar American case[43] involving a claim by a kidney donor against a surgeon who had negligently damaged his father's kidney, the son's argument that he was owed a duty of care as a 'rescuer' failed. Nevertheless, *Urbanski* was recently grouped by the Ontario Court of Appeal[44] with the decisions of *Spillane* and *Ahmed*, as examples of an 'evolving area' of where a doctor *may* owe a duty to a non-patient for harm arising out of a HCP's negligent treatment of a patient.

Hence, non-patient suits against HCPs can potentially arise where that non-patient is injured or killed by a mentally-unhinged patient, or by a physically-impaired patient, or (more rarely) where the injury occurs by reason of a medically-caused physical injury to the patient himself. Whether, and if so, why, English law would, or should, find that a HCP owes a duty of care to a non-patient arising out of the three scenarios considered in this Section, will form the basis of the analysis in Section C.

C CONSTRUCTING (AND DECONSTRUCTING) A DUTY OF CARE

Sixty years after the trial judge declared to the jury in *Holgate v Lancashire Mental Hospitals Board, Gill and Robertson*[45] that prison doctors could owe a duty of care to a woman harmed by a released mental patient, the Court of Appeal was not quite so keen to endorse the notion. In *Palmer v Tees HA*, Stuart-Smith LJ held that *Holgate* 'occurred at a time when the essential elements of a duty of care were much less clearly defined than is the position today',[46] and Pill LJ bluntly remarked that, '*Holgate* cannot be relied upon to establish an arguable case'[47] on behalf of murder victim Rosie Palmer, and her mother.

Courts are, nowadays, far more careful in their articulation of the basis upon which any defendant should be liable to some stranger for harm done by some person within the defendant's control, and the case of non-patient suits against HCPs is no exception. However, as will be seen shortly, the results of the duty of care analysis has not always netted entirely consistent results.

By reference to the case law presented in Section B, this Section explores how the elements of the tri-partite framework in *Caparo Industries plc v Dickman*[48] have been answered (explicitly or implicitly) in the novel scenario of non-patients seeking to render a HCP liable for failing to medically supervise/treat/control a physically- or mentally-impaired patient. Although there is a relative paucity of English case law on the subject, the analysis undertaken herein is intended to provide some guidance, should equivalent cases to those canvassed in Section B be brought before English courts in the future.

In a nutshell, the delineation of a duty of care to third parties in the health context generally, and in the context of harm done by the so-called 'dangerous patient' in particular, is difficult to state with much certainty, and reasonably hard to prove.

1. Reasonable foreseeability of harm

Where the HCP is treating a 'dangerous patient', the first of Lord Bridge's requirements in *Caparo*—reasonable foreseeability of harm to the non-patient—would ordinarily appear to be a formality. Occasionally, however, the element has given rise to controversy or comment.

For example, of the unusual scenario in *Urbanski* (where the father donated a kidney to his daughter, who lost hers because of the negligence of her surgeon), Klar has noted[49] that 'the goal of compensation has overtaken Lord Atkin's neighbour principle,' and has suggested that the notion that a kidney transplantation was an expected and anticipated result for a person whose own kidneys were lost, and that it would be entirely 'foreseeable' that a family member would agree to give up one of their kidneys for the benefit of a relative who was in need of one, was perhaps a stretch.

Additionally, where a patient had no history of prior dangerous conduct that would alert a HCP to the foreseeability of harm to another, the element may fail. As the British Columbia Supreme Court put it in *C (CL) v Lions Gate Hospital*, if the patient is an 85-year-old who had, prior to the incident, presented merely as a 'confused elderly man ... who found it difficult to settle down and wandered', his aggressive behaviour towards a third party could hardly have been forseen.[50] In *Robertson v Adigbite* too, Macaulay J held that '[b]ased on all that was known about [the disabled patient, A] there was no reason to foresee a likely risk that [he] would assault other shoppers at the Costco store.'[51] To hold that either of these assaults on the non-patients constituted reasonably foreseeable harm would be legally wrong, because it would 'elevate the principle of foreseeability to that of a guarantee against "unpredictable" and "unexpected" intrusions.'[52] Other Canadian non-patient suits have occasionally also failed on the basis that foreseeability of harm could not be proven, given the patient's behaviour and/or medical diagnosis prior to the incident.[53]

However, foreseeability of harm has not generally been controversial in the cases considered in this chapter, given the impairment under which the patient is labouring, and the dangers posed by such a patient to third parties.

Of course, the enquiry does not, and cannot, end there. Mentally-ill or physically-impaired patients often cause the relevant damage when mixing with the public or a cross-section of it, and as Stocker LJ stated in *Jones v Wright*, '[s]ome limitations must be put upon what is reasonably foreseeable if a duty of care is not to be owed to the whole world at large'.[54] The 'legal proximity' and 'legal and public policy' limbs serve that purpose, and attention will now turn to those requirements.

2. The requisite proximity between healthcare professional and non-patient

The court will search for the requisite nexus, or proximity, between the HCP and the non-patient. That may ultimately depend upon the circumstances as between patient and HCP, and as between patient and non-patient, **but** it is the overall quality of the relationship between HCP and non-patient that determines the issue (i.e., the hypotenuse of Figure 1.1[55]).

In seeking to establish this close and direct relationship, a non-patient will have regard to the following factors (none of which is being put forward here as being conclusive or definitive, but all of which may be relevant, depending upon the circumstances of the particular case):

Degree of control and/or warnings

The degree of control that the HCP can exercise over the patient's actions (including the provision of warnings), *or* the warnings that the HCP could reasonably have provided to the *non-patient directly* to guard him against the harm that befell him, will be highly relevant to the duty of care enquiry, in the case of harm done by physically-disabled or mentally-ill patients.[56]

As later discussion of *Tarasoff* will show, the much more extensive American jurisprudence on the topic has drawn a marked and crucial distinction between these two factors—warning the non-patient, and the ability to control the patient—in order to decide what (if any) duty should be cast on the HCP. However, they are dealt with under one heading herein, principally because they tended to be conflated in the leading English authority of *Palmer v Tees HA*. Re warning: the psychiatrists employed by Tees HA who were treating psychotic patient, Mr Armstrong (A), owed no duty to Rosie Palmer, the little girl whom he murdered, because, as Stuart-Smith LJ asked, 'what [could] the defendant ... have done to avoid the danger?'.[57] They could not have warned the family of every child living in the vicinity of A; and once released into community care, then any form of warning to potential victims, or of controlling the actions of A, ranged between 'of doubtful effectiveness' and utterly infeasible: 'the most effective precaution cannot be undertaken as the defendant does not know who to warn'.[58] Re control: the other principal protective measure—the involuntary detention of A—was no option either, given the 'considerable restrictions' which applied to the procedure. It would have had 'doubtful effectiveness' in any event, given the time that elapsed between the confessions by A of his violent fantasies and the murder itself. All of this pointed to a decision that it would be 'unwise to hold that there is sufficient proximity.'[59]

Once released into the community, or while under out-patient care, the degree of control over a psychiatric patient lessens considerably. The patient may not be taking his medication under close supervision, or maintaining constant contact with his HCP, or abstaining from alcohol or other drugs, perhaps, in the 'outside setting'. This factor was crucial in a trio of New Zealand cases which denied any duty of care towards the non-patients by the respective HCPs. In *Van der Wetering v Capital Coast Health*,[60] re the released patient who shot dead four people on his property including his own father, Master Thomson remarked that there was no way of controlling Van Der Wetering's behaviour, other than by obtaining a compulsory detention order; in *Ellis v Counties Manukau District Health Board*,[61] Potter J noted the importance of control or the *ability to exert control* on the HCP's part before a duty of care can arise; and in *Maulolo v Hutt Valley Health Corp Ltd*,[62] where the released patient shot dead his girlfriend while in community care, a similar point was made.

On the other hand, patients who are *detained* when they harm the third party non-patient probably expose the defendant doctor/hospital to a more likely finding that the defendants owed that claimant a duty of care. For example, in the New Zealand case of *S v Midcentral District Health Board (No 2)*,[63] in which an outpatient S was raped by a compulsory inpatient (P), the fact that P was an in-patient rendered him subject to far greater controls than had existed for the outpatients or voluntary patients in *Palmer*, *Maulolo* and *Van Der Wetering*. In *Ellis*, the fact of detention was explained as being an important distinguishing feature that contributed to a positive duty of care finding in *Midcentral*.[64]

The 'odd one out' of these Commonwealth decisions, regarding mentally-ill patients, is that of *Holgate v Lancashire Mental Hospitals Board, Gill and Robertson*[65]—and given the emphasis that is now placed upon the degree of control which the HCP could reasonably exercise over the dangerous patient, it is difficult to see how the decision can be considered correct, were it to be decided by an English court today.[66]

Finally, the ability for a HCP to provide practical warnings to the non-patient directly may be impossible in the context of the dangerous patient, given how often it is a member of the public who is injured or killed (recalling the comments of Stuart-Smith LJ in *Palmer*, above—a further example of a duty of care failing for this reason is provided by *Robertson v Adigbite*[67]). However, where the HCP was in a position to warn *the patient* of the dangers of medical treatment or medication that could render that patient prone to incapacity while driving, that factor has clearly influenced American courts to find a relevant duty in favour of a non-patient who was killed or injured by the ill patient.[68]

Vulnerability of the non-patient vis-à-vis the HCP

Relevant case law suggests that a HCP's information monopoly is a factor that *may* render a non-patient 'vulnerable' in a legal sense, where that non-patient is harmed by a patient. A HCP may have such a monopoly in two scenarios.

First of all, the HCP may have crucial information about the dangers posed by a patient, about which the non-patient knows nothing, and simply cannot ascertain for himself from any other source. Some case law expressly notes this point to be significant when trying to establish a nexus between a HCP and a third party injured by a mentally-ill patient.[69] For example, in *S v Midcentral District Health Board (No 2)*,[70] the violent sexual predatoriness of patient P was well-documented and known to the treating psychiatrists, a factor which contributed to the finding of a duty of care towards the co-patient S. The factor has been most inconsistently treated, however—given the admission by Armstrong to his psychiatrist that he felt driven to sexually abuse a young child in an interview prior to his release, *Palmer* is difficult to square with *Midcentral* on this point. However, the cases are probably more reconcilable on the basis of the geographical and temporal proximity present in *Midcentral* and entirely absent in *Palmer* (as discussed shortly).

In reality, the very nature of the medical relationship will inevitably entail that the HCP holds information about the physical or mental disabilities of the patient which was not known to external parties, such as the non-patient eventually harmed. Hence, it is arguable that the HCP's mere monopoly on information about the patient is not, and should not be, a weighty factor in the matrix of factors pointing towards a duty of care on the HCP's part.

Secondly, the HCP's greater knowledge of the medication or medical treatment which he has administered to a patient, and how that could adversely affect the patient physically, has proven to be a factor of some importance, where physically-disabled patients have harmed third parties. For example, in *Cram v Howell*,[71] the Indiana Superior Court held that the doctor who administered to his patient a vaccination which caused the patient to lose consciousness while driving, owed a duty to the injured non-patient, because the doctor knew (and the patient did not) that the immunisation could cause repeated loss of consciousness in some people. By failing to inform the patient of that information, the HCP (indirectly) rendered the non-patient vulnerable.

Temporal and geographic proximity

A lack of temporal proximity between the HCP's alleged breach, and the harm suffered by the non-patient, has proven to be a fairly significant factor tending against a duty of care—especially in those unfortunate cases in which a mentally-ill patient wreaks havoc and causes tragedy some considerable time after his allegedly negligent release.

For example, in *Palmer* (where A's murder of Rosie Palmer occurred just over a year from his release), Pill LJ observed that 'the passage of time and distance' between the two events had the consequence of no duty of care.[72] In *Maulolo v Hutt Valley Health Corp Ltd* too (where the patient murdered his girlfriend just over a year later after release), no duty of care was owed either—with the court noting that large time-spans also permit of 'several causative steps', including unpredictable human behaviour, between the HCP's conduct and the eventual tragedy.[73]

Moreover, the fact that the harm done by the patient occurred at a place which was geographically remote from the HCP's province of control has been specifically noted in some non-patient cases to militate against any duty of care being owed.

In *Van Der Wetering v Capital Coast Health* (the fatal barbeque case), the fact that '[t]he events giving rise to the injuries took place well away from the defendant's premises ... [meant that the deceased non-patients] could not sensibly suggest that they relied on the [doctor or health authority] not to cause harm to them and/or to protect them from its occurrence'.[74] The point was also made in *Maulolo*[75] and *Palmer*,[76] two cases of psychiatrically-ill patients running amok well away from the medical facility where they had previously been treated.

This is one factor in which the Canadian cases concerning physically-disabled patients whose dangerous driving has harmed or killed strangers appears to go further than English and New Zealand jurisprudence. If the lack of geographic proximity were as consistently applied as it was in *Van der Wetering*, *Palmer* and *Maulolo*, then the fact that a car accident between the patient and non-patient occurred some distance away from the defendant hospital's mental ward could not have possibly founded a duty of care in the Ontario case of *Wenden v Trikha*, for example—yet the court held the question open for another day.[77] In fact, a possible duty to the motoring public was referred to ('[i]f it could be said that the danger posed and foreseen was to members of the motoring public, then the plaintiffs may have been persons who fell within the requisite proximate relationship to the hospital and Dr Yaltho and persons whom they should reasonably foresee would suffer damage by reason of the actions of Trikha'[78]). It has been judicially noted by one Canadian judge[79] that Canadian jurisprudence may extend the boundaries of a duty of care more widely than the English jurisdiction does—and indeed, a lack of geographic proximity is an example of one nexus link that may be in England's bailiwick but not in Canada's.

Knowledge of the non-patient's identity

Very few cases resemble the tragic events of *Tarasoff v Regents of the University of California*,[80] where Mr Poddar specifically told his psychotherapist that he intended to kill Tatiana Tarasoff—and then did precisely that. The action in negligence was permitted by the California Supreme Court to proceed, because a 'special relationship' existed between psychotherapist and non-patient victim.

In English law, then, if the HCP knows of the identity of a non-patient who is potentially at risk from a mentally-ill patient's acts before the threat comes to fruition, is this sufficient, *of itself*, to fix the relationship between HCP and non-patient with the requisite proximity to base a duty of care? On the present state of authorities, the answer is, perhaps surprisingly, 'no'. In other words, were a *Tarasoff*-type case to arise in English law, it is **not** an automatic proposition of law that the HCP *would* owe a duty to the pre-identified victim. Four particular authorities support that assertion.

Firstly, in *Palmer v Tees HA*,[81] Pill LJ posed the hypothetical example: suppose that a psychotic patient says, 'after release from this mental facility, I will kill Y'. His Lordship said that he 'saw force' in the argument that whether the identity of a victim 'is known *ought not* to determine whether the proximity test is passed. It is forcefully argued that the difference between the threat "I will kill Y" and the threat "I will kill the first bald-headed man I meet" ought not to determine whether a duty is placed upon a defendant, though it would obviously go to the extent of the duty and the measures necessary to discharge it.'[82]

As the facts and outcome of *Palmer* made plain, the problem for Y (the non-patient) is that proximity is a nuanced enquiry—even if a patient were to say to a HCP, 'I'm going to kill Y after I'm out of here', other factors—geographic and temporal proximity, the degree of control over the patient, the ability to take precautions to prevent the harm to Y, or local 'environmental' influences—will also be highly relevant to the proximity enquiry. Some of these may well offset the fact that the identity of the unfortunate victim was known to the defendant HCP.

Secondly, the dreadful case of *Osman v Ferguson*[83] is probably the closest English equivalent to *Tarasoff*.

> In *Osman v Ferguson*, a schoolteacher Mr Paget-Lewis (P) formed an unhealthy attachment to a 15-year-old male pupil, Ahmed Osman (O), harassed him and his family repeatedly, made unfounded accusations of a sexual nature against the boy, changed his name to that of the boy's, and damaged and defaced the family's property and car. The police were intimately aware of the harassment and interviewed P, at which point P told the police that the loss of his job was distressing, and there was a danger that he would do something criminally insane. Almost a year after the campaign of harassment had begun, P followed O and his family to their flat, shot and severely injured O, and killed O's father. **Held:** the action by O and O's father's estate against the police was struck out as disclosing no reasonable cause of action.

In this case (and unlike *Palmer*), there was an 'arguable case' that 'a very close degree of proximity amounting to a special relationship' between the family and the police was established (clearly, the identity of the claimant victims was well-known to the police).[84] The court concluded, however, that it would be against public policy to impose such a duty on the police. The public policy reasons canvassed in *Osman* which negated a duty of care were derived from earlier case law arising from the police's investigations of the 'Yorkshire Ripper' murders[85]—and more recently, these policy reasons were again approved by the House of Lords in a third case of crucial significance to the present issue of a pre-identified victim.

In *Van Colle v Chief Constable of the Hertfordshire Police; Smith v Chief Constable of Sussex Police*,[86] persistent and serious threats were made against the claimant by his former partner, following a relationship break-up. That claimant was eventually attacked and seriously injured by his former partner, and sued the police for failing to take reasonable precautions to prevent the attack:

> In *Van Colle/Smith* (which comprised two appeals heard together), the question was whether, if the police are alerted to a threat that D may kill or inflict violence on V, and the police take no action to prevent that occurrence, and D does kill or inflict violence on V, may V or his relatives obtain civil redress against the police? Ongoing threats were made against Stephen Smith (S) by his former partner (Gareth Jeffrey, J) following the break-up of their relationship. S provided police officers with details of J's previous history of violence, J's home address and the contents of the messages. The officers did not look at the messages of threats, or complete a crime form or

take a statement from S. However, they took steps to trace the calls, liaised among other police officers and informed S of the progress of that investigation. S was then attacked at his home by J and sustained severe and continuing injuries. He sued the police in negligence for the officers' failure to protect him from the attack. **Held:** the action was struck out as disclosing no cause of action against the police.

The final authority of crucial importance to the issue of a pre-identified victim arose, not against a health authority or the police, but against a public housing authority.

In *Mitchell v Glasgow CC*,[87] Mr Drummond (D) and Mr Mitchell (M) had been council tenant residents since the 1980s, and during which time the neighbours got along very badly, due to D's anti-social behaviour (e.g., playing loud music during the night, smashing M's windows with an iron bar). D was arrested and jailed during this period for his behaviour, and he regularly threatened to kill M, and that he would be 'dead meat'. Other tenants heard D threaten M in this way. The Council warned D that if he persisted in this conduct they would take action to recover possession of his house, but the threats towards M and other neighbours continued at least once a month. In July 2001, the Council invited D to a meeting to discuss another violent incident involving D, and about a notice of proceedings for recovery of possession that had been served on him. D attended the meeting, lost his temper, became abusive, and meeting lasted less than an hour. He went straight home, and thereafter battered M with an iron bar or stick, causing serious injuries from which M died 10 days later in hospital. M's estate sued the Council, alleging that it did not warn M that they had summoned D to the meeting, nor did they make any attempt to warn either him or the police about his behaviour at the meeting or of any possible risk of retaliation against M as a result of it. M's estate alleged that, if M had been given these warnings, M would have kept out of D's way and would not have died. **Held:** the action in negligence could not succeed. There was no duty on the Council to prevent the risk of harm being caused to M by the criminal act of D, a third party, which the Council did not create and had not undertaken to avert.

As Lord Bingham remarked in *Mitchell*, a duty on a defendant to warn a person that he is at risk of injury as the result of the criminal act of another only arises when the defendant 'has by his words or conduct assumed responsibility for the safety of the person who is at risk.'[88] Lord Brown added that, in this case, 'there will be very few occasions on which a bare duty by A to warn B of possible impending violence by C will arise'.[89] Furthermore, given that the Council 'cannot in any meaningful sense be said to have created the risk of injury that foreseeably arose here, or to have assumed specific responsibility for [Mr Mitchell's] safety from [Mr Drummond], the contention that the Council was under a positive duty to warn [Mr Mitchell] and that the Council is liable for [Mr Mitchell's] death because of a mere omission to do so appears to me plainly unsustainable.'[90]

Hence, in *Palmer*, Pill LJ's example may have been only hypothetical, but in each of *Osman*, *Van Colle/Smith* and *Mitchell*, a victim was killed (or seriously injured) by a person whose propensities for violence were well-known to relevant public authorities, and where the victims were also well-known to the defendants, before the horrific events in each case occurred.

In combination, these four authorities tend to suggest that a HCP's knowledge of a non-patient's identity does not, of itself, give rise to a duty of care on the part of the HCP to protect or to warn the intended victim against the threat of danger posed by a dangerous patient. If the closeness of a landlord–tenant relationship was not sufficient in *Mitchell*, it also suggests that a HCP would similarly rarely assume such responsibility to a stranger living in the public domain, and distant in time and space from the HCP's sphere of influence and activity.

Notably, exceptions to the no-duty-to-warn/protect-third-parties rule *have* arisen in English law—where, say, the relationship between defendant and party doing the harm was jailor–custodian (one of real supervision and control over the actions of that party), or where the defendant armed the party doing the harm with a gun or other weapon that was used against the third party. However, these are very unusual scenarios, quite different from the landlord in *Mitchell*, and the HCP dealing with an out-patient in *Tarasoff* and *Palmer*.

Hence, on the basis of the authorities considered in this section, were a *Tarasoff*-type case to arise in England, the mere fact that the victim was pre-identified is not conclusive. It is only one of a matrix of factors which tend to show, or to disprove, proximity between the mental HCP and the third party victim.

The non-patient within an identifiable class, or 'at special risk'

Of course, the *Tarasoff*-type case is (thankfully) quite rare. Far more often, the HCP does not know the identity, or even of the existence, of the non-patient whom his patient maims or kills, in consequence of physical impairment or mental illness.

A HCP may owe a duty to that unknown non-patient if the non-patient was one of an identifiable class who was *at special risk* from the patient. However, if the non-patient was merely one of the vast number of general public members who was at risk, with no distinguishing feature separating out that non-patient from the public (apart from the fact that the non-patient was the one harmed), then no requisite proximity will be found, according to English and Commonwealth case law. That 'special risk' factor has been translated to the HCP–non-patient context.[91] Its absence is the factor 'that so often tells against a finding of proximity', as the New Zealand High Court put it.[92]

From an analysis of relevant English and Commonwealth case law summarised in Section B, five propositions are evident, as to who is, and is not, 'at special risk' from a patient.

First, where the dangerous patient happens to coincidentally come across the third party victim in public, then that victim is not at special risk—he was just in the wrong place at the wrong time. For example, in *Robertson v Adigbite*,[93] the British Columbia Supreme Court concluded that, even if it were reasonably foreseeable that A, the disabled man, would react aggressively while on a shopping trip (which it was not), it could not be said that the shoppers at the Costco store were members of a small readily identifiable class who stood in a higher risk category than the general public. Rather, Mr Robertson, the person attacked, stood in the same position of risk as any member of the public. It is on the same basis that, arguably, a duty of care should **not** have been conceded in *Partington's* case[94]—Mrs Partington's unfortunate encounter with patient Claudia was entirely coincidental.

Secondly, where the non-patient falls within an identifiable class of close relatives of the patient, that may assist to establish special risk. For example, in *Ahmed v Stefaniu* (the case in which the discharged mental patient killed his sister, with whom he lived after his release),[95] the treating psychiatrists did not know with whom the patient was to live after his release, yet, a duty was still capable of being owed by the HCPs to the sister, for she was one of a small identifiable class at risk. Additionally, those strangers who come within close temporal and physical proximity to the patient *at the time of the alleged medical breach* are probably distinguishable from the general public because they are in heightened danger, and the scope of the class is necessarily delimited by physical and temporal boundaries. The rape victim in *S v Midcentral District Health Board (No 2)*[96] fell within that category.

Thirdly, for the purposes of English law, a legacy of *Palmer* is that, as between HCP and stranger, a 'special risk' that turns upon a targeted demographic is going to be difficult to establish. The class of children of whom Rosie Palmer was one (analogous to the class of 'bald-headed men' given by Pill LJ) did not constitute sufficient 'at special risk' status for that victim— notwithstanding that she lived in close geographic proximity to Mr Armstrong and fitted the profile of those at risk from his violent sexual fantasies. In this regard, the hypothetical example provided by Cory J in the Canadian case of *Smith v Jones* ('it may be sufficient to engage the duty to warn if a class of victims, such as little girls under five living in a specific area, is clearly identified [rather than a specific individual]'[97]) does not represent current English law.

Fourthly, if a patient harms another road user, English jurisprudence would probably demonstrate more conservatism than the potentially long bow that has been drawn by some Canadian decisions—in *Spillane v Wasserman*[98] (the case of the epileptic driver who hit a bicycle rider), a duty of care was owed by the HCP to the non-patient; and in *Wenden v Trikha*[99] (the case of the student who thought his car was a time capsule), the Alberta Queen's Bench was not prepared to rule out a duty of care between his treating HCPs and the pregnant woman whom he seriously injured when driving his car through a red light. Clearly, where a physically-disabled or mentally-disturbed patient kills or injures a stranger because of his erratic driving, absolutely no knowledge of the identity of the stranger can be attributed to the treating HCPs, except that the stranger fell within that wide class of road users. It is *most* unlikely that an English court would attribute to these Canadian classes any 'special risk' necessary to uphold a duty of care.

As the court did not need to rule on the duty of care question in *Wenden v Trikha*, Canadian commentary has since tended to ascribe quite different viewpoints as to the significance of the decision. On the one hand, Evans categorically states that, 'under Canadian case law, [medical] practitioners have no legal duty to warn a third party'.[100] On the other hand, Flanagan comments of *Wenden* that a doctor may be liable, under Canadian law, for foreseeable injury caused to a wide class of potential third parties by a patient,[101] while Picard and Robertson concur that it 'seems likely that ... a Canadian court would endorse the general principles underlying the [*Tarasoff*] decision.'[102] In the writer's view, at the very least, the Canadian authorities to date tend to suggest that the test of 'special risk' is construed far more favourably in Canada than in England, and that the preparedness of Canadian courts to find a duty of care in respect of 'dangerous patients' is more obvious than it is, at present, in English law (this is a viewpoint which has also been put by one Canadian judge[103]). As noted in Chapter 2, in *Carmarthenshire CC v Lewis*,[104] a defendant kindergarten was liable to Mr Lewis, a third party road user, who was killed when a young child wandered out into a road adjacent to the kindergarten, but that decision rested on the test of reasonable foreseeability, well before proximity and public policy were adopted as such strong 'control mechanisms' in *Caparo*. If Rosie Palmer was not at special risk by merely living near Armstrong, it is difficult to see how a road user who happens to cross paths with a delusional patient driver would be either, so far as the English courts are concerned.

Fifthly and finally, also unlikely to be 'at special risk' is that class of persons who come within the patient's orbit at some point in the future, after the alleged medical breach has occurred. Courts in England and elsewhere have been less-than-sympathetically inclined to third parties who did not know the patient at all at the time of the breach. This factor has been important in cases where the claimant stranger has alleged pure economic loss caused by the medical breach;[105] and it is equally applicable to patients who cause personal injury to strangers. For example, in *Maulolo v Hutt Valley Health Corp Ltd*,[106] the patient killed his girlfriend about a year after his release from a psychiatric institution where he had been an inpatient for schizophrenia. The relationship commenced after the patient's release. No duty was owed, in part because it was impossible (said the court[107]) to distinguish the girlfriend from the public at large.

As McIvor has noted,[108] the requirement of proving that the claimant is 'at special risk' instead of being simply a random member of the public allows the court 'to exclude all but the most exceptional of cases'—and *Palmer* was not that sort of 'exceptional case'. Actually, the fact that Rosie Palmer failed in her negligence action is not particularly surprising, given the lack of proximity factors which the English courts hold to be so crucial to the construction of a duty of care—the outpatient setting, the lack of temporal or physical proximity between HCP and victim, the lack of control over Armstrong, the inability to warn the Palmers, in combination with the lack of 'special risk' on the victim's part. Also, the class of whom the little girl was one was too large to sit comfortably with most other English jurisprudence concerning third party claims (with the exception of the pre-*Caparo* decision of *Lewis v Carmarthenshire CC*).

Intervening reactive measures: reporting the patient

If a HCP's breach was that he failed to take a certain step, and performing that step would have both met the standard of reasonable care and would have almost certainly protected the non-patient from the harm that eventuated, then a finding of proximity between the HCP and non-patient is more likely. Termed by Ontario judge, Cullity J, as a 'foreseeable reactive measure ... [that] could possibly affect the issue of proximity',[109] it will go by the name of causal proximity in this section. Such a 'step', in the context of this chapter, may encompass reporting the patient's infirmities to an external authority such as the Driver and Vehicle Licensing Agency (DVLA).

In fact, the GMC recommends that a HCP report to the DVLA if a patient is medically unfit to drive, and that the HCP should 'make every reasonable effort to persuade them to stop' driving.[110] The DVLA Guidelines themselves advise the HCP to disclose to a medical adviser at DVLA if a patient continues to drive.[111] It follows that if the DVLA would have intervened, and the doctor's conduct in not reporting deprived the non-patient of that 'reactive measure' that would have prevented the harm from occurring, then causal proximity may be established.

Canadian authority confirms that, when legislation imposes a *duty* on a HCP to report that a patient is medically unfit to drive, and the HCP fails to do so, that can lead to civil liability towards a non-patient.[112] For example, in *Spillane v Wasserman*,[113] the patient's GP failed to report to the Registrar of Motor Vehicles that his patient, suffered epileptic night and daytime seizures, as statutorily required[114]—and Mrs Spillane, the widow of the road user that the patient killed, successfully alleged that the GP owed her husband a duty of care on this basis.[115] Had the GP reported the patient's physical impairment to the Registrar, the patient would have been de-licensed, and it would have then been unlikely that he would have been driving. In legal language, the Registrar would have taken the intervening steps necessary to protect Mr Spillane from harm. Other non-patient suits also indicate that a statutory obligation to report a patient's medical condition to a public authority is highly relevant to the duty question, because '[t]he statutory background can raise wider policy issues, and the boundary between proximity and policy can merge.'[116]

What, though, if the HCP is merely advised to report the patient, under professional guidelines—does this still support the existence of a duty to non-patients who may be harmed by the omission of the HCP to report? Interestingly, this precise question was left open in the Canadian case of *Bakker v Van Sentan*.[117] No English case has yet constructed a 'duty of care to protect' from HCP to non-patient, on the basis of professional guidelines (and of course, such guidelines do not have the force of law[118]).

That completes the proximity factors that have arisen to date in non-patient suits against HCPs arising out of the actions of a physically-impaired or mentally-ill patient. Additionally, if a non-patient is harmed or killed by such a patient, a suit against the HCP is likely to run into a number of policy reasons negating a duty of care. These are the subject of consideration in the following Section.

3. The relevant policy factors in the context of dangerous patients

It is really in the area of public policy that the prospect of casting a duty on a HCP to avoid or to minimise injury to non-patients brought about by a dangerous patient becomes most troublesome (or, as Healy puts it, '[t]he issues are as complicated as they are unpalatable'[119]).

The policy reasons against an affirmative duty to warn

English law is notoriously hesitant to impose a positive duty to act where the essential rubric of the allegation is that the defendant failed to act to prevent harm befalling the claimant. This has important ramifications, should any similarly-themed action be brought against a HCP for failing to warn a third party about the risks posed by a mentally-ill or physically-disabled patient.

In the previously-mentioned case of *Mitchell v Glasgow CC*,[120] the House of Lords articulated a number of reasons why, in the situation of a victim tenant who was killed by an anti-social fellow-tenant, the Council had no duty to warn the putative victim of the threat posed by the killer. *Mitchell* has some striking resemblances to *Tarasoff*, and as such, the views expressed by the House of Lords strongly suggest that, were a *Tarasoff*-type case to arise in English law, it would be decided against the victim for policy reasons (and, hence, opposite to the way in which the Supreme Court of California determined the case). Lord Hope's policy reasons in *Mitchell*[121] (which drew upon *Van Colle/Smith*[122] and other cases[123]), and with which the other Lords expressly agreed,[124] are outlined in Table 3.1.

Conflicts of duties to patient and to non-patient

Any conflict of duties (actual or potential) between that owed to the HCP's patient and that owed to the non-patient, will likely preclude a duty to the non-patient. A HCP will not be permitted to place the stranger's interests above those of his patient.

However, if it can be argued that whatever is required of the HCP to discharge his duty to his patient would *also* discharge any duty to the non-patient, the duties are coincident, and no conflict arises. Notably, the English Court of Appeal was invited to follow this line of reasoning in *Palmer v Tees HA*.[125] Mrs Palmer argued that the duty imposed on Tees HA was, not to warn her and Rosie *per se* of the dangers posed by psychotic patient Mr Armstrong (A), but to provide adequate medical treatment for A to reduce the risk of his killing a child, and/or to stop him from being released from hospital whilst he posed a risk. It was argued that this duty *coincided* with the duty to Rosie Palmer and her mother to prevent a mentally-ill person in A's position from injuring those who lived in close proximity with him. However, the Court of Appeal declined to accept this line of argument, and no such duty was owed. Of course, and separately, the Court of Appeal would not countenance, in *Palmer*, any duty on the doctors to warn third parties about A (even had they known who to warn).

Table 3.1   The policy reasons against a duty to warn a third party who is threatened by another

- the implication of such a duty for other cases was 'complex and far reaching'—it could be cast on many. If the Council, as social landlord, was under a duty, wouldn't, say, a social worker who heard the threats issued by D be under a duty to warn a potential victim too?
- obversely, *to whom* would this duty to warn be owed? Others in the neighbourhood had complained to the Council about D's behaviour too. Surely the duty would be owed to all of them—or none. The size of the putative class could be problematical in all such contexts. [This policy factor is revisited later in the Section.]
- a duty to warn is not necessarily a one-off message—it may require the defendant (the Council here) to determine, step by step at each stage, whether or not the actions that they proposed to take in fulfilment of their responsibilities as landlords required a warning to be given, and to whom. Hence, how any defendant in this position would feasibly discharge the duty could be problematical.
- it would lead to defensive practices and delay—defendants may have to defer taking certain steps until the warning had been received by everyone, and an opportunity given for it to be acted on.
- paradoxically, 'the more attentive they were to their ordinary duties [regarding the dangerous party], the more onerous the duty to warn others would become' for defendants, because with intervention would come awareness and control.
- it was 'desirable too that social landlords, social workers and others who seek to address the many behavioural problems that arise in local authority housing estates and elsewhere, often in very difficult circumstances, should be safeguarded from legal proceedings arising from an alleged failure to warn those who might be at risk of a criminal attack in response to their activities. Such proceedings, whether meritorious or otherwise, would involve them in a great deal of time, trouble and expense which would be more usefully devoted to their primary functions in their respective capacities'—and the same could be said of proceedings against HCPs and health authorities who deal with difficult cases of the mentally-ill and violently-predisposed (this point was made at first instance in *Palmer v Tees HA*[126]).
- if there was a duty to warn imposed upon defendants such as the Council here, then defensive measures against the risk of legal proceedings 'would be likely to create a practice of giving warnings as a matter of routine. Many of them would be for no good purpose, while others would risk causing undue alarm'. The risk of such warnings losing their effect, should they be given as a matter of course, would arise in medical cases too.

The duty of confidentiality to the patient

What of a HCP's duty of confidentiality to his mentally- or physically-impaired patient? Surely any duty to warn a non-patient of the potential threat posed by the patient would conflict with this duty of confidentiality?

The issue has not, as yet, arisen for decision in England. The leading English cases on a HCP's duty of confidentiality have concerned HCPs who *voluntarily* acted by giving information about a mentally-ill patient to a third party, in order to protect the public against that dangerous patient.

In *W v Egdell*,[127] W, a paranoid schizophrenic, shot four members of a neighbouring family. He shot another neighbour who had come to investigate the shooting, and then drove off in his car, throwing hand-made bombs as he did so. Later the same day W shot two more people. Five of his victims died of their injuries. W pleaded guilty to manslaughter on the ground of diminished responsibility, and was held in a secure hospital for 12 years, before seeking a transfer to a regional secure unit, a move opposed by the Secretary of State and the defendant, an independent psychiatrist who had to review and report on W. The report, which described W's continuing violent fantasies and interests in bomb-making activities, was prepared for the mental health review tribunal; but the psychiatrist also sent the report (against W's wishes) to the medical officers who were treating W at the secure hospital. **Held**: there was no breach of the duty of confidentiality in this case.

In *R v Crozier*,[128] a mentally-ill patient of the psychiatrist attacked his sister with an axe. The patient pleaded guilty to attempted murder, and the treating psychiatrist prepared a report on the patient for sentencing purposes. The report was not made available at sentencing, and nine years' imprisonment was ordered. The psychiatrist then gave his report to the Crown, and with this, the Crown achieved a longer sentence. The patient alleged breach of confidentiality. **Held:** the disclosure of the report to the Crown was upheld; the psychiatrist was not liable for breach of confidentiality.

In *Egdell*, the Court of Appeal held that, in a contest of two public interests in this case, 'the information in the [psychiatrist's] report was relevant information, and the public interest in its restricted disclosure to the proper authorities outweighed the public interest that the [W's] confidences should be respected'.[129] In *Crozier* too, there was a 'stronger public interest'[130] in disclosing a psychiatric report about the patient (i.e., an interest stronger than the interest in maintaining doctor–patient confidentiality). (The 'public interest exception' to a HCP's duty of confidentiality has been considered in detail by other commentators,[131] and will not be discussed further herein.)

However, for present purposes, the courts in both *Egdell* and *Crozier* did **not** suggest that a psychiatrist who was treating a violent patient was under *any duty* to inform or protect a potential victim.[132] No statement in the judgments goes that far. The courts did not purport to address the independent question of whether, and if so in what circumstances, a duty can be owed by a HCP to a third party—and the outcomes of the two cases certainly do not automatically imply that the psychiatrists owed any specific duty of care to any member of the public who may have been injured by their patients. Hence, the cases do not provide much assistance in answering the question the subject of this chapter.

However, in *Tarasoff*,[133] where a duty to warn the victim Tatiana Tarasoff and her parents of the threat posed by Mr Poddar *was* upheld by the California Supreme Court, the issue of the two conflicting duties—confidentiality to patient, and protection to victim—had to be squarely addressed. The psychotherapist had vehemently argued that to require him to give a warning would entail the revelation of confidential communications, and that this would constitute a breach of trust, would deter violence-prone persons from seeking therapy, and would hamper the treatment of other patients. Essentially (it was submitted), if the law could compel disclosure of some psychotherapeutic communications, 'psychotherapy could no longer be practiced successfully'.[134] The Supreme Court of California disagreed. It dealt with the breach-of-duty-of-confidentiality in four points.

First, it regarded the possible adverse effects of a duty to warn upon the practice of psychotherapy in California as being 'dubious', and unsupported by evidence.[135] This forecast was supported by later empirical studies which showed that the *Tarasoff*-induced obligation of disclosure in exceptional circumstances—and the consequential inability of HCPs to promise absolutely confidential treatment—did not 'signal the downfall of effective therapeutic relationships as the critics had prophesied'[136] nor signal the 'psychiatric Armageddon'.[137] Secondly, the duty to disclose arose to protect the public interest of 'safety from violent assault', and hence, the duty of confidentiality owed to patients in respect of patient–psychotherapist communications 'must yield to the extent to which disclosure is essential to avert danger to others. The protective privilege ends where the public peril begins'.[138] Thirdly, the duty to warn was perceived to be an exceptional detraction from the ordinarily-applicable duty of confidence. Hence, they were not to be 'encouraged routinely', and had to be discreet, to 'preserve the privacy of his patient to the fullest extent compatible with the prevention of the threatened danger'.[139] Lastly, the duty to warn upon a HCP was cast by the court as a further protection against what it termed a 'risk-infested society', where citizens are living in a 'crowded and computerized society [which] compels the interdependence of its members', which itself was in the public interest.[140]

In the absence of any successful *Tarasoff*-type case to date, English law has not yet had to consider whether a duty to warn/protect would similarly trump the duty of confidentiality which a HCP owes to a patient, even to a violently-predisposed patient.

The size of the class

This factor is closely related to the 'at special risk' proximity factor. No 'special risk' is likely to mean that the class of persons of whom the unfortunate victim was one is simply too large under English law. This problem, of course, particularly arises if no specific threat was made by the patient against any person or if a physically-impaired patient mingles freely with the general public while generating havoc. The spectre of indeterminate liability—derived from Cardozo CJ's famous dicta[141]—has been just as frequent a visitor to stranger claims considered in this chapter as with other non-patient suits.

For example, the potential size of the class, of which the non-patient was one, was referred to as a factor in *Palmer v Tees HA*[142]—and the New Zealand cases of *Maulolo v Hutt Valley Health Corp Ltd*,[143] and *Ellis v Counties Manukau District Health Board*[144] reflect a similar concern. In none of these was a duty of care owed by HCP to the non-patient.

Of course, the exception to this—where the class of whom the non-patient was one was huge—occurs in the North American cases in which the HCP failed to inform the patient of the effects of medication or medical treatment, and that patient then harms a road user (such as *Myers v Quesenberry*[145]). The road user class in *Wenden v Trikha* has already been referred to.[146] This class of road users virtually equates to the general public. In *Healey v Lakeridge Health Corp*, however, Cullity J refused to countenance the size of the class of road users as precluding a duty of care on the part of a HCP (in dicta):

> I do not think liability should be considered to be objectionably indeterminate simply because, in theory, any member of the public could have come in contact with AB [the patient]. The possibility that any member of the public could be on a highway at a particular time is not considered to be inconsistent with duties of care owed to such persons by the drivers of motor vehicles.[147]

It remains to be seen whether an English court would be prepared to take such a pragmatic view towards the issue, were a case similar to *Myers v Quesenberry* to arise for consideration, where the injured non-patient was one of the class of road users at risk from the physically-impaired patient.

Patient self-responsibility

In the case of physically-disabled patients (and for those mentally-ill patients who retain a measure of personal autonomy and decision-making capacity), these patients already know that they suffer from their impairment. If, say, an epileptic driver knows that he suffers from seizures, and if the law has to balance the patient's responsibility for the non-patient's misfortune against the burden of imposing liability upon HCPs to the non-patient, then some judges plainly think that the burden of protecting the non-patient is better left with the patient. Any warnings that a HCP may give that patient not to drive, may be, in the words of the Supreme Court of Texas—

> incremental, but the consequences of imposing a duty are great. The responsibility for safe operation of a vehicle should remain primarily with the driver who is capable of ascertaining whether it is lawful to continue to drive once a disorder such as epilepsy has been diagnosed and seizures have occurred. Accordingly, we decline to impose on physicians a duty to third parties to warn an epileptic patient not to drive.[148]

In reality, the fact of patient autonomy and self-determination can count against the patient in other legal contexts too (e.g., in the attribution of contributory negligence). In the same way, it is submitted that the factor should be equally applicable when determining upon whom, of two potential parties, a duty of care should be imposed. It is in cases of the physically-disabled patient who understands the nature of his impairment and who fully appreciates the risk which he poses to other road users, that this factor probably warrants its highest consideration.

The wider consequences of a duty upon the delivery of health services to a community

Finally, it is worth noting one particular policy reason that was raised in the Alabama case of *Taylor v Smith*,[149] which concerned the drug-addicted patient who was involved in a car accident with Mrs Taylor while on the way home from out-patient methadone treatment.

The Supreme Court of Alabama held that the administration of methadone by the HCP to an outpatient who had consistently tested positive for other drugs during the treatment programme, was an 'affirmative act' which, in the absence of strong countervailing public-policy reasons, gave rise to a duty to non-patient motorists who may be injured in a car accident with the patient.[150] The HCP, however, argued that he ought to owe no duty to non-patients in these circumstances, as a matter of public policy, because it would 'necessarily end out-patient methadone treatment in Alabama,' with a consequent increase in substance abuse. He contended that 'it would not only be reasonably foreseeable, but an altogether certainty, that [patients such as Ms Ennis] would seek drugs illegally, in an unsupervised and unmonitored setting, leaving society to deal with the costs and dangers attendant to such illegal activity'.[151] Ultimately, the Supreme Court found this argument 'unpersuasive', because in this case, the patient had continued with substance abuse throughout her treatment in any event. Besides, the circumstances involved such a high potential for severe personal injury, death, and property damage to non-patients that the policy considerations cited by Dr Smith in this case 'did not justify the risk of releasing a dangerously medicated patient upon the highways of Alabama, without potential liability to the physician who directly administered the medication.'[152]

However, the case does raise the spectre of policy reasons being couched in the particular context of what any duty of care to non-patients could mean for the *delivery of health services more generally*. While this line of argument was unsuccessful in *Taylor*, and a duty to the non-patient was found, what a duty could mean for the wider community generally was effective in causing the House of Lords to find no duty of care against the local authority in *Mitchell v Glasgow CC*.[153] Albeit that this was a different context—a suit against the council for failing to protect one tenant from the murderous activities of another tenant—the impact which a duty of care towards Mr Mitchell would have upon social landlords and social workers more generally, was specifically cited by the House of Lords as a reason for discounting any duty at all.[154]

Thus, this policy reason may come to feature in an appropriate non-patient suit brought against a HCP in English law in the future.

4. How would *Tarasoff* be decided in English law today?

In light of the proximity and policy factors outlined in the previous sections 2 and 3, respectively, the question should be squarely addressed: would English law impose any duty to protect/warn towards a pre-identified *Tarasoff*-type victim? It has previously been mooted by other commentators that *Palmer* leaves the door slightly ajar for that possibility.[155]

However, the possibility is really quite remote, in this author's view. Dicta from *Palmer* itself; the outcome of *Osman v Ferguson*; and the more recent House of Lords authorities of *Van Colle/Smith* and *Mitchell* (albeit arising in the non-medical context) all indicate strongly that any duty of care owed by a HCP towards a non-patient victim would be most unlikely, even where the victim was an identified (or a clearly identifiable) individual. The fact that there may be a real risk, a foreseeable risk, of harm to the third party if the HCP does not warn the third party is, of course, not conclusive—'the question is one of fairness and public policy'.[156] The proximity and policy factors discussed previously point, in the main, against such a duty, as do the difficulty in even casting the duty (to protect, to warn, or both?), and the continuing influence of the 'mere omissions' rule in English law.

Only if a very unusual set of circumstances were to be present *might* a duty of care be found:

- if a threat was made to the HCP about a pre-identified victim (i.e., analogising *Osman* on proximity, and distinguishing *Palmer*);
- if the threat made by the patient was serious, grave, and indicated that the person or life of the non-patient was endangered—as opposed to oft-repeated but empty threats (analogising *Osman*, and distinguishing *Mitchell*);
- if there was a clear avenue by which the HCP could warn the non-patient of the pending threat (i.e., again distinguishing *Palmer*);
- if the harm to befall the non-patient occurred very close in time to the act of the HCP's breach towards the patient (distinguishing *Van Colle/Smith* and *Palmer*); and
- if the HCP (or medical authorities) were in a position to control/supervise the patient (which probably excludes out-patient settings of the type in *Palmer*, and may require that the HCP was in a position to arrange for the compulsory detention of the patient prior to the attack on the non-patient).

Even were a duty to be cast on the HCP, however, it would probably be restricted in two respects, in light of the House of Lords' decision in *Mitchell*. First, the Lords treated the argument, that the Council had a duty to warn the potential victim Mr Mitchell, with a distinct lack of enthusiasm—for policy reasons which can be analogised to the medical context rather easily. In light of that, it is submitted that, were a *Tarasoff*-type scenario to arise for judicial consideration in England, the duty on the HCP's part would probably be framed no wider than a *duty to control* the dangerous patient (if that were indeed lawfully possible), rather than a duty to warn the non-patient. As will be discussed shortly in Part D, how the particular duty cast upon the HCP is framed has become a thorny and divided issue in US jurisprudence.

Secondly, *Mitchell* suggests that, even were a HCP to be told by a patient that he wished to kill a non-patient, the HCP may be under no duty to inform *the police* of that warning. In *Mitchell*, it was one of Mr Mitchell's estate's claims that the Council failed to keep the police informed of the steps which they proposed to take against D, and failed to alert the police that a meeting had been arranged for that day. Neither allegation was successful. In that respect, English law may again march to a different drum from the Californian Supreme Court in *Tarasoff*—for, in that case, it was held the HCP did not do enough to discharge his duty to Tatiana Tarasoff, by notifying the Berkeley campus police of the threats made by Mr Poddar. It is likely that, were the English courts to hear such a case, there would be no affirmative duty upon the HCP to undertake even that step.

5. Patients who kill a non-patient, and art 2 of the Convention

Where a non-patient is killed by a patient who is under the care of a public health authority (e.g., NHS Trust) and its employees, this section briefly considers, for the sake of completeness, a potential claim which the non-patient's estate (or the non-patient's close relatives) may seek to bring against the Trust for a contravention of the state's positive obligation under art 2 of the Convention to protect the deceased non-patient's right to life.[157]

Section 6(1) of the Human Rights Act 1998 provides that it is unlawful for a public authority to act in a way that is incompatible with a Convention right. The acts and omissions of a NHS hospital's medical staff are capable of engaging the responsibility of the state under art 2.[158] The non-patient's relatives, will be entitled to obtain a judicial remedy against an NHS Trust, under s 8 of that Act, if they can establish that the Trust (or its employees) acted in a way that was incompatible with the deceased non-patient's Convention rights.[159]

There have not, as yet, been any cases considered in England whereby the estate of a non-patient who was killed by a mentally-ill or physically-impaired patient has brought an action against the relevant NHS Trust. *Palmer v Tees HA*[160] pre-dated the implementation of the Convention,[161] which precluded any discussion of art 2's application to those tragic facts. Rather, one type of art 2 suit that *has* been brought (by patients' relatives) against medical authorities to date has concerned suicide patients who were being treated for depression at a NHS medical facility, and whose suicides were allegedly the result of negligence on the part of NHS-employed staff, or as a result of some systemic breach by the NHS Trust.[162] Another type of art 2 suit arising in medical negligence has occurred where a patient died in a NHS hospital, allegedly due to mis-diagnosis and/or mistreatment of his condition, and a breach of the state's obligation to protect that patient's life was claimed.[163] However, neither of these are particularly helpful for the scenario which is the subject of this chapter—*viz*, the death of a non-patient at the hands of a patient.

Article 2 enjoins the state, not only to refrain from the intentional and unlawful taking of life (a scenario which is not relevant for present purposes), but also to take appropriate steps to safeguard the lives of those within its jurisdiction.[164] It is this latter positive obligation cast upon the state which is most important for any non-patient suit against an NHS Trust, arising from a patient's behaviour—for, in certain well-defined circumstances, art 2 may imply a positive obligation on an NHS Trust to take *preventive operational measures* to protect an individual whose life is at 'real and immediate risk ... from the criminal acts of a third party.'[165] The state will have contravened that obligation if it 'failed to take measures within the scope of [its] powers which, judged reasonably, might have been expected to avoid that risk.'[166] Hence, it may be claimed that, by failing to advise a non-patient of, or otherwise protect the non-patient from, the dangers posed by a mentally-unhinged or physically-disabled patient undergoing NHS treatment, the NHS Trust (and its employees) acted in a way that was incompatible with the non-patient's right to life.

In *Mitchell*, an art 2 claim against the Glasgow CC, for failing to protect Mr Mitchell from the murderous acts of Mr Drummond, failed[167]—as did similar claims brought in *Van Colle*[168] and *Osman*[169] against the relevant police authorities in respect of the murders committed in those cases—the murder of a police witness by a police suspect, and the murder of a student's father by that student's former teacher, respectively. Although arising from a non-medical context, these authorities usefully inform as to the likely future prospects of an art 2 claim, should such a claim ultimately be brought against a health authority in respect of a patient's murderous acts. It is, perhaps, the failure of the art 2 claim by Mr Mitchell's estate against the Glasgow CC that is the most interesting of all, for present purposes—because of the parallels which can be drawn between a public housing authority and an NHS Trust. Both of them have troubled, incapacitated or disturbed persons within their sphere of activity, and neither of them is 'in the business' of preventing or suppressing criminal activity. Arguably they are closely analogous.

There were, essentially, three reasons given by Lord Rodger as to why no positive operational duty arose on the part of the Council to prevent the harm that befell Mr Mitchell. First, Mr Mitchell and the Council were not in any sort of relationship that could give rise to an assertion that the public authority had a positive duty to protect Mr Mitchell from criminal assaults—their relationship was best characterised as social landlord and tenant, but with nothing approaching care and control by the Council over Mr Mitchell.[170] Secondly, there was no 'real and immediate risk' to Mr Mitchell's life that would have triggered an obligation on the part of the state. At the precise point at which such a risk supposedly arose (about an hour after the meeting between Mr Drummond and the Council officers), no Council officers were present nor were they under any duty to be present.[171] Thirdly:

> councils and housing associations etc do not have, and are not meant to have, the resources, staff or powers to take effective steps to prevent such crimes. On the contrary, they are resourced on the basis that they are landlords operating within a society where the responsibility for preventing violent crime *lies with the police*, who, in their turn, are given the resources, training and powers to do the job. Costly duplication of the work of the police is neither necessary nor indeed desirable.[172]

These reasons as to why art 2 did not have relevance to a local council arguably have just as much resonance for a health authority, whose employees are treating mentally-ill or physically-disabled patients as out-patients. Neither public authority is funded by the state to prevent criminal violence. Moreover, expressions of violent fantasies on the part of patients, which they then do not act on for some considerable period—two months in *Tarasoff*, 12 months in *Palmer* and *Maulolo*—will render the 'real and immediate risk' test difficult to satisfy. As Lord Hope said, '[t]he test that the [claimant] must satisfy is a high one'[173]—and on the basis of *Mitchell*, it is doubtful that the facts of *Palmer* would have given rise to an operational obligation on the part of the relevant health authority either.

Previously, it has been suggested by commentators that the implementation of art 2 into English jurisprudence was a portent of a developing and wider duty-to-protect than had hitherto existed in English domestic law,[174] that it 'helped create a judicial environment that will be more sympathetic' to *Tarasoff*-type claims',[175] and that it 'has opened the door to the introduction of a doctrine analogous to *Tarasoff* in the United Kingdom'.[176] However, in this author's view, these aspirations have been dealt a severe (although perhaps not, as yet, a fatal) blow—in respect of both claims in negligence, and for violation of art 2's obligation on the state to protect life—in light of the House of Lords' stance in *Mitchell*. There seems to have been little judicial willingness to extend the scope of liability in that fashion, or to trump conservative legal principle with the undoubted sympathy that such tragedies naturally elicit.

It is now appropriate to take a closer look at the *Tarasoff* decision, and to consider how (and why) it has been expanded, or contracted, or even rejected outright, by various US state courts and legislatures.

D THE TREATMENT OF *TARASOFF* IN THE UNITED STATES: LESSONS FOR ENGLAND?

Academically, *Tarasoff v The Regents of the University of California* [177] has been described as 'one of the single most celebrated cases in the recent history of American tort law',[178] its 'most influential ruling in mental disability law',[179] and 'the subject of immense legal commentary'.[180] Judicially, it has been termed as a 'landmark case'[181] and historically significant: '[i]n the more than 30 years since this seminal decision, *Tarasoff*-type duties have been widely accepted throughout the country and imposed through either the common law or by statute'.[182]

A 30th anniversary symposium on the case[183] shows that vehement criticisms continue—and these are just the legal arguments. The economist, Ginsberg, for example, has argued[184] that, whatever version of the *Tarasoff* duty is analysed, from an economic perspective, it is untenable—'no version induces both the therapist and the potential victim to behave in a socially desirable way in all cases. Further, some versions fail to induce socially desirable behavior in any case'.

In Section C, the view was expressed that, should the tragic facts of *Tarasoff* arise for determination in an English court, there would likely be a judicial reluctance to cast any duty upon the HCP in favour of the non-patient. The boundaries defining a duty of care in English law would most probably preclude liability from arising. However, *were* a *Tarasoff*-type principle to be considered for English law, a consideration of American jurisprudence—from both judicial pronouncements and academic commentary—suggests that there are **eight** important lessons to be learnt.[185] Dealing with each in turn:

1. What does a *Tarasoff*-type duty actually require a healthcare professional to do?

An ongoing bone of contention is the extent of the duty of reasonable care which is imposed upon HCPs by *Tarasoff*—what is it a duty to actually *do*? In this, US courts have tended to differ markedly.[186]

The narrow interpretation

To reiterate, in *Tarasoff*, the California Supreme Court held that the *general rule* is that there is ordinarily no duty to control a third party's conduct to prevent harm to another individual. Hence, liability will not be imposed where the avoidance of foreseeable harm requires a defendant to control the conduct of another person. However, a mental HCP owes a duty to use reasonable care to protect third parties endangered by his patient where that HCP has a 'special relationship' with either the person whose conduct needs to be controlled (the patient) or the foreseeable victim of that conduct (the third party victim).[187] In *Tarasoff* itself, the 'special relationship' existed between the psychotherapist and Mr Poddar, which was enough to 'support affirmative duties for the benefit of third persons', that third party being Tatiana Tarasoff.

From the outset, the decision in *Tarasoff* itself threw the scope-of-duty question into sharp relief. The majority in that case phrased a (incredibly wide) duty on the HCP to use reasonable care to prevent danger befalling the non-patient:

> When a therapist determines, or pursuant to the standards of his profession should determine, that his patient presents a serious danger of violence to another, he incurs an obligation *to use reasonable care to protect the intended victim against such danger*. The discharge of this duty may require the therapist to take one or more of various steps, depending upon the nature of the case. Thus it may call for him to warn the intended victim or others likely to apprise the victim of the danger, to notify the police, or to take whatever other steps are reasonably necessary under the circumstances. [and] once a therapist does in fact determine, or under applicable professional standards reasonably should have determined, that a patient poses a serious danger of violence to others, he bears a duty to *exercise reasonable care to protect the foreseeable victim of that danger*.[188]

However, in *Thompson v County of Alameda*,[189] the California Supreme Court later narrowed this ruling significantly. There was only a duty on the HCP to warn a 'readily identifiable victim' of the violent intentions of his patient. *Tarasoff* did **not** impose an affirmative duty to warn whenever a patient made 'non-specific threats of harm directed at non-specific victims'—under the narrow *Thompson* ratio, the intended third party victim had to be 'foreseeable' and 'readily identifiable'. Of course, this fact scenario was not present in *Thompson* itself—the young murder victim killed by his neighbour, F, was not 'targeted', but was merely one of the neighbourhood children who was at risk from F's murderous intent. Moreover, the required step on the HCP's part was a duty to warn the intended victim (or others who could reasonably implement protective measures regarding the intended victim). In *Thompson*, however, the Californian Supreme Court pointed to the difficulty in giving an adequate warning to the parents of the potential young victims ('[w]e are skeptical of any net benefit which might flow from a duty to issue a generalized warning of the probationary release of offenders'[190]).

Some courts have precisely followed the narrow duty cast by *Tarasoff*, and have gone no further than that.[191] However, others have been far more 'adventurous'.

A duty to warn the victim, or others, where the victim falls within a class of potential victims

Some American courts have been prepared to impose upon a HCP a duty to warn a person who falls within an identifiable 'class of potential victims'. In appropriate cases, this warning should be conveyed to the victim himself, or to others who could be expected to implement protective measures for the intended victim.

In the following illustrative cases, the relevant classes were, respectively, the patient's co-employees and the patient's future clients:

In *Logan v Smith*,[192] the patient, Mr Beck (B), killed four people who worked with him at the Connecticut Lottery Headquarters, and then killed himself. Prior to the murders, B had been treated by Dr S, psychiatrist. At these sessions, B had stated that he was very agitated at work, that he was experiencing harmful and dangerous thoughts, that he was angry and enraged at work about what he perceived to be a lack of support, and that his employer was trying to make his life miserable. B showed increased agitation and paranoia about his work and his colleagues, and told Dr S that he had contacted the Attorney General, the State Police, the Governor's office and the FBI, concerning his problems at work. The estates of the victims sued Dr S, alleging a negligent failure to warn. **Held**: there was a basis for alleging a duty to warn on Dr S—because B had made threats against a specifically identifiable group, his fellow employees at the Lottery Commission, and the murdered victims were members of that group.[193] The motion to strike out the claim failed.

In *Almonte v New York Medical College*,[194] the third party, Denny Almonte (A), was a 10-year-old boy who was diagnosed to be borderline mentally-retarded, and who was having suicidal thoughts. A was referred to a hospital crisis centre for psychoanalytical treatment, and was assigned to Dr DeMasi (M), a psychiatric post-graduate student/resident at a medical college. A was allegedly sexually assaulted and threatened by M. To become a psychoanalyst, as M wished to, it was compulsory to undergo psychoanalysis. Dr Ingram was M's analyst. During the sessions, M told Dr I that he was a paedophiliac. Dr I was aware that M intended to enter child psychiatry as a profession, but Dr I did not attempt to prevent M from treating children, or to prevent M's promotion to a position of responsibility. A sued both college and Dr I for a negligent failure to warn M's future patients who could be at risk from his paedophiliac tendencies. **Held:** the motion to strike out the claim failed; there was an arguable duty to warn here.

In *Almonte*, the court did not actually state that Dr Ingram should have warned Denny's parents of the threat posed if their son were to be treated by DeMasi. Rather (said the court), if, per *Tarasoff*,[195] the duty to warn could be discharged by 'warn[ing] the intended victim or others likely to apprise the victim of the danger', then Dr Ingram could have warned *the college* of the potential problem posed to young patients of DeMasi (i.e., the class of victims of whom Denny was one). Then, the college could have taken steps to warn *the hospital crisis centre*, where Denny was being treated.[196]

Either way, the duty to warn arose in these cases where the non-patient was not pre-identified by name, but was merely one of a class. The fact that they were not struck out, and *Palmer* was, demonstrates the gulf that exists between some US law and the English position.

A duty to warn in respect of any foreseeable victim, even absent a threat

An even wider construction of the *Tarasoff* principle holds that a HCP is under a duty towards *any foreseeable victim* who is within the zone of probable danger from the patient, even if there has been no specific threat to that victim.[197]

It has been judicially remarked[198] that, although *Tarasoff* involved a specifically identifiable victim, other courts have found a duty to all foreseeable victims, including members of the general public. To English lawyers, the possibilities that such a wide holding can lead to may appear to be truly startling:

> In *Rivera v New York City Health and Hospitals Corp*,[199] the patient, Mr Perez (P), who was a homeless and mentally-ill man, pushed Mr Rivera (R) onto the subway tracks in front of an oncoming train at 51st Street Lexington Avenue subway station. R lost both legs. At the time, P was receiving medical care and other assistance from three medical facilities and from two homeless shelters. R sued the relevant HCPs and homeless shelters for his personal injuries, arguing that the homeless shelters' staff and HCPs were negligent in failing to protect the public from P. **Held:** no motion to strike out against the HCPs would be granted; an arguable duty of care to warn existed.

The court concluded that 'no bright-line rule' existed as to whether HCPs had a duty to prevent their patients from injuring others in the general public, but instead, each case turned on its own facts. Notably, there was no specific threat made here by Mr Perez, or even to the wide class of which he was a member.

Of course, if there is to be a duty towards those who are foreseeably at risk of harm from the patient, but who are not readily identifiable, then no matter how many potential victims that may be, any obligation to warn becomes fanciful. *Who* to warn? Far more likely, in that context, is a duty upon the HCP to *control* the actions of the patient—which also goes beyond the strict ratio of *Tarasoff*. Yet, that precise duty has been upheld, as noted in the next point.

A duty to control (i.e., detain) the patient

Tarasoff itself cast on the HCP a general duty to protect the non-patient, which might require him (said the California Supreme Court) to take 'one or more of various steps, [say] ... to warn the intended victim of the danger, to notify the police, or to take whatever other steps are reasonably necessary under the circumstances.'[200]

Some courts have interpreted that truly widely, such as casting a duty on the HCP to arrange for involuntary detention of the patient:

> In *Lipari v Sears, Roebuck & Co*,[201] the patient, Mr Cribbs (C), bought a shotgun from a Sears store, went to a nightclub, and fired it into a crowded dining room, killing Mr Lipari (L) and seriously injuring his wife. Prior to this, C had been committed to a mental institution, and had been receiving psychiatric care from the Veterans Administration (VA). Shortly after purchasing the gun, C resumed participation in psychiatric day care treatment at the VA, but a month before the murders, C removed himself from this treatment, against the advice of his doctors. It was alleged that the VA's treatment of C was negligent because the VA knew or should have known that C was dangerous to himself and others, and because the VA, despite this knowledge, failed to initiate measures and procedures that were 'customarily taken or initiated for the care and treatment of mentally ill and dangerous persons'. **Held:** the motion to strike out the claim failed; there was an arguable basis for a duty of care owed by VA towards L.

VA specifically challenged L's claim on the basis that it was one thing to uphold a HCP's duty to third persons that was based upon warning potential victims of his patient's dangerous propensities (as *Tarasoff* had held)—but it was quite another to uphold a duty in this case, where the VA had no idea who to warn in respect of C's mental state. Mr Cribbs had never, in the presence of his therapist, threatened to kill anyone, much less Mr Lipari. However, the District Court of Nebraska was content to allow the claim to proceed, on the basis that '[i]t is not unfair to require the psychotherapist to take those precautions which would be taken by a reasonable therapist under similar circumstances', and that this *could* require an attempt to detain a patient, or to take some precautions other than warnings.[202]

Unsurprisingly, there has been opposition, both judicially and academically, to the notion of imposing on a HCP a duty of care, the scope of which is to protect an intended victim by compulsorily detaining the patient. For example, in *Tarasoff* itself, one of the intervenors had suggested that a HCP who realises that he is dealing with a dangerous patient should not be under any duty to warn the intended victim (even assuming that such a victim was identified), but rather, should set procedures in motion for involuntarily detaining the patient. The Supreme Court of California rejected this, however, noting that '[t]he giving of a warning ... would in many cases represent a far lesser inroad upon the patient's privacy than would involuntary commitment.'[203] Indeed, some judges in the US have starkly disagreed with the *Tarasoff* ratio[204] as representing a wrong step in the law, principally because the notion of casting a duty on a HCP to *control* a third party to prevent his doing damage to a non-patient was infeasible. The Florida Court of Appeal decision in *Boynton v Burglass*[205] was one such case—Judge Jorgenson stated that, while other jurisdictions had chosen to follow *Tarasoff*, 'we reject that "enlightened" approach.'[206]

> In *Boynton v Burglass*, Mr Blaylock, who was an outpatient of Dr Burglass, the defendant psychiatrist, shot and killed Mr Boynton. The HCP was sued in negligence, with Mr Boynton's estate alleging that Dr Burglass failed to hospitalize Mr Baylock, failed to warn Mr Boynton or the police that Mr Blaylock was violence-prone and had threatened serious harm to Mr Boynton, and failed to prescribe the proper medications for Mr Blaylock. **Held:** no liability in negligence made out.

Judge Jorgenson considered that the *Tarasoff* principle implied that the HCP, on whom the duty was imposed, has the ability or the right to control the patient's behaviour—and yet, many relationships between psychiatrist and patient lack that crucial element of control (and, certainly, the outpatient–doctor relationship in *Boynton* lacked that control).[207] The *Boynton* court noted that the *Tarasoff* majority judgment was vague: 'by entering into a doctor–patient relationship, the therapist becomes sufficiently involved to assume some responsibility for the safety [of patient and third party victim whom he knows to be threatened]'.[208] Yet (asked Judge Jorgenson), how does *control* follow from this statement?

As examples of academic criticism: McClarren argues that: it can be contrary to the public policy of providing the mentally-ill within the community with supportive, rather than punitive, medical treatment; it could lead to 'the incarceration of hundreds of innocent, non-dangerous mental patients'; the potential for increased costs resulting from increased detention and hospitalisation would be 'staggering'; and there may be statutory restrictions on involuntary detention which the HCP could not satisfy in any event.[209] Hubbard further points out[210] that, even had the therapist succeeded in having Poddar involuntarily detained under the relevant mental health laws, that confinement could not last indefinitely, and, absent more odd conduct by the patient, almost certainly would not have continued throughout the intervening two months before Tatiana Tarasoff was actually murdered.

A duty to control the patient more tangentially

The duty to control the patient may take some form other than detention, according to some American decisions. It could, for example, put in place restrictions on the patient in the workplace.

In *Almonte v New York Medical College*[211] (facts outlined previously), one of the reasons that Denny Almonte's suit was permitted to proceed against the college and Dr Ingram was that there was an arguable basis upon which to find that Dr Ingram owed a duty to control Dr DeMasi's conduct. The District Court of Connecticut considered that Dr Ingram's relationship with the attacker, DeMasi, was 'not solely that between a psychiatrist and a voluntary patient', but rather, 'Ingram was DeMasi's instructor as well as his analyst, and thus had official authority or control over DeMasi that does not exist in the usual analyst-voluntary patient relationship.' This was a cogent basis, said the court, upon which to distinguish other cases[212] in which courts had rejected a duty to control owed to the public by a psychiatrist. Here, Dr Ingram could have steered DeMasi away from child psychiatry, or redirected DeMasi's professional development.

A continuum of duties?

In light of the above, it is unsurprising, then, that some American commentators have criticised the conflicting duties, the ambiguities associated with each type of duty, and the lack of sufficient guidance provided by the law to allow HCPs to avoid liability.[213] The *Tarasoff* principle has been developed into a true patchwork quilt of legal principle, with one recent court noting, with some exasperation, that—

> [t]here have been a variety of different approaches; some courts treated both warning a potential victim and controlling a dangerous patient as options under one duty to protect, while other courts have reasoned that *warning* victims and *controlling* patients are separate duties, each with different requirements that trigger the respective duty.[214]

In a perceptive analysis of the variations which have emerged in the interpretation of the *Tarasoff* principle, Waller proposes[215] that, in essence, the duty on a HCP to protect third parties from a dangerous patient generates a range of potential duties, or 'a continuum which depends on the circumstances'.[216] Waller suggests that the following matrix could be adopted:

Table 3.2   Waller's Matrix of the Duty to Protect

Setting/Victims	'Readily identifiable victims'	'Foreseeably endangered victims'
Outpatient setting	Duty to warn	Duty to involuntarily detain
Inpatient setting	Duty to continue detention plus a duty to warn	Duty to continue detention

As Waller notes, 'the most difficult scenario is the outpatient with violent propensities who has not threatened anyone in particular'[217]—an observation which has been similarly borne out, in English law, by the decision in *Palmer v Tees HA*.[218]

The uncertainty as to what, precisely, a *Tarasoff*-type principle *expects* of a HCP—and the particularly blurred analysis of whether a 'duty to protect' entails a duty to warn or a duty to control, or both—renders the principle a cautionary tale for other jurisdictions. This is, perhaps, its most important lesson for English law.

2. A matter for statute?

As canvassed in the previous point, some US courts have refused to follow *Tarasoff*. When confronted with the opposing viewpoints between that case, and *Boynton's* case, the Court of Appeal of Florida (in refusing to depart from *Boynton*) stated that the whole problem of when a HCP should be liable to a non-patient for the harm rendered by his dangerous patient was better left to the legislature—because this was a societal problem, and one that was ill-suited to the 'more limited fact-finding resources' at a court's disposal. Instead:

> If our society has progressed (or regressed) to such a point that there should now be recognized new causes of action where none have existed before, we conclude that it is the better part of judicial wisdom to await the establishment of such causes of action by legislative action after input as to all the variables from competing elements of society.[219]

In fact, in some US state jurisdictions, the legislatures have sought to codify the ratio in *Tarasoff*, although the wording of the statutes differ considerably.[220] For example, the Michigan Mental Health Code[221] provides as follows, in s 946 (extract):

---

(1) If a patient communicates to a mental health professional who is treating the patient a threat of physical violence against a reasonably identifiable third person and the recipient has the apparent intent and ability to carry out that threat in the foreseeable future, the mental health professional has a duty to take action as prescribed in subsection (2). Except as provided in this section, a mental health professional does not have a duty to warn a third person of a threat as described in this subsection or to protect the third person.

(2) A mental health professional has discharged the duty created under subsection (1) if the mental health professional, subsequent to the threat, does one or more of the following in a timely manner:

    (a) Hospitalizes the patient or initiates proceedings to hospitalize the patient under chapter 4 or 4a.

    (b) Makes a reasonable attempt to communicate the threat to the third person and communicates the threat to the local police department or county sheriff for the area where the third person resides or for the area where the patient resides, or to the state police.

Introduced in 1989, the purpose of the Michigan statute was, apparently, to limit the liability of mental health practitioners from wider interpretations which *Tarasoff* had yielded.[222]

Hence, according to the Michigan Court of Appeal in *Dawe v Bar-Levav and Associates PC*,[223] a HCP only has a duty to warn a third party of the danger posed by his patient or to hospitalise the patient if four criteria are met: (1) the HCP is presently treating a patient, (2) the patient communicates a threat of physical violence to the HCP, (3) the threat of physical violence is directed against a readily identifiable third person, and (4) the patient has the apparent intent and ability to carry out the threat in the foreseeable future.[224]

This limiting effect of Michigan's statute has been clearly evident in a number of tragic cases. The four criteria referred to above are conveniently illustrated by the following cases:

In *Dawe v Bar-Levav and Associates PC*,[225] the patient, Joseph Brooks (B), had been a former patient of Dr B-L. B came to the psychiatrist's surgery, where he had previously received treatment some three months previously, and shot and killed Dr B-L, and then proceeded to the back of the office and fired into the group therapy room, killing one patient and wounding others, including Dawe (D), the non-patient (for present purposes). After firing dozens of rounds into the room, B committed suicide. D sued the psychiatrists who operated the surgery, alleging that B had made threatening statements to them about 'fantasizing about murdering', and had also delivered a manuscript to the surgery in June which could allegedly have been construed as a threat of violence against other members who participated in his group therapy sessions, including D. **Held:** the psychiatrists were not liable. B was not presently being treated by the surgery; and had not communicated a sufficiently-clear 'threat of physical violence' against D to the psychiatrists.

In *Jenks v Brown*,[226] Mr Jenks (J) had a son, born of his marriage to his wife (DL). The couple subsequently divorced. That son was kidnapped by his wife (the couple were, at that time, divorced). For a lengthy period, DL had received psychiatric treatment from the psychiatrist Dr B, during which she allegedly said that she intended to kidnap her child and take him 'underground'. J alleged that Dr B owed him a duty of care under the statute. **Held**: no liability attached to the psychiatrist. The threat made by DL was not against J, but potentially against *the child*. The child was a 'reasonably identifiable third person', but he was not the person suing. (Hence, the court did not need to deal with the potentially thorny issue of whether a threat to kidnap constituted a threat of physical violence.[227])

In *Swan v Wedgwood Christian Youth and Family Services Inc*,[228] Harry Swan (S), the non-patient, was killed by his live-in girlfriend's 16-year-old son, Clyde LaPalm (CL), the patient. CL had a long history of behavioural problems and in-patient treatment. After criminal proceedings for various offences, CL was transferred to a 'secure residential program' at Wedgwood which specialised in adolescents who had serious emotional or behavioural problems and were difficult to place. While there, CL showed good progression, and he had handled visits from his mother and S well. Hence, it was decided that CL could make a visit to his mother's home for five days. While there, CL tried to set fire to a truck and to a house, jumped from the second floor window of his mother's home, and briefly set fire to himself. His mother rang the psychiatric facility and was told that CL did not require immediate psychiatric attention, but the incident would be discussed when CL returned to Wedgwood. After the call, S advised CL to 'calm down', whereupon CL punched and attacked S, dropping a microwave oven and a television on S. S died of blunt trauma to the head, and his estate sued the Wedgwood HCPs in negligence. **Held:** no liability arose. CL had communicated no threat against S, and at the time the decision was made to release, had no apparent intent to harm others in any event.

Important phrases in the statute, such as 'a reasonably identifiable third person' and 'a threat of physical violence', are statutorily-undefined (and Michigan's statute is typical in that regard).

The two sentiments expressed in this section—that statute best curbs the potential excesses of a *Tarasoff*-type principle, and that imposing any such duty on HCPs should be a matter for Parliament, given societal concerns over the treatment of the mentally-ill and physically-disabled—are of potential interest to English law-makers.

3. Judicial rejection of the *Tarasoff* principle: policy and distinctions

It will be recalled that, in the Florida decision in *Boynton v Burglass*,[229] the majority stated that, while other jurisdictions had chosen to follow *Tarasoff*, 'we reject that "enlightened" approach.'[230] One reason for that view was that the very nature of psychiatry meant that any duty cast upon the HCP would be unfair and unworkable, and that no such duty should be imposed, as a matter of policy. The majority had regard to what it considered to be the 'inexact science' of psychiatry and the 'largely mysterious' internal workings of the human mind. It drew contrasts between 'a physician's diagnosis, which can be verified by x-ray, surgery, etc., [and] the psychiatrist [who] cannot verify his diagnosis, treatment or predicted prognosis except by long-term follow-up and reporting'.[231] The very ability of the psychiatrist to predict future violent behaviour depended upon 'the clarity of his crystal ball. Because of the inherent difficulties psychiatrists face in predicting a patient's dangerousness, psychiatrists cannot be charged with accurately making those predictions and with sharing those predictions with others. Therefore, we decline to charge Dr Burglass with such a duty.'[232] Hence, any duty on a psychiatrist or other mental health worker to warn the victim or to notify the police would be 'unreasonable and unworkable'.[233]

Academic commentary has also emphasised this point. For example, Slovenko[234] draws attention to the fact that, in *Tarasoff*, the American Psychiatric Association (APA) itself took the position in its *amicus curiae* brief at the trial[235] that a psychotherapist should not be obliged to report a patient who presents a 'serious danger' because the psychotherapist is not a reliable predictor (although, ironically, in *Tarasoff* itself, the psychotherapist *did* accurately predict that Mr Poddar would commit murder). Slovenko himself posits the view that whether a person poses a 'serious danger' is a value judgment, not defined by law or by the APA's Diagnosis and Statistical Manual of Mental Disorders, and that, '[i]n managing a psychiatric ward, psychiatrists do not predict much; they simply loosen the controls a bit and see what happens.'[236]

Very recently, in April 2009, and as a case of first impression in that state jurisdiction, the Supreme Court of Rhode Island also refused to impose a *Tarasoff*-type duty (a mental patient struck a non-patient stranger with a metal crow bar in a dry-cleaning store, causing the victim to suffer extensive head and brain injuries) in *Santana v Rainbow Cleaners Inc*.[237] When read in combination with *Boynton*, it is clear that a number of policy concerns underpin these refusals to follow *Tarasoff*. These include the following:

- to impose such a duty on the psychiatrist would 'wreak havoc' with the doctor's ethical duty of confidence owed to the patient, especially where '[c]onfidentiality is the cornerstone of the psychiatrist-patient relationship'.[238] Not only would it destroy the relationship of trust and confidence between the parties, but it could interfere in practice with the psychiatrist's other work, given that much psychiatric work encourages the patient 'to freely vocalize his fantasies, repressed feelings, and desires. Requiring psychiatrists to warn potential victims every time a patient expresses feelings of anger towards someone would seriously interfere with the treatment, both because of the breach in confidentiality and the practical problem of determining whether a patient really intended to carry out his violent feelings';[239]
- given the nature of the relationship between a voluntary outpatient and a community mental health centre that treated the patient, it is impossible for the HCPs to control the conduct of the patient in an outpatient setting;[240] and
- to impose a *Tarasoff*-duty would lead to defensive treatment of the mentally-ill (e.g., the overcommitment and more frequent involuntary detention of patients), as HCPs 'operated under the increased fear of potential liability'.[241]

Academic commentary emanating from the US frequently points to the policy reasons that render *Tarasoff* an unworkable doctrine. As Harmon notes, conflicts of duties of the HCP towards patient and victim, and the policy issues surrounding doctor–patient privilege and public safety, remain hotly-debated issues;[242] while Nicastro remarks that the practical consequence of *Tarasoff* has been to ensure that HCPs must be 'forever looking over their shoulders', recording not only their treatment of the patient, but what warnings or what other protective steps have been taken for a potential victim's safety (i.e., defensive psychiatry prevails).[243] Annas concludes that the spectre of liability under *Tarasoff* encourages in-patient rather than out-patient treatment, and likens psychiatrists to police.[244]

Moreover, rather than rejecting *Tarasoff* out of hand, courts have sometimes taken a 'distinguish at all costs' approach to the problem. As Patterson points out,[245] in *Matt v Burrell Inc*,[246] the Court of Appeals of Missouri 'went to great lengths to find no liability' on the part of the HCPs there. The mental patient had told staff of a mental health care facility that she intended to kill herself 'by wrecking her car'. When she attempted to do just that, by colliding with the non-patient's car, one of the grounds for rejecting any duty of care on the part of the medical staff towards the non-patient was that the patient did not say that she intended to wreck her car 'by colliding with another vehicle'!

Hence, when American courts have disliked *Tarasoff*, they have tended to either rely upon policy reasoning which is entirely reminiscent of English views in *Palmer*, *Osman* and their progeny; or they have used hairs-breadth distinctions to circumvent the principle altogether.

4. Other expansions of the *Tarasoff* principle

The applications of the *Tarasoff* doctrine in US jurisprudence rather calls to mind the notion that, once the dyke is breached, floods will follow.

For example, the gap between the patient's threat and his act towards a third party was about two months in *Tarasoff*, but it was *ten years* in the following case:

> In *Jablonski ex rel Pahls v US*,[247] Mr Jablonski (J), a mental patient at a veteran's administration hospital, murdered his female partner, Ms Kimball (K) on 16 July 1978. J had never threatened his girlfriend, although K herself had told J's treating therapist that she felt 'insecure' around J and was 'concerned' about his behaviour, particularly towards her mother, which had been unpleasant and potentially violent (J had threatened K's mother and had allegedly attempted to rape her, which was the incident that lead to the psychiatric evaluation at issue). The hospital records of J's prior treatment revealed that, in 1968, he had received extensive care at an Army hospital in El Paso, where he had had 'homicidal ideation toward his wife', that on numerous occasions he had tried to kill her, that he 'had probably suffered a psychotic break and the possibility of future violent behavior was a distinct probability'. **Held:** the HCPs were liable in negligence to K's estate, for failing to adequately warn K or obtain J's past medical records.

This decision demonstrates a number of extensions, quite apart from the period of time between threat and harm done. The court itself admitted that this was no *Tarasoff*-specific case: '[u]nlike the killer in *Tarasoff*, Jablonski made no specific threats concerning any specific individuals. Nevertheless, Jablonski's previous history indicated that he would likely direct his violence against Kimball. He had raped and committed other acts of violence against his wife. His psychological profile indicated that his violence was likely to be directed against women very close to him. This, in turn, was borne out by his attack on [the deceased's mother].'[248] Apart from the 'threat' being ascertained from historical records, the non-patient was just one of a class of potential victims here ('women very close to the patient'); and as Thomas notes,[249] the case illustrated a further expansion of the *Tarasoff* principle, in that J's psychiatric evaluation was performed at the emergency department of a hospital, thus casting the duty to protect upon a psychiatrist, even in an *emergency* situation.

Further, in *Tarasoff*, there was a threat of intentional violence. However, its principle has also been applied where a patient had **no** such tendencies, but simply could embark on 'unpredictable' conduct or recklessness. Where that could have, as its tragic by-product, the death or injury of another, a duty on the HCP has been cast:

> In *Petersen v State of Washington*,[250] Larry Knox (K), a psychotic and schizophrenic patient, ran a red light, hit the car driven by Ms Petersen (P), and severely injured her. At the time of the accident, K was on probation for a second degree burglary conviction, and the conditions of his probation were that he participate in mental health counseling and refrain from using controlled substances. Five days before the accident occurred, K had been released from hospital, where he had been receiving psychiatric care, since self-mutilating about a month earlier. K told his treating doctors that he had taken the drug 'angel dust' during the previous year, and also just prior to the incident in which he emasculated himself. Medical opinion was that K's 'schizophrenic symptomatology was due primarily to the use of angel dust', and K was prescribed an antipsychotic medication. P sued K's treating HCPs, arguing that K was under the influence of drugs at the time of the accident (it was later learned that K had flushed the medication he received from the hospital down a toilet), and that he should have been detained or better supervised. **Held:** negligence was proven, and a duty was owed to P, as someone who might foreseeably be endangered by K's drug-related mental problems.

Hence, Mr Knox was treated as a 'potentially dangerous person [whose] behaviour would be unpredictable'—and that was sufficient to invoke the *Tarasoff* principle. As McClarren notes,[251] *Petersen* was significant for several reasons, among them, that no American court had held a HCP liable, before this, for harm caused by a mentally-ill patient's unintentional negligent act.

A *Tarasoff*-type duty to warn has even been invoked where what was threatened was, not the non-patient himself but the non-patient's property—i.e., when a HCP who knows (or should have known) that his patient posed a serious risk of danger to that property.

> In *Peck v The Counseling Service of Addison County*,[252] the patient, John Peck (P), 29, set fire to his parents' barn, and it was completely destroyed. At the time of this incident, P was an outpatient of a counseling centre, under the treatment of a counselor-psychotherapist. A week prior, P, who was living at home with his parents, had an argument with his father. During this argument, his father called him 'sick and mentally ill' and told him he should be hospitalised. P packed his suitcase, went to the Counseling Service, and told his therapist that he had had a fight with his father, that he was upset with his father, and that 'he didn't think his father cared about him or respected him', and that he 'wanted to get back at his father'. When asked how, P said, 'I don't know, I could burn down his barn.' After the therapist and P discussed the possible consequences of such an act, P promised the therapist not to burn down his father's barn. Believing that P would keep his promise, the therapist did not disclose the threats to any other staff member of the Counseling Service or to the claimant parents. **Held:** therapist was liable in negligence (subject to finding of contributory negligence).

Some interpretations of the *Tarasoff* doctrine have also widened it to include scenarios where the HCP ought to have known of the threat of harm to the non-patient, not from the patient himself, but from some *other concerned third party*:

> In *Ewing v Goldstein*,[253] the patient, Mr Colello (C), a former member of the Los Angeles Police Dept, was treated by Dr G, a marriage and family therapist, for work-related emotional problems, and for problems concerning his former girlfriend, Diane Williams (W). C told his father that he was considering causing harm to W's new boyfriend, Mr Ewing (E). C told his father that he was extremely depressed over the fact that W was 'seeing someone else', and that he thought that he would 'kill the kid' (meaning E). C's father contacted Dr G by phone, and told him what his son had said. At the instigation of C's parents and Dr G, C was hospitalised for psychiatric treatment, but was discharged after only a day, despite his parents' and Dr G's concerns. The following day, C murdered E and then committed suicide. E's parents sued Dr G, for a negligent failure to warn E of the communication (from C's father) that C had threatened to kill or cause serious physical harm to E. **Held:** a triable issue of negligence existed, and Dr G was not entitled to summary judgment.

The trial court had originally found for the hospital and Dr Goldstein because 'the patient himself' had not communicated the threat to the therapist',[254] but this was overturned on appeal. Although the case actually turned upon the interpretation of the *Tarasoff*-driven provisions of the California Civil Code,[255] the outcome of this case has been heavily criticised by commentator Smith, who argues that, in establishing an expanded duty to warn, the court failed to define what relationship is required between the patient and the divulger of the information in order to trigger the duty to warn; and the decision 'asks the therapist not only to be able to assess the risk of violence with the patient in front of him or her, which is an uncertain endeavor to begin with, but also to potentially act on a violence risk assessment based on a third-party communication about the patient. This added level of complexity imposed upon the already difficult business of risk assessment could move prediction from the realm of challenging to mere guesswork ...'.[256]

A final expansion to be mentioned in this section concerns upon whom the duty is to be cast. Commentator Williamson[257] makes the point that, given how widely the *Tarasoff* doctrine has been applied, '[t]aken together, the post-*Tarasoff* cases suggest that a duty to protect may be imposed on: (1) *any professional*, (2) who knows or should know that a client or customer poses a serious danger of harm to any number of foreseeable victims, and (3) who is able to take reasonable steps to protect the third party or parties.' That being so, Williamson asks why the doctrine should not extend, say, to employers who are aware of the disturbed behaviour of one of their employees; or to a university professor who is aware that a student is seriously disturbed—scenarios which are a world away from the original *Tarasoff* tragedy.

Of course, being a matter of state rather than federal law, although almost every US state jurisdiction has made either a common law or statutory rule to deal with the duty imposed upon the HCP in respect of dangers posed by mentally-ill patients, the rules vary enormously—as Harmon says, 'from the precise to the general, and cover[ing] a variety of violent intentions: from third parties, to suicides, to real property'.[258]

Hence, in light of the above extensions to the *Tarasoff* principle, plus the various incarnations of how the duty can be cast that were examined in Section 1 above, the author agrees wholeheartedly with Thomas that English jurists would be 'wise to note that many courts in the United States have struggled to confine the *Tarasoff* doctrine. Attempts to place reasonable limits on the duty have been fraught with difficulty.'[259]

5. What responsibility (if any) should the non-patient bear?

A further notable feature of the *Tarasoff* principle is that there is no real consistency as to how the law treats the unfortunate non-patient who knew the mentally-ill patient, and who thus had some awareness of the propensity for danger posed by the patient.

On the one hand, such knowledge will serve to preclude any duty to control/warn on the HCP's part in the non-patient's favour—casting a burden of 'self-protection' upon the non-patient himself:

> In *Heltsley v Votteler*,[260] Lola Hansen (X) was a patient of Dr V, a Marshalltown psychiatrist. While still Dr V's patient, X drover a car over the victim, Ms Heltsley (H), the non-patient, in a Marshalltown park. X had suffered from serious mental illness, manifesting by agitated, compulsive and aggressive behavior over a period of more than two years. X threatened people who bid against her at used furniture auctions, and purchased large quantities of furniture that she and her husband did not need and could not afford. X and H became friends through their association at auctions. However, X had on previous occasions threatened to kill her husband and H, she had run down both twice, and when H initiated X's commitment to a mental hospital, X told H that she would kill her. H sued Dr V in negligence for the injuries caused by X's attack. **Held:** summary judgment was granted in Dr V's favour.

The court concluded that a *Tarasoff*-type duty should not be imposed when the foreseeable victim knew of the danger posed by the patient—which this victim surely must have done, given the threats and assaults directed towards her. Other cases have also attributed a finding of no-duty to the principle, at least in part, that the non-patient knew about the patient's mental illness, and of its dangerous manifestations.[261]

On the other hand, there is considerable room for uncertainty as to how knowledge on the non-patient's part should be treated at law. For example, in the previously-considered case of *Jablonski ex rel Pahls v US*,[262] Mr Jablonski, the patient, had shown violent and aggressive behaviour towards his girlfriend's mother, and the defendant psychiatrist argued that the 'signs of potential violence' were clearly evident. Indeed, the non-patient girlfriend (whom Mr Jablonski ultimately murdered), had received a number of warnings about his propensity for violence and danger—and from a number of sources, from staff members at a psychological hotline, from her lawyer and her priest, and from her mother. However, *still* a duty of care was owed to her, as a non-patient, by Mr Jablonski's psychiatrist.

It is submitted that, were a *Tarasoff*-type duty to be implemented into English law (which is highly doubtful), then a finding of contributory negligence on the part of the non-patient in appropriate cases, rather than a complete negation of any duty of care, would appear to be the more measured compromise.

6. Defining the trigger for the *Tarasoff* duty

Academic opinion has often, stridently, noted the uncertainty that arises as to when a HCP is supposedly under a *Tarasoff*-type duty. According to *Tarasoff* itself, it was to arise '[w]hen a therapist determines, or pursuant to the standards of his profession should determine, that his patient presents a serious danger of violence to another'.

However, as both Twerski[263] and Harmon[264] point out, just what type of 'threat' or 'warning' triggers the duty on the HCP has been little judicially-analysed. As a result, they are poorly-defined and difficult to predict—to quote Twerski, 'what if instead of a direct threat to kill Tatiana, Poddar had told the psychiatrist that in the distant future, two, three, or 10 years hence, he would find a way to hurt Tatiana and hold her accountable for all the pain she had caused him? Would the California court still have found a duty to warn Tatiana of Poddar's threat? What threshold of danger and how imminent must the threat be to trigger a duty to warn?'

Furthermore, an expert in psychiatry, Mossman, has argued that *Tarasoff* assumes that a therapist's judgment can take the form of binary, 'yes-or-no' assessments about whether 'a serious danger of violence' exists, whereas that is not how psychiatry operates: '[a]t best, therapists know about probabilities or (more often) degrees of relative risk. This means that what must trigger a therapist's decision to take protective action can only be the therapist's perception of a sufficient likelihood that violence will occur—not a yes-or-no determination by the therapist that a "serious danger of violence" has presented itself.'[265]

Additionally, Simon[266] observes that the relationship between the *Tarasoff* doctrine and the American Psychiatric Association's *Principles of Medical Ethics with Annotations Especially Applicable to Psychiatry*[267] has not always been plain, with one version justifying a breach of patient–doctor confidentiality when the danger presented by P was considered to be 'imminent', and with another version replacing it with 'significant' after one trial descended into a debate among experts as to what 'imminent' actually meant—and all of this in circumstances where, in *Tarasoff* itself, the word 'imminent' was not used at all. It is unhelpful if professional guidelines change and, further, if they are very difficult to apply in practice.

Hence, the level of dangerousness which should trigger a *Tarasoff*-type duty, and how a reasonable HCP is always expected to recognise that, constitute important concerns about the rule.

7. The problem of proving breach in a *Tarasoff* scenario

Even if a duty to warn/protect should be proven to exist, it must be emphasised that the remainder of the negligence action may not succeed.

As noted in Chapter 2,[268] the law expects reasonableness, not perfection. Preventing patients from running amok may simply be beyond the resources or capacity of the defendant, or counter-measures may have been unnecessary for a reasonable HCP to implement. The *Tarasoff* principle also raises particular concerns when the victim is not precisely pre-identified. What lengths is the HCP expected to go to, in order to discharge the standard of reasonable care? The *Tarasoff* court itself left the question open in an unsatisfactory manner:

> [w]e recognize that in some cases it would be unreasonable to require the therapist to interrogate his patient to discover the victim's identity, or to conduct an independent investigation. But there may also be cases in which a moment's reflection will reveal the victim's identity.[269]

Some commentators have been critical of allowing the action against the psychotherapist to proceed, on the basis that *Tarasoff* renders the question of proof of breach extremely uncertain,[270] while others have pointed to the difficulty of proving breach when the difficulties in 'predicting dangerousness' are so manifest.[271]

Indeed, this problem of proving breach on the part of a HCP who is dealing with a dangerous patient has already been well-illustrated in relevant Commonwealth law. In the English case of *Partington v London Borough of Wandsworth*,[272] Schiemann J emphasised that the assessment of what was reasonable supervision on the part of the Council's careworker required the court to balance what '[was] best for the handicapped person with what [was] best for the rest of the world.' The patient, Claudia, was not running or thrashing her arms in a way which would obviously have alerted the careworker that anything was wrong or that an attack on Mrs Partington was imminent. Similarly, in the Canadian case of *Wenden v Trikha*, the court was, on the evidence, 'satisfied that ... all the hospital staff, acted appropriately and were not in breach of any duty they may have owed to Trikha or to anyone else.'[273]

Hence, the difficulties in proving these negligence suits are by no means limited to proving that a duty of care was owed in the first place.

8. Proving a causal link may be difficult

Finally, there may be a considerable difficulty, under the *Tarasoff* principle, in proving that the HCP's failure to act caused the damage complained of, *viz*, the injury to or murder of the non-patient.

First, the damage to the non-patient may have occurred in any event, on the balance of probabilities, even had the HCP discharged the duty which the law imposed on him. As Thomas points out,[274] the court in *Tarasoff* avoided any analysis of causation, but it is 'far from clear' that causation would have been proven there on but-for principles. To do so, Tatiana Tarasoff would have to prove that, had Dr Moore given a suitable warning of the threat posed by Mr Poddar, she could have taken steps that, more probably than not, would have averted the danger, and the murder. But even if the young woman and her parents had been forewarned, Mr Poddar may still, on the balance of probabilities, have killed the object of his obsession. One American commentator calls the *Tarasoff* case 'peculiar', precisely because it is unclear what a warning to the victim would have achieved—'[t]he information is of limited value to the victim because, in most big cities, such a threat will not trigger police protection'.[275]

Similarly, in *Thompson v County of Alameda*[276]—where Jonathan was murdered by his neighbour, the mentally-ill patient, James F, in the garage next door—the Californian Supreme Court observed that, even if direct and precise warnings had been given, they would have had little effect:

> the generalized warnings sought to be required here would do little to increase the precautions of any particular members of the public who already may have become conditioned to locking their doors, avoiding dark and deserted streets, instructing their children to beware of strangers and taking other precautions. By their very numbers the force of the multiple warnings required to accompany the release of all probationers with a potential for violence would be diluted as to each member of the public who by such release thereby becomes a potential victim. Such a warning may also negate the rehabilitative purposes of the parole and probation system by stigmatizing the released offender in the public's eye.[277]

As a second difficulty, the allegation against the HCP in the context of where a dangerous mentally-ill patient injures or kills a non-patient inevitably entails an 'omission to act'. As canvassed earlier in Chapter 2,[278] omissions are treated differently in English law, and while a causal link can be established in such circumstances (according to the analysis outlined in that earlier chapter), it will be a weaker causal link that will be countenanced, whereby the HCP created the opportunity for the harm to occur.

Thirdly, there is the possibility that the dangerous patient himself will have been taken to have committed some intervening act by reason of his own behaviour, which severs the linkage between the HCP's omission and the non-patient's damage. English commentators Morris and Adshead explain that the chain of causation between the HCP's breach and the crime committed by the patient—

> may be so long that liability can no longer be imposed on the original health care providers. Many violent crimes are committed for reasons other than mental illness—alcohol or emotional distress are just as significant factors. In those cases, while it might be said that the crime would not have been committed had the patient been in hospital (although it might still have been), the discharge of the patient, negligent or otherwise cannot be the cause of the offence. Where there has been an intervening event, or the chain of causation is long, liability cannot be imposed. Otherwise detention in hospital might be justified solely for the purpose of preventing crime.[279]

Again, the point must be reiterated—proving the existence and scope of the duty to be cast upon the HCP is only part of the non-patient's legal challenge under a *Tarasoff*-type principle.

E CONCLUSION

This chapter has concentrated upon the intricacies of seeking to prove that a HCP owes a duty of care to the stranger who is harmed by a physically-impaired or mentally-ill patient.

The numerous critiques as to *Tarasoff*-type duty's scope and meaning which have been canvassed in this section, render the doctrine, for English jurists, one of great fascination and interest, perhaps in the way that a Great White Shark is fascinating and interesting—best observed from very long range. Rather than imposing any affirmative duty on a HCP in favour of a non-patient, it is submitted that discretionary disclosure (as practised in *Egdell* and *Crozier*) should be encouraged. English law shows every sign of maintaining the strict and conservative stance that mandatory duties to warn/protect third parties ought to be rejected, particularly in light of *Palmer v Tees HA* and light of the post-*Palmer* jurisprudence of *Osman*, *Van Colle/Smith* and *Mitchell*.

Perhaps the most important lesson of *Tarasoff* for English law-makers is that, if it is ever to be introduced, it is crucial that the *scope of the duty* be clearly stated. In any tri-partite scenario involving HCP, patient and third party victim, an essential legal question is whether any potential duty on the part of the HCP should be directed towards the patient himself, or to the third party, or both. (Precisely the same problem arises in respect of the contraction or inheritance of disease, which is considered next in Chapter 4.) To construe the HCP's duty as one owed to the patient, to control, advise, and so on—which has the *by-product* of protecting the third party too—is the tack which the lawyers representing Rosie Palmer tried, but which met with little success. On the other hand, to impose a duty on the HCP which requires proactive conduct *vis-à-vis* the third party, may impose a duty of care which is impossible for a *reasonable* HCP to discharge.

There is no doubt that suits by persons who are strangers to the doctor–patient relationship continue to present as evolving and novel claims. Battle-lines will frequently be drawn—on the one side, the non-patient will argue that a HCP can owe a duty of care directly to him, in respect of the treatment of his patient, and on the other side, the HCP will frequently argue that he cannot owe general obligations to non-patients (and that the only cases that supported any such wider duty were HCPs who are employed to carry out examinations of employees and insureds).[280]

In England, this is an area which seems ripe for further claims to potentially emerge— although *Palmer* (itself arising in the medical context) and post-*Palmer* jurisprudence (which arose in other contexts involving public authorities) suggest that negligence will be increasingly difficult to prove, whether or not the non-patient harmed by the patient was pre-identified, or was merely a 'chance encounter' with the patient.

Finally, it remains a theoretical possibility that, where a patient kills another while under medical treatment or supervision, it may be claimed that the NHS Trust under whose care the patient was, violated the victim's art 2 Convention rights. Such a case has yet to be brought. However, the fact that the courts have denied victim claims in *Osman*, *Van Colle* and *Mitchell*, renders such a claim problematical.

ENDNOTES

1. [1937] 4 All ER 19 (QB).
2. *Home Office v Dorset Yacht Co Ltd* [1970] AC 1004 (HL) 1062–63 (Lord Diplock).
3. [1990] 2 AC 605 (HL) 617–18 (Lord Bridge).
4. 17 Cal 3d 425, 551 P 2d 334, 131 Cal Rptr 14 (Cal 1976). This was a majority decision, with the majority comprising Tobriner J, with whom Wright CJ, Sullivan and Richardson JJ agreed; with a separate concurring and dissenting opinion by Mosk J; and Clark J and McComb J dissented.
5. *JD v East Berkshire Community Health NHS Trust* [2005] UKHL 23, [2005] 2 AC 373, [46] (Lord Bingham).
6. [2000] PIQR P1 (CA). It was noted that the claimant's counsel 'referred to a number of American cases': at P12.
7. *JD v East Berkshire Community Health NHS Trust; RK and MAK v Dewsbury Healthcare NHS Trust; RK and AK v Oldham NHS Trust* [2005] UKHL 23, [46] ('In some American jurisdictions it has been accepted that a doctor may owe a duty to a person who is not his patient: see, for example, *Tarasoff*'); *W v Egdell* [1990] Ch 359, 415 ('[counsel] referred to the American case of *Tarasoff* as an example of extreme circumstances and submitted that only in the most extreme circumstances could a doctor be relieved from observing the strict duty of confidence imposed upon him by reason of his relationship with his patient').
8. e.g.: *Clunis v Camden and Islington HA* [1998] QB 978 (CA); and the cases referred to in Ch 1, nn 83 and 84.
9. See the cases referred to in Ch 1, n 85.
10. As noted in, e.g.: I Freckelton and K Petersen (eds), *Controversies in Health Law* (Federation Press, Sydney, 1999) 155.
11. [1937] 4 All ER 19 (Liverpool Summer Assizes).
12. QB, Schiemann J, 3 Nov 1989.
13. [1999] EWCA Civ 1533, (1998) 39 BMLR 35, [2000] PNLR 87.
14. Mrs Palmer's claim was for pure psychiatric illness, and is considered in detail in Ch 8.
15. As to whether pursuing the tort of misfeasance in public office against the health authorities would have benefited the claimants in *Palmer*, see: J Mason and G Laurie, 'Misfeasance in Public Office: An Emerging Medical Law Tort?' (2003) 11 *Med L Rev* 94 (the authors conclude that the chances would be 'slim'). Jones agrees, proposing that English courts would probably be reluctant to see claims based on misfeasance brought against the NHS: M Jones, *Medical Negligence* (4th edn, Sweet & Maxwell, London, 2008) 168, fn 458. As to whether the right to strike out in this case was compatible with art 6 of

the ECHR, see, e.g.: D Fairgrieve and P Craig, '*Barrett*, Negligence and Discretionary Powers' [1999] *Public Law* 626; N Beresford, 'Taxonomy in the Court of Appeal' (2000) 116 *LQR* 205.

[16] See too, for relevant observations—in Canada: *Lawson v Wellesley Hosp* [1978] 1 SCR 893, (1978), 76 DLR (3d) 688 (SCC) (Lawson, a non-psychiatric patient, assaulted in hospital corridor by psychiatric patient in unprovoked and sudden attack; sued hospital in negligence, for permitting a mentally-ill patient, with known propensities to violence, to be at large in hospital premises without adequate control or supervision of his movements; as a preliminary point of law as to whether third party could bring suit against hospital for acts of one of its patients, action could proceed; no detailed analysis of legal relationship between hospital and L, except for statement of Laskin CJ: 'at common law a hospital, especially one providing treatment for mentally-ill persons, would be under a common law liability if, by reason of its failure to provide adequate control and supervision, injury occurred to third persons by reason of the conduct or behaviour of a patient ... The next question is whether or not it can be said that a hospital or psychiatrist or both owe a like duty of care to persons who are not their patients.' Also: See, also: *Tanner v Norys* [1980] 4 WWR 33 (Alta CA), leave to appeal to SCC ref'd: 33 NR 354 (note) (SCC) (psychiatrist might be liable to third party if patient actually carried out threat against that third party); *Stewart v Freeland* [2006] OJ No 4581 (Ont CA) (involuntary mental patient eloped from hospital and killed mother shortly after; hospital had delayed notifying police of elopement; psychiatrist applied for summary judgment on limitation point, but action permitted to continue to trial); *Campbell Estate v Fang* (1994), 116 DLR (4th) 443, (1994), 21 Alta LR (3d) 1 (CA) (GP prescribed Tylenol, Halcyon and Valium for patient, who subsequently killed C in a violent murderous rage; Mrs C learned of GP's treatment and drug prescriptions given to patient during sentencing hearing; Mrs C sued GP, alleging that, given patient's medical history, he was likely to turn violent and murderous if negligently prescribed that medication; extension-of-limitation-period application successful).

[17] (2006), 275 DLR (4th) 101 (Ont CA), leave to appeal to SCC dismissed: (SCC, 5 Apr 2007). The issue of whether Dr S owed the husband a duty of care was not at issue on appeal: at [26]. For case comment, see: R Bland, '*Ahmed v Stefaniu*' (2007) 28 *Health Law Canada* 25.

[18] *ibid*, [22].

[19] (1991), 116 AR 81 (Alta QB), amended: (1991), 118 AR 319 (Alta QB), additional reasons: (1992), 6 CPC (3d) 15 (Alta QB), aff'd: (1993), 135 AR 382 (CA), leave to appeal ref'd: (1993), 149 AR 160 (note) (SCC). See, for comment: J Sestito, 'The Duty to Warn Third Parties and AIDS in Canada' (1996) 16 *Health Law Canada* 83; D Smith, '*Wenden v Trikha* and Third Party Liability of Doctors and Hospitals: What's Been Happening to *Tarasoff?*' (1995) 4 *Health L Rev* 12; D Truscott and K Crook, '*Tarasoff* in the Canadian context: *Wenden* and the Duty to Protect' (1993) 38 *Canadian J of Psychiatry* 84; L Ferris, 'In the Public Interest: Disclosing Confidential Patient Information for the Health or Safety of Others' (1998) 18 *Health Law Canada* 119.

[20] *ibid* (Alta QB) [92].

[21] *ibid*, [94].

[22] See too, for further Canadian authorities of interest: *Molnar v Coates* (1991), 5 CCLT (2d) 236 (BCCA) (action against HCP), and later, against the hospital directly: (1993), 50 WAC 246 (BCSC) (out-patient attacked his sister, seriously injuring her; sister sued patient's psychiatrist, alleging a failure to monitor patient and his medication levels competently; claim failed); *Kines Estate v Lychuk Estate* (1996), 10 WWR 426, 112 Man R (2d) 71 (QB) (former psychiatric patient shot and killed third party; estate sued patient's psychiatrists in negligence; claim struck out as disclosing no cause of action; no duty of care owed to victim by psychiatrists).

[23] [2002] NZAR 375 (HC). For case comment, see, e.g.: W Brookbanks, 'Liability for Discharged Psychiatric Patients' [2002] *NZLJ* 199.

[24] NZHC, Master Thomson, 19 May 2000.

[25] [2000] BCSC 1189, (2000), 2 CCLT (3d) 120.

[26] (1988), 52 Man R (2d) 20 (QB), appeal dismissed: (1988), 55 Man R (2d) 188 (CA).

[27] 17 Cal 3d 425, 551 P 2d 334, 343, 131 Cal Rptr 14 (Cal 1976).

[28] The criminal proceedings in this case, which provide more background to the events leading to the murder, are reported as: *People v Poddar*, 10 Cal 3d 750 (Cal 1974). The civil case was eventually

settled out of court, as noted in: G Annas, *The Rights of Patients* (3rd edn, Southern Illinois U Press, Carbondale, 2004) 257.

29   27 Cal 3d 741, 614 P 2d 728, 167 Cal Rptr 70 (Cal 1980).

30   (1992), 13 CCLT (2d) 267 (Ont Gen Div), additional reasons at: (Ont Gen Div, 1 Apr 1993), aff'd: (1998), 41 CCLT (2d) 292 (Ont CA). For an American equivalent, involving treatment of an epileptic patient, see, e.g.: *Duvall v Goldin*, 139 Mich App 342, 362 NW 2d 275 (1984) (duty owed by psychiatrist to non-patient).

31   [2003] ABQB 804.

32   *ibid*, [56], citing many of the cases referred to elsewhere in this Section.

33   [1994] CanLII 517 (Ont CA).

34   For further cases and commentary, see, e.g.: L Gostin *et al*, *Law, Science and Medicine* (3rd edn, Foundation Press, New York NY, 2005) 776; Annotation, 'Liability of Physician, for Injury to or Death of Third Party Due to Failure to Disclose Driving-Related Impediment', 43 ALR (4th) 153. For further cases in which the relevant HCP did, or could, owe a duty of care to a non-patient who was harmed by the patient driver, see, e.g.: *Cram v Howell*, 680 NE 2d 1096 (Ind 1997); *Wilschinsky v Medina*, 775 P 2d 713 (NM 1989) (injection of drugs); *MacPhail v Desrosiers* [1998] NSJ No 353, aff'd: 1998 Carswell NS 497 (NSCA) (fainting after abortion).

35   892 So 2d 887 (SC Ala 2004).

36   144 Cal App 3d 888, 193 Cal Rptr 733 (App Ct 1983). For another diabetic case, see, e.g.: *Hardee v Bio-Medical Applications of SC Inc*, 370 SC 511, 636 SE 2d 629 (SC 2006) (patient a Type 1 Insulin-dependent diabetic who required hemo-dialysis treatment three times a week; after completion of treatment, patient customarily drove home; on one occasion, minutes after treatment ended, patient lost control of car and collided with the Hardees; patient killed and Hardees seriously injured; duty of care owed by HCP to Hardees to warn patient of risks of driving).

37   680 NE 2d 1096 (Ind 1997).

38   *Schmidt v Mahoney*, 659 NW 2d 552 (Iowa 2003).

39   *Forlaw v Fitzer*, 456 So 2d 432 (Fla 1984).

40   *Praesel v Johnson*, 967 SW 2d 391 (Tex 1998).

41   Adopting the facts and reasoning of: *Young v Wadsworth*, 916 SW 2d 877 (Mo Ct App ED 1996), and a key reason in *Praesel v Johnson*, *ibid*, for denying a duty of care. See, too, e.g.: *Calwell v Hassan*, 260 Kan 769, 925 P 2d 422 (1996) (doctor treated patient for daytime drowsiness; injury caused to non-patient; no duty to warn patient not to drive, where patient knew she might become drowsy or fall asleep while driving).

42   (1978), 84 DLR (3d) 650 (Man QB).

43   *Moore v Shah*, 90 AD 2d 389, 458 NYS 2d 33 (3d Dept 1982).

44   *Paxton v Ramji* [2008] ONCA 697, (2008), 299 DLR (4th) 614 (Ont CA) [58].

45   [1937] 4 All ER 19 (Liverpool Summer Assizes).

46   [1999] EWCA Civ 1533, [28].

47   *ibid*, [no pp]. For further judicial criticism of the case: *Home Office v Dorset Yacht Co Ltd* [1970] AC 1004 (HL) 1040–41 (Lord Diplock) 1031 (Lord Morris). Indeed, the citation by the authors, E Picard and G Robertson, *Legal Liability of Doctors and Hospitals in Canada* (4th edn, Thomson Carswell, Toronto, 2007) 220, that *Holgate* is authority for the proposition that, where a mentally-ill patient harms a non-patient, 'there is little doubt that the doctor and the hospital owe a duty of care to the third party', is perhaps rather hopeful, given the criticism of *Holgate* in subsequent English decisions.

48   [1990] 2 AC 605 (HL) 617–18 (Lord Bridge).

49   L Klar, 'The Role and Fault of Policy in Negligence Law' (1996–97) 35 *Alberta L Rev* 24, (accessed online, no pp available). Also referenced, with similar questioning, in: A Linden, L Klar and B Feldthusen, *Canadian Tort Law: Cases, Notes and Materials* (13th edn, Lexisnexis Canada Inc, Toronto, 2009) 410. Cf, however: M Jones, *Medical Negligence* (4th edn, Sweet & Maxwell, London, 2008) 145, who considers the donation by close family members to be 'clearly more foreseeable as potential donors, who would feel a greater sense of moral obligation to the patient'.

50   (2001), 95 BCLR (3d) 347 (SC) [40]–[41]. This was a *patient* suit against the hospital for the behaviour of a co-patient, but the principle applies regardless.

51   [2000] BCSC 1189, (2000), 2 CCLT (3d) 120, [64].

52   *C (CL) v Lions Gate Hosp* (2001), 95 BCLR (3d) 347 (SC) [54].

53   e.g.: *Mustafic v Smith* (1988), 52 Man R (2d) 20 (QB), aff'd: (1988), 55 Man R (2d) 188 (CA), leave to appeal ref'd: (1989), 60 Man R (2d) 80 (note) (SCC); and *Molnar v Coates* (1991), 5 CCLT (2d) 236 (BCCA).

54   [1991] 3 All ER 88 (CA) 114.

55   See p 4.

56   See, for similar comment: *Wenden v Trikha* (1991), 28 ACWS (3d) 135 (Alta QB) [74]–[80].

57   [1999] EWCA Civ 1533, [32].

58   *ibid*, [32], cf. the mechanic who fails to fix brakes, per Stuart-Smith LJ at [24]–[25].

59   *ibid*.

60   NZHC, 19 May 2000.

61   [2006] NZHC 826, [2007] 1 NZLR 196, 288.

62   [2002] NZAR 375 (HC).

63   [2004] NZAR 342 (HC) [28], [44].

64   *Ellis v Counties Manukau District Health Board* [2006] NZHC 826, [2007] 1 NZLR 196 (HC) [137]–[139], [141]–[145], [160]–[163].

65   [1937] 4 All ER 19 (Liverpool Summer Assizes).

66   For further academic doubts about *Holgate*, see, e.g.: D Miers, 'Liability for Injuries Caused by Violent Patients' [1996] *JPIL* 314, 317, 323, citing also: B Hoggett, *Mental Health Law* (Sweet & Maxwell, London, 1990) 247, and A Parkin, 'Discretion and Resources in Mental Health Provision' (1991) 141 *NLJ* 1453; F Morris and G Adshead, 'The Liability of Psychiatrists for the Violent Acts of their Patients' (1997) 147 *NLJ* 558, 575; C McIvor, *Third Party Liability in Tort* (Hart Publishing, Oxford, 2006) 133, fn 121; N Beresford, 'Taxonomy in the Court of Appeal' (2000) 116 *LQR* 205, 206.

67   [2000] BCSC 1189, (2000), 2 CCLT (3d) 120.

68   e.g,, *Myers v Quesenberry*, 144 Cal App 3d 888, 193 Cal Rptr 733 (App Ct 1983); *Hardee v Bio-Medical Applications of SC Inc*, 370 SC 511, 636 SE 2d 629 (SC 2006) (both diabetic cases).

69   Noted, e.g., in: *AAA v BBB* [2005] WASC 139, [80] (but this was not such a case).

70   [2004] NZAR 342 (HC) [28], [44].

71   680 NE 2d 1096 (Ind 1997).

72   [1999] EWCA Civ 1533, (accessed online, no pp available).

73   [2002] NZAR 375 (HC) [21]–[23], and [36].

74   (NZHC, 19 May 2000, Master Thomson) 19–20.

75   [2002] NZAR 375, [29].

76   [1999] EWCA Civ 1533, [25], with Stuart-Smith LJ drawing a contrast with *Home Office v Dorset Yacht Co Ltd* [1970] AC 1004 (HL), where 'the plaintiff's boat was readily to hand'.

77   (1991), 116 AR 81 (Alta QB) [94] (but no liability—no breach), aff'd (1993), 14 CCLT (2d) 225 (Alta CA).

78   *ibid*, [94].

79   *Healey v Lakeridge Health Corp* (2006), 38 CPC (6th) 145 (Ont SCJ) [71] (Cullity J).

80   17 Cal 3d 425, 551 P 2d 334 (1976).

81   [1999] EWCA Civ 1533, (1998) 39 BMLR 35.

82   *ibid*, (accessed online, no pp available).

83   [1993] 4 All ER 344 (CA). Application for leave to appeal to HL was refused. An action against P's psychiatrist Dr Ferguson was abandoned.

84   *ibid*, 350 (by majority, Beldam LJ reserving the question).

85   *Hill v Chief Constable of West Yorkshire* [1989] AC 53 (HL).

86   [2008] UKHL 50, [2009] 1 AC 225 (HL).

87   [2009] UKHL 11, [2009] 2 WLR 481 (HL).

88   *Mitchell v Glasgow CC* [2009] UKHL 11, [29].

89 *ibid*, [81], [83], and citing, (at [18]) the exceptional cases where a duty of care by defendant to third party for the acts committed by the criminally-minded was upheld: *Home Office v Dorset Yacht Co Ltd* [1970] AC 1004 (HL); and *A–G of the British Virgin Islands v Hartwell* [2004] UKPC 12, [2004] 1 WLR 1273.

90 *ibid*, [83].

91 *Wenden v Trikha* (1991), 28 ACWS (3d) 135 (Alta QB) [54], [56], [63], aff'd (1993), 14 CCLT (2d) 225 (Alta CA), and cited in, eg: *Healey v Lakeridge Health Corp* (2006), 38 CPC (6ᵗʰ) 145 (Ont SCJ) [47], [53].

92 *Ellis v Counties Manukau Dist Health Board* [2006] NZHC 826, [2007] 1 NZLR 196, [164] (Potter J).

93 [2000] BCSC 1189, (2000), 2 CCLT (3d) 120.

94 *Partington v Wandsworth LBC* (QB, 3 Nov 1989).

95 (2006), 275 DLR (4ᵗʰ) 101 (Ont CA), leave to appeal to SCC dismissed: (SCC, 5 Apr 2007).

96 [2004] NZAR 342 (HC).

97 [1999] 1 SCR 455, [59].

98 (1992), 13 CCLT (2d) 267 (Ont Gen Div), additional reasons at: (Ont Gen Div, 1 Apr 1993), aff'd: (1998), 41 CCLT (2d) 292 (Ont CA).

99 (1991), 116 AR 81 (Alta QB). According to J Van Exan, 'The Legal and Ethical Issues Surrounding the Duty to Warn in the Practice of Psychology' [2004] *Windsor Rev of Legal and Social Issues* 123, 130, '*Wenden v Trikha* most closely resembles the *Tarasoff* decision'.

100 D Evans, *The Law, Standards, and Ethics in the Practice of Psychology* (2ⁿᵈ edn, Emond Montgomery Publications Ltd, Toronto, 2004) 202.

101 W Flanagan, 'Genetic Data and Medical Confidentiality' (1995) 3 *Health LJ* 269, [22].

102 E Picard and G Robertson, *Legal Liability of Doctors and Hospitals in Canada* (4ᵗʰ edn, Thomson Carswell, Toronto, 2007) 38.

103 See *Healey v Lakeridge Health Corp* (2006), 38 CPC (6ᵗʰ) 145 (Ont SCJ) [71] (Cullity J) ('The decision in *Spillane* appears to extend even further the potential range of relationships giving rise to a duty of care and, in *Wenden*, the court was, at least, prepared to contemplate the possibility of a similar extension. It is not clear to me that the English authorities would go that far'). Leading English commentator Jones agrees that an English court would be unlikely to find a duty of care owed by the hospital on *Wenden v Trikha*-type facts: M Jones, *Medical Negligence* (4ᵗʰ edn, Sweet & Maxwell, London, 2008) 170–71.

104 [1955] AC 549 (HL).

105 *Goodwill v British Pregnancy Advisory Service* (1996) 31 BMLR 83 (CA) 88, 91 (discussed in Chapter 7).

106 [2002] NZAR 375 (HC). The claim was brought by the relatives of the murdered girlfriend.

107 *ibid*, [23], [26]–[27]. Subsequently, according to *Couch v A-G* [2008] NZSC 45, [106], the statement in *Maulolo v Hutt Valley Health Corp*, of 'the ability of the defendant to identify the victim', was a 'similar idea to that captured by the special risk test'. The case was particularly startling: the patient was released by a doctor who was fraudulently passing herself off as a qualified psychiatrist (but the release was legally effective nonetheless); and the last contact that the mental health worker who was assigned to care for P in the community had had with his patient was the day of the release, more than a year before the murder.

108 C McIvor, 'The Positive Duty of the Police to Protect Life' (2008) 24 *PN* 27, 32. For further academic discussion/criticism of the proximity analysis in *Palmer*, see, e.g.: J Ellis Cameron-Perry, 'Homo Ludens: *Jolly v Sutton LBC*' (2000) 24 *SLT* 189; D Miers, 'Liability for Injuries Caused by Violent Patients' [1996] *JPIL* 314, 320; 'Negligence: Duty of Care: Health Authorities' [1999] *JPIL* 326, 327–28.

109 *Healey v Lakeridge Health Corp* (2006), 38 CPC (6ᵗʰ) 145 (Ont SCJ) [71].

110 See GMC, *Confidentiality: Reporting Concerns About Patients to the DVLA or the DVA* (Oct 2009), and the discussion in Chapter 2, p 43.

111 DVLA, *For Medical Practitioners: At a Glance Guide to the Current Medical Standards of Fitness to Drive* (Drivers' Medical Group, Feb 2008) 4, citing: *Confidentiality: Protecting and Providing Information, ibid.*

112 E Picard and G Robertson, *Legal Liability of Doctors and Hospitals in Canada* (4th edn, Thomson Carswell, Toronto, 2007) 31–32.

113 (1992), 13 CCLT (2d) 267 (Ont Gen Div), additional reasons at: (Ont Gen Div, 1 Apr 1993), liability aff'd but apportionment varied in: *Spillane v Wasserman* (1998), 41 CCLT (2d) 292 (Ont CA).

114 Highway Traffic Act, RSO 1980, c 198, s 177(1).

115 (1998), 41 CCLT (2d) 292 (Ont CA) (doctors' contribution reduced from 40% to 5%; patient 'failed to report some seizures to the appellants, neglected to take his medication, and falsified his license renewal application—all deliberately': at [6]. Also: *Toms v Foster* [1994] CanLII 517 (Ont CA).

116 *Ellis v Counties Manukau Dist Health Board* [2006] NZHC 826, [2007] 1 NZLR 196, [165], citing: *Rolls-Royce New Zealand Ltd v Carter Holt Harvey Ltd* [2005] 1 NZLR 324 (HC) [64].

117 [2003] ABQB 804, [59], referring to: Motor Vehicle Administration Act, RSA 1980, c M-22, s 14(2), which only entitled a physician to report on medical conditions affecting a person's ability to operate a motor vehicle, but did not require a physician to do so—in contrast to the Ontario regime at issue in *Spillane, ibid.*

118 See Chapter 2, pp 41–43.

119 J Healy, *Medical Negligence: Common Law Perspectives* (Sweet & Maxwell, London, 1999) 47.

120 [2009] UKHL 11, [2009] 2 WLR 481.

121 *ibid*, [27]–[28].

122 [2008] UKHL 50, [2009] 1 AC 225.

123 *viz,: Hill v Chief Constable of West Yorkshire* [1989] AC 53 (HL) 63 (Lord Keith) 65 (Lord Templeman); *Phelps v Hillingdon LBC* [2001] 2 AC 619 (HL) 672–74 (Lord Clyde), and earlier: [1998] EWCA Civ 1686, [65] (Stuart-Smith LJ); *McFarlane v Tayside Health Board* [2000] 2 AC 59 (HL) 83 (Lord Steyn); *X (Minors) v Bedfordshire CC* [1995] 2 AC 633 (CA) 661–63 (Sir Thomas Bingham MR), and on appeal: [1995] 2 AC 633 (HL) 749–51 (Lord Browne-Wilkinson); *Alexandrou v Oxford* [1993] 4 All ER 328 (CA); *Osman v Ferguson* [1993] 4 All ER 344 (CA).

124 *Mitchell* [2009] UKHL 11, [44] (Lord Scott), [72] (Lord Rodger), [73] (Baroness Hale), [83] (Lord Brown).

125 [1999] EWCA Civ 1533, (1998) 39 BMLR 35.

126 *Palmer v Teeside HA* (1998) 45 BMLR 88 (QB) 101–2 (Gage J).

127 [1990] 1 Ch 359 (CA).

128 (1990) 8 BMLR 128 (CCA). Cf: *X (HA) v Y* [1988] 2 All ER 648 (QB) (not in public interest to allow newspaper to publish any information obtained through a breach of confidence from medical records of AIDS sufferers, where two such sufferers were GP's in general practice).

129 [1990] 1 Ch 359 (CA) 416 (Sir Stephen Brown P) 419 (Bingham LJ). The quote is taken from the headnote.

130 As the court put it in *R v Crozier* (1990) 8 BMLR 128 (CCA).

131 e.g.: R Gilbar, 'Medical Confidentiality Within the Family: The Doctor's Duty Reconsidered' (2004) 18 *Intl J of Law, Policy and the Family* 195; A Abadee, 'The Medical Duty of Confidentiality and Prospective Duty of Disclosure: Can They Co-exist?' (1995) 3 *JLM* 75; W Herdy, 'Must the Doctor Tell?' (1996) 3 *JLM* 270; L Skene, 'Genetic Secrets and the Family: A Response to Bell and Bennett' (2001) 9 *Med L Rev* 162; K Doran, 'Medical Confidentiality: The Role of the Doctrine of Confidentiality in the Doctor–Patient Relationship' (1997) 3 *Medico-Legal J of Ireland* 21; B Mahendra, 'Medical Disclosure and Confidentiality' (2001) 151 *NLJ* 10; S Keeling, 'Duty to Warn of Genetic Harm in Breach of Patient Confidentiality' (2004) 12 *JLM* 235; L Edozian, 'Disclosure of Medical Information when a Patient Presents a Danger to Others: Duty or Discretion?' (2001) 7 *Clinical Risk* 224.

132 A point also noted by, e.g.: F Morris and G Adshead, 'The Liability of Psychiatrists for the Violent Acts of their Patients' (1997) 148 *NLJ* 558, 558; M Thomas, 'Expanded Liability for Psychiatrists: *Tarasoff* Gone Crazy?' [2009] *J of Mental Health Law* 45, 50; C Jones, 'Tightropes and Tragedies: 25 Years of *Tarasoff*' (2003) 43 *Medicine, Science and the Law* 13.

[133] *Tarasoff v The Regents of the Uni of California*, 17 Cal 3d 425, 131 Cal Rptr 14 (Cal 1976).

[134] *ibid*, 440.

[135] *ibid*.

[136] A Garton, 'Reconciling the Incongruous Demands of Therapist–Patient Confidentiality and Falsely-Accused Third Parties' (2007) 37 *Cumberland L Rev* 77, 108, quoting the study undertaken by: D Shuman and M Weiner, 'The Privilege Study: An Empirical Examination of the Psychotherapist–Patient Privilege' (1982) 60 *North Carolina L Rev* 893, 915. See, too: D Givelber, '*Tarasoff*: Myth and Reality: An Empirical Study of Private Law in Action' (1984) *Wisconsin L Rev* 443.

[137] D Givelber, 'The *Tarasoff* Controversy: A Summary of Findings from an Empirical Study of Legal, Ethical, and Clinical Issues' in J Beck (ed), *The Potentially Violent Patient and the Tarasoff Decision in Psychiatric Practice* (1985) 37.

[138] 17 Cal 3d 425, 441–42 (Cal 1976).

[139] *ibid*, 441.

[140] *ibid*, 442.

[141] i.e., imposing 'liability in an indeterminate amount for an indeterminate time to an indeterminate class' in *Ultramares Corporation v Touche*, 174 NE 441, 444 (1931).

[142] [1999] EWCA Civ 1533.

[143] [2002] NZAR 375 (HC) [34].

[144] [2006] NZHC 826, [2007] 1 NZLR 196, [132], [147]. See, further, W Brookbanks, 'Liability for Discharged Psychiatric Patients' [2002] *NZLJ* 199, 201.

[145] 144 Cal App 3d 888, 193 Cal Rptr 733 (1983).

[146] See p 65.

[147] (2006), 38 CPC (6th) 145 (Ont SCJ) [75].

[148] *Praesel v Johnson*, 967 SW 2d 391, 398 (Tex 1998).

[149] 892 So 2d 887 (Ala 2004).

[150] *ibid*, 895.

[151] Cited from the defendant's brief, at *ibid*, 895–96.

[152] *ibid*, 897.

[153] [2009] UKHL 11, [2009] 1 AC 874.

[154] As noted in Table 3.1 above.

[155] e.g.: J Dawson, 'Randomised Controlled Trials of Mental Health Legislation' (2002) 10 *Med L Rev* 308, 310 ('[e]ven in England there is a chance that HCPs may be found liable to a person harmed, where injuries are clearly foreseeable to specific individuals in the immediate proximity of the patient'); M Jones, *Medical Negligence* (4th edn, Sweet & Maxwell, London, 2008) 166 (whether *Tarasoff* would be followed in England 'remains debatable'); J Mason, 'The Legal Aspects and Implications of Risk Assessment' (2000) 8 *Med L Rev* 69, 75 ('the door to liability ... is certainly not closed'); F Morris and G Adshead, 'The Liability of Psychiatrists for the Violent Acts of their Patients' (1997) 147 *NLJ* 558, 575 ('[w]hen a patient identifies a proposed victim, the proximity of the relationship *may* be established': emphasis added); D Miers, 'Liability for Injuries Caused by Violent Patients' [1996] *JPIL* 314, 320 ('Much would depend on the patient's clinical history, the credibility of the threat, the amenability of the patient's condition to treatment and of the patient's reliability concerning compliance with a medication regime').

[156] *Mitchell v Glasgow CC* [2009] UKHL 11, [2009] 1 AC 874, [26] (Lord Hope).

[157] Art 2(1) provides: 'Everyone's right to life shall be protected by law. No one shall be deprived of his life intentionally save in the execution of a sentence of a court following his conviction of a crime for which this penalty is provided by law.'

[158] *Mitchell v Glasgow CC* [2009] UKHL 11, [2009] 1 AC 874, [66].

[159] See Chapter 1, p 11.

[160] [1999] EWCA Civ 1533, [2000] PIQR P1.

[161] The European Convention for the Protection of Human Rights and Fundamental Freedoms 1950 (as set out in Sch 1 to the Human Rights Act 1998) came into force in October 2000.

[162] *Rabone v Pennine Care NHS Trust* [2009] EWHC 1827 (QB); *Savage v South Essex Partnership NHS Foundation Trust* [2008] UKHL 74, [2009] 1 AC 681. Both claims failed, for reasons explored in: R Mulheron, 'Deaths, Medical Negligence, and Art 2 of the Convention: Some Emerging Themes' [forthcoming, 2010].

[163] *Powell v UK* (2000) 30 EHRR CD 362 (ECtHR) (the claim failed).

[164] *Osman v UK* (2000) 29 EHRR 245 (ECtHR) [115]. Discussed further in Chapter 1.

[165] *ibid*, [116].

[166] *ibid*.

[167] *Mitchell v Glasgow CC* [2009] UKHL 11, [2009] 1 AC 874, [30]–[34] (Lord Hope), [45] (Lord Scott), [64]–[71] (Lord Rodger), [78] (Baroness Hale), [85] (Lord Brown).

[168] *Smith v Chief Constable of Sussex Police; Van Colle v Chief Constable of Hertfordshire* [2008] UKHL 50, [2009] 1 AC 225, [28]–[39] (Lord Bingham), [65]–[71] (Lord Hope), [84]–[87] (Lord Phillips), [105] (Lord Carswell), [114]–[118] (Lord Brown). The fact scenario involving Stephen Smith's attack by his former partner has been considered previously: at p 75, 76. In the *Van Colle* case, the claim was brought under ss 6 and 7 of the HRA, in reliance on arts 2 and 8 of the Convention, and no claim was made under the common law in negligence. In *Smith*, on the other hand, the claim was brought in negligence, and no claim was made for violation of a Convention right.

[169] *Osman v UK* (2000) 29 EHRR 245 (ECtHR).

[170] *Mitchell v Glasgow CC* [2009] UKHL 11, [2009] 1 AC 874, [69].

[171] *ibid*, [67]. Nor was there any 'real and immediate risk' made out in either *Osman v UK* (2000) 29 EHRR 245 (ECtHR) [121] or in *Van Colle* [2008] UKHL 50, [2009] 1 AC 225 (HL) [36], [39], [71], [86].

[172] *ibid*, [70] (emphasis added).

[173] *ibid*, [31].

[174] A Hubbard, 'The Future of "The Duty of Protect": Scientific and Legal Perspectives on *Tarasoff's* Thirtieth Anniversary' (2006) 75 *U of Cincinnati L Rev* 429, 441–42.

[175] M Perlin, '"You Got No Secrets to Conceal": Considering the Application of the *Tarasoff* Doctrine Abroad' (2006) 75 *U of Cincinnati L Rev* 611, 625.

[176] M Thomas, 'Expanded Liability for Psychiatrists: *Tarasoff* Gone Crazy?' [2009] *J of Mental Health Law* 45, 50.

[177] 17 Cal 3d 425, 131 Cal Rptr 14, 551 P 2d 334 (1976). As Lake describes, '[t]he previous opinion [in 1974, *Tarasoff I*] was vacated after rehearing. When the court ruled in *Tarasoff I* that a therapist who has reason to believe that a patient will harm another must warn the endangered person, there was, according to some accounts, an "outraged reaction". Some believe that the reaction to this holding drove the court to rehear the case': P Lake, 'Revisiting *Tarasoff*' (1994) 58 *Albany L Rev* 97, fn 1, citing: V Merton, 'Confidentiality and The "Dangerous" Patient: Implications of *Tarasoff* for Psychiatrists and Lawyers' (1982) 31 *Emory LJ* 263, 294.

[178] Lake, *ibid*, 97.

[179] D Mossman, 'Critique of Pure Risk Assessment or Kant Meets *Tarasoff*' (2006) 75 *U Cincinatti L Rev* 523, 524.

[180] A Harmon, 'Back from Wonderland: A Linguistic Approach to Duties Arising from Threats of Physical Violence' (2008) 37 *Capital U L Rev* 27, fn 23.

[181] *Schuster v Altenberg*, 424 NW 2d 159, 167 (Wis 1988).

[182] *Santana v Rainbow Cleaners Inc*, 969 A 2d 653, 660 (Rh Is 2009). The recognition or rejection of a *Tarasoff* duty is a matter of state, not federal, law.

[183] A Hubbard, 'The Future of "The Duty to Protect": Scientific and Legal Perspectives on *Tarasoff's* Thirtieth Anniversary: Symposium', and other papers from the Symposium, reported in (2006) 75 *U of Cincinnati L Rev*.

[184] 'Therapists Behaving Badly: Why the *Tarasoff* Duty is not Always Economically Efficient' (2007) 43 *Willamette L Rev* 31.

[185] What follows in this section does not purport to comprehensively canvas the huge number of *Tarasoff*-spawned US cases, concerning harm done to third parties by mentally-ill patients. The cases discussed herein are chosen for illustrative purposes, to highlight the interpretative difficulties that emerged under

this contentious principle of law. For discussion of further and different case law, see, e.g.: Annotation, 'Liability of One Treating Mentally Afflicted Patient for Failing to Warn or Protect Third Persons Threatened by Patient', 83 ALR 3d 1201; M Firestone, 'Psychiatric Patients and Forensic Psychiatry' in S Sanbar (ed), *Legal Medicine* (7th edn, American College of Legal Medicine Textbook Comm, Mosby Elsevier, 2007) ch 67; 'R Patterson, *Harney's Medical Malpractice* (4th edn, Lexis Law Publishing, Charlottesville VA, 1999) Section 10.5; S Pegalis, *The American Law of Medical Malpractice*, vol 1 (3rd edn, Thomson West, Eagan MN, 2005) Section 3.16.

[186] For a recent judicial summary of the 'variety of different approaches' adopted by courts and statutes, see, e.g.: *Santana v Rainbow Cleaners Inc*, 969 A 2d 653 (Rh Is Sup Ct, 30 Apr 2009).

[187] 551 P 2d 334, 343 (1976).

[188] 551 P 2d 334, 340, 345 (Cal 1976) (Tobriner J) (emphasis added).

[189] 27 Cal 3d 741, 759, 614 P 2d 728, 738, 167 Cal Rptr 70, 80 (Cal 1980).

[190] *ibid*, 755–56. Also see discussion in, e.g.: *Bradley v Ray*, 904 SW 2d 302, 307 (Miss 1995).

[191] e.g.: *Bardoni v Kim*, 390 NW 2d 218 (Mich 1986); *Peck v Counseling Service*, 146 Vt 61, 499 A 2d 422 (Vt 1985); *McIntosh v Milano*, 168 NJ Super 466, 403 A 2d 500 (NJ 1979); *Hasenei v US*, 541 F Supp 999 (D Md 1982); *Leedy v Hartnett*, 510 F Supp 1125 (MD Pa 1981); *Cairl v State*, 323 NW 2d 20 (Minn 1982).

[192] 2001 LEXIS 2231 (Conn Sup Ct, 7 Aug 2001).

[193] *ibid*, 11.

[194] 851 F Supp 34 (D Conn 1994).

[195] *Tarasoff v The Regents of the Uni of California*, 551 P 2d 334, 340 (1976).

[196] 851 F Supp 34, 41 (D Conn 1994).

[197] e.g.: *Lipari v Sears, Roebuck & Co*, 497 F Supp 185, 194–95 (D Neb 1980); *Shively v Ken Crest Centers for Exceptional Persons*, 2001 Del Super LEXIS 58 (Del Super 2001); *Estates of Morgan v Fairfield Family Counseling Centre*, 77 Ohio St 3d 284, 673 NE 2d 1311, 1324–26 (1997); *Hamman v County of Maricopa*, 161 Ariz 58, 775 P 2d 1122, 1128 (1989); *Schuster v Altenberg*, 424 NW 2d 159, 166 (1988); *McIntosh v Milano*, 168 NJ Super 466, 403 A 2d 500, 511–12 (NJ Super Ct 1979); *Cain v Rijken*, 700 P 2d 1061 (1985).

[198] *Rivera v New York City Health and Hosp Corp*, 191 F Supp 2d 412, 421 (2002), also citing the cases, *ibid*.

[199] *ibid*.

[200] *Tarasoff v The Regents of the Uni of California*, 551 P 2d 334, 340, 345 (Cal 1976).

[201] 497 F Supp 185 (D Neb 1980).

[202] *ibid*, 193.

[203] 551 P 2d 334, fn 14 (Cal 1976), referring to the brief put forward by Amicus.

[204] e.g.: *King v Smith*, 539 So 2d 262, 264 (Ala 1989); *Santa Cruz v Northwest Dade Community Health Center Inc*, 590 So 2d 444, 445 (Fla App 1991); *Thapar v Zezulka*, 994 SW 2d 635, 638 (Tex 1999); *Nasser v Parker*, 249 Va 172, 455 SE 2d 502, 505–6 (Va 1995).

[205] 590 So 2d 446 (Fla 3d DCA 1991).

[206] *ibid*, 448.

[207] *ibid*, 449.

[208] *Tarasoff v The Regents of the Uni of California*, 551 P 2d 334, 349 (Cal 1976).

[209] G McClarren, 'The Psychiatric Duty to Warn: Walking a Tightrope of Uncertainty' (1987) 56 *U Cincinnati L Rev* 269, 284–85.

[210] A Hubbard, 'The Future of "The Duty to Protect": Scientific and Legal Perspectives on *Tarasoff's* Thirtieth Anniversary: Symposium'.

[211] 851 F Supp 34 (D Conn 1994).

[212] e.g.: *Brady v Hopper*, 570 F Supp 1333, 1338 (D Colo 1983), aff'd: 751 F 2d 329 (10th Cir 1984); *Currie v US*, 644 F Supp 1074, 1080–84 (MDNC 1986), aff'd: 836 F 2d 209 (4th Cir 1987).

[213] M Hall *et al*, *Health Care Law and Ethics* (7th edn, Aspen Pub Wolters Kluwer, New York NY, 2007) 195.

[214] *Santana v Rainbow Cleaners Inc*, 969 A 2d 653, 660 (Sup Ct Rh Is, 31 Apr 2009).

215   T Waller, 'Application of Traditional Tort Law Post-*Tarasoff*' (1997) 31 *Akron L Rev* 321.

216   *ibid*, 340, citing: *Perreira v State*, 768 P 2d 1198, 1209–14 (Colo 1989). See, also, on this point: M Quattrocchi and R Schopp, 'Tarasaurus Rex: A Standard of Care That Could Not Adapt' (2005) 11 *Psychology, Public Policy and Law* 109; A Felthouse and C Kachigan 'To Warn and to Control: Two Distinct Legal Obligations or Variations of a Single Duty to Protect?' (2001) 19 *Behavioral Sciences and the Law* 355.

217   *ibid*, 340.

218   [1999] EWCA Civ 1533, (1998) 39 BMLR 35.

219   *Green v Ross*, 691 So 2d 542, 542–43 (1997). In 1988, Florida's legislature introduced legislation (455.2415, Florida Statutes (1989)) that permitted psychiatrists to 'disclose patient communications', but did not compel such disclosure. Hence, that legislation would not have rendered the outcome of this case any different, said the majority, even had the legislation been retrospective, which it was not.

220   These statutes are conveniently listed in *Bradley v Ray*, 904 SW 2d 302 (1995), which notes that, at that time, 15 states had enacted such legislation, including California, the source jurisdiction of the *Tarasoff* rule.

221   MCLS § 330.1946 (2009).

222   Noted in: *Jenks v Brown*, 219 Mich App 415, 417, 557 NW 2d 114, 117 (2006), citing: House Legislative Analysis, HB 4237, 11 Jul 1989.

223   279 Mich App 552, 761 NW 2d 318 (Mich Ct App, 10 Jul 2008). At the time of writing, leave to appeal has been granted in this case: *Dawe v Dr Reuvan Bar-Levav & Assocs PC*, 2009 Mich LEXIS 1615 (Mich, 3 Aug 2009).

224   *Dawe*, *ibid*, 558–59 (2008).

225   *ibid*. See too: *Reh v Laskowski*, 2009 Mich App LEXIS 389 (Mich Ct Apps, 24 Feb 2009) (psychotic patient threatened said he 'wanted to kill white people'; later tried to kill white employees at a nearby learning center; held that, merely because they were Caucasian and worked geographically close did not make victims 'reasonably identifiable third persons'; 'white people' represented everyone with white skin, i.e., a huge group).

226   219 Mich App 415, 557 NW 2d 114 (1996).

227   *ibid*, 417.

228   230 Mich App 190, 583 NW 2d 719 (1998).

229   590 So 2d 446 (Fla 3d DCA 1991).

230   *ibid*, 448.

231   *ibid*, citing, in that regard, *Nesbitt v Community Health of South Dade Inc*, 467 So 2d 711, 717 (Fla 3d DCA 1985), quoting T Almy, 'Psychiatric Testimony: Controlling the 'Ultimate Wizardry' in Personal Injury Actions' (1984) 19 *The Forum* 233, 243; and *Hasenei v US*, 541 F Supp 999, 1011 (D Md 1982).

232   *ibid*, 450.

233   *ibid*.

234   R Slovenko, 'Surveying the Attacks on Psychiatry in the Legal Process' (1996) 1 *Intl J of Evidence and Proof* 48, 67.

235   33 Cal App 3d 275, 108 Cal Rptr 878 (1974).

236   Slovenko, *ibid*, 68.

237   969 A 2d 653 (Rh Is Sup Ct, 30 Apr 2009).

238   *Boynton*, 450–51.

239   *ibid*, 451, citing: S Wolfe, 'The Scope of a Psychiatrist's Duty to Third Persons: The Protective Privilege Ends Where the Public Peril Begins' (1984) 59 *Notre Dame L Rev* 770, 785–86.

240   *Rainbow Cleaners*, 665–66.

241   *ibid*.

242   A Harmon, 'Back from Wonderland: A Linguistic Approach to Duties Arising from Threats of Physical Violence' (2008) 37 *Capital U L Rev* 27, 77–80.

243   D Nicastro, 'Case Focus: Physician Liability to Non-Patients' (2007)' (2008) 52 *Boston Bar J* 20, 21, citing a statement from the Chief Justice in: *Coombes v Florio*, 450 Mass 182 (2007).

[244] G Annas, *The Rights of Patients* (3rd edn, Southern Illinois U Press, Carbondale, 2004) 257. However, this
       author ultimately agrees with the *Tarasoff* doctrine: 'when the life of another can be saved by breaching
       a confidence, the disclosure is limited, and there is no reasonable alternative for accomplishing the
       same objective, courts (and society in general) will properly have little difficulty mandating disclosure
       to someone who can prevent the harm': at 257.

[245] R Patterson, *Harney's Medical Malpractice* (4th edn, Lexis Law Pubg, Charlottesville VA, 1999) 289,
       fn 80.

[246] 892 SW 2d 796 (Mo App 1995).

[247] 712 F 2d 391 (9th Cir 1983).

[248] *ibid*, 398.

[249] M Thomas, 'Expanded Liability for Psychiatrists: *Tarasoff* Gone Crazy?' [2009] *J of Mental Health
       Law* 45, 48.

[250] 100 Wn 2d 421, 671 P 2d 230 (Sup Ct Wash, 1983).

[251] G McClarren, 'The Psychiatric Duty to Warn: Walking a Tightrope of Uncertainty' (1987) 56 *U
       Cincinnati L Rev* 269, 276.

[252] 146 Vt 61, 499 A 2d 422 (Sup Ct Vt, 1985).

[253] 120 Cal App 4th 807, 15 Cal Rptr 3d 864 (Cal CA, 2004).

[254] Noted in: *Ewing v Northridge Hosp Medical Center*, 16 Cal Rptr 3d 591, 593 (Cal Ct App 2004).

[255] California Civil Code, s 43.92, which states that, to initiate the duty to warn, the patient must
       communicate to the therapist 'a serious threat of physical violence against a reasonably identifiable
       victim or victims'.

[256] G Smith, '*Ewing and Goldstein* and the Therapist's Duty to Warn in California' (2006) 36 *Golden Gate
       U L Rev* 293, 301–2, 313. See also, for further criticisms of the case: D Edwards, 'Duty-to-Warn—Even
       if it May Be Hearsay? The Implications of a Psychotherapist's Duty-to-Warn a Third Person When
       Information is Obtained From Someone Other Than His Patient' (2006) 3 *Indiana Health L Rev* 171;
       A Harmon, 'Back from Wonderland: A Linguistic Approach to Duties Arising from Threats of Physical
       Violence' (2008) 37 *Capital U L Rev* 27, 77–80.

[257] B Williamson, 'The Gunslinger to the Ivory Tower Came: Should Universities Have a Duty to Prevent
       Rampage Killings?' 60 (2008) *Florida L Rev* 895, 906, and 912–13. See, for another interesting
       perspective of potential liability of education institutions under the *Tarasoff* principle: M Gilbert,
       '"Time-Out" for Student Threats?: Imposing a Duty to Protect on School Officials' (2002) 49 *UCLA L
       Rev* 917.

[258] A Harmon, 'Back from Wonderland: A Linguistic Approach to Duties Arising from Threats of Physical
       Violence' (2008) 37 *Capital U L Rev* 27, 30.

[259] M Thomas, 'Expanded Liability for Psychiatrists: *Tarasoff* Gone Crazy?' [2009] *J of Mental Health
       Law* 45, 55.

[260] 327 NW 2d 759 (1982).

[261] e.g.: *Rogers v South Carolina Dept of Mental Health*, 297 SC 363, 377 SE 2d 125 (Ct App 1989)
       (patient killed sister; no duty of care).

[262] 712 F 2d 391 (9th Cir 1983).

[263] 'The Cleaver, the Violin, and the Scalpel: Duty and the Restatement (Third) of Torts' (2008) 60 *Hastings
       LJ* 1, 12.

[264] 'Back from Wonderland: A Linguistic Approach to Duties arising from Threats of Physical Violence'
       (2008) 37 *Capital U L Rev* 27, 30–31.

[265] 'Critique of Pure Risk Assessment or Kant Meets *Tarasoff*' (2006) 75 *U Cincinatti L Rev* 523, 545,
       567–68.

[266] 'The Myth of "Imminent" Violence in Psychiatry and the Law' (2006) 75 *U Cincinnati L Rev* 631.

[267] This guidance was revised in 2009, and is available at: <http://www.psych.org/MainMenu/
       PsychiatricPractice/Ethics/ResourcesStandards/PrinciplesofMedicalEthics.aspx>.

[268] See Chapter 2, p 47.

[269] 17 Cal 3d 425, 551 P 2d 334, fn 11 (Cal 1976).

270   B Williamson, 'The Gunslinger to the Ivory Tower Came: Should Universities Have a Duty to Prevent Rampage Killings?' (2008) 60 *Florida L Rev* 895, 912–13.

271   J Areen *et al*, *Law, Science and Medicine* (Uni Casebook Series, Foundation Press, Mineola NY, 1984) 427, noting the jury's finding that the defendant psychiatrist had not deviated from a reasonable standard of conduct in failing to control the actions of psychiatric patient who murdered his former girlfriend, in *McIntosh v Milano*, 168 NJ Super 466, 403 A 2d 500 (NJ 1979); G Robertson, *Mental Disability and the Law in Canada* (2nd edn, Thomsen Carswell, Toronto, 1994) 455–58; E Picard and G Robertson, *Legal Liability of Doctors and Hospitals in Canada* (4th edn, Thomson Carswell, Toronto, 2007) 220.

272   QB, Schiemann J, 3 Nov 1989.

273   (1991), 116 AR 81 (Alta QB) [92].

274   M Thomas, 'Expanded Liability for Psychiatrists: *Tarasoff* Gone Crazy?' [2009] *J of Mental Health Law* 45, 53–54.

275   E Richards and K Rathbun, *Medical Care Law* (Aspen Publishers, Gaithersburg, MD, 1999) 332.

276   27 Cal 3d 741, 614 P 2d 728 (Cal 1980).

277   *ibid*, 755.

278   See Chapter 2, pp 43, 44.

279   F Morris and G Adshead, 'The Liability of Psychiatrists for the Violent Acts of their Patients' (1997) 147 *NLJ* 558, 575.

280   See, e.g., the opposing positions in: *Stone v Hipp* (Ont SCJ, Harris J, 17 Mar 2008) [8] (non-patient husband's claim against psychiatrist allowed to proceed to trial; an evolving area, with a duty of care possible).

Chapter 4

Contraction or Inheritance of Disease by Non-Patients from Patients

A INTRODUCTION

1. Introducing the two facets of disease liability

Where a HCP is treating a patient for an infectious or communicable disease, it may be alleged that the patient transmitted the disease to a non-patient, because the HCP mis-diagnosed the disease, thus allowing the disease to spread, or because the HCP correctly diagnosed the disease but failed to employ either adequate warnings or precautionary measures to stop the spread.

Alternatively, suppose that a HCP treats a patient with an hereditary condition or disease. A biological relative of the patient, who later learns about his genetic predisposition to that particular condition/disease, may assert that the patient's HCP, who knew (or should have known) of the predisposition, owed *him*—the relative—a duty to either warn him directly of that fact, or to warn the patient that the genetic information should be passed on to the relative so that he could be promptly tested and/or treated. Had either of these warnings been given, then the non-patient relative may have chosen to have, say, an elective hysterectomy, mastectomy or oophorectomy.[1]

This chapter considers whether (and, if so, why) a HCP, in either of these scenarios, can be liable in negligence for failing to avoid or to minimise the non-patient's suffering the disease or condition.

So far as the author's searches can ascertain, there has been limited English litigation on the first of these conundrums, and none at all which directly addresses the issue in the second scenario. What authorities there are in England—and a smattering of cases in other jurisdictions, selected for their interesting insights upon the issue—are summarised in Section B. The different ways in which a duty of care may be legally cast are discussed in Section C, while the legal issues which have arisen, when seeking to construct a duty of care owed by the HCP to a non-patient in these scenarios, are discussed in Section D. Section E then canvasses some of the arguments which have tended to either prove, or disprove, a causal link between the HCP's breach in relation to the diseased patient, and the non-patient's suffering the disease. Section F concludes.

Transmission and inheritance of a disease raise relatively similar legal problems to each other, particularly in respect of the existence (if any) of a duty of care on the part of the HCP. One American legal research committee remarked that while genetic diseases and communicable diseases are not 'strictly analogous', their only major difference is that transmission in the former case is 'vertical', and in the latter case, it is 'horizontal'.[2] Certainly, the two scenarios share many common features. From a public health perspective, the types of non-patients at risk of contagious or genetic diseases are often easily identifiable; the involvement of the patient in this context is purely accidental or inadvertent (by contrast with other types of 'dangerous patients', considered in the previous chapter, whose mental or physical afflictions result in their positive acts of harm to the non-patient—albeit that both judicial decision-making[3] and academic commentary[4] have illustrated the cross-over of principle in these areas of third party medical negligence liability);

substantial harm posed by the patient to the smaller or wider community may be capable of being averted by prompt warning and monitoring; the allegation against the HCP in both cases also tends to be one of *omission* to act, and hence, the question at law becomes whether there was a 'special relationship' as between the non-patient and the HCP, sufficient to support the imposition of the affirmative duty to act for the benefit of the non-patient; and the HCP's duty of confidentiality to the patient will frequently be at issue, regardless of whether the patient is suffering a transmissible disease or genetic condition.[5]

Moreover, the subject matter of this chapter concerns evolving areas of negligence liability in which courts and commentators are feeling their way. In relation to genetic information which foreshadows a propensity or certainty of illness or disease for a non-patient, leading commentators have long called the potential liability which a doctor bears towards that non-patient 'a looming area of medico-legal controversy'.[6] On the same note, in the leading cases of transmission-of-disease-from-patient-to-others in Canada (in 2006)[7] and the United States (in 1993),[8] the respective courts observed that the cases before them were ones of first impression, in which there were no precedents establishing a duty of care on the part of the defendant HCPs to any non-patient (whether it be close family members or members of the public) to whom undiagnosed, or mis-diagnosed, infections were transmitted by a patient.

For these various reasons, it is convenient to consider both the contraction and inheritance of disease by non-patients, and the potential liability of a patient's HCP towards those parties, in the one chapter.

2. What the chapter does not cover

Given the many complex legal issues associated with disease-motivated litigation, it is perhaps prudent to mark out the limits of this chapter.

First, it excludes from consideration the ethical and legal dilemmas for clinicians and medical researchers, arising from genetic research (e.g., in relation to genetic or hospital research[9] or human genome projects[10]). Also excluded from consideration are medical investigations conducted for the purposes of eliminating or identifying suspects in criminal investigations. In any of these contexts, information may arise about a subject, which flags that biological relatives could face disease/ illness or adverse medical conditions (such as infertility). Whether a clinician, medical researcher or other HCP bears an affirmative duty to disclose genetic test results to a third party in these circumstances, and other ethical dilemmas, have been oft-debated by relevant ethics committees and working groups[11] and by academics,[12] but fall outside the scope of this chapter. Rather, the chapter concentrates upon the type of scenario whereby a GP or hospital doctor is treating a patient who has a disease, and where there is a foreseeable risk that a non-patient (family member, hospital visitor, etc.) may suffer that disease too.

Secondly, the chapter does not deal with the transmission of diseases *from one treated patient to another treated patient*, due to allegedly poor hygiene practices or defective infection control practices on the part of the HCP or health authority. There have been cases, in England[13] and elsewhere,[14] in which a number of patients contracted illness or disease from each other (or who were exposed to that risk) after all undergoing medical treatment at the hands of the HCPs. However, these cases in which all the parties were the defendant's patients do not raise the same difficulties in proving liability in negligence as the true non-patient suit does, and hence, are not sufficiently analogous to warrant close attention in this chapter.

Finally, the chapter does not deal with the issue of pre-natal genetic testing, and the various claims that could feasibly result, should a HCP's patient give birth to a child who bears an hereditary illness. In this scenario, both parent and child are considered to be the doctor's patients, and hence, their claims (for wrongful birth or wrongful life, respectively) fall outside the scope of this book.[15]

B RELEVANT DISEASE-RELATED SCENARIOS

Figure 4.1 illustrates the principal conundrum at issue in this chapter, *viz*, whether the HCP owes a direct and independent duty to a claimant suffering from a disease who was never the HCP's own patient:

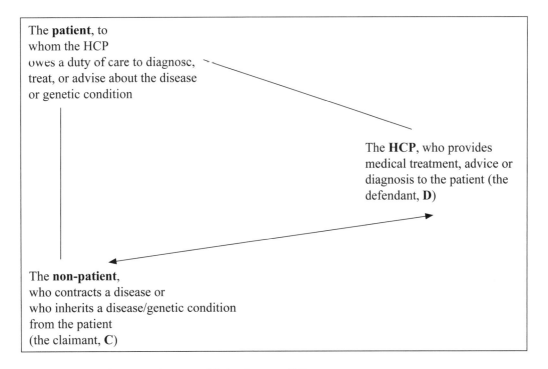

The **patient**, to whom the HCP owes a duty of care to diagnose, treat, or advise about the disease or genetic condition

The **HCP**, who provides medical treatment, advice or diagnosis to the patient (the defendant, **D**)

The **non-patient**, who contracts a disease or who inherits a disease/genetic condition from the patient (the claimant, **C**)

Figure 4.1   HCPs and the spread/inheritance of disease

Dealing with the relevant scenarios in turn:

1. Contagious or communicable diseases

This section deals with contagious or communicable diseases (other than sexually-transmitted diseases, which comprise the focus of Section 2). Where disease, such as scarlet fever or tuberculosis, has spread from a patient to others, due to a HCP's mis-diagnosis, or mis-treatment or mis-management of the disease, those 'others' have variously comprised a wide range of claimants—from family members living with the patient, to neighbours, to carers, to members of the public such as hospital visitors.

It remains an unresolved question in England as to whether a HCP owes a duty to any such non-patients to avoid or minimise loss and damage on their part caused by their contracting a disease. The most relevant English case concerned family members:

> In *Evans v Liverpool Corp*,[16] patient E, a six-year-old boy, suffered an attack of the highly-infectious disease of scarlet fever. He was discharged from a fever hospital in Liverpool by the defendant, a visiting physician working at the hospital. E appeared well at the point of discharge, except for a small sore at the corner of his mouth. Within a week, all three of his siblings had developed scarlet fever. Their father, the claimant Mr E, sued the hospital which employed the physician, seeking to recover the expenses to which he was put in caring for them all. **Held:** the claim against the hospital ultimately failed, because the hospital was not vicariously liable for the wrongdoing of the physician (but a lack of reasonable care on the physician's part was found, given the sore at the date of discharge[17]).

As subsequently remarked upon in a later English case,[18] the judgment in *Evans* was confined to the narrow question of whether or not the hospital was vicariously liable for the proved negligence of the visiting physician—it was not, because the physician was not sufficiently of 'employee' or 'servant' status to warrant a finding of vicarious liability on the hospital's part.[19] The physician himself was not sued directly for negligence, and it is difficult to glean from the judgment any obiter proposition that the physician's own duty *could* extend to the patient's family members, as non-patients.

Given its narrow ratio, the decision in *Evans* was judicially perceived to be less-than-helpful in a subsequent Irish transmission-of-disease case:

> In *Denneny v Kildare County Board of Health and Public Assistance*,[20] patient Carmel, a young girl, was admitted to a fever hospital suffering from scarlet fever. She was discharged on Christmas Eve 1933 by the medical officer in charge, who considered that infection had ceased. However, Carmel turned out to be still infectious, and each of her siblings contracted scarlet fever from Carmel. Her sister Caroline died in February 1934 from the disease. Their father brought an action, alleging that he had suffered loss by reason of medical expenses, and in his business. Among other things, it was argued that the operators of the hospital were negligent in failing to fulfil their statutory and common law duty not to discharge an infectious person to the danger of the public, of which the claimant father was a member. **Held:** the claim was struck out on the basis that the action, as framed, was 'unsustainable'.

Hanna J held that, while it was not necessary to decide the point, it would be an 'extraordinary result' if the father's case could be feasible, because 'not only would everyone of the three persons who took scarlatina from the little girl be entitled to bring an action against the Board of Health, ... but, if there had been an epidemic, the whole neighbourhood might have had an opportunity of bringing actions against them.'[21] Of the earlier *Evans* decision, Hanna J merely said that, 'when that case is fully considered, it will be found that the Judge negatived such a general right in the community or the public'.[22] These concerns about the potential 'floodgates' of non-patient claimants do not pertain to the question, though, as to whether a duty of care *could* be owed to Carmel's siblings, as non-patients who had contracted scarlet fever themselves.

Hence, there is no English authority as yet which holds that a HCP owes a duty of care to a non-patient who contracts a contagious or communicable disease from the HCP's patient.

By contrast, a number of more recent North American authorities shed a far more positive light upon the viability of these types of non-patient claims. The leading Canadian decision arose from a certification application in class proceedings,[23] where the only relevant question for the Ontario Superior Court of Justice was whether a cause of action by the classes of non-patients was evident on the pleadings:

> In *Healey v Lakeridge Health Corp*,[24] patient AB died from tuberculosis in October 2003. Three particular groups of claimants brought claims against the hospital at which he died and against the respirologist who treated him prior to his death. The alleged breaches included: failing to diagnose TB; prescribing drugs that triggered or exacerbated TB without first ruling out a diagnosis of TB; failing to warn the claimants of the risk of exposure to TB; and failing to report AB's infection to public health authorities in a timely manner. The three groups of non-patients consisted of: those who were infected with TB by their contact with AB in the hospital (the infected claimants); those who were exposed to TB through contact with one of the infected persons (the cross-infected claimants); and those who never tested positive for TB but who were advised by the public health authority that they may have contracted TB and needed to have tests undertaken (the uninfected claimants).[25] (The uninfected claimants brought fear-of-the-future claims, and their claims are dealt with separately in a later chapter.[26]) **Held:** the infected non-patient sub-class was permitted to go forth to trial, because the pleadings disclosed an arguable cause of action on their behalf;[27] but the cross-infected non-patient sub-class was not permitted to proceed.

United States authority has long held that a HCP can owe a duty of care to third parties who were in 'dangerous proximity' to a patient who was afflicted with a communicable disease.[28] As Kovalesky notes,[29] this duty to non-patients well and truly pre-dates the better known and *Tarasoff*-inspired duty to non-patients arising from the actions of mentally-ill patients. The leading authorities show some mixed results, however:

> In *Bradshaw v Daniel*,[30] patient Elmer Johns (EJ) visited a hospital emergency room complaining of headaches, muscle aches, fever, and chills. He was diagnosed with and treated for the latter stages of Rocky Mountain Spotted Fever. EJ's condition rapidly deteriorated, and he died the next day. The defendant treating doctor, Dr D, communicated with EJ's wife, Genevieve (GJ), during EJ's treatment, but never advised her of the risks of exposure to Rocky Mountain Spotted Fever, or that the disease could have been the cause of EJ's death. A week after her husband's death, GJ presented at the emergency room of another hospital, with similar symptoms of chills, fever, mental disorientation, nausea, lung congestion, myalgia, and swelling of the hands. She was admitted to hospital and treated for Rocky Mountain Spotted Fever, but she died three days later. Her son sued, alleging that Dr D was negligent in failing to advise GJ that her husband died of Rocky Mountain Spotted Fever, and that in failing to warn her of the risk of exposure, caused her death. Dr D argued that he owed GJ no legal duty because of the absence of a patient–doctor relationship. **Held** (by the Supreme Court of Tennessee, reversing the lower Court of Appeals): Dr D had a duty to warn his patient's wife, GJ, of the risk to her of contracting Rocky Mountain Spotted Fever, when he knew, or should have known, that his patient EJ was suffering from the disease.

> In *Gammill v US*,[31] patient Mrs Johnson was diagnosed as having infectious hepatitis and gastroenteritis by Dr Hamilton, a civilian doctor at Fort Carson military base. Her two small

children, Christie and Stephanie, were cared for by Ms Ladonna Gammill, wife of Lawrence Gammill (LG), and mother of Cynthia Gammill (CG). Neither child showed symptoms of serious illness. However, seven days later, Stephanie was diagnosed with hepatitis, and Dr H recommended that the whole Johnson family receive gamma globulin inoculations. Neither Dr H nor the staff at Fort Carson notified the public health authorities of the hepatitis in the Johnson household (which was required by Colorado law and by army regulations regarding communicable diseases at Fort Carson). Over a week later, LG was diagnosed (by the Gammill's family physician) with hepatitis, as was CG. LG was hospitalised and then ill at home for five months. Stephanie Johnson was the likely source of infection in the Gammill family. According to the evidence, the Gammills would likely have been contacted by the county health department within 24–72 hours if that department had been properly notified by Dr H, and if the Gammills had been contacted within that time period, they would have had several days to receive effective gamma globulin inoculations. **Held:** Dr H owed no duty of care to either LG or CG as non-patients/third parties, and their actions were struck out.

In *Candelario v Teperman*,[32] patient Ms Diaz (D) was diagnosed as having hepatitis C in 1992, and, until her death in 1994, was treated for the disease by the defendant, Dr T, at the New York University Medical Centre. At times between her diagnosis and her death, D was released from the hospital and was cared for by the claimant, her daughter Carmel Candelario (CC), at their home. In the course of caring for her mother, CC allegedly came into contact with her mother's bodily fluids which were capable of transmitting the virus that causes hepatitis C. In 1997, CC was diagnosed as having hepatitis C, and sued Dr T, alleging that she contracted hepatitis C because T, although aware that CC was caring for her mother, failed to warn CC of the contagious nature of hepatitis C and failed to instruct her to take precautions. **Held:** Dr T was entitled to summary judgment dismissing the complaint; as a matter of law, Dr T could not be liable to CC who had not been his patient.

In *Crawford v Wojnas*,[33] the patient infant, Melissa Crawford, was administered a live polio vaccine by the defendant GP, Dr W. Unfortunately, the vaccine mutated in the child's body, and the polio virus spread to the mother, Mrs Sheri Crawford (SC, the non-patient), causing her paralysis. SC sued Dr W, alleging that he owed her a duty to disclose risks and alternatives about treatment for the patient (*viz*, killed and inactivated polio vaccine, which expert evidence stated was rarely used in the US but was a risk-free alternative for third parties who came in close contact with the infant, such as parents). **Held:** no duty of care was owed to SC by Dr W.

The precise reasons for these varying conclusions are canvassed in Section D, when the specifics of establishing or disproving a duty of care are analysed.

As a variation on the theme, there may be the 'odd situation' in which the HCP mis-diagnoses that the patient has an transmissible illness, and counsels the patient to convey the (wrong) information to a non-patient, which ultimately causes the non-patient some type of *psychiatric* injury. The scenario, whilst unusual, occurred in one classic American case:

In *Molien v Kaiser Foundation Hosp*,[34] patient Mrs M was mis-diagnosed by her GP as having syphilis, and the GP advised Mrs M to tell her husband (Mr M, the non-patient) that he might be infected and to be tested. The wife became suspicious and upset that her husband had engaged in extra-marital sexual activities. This ultimately lead to the break-down of the marriage, following which Mr M sued his wife's GP for his emotional distress and other damages flowing from the divorce. **Held:** the claim succeeded; the GP was liable to the husband for the negligent infliction of mental distress, on the basis that the harm to the non-patient husband was 'reasonably foreseeable'.

As some American commentators have noted,[35] *Molien* casts a rather onerous duty on a HCP, for it leaves him exposed to liability for any mental injury suffered by non-patients/third parties by reason of the wrong information being conveyed about the patient's medical situation. For English purposes, such a proposition has something of an equivalent, in *Farrell v Avon HA*,[36] in which a non-patient father was negligently, and wrongly, told that his baby, the defendant's patient, had died in birth, and where the father recovered for the recognisable psychiatric injury suffered from this traumatic event. The principles associated with recovery of pure psychiatric injury are examined later in Chapter 8.

In summary, non-patient suits against HCPs for damages for personal injury and consequential damage resulting from the transmission of contagious/communicable diseases from patient to non-patient have been countenanced in North America; but there have been no such cases emerging in English law as yet.

2. Sexually-transmitted diseases

A spouse or partner of the patient may contract a sexually-transmissible disease from the patient, raising the question as to whether the patient's HCP can owe a duty of care to that non-patient spouse or partner:

> In the Ontario decision of *Pittman Estate v Bain*,[37] patient Mr Pittman (P) contracted HIV from a contaminated blood transfusion received during cardiac surgery. Although his GP, Dr B, was later notified that the blood might have been infected and that P should be tested, Dr B never revealed this information to P, who then unwittingly transmitted the virus to his wife Rochelle (Mrs P, the non-patient). Dr B was concerned about the effect that any such news would have on P's mental and cardiac condition, and he thought (incorrectly) that P was not in sexual relationship with his wife, and so withheld the information about the HIV status from P. After P's death, his wife tested HIV-positive. **Held:** ultimately, Mrs P recovered compensation ($469,317).

The judicial reasoning in *Pittman v Bain* is, unfortunately, less than clear. A duty of care was undoubtedly owed by the GP to P, his patient. In respect of any duty owed by GP to non-patient Mrs P, however, Lang J of the Ontario General Division was not convinced: '[i]n this context, it is unnecessary for me to determine whether Dr Bain had an independent duty to Mrs Pittman, because Dr Bain did have an obligation to tell Mr Pittman [of his HIV status], and if he had told Mr Pittman, the evidence established that Mr Pittman would have told his wife'.[38] Thus, the compensation recovered by Mrs P was expressly *not* awarded on the basis of an independent separate duty owed towards her—a point which was judicially reiterated, more recently, in *Healey v Lakeridge Health Corp*.[39] However, some commentators disagree, and consider that a duty of care *must* have been owed to Mrs P, in order for her to recover any compensation at all,[40] while another has suggested that there is sufficient doubt surrounding what *Pittman v Bain* stands for, that any duty cast on the HCP should be left to the legislature.[41]

By contrast, the decisions canvassed below are more transparent than *Pittman* because, in each case, it was expressly held that the defendant HCP **did** owe an independent duty of care to the non-patient.

Two leading Australian decisions concerned the transmission of HIV to each of the respective non-patient wives, in whose favour a duty of care was found:

In *BT v Oei*,[42] patient AT was treated by his GP Dr O for Hepatitis B in 1992. AT told Dr O that he was not an IV drug user, but that he had engaged in casual relationships in the past. AT started a relationship with his partner, BT (the non-patient), in 1992. At the start of the relationship, AT told BT that he had Hepatitis B. From the end of 1991, AT was treated by Dr O off and on for fever, aches, pains and other symptoms of illness, and diagnosed with various possible illnesses, including gastro-enteritis. When AT was finally referred by Dr O to a specialist in 1994, and a HIV antibody test requested, AT was diagnosed as HIV-positive. Dr O was held to be negligent in failing to diagnose AT as likely to be suffering from HIV illness (in light of his history and symptoms), or to counsel him (adequately or at all) to undergo an HIV antibody test. BT, who was living with AT as his de facto wife (they subsequently married in 1994), also contracted HIV (probably around January 1993). AT eventually died of liver failure, unrelated to his HIV illness. It was common ground that Dr O owed a duty of care to AT as his patient. However, the question was whether Dr O also owed a duty of care to BT as his patient's sexual partner. **Held:** Dr O did owe BT an independent duty of care.[43] According to Bell J, '[t]here is no suggestion that the obligation on the doctor extends beyond the provision of adequate advice to the patient.'[44] Rather, it was to provide patient AT with appropriate and adequate advice about the diagnosis and warnings associated with the deadly HIV virus.

In *Harvey v PD*,[45] both the claimant PD and her partner FH attended a joint consultation with the defendant GP Dr H, so that both could have blood tests to ensure that neither were HIV carriers, prior to their marriage. PD received her blood tests results (which showed her to be HIV-negative), not from the GP but from the surgery receptionist. PD requested a copy of FH's pathology report, in light of the earlier joint consultation with the GP, but was told by the receptionist that she was not entitled to FH's, but only to her own. In fact, FH's blood tests showed him to be HIV-positive, but FH misled the claimant into believing that his tests were, like hers, negative. PD subsequently contracted HIV from FH, and sued Dr H, alleging that he failed to take sufficient steps to inform her of the fact that FH was HIV-positive, particularly in light of the concerns which PD expressed in the joint consultation, to the effect that the information was of great importance to them both. **Held:** a duty of care was owed by Dr H to PD. As it was not possible for the GP to have warned the claimant PD that her partner was HIV-positive, since such disclosure was prohibited by relevant legislation,[46] the duty owed to PD was said to be a separate and independent duty to protect her, which could have been discharged by telling FH to warn PD directly; by referring him for counselling; or by informing the Director-General of the Department of Public Health, which was allowed if a HIV-positive person was putting third parties at risk.[47]

Similarly, two well-known American decisions support an independent duty being owed to the non-patient who acquired a sexually-transmitted disease from the HCP's patient:[48]

In *Reisner v The Regents of the Uni of California*,[49] patient Jennifer Lawson (JL) was a 12-year-old girl who had received a blood transfusion. The day after this, her doctor, Dr F, discovered the blood was contaminated with HIV antibodies. Although the same doctor continued to treat JL, he never told her or her parents about the tainted blood. Three years later, JL started dating Daniel Reisner (DR) and they commenced a sexual relationship. Two years later, Dr F told JL she had AIDS and JL told DR. A month later, aged 17, JL died of AIDS. Shortly thereafter, DR discovered he was

HIV-positive. DR sued JL's doctor in negligence. **Held**: Dr F owed a duty of care to the non-patient DR. 'Daniel does not claim Defendants had to warn him, only that they had to warn Jennifer or her parents, "others [who were] likely to apprise [him] of the danger" (and, of course, did just that when they learned of it).'[50]

In *Di Marco v Lynch Homes-Chester County Inc*,[51] patient Ms Viscichini (V), a blood technician, suffered a needle stick injury while taking blood from a Hepatitis B carrier in a nursing home. When V learned the patient had hepatitis, she immediately sought treatment from two doctors, both of whom told her that, if she remained symptom-free for six weeks, it would mean she had not been infected by the hepatitis virus. Although she was not told to refrain from sexual relations for any period of time, she did so until eight weeks after exposure. As she had remained symptom-free during that time, she then resumed sexual relations with her boyfriend, Mr Di Marco (DM), the non-patient in this scenario. Three months after exposure, V developed Hepatitis B and, three months after that, DM was diagnosed as having the same disease. DM sued V's doctors, claiming they were negligent in not warning V that, if she had sexual relations within six *months* of exposure (not six weeks, as advised), then she could infect her sexual partner. **Held**: the doctors owed a duty of care to DM. According to the Supreme Court of Pennsylvania, the duty would be discharged by explaining to V the precautionary steps that should be taken to prevent the spread of Hepatitis B to others, including DM.[52]

Notably, none of the abovementioned cases advocated that the HCP owed a duty to warn the sexual partners, directly, of steps that should be taken to guard against the contracting of disease—an issue to which attention will return in Section C.

Thus far, no English case has arisen to form part of this cadre of non-patient suits.

3. Inherited diseases and conditions

Regarding the problem of inherited diseases, and whether a HCP can be under a duty to breach confidentiality in order to warn other members of the patient's family (and the HCP's non-patients) of their genetic predisposition to illness or disease, two American cases are the leading examples of an extended judicial outlook in which, in both cases, the relevant HCPs owed a duty of care to their patient's children.

In *Pate v Threlkel*,[53] patient Marianne New was diagnosed with a genetic disease, medullary thyroid carcinoma, in 1987, and was treated by Dr T for that condition. Her daughter Heidi Pate (HP, the non-patient) was diagnosed in 1990 with the same condition, which was genetically-transmissible. HP sued her mother's physician for not warning her mother that HP might be at risk from developing the disease. HP alleged that, had she been warned, she could have taken preventative action to cure the condition (specifically, she argued that she would have been tested to determine whether she had inherited the disease and whether she needed early preventative treatment). **Held**: a duty of care to HP *did* exist, which duty could be met by warning the patient mother that her biological children should seek medical care.[54]

The duty cast by the Supreme Court of Florida was rather limited—it acknowledged that '[t]o require the physician to seek out and warn various members of the patient's family would often be difficult or impractical and would place too heavy a burden upon the physician. Thus, we emphasise that in any circumstances in which the physician has a duty to warn of a genetically transferable disease, that duty will be satisfied by warning the patient'.[55] Thus, again the HCP had no duty to warn the patient's children directly.

However, whether that more burdensome duty *could* be cast on the HCP was revisited in the following decision:

> In *Safer v Estate of Pack*,[56] physician Dr P had treated his patient, Mr Robert Batkin (RB), for retro-peritoneal cancer (multiple polyposis of the colon). RB ultimately died of cancer, eight years after the initial diagnosis, and following extensive treatment and surgery. The patient's daughter Donna Safer (DS, the non-patient) was 10 when her father died. Then, 26 years later, in 1990, DS was also diagnosed with polyposis of the colon. She underwent a total abdominal colectomy and other surgery, and chemotherapy. In 1991, DS obtained her father's medical records and learnt that her father had suffered from polyposis. She sued Dr P, alleging that he had breached his duty of care in failing to warn of the hereditary risk to her health, and that failure to discharge this duty had deprived her of the chance for monitoring, early detection and treatment. **Held**: there was a duty imposed on Dr P to warn of the genetic condition, and the case was sent back to trial for further hearing.

The New Jersey Superior Court Appellate Division expressly distinguished *Pate*[57] and left open the possibility of a more robust duty: a duty *to warn genetic relatives directly*. Specifically, '[i]n terms of foreseeability especially, there is no essential difference between the type of genetic threat at issue here and the menace of infection, contagion or a threat of physical harm',[58] and that '[w]e decline to hold as the Florida Supreme Court did in *Pate v Threlkel* that, in all circumstances, the duty to warn will be satisfied by informing the patient. It may be necessary, at some stage, to resolve a conflict between the physician's broader duty to warn and his fidelity to an expressed preference of the patient that nothing be said to family members about details of the disease.'[59]

Again, the abovementioned US authorities about inherited diseases are yet to find any counterpart in English jurisprudence.

C THE KEY DUTY OF CARE QUESTION

Clearly, the authorities canvassed in Section B confirm that, across the jurisdictions which form the basis of this comparative study, a duty of care *has* been cast upon a HCP in favour of a non-patient who has acquired or inherited disease from the HCP's patient—although, again, the relative dearth of English case law must be reiterated.

However, were the issue to be litigated in England in the future, experience from elsewhere shows that (as with that other category of 'dangerous patient' considered earlier in Chapter 3) the *content* or *scope* of any such duty is a key question. In this section, four points will be discussed: the weak form of any duty of care to the non-patient in disease cases; the robust form of any such duty; the case which has been put by various law reform opinion and academic commentary as to why *no duty at all* should be owed to a non-patient in respect of inherited diseases; and, finally, the likely direction which English law would follow in delineating the scope of the duty in disease cases.

1. The weak form of duty

The weak form of duty allows the defendant HCP to discharge his duty to the non-patient *by dealing with the patient alone*—to inform the patient about the nature of the disease and its treatment; to diagnose and treat and put in place measures to effectively 'cocoon his disease'; to counsel the infected patient on how to avoid the transmission of the virus; and, most crucially, to counsel and advise the patient to warn a non-patient about the disease so as to enable that non-patient to take steps to protect himself.

This conduct satisfies the duties owed to the patient *and* to the non-patient simultaneously, and is a weaker duty of care[60] insofar as the non-patient is concerned (weaker, because it depends upon **no** proactive step being taken by the HCP towards the non-patient himself).

Of the cases canvassed in Section B, this was by far the more popular tack adopted by the relevant courts—it was preferred, e.g., in *Pate v Threlkel, BT v Oei, Harvey v PD, Di Marco v Lynch Homes-Chester County Inc, Reisner v The Regents of the University of California*, and in the TB case of *Healey v Lakeridge Health Corp*. In *Reisner*, it was succinctly put: '[o]nce the physician warns the patient of the risk to others and advises the patient how to prevent the spread of the disease, the physician has fulfilled his duty—and no more (but no less) is required'.[61]

The relative 'popularity' of the weak form of duty is undoubtedly due to three factors as were explored in Chapter 3.[62] First, it is far less burdensome for HCPs to discharge, and avoids awkward questions of what effort the HCP must plough into the task of seeking out and warning third parties, particularly where a large class of potential non-patients looms. Secondly, it is more likely to avoid the HCP's having to breach his duty of confidentiality, in order to satisfy his conflicting duty to the non-patient. It will be recalled that, in *BT v Oei*,[63] the GP who omitted to arrange a HIV test for his patient, AT, owed a separate and independent duty to warn AT's defacto wife, BT (the non-patient), but the New South Wales Supreme Court explicitly held that the content of the GP's duty to BT was *not* to warn BT. Rather, the duty to BT (and to any other sexual partner of AT) would have been discharged by the diagnosis and provision of proper advice to patient AT. These duties were *aligned*, or 'coincident'.[64] This approach renders conflicts more theoretical than real: '[i]n such a circumstance it is difficult to see how, as a matter of practical reality, a conflict could arise.'[65] Thirdly, under the weak form of duty, there are definite limits to what conduct the law will expect of the HCP in respect of his dealings with the patient. For example, in *Di Marco*[66] (the case of the hepatitis-infected nursing home technician who inadvertently transmitted the disease to her husband), the court did not hold that the wife's doctors had a duty to *control their patient's conduct*—rather, it emphasised that the duty was limited to advising her, competently, of how she should act in order not to transmit a communicable disease.

2. The robust form of duty

The option which infuses a duty of care with a more robust flavour—dependent as it is upon proactive warnings or other reasonable steps being taken *towards the non-patient directly* to protect the non-patient from suffering harm from a disease manifesting—is obviously a more burdensome duty on the HCP.

It is one which the Ontario General Division shied away from imposing in *Pittman v Bain*, and which the Supreme Court of Florida explicitly refused to countenance in *Pate v Threlkel*.

However, it has judicial support in American jurisprudence, as evidenced by the inheritance-of-disease case of *Safer v Estate of Pack*, and the transmission-of-disease case of *Bradshaw v*

Daniel. In the latter, the Supreme Court of Tennessee explicitly stated that a HCP may be liable in negligence to a non-patient infected by a patient 'if the physician ... fails to warn family members or others who are foreseeably at risk of exposure to the disease.'[67] Hence, there was a duty on Dr Daniels to warn Genevieve Johns, as an 'identifiable third person in the patient's immediate family' of the foreseeable risks emanating from Elmer Johns' illness.[68] In *Safer*, the group of third parties to be identified was similarly small and 'easily identified'—the biological children of Mr Batkin.[69]

There are, in particular, three reservations about the robust form of duty which have been raised in the judicial and academic literature concerning disease scenarios. Although these have often been raised in the context of any duty to warn non-patients directly of a patient's genetic information, they have resonance for transmission-of-disease cases too.

(a) A corresponding duty of confidentiality?

First of all, does a duty to warn non-patients about the risk of their contracting disease raise an ancillary *duty of confidentiality*? It is one thing to owe a duty of confidentiality to one's own patient, but if there is to be a duty cast upon HCPs to warn non-patients of a patient's disease, should there be a corresponding duty of confidentiality imposed upon the HCP towards those non-patients too? Suppose that a HCP becomes aware, from his dealings with the patient or with the non-patient, that the non-patient is HIV-positive, or has a genetic condition—is that HCP obliged to keep all such information confidential (to the extent that the law permits), just as he would if the sufferer was his own patient?

In such circumstances, a duty of confidentiality would be owed to the non-patient in accordance with the statement by the House of Lords that, as a 'well-settled principle of law', where one party (here, the HCP) acquires confidential information by virtue of his relationship with another, in circumstances importing a duty of confidence, the confidant will not be at liberty to divulge that information to a third party without the consent, or against the wishes, of that other.[70]

Laurie, for example, notes that if some forms of genetic information also reveal significant information about the genetic constitution of relatives, then—

> [o]n an objective analysis ... those who receive this information might owe a duty of confidence not only to the initial source, but also to the blood relatives of that person. On a strict application of the law, the duty is owed to the collective, and therefore it is for the collective to decide when, and how, disclosures of the confidential information should be made. But, it is not at all clear how workable this would be in practice, either in terms of seeking to protect collective confidentiality, or in determining to which family members a duty would be owed.[71]

Arguably, there *ought* to be a corresponding duty of confidentiality owed by the HCP towards those same non-patients, if the law were to insist upon a robust form of duty on the HCP to warn or protect non-patients—otherwise, one without the other would rob their relationship of its trust and confidence. However, as Laurie suggests, entering these particular legal waters entails a lack of definition and certainty—especially where the duty of confidentiality owed by HCP *to his own patient* is not an absolute duty.

(b) The onerous task cast upon the healthcare professional

The burdens imposed upon a HCP under a robust form of duty to warn or to protect the non-patient directly can essentially be summarised in three words: who, why, and when?

Under the weak form of duty in disease cases, it is essentially the *patient's* responsibility—as the last linkage in the chain of information conveyance—to protect the non-patient from harm. In *BT v Oei*, for example, it was patient AT who would have been expected to pass on the information about HIV testing and protection against the virus to his wife BT, had the defendant GP instructed a HIV antibody test to have been performed on AT. Leading academic opinion in England similarly advocates *against* any duty upon HCPs to warn non-patients directly of a patient's genetic information, because, morally-speaking, it is the patient himself who should be bearing that burden. For example, Brazier contends[72] that to impose a duty to warn on a HCP should, at best, take the reduced form of warning his patient that genetic information should be passed on to relatives. After that—

> [i]f it is *my* relatives who are at risk because of our heritage, the responsibility to act to protect those family members is primarily mine. Professionals can and should inform and advise me to assist me to discharge my ethical responsibilities. I cannot shuffle off responsibility to them. They should not be forced to act as moral policemen.[73]

Some American commentary shares the view that educating and counselling *patients*, rather than imposing any duty to warn upon a HCP, is far preferable.[74]

As a further plank against any robust form of duty in disease cases, it has also been pointed out that it cannot be assumed that the cadre of non-patients at risk from the patient's diseased condition may necessarily be a small one: '[a] universal duty to warn would make the patient–physician relationship subservient to a more diffuse public health obligation, benefiting an unspecified number of non-patients'.[75] It not difficult to imagine the various dilemmas which could arise about *which* relatives/non-patients should be owed a duty, and how much effort should be made on the part of the HCP to inform these relatives.

Moreover, when would such a duty apply? If the non-patient was a very young child, as Donna Safer was (only 10 years old) at the time of the diagnosis of hereditary disease in the patient, should the HCP's duty to warn and protect arise then, or later (e.g., upon majority, or perhaps at an age when the condition may be particularly prone to manifest)? As some American commentators have put it, 'is it appropriate to inform a child of his genetic characteristics, especially those that might predict disease, an increased susceptibility to disease, or developmental limitations or capacities?'[76]

To the contrary, however, American commentator Dworkin refutes the 'burdensome' tag, arguing that the robust form of duty towards non-patients, arising from 'dangerous patients' of all kinds, should not be 'over-egged':

> The concern that doctors will be overburdened is mistaken. It proceeds from forgetting that duties are obligations to make reasonable efforts to achieve certain ends, not obligations to achieve them. The duty on the psychotherapist in *Tarasoff* was not a duty to warn the intended victim. It was a duty to make a reasonable effort to warn her. That is a very different and less burdensome thing. Similarly, in the genetic and communicable disease contexts, recognizing that doctors owe duties to persons in addition to their patients means only that they must treat such persons reasonably ... Doctors only have to try to warn third parties if the third party can take some meaningful action based on the warning to protect himself or someone close to him. Doctors only have to make reasonable efforts to warn third parties.[77]

Given the number of arguments of policy and legal principle that are put forward for rejecting any duty at all in favour of non-patients where genetic information is concerned (canvassed below in

Section 3, undoubtedly many would refute the suggestion that a robust duty of care by HCP to non-patient is not, ultimately, all that difficult to discharge.

(c) A fragile or unwilling patient

What if the diseased patient cannot be informed or relied upon, or is simply unable, to pass the information on to the non-patient—in the event that the non-patient/s are identified or easily identifiable? The weak form of duty depends upon the HCP dealing exclusively with the patient, so as to discharge any duty that the HCP owes to the non-patient. If the patient is unable or unwilling to pass on any such information to the non-patient, then there is then no question of the weaker duty being fulfilled. Should this, of itself, be grounds for imposing the strong version of the duty on the HCP, forcing him to liaise directly with the non-patient so as to warn/advise/protect?

This proposition was pleaded in the live polio vaccine case of *Crawford v Wojnas*[78] in which the non-patient mother was left paralysed, but was unsuccessful. The court concluded that, since the HCP's duty to disclose information about inherent risks associated with a medical treatment was patient-oriented, then that HCP should not be liable for failing to disclose risks and information about alternative forms of treatment to third parties.[79] Hence, the doctor who administered the live vaccine to the patient, an infant child, was under no duty to warn the mother separately of the possibility of the vaccine mutating and spreading to her.

In fact, in any scenario involving a diseased patient, it becomes a hypothetical enquiry as to what a patient would have done under the weak form of duty, if the HCP had warned the patient of the risks which he posed to non-patients. Would the patient have actually taken steps to act in the non-patient's best interests? Courts have generally been prepared to adopt a benevolent attitude towards the patient in that regard—accepting that any warnings given by the HCP would not have been futile, and would have been heeded and acted upon by the patient. In relationships of close intimacy, the court's preparedness to find that the patient would have taken appropriate steps to warn or inform the non-patient is understandable—recall, for example, Lang J's comment, in *Pittman v Bain*, that if Dr Bain had told Mr Pittman of his HIV infection, 'the evidence established that Mr Pittman would have told his wife'.[80] However, even in other contexts where the non-patients were strangers to the patient, courts have been prepared to find that the patient would have 'done the right thing' and followed the HCP's advice to curb his conduct in order to protect third parties. At least, that tack has been adopted in the context of other 'dangerous patients'. For example, in the Californian case of *Myers v Quesenberry*,[81] where the patient driver hit a pedestrian bystander while under emotional distress and while suffering a diabetic attack, the Court of Appeals explained:

> As a practical matter, the doctors here could not have effectively warned [pedestrian non-patient] Myers of the danger presented by Hansen's driving ... However, they could easily have warned Hansen not to drive because of her irrational and uncontrolled diabetic condition ... this probably would not have been a futile act. Having otherwise complied with her doctors' professional recommendations, Hansen presumably would have continued to follow their advice had they warned her not to drive ... we cannot factually presume Hansen would have ignored the doctors' warning.[82]

It is submitted that, because a diseased patient cannot be relied upon to convey a warning to the non-patient or to curb his own conduct so as to protect a class of non-patients, is no grounds for insisting upon a robust form of duty upon the HCP. Rather, if a HCP fails to warn a patient of the risks posed by his diseased condition, under the weak form of duty, and if it is established that, on the balance of probabilities, the patient would or could not have warned, or otherwise protected, the non-patient from the disease, then that will defeat causation, and no liability should be found on the part of the HCP. The problems of establishing a causal link in disease cases are further explored in Section E.

3. The particular problem of genetic information: the case against any duty of care at all

It has been oft-pointed out that genetic information about a patient is not the same as other medical information. The medical condition is transmitted from patient to others only by way of procreation, so it is 'unique', in the sense that there is a 'highly-variable propensity for the condition to be shared by members of a family who are biologically related.'[83] Also, by the very nature of the problem, relatives are often involved in a patient's misfortune. Hence, information about a patient's genetic condition possesses several characteristics that renders it of great pertinence to non-patients, either for positive or for negative reasons.

Skene,[84] Ball and Bennett,[85] and Laurie[86] collectively note these distinguishing features as follows:

- relatives may need to be tested, where there is no direct test for the gene itself and a marker, or linkage, test is required for identification;
- even if relatives are not tested, a patient's genetic diagnosis may need to be verified by relatives providing information, or by others who provide information about relatives;
- genetic information can be hard to comprehend, and relatives are often called upon to support or assist the patient;
- for many genetic conditions, the diagnosis is not certain, but merely is a sign of propensity, meaning that relatives themselves may have to live with negative and uncertain prospects;
- genetic abnormalities constitute sensitive information, and people can react differently to such information, e.g., by blaming themselves or others, by showing jealousies where one relative 'missed' the condition, by 'survivor guilt' complexes on the part of those who are not marked out, or fear-of-the-future conditions developing in those whose genetic make-up does show a propensity for onset of illness; and
- a genetic test may reveal information about relatives which they never would wish to have known, or for which they themselves did not seek testing.

Given this volatile mix, it comes as no surprise that there is a powerful school of thought that no duty, either to disclose genetic information to a non-patient (the robust form of duty) or to counsel a patient to convey such information to a non-patient (the weak form of duty), should ever be imposed on a HCP.

For example, in its review of the protection of human genetic information in 2002–3,[87] the Australian Law Reform Commission did not endorse the judicial development of a duty being imposed upon HCPs with respect to family non-patients at risk of genetic disorders—quite the reverse.[88] In the Commission's opinion, regardless of whether the duty was couched as a direct duty to act towards the non-patient (by giving warnings) or as a duty to the patient to convey the warnings himself to the non-patient, it was riddled with potential difficulties. Notable academic commentary on the subject, from England[89] and elsewhere,[90] has concluded similarly.

The arguments against any duty of care being imposed in the context of inheritable diseases (drawn from both the Commission's reports and the abovementioned academic commentary) are summarised in Table 4.1.

It is interesting to also canvass the views of a medically-qualified commentator on the subject. Clayton, a US commentator who is both medically and legally-qualified, makes three cogent points[91] as to why *either* of the duties cast by *Safer* and *Pate* are, practically-speaking, of considerable burden to those who practise medicine. First, patients are complex beings, and it is perfectly possible that a patient will not consent to his genetic information being broadcast to even close family members, which leaves the HCP in an invidious position—is he exculpated under the weak form of duty per *Pate* because he counselled the patient to convey the information, or is he liable under the robust form of duty in *Safer* because he did not go ahead and warn the family members directly? American law on this remains unclear. Secondly, one of the duties on the part of the HCP is to warn a patient of risks and information that would enable that patient to make reasoned decisions about his *own* health care. It is quite an extension to cast an onus on the HCP to give the patient enough information *to enable that patient to help others*. Thirdly, Clayton argues that if it is legally correct that HCPs should not have a duty to directly warn individuals who are not their patients about disease risks, then they should not be subjected to a type of 'indirect liability' (via the weak form of duty) either.

The arguments are, of course, not entirely one-sided. Imposing some form of duty of care upon the HCP towards non-patients who suffer from a genetic predisposition to injury is supported on the basis that it would only be an exceptional duty—only applicable where the patient's HCP was (or reasonably ought to have been) aware that the non-patient was at *realistic (or even high) risk of serious personal injury or death*, and knew that, by disclosing the information, he could have prevented that serious physical harm to the non-patient, on the balance of probabilities.[92]

Moreover, where hereditary disease is concerned, some commentators have advocated that a duty to non-patient family members to disclose any genetic information that confirms that a family member is, or is likely to be, at risk of disease, should be mandated. This is on the basis that the biological family is a special unit within society, inextricably bound by its genetic information. For example, Gilbar posits the view[93] that, if English jurisprudence were to adopt a 'shared decision-making model [in which] the process of decision-making is not given solely either to the patient or the doctor but is one of discussion together', then non-patient relatives should figure more prominently, in both the drafting of professional medical guidelines and in the law of medical negligence, than they currently do. Were that the case, then a duty of care by a HCP to a non-patient may fit in somewhat more easily than it currently does in English law because, 'in considering disclosure, the interests of family members will be dealt with, as this model recognises their involvement and their prominent role in the patient's care, whether or not they are present in the examination room'.[94] These comments have particular resonance in the case of hereditary diseases. Skene also points out[95] that the model of shared genetic information among blood relatives—which rejects the concept of an individual patient's rights in favour of 'a wider responsibility and communal concern'—has found favour with some ethical working groups in England.[96] Skene argues that a 'family-centred approach' has several advantages, in that it develops a 'family pedigree'; has its primary focus upon health promotion; reflects the reality that many doctors and patients support sharing information within families; is already practised informally; and is defensible when considering that suits by patients for disclosure (or by non-patients for non-disclosure) are very rare, and likely to remain so.[97] American commentators have also frequently pointed out[98] that the practical consequence of *Safer v Pack* and *Pate v Threlkel* is that HCPs owe some form of duty of care to the entity called the 'genetic family' in that jurisdiction.

Table 4.1   Arguments against recognition of any duty of care in genetic condition scenarios

---

- warning the patient's relatives will not prevent them from having the gene: they already have it. Any failure to inform that relative (whether by the HCP or by the patient) does not *cause* the relative's harm—and if **a causal link cannot be made out**, it countenances against any duty of care being owed;
- the **potential psychological, financial, or social harm**, should a warning about genetic information be given to the non-patient, can be significant—the relative could be highly distressed, could incur wasted expenditure, or could make certain choices to his ultimate detriment. As Skene succinctly states: 'The existence of a mutation in the family may influence life and health insurance, employment, loans, marriageability, reproductive choices, adoption, school admission, and suicide';
- perhaps the **relative did not want to know** what fate could/would befall him—this wish should be respected;
- if the genetic condition has **no cure or preventative medical measure available**, then what good would the imposition of a duty of care achieve? 'There are very few genetic conditions for which a cure exists', according to Bell and Bennett. Hence, how would a HP discharge the duty, other than to convey information, that the non-patient had an incurable condition to look forward to?
- **genetic tests can be unreliable or non-specific**—again, as Bell and Bennett explain, 'given how many genetic diseases are multifactorial, test results from relatives may have limited reliability'—should a duty to warn a relative (whether cast upon HCP or patient) ever be set in such circumstances?
- patients may be **discouraged from seeking genetic testing** if relatives could then obtain the information via the imposition of a duty to warn cast upon either HCP or patient;
- a HCP must act in his patient's best interests, which may be furthered by maintaining a **harmonious relationship with key family members**—and this relationship may be impaired if a duty was cast upon the HCP to either warn the relative directly or request that the patient do so;
- it may be difficult to decide whether a **threshold of seriousness of injury or disorder** should govern who is owed the duty. What if the genetic disorder is only trivial? Such uncertainty causes reservations about whether any duty to disclose to the non-patient should ever be imposed on a HCP in these circumstances;
- whatever duty may be cast upon a HCP to protect non-patients from the actions of mentally-ill or psychotic patients, the dangers posed by genetic risks are **less obvious and overt**, and less deserving of any duty of care being cast upon the HCP;
- **litigation by a relative** against a HCP for failing to warn of an inherited condition was **unlikely** because 'single gene disorders that cause immediate effects are rare' in any event (per Skene), and hence, the difficulties of delineating a duty of care upon a HCP is not 'worth the candle', given the rarity of any likely litigation;
- to impose *any* duty on the HCP to protect a relative's interests would **damage the HCP–patient relationship**, given the already-existing duty of confidentiality owed to the patient.

However, this approach has its fierce critics. For example, Bell and Bennett discount[99] what they term the 'communitarian approach', arguing that 'genetic filiation is not enough in itself to warrant setting aside important legal and ethical protections', *viz*, the traditional patient-oriented right to confidentiality; and furthermore, the interest of relatives of patients in not knowing genetic information (the 'right not to know') also needs to be respected.

Hence, clearly the question of whether a HCP ought to owe any duty of care to a non-patient, in the case of a hereditary disease for which he is treating his own patient, is just as controversial a question as the scope of that duty, if owed.

4. Summary: weak or robust form of duty?

Of the two forms of possible duty—weak or robust—which is English law likely to favour in disease cases?

It will be recalled from Chapter 3 that, in the case of harm done to a third party by a psychotic patient in *Palmer v Tees HA*,[100] the English Court of Appeal was invited to accept the line of reasoning that the duty imposed on the defendant health authority was, not to warn non-patients Mrs Palmer and Rosie about the dangers posed by psychotic patient Mr Armstrong, particularly towards small children, but to provide adequate treatment for Armstrong and to stop his release whilst he posed a risk to children. The court rejected this argument, and no duty was owed to either of these claimants. That *Palmer* would not countenance even this weak form of duty upon Armstrong's psychiatrists, let alone a more robust duty to warn third parties about Armstrong (even had they known who to warn), is, in this author's opinion, highly significant in the context of inherited or transmissible diseases, and any duty which HCPs may owe to biological relatives.[101]

Moreover, the robust version of the duty, if applicable, imposes a *duty* (and not merely an entitlement) on the HCP to breach the duty of confidentiality owed to his patient, and to share information about the patient with a third party. As has been discussed elsewhere in this book,[102] there are circumstances in which English law has held that a breach of a patient's confidences is *justified* (in the case of a 'dangerous patient' suffering from mental frailty or psychosis)—but these decisions have, to date, not *mandated* the HCP's disclosure of a patient's condition to enable the protection of a third party. In this author's view, it is extremely unlikely that English courts would compel disclosure to a non-patient, in the context of a patient's communicable disease or genetic information, either. It is one thing for the law to say that a HCP has a discretion to warn about information concerning his patient, where that step is thought necessary to protect the non-patient from harm. It is entirely another matter to burden the HCP with a *duty* to do so.

Some of the previously-mentioned difficulties—that a duty to disclose genetic information to a non-patient would force the HCP to become the moral arbiter of how families/patients should conduct themselves, and that a duty to warn non-patients directly could invoke an obverse duty to protect the confidentiality of information concerning non-patients—are other significant counter-punches to any contention that a HCP should be under a proactive duty to warn non-patients of the dangers posed by patients with hereditary or transmissible illness.

Finally, a robust duty to warn the non-patients directly was employed in the American cases of *Safer v Pack* and in *Bradshaw v Daniel*, but in both cases, the non-patient class was extremely small, easily identified and accessible to the HCP. In any event, this robust duty was surely unnecessary when a weak form of duty would have done. As a matter of policy, this must be especially so, where the patient suffering from disease is reasonably equivalent to the *physically-* disabled patient—able to exercise personal autonomy and self-determination so as to protect the non-patient himself, if he so chooses.

For these various reasons, the author agrees with other commentary that the prospect of English law imposing a robust form of duty on HCPs in disease-related litigation is 'slight'.[103] If a duty towards a non-patient to avoid or minimise injury is to be countenanced at all, then of the two options, the weak form of duty is likely to be the highest form that such a duty would take. In the case of genetic conditions, the *Pate v Threlkel*-type solution would be more amenable to English courts than the *Safer v Estate of Pack* alternative, and in *all* cases, the 'less bold' solution would be the most that could be expected: that a HCP would have a duty to advise the patient of the risk to others posed by his transmissible or genetically-disposed illness or disease, to advise the patient how to prevent the spread of the disease, and to provide the patient with information that should be given to others—in the words of *Reisner*, 'no more (but no less) is required'.[104]

If a duty of care is to be recognised at all, then as with all third party relationships, the most difficult aspect of the non-patient's suit against a HCP in disease cases is whether he shares a sufficiently proximate, (close and direct) relationship with the HCP; and whether it is 'fair, just, and reasonable' to impose a duty of care on the HCP towards a person who is not his patient. The following Section examines the particular issues which have arisen in proving or debunking a duty of care in disease cases.

D CONSTRUCTING (AND DECONSTRUCTING) A DUTY OF CARE

Foreseeability of personal injury is not likely to be a difficulty, where a non-patient contracts[105] or inherits[106] a disease from a patient. Jones points out that the reporting duties contained in the Public Health (Control of Disease) Act 1984, ss 10 and 11, mean that foreseeability of injury to third parties will be 'virtually a foregone conclusion in respect of [the nominated] diseases', should such a case arise in England.[107]

Foreseeability does not define the boundaries of liability, however. It may be perfectly foreseeable that, if a GP does not diagnose a child's illness as rubella, that child will continue to attend school, may spread the disease to a classmate, that classmate's mother may be pregnant, that mother may herself contract rubella, and that mother may then give birth to a severely disabled child—that chain is foreseeable.[108] However, proximity and policy circumscribe the limits of liability, and in disease cases, both are likely to be contentious.

1. Proximity factors

Where the non-patient has succeeded in establishing a duty of care, or at the very least, has shown a cause of action on the face of the pleadings in cases of inherited and transmissible diseases sustained by that non-patient, several common factors emerge from the case law. Dipping into the basket of proximity factors outlined earlier in Chapter 2, in the specific scenario the subject of this chapter:

The vulnerability of the non-patient

Non-patients at risk of manifesting disease are vulnerable, because generally they have to rely upon HCPs who are in a stronger position *by virtue of the information* that they possess about the diseased patient, and about which the non-patient knows nothing and cannot ascertain for himself.[109]

For example, in the Australian case of *BT v Oei*,[110] BT, as AT's sexual partner, was in no position to know that AT was infected with HIV. She could only have been protected against that knowledge if AT had been competently diagnosed and treated by his GP. AT was unaware of his HIV status; the GP's specialist knowledge and training equipped him to identify the risk that AT had contracted HIV; and that failure to diagnose and adequately counsel AT to undertake an HIV antibody test exposed BT to the real risk of contracting the fatal disease, without her ability to detect AT's HIV status herself.[111] The result in the American decision of *Bradshaw v Daniel*[112] (concerning the spread of Rocky Mountain fever to the patient's wife, who died as a result) was not explained by the court in those terms, but commentator Parker justifies why the wife's estate succeeded on that basis: 'the relationship puts the physician in a position to know of a risk that may not be obvious to others [such as the patient's family]'.[113]

Reliance by the non-patient

In the successful non-patient suits mentioned in the previous point, the non–patients themselves did not know of what (if anything) the patient had been told about his illness. Hence, it cannot be said that these non-patients explicitly relied upon the defendant HCPs to advise/counsel/warn their patients, concerning the transmission of disease—theirs was an implied reliance only.

Actual reliance, however, was present in *Di Marco v Lynch Homes-Chester County Inc*, the case in which the patient technician was pricked with a Hepatitis-contaminated needle, and thereafter infected her husband. One of the key features for the Pennsylvania Supreme Court, in finding for the non-patient husband, was that he was aware of the (incorrect) information which had been provided to his wife by the two defendant doctors, about the need for sexual abstinence for a 6-week period, and that he had relied and acted upon this advice.[114] As Kiely observes,[115] the court did not deal with the issue of whether the doctors would have owed a duty of care, if the husband had never been told by his wife of the medical advice given to her.

However, either form of reliance will undoubtedly be sufficient in English law in this context, such that a duty of care may arise where the non-patient cannot prove actual reliance upon what the HCP told the patient about the disease and the precautions that should be taken in respect of it.

Knowledge of the identity of the non-patient, or as one of an identifiable class

It is useful, but not necessary, to a finding of proximity between HCP and non-patient, that the HCP knew the identity of the non-patient. However, not every HCP will be liaising with the non-patient wife, as his patient passes through serious illness and ultimately dies, as occurred in *Bradshaw v Daniel*.

The fact that the HCP does not know the actual identity of the non-patient is not, however, fatal to the non-patient suit in English law. In the non-patient suit in *McFarlane v Tayside Health Board*,[116] a wrongful conception case where a negligently-performed sterilisation was performed on Mr McFarlane, the surgeon had never met the non-patient wife; and more generally, the House of Lords held, in *Dorset Yacht Co Ltd v Home Office*,[117] that a duty of care is still capable of being owed by a defendant to a third party, if the third party was one of an identifiable class of persons at risk from the defendant's acts or omissions. In each case, the identifiable classes were those of present sexual partners and closely-proximate property owners, respectively. Hence, the defendant's lack of knowledge of the identity of the harmed third party is not a barrier to a successful imposition of a duty of care.

Consistently with this, in several disease-related non-patient suits emanating from other jurisdictions, the successful non-patient formed one of an identifiable class. These classes have included, e.g.:

- a class comprising the biological family members of a patient with a genetic disorder—in *Pate v Threlkel*,[118] the Supreme Court of Florida held that the HCP's duty to Heidi Pate, the patient's daughter, was 'obviously for the benefit of *certain identified third parties* and the physician *knows of the existence of those third parties*, [and hence] the physician's duty runs to those third parties'); while the Superior Court of New Jersey pointed to the fact that, in *Safer v Estate of Pack*, '[t]he individual or group at risk is easily identified';[119]

- a class of current sexual partners of the patient—in *BT v Oei*,[120] the GP did not know who AT's partner was, but the class of whom non-patient BT was the only member was one which was identifiable and known to the GP;
- a class of hospital visitors exposed to an infected hospital patient—in *Healey v Lakeridge Health Corp*,[121] the identity of the infected hospital visitors who were exposed to the patient's TB infection was even more of an unknown quantity to his treating respirologists, but they were capable of forming an identifiable class.

Whilst not conclusive, easily identifiable classes such as these will certainly assist to establish proximity between HCP and non-patient.[122]

By contrast, the following classes, of whom the non-patient was one, were too large, unknown, and amorphous, to warrant a duty being imposed (and English courts would be likely to hold the same):

- a class of persons exposed to infected hospital visitors—in *Healey*, this class was not certified by Cullity J as being appropriate for class action treatment, given that no duty of care would be owed by the respirologist and hospital to this large and unidentifiable group of non-patients;
- a class of casual carers of a diseased patient, and the carer's family—the United States Court of Appeals for the Tenth Circuit was unprepared to find that Dr Hamilton owed the Gammills, who suffered from infectious hepatitis after 'babysitting' patient Lauralee Johnson, any duty of care in *Gammill v US*.[123] It was only prepared to hold that the doctor could be under 'a much more limited duty ... to warn a patient's family, treating attendants, or other persons likely to be exposed to the patient, of the nature of the disease and the danger of exposure ... at the bare minimum the physician must be aware of the specific risks to specific persons before a duty to warn exists.'[124] In this case, though, Dr Hamilton did not know the Gammills, did not know that his patient had been cared for them, and hence, was unaware of their risk of exposure to hepatitis. To impose a duty upon the HCP in these circumstances would constitute an 'unreasonable burden upon physicians'.[125]

Of course, in its 'weak form', any duty to the non-patient is discharged by the HCP dealing with *the patient*—which obviates the need for the HCP to find out who unknown, but identifiable, third parties might be. Hence, in practical terms, it matters not whether the non-patient is or is not actually known to the HCP.

In summary, knowledge of the existence of the non-patient, as one of an *identifiable class* of person who could contract or inherit disease from the patient, is likely to be necessary in a successful English suit. Knowledge of the non-patient's identity, however, will not be required.

Causal proximity between HCP's conduct and the non-patient's damage

What if the HCP's breach precluded a step which, had it occurred, would have almost certainly protected the non-patient from contracting the disease that he eventually suffered from? That intervening step has been termed, in *Healey v Lakeridge Health Corp*, as a 'foreseeable reactive measure ... [that] could possibly affect the issue of proximity.'[126] Equally, this may be given the label of 'causal proximity'.

Hence, had the GP in *BT v Oei*[127] conducted a HIV test on his patient and warned him of the fact that he had the disease, the evidence was that the patient *himself* would have taken precautions to prevent the spread of the disease to his partner; and *Pittman Estate v Bain*[128] demonstrated the same point. Similarly, in *Healey* itself, had the specialists or hospital notified the public health authorities of patient AB's active tuberculosis as statute required for any reportable disease, the Department of Public Health would have taken steps to prevent exposing the non-patient visitors to the risk of TB.[129] Hence, in these cases, either the patients themselves, or the relevant public health authorities, respectively, would have taken the intervening steps necessary to protect the non-patients from harm.

Non-patient was 'at special risk'

Where unknown to the HCP, a non-patient affected by disease acquired from the patient will have to prove that the class, of whom he was one, was sufficiently defined—and the wider the class, the greater the need for the non-patient to prove a 'special risk' over and above that faced by *the general public*.

A non-patient may seek to argue that, under the weak form of duty, it should be immaterial how big the class of potential non-patients may be, because if it is not *he* that should have been warned of the patient's disease, but the patient himself, then it should not matter how big was the class, of whom the non-patient was one. (This was, after all, one of the justifications put forward previously as to why the class of non-patients, of whom the claimant was one, only needs to be *identifiable* to the HCP, without personal knowledge of the non-patient himself.) This was, essentially, the view that the Court of Appeal of California reached in upholding the non-patient suit in the HIV case of *Reisner v The Regents of the University of California*,[130] when dealing with the class of future sexual partners of Jennifer Lawson, of whom Daniel Reisner was one.

However, such an argument is likely doomed to fail in English law (and the outcome in *Reisner* would probably not be replicated in England). As discussed previously in this book,[131] proof that the claimant was 'at special risk' is a common thread throughout third party claims in English law. On this basis, the class of future sexual partners was specifically rejected, in *Goodwill v British Pregnancy Advisory Service*,[132] as equating to a wide, amorphous class comprising the public-at-large. The decision, involving a non-patient who formed an intimate relationship with the patient after the alleged breach occurred on the part of the HCP, occurred in the context of a *pure economic loss claim* by a non–patient—but it is most unlikely that the greater importance accorded to personal injury over pure economic loss would cause a change in this principle. After all, in a separate context of police defendants, Jacqueline Hill, who was the final murder victim of the 'Yorkshire Ripper', suffered the most unimaginable personal injury of all, yet she was not deemed to be at special risk, any more than was the general female public.[133] Moreover, the fact that the defendant HCP may have foreseen that the patient would enter into an intimate relationship and expose a non-patient to the risk of contracting a disease would not be sufficient, given that reasonable foreseeability of harm is not conclusive of the duty question under English law.

Hospital visitors exposed to an ill patient constitute another large class—approaching that of general public—yet the Canadian authority of *Healey* certainly supports the view that such visitors can constitute a feasible non-patient class with sufficient legal proximity to a negligent HCP,[134] if the visitors acquire disease from that unfortunate patient. Another Canadian judge has remarked, *obiter*, that a hospital's duty of care could 'quite readily extend ... to persons who were on the premises of a hospital on business, or who were simply visiting other patients' in the hospital.[135] It is difficult to find English or other Commonwealth authority that has been prepared to go this far—although the 'special risk' demanded by English law could well be provided by the fact that the closed environment of a hospital, and the risks posed within that environment, mark out visitors as being vulnerable to disease, harm from patients, and the like.

Hence, even under the weak form of duty which merely requires the HCP to act in relation to the diseased patient, if the non-patient is a member of a class of persons at risk of harm from the HCP's acts or omission, which class is too big and too amorphous, that factor will derail the non-patient suit.

Physical and temporal proximity

Almost inevitably, there will be a close physical proximity between patient and the non-patient claimant, in order that the transmission of disease occurred in the first place (e.g., close physical intimacy in the HIV cases of *BT v Oei* and *Pittman v Bain*, close daily proximity between ill husband and non-patient wife in the Rocky Mountains fever case of *Bradshaw v Daniel*; and physical proximity between hospital patient and hospital visitors in *Healey*). Obversely, in *Healey*, the cross-infected non-patients failed to establish a cause of action against the HCP, partly due to their lack of physical proximity with the patient.

Some degree of temporal proximity, between the HCP's negligent act or omission and the non-patient's damage, will also be required. As seen in Chapter 3, in other 'dangerous patient' contexts where the non-patient suffered harm almost a year after the health authority's breach (e.g., *Palmer v Tees HA*[136] and *Maulolo v Hutt Valley Health Corp Ltd*[137]), proving a duty of care in favour of the non-patient was an impossible task. In the context of pure economic loss, the lack of temporal proximity was also used in *Goodwill v British Pregnancy Advisory Service*[138] to rule out, as un-proximate victims, the patient's future sexual partners. Notably, a considerable time lag between when the HCP's breach occurred and when the non-patient's damage manifested by his relationship with the patient was specifically rejected by the *Reisner* court[139] as being of any relevance—but were a similar case to come before the English courts, it is submitted that *Reisner* would not be decided in the same way. *Palmer* and *Goodwill* suggest that a lack of temporal proximity would count against the non-patient's prospects of establishing a duty of care.

2. Public policy considerations

The third element of the *Caparo* analysis applicable to novel negligence scenarios—involving considerations of policy—has featured in disease-related non-patient claims against HCPs. Five have emerged as being of particular relevance to the question as to whether it would be unfair, unjust and unreasonable to impose a duty upon the HCP towards the non-patient who has contracted/inherited a disease:

Conflict with the duty of confidentiality towards the patient

If patients perceive that a HCP has a duty to inform non-patients of the patient's illness, or if the HCP seeks to persuade the patient to disclose that fact to the non-patient, patients may distrust the capacity of their doctors to keep their medical information confidential. They may not present themselves for medical treatment at all, potentially compromising not only their own health, but that of the public. Discouraging would-be patients from coming forward for treatment for genetic conditions or for communicable diseases would be an unacceptable by-product of a duty owed by

HCP to non-patient. As Rose J put it in *X HA v Y*, '[i]n the long run, preservation of confidentiality is the only way of securing public health'.[140]

Academic commentary has also emphasised that any affirmative duty upon a HCP to disclose information about diseases being borne by a patient must be wrong—it 'undermines the very principles of the doctor-patient relationship. Knowing that private medical information may be revealed will discourage individuals from seeking medical treatment or prevent them from being candid with their physician.'[141]

However, these concerns can be met by two ripostes. First, and as discussed in Chapter 2,[142] the duty of confidentiality is not absolute—English law is certainly prepared to uphold an *ability* to directly warn a non-patient of disease, should it be shown that the public interest favours disclosure to that non-patient (be it a family member, a close associate of the patient, or members of the general public); and the GMC's own Guidelines exhort HCPs to breach confidentiality in exceptional cases where failing to disclose could 'expose others to risk of death or serious harm'.[143]

Secondly, the weak form of duty on the HCP avoids the prospect of conflict. If what is required of the HCP to discharge his duty to his patient (i.e., to stress to the patient about the potential relevance of the patient's confidential genetic information to other blood relatives, or to counsel a HIV-positive patient about the precautionary steps that he should adopt in relation to his sexual partner) would *also* discharge any duty to non-patient (i.e., a duty to minimise or avoid injury to that non-patient caused by the inheritance of propensity for disease from the patient, or a duty to take precautionary steps regarding the patient's sexual partner), the duties are *aligned*, and no conflict arises. The point was underscored in *BT v Oei*,[144] for example, where the GP owed a duty to the non-patient who contracted HIV from the patient, on the basis that the content of the GP's duty to BT would have been discharged by the diagnosis and provision of proper advice to patient AT. These duties to both patient and non-patient were 'coincident',[145] rendering a conflict unlikely as a 'practical reality.'[146]

Hence, as a matter of policy, any duty of care owed by a HCP to the non-patient is more likely if the scope of the duty is *read down* to the weak form.

The size of the class

The class of non-patients (of whom the claimant is one) at risk from the HCP's acts or omission in relation to a diseased patient, cannot give rise to the spectre of indeterminate liability on the HCP's part[147]—classes which are potentially excessive in size and uncertain in character render any duty to the non-patient unlikely. (As pointed out in Chapter 3, this factor is closely linked to the requirement that, for wide classes, the non-patient must prove that he was 'at special risk'.) This policy factor has proven important in the context of disease-related non-patient litigation.

On the one hand, in the Canadian case of *Healey v Lakeridge Health Corp*,[148] Cullity J considered that the *cross-infected* class of claimants (those cross-infected with tuberculosis by exposure to those in the community who had come into contact with AB before he died of TB) was potentially 'ever-widening' and problematical, and that class was not certified as being able to go forth as a class action. Moreover, the early case of *Evans v Liverpool Corp*[149] was decried by the Irish High Court in *Denneny*[150] as **not** standing for the proposition that a duty of care could be owed by a HCP to members of the public, if a patient's negligent treatment exposed the public to the disease from which the patient was suffering.

On the other hand, in the successful non-patient suit in *BT v Oei*, the court expressly noted that the GP was **not** exposed to indeterminate liability, given that the non-patient class comprised the patient's current sexual partner/wife;[151] and in *Healey*, the class of *infected* persons (hospital visitors) could claim an arguable duty of care owed to them by the hospital/respirologist, because there was no 'spectre of indeterminate liability'.[152] Even though the class was obviously much larger than that which the court was concerned with in *BT*, Cullity J rationalised an arguable duty of care on the basis that the source of these non-patients' infections was a patient being treated at a health centre, and the number exposed within or by visiting this centre during the time of AB's treatment was limited.

The effect of statutory provisions or professional guidelines encouraging or compelling disclosure about disease

Statutory provisions or professional guidelines which mandate a HCP to report information to public authorities about the disease being suffered by a patient, or which require the HCP to convey certain advice about the disease to the patient himself, may contribute towards a finding of a duty of care to the non-patient.

In *BT v Oei*, the defendant GP was bound by s 12(1) of the Public Health Act 1991 (NSW) which required a medical practitioner, who believed on reasonable grounds that his patient was suffering from a sexually transmissible medical condition, to inform *his patient* of the patient's statutory responsibility to warn prospective sexual partners of his condition.[153] Bell J concluded that:

> a consideration of public policy reflected in the statutory obligations placed upon medical practitioners with respect to the treatment of and supply of information to patients with sexually transmissible medical conditions, ... to my mind makes the imposition of the duty appropriate in the circumstances of this case.[154]

A similar obligation does not apply to English medical practitioners, although, as discussed in Chapter 2,[155] the Public Health (Control of Diseases) Act 1984[156] requires a HCP to notify the relevant health authority when he suspects that his patient suffers from a notifiable disease.

A discretion to notify others of a patient's transmissible or hereditary disease is widely supported in England. The GMC's Guidelines have already been mentioned.[157] The Human Genetics Commission of England[158] states that there may be cases for disclosing sensitive genetic information 'where it is in the interest of the patient, of relatives, or of the wider public'. The Nuffield Council on Bioethics[159] provides that, where genetic screening revealed information that could have 'serious implications for relatives of those who have been screened', then 'HCPs should seek to persuade individuals, if persuasion should be necessary, to allow the disclosure of relevant genetic information to other family members', and that, if the subject refuses, then '[i]n such exceptional circumstances, the individual's desire for confidentiality may be overridden. The decision can only be made case by case.'[160] The British Medical Association has cited the discretion of the HCP to inform relatives of genetic information in exceptional circumstances, but has disavowed any legal duty to do so on the part of the HCP.[161] No English case has yet constructed a duty of care, from HCP to non-patient, on the basis of such guidelines, and it must be reiterated that they do not have the force of law. Moreover, the abovementioned guidances all pertain to a *justified* disclosure by a HCP in order to protect third parties—not a *mandatory* duty to disclose or to otherwise protect non-patients.

Nevertheless, it is open to a court (as occurred in *BT v Oei*) to consider the policy behind the text of statutory provisions or professional guidances when deciding whether the HCP and non-patient were legally proximate, and whether it is fair, just and reasonable, that a duty of care should be imposed.

The higher importance of public health

As a policy reason in favour of finding a duty of care towards a non-patient, on the part of the HCP who is treating a patient for a communicable or contagious disease, a non-patient claimant may seek to point to the importance of public health, and the disaster that can be wrought to a community by inadequate infection controls.

Indeed, this argument has found favour in leading American cases in which a HCP's duty to the non-patient was upheld, e.g.: in the AIDS case of *Reisner* ('the facts of this case compel a conclusion designed to encourage the highest standard of care concerning communicable and infectious diseases'[162]); and in the Hepatitis case of *Di Marco* ('[c]ommunicable diseases are so named because they are readily spread from person to person. Physicians are the first line of defense against the spread of communicable diseases, because physicians know what measures must be taken to prevent the infection of others ... Such precautions are taken not to protect the health of the patient, whose well-being has already been compromised, rather such precautions are taken to safeguard the health of others'[163]). Similarly, in *BT v Oei*, Bell J suggested that the incurrence of physical ill-health to a non-patient (and an ancillary liability imposed upon HCPs who fail to act reasonably to prevent that incurrence) is considerably more significant than scenarios in which a non-patient merely suffers pure economic loss.[164]

The ability for disease to do harm to society at large, and for HCPs to play a significant part in halting its spread, marks this type of non-patient suit out as being somewhat different. To date, no English case has expressly acknowledged this factor as being significant, but it is suggested that it could feature prominently, should such litigation be instituted in the future.

What would imposing a duty of care achieve?

In Jacqueline Hill's estate's suit against the West Yorkshire Police,[165] for failing to protect her from the murderous activities of the Yorkshire Ripper, one of the reasons for denying a duty of care was that it would achieve little. As the House of Lords memorably put it, were a duty of care to be imposed on the police to protect the claimant, then 'the court would have to decide whether an inspector is to be condemned for failing to display the acumen of Sherlock Holmes and whether a constable is to be condemned for being as obtuse as Dr Watson ... But that finding would not help anybody or punish anybody.'[166]

Similarly, when Daniel Reisner contracted the HIV virus from his partner, Jennifer Lawson, and sued Jennifer's doctor for failing to inform Jennifer of her positive HIV status,[167] the defendants argued that this non-patient suit would achieve no long-term good. Literally billions of dollars were being invested in the scientific research of HIV/AIDS, and imposing negligence liability upon individual HCPs would not speed up the search for better detection, treatment, and a cure. The Court of Appeal of California said, however, that the defendants 'miss the point', and that while tort liability for failing to warn Jennifer to convey information to non-patient Daniel 'may not hasten the day when AIDS can be cured or prevented, it may, in the meantime, protect one or more persons from unnecessary exposure to this deadly virus.'[168]

This is clearly an area where reasonable opinion about policy will differ—where some will consider that the very purpose of tort law is both to deter negligent practices, and to put the claimant in the position as if the tort had not been committed, so far as money can do it; while others will consider that not every civil wrong will have a remedy.

E PARTICULAR CAUSATION CONUNDRUMS IN DISEASE-RELATED SCENARIOS

The non-patient suffering from disease will have to establish proof of some damage which was caused by the HCP's act or omission—an essential element in the claim in negligence. Significant causal conundrums may arise in this type of non-patient suit against a HCP.

1. No positive act by the healthcare professional regarding the inheritance or spread of disease

If a HCP fails to disclose/warn/counsel, etc (either to the non-patient directly, or to the patient), about a patient's genetic predisposition to disease, it cannot be said that the HCP caused the non-patient's harm in any positive sense—when the non-patient already had the relevant gene. In that sense, as the trial judge observed in *Safer v Estate of Pack*, non-patient suits based upon genetic diseases are different from those arising out of both infectious diseases and threats of harm from mentally-ill patients: 'the harm is already present within the non-patient child.'[169] Commentator Suter expressed the point this way: 'individuals with disease genes do not put relatives at risk by carrying the gene. Their relatives have no risk of becoming carriers; they only have the risk of *finding out* that they are carriers.'[170]

Interestingly, a similar line of reasoning—that the HCP did nothing to positively cause the non-patient's illness—has been applied by some American courts as a means of limiting a HCP's liability in negligence in the case of communicable diseases too. For example, in *Candelario v Teperman*,[171] the reason that Dr Teperman was not negligent towards Mrs Candelario, who contracted Hepatitis while caring for her mother, was that 'there is no allegation or evidence that any treatment Dr Teperman administered to [the patient] mother caused plaintiff to become infected with hepatitis C.'[172] In other words, liability could only be established when the HCP's *treatment of the patient* caused the non-patient's injury in some positive way. The reasoning has been followed more recently in the same jurisdiction.[173] Hence, allegations that a HCP was negligent in failing both to warn patients and third parties of the risk of exposure to a disease, and to isolate the patient, are not sufficient to establish causation under this approach.

In English law, however, a causal link could be established, based upon a HCP's omission to act (to warn or disclose) in relation to the patient, in the sense that 'it deprives third parties of a chance to avail themselves of any therapies or cures'[174] (assuming that such cures or therapies are available). As discussed in Chapter 2,[175] a weaker causal link of this type—the mere creation of an opportunity to do harm—has been successfully used in the case of omissions to act in other cases, both within and outside the medical context.

Moreover, in the context of wrongful birth cases,[176] parental claimants may successfully sue a doctor for the damages resulting from the birth of a disabled child, where the substance of the suit is that the HCP failed to detect an already-existing condition in their child *in utero* (say, spina bifida) or failed to carry out pre-natal DNA testing (which would have identified, say, a severe hereditary blood disease), thereby depriving those parental claimants of the opportunity to choose a lawful abortion of the foetus. By analogy with these naturally-occurring conditions, a non-patient would seek to argue that an existing abnormality in his genetic make-up should be disclosed to him to enable him to seek the opportunities that medical treatment may offer, by which to avoid or minimise his personal suffering.

2. The linear chain of causation

In *Reisner v The Regents of the University of California*, the Californian Court of Appeal pointed out that, for Daniel Reisner (the partner of the patient who had acquired AIDS via blood transfusion) to succeed, he had a formidable causal challenge:

> Daniel will also have to prove causation—not just that Jennifer would have told him about her illness and that he would then have refrained from intimate contact with her, but also that he could not have acquired the disease elsewhere.[177]

Hence, in disease cases, where the weak form of duty is upheld, the non-patient will usually have to prove *three* causal links in the chain, in order to establish that the HCP's omission to disclose/warn/counsel the patient caused his harm:

   i. That the patient would have conveyed the information about his disease to the non-patient in order to afford the non-patient the opportunity to protect himself;
  ii. That the non-patient would indeed have adjusted his conduct or position so as to protect himself; and
 iii. That the non-patient would not have acquired the disease from some other source (unnecessary to prove in cases of hereditary disease).

Each of these linkages must be proved on the balance of probabilities.

(a) The patient's own conduct

Point (i) focuses upon the *patient's* conduct (what the patient would have hypothetically done). Three points are relevant.

First, as alluded to in the passage from *Reisner* and in other authorities,[178] under the weak form of duty, if the patient would have probably declined to inform blood relatives, sexual partners, etc, of the information given to him by the HCP, then this should excuse the HCP from any liability—on the basis that the more immediate, or proximate, cause of the non-patient's injury was the patient's own conduct. (Indeed, some commentators have flagged the possibility of an action by the non-patient *against the patient* in these circumstances[179].) It has long been accepted in English law that unreasonable or deliberate (rather than merely mischance) behaviour on the part of a third party (the patient in this case) can sever the causal link between the defendant's conduct and the claimant's damage.[180]

Secondly, under the robust form of the duty of care, it will be the HCP's failure to notify the *non-patient* of the patient's medical condition that will be alleged to be the cause of the non-patient's harm. What if the patient, though, expressly tells his HCP that under no circumstances is his medical condition to be discussed with family members? This potential problem was flagged in *Safer v Estate of Pack*, but the court did not resolve the issue because the evidence did not suggest that sort of problem existed in this case.[181] As well as creating ethical problems for the HCP (articulated by Clayton previously[182]), this dilemma would also raise significant causation problems for a non-patient.

Thirdly, in *Safer v Estate of Pack*, the trial judge pointed out that, in hereditary disease cases brought by non-patients, it was not possible to point to any positive action by the patient— the non-patient's harm was not 'introduced by a [mentally-ill] patient who was not warned to stay away. The patient is taking no action in which to cause the child harm'.[183] In the *Tarasoff*-type scenario, where the patient threatens to kill the non-patient, and then does so, there is what has been termed a 'linear relationship of cause and effect',[184] whereas that type of linear relationship is absent in hereditary disease cases. Academic commentary has also pointed out that if some positive harmful action on the part of the HCP's patient is a criterion for liability, then causation should fail.[185] However, in such cases, it must be reiterated that the essential causal question is: would the non–patient's harm have been suffered, but for the HCP's omission? If it can be shown that *the patient would have acted differently* towards the non-patient, had the patient been advised/counselled/treated reasonably and competently by the HCP, then the causal link in (i) above will be established (as it was, for example, in *Pittman Estate v Bain*[186]).

(b) The non-patient's conduct

Point (ii) focuses upon what the *non-patient* would have done, hypothetically, once warned or informed by the patient. If the non-patient would have taken steps to avoid or minimise the risk of harm arising from the patient's disease, then the second causal link will be made out.

The analysis of causation in *BT v Oei* demonstrates this linkage well. It will be recalled that BT, who contracted HIV from her partner, patient AT, established a weak form duty of care: AT's GP ought to have arranged a HIV antibody test for AT and, thereafter, ought to have counselled AT to take appropriate steps to protect BT from contracting the virus. Bell J concluded that the causal links were made out:

> Had AT known he was HIV positive and had he received adequate counselling concerning the transmission of HIV and safe sex practices would he have taken measures to protect BT from risk of infection? The expert evidence strongly suggests that he would. Dr Furner, whose expertise in the area of dealing with people who are HIV positive I accept without reservation, stated that it is generally accepted that a very high percentage of persons (of any sexual orientation) if adequately counselled will both notify their sexual partner and change their sexual practices so as not to place their sexual partner at risk ... I therefore find that had AT been appropriately counselled as at December 1992 he would have undergone an HIV antibody test. Such a test would have shown he had contracted HIV. Proper advice would have brought home to him the need to protect his partner from risk of infections and the means to do so. The couple would not have engaged in unprotected sexual relations thereafter ... The defendant's negligent failure to properly advise AT with respect to a possible diagnosis of HIV and the need for an antibody test materially contributed to the plaintiff's infection with the virus.[187]

On the other hand, if the non-patient could have done nothing different, because the condition or illness confronting that non-patient had no prospects of a cure, then the damage suffered by the non-patient would have been suffered anyway, and hence, the HCP's failure to warn/disclose of the patient's illness did not cause the damage complained of by the non-patient. In the case of hereditary disease, if it was not possible to reduce the risk of injury to be caused by the genetic disorder—should the disorder have no cure or avenue of alleviation—the causal chain will fail at this point.[188]

A similar problem—that the non-patient probably could not have averted the damage—can arise in the case of transmitted diseases too. For example, in *Gammill v US*,[189] the claim was struck out as disclosing no cause of action because no duty of care was owed by the HCP to the baby-sitters who contracted Hepatitis from the patient child. Furthermore, the district court denied that there was any causal connection between the HCP's conduct and the resulting injury to the baby-sitters, on the following basis:

> if the physician had notified the appropriate health authorities of the hepatitis in the Johnson family pursuant to the statute, the health officials would have had to investigate the matter, find the Gammills had contact with the Johnson baby for three to four hours before she was diagnosed as having the disease, and seek out and advise the Gammills to receive gamma globulin inoculations. Later the Gammills on their own initiative would have had to actually receive the shots. Note that all this activity would have had to have been accomplished within the relatively short time span of a couple of days, for the plaintiffs were already infected with hepatitis ... seven days before ... the doctor was under the duty to report the diagnosis. [and] ... even if the inoculations were given to the plaintiffs, they still would have become sick with the disease—inoculation would serve only to lessen the degree of sickness.[190]

(c) Infection from some other source

Point (iii) concentrates upon the question of whether the non-patient could have acquired the disease from some source other than the patient. Where the non-patient is one of a class of cross-infected persons, for example (persons who were not exposed to the patient himself, but to persons infected by the patient), there may be a myriad of other possible exposures that could be blamed for the transmission to the non-patient. According to the court in *Reisner*, Typhoid Mary was so named because, in the early 1900s, Mary Mallon, an Irish cook working in the United States, was a typhoid carrier who, herself immune to the typhoid bacilli, unwittingly infected virtually everyone with whom she came in contact. There were 51 cases of direct infection, but countless others who were cross-infected.[191] The *Reisner* court pointed out that the cross-infecteds would face formidable causation difficulties, in proving that they probably would not have suffered the contagious disease from some source other than Mary Mallon.[192]

F   CONCLUSION

In the case of transmissible diseases, directly-relevant English authorities are thin (although, as *Evans v Liverpool Corp*[193] shows, the scenario has arisen for tangential judicial consideration), while there is a paucity of English case law concerning suits by family members against HCPs regarding inheritable diseases. Nevertheless, the range of case law to which reference has been made in this chapter has portents for a likely greater incidence of disease-related litigation in the future for English courts.

It has been pointed out[194] that, in an area which has developed as quickly as the field of genetic information, the common law suffers from a distinct disadvantage. It is a reactive mechanism, so it takes time to reflect changes in science or health policy. Hence, the lag between scientific policy and the casting of legal duties upon HCPs is said to be 'particularly apparent'. Nevertheless, courtrooms are where these disputes ultimately end up, particularly in cases of first impression as these would be in English law. On that score, and while notably not expressing any view upon whether a HCP should be under a duty to warn family members of the risk of inheritable disease, the Australian judge, Justice Michael Black, has noted that:

> It is in the courts that our society sometimes plays out its most complex, emotive and seemingly unresolvable conflicts. The revolutions in genetics and biotechnology are bound to give rise to these conflicts in the future.[195]

Of course, given the controversy surrounding genetic privacy, it is always open to the legislature to decree if/when such information should be disclosed to non-patients, as several US states have done.[196]

There is little prospect of English law burdening a HCP with a duty to warn non-patients directly of the risk of hereditary or transmissible disease. No case to date has imposed upon a HCP a duty to directly warn a non-patient of some risk posed by the HCP's knowledge of the patient in *any* context involving so-called 'dangerous patients'. The more likely duty to emerge in English law—if one is to be cast upon the HCP at all—is a duty to diagnose the patient's illness correctly, and then to counsel the patient to inform others who are closely associated with the patient who may be at risk from the disease, whether by contraction or inheritance of the disease. Regardless of the type of duty imposed (weak or strong), foreseeability of personal injury on the non-patient's part is not likely to present any problems in the duty analysis, but the other elements of proximity and public policy will be vested with difficulty.

In the meantime, the guideline in the Appendix, '*Potential Liability to Non-Patients and Third Parties: A Synopsis for Healthcare Professionals*', seeks to outline, for the benefit of HCPs, the key points that arise in this difficult field of potential medical liability for inherited and communicable diseases suffered by non-patients.

ENDNOTES

1   The surgical removal of the uterus, breast, or ovary, respectively.
2   Comm for the Study of Ethical Problems in Medicine and Biomedical and Behavioural Research, *Screening and Counseling for Genetic Conditions: A Report on the Ethical, Social and Legal Implications of Genetic Screening, Counseling and Education Programs* (Washington, Feb 1983) 44.
3   Several US decisions involving transmission of disease undertake an analysis by reference to a *Tarasoff*-type duty to protect non-patients from harm done by a mentally-ill or psychotic patient, e.g.: *Bradshaw v Daniel*, 854 SW 2d 865, 870–72 (SC Tenn 1993); *Reisner v The Regents of the Uni of California*, 31 Cal App 4th 1195, 1198–99, 37 Cal Rptr 2d 518 (Cal Ct App 1995); and in the disease case of *Healey v Lakeridge Corp* (2006), 38 CPC (6th) 145 (Ont SCJ), the court referred to the mentally-ill patient case of *Wenden v Trikha* (1991), 116 AR 81 (Alta QB) or analogous purposes.
4   e.g.: M Kovalesky, 'To Disclose or not to Disclose: Determining the Scope and Exercise of a Physician's Duty to Warn Third Parties of Genetically-Transmissible Conditions' (2008) 76 *U Cincinnati L Rev* 1019, 1029–31; M King, 'Physician Duty to Warn a Patient's Offspring of Hereditary Genetic Defects: Balancing the Patient's Right to Confidentiality Against the Family Member's Right to Know: Can or Should *Tarasoff* Apply?' (2000) 2 *Quinnipiac Health LJ* 1.
5   See, e.g., the discussion in: R Cole, 'Authentic Democracy: Endowing Citizens with a Human Right in their Genetic Information' (2005) 33 *Hofstra L Rev* 1241, 1253–54, citing: the observations of Judge Kestin in *Safer v Estate of Pack*, 677 A 2d 1188, 1192 (NJ Super Ct App Div 1996).
6   D Bell and B Bennett, 'Genetic Secrets and the Family' (2001) 9 *Med L Rev* 9, 9.
7   *Healey v Lakeridge Health Corp* (2006), 38 CPC (6th) 145 (Ont SCJ) [41]–[42] ('[t]he question has obvious importance that extends beyond the specific facts of this case. Counsel have been unable to refer me to any Canadian authorities in which physicians or hospitals have been found to owe a duty of care to members of the public to whom undiagnosed, or mis-diagnosed, infections are transmitted by a patient').

[8] *Bradshaw v Daniel*, 854 SW 2d 865, 870 (SC Tenn 1993) ('[i]nsofar as we are able to determine, there is no reported decision from this or any other jurisdiction involving circumstances exactly similar to those presented in this case').

[9] See, generally, the special issue of (2007) 18 *King's LJ*, containing the symposium papers relating to: 'Governing Genetic Databases: Collection, Storage and Use' (Ethox Centre, Uni of Oxford, 2007). Also, for some judicial discussion, see, e.g.: *Blaz v Michael Reese Hosp Foundation*, 74 F Supp 2d 803 (ND Ill 1999) (hospital research programme to investigate risks of hospital's previous radiation treatments; former patient developed neural tumours; duty on researcher to warn former patient of 'strong connection' between radiation treatment and such tumours).

[10] For information on the Human Genome Project, which was completed in 2003 and which was a 13-year project co-ordinated by the US Dept of Energy and the National Institutes of Health, with significant input from the Wellcome Trust (UK), see: <http://www.ornl.gov/sci/techresources/Human_Genome/home.shtml>.

[11] See, e.g.: Nuffield Council on Bioethics, *The Forensic Use of Bioinformation: Ethical Issues* (Sep 2007), especially ch 3; and earlier, by the same Council, *Genetic Screening and Ethical Issues* (Dec 1993), especially ch 5; J Yates *et al*, *Report of the Clinical Genetics Soc Working Party on DNA Banking, Guidelines for DNA Banking* (1989) 26 *J of Med Genetics* 245; *Report of the Comm on the Ethics of Gene Therapy (the Clothier Comm)* (Cm 1788, 1992); House of Commons Science and Technology Comm (Shaw Comm), *Third Report, Human Genetics: The Science and its Consequences*, Vol 1 (1995).

[12] e.g.: R Furman, 'Genetic Test Results and the Duty to Disclose: Can Medical Researchers Control Liability?' (1999) 23 *Seattle U L Rev* 391; P Case, 'Confidence Matters: The Rise and Fall of Informational Autonomy in Medical Law' (2003) 11 *Med L Rev* 208, III and IV; L Skene, 'Patients' Rights or Family Responsibilities?—Two Approaches to Genetic Testing' (1998) 6 *Med L Rev* 1; D Madden, 'Ethical and Legal Issues in Psychiatric Genetics Research' [2004] *Medico-Legal J of Ireland* 38.

[13] e.g., *Lindsey CC v Marshall* [1937] AC 97 (HL) (patient in maternity home suffered puerperal fever and removed to hospital; new patient admitted to home after disinfectant practices also caught the fever); *AB v Tameside and Glossop HA* (1996) 35 BMLR 79 (CA) (health authorities learnt that former health care worker, who had been involved in obstetric treatment, tested HIV-positive and that female patients of health care worker at very remote risk of infection from that source).

[14] e.g., in Canada, by means of two class actions: *Anderson v Wilson* (1999), 44 OR (3d) 673, 175 DLR (4th) 409 (Ont CA) (several patients contracted hepatitis B after undergoing tests at defendant's medical clinic; tests allegedly performed by hepatitis-positive technician); *Rose v Pettle* (2004), 43 CPC (5th) 183 (Ont SCJ) (patients contracted skin infection, Mycobacterium abscessus, allegedly attributable to course of acupuncture treatments administered by defendant without use of disposable needles). In the US, e.g.: *Hofmann v Blackmon*, 241 So 2d 752 (1970); *Helman v Sacred Heart Hosp*, 62 Wash 2d 136, 381 P 2d 605 (1963) (staphylococcus infection spread from one patient to hospital roommate; sterile techniques allegedly not followed by staff).

[15] See Chapter 1, pp 15–16.

[16] [1906] 1 KB 160 (KB).

[17] According to an earlier jury verdict: *ibid*, 161 (as described by Walton J).

[18] *Gold v Essex CC* [1942] 2 KB 293 (CA) 300.

[19] [1906] 1 KB 160 (KB) 166 ('It is contended that the doctor was the servant of the [local authority responsible for the hospital] for the purpose of discharging the child, and that they are liable for the negligence of their servant, but the terms of his appointment, and the rules under which he acted, do not bear out this contention').

[20] [1936] 1 IR 384 (HC).

[21] *ibid*, 399–400.

[22] *ibid*, 400.

[23] Pursuant to the Class Proceedings Act, 1992, SO 1992, c C 6.

[24] (2006), 38 CPC (6th) 145 (Ont SCJ).

[25] See the class definition set out in *ibid*, [18].

[26] Chapter 9.

27 The certification criterion contained in s 5(1)(a) was of most relevance to the present enquiry, although the other four certification criteria contained in s 5(1) were also extensively discussed in the judgment.

28 For early US authority, more contemporaneous with *Evans* and *Denneny*, see, e.g.: *Davis v Rodman*, 227 SW 612, 614 Ark 1921) (physician under duty to exercise reasonable care to prevent the spread of typhoid); *Jones v Stanko*, 160 NE 456, 458 (Ohio 1928) (physician liable for injuries incurred by next-door neighbour who contracted black smallpox as result of doctor's failure to warn); *Skillings v Allen*, 173 NW 663 (Minn 1919) (doctor under duty to use due care in advising patient's parents about possible transmission of scarlet fever); *Edwards v Lamb*, 45 A 480, 484 (NH 1899) (doctor liable for failing to warn patient's wife of possibility of infection), all cited in: *Bradshaw v Daniel*, 854 SW 2d 865, 871 (Tenn 1993). See, further: Annotation, *Liability of Doctor or Other Health Practitioner to Third Party Contracting Contagious Disease from Doctor's Patient* 3 ALR 5th 370.

29 M Kovalesky, 'To Disclose or not to Disclose: Determining the Scope and Exercise of a Physician's Duty to Warn Third Parties of Genetically-Transmissible Conditions' (2008) 76 *U Cincinnati L Rev* 1019, 1023.

30 854 SW 2d 865 (Tenn 1993). The fact that Rocky Mountain Spotted Fever is not 'contagious in the narrow sense that it can be transmitted from one person to another' was irrelevant, and did not negate any duty of care owed by a HCP to a non-patient who contracted that disease from the HCP's patient. Provided that a non-patient was 'at risk of contracting disease' (here, the disease affected rodents and mammals, and was transmitted to humans via the bites of infected ticks), that was sufficient. The issue of a HCP's liability towards third parties could arise not only in relation to strictly contagious diseases.

31 727 F 2d 950 (10th Cir 1984).

32 789 NYS 2d 133 (App Div 2005).

33 51 Wash App 781, 754 P 2d 1302 (1988).

34 27 Cal 3d 916, 616 P 2d 813 (Cal 1980).

35 E Richards and K Rathbun, *Medical Care Law* (Aspen Publishers, Gaithersburg Maryland, 1999) 317.

36 [2001] Lloyd's Rep Med 458 (QB).

37 (1994), 112 DLR (4th) 257 (Ont Gen Div).

38 *ibid*, 401.

39 (2006), 38 CPC (6th) 145 (Ont SCJ) [45].

40 Picard and Robertson note that 'it must follow from the [*Pittman*] decision that an independent duty of care was owed to Mrs Pittman, otherwise no liability could have been imposed; she would not have been able to rely on a duty of care owed to her husband': E Picard and G Robertson, *Legal Liability of Doctors and Hospitals in Canada* (4th edn, Thomson Carswell, Toronto, 2007) 182, and 222, fn 66.

41 J Sestito, 'The Duty to Warn Third Parties and AIDS in Canada' (1996) 16 *Health Law in Canada* 83, 91.

42 [1999] NSWSC 1082. For case comment, see, eg: D Hirsch, 'Doctor's Duty of Care to a Patient's Sexual Partner' (1999) 8 *Aust Health Law Bull* 53; M Lynch, 'Doctors' Duties and Third Parties' (2000) 7 *JLM* 244; A Langford, 'Doctors' Liabilities to Third Parties' (2001) 75 *Law Institute J* 74; J Devereux, 'Negligence' (2000) 7 *JLM* 249.

43 BT, who was very ill at the time of trial, was awarded $160,000 in general damages.

44 [1999] NSWSC 1082, [97].

45 [2004] NSWCA 97, (2004) 59 NSWLR 639.

46 Pursuant to the Public Health Act 1991 (NSW), s 17, discussed at *ibid*, [63].

47 Pursuant to the Public Health (General) Regulation 1991 (NSW), s 10 then operative. For discussion, see, e.g.: B McSherry, '*PD v Harvey and Chen*' (2003) 11 *JLM* 18; L Skene, *Law and Medical Practice: Rights, Duties, Claims and Defences* (2nd edn, Lexisnexis Butterworths, Sydney, 2004) 218.

48 For lesser-known cases concerning non-patient suits for HIV-transmission, see, e.g.: *Lemon v Stewart*, 111 Md App 511, 682 A 2d 1177 (1996) (no duty to inform members of patient's extended family of the patient's HIV-positive status); *NOL v Dist of Columbia*, 674 A 2d 498 (DC 1995) (no duty to patient's husband to disclose patient's HIV-positive status).

49 31 Cal App 4th 1195, 37 Cal Rptr 2d 518 (Cal Ct App 1995).

50 *ibid*, 1199.

51   525 Pa 558, 583 A 2d 422 (1990). Applied in, e.g.: *CW v Cooper Health Sys*, 906 A 2d 440 (NJ Super Ct 2006).

52   Previously, the trial judge in *Di Marco* had held that the doctors owed Mr Di Marco no duty of care because of no privity between doctor and non–patient (although it was suggested that the result may have been different, and a duty owed, where the patient and the non-patient were married): *ibid*, 423.

53   661 So 2d 278 (SC Fla 1995).

54   Reversing *Pate v Threlkel*, 640 So 2d 183, 186 (Fla Dist Ct App 1994), which had denied any duty of care.

55   661 So 2d 278, 282 (SC Fla 1995).

56   291 NJ Super 619, 677 A 2d 1188 (App Div 1996).

57   *ibid*, 627.

58   *ibid*, 625–26.

59   *ibid*, 627.

60   The terminology adopted in other academic commentary too, e.g.: P Case, 'Confidence Matters: The Rise and Fall of Informational Autonomy in Medical Law' (2003) 11 *Med L Rev* 208, fn 18, citing, *inter alia*, *BT v Oei*. See too: D Bell and B Bennett, 'Genetic Secrets and the Family' (2001) 9 *Med L Rev* 130, 151–52.

61   *Reisner v The Regents of the Uni of California*, 37 Cal Rptr 2d 518, 523 (Cal Ct App 1995).

62   See Chapter 3, pp 80–85.

63   [1999] NSWSC 1082.

64   *ibid*, [98].

65   *ibid*, [95].

66   525 Pa 558, 583 A 2d 422 (1990).

67   854 WE 2d 865, 871 (Tenn 1993), citing, e.g., dicta in: *Gammill v US*, 727 F 2d 950, 954 (10th Cir 1984).

68   The phrase used at *ibid*, 872.

69   677 A 2d 1188, 1192 (NJ Super Ct App Div 1996).

70   *A-G v Guardian Newspapers (No 2)* [1990] 1 AC 109 (HL) 215.

71   G Laurie, *Responses to the 'Whose hands on your genes?' Consultation*, available at: <http://www.hgc. gov.uk/Client/Content_wide.asp?ContentId=424>.

72   M Brazier, 'Do No Harm—Do Patients have Responsibilities Too?' (2006) 65 *CLJ* 397.

73   *ibid*, 413 (original emphasis).

74   C Hook *et al*, *Primer on Medical Genomics Part XIII: Ethical and Regulatory Issues* (2004) 79 *Mayo Clinical Procedure* 645, 646, as reproduced in: L Gostin *et al*, *Law, Science and Medicine* (3rd edn, Foundation Press, New York NY, 2005) 79.

75   K Offit *et al*, 'The "Duty to Warn" a Patient's Family Members about Hereditary Disease Risks' (2994) 292 *J of the American Medical Assn* 1469, as reproduced in: L Gostin *et al*, *ibid*, 77.

76   B Furrow *et al*, *Health Law: Cases, Materials and Problems* (6th edn, Am Casebook Series, Thomson West St Paul MN, 2008) 1366. Others ask whether, for a child non-patient, the HCP should be compelled to disclose to a different third party, such as a parent, or a court, or other public authority: A LaFrance, *Bioethics: Health Care, Human Rights and the Law* (2nd edn, LexisNexis Publishing, Newark NJ, 2009) 993.

77   R Dworkin, 'Getting What We should from Doctors: Rethinking Patient Autonomy and the Doctor-Patient Relationship' (2003) 13 *Health Matrix* 235, 277–78.

78   51 Wash App 781, 754 P 2d 1302 (1988).

79   *ibid*, 783.

80   (1994), 112 DLR (4th) 257 (Ont Gen Div) 401.

81   144 Cal App 3d 888, 193 Cal Rptr 733 (1983). See too, on this point: *Hardee v Bio-Medical Applications of SC Inc*, 370 SC 511, 516 (SC 2006).

82   *ibid*, 892–93.

83   D Bell and B Bennett, 'Genetic Secrets and the Family' (2001) 9 *Med L Rev* 130,130. See also: S Keeling, 'Duty to Warn of Genetic Harm in Breach of Patient Confidentiality' (2004) 12 *JLM* 235, 237.

84   L Skene, 'Patients' Rights or Family Responsibilities? Two Approaches to Genetic Testing' (1998) 6 *Med L Rev* 1, 6.

85   D Bell and B Bennett, 'Genetic Secrets and the Family' (2001) 9 *Med L Rev* 130, 130.

86   G Laurie, 'The Most Personal Information of All: An Appraisal of Genetic Privacy in the Shadow of the Human Genome Project' (1996) 10 *Intl J of Law, Policy and the Family* 74, 82.

87   Contained in the ALRC publications: *Protection of Human Genetic Information* (Issues Paper 26, 2002), especially [8.66]; *Protection of Human Genetic Information* (DP 66, 2002), especially [18.53]; *Essentially Yours: The Protection of Human Genetic Information in Australia* (Rep 96, 2003), especially [21.46]–[21.51]. See also the reports, American Society of Human Genetics and the American College of Medical Genetics, 'Points to Consider: Ethical, Legal, and Psychosocial Implications of Genetic Testing in Children and Adolescents' (1995) 57 *Am J of Human Genetics* 1233, 1234–36; and: by the Society's Social Issues Sub-Committee on Familial Disclosure, 'Professional Disclosure of Familial Genetic Information' (1998) 62 *Am J of Human Genetics* 474.

88   ALRC (Rep 96, 2003), *ibid*, [21.51].

89   G Laurie, 'The Most Personal Information of All: An Appraisal of Genetic Privacy in the Shadow of the Human Genome Project' (1996) 10 *Intl J of Law, Policy and the Family* 74, 84, and by the same author: 'Obligations Arising from Genetic Information: Negligence and the Protection of Familial Interests' (1999) 11 *CFLQ* 109; J McHale, 'Genetic Screening and Testing the Child Patient' [1997] *CFLQ* 33, I Brown and P Gannon, 'Confidentiality and the Human Genome Project: A Prophecy for Conflict', in S McLean, *Contemporary Issues in Law and Medicine* (Dartmouth, London, 1995); K Liddall and A Hall, 'Beyond Bristol and Alder Hey: The Future Regulation of Human Tissue' (2005) 12 *Med L Rev* 170, 185–86; M Brazier, 'Do No Harm—Do Patients have Responsibilities Too?' (2006) 65 *CLJ* 397, 412.

90   D Bell and B Bennett, 'Genetic Secrets and the Family' (2001) 9 *Med L Rev* 130, 149–52; L Andrews, 'The Genetic Information Superhighway: Rules of the Road for Contacting Relatives and Recontacting Former Patients' in B Knoppers (ed), *Human DNA: Law and Policy* (Kluwer Law International, The Hague, 1997) 133, 136–38; L Skene, 'Patients' Rights or Family Responsibilities? Two Approaches to Genetic Testing' (1998) 6 *Med L Rev* 1, 29–30; B McGivern, 'Tortious Liability for (Selected) Genetic Harm: Exploring the Arguments' (2002) 10 *Torts LJ* 41, 48; P Florencio and E Ramanathan, 'Secret Code: The Need for Enhanced Privacy Protections in the United States and Canada to Prevent Employment Discrimination Based on Genetic and Health Information' (2001) 39 *Osgoode Hall LJ* 77, fn 59, citing also, for a similar view: W Flanagan, 'Genetic Data and Medical Confidentiality' (1995) 3 *Health LJ* 269, 287; S Suter, 'Whose Genes Are These Anyway? Familial Conflicts over Access to Genetic Information' (1993) 91 *Michigan L Rev* 1854, 1881–82. For judicial commentary on the ALRC's final report, see: The Hon Michael Black, 'Genetics in the Courtroom' (2003) 26 *U of New South Wales LJ* 755.

91   E Clayton, 'What should the Law Say about Disclosure of Genetic Information to Relatives?' (1998) 1 *J Health Care L and Policy* 373, 388–90.

92   The position put, or noted, in, e.g.: W Flanagan, 'Genetic Data and Medical Confidentiality' (1995) 3 *Health LJ* 269, [35]; C Ngwena and R Chadwick, 'Genetic Diagnostic Information and the Duty of Confidentiality' [1993] *Med Law Intl* 73; R Gilbar, 'Medical Confidentiality within the Family: The Doctor's Duty Reconsidered' (2004) 18 *Intl J of Law, Policy and the Family* 195; P Case, 'Confidence Matters: The Rise and Fall of Informational Autonomy in Medical Law' (2003) 11 *Med L Rev* 208; M Bottis, 'Comment on a View Favouring Ignorance of Genetic Confidentiality' (2000) 7 *Euro J of Health Law* 173.

93   Gilbar, *ibid*, 206–7.

94   *ibid*.

95   L Skene, 'Patients' Rights Or Family Responsibilities?—Two Approaches To Genetic Testing' (1998) 6 *Med L Rev* 1, 32–35, discussing the legal /rights/privacy model, and the medical familial model.

96   *ibid*, citing, at fn 3, *Ethical Issues in Clinical Genetics* (Chair, Martin Bobrow, Paediatric Research Unit, Guy's Hospital, London, Oct 1991).

97   L Skene, 'Legal Regulation of Genetic Testing: Balancing Privacy and Family Interests' in A Iltis *et al* (eds), *Legal Perspectives in Bioethics* (Routledge Taylor & Francis, New York NY, 2008) ch 12, esp 209

('the law must ... take a "familial" approach when considering the privacy of genetic information, as distinct from the "individual rights" approach that is common in western liberalism').

[98]　e.g.: J Dolgin, 'Biological Evaluations: Blood, Genes, and Family' (2008) 41 *Akron L Rev* 347, 393–94, and by the same author: 'The Evolution of the "Patient": Shifts in Attitudes About Consent, Genetic Information, and Commercialization in Health Care' (2005) 34 *Hofstra L Rev* 137; M Kovalesky, 'To Disclose or not to Disclose: Determining the Scope and Exercise of a Physician's Duty to Warn Third Parties of Genetically-Transmissible Conditions' (2008) 76 *U Cincinnati L Rev* 1019, 1029–31; S Suter, 'Whose Genes Are These Anyway?: Familial Conflicts Over Access to Genetic Information' (1993) 91 *Michigan L Rev* 1854.

[99]　D Bell and B Bennett, 'Genetic Secrets and the Family' (2001) 9 *Med L Rev* 130, 132.

[100]　[1999] EWCA Civ 1533, [2000] PNLR 87.

[101]　As noted, too, in: D Bell and B Bennett, 'Genetic Secrets and the Family' (2001) 9 *Med L Rev* 130, 152–53.

[102]　See pp 81–83, citing, e.g.: *W v Egdell* [1990] Ch 359 (CA); *R v Crozier* [1991] Crim LR 138 (CCA).

[103]　G Laurie, *Genetic Privacy* (CUP, Cambridge, 2002) 270.

[104]　31 Cal App 4th 1195, 1203, 37 Cal Rptr 2d 518, 523.

[105]　e.g., *Bradshaw v Daniel*, 854 SW 2d 865, 872 (SC Tenn 1993) (there were foreseeable risks for 'identifiable third persons in the patient's immediate family' emanating from the patient's Rocky Mountains fever).

[106]　e.g., *Pate v Threlkel*, 661 So 2d 278, 282 (1995) (in the case of genetic diseases inherited by a non-patient, biological relatives 'fall within the zone of foreseeable risk').

[107]　M Jones, *Medical Negligence* (4th edn, Sweet & Maxwell, London, 2008) 155.

[108]　Hypothetical example given by Clarke JA in *X and Y v Pal* (1991) 23 NSWLR 26 (CA), and also referred, *ibid*, 154. See too: S Keeling, 'Duty to Warn of Genetic Harm in Breach of Patient Confidentiality' (2004) 12 *JLM* 235, 237.

[109]　Noted in: *AAA v BBB* [2005] WASC 139, [80] (but this was not such a case). See too Keeling, *ibid*, 242.

[110]　[1999] NSWSC 1082.

[111]　*ibid*, [98].

[112]　854 WE 2d 865 (Tenn 1993).

[113]　C Parker, 'Camping Trips and Family Trees: Must Tennessee Physicians Warn their Patients' Relatives of Genetic Risks?' (1998) 65 *Tennessee L Rev* 585, 597.

[114]　559 A 2d 530, 535 (1989).

[115]　T Kiely, *Modern Tort Liability: Recovery in the '90s* (John Wiley & Sons, New York, 1990) 319–20.

[116]　[2000] 2 AC 59 (HL).

[117]　[1970] AC 1004 (HL).

[118]　661 So 2d 278, 282 (Fla 1995).

[119]　677 A 2d 1188, 1192 (NJ Super Ct 1996).

[120]　[1999] NSWSC 1082.

[121]　(2006), 38 CPC (6th) 145 (Ont SCJ).

[122]　A point also made in, e.g.: W Flanagan, 'Genetic Data and Medical Confidentiality' (1995) 3 *Health LJ* 269, [23]; D Bell and B Bennett, 'Genetic Secrets and the Family' (2001) 9 *Med L Rev* 130, 150.

[123]　727 F 2d 950 (10th Cir 1984).

[124]　*ibid*, 954, citing, in particular: *Davis v Rodman*, 227 SW 612 (Ark 1921).

[125]　*ibid*.

[126]　(2006), 38 CPC (6th) 145 (Ont SCJ) [71].

[127]　[1999] NSWSC 1082.

[128]　(1994), 112 DLR (4th) 257 (Ont Gen Div).

[129]　[2006] OJ No 4277 (SCJ) [72].

[130]　31 Cal App 4th 1195, 37 Cal Rptr 2d 518 (Cal Ct App 1995).

[131]　See Chapter 2, pp 45–46, and Chapter 3, pp 77–79.

[132]　(1996) 31 BMLR 83 (CA).

[133]　*Hill v Chief Constable of West Yorkshire* [1989] AC 53 (HL).

134 At least, the class survived a 'cause of action' test, under s 5(1)(a) of the Class Proceedings Act, SO 1992, c 6.
135 *Wenden v Trikha* (1991), 116 AR 81 (Alta QB), aff'd (1993), 14 CCLT (2d) 225 (Alta CA) [69] (Murray J).
136 [1999] EWCA Civ 1533, (1999) Lloyd's Rep Med 351.
137 [2002] NZAR 375 (HC) [34].
138 (1996) 31 BMLR 83 (CA).
139 *Reisner v The Regents of the Uni of California*, 31 Cal App 4th 1195, 1201, 37 Cal Rptr 2d 518 (1995). The defendants pointed to the lack of an 'immediate temporal connection', given the three years' lapse between when Jennifer's doctor did not disclose the information about the blood contamination, and Daniel's injury, but the court stated that '[w]e reject Defendant's euphemistic efforts to limit liability on an artificial and immaterial basis'. Nor was a three-year gap significant in: *Candelario v Teperman*, 789 NYS 2d 133 (App Div 2005).
140 [1988] 2 All ER 648 (QB) 653.
141 e.g.: M King, 'Physician Duty to Warn a Patient's Offspring of Hereditary Genetic Defects: Balancing the Patient's Right to Confidentiality Against the Family Member's Right to Know: Can or Should *Tarasoff* Apply?' (2000) 2 *Quinnipiac Health LJ* 1, 38. Cf: L Deftos, 'Genomic Torts: The Law of the Future: The Duty of Physicians to Disclose the Presence of a Genetic Disease to the Relatives of Their Patients with the Disease' (1997) 32 *U San Francisco L Rev* 105, 131 (referring to 'substantial and surprisingly consistent support from medical, scientific, and legal bodies for allowing disclosure of genetic information to third parties under some circumstances').
142 See Chapter 2, pp 41–43.
143 GMC, *Confidentiality* (2009) [53].
144 [1999] NSWSC 1082. See, too, on the same point.: *McDonald v Sydney South West Area Health Service* [2005] NSWSC 924, [68]; and *AAA v BBB* [2005] WASC 139, [81] ('A medical practitioner treating a patient in respect of a sexually transmissible disease might conceivably be liable to a sexual partner of the patient if such a person is foreseeably at risk of injury but that would be because there is no conflict between the duty owed to the patient and the obligation to the person at risk').
145 *ibid*, [98].
146 *ibid*, [95].
147 i.e., imposing 'liability in an indeterminate amount for an indeterminate time to an indeterminate class' in *Ultramares Corporation v Touche*, 174 NE 441, 444 (Ct App 1931). Also: *Jones v Wright* [1991] 3 All ER 88 (CA) 114 (Stocker LJ): 'Some limitations must be put upon what is reasonably foreseeable if a duty of care is not to be owed to the whole world at large'.
148 (2006), 38 CPC (6th) 145 (Ont SCJ) [76].
149 [1906] 1 KB 160.
150 [1936] 1 IR 384 (HC).
151 e.g.: *BT v Oei* [1999] NSWSC 1082.
152 [2006] OJ No 4277 (SCJ) [75].
153 Discussed in: [1999] NSWSC 1082, [92]–[94].
154 [1999] NSWSC 1082, [98]. Followed, in a different context of where a patient had not previously presented at a surgery, but whose wife sought, unsuccessfully, an appointment for her husband before his death of a brain haemorrhage: *Alexander v Heise* [2001] NSWSC 69.
155 See Chapter 2, p 41.
156 c 22, s 11 (in force 26 Sep 1984). The list of 'notifiable diseases' is contained in s 10, and includes cholera, small pox and typhus. See too, The Public Health (Infectious Diseases) Regulations 1988 (SI No 1546).
157 See n 143 above, and Chapter 2, p 43.
158 Human Genetics Comm, *Inside Information: Balancing the Interests in the Use of Personal Genetic Data* (Dept of Health, London, 2002) [3.68]. For information about the ongoing work of the Commission, see: <http://genome.wellcome.ac.uk/doc_WTD021009.html>, and <http://www.hgc.gov.uk/Client/index.asp?ContentId=1>.
159 *Genetic Screening and Ethical Issues* (Dec 1993), recommendation 10.9.

[160] *ibid*, recommendation 10.10.

[161] BMA, *Human Genetics: Choice and Responsibility* (OUP, Oxford, 1998) 69–70.

[162] 31 Cal App 4th 1195, 1201, 37 Cal Rptr 2d 518, 521–22. See too: *CW v Cooper Health Sys*, 906 A 2d 440, 452 (NJ Super Ct 2006) ('[t]he imposition of this duty of care upon health care providers also promotes sound public policy ... HIV and AIDS is not just a personal tragedy, but a burgeoning public health crisis').

[163] 583 A 2d 422, 424–25 (1990).

[164] [1999] NSWSC 1082, [87].

[165] *Hill v Chief Constable of West Yorkshire* [1987] UKHL 12, [1989] AC 53 (HL).

[166] *ibid*, 64 (Lord Templeman).

[167] *Reisner v The Regents of the Uni of California*, 31 Cal App 4th 1195, 37 Cal Rptr 2d 518 (App Ct 1995).

[168] *ibid*, 1203.

[169] As quoted at: *Safer v Estate of Pack*, 291 NJ Super 619, 623–4 (NJ Super Ct App Div 1996).

[170] S Suter, 'Whose Genes Are These Anyway? Familial Conflicts Over Access to Genetic Information' (1993) 91 *Michigan L Rev* 1854, 1881.

[171] 789 NYS 2d 133 (App Div 2005).

[172] *ibid*, 135, relying on: *McNulty v City of New York*, 792 NE 2d 162 (2003) (no duty to warn patient's friend to seek medical treatment after contact with patient suffering from infectious meningitis; friend contracted disease).

[173] *Spina v Jack D Weiler Hosp of the Albert Einstein College of Medicine*, 813 NYS 2d 406, 407 (App Div 2006).

[174] Noted in, e.g.: G Laurie, 'Obligations Arising from Genetic Information: Negligence and the Protection of Familial Interests' [1999] *CFLQ* 109, [no pp available]; A Grubb, 'HIV Transmission: Doctor's Liability to Future Partner' (2007) 5 *Med L Rev* 250, (accessed online, no pp available).

[175] See Chapter 2, pp 49–50.

[176] e.g.: *Farraj v King's Healthcare NHS Trust* [2006] EWHC 1228 (QB); *Salih v Enfield HA* [1991] 3 All ER 400 (CA); *Anderson v Forth Valley Health Board* (1998) 14 BMLR 108 (QB); *Rand v East Dorset HA* [2000] Lloyd's Rep Med 181 (QB); *Hardman v Amin* [2000] Lloyd's Rep Med 498 (QB); *Groom v Selby* [2001] EWCA Civ 1522, (2002) 64 BMLR 47.

[177] 31 Cal App 4th 1195, 1204, 37 Cal Rptr 2d 518, 523 (1995).

[178] See, e.g., the discussion in: *CW v Cooper Health Sys*, 906 A 2d 440, 451 (NJ Super Ct 2006).

[179] e.g.: M Brazier, 'Do No Harm—Do Patients have Responsibilities Too?' (2006) 65 *CLJ* 397, 410–11; G Laurie, 'Obligations Arising from Genetic Information: Negligence and the Protection of Familial Interests' [1999] *CFLQ* 109.

[180] *Knightley v Johns* [1982] 1 WLR 349 (CA) (motor vehicle accident occurring in one-way tunnel).

[181] 677 A 2d 1188, 1192–93 (NJ Super Ct 1996).

[182] E Clayton, 'What should the Law Say about Disclosure of Genetic Information to Relatives?' (1998) 1 *J Health Care L and Policy* 373, 388–90.

[183] As quoted at: *Safer v Estate of Pack*, 291 NJ Super 619, 623–4 (1996).

[184] J van Exan, 'The Legal and Ethical Issues Surrounding the Duty to Warn in the Practice of Psychology' (2004) 18 *Windsor Rev of Legal and Social Issues* 123.

[185] G Laurie, 'Obligations Arising From Genetic Information: Negligence and the Protection of Familial Interests' [1999] *CFLQ* 109 (accessed online, no pp available); W Flanagan, 'Genetic Data and Medical Confidentiality' (1995) 3 *Health LJ* 269, [30].

[186] (1994), 112 DLR (4th) 257 (Ont Gen Div).

[187] [1999] NSWSC 1082, [181], [183].

[188] See, e.g., M Brazier, 'Do No Harm—Do Patients have Responsibilities Too?' (2006) 65 *CLJ* 397, fn 72.

[189] 727 F 2d 950 (10th Cir 1984).

[190] *ibid*, 952–53.

[191] *Reisner v The Regents of the Uni of California*, 31 Cal App 4th 1195, 37 Cal Rptr 2d 518, fn 6 (1995).

[192] *ibid*, 1204. In *Healey v Lakeridge Health Corp* (2006), 38 CPC (6th) 145 (Ont SCJ), no duty of care towards the class of cross-infected non-patients was owed, and potential causal problems for this class did not arise for consideration.

[193] [1906] 1 KB 160 (KB).

[194] T Caulfield, 'Testing Adolescents for the Alzheimer Gene: Tensions in Law and Policy' (1997) 25 *Manitoba LJ* 31, [29].

[195] The Hon Michael Black, 'Genetics in the Courtroom' (2003) 26 *U of New South Wales LJ* 755, 'Conclusions'.

[196] For discussion of these enactments, see, e.g.: M Kovalesky, 'To Disclose or not to Disclose: Determining the Scope and Exercise of a Physician's Duty to Warn Third Parties of Genetically-Transmissible Conditions' (2008) 76 *U Cincinnati L Rev* 1019, 1031–33; G McAbee *et al*, Physician's Duty to Warn Third Parties About the Risk of Genetic Diseases' (1998) 102 *Pediatrics* 140. For interesting discussion of genetic harm, see S Keeling, 'Duty to Warn of Genetic Harm in Breach of Patient Confidentiality' (2004) 12 *JLM* 235, 250–53.

Chapter 5

'Bad Samaritan' Liability: Failing to Assist Non-Patients

A INTRODUCTION

In the biblical text,[1] when the 'good Samaritan' stopped to assist a man who had been assaulted and robbed, and gave what emergency medical treatment he could, presumably the Samaritan had no concerns about thereafter being sued, should the treatment not have succeeded! The parable resonates quite differently in the modern age, however—when many HCPs are so concerned about the possibility of being liable in negligence for rendering emergency medical aid, that they may avoid doing so altogether.

This chapter does not deal with the legal position of the Good Samaritan who *assists* in a medical emergency (that is the subject of consideration in Chapter 6). Rather, this chapter focuses upon the 'Levite of the parable'—in other words, upon the HCP who, for whatever reason, chooses to 'look the other way'. The HCP has no antecedent relationship with that victim (the non-patient)—they are true 'strangers' to each other; the HCP perceives an urgent medical situation or emergency; he may, or may not, have a medical specialism particularly suited to deal with the victim's emergency; and he declines or refuses to assist.[2]

There is no suggestion that *mal fides* prompts this hesitancy to get involved, nor that it occurs frequently. Indeed, empirical evidence in England suggests quite the opposite—that the vast majority of doctors *have* acted as Good Samaritans.[3] However, one of the assumptions underpinning the chapter is that hesitancy on the part of HCPs to get involved does exist 'in the real world', for valid and understandable reasons. Whether due to tiredness or exhaustion, worry about litigation, inconvenience, pressures of other work, concerns about not having the correct protective gloves or equipment, being on holiday or 'off-duty',[4] HCPs have openly admitted to concerns about acting as Good Samaritans.[5]

The aim of this chapter, in the first instance, is to examine the position, at common law, of that tired, worried, busy, or off-duty HCP who does not assist. The common law is reluctant to impose a *compulsion* upon a HCP to intervene to assist a stranger in medical need. However, some exceptions **do** exist—and some significant common law jurisprudence from elsewhere, involving the HCP bystander, provokes the question of whether those exceptions should, or could, be widened in English law. These topics are dealt with in Sections B and C, respectively.

Meanwhile, England has no legislation which attempts to transpose 'the moral duty or humanitarian spirit which motivated the good Samaritan'[6] into a *legal duty* upon HCPs to assist those in medical emergencies. Disciplinary sanctions may arise, but there is no question of civil or criminal sanction against the bystander. However, that is precisely what has been implemented in some other common law (and civil) jurisdictions, with a potential for these provisions to be used against HCPs. This somewhat startling scenario is considered in Section D.

Thereafter, the chapter will refer, in Section E, to two causal conundrums which inevitably arise for consideration, should a duty to assist/rescue be applied to a HCP more prevalently than English law presently countenances. Section F concludes.

The topicality of Samaritan law, in general, has been highlighted by the fact that the Irish Law Reform Commission has recently conducted an important consultation on the topic, asking whether any legislation should be introduced in respect of both Bad and Good Samaritans.[7] The potential lessons of any such legislation for England will be considered throughout this chapter and next.

B NO COMMON LAW DUTY TO ASSIST A STRANGER IN A MEDICAL EMERGENCY

Under English law, there is no common law duty imposed upon a bystander to intervene and to offer assistance to a stranger requiring medical treatment. This general proposition has been incontrovertibly set by the House of Lords—

> The very parable of the good Samaritan ... illustrates, in the conduct of the priest and of the Levite who passed by on the other side, an omission which was likely to have as its reasonable and probable consequence damage to the health of the victim of the thieves, but for which the priest and Levite would have incurred no civil liability in English law (*Home Office v Dorset Yacht Co Ltd*[8]).

—and, in the context of HCPs who choose not to intervene or to assist, the common law is equally plain:

- The 'doctor in the house' who volunteers to assist a lady in the audience who, overcome by the drama or by the heat in the theatre, has fainted away, is impelled to act by no greater duty than that imposed by his own Hippocratic oath (*In re F (Mental Patient: Sterilisation)*.[9]
- a doctor, of course, is not obliged, *merely because he is a doctor*, to provide ... medical treatment (*R (on the application of Burke) v GMC*).[10]
- a doctor who happened to witness a road accident will very likely go to the assistance of anyone injured, but he is not under any legal obligation to do so, save in certain limited circumstances which are not relevant [...] and the relationship of doctor and patient does not arise (*Capital and Counties plc v Hampshire CC*).[11]

Interestingly, although both *In re F*, and more recently, the Irish Law Reform Commission,[12] put great store by what the Hippocratic Oath may require from a moral point of view, one American court was not prepared to concede that the Oath indeed had that effect—'[e]ven the Hippocratic Oath, by which every doctor is morally bound, assumes a pre-existing relationship of patient and physician.'[13]

Hence, the general common law position is that a HCP is under no duty to attend upon a person who is sick, even in an emergency, if that person is one with whom the HCP is not, and has never been, in a formal professional relationship. To such a rule, there are common law exceptions, which will be considered later in Part C. Meanwhile, however, some further attention to this important general rule is warranted.

1. The no-duty-to-assist rule illustrated in medical scenarios

No cases have arisen for judicial determination in England thus far, where a HCP has been sued successfully for failing to assist a stranger in medical need, so far as the author's searches can ascertain. However, a claimant has sought to push the boundaries of when a HCP will be legally required to assist a non-patient.

> In *Bishara v Sheffield Teaching Hosp NHS Trust*,[14] the following alleged facts and respective parties' divergent positions are taken from the interlocutory skirmishes in the case.[15] Ms Bishara (B), a young house doctor in a dental surgery, met with an older colleague (the regional postgraduate dental dean), Dr F, for a 'career chat'. The interview did not go particularly well. B became upset and (according to her legal claim) then fell ill with migraine towards the end of the meeting. At this point, the evidence of the parties diverged considerably. B alleged that she asked Dr F to call an ambulance, but he did not do so, simply terminating the interview and leaving her in a state of collapse on the stairs outside his office, where she remained for some four hours. Dr F, on the other hand, strongly denied these allegations, alleged that the first that he knew of B's ill condition was after the interview, when he was told that she was sitting on the stairs, and that from then onwards, Dr F and his staff did all they possibly could to get help for her. **Held:** summary judgment in Dr F's favour disallowed; matter sent for trial.

The lower court[16] had granted Dr F summary judgment, on the basis that Ms Bishara's claim had no real prospect of success. This result came about (it was held) because no duty of care could be owed by Dr F to Ms Bishara—even if her version of events was believed (and that would be highly contested), 'her case is simply a claim against a bystander for not helping and so is, on principle, beyond the pale of the law of negligence'[17] (as the defendant NHS Trust put it on behalf of its employee, Dr F). However, on appeal, Sedley LJ considered that it was not possible to say that, legally speaking, no duty of care could be owed by Dr F in these circumstances (although whether that was proven would, of course, be a matter for trial). Hence, the Trust's application for summary judgment was a 'false economy', and the matter had to be re-entered for trial.[18] In particular, Sedley LJ remarked that, on the three-fold principles of reasonable foreseeability, proximity and public policy espoused in *Caparo Industries plc v Dickman*,[19] it was 'arguable (I put it no higher) ... that the particular situation was one of sufficient proximity to take Dr F out of the role of bystander and to require him to take such steps as were reasonable to protect [Ms Bishara's] wellbeing.'[20] Without coming to any concluded view on the point, the proximity factors in this case were said to *possibly* amount to:

- the circumstances out of which the complaint of injury arose (a stressful career meeting);
- the relationship between the parties (the HCP was a colleague in a supervisory role, conducting that career meeting);
- a request for medical assistance made by the alleged victim, which was allegedly refused (the evidence on this point would be crucial, should the matter proceed to trial); and
- the continuing physical proximity between the HCP and the alleged victim during the period that the illness manifested/continued.[21]

On the subject of the third *Caparo* limb, that of policy, Sedley LJ stated that 'whether the case is one of simple omission and therefore excluded as a matter of policy from the arena of tort liability, has to be decided in the light of the facts.'[22]

It should be emphasised that this decision falls well short of casting any duty on the part of a HCP to come to a victim's assistance, entailed no proof of wrongdoing on the relevant HCP's part whatsoever, and no further litigation in the case has been reported since.[23] It is of interest, however, as a rare instance of a medically-related alleged omission-to-act claim in English litigation.

Moving off-shore, the no-duty-to-assist principle has arisen in Canadian medico-legal case law:

> In the Ontario case of *Stevenson v Clearview Riverside Resort*,[24] a group of ambulance attendants and their friends went to a beach for a volleyball tournament and a party. Just before midnight, one of their group, 27-year-old Chris Stevenson (S), dived from a wooden dock into the Nottawasaga River, where the water was only inches deep, broke his neck, and suffered quadriplegia. Three of his friends were sitting on the dock at the time, and thought that S was 'kidding' when he was floating face down in the river for a period, until one of them jumped in to turn him over to save him from drowning. Another of the trio, D, was sued in third party proceedings, allegedly for not providing advice to leave S floating in the water after he had been turned over, until the ambulance attendants arrived. The specific allegation raised against D was that, as a trained ambulance officer, she 'failed to take reasonable steps to protect the plaintiff from further injury to his spinal cord, and that she failed to act, or assist or verbally instruct those who were involved in the rescue of the plaintiff, despite her training and experience.' **Held:** the claim against D could not proceed to trial.

The Superior Court of Justice reiterated that, in the absence of some antecedent relationship between HCP and person in need of medical attention, the common law does not compel rescue:

> Canadian law has long recognized the common law principle that there is no positive duty to rescue unless a special relationship exists ... As a matter of law it is clear that there is no obligation on D to participate in the rescue. An off-duty ambulance attendant at a private party cannot be in a category of persons with 'special duty' ... there is no liability attached to a person who stands by while another is in peril in the absence of a special relationship ...[25]

The two other friends of Mr Stevenson who participated in the rescue, and who had no medical training, were also sued in negligence in third party proceedings—but they were treated as 'good Samaritans', because they voluntarily assisted Mr Stevenson by removing him from the water and helping his breathing. They are deferred to Chapter 6 for consideration (the claims against them in negligence were also dismissed).

Hence, while the odd scenario does arise, instances of litigation even being brought against HCPs who allegedly act as mere bystanders are very rare, in either English or Commonwealth case law.

Why the common law adopts the liberal view which it does towards 'bad Samaritans' has been attributed to a mixture of history, economics, societal culture, and the difficulty in moderating the morals which should govern human nature by the 'blunt instrument' of legal doctrine.

2. Reasons for the no-duty-to-assist rule

Cardozo J once said, 'Danger invites rescue. The cry of distress is the summons to relief'.[26] However, it is an invitation which can be refused, and a cry which can be ignored, according to the English common law. Several justifications have been *judicially* put forward in support of the common law's no-duty-to-assist stance. Drawn from English, Canadian, Australian, Scottish and American decisions (which have arisen in all types of non-medical and medical contexts), they are summarised below.

Although it is undoubtedly true that many of these arguments supporting the common law rule were not made within the context of a failure to give emergency medical treatment at all,[27] it is, nevertheless, important to appreciate how judicially oft-cited, and numerous, the arguments are—thereby placing this common law rule in almost 'immutable and sacrosanct' territory. As the following discussion demonstrates, however, most of these viewpoints have attracted some sharply-worded contrary opinion:

The wrong is an omission

As already canvassed in Chapter 2,[28] the common law does not, generally speaking, impose liability for what are considered to be 'pure omissions' or 'mere omissions'[29]—which, in the present context, includes a failure of a HCP to assist an injured person with whom he has no antecedent relationship.

Some judicial examples of lawful 'Bad Samaritan'-type activity may sound rather startling. Failing to stop a blind stranger stepping out in front of busy traffic is not actionable, whereas the positive act of carelessly bumping into, and propelling him in front of, the traffic, may well give rise to actionable negligence.[30] A person is under no duty to shout a warning to a stranger who is not paying attention and is about to walk over a cliff edge.[31] It is legally permissible to eat lunch on a beach while watching another beach-goer drown.[32] An observer can watch a neighbour's goods being destroyed by rain, when minimal effort would have salvaged them.[33] Absent a pre-existing responsibility for the child, a fit strong adult can watch that child drown in shallow water, although the child was easily able to be hauled to safety.[34]

Therefore, while it is true that the law's reluctance to impose affirmative duties may have the unfortunate consequence of actually sanctioning a defendant's 'wilful indifference to the safety of others', nevertheless, the resistance to affirmative duties to help stems from the moral and political value-judgment that 'it is usually considered worse to do harm than to fail to help'.[35]

Two issues are legally *irrelevant*, and do not, of themselves, establish any duty of care on a HCP to assist a victim in need. First, it does not matter that a HCP's failure to assist is contrary to what a reasonable body of medical opinion considered should have been done.[36] In other words, it does not assist to prove a duty that breach may be made out. Secondly, the mere fact that a HCP's lack of intervention could foreseeably result in injury or death for the victim does not create a legal obligation, or duty, to assist either. As explained earlier in Chapter 2,[37] under the tri-partite *Caparo* test, foreseeability of harm is only one element necessary to establish a duty on the HCP's part to exercise care towards a non-patient—the victim must establish sufficient proximity between the HCP and himself too. Exceptionally, this may be possible, as Section C describes, but it will be a rare thing. As Norris notes, had a warning been shouted to a cliff-top walker about to plunge to his death, '[he] would have looked up and saved himself. So why have I no responsibility for them in law? All I had to do was be neighbourly and/or careful: is that too much to ask? The explanation can only be that ... the law imposes no duty of care ... [because] I have assumed no responsibility to the unfortunate victim [and] the victim has not relied on me.'[38] Readers are referred back to Chapter 2 for a fuller discussion of the roles which 'assumption of responsibility', and 'reliance' by the claimant upon the skill or care of the defendant, continue to play in the development of a duty of care analysis, especially insofar as novel third party claims scenarios are concerned. These will be explored shortly in Section C, when the exceptional 'duties to assist' on HCPs are discussed.

Finally, it has sometimes been said that the division between an act (where a duty attaches) and an omission (where it does not, generally speaking) is meaningless, blurry, and lacks a consistent definition. For example, what really happens when a driver hits another car which is stopped at a red light? Is it the positive act of driving, or the omission to keep a proper lookout and to brake in time?[39] In *Stovin v Wise*, Lord Hoffmann sought to answer this criticism of the common law's stance, by admitting that '[o]f course it is true that the conditions necessary to bring about an event always consist of a combination of acts and omissions', but that the law of negligence 'distinguish[es] between regulating the way in which an activity may be conducted, and imposing a duty to act upon a person who is not carrying on any relevant activity [at all]'.[40] It is only in the *latter* case that the English common law will not impose a duty to act carefully. However, the blurred lines between acts and omissions do not trouble us in this chapter, for we are considering the type of scenarios where the HCP does not assist a non-patient *at all*—where, say, a HCP does not respond to a call to help Lord Goff's fainted theatre patron.[41] That is, in legal terms, a pure omission; and, ordinarily, no duty of care will attach to the HCP in those circumstances.

A literal interpretation of Lord Atkin's neighbour principle

Lord Atkin's classic statement in *Donoghue v Stevenson*—'[t]he rule that you are to love your neighbour becomes in law, *you must not injure your neighbour*'[42]—has been taken literally by some judges, who consider[43] that Lord Atkin contemplated the neighbour principle as requiring defendants to take reasonable care to avoid doing some positive act that might cause injury to another. That expression did not intend to impose a duty on defendants to protect persons against injury—whether that harm presented from the defendant himself, from some third party, or from some naturally-occurring accident—merely where the defendant *did nothing* to prevent the injury from happening. Recently, in *Mitchell v Glasgow CC*, Lord Scott expressly cited and relied upon Lord Atkin's neighbour principle to again reiterate that 'it is accepted ... that the Pharisee who passed by the injured man on the other side of the road would not, by his failure to offer any assistance, have incurred any legal liability ... The Pharisee, both in England and Wales and in Scotland, would have been in breach of no more than a moral obligation.'[44]

Of course, reliance upon particular passages and phrases of Lord Atkin's speech can point quite the other way, given that his Lordship also referred to the duty to 'take reasonable care to avoid acts *or omissions* which you can reasonably foresee would be likely to injure your neighbour'.[45] Additionally, much of Lord Atkin's 'neighbour principle', based as it was upon the foreseeability of harm to one's neighbour and an undefined concept of proximity, has been substantially revamped and reworked by later authorities[46]—rendering reliance upon specific phrases of the judgment (one way or the other) less-than-ideal.

The importance of individual liberty

The no-duty-to-rescue/assist rule has been upheld on the basis that to insist upon rescue would sit uncomfortably with the individual liberty of doing as one chooses—provided one does not *do harm* to other people.[47] In *Stovin v Wise*, the House of Lords said that, '[i]n political terms, it is less of an invasion of an individual's freedom for the law to require him to consider the safety of others in his actions than to impose upon him a duty to rescue or protect.'[48] Relatedly, to impose such a duty would place would-be interveners under an 'intolerable burden' to be on the look-out to prevent all foreseeable harm.[49]

This argument proved a 'clincher' for the Irish Law Reform Commission in its report on Samaritan law. It maintained that 'the imposition of a positive duty to intervene would constitute too great an infringement of an individual's freedom, an important feature of the common law.'[50]

In rebuttal, however, Silver contends[51] that, although the law 'should not be in the business of coercing kindness', the fact remains that to insist that people in society restrict their own freedoms and choices for the benefit of others has many precedents, and that the benefit to society where individuals do have their freedoms restricted can outweigh the individual cost of bearing that restriction. Silver cites laws that require parents to send their children to school, laws that require employers to provide safe systems of work, and laws that require the wearing of seatbelts or bicycle helmets, as examples—and 'in much the same way, the *benefit* provided by a legal rescue duty— the saving of lives—justifies the deprivation of our freedom to remain passive in emergencies.'[52] McIvor also gives the 'individual liberty' argument short shrift, noting that a duty of positive action is not unduly restrictive if, 'in utilitarian terms ... the overall effect is to maximise liberty'.[53]

A large class of potential defendants

Where one fails to intervene to help someone in danger or distress, then many others may have 'looked the other way' too. Hence, any duty to assist 'may apply to a large and indeterminate class of people who happen to be able to do something.'[54] In that case, a successful suit by the victim against *all* those onlookers could impose a considerable burden upon insurers, possibly giving rise to very large numbers of claims, and for large amounts of damages.[55]

Those who favour the imposition of a duty-to-assist rule, however, remain unconvinced by this argument, with Silver, for example, remarking: 'There is no reason to limit individual liability simply because others have simultaneously engaged in the same unacceptable conduct. When a group of persons commits a robbery, for example, each is no less morally or legally responsible than if he had acted alone.'[56]

'Why pick on me?'

This is the obverse of the previous point. If, out of a group of onlookers who were capable of rendering assistance but who did not, the victim sues *one* onlooker only (the one with the 'deepest pocket', or against whom the victim has a vendetta, perhaps), then this gives rise to a 'moral' dilemma, or the 'why pick on me?' argument, as Lord Hoffmann termed it.[57]

Of course, the contrary argument is—'why not?'. Legal practice is littered with examples of where a claimant carefully chooses which, from a number of potential defendants, he prefers to sue—and several motivations, whether they be financial, personal, or tactical, may prompt that choice. If a defendant believes that another was responsible for the harm caused to the claimant, third-party proceedings are available to draw in another to the litigation. As the Irish Commission noted, the 'why one and not another defendant' problem here is as solvable as it is in ordinary negligence cases where there are multiple defendants.[58]

Expending money not justifiable

In blunt economic terms, the common law cannot justify a rule that requires a bystander, who is not involved with the stranger's activities *and* who has not created the danger himself through his own wrongdoing, to spend money on behalf of the stranger's rescue.[59] The possibility of a duty-to-assist being applied in circumstances which would put the bystander to expense to carry out the rescue is a deterrent to recognising such a duty at all.

Academic commentators such as McInnes[60] and Williams[61] argue, however, that HCPs have been permitted to recover their expenses and reasonable remuneration incurred in rescuing another's life (even when such rescue is unfortunately unsuccessful) in Canada and in the US, and that English law should also recognise a restitutionary claim for such expenses as a matter of course. In the medical context, it is interesting to note a recent decision of the Court of Quebec Small Claims Division, in *Coopersmith c Air Canada*:[62] The court had to decide an important, and hitherto unresolved, point of law—'[w]hen a physician travelling on an international flight assists another passenger in need of medical attention at the insistence of the person in charge of the cabin, is the physician entitled to a reward from the airline for this service?' The court answered this, 'yes', and Dr Coopersmith, who tended to three passengers during the course of the flight, recovered Can\$1,000. The court reaffirmed that Dr Coopersmith was not under a legal obligation to act as a Good Samaritan during the course of the flight.[63] However, where HCPs do so, the court adjudged that airlines are required to pay those HCPs for their medical work, and for any loss of enjoyment of the flight or their travel as a result of the flight.[64] Were the principle of this judgment to be widely endorsed in English law, then a corresponding affirmative duty-to-assist may be more tenable.

Exposure to danger not justifiable either

There is also the delicacy of imposing an affirmative duty to intervene when, as the Irish Law Reform Commission frankly remarks, 'a rescue, by definition, will usually entail some element of danger—both for the stranger and the good Samaritan.'[65]

In fact, this sobering reality has been well-illustrated in English law in the past:

> In *Baker v TE Hopkins & Son Ltd*,[66] TE Hopkins, a building company, was engaged to clear a deep well of water, which was done by means of a petrol-driven pump. The operation of the pump created a haze of fumes in the well, including a dangerous concentration of the colourless gas, carbon monoxide. Two workers went down into the well regardless (and despite instructions from the foreman to wait for extra assistance), and were overcome by the poisonous gas which rendered them unconscious. Dr Baker was called to the site, and was lowered into the well, with a rope tied to his body, in order to see if he could rescue the men (even though he was also warned not to enter the well). Efforts to then pull Dr B to the surface failed, because the rope which was tied to him became caught in a downpipe. By the time that it could be disentangled by personnel arriving from the fire brigade with suitable breathing apparatus, Dr B had died (as had the two workmen). **Held:** Hopkins were liable in negligence for the death of Dr B, because it was a natural and proper consequence of Hopkins' negligence towards the two workmen that someone would attempt to rescue them, and Hopkins should have foreseen the potential dire consequences of any rescue attempt.

Of course, there was no question of Dr Baker having been under a *legal* duty to respond to the summons for help, with the court noting that his motives for acting as he did were sourced in altruism and humanity: 'the late Dr Baker acted as he did in an urgent and passionate desire to do everything that he could, even at great risk to himself, to preserve human life.'[67]

Silver, who advocates for a duty-to-assist rule, however, points out[68] that any duty-to-rescue rule would surely stop short of requiring any bystander to be forced to imperil his own life for the sake of a stranger, and that it should be possible to frame a rule that suspends such a duty if a rescue would entail, for the bystander, a risk of serious bodily harm, damage to health or to property, or risk of interference with obligations to third parties. Ashworth also observes that the law should stop short of imposing any duty that obliges a rescuer to place himself in actual *or even perceived* danger.[69]

In its consultation, the Irish Commission asked whether a duty-to-assist ought to be imposed in so-called cases of 'easy rescue', i.e., a rescue that does not impose expense, danger, or undue inconvenience upon the bystander.[70] Ultimately, however, the Commission recommended against any such duty, principally because of its 'uncertain nature'.[71] What was 'easy' would be subjective, and dependent upon the particular onlooker concerned; requiring some 'least effort' standard may benefit the victim very little, if at all; and defining and identifying the borderline between an 'easy' and a 'difficult' rescue 'would pose a virtually impossible task'.[72] Duxbury, on the other hand, remarks that the problem with an 'easy rescue' principle is, not its uncertainty, but its enforceability: '[t]he strongest swimmers at the beach are the ones who should be able to save the plight of the drowning child by making only a slight or moderate sacrifice. But if, for whatever reason, the strongest swimmers do not reveal their hands, it will probably be impossible to show that anyone is in breach of their legal duty.'[73]

Altruistic qualities undermined

Would the admiration which the court, and the public, felt for rescuers in Dr Baker's position ('a brave and humane doctor', as Barry J described him[74]) be undermined if Dr Baker had been compelled by law to turn up at the well and do what he could to assist? And while kindness and sympathy may motivate selfless behaviour towards the ill and injured, is it the place of the law to compel these sentiments?

In a rather bleak judgment, Judge Ware was driven to say in an old American case (where a number of persons floating at sea were passed by 'in one of the most frequented parts of the American seas', leaving many of them to a 'watery grave') that the bystanders who continually passed by may not have understood that 'sometimes even in godliness there is gain', but rather, it might have been necessary to 'tempt them by the allurements of pecuniary profit, if they can be led by no other, to acts of humanity and mercy.'[75] To turn that proposition around: rather than pecuniary *temptations* to encourage rescue, should the common law recognise a general duty-to-rescue principle that would financially *punish* those who omitted to rescue (via an award of damages)?

Clearly, the common law has **not** considered it correct to compel altruism. Indeed, the Irish Commission reiterated that any duty to intervene is 'morally motivated', to transform it into a legal duty 'would be to deprive it of its altruistic quality',[76] and that 'while altruism plays an important part in the formation of legal principles, the concept of forced volunteerism appears to be a contradiction in terms.'[77]

An historical perspective

One American court has attributed the common law's longstanding lenient treatment of the bystander to the age of accident-prone industrialisation: '[a] sense of rugged individualism, combined with the harsh realities of industrialization, formed an impenetrable shield of immunity around all who failed to help, even those who could, with the greatest of ease, prevent the most violent and senseless of deaths.'[78]

Obversely though, if legal doctrine is truly a product of timing, then it has been contended that a duty-to-assist rule is even *more* warranted in the modern on-the-move society, when support and community networks are much-diminished—'[a]s the bonds among community members weaken, so must the social pressure and individual desire to assist members in distress. A legal duty to rescue would, in part, replace the waning social duty.'[79]

Some exceptional circumstances do exist

As the House of Lords has pointed out,[80] it is not true to say that the English common law creates an immunity around **all** those who fail to act—there are a number of 'special relationships' where the law *does* recognise a duty to protect the person or property of another in certain circumstances, breach of which will give rise to liability in negligence.

For example, positive duties to protect or avert harm or rescue *are* imposed, variously, upon occupiers (towards visitors and trespassers[81]), upon the police (towards prisoners in custody who are at risk of suicide[82]), upon those in control of a dangerous thing on or near a roadway (towards other road users[83]), and upon a landowner (towards an adjoining landowner, in respect of a fire hazard created on the former's land[84]). These are established, and exceptional, bases upon which there may be a duty to take positive steps to protect others from harm or to rescue their persons or property.

However, the law has been reluctant to expand these 'special relationships'. As Todd remarks, development of any duty-to-assist has been restricted, partly because 'the courts have been fearful of introducing a new and unpredictable area of responsibility'.[85] Certainly, to date, a HCP–stranger in medical need has not been considered to be a relationship to warrant exceptional treatment (subject to the discussion in Section C below).

Additional factors

The previously-mentioned reasons can be sourced from various judgments, but in addition to those, at least five other justifications for the no-duty-to-assist rule have been advanced by academic commentators.[86]

First, any such rule would foster instances of 'officious meddling' by 'do-gooders' in the affairs of strangers, but on the other hand, would not foster an enormous increase in rescue efforts, given the number of uncoerced rescues that already happen at the hands of such 'do-gooders'. Secondly, were a duty-to-assist rule a reality, then rescues and assistance would be rendered chaotic by 'too many rescuers' and by overly defensive and protective measures being invoked, all with the aim of avoiding the threat of legal action. Thirdly, the bystanders at risk from legal action under a duty-to-assist rule could be difficult to trace after the event, if there were few or no witnesses to the incident. Those who feared that they might have breached a duty-to-rescue rule would be unlikely to co-operate with authorities in any later investigations of the incident, thus rendering the enforceability of such a duty very problematic. Fourthly, people might take foolish or unnecessary risks if they were aware that bystanders were under a legal duty to assist them. Fifthly, if a duty-to-assist were to be the law, then the reluctant rescuers would carry its impact, and because the quality of rescue efforts by reluctant rescuers generally would be of lower quality than that of purely voluntary rescuers, that could be to the detriment of the person in peril.

Finally, in his excellent review of the French duty-to-rescue rule, Tomlinson argues[87] that any duty-to-assist rule is both unnecessary and even inappropriate in the modern era of state-organised and publicly-funded co-ordinated emergency services. For one thing, '[n]o longer do onlookers summon the nearest doctor to aid a person in peril, but they contact emergency medical services to transport the victim to the nearest hospital with the highest technologically-advanced equipment available to treat emergency patients. It is the rare case where the passer-by or the nearest physician can do something significant to assist a person in peril'. Moreover, argues Tomlinson, '[c]itizens, aware of the benefits modern medicine offers, now expect the State to assume responsibility for organizing emergency medical services. Rescue has become the job of professionals. All of us contribute to paying for those services through our taxes.' All of this diminishes a need for a duty-to-assist to be imposed upon the HCP.

In summary: when considered in combination, the historical, cultural, and doctrinal reasons advanced above seem destined to give rise to the conclusion that a mandatory general duty-to-rescue principle is unlikely to feature in English common law (subject to point 3 below). This is notwithstanding that some judges consider its absence to be one of the common law's more 'notorious'[88] and 'perverse'[89] aspects, and that it could eventually become 'repugnant to modern thinking'.[90]

3. The relationship between the Convention and the no-duty-to-assist rule

Two points arise for brief discussion, concerning the interplay between the common law's no-duty-to-assist rule, and the implementation of the European Convention on Human Rights into English jurisprudence.

First, as mentioned in Chapter 1,[91] courts themselves are public authorities, pursuant to s 6(3) of the Human Rights Act 1998 (HRA), and hence, they must ensure that English common law is compatible with the Convention's obligations, even when adjudicating on disputes between purely private parties (the so-called 'horizontal effect' of the HRA). Hence, Brazier has argued that art 2 of the Convention (which provides that '[e]veryone's right to life shall be guaranteed by law') may require the common law rule to be revisited, and that a reluctance to uphold affirmative duties to act towards strangers does not sit comfortably with art 2:

> One beneficial consequence of an emphasis on rights is that the English courts may well at some point have to revisit a duty to rescue. A legal system which imposes no responsibility to provide even easy rescue may not conform to art 2 of the Human Rights Convention. My right to life may impose duties on my fellow citizens.[92]

Williams adds that art 3 (which provides that '[n]o one shall be subjected to torture or to inhuman or degrading treatment or punishment') may be relevant in this context too, so that a denial of emergency medical assistance to a victim may amount to inhuman and degrading treatment towards that party.[93] Wright further argues that the right enshrined in art 8 (respect for private and family life) could arguably be achieved by the imposition of criminal sanctions without a compulsory duty to rescue being recognised in tort, although 'there is something distinctly unattractive about a legal system which denies redress where it can be shown that physical injury or death could have been avoided through the provision of assistance which would have involved no risk to the rescuer.'[94]

Secondly, and as was mooted in Chapter 1,[95] it may be possible for a non-patient to allege that, failing some intervention to assist on the part of a health authority (or its employed HCPs), he is entitled to obtain a judicial remedy, if it can be established that the health authority acted in a way that was incompatible with the victim's Convention rights. Allen poses[96] an interesting theory as to why the state's operational duty to protect the life of a specified individual may be engaged, if a NHS-employed HCP, while acting in the course of his employment, observes Lord Keith's cliff-top walker[97] stride over the cliff to his death, and fails to shout any warning or otherwise prevent the tragedy. Allen's argument (which is put forward as 'one school of thought') follows these lines:

- the HCP is required to act compatibly with art 2, because he is performing a function of a public nature while acting in the course of his employment;
- the obligation applies in the context of any activity, whether public or not, in which the right to life may be at stake, as it is in this cliff-top scenario;
- the HCP is aware of a real and immediate risk to the walker's life, per the test articulated in *Osman v UK*, by which an operational duty can be imposed upon the state to protect the life of a specified individual such as the walker, if that victim can show that the HCP knew, or ought to have known, when he was observing the walker, of a 'real and immediate risk' to the walker's life;[98]
- it is therefore arguable that the operational duty to protect life would be triggered in the circumstances, because it is a 'free-standing concept, self-supporting in nature, one that bites whenever the *Osman* elements are met';[99]
- hence, the HCP would be obliged to do all that he could to avert the walker's plunge to death, so that merely standing by and observing what was about to happen would violate that person's right to life.

Allen rightly posits that this outcome 'would mark a radical departure from the common law stance.'[100]

However, a non-patient's potential action for violation of a Convention right, in respect of a HCP's failure to intervene to protect the life of that stranger in a medical emergency, has not been considered since the Convention's implementation in English law (unsurprisingly, given how very few 'Bad Samaritan'-type cases have been instituted at all in English law); and the impact (if any) of arts 2 or 3 upon the common law's general no-duty-to-assist rule has also yet to be judicially considered.

To most general rules, of course, there are exceptions. Attention will now turn to those scenarios in which, unusually, the common law **has** imposed upon a HCP a duty to assist a stranger in medical need. These scenarios range from the fully-expected to the highly-controversial.

C   EXCEPTIONAL SCENARIOS: A COMMON LAW DUTY TO ASSIST STRANGERS IN MEDICAL EMERGENCIES

The no-duty-to-rescue rule is so startling in its potential application to medical scenarios involving an unwilling HCP that, almost inevitably, there are instances where courts have found that a HCP *is* under a common law duty to assist another who is in medical need and with whom the HCP has never, previously, had a professional relationship. Three exceptional scenarios are examined below.

1. Requests for medical treatment at A&E facilities

The point at which *hospital doctors* owe a duty of care towards those who present themselves at a hospital for medical treatment is governed by the common law in England. The National Health Service (General Medical Services Contracts) Regulations 2004,[101] which stipulate who are 'patients' and the procedures to be followed for registering patients with a doctor, etc.,[102] apply only to GPs, and not to hospital doctors.[103]

For hospital doctors, a duty of care arises at common law at the point when a person in need of medical assistance is 'accepted for treatment'.[104] In other words, 'once a patient has been received or admitted into a National Health Service hospital, the duty to provide (and thereafter to go on providing) treatment arises, whether the patient is competent or incompetent, conscious or unconscious'.[105]

Three points about this common law exception, which imposes a duty-to-assist on hospital doctors, are pertinent.

First of all, the point of 'acceptance' may occur (and a duty of care may hence attach) without a hospital doctor in A&E/casualty actually laying eyes, let alone hands, on the victim:

> In *Barnett v Chelsea and Kensington Hospital Management Committee*,[106] three night-watchmen presented themselves to a casualty department, complaining to a nurse on duty that they had been vomiting for three hours after drinking tea. One of them, Mr Barnett (B), was so poorly that he lay down on the chairs. The on-duty casualty officer was himself vomiting and sick upstairs on the second floor of the hospital, and the nurse rang through to him, reporting the men's complaints. In a reference to the fact that it was New Year's Eve, the A&E officer replied, 'Well, I am vomiting myself and I have not been drinking. Tell them to go home and go to bed and call in their own doctors'. The men left the casualty department, and B died five hours later from poisoning by arsenic (an inquest held that the arsenic had been introduced into the tea by person or persons unknown). One of the issues for the court was whether or not the A&E officer owed any duty of care to B, when he had not actually sighted B. **Held:** a duty of care was owed (however, B's estate ultimately failed in its claim because, even had B been admitted to the hospital wards and treated with all care, B would have died, because the antidote to arsenic poisoning could not have been given in time, given the delay in seeking treatment).

A duty was found, because of a combination of factors: the casualty department was open and receiving patients; Mr Barnett presented himself complaining of illness or injury for the very purpose for which the A&E department offered its services; the symptoms of long-term vomiting warranted an examination of the watchmen by the A&E officer, rather than leaving any such observation to the nurse on duty, however experienced she might be; and (in modern duty of care parlance), the advice which the A&E officer gave to see their own GP's if their symptoms persisted (no matter how rudimentary) demonstrated an assumption of responsibility for the their care and treatment. In all the circumstances, Nield J was satisfied that there was 'such a close and direct relationship between the hospital and the watchmen that there was imposed upon the hospital a duty of care which they owed to the watchmen.'[107]

Secondly, jurisprudence from Canada indicates that a duty can attach to *off-duty* doctors in A&E just as firmly as to their on-duty colleagues:

> In *Egedebo v Windermere District Hosp Assn*,[108] the victim, Mr Egedebo (E), alleged that, as a result of the lack of medical treatment provided by doctors while he was a patient at a hospital,

he became a triplegic (paralysis in both legs and his right hand and arm). E visited the casualty department of his local hospital just before midnight, suffering from burning sensations in his chest, and unable to move his legs. No doctor was available to attend to him, because they were all involved in a Caesarean section in the operating room. He was taken to the hospital's emergency room, where the nurses performed an ECG. Shortly after 12:30 am, one of the nurses saw Dr S and told him that there was a patient with a possible cardiological problem. Dr S replied that he was not on call. Another doctor was the physician on call, but he was administering anaesthetic in the operating room until 1:50 am. Eventually, E was transferred to another hospital, where the correct diagnosis was made that he had suffered a rupture of a congenital vascular (arterial-venous) malformation of the spinal cord, giving rise to his grievous injuries. Part of E's case was that Dr S had a duty to attend to him while he was in the emergency room, notwithstanding that he was 'off-duty' at the time. **Held:** Dr S owed E a duty to treat (however, the case ultimately failed, due to a failure of the requisite causal link between breach and the triplegia suffered).

The combined reasons for finding the requisite duty of care were that: the nurse had informed Dr S that Mr Egedebo may be suffering from a potential life threatening condition; whilst he was not 'on call', Dr S was still on duty at the hospital itself; he knew (or ought to have known) that the physician on call was in the operating room at that time; he knew (or ought to have known) that *all* the other physicians available were in the operating room; the Code of ethical conduct of the medical profession in British Columbia required him to check on a person presenting with the victim's symptoms; and the HCP was not himself faced with a situation that forced him to make a choice between two patients who were in life threatening emergencies.[109] Commentators Picard and Robertson have explained the result in *Egedebo* as arising from 'the principle of "holding out"', which they describe in these terms:

> a hospital with an emergency department holds itself out as being willing and able to render emergency treatment, and this implied undertaking is relied upon by those who come to the emergency department seeking attention. This combination of undertaking and reliance is sufficient to give rise to a duty on the part of the hospital to render emergency care.[110]

A similar viewpoint would likely be taken by an English court, were the same situation to arise in an English hospital. As noted by one leading English text, 'in principle, the duty exists because of the holding out by the doctor that he is there to deal with emergency cases that present themselves.'[111] In *Barnett*,[112] Nield J noted that if a casualty department of a hospital closes its doors and says no patients can be received, then there would be no duty of care owed by any of the members of that facility towards a person attending casualty—but conversely, it follows that, wherever an emergency department *is* open to receive patients, 'without hindrance', then a duty arises to treat anyone who presents.[113]

Thirdly, while the common law is willing to cast a duty on sick and off-duty doctors in A&E facilities to treat strangers, the duty is not a blanket one, according to English dicta. Suppose that the receptionist at A&E discovers that the person who presents (the victim), is already seeing his GP about a medical problem, and merely wants a second opinion from an A&E doctor, so the victim is sent away without being seen by any HCP. Alternatively, suppose that the victim has a small cut which a nurse in A&E can easily treat without calling on the services of the A&E doctor on duty, so the doctor does not see the victim. These hypothetical scenarios were cited by Nield J in *Barnett* as examples of where an A&E doctor would **not** be held to owe a duty of care to either see or to examine the victim. 'It is not ... the case that a casualty officer must always see the caller at his department. Casualty departments are misused from time to time.'[114]

Hence, in summary, the first common law duty-to-assist imposed upon HCPs towards strangers is not an especially surprising one—A&E medical staff owe a duty to assist anyone who presents at an A&E facility for medical treatment (subject to the third point noted above).

2. An emergency request, an affirmative undertaking, and reliance

Even if the HCP has no pre-existing relationship with a person in need of medical assistance, a duty of care will arise on the HCP's part towards that non-patient, under English common law, where:

- the non-patient *requests* medical assistance from the HCP;
- there is a reciprocal and affirmative *undertaking* given by the HCP to provide that assistance; and
- the non-patient *relies* on the HCP, in the sense that he adjusts his position in the expectation that the assistance will be forthcoming.

In *Capital and Counties plc v Hampshire CC*, Stuart-Smith LJ observed that, '[a]s a general rule a sufficient relationship of proximity will exist when someone possessed of special skill undertakes to apply that skill for the assistance of another person who relies upon such skill and there is direct and substantial reliance by the plaintiff on the defendant's skill.'[115]

In fact, *Capital and Counties* was not a case involving HCPs at all (but, rather, the fire brigade[116]). However, the fixing of a duty of care to assist, as between a HCP and a stranger, has been tangentially illustrated by the case of the ambulance service which was requested to respond to a 999 call:

> In *Kent v Griffiths*,[117] the victim, Mrs Kent (K), was pregnant, when she suffered a serious asthma attack at her home. Her GP was summoned, and assessed that K was in urgent need of transfer to the casualty section of the hospital (where she was expected). An emergency 999 call was placed by her visiting GP at 4.25 pm, and accepted by the ambulance service operator. When no ambulance turned up, there were two follow-up calls made (at 4.38 pm and 4.54 pm), in which the operator again assured that an emergency ambulance was 'on its way'. The ambulance arrived at 5.05 pm, and K arrived at hospital at 5.17 pm. K suffered a respiratory arrest during the journey. K suffered a miscarriage and brain damage as a result of the delay in reaching hospital. The trial judge found that the record prepared by a member of the ambulance crew was deliberately falsified to indicate that the time of arrival at K's home was not 5.05 pm, but 4.47 pm. No satisfactory explanation for the ambulance taking 34 minutes to travel 6.5 miles from its base to K's home was ever given. **Held:** the ambulance service owed a duty of care to assist the victim, K (K was awarded damages of over £370,000; claim in negligence against K's GP was dismissed).

There were essentially four reasons as to why a duty to assist a stranger such as Mrs Kent applied to the ambulance—and this reasoning arguably has significant impact for all HCPs practising in England.

First, while there may have been no antecedent relationship between Mrs Kent and the ambulance before the event, a legal relationship between them 'crystallised' when the first 999 call was accepted: 'The *acceptance of the call* in this case established the duty of care', said Lord

Woolf MR.[118] At that point, there was a legal assumption of responsibility on the ambulance's part. Therefore, the very facts of *request*, and *affirmative response*, appear to have fixed the duty of care, without more—a point which has been made in academic commentary since.[119] However, to add to that, *reliance* on the victim's part was proven because, but for the acceptance of the 999 call, K's husband would have driven her to casualty and she would have arrived prior to the respiratory arrest (i.e., 'if an ambulance service is called and agrees to attend the patient, those caring for the patient normally abandon any attempt to find an alternative means of transport to the hospital'[120]). Although such reliance is relevant to proving the causal link, it is submitted that Mrs Kent's specific reliance on the ambulance was an integral part of her success in this case, and buttressed a finding that an affirmative duty to assist existed on the ambulance's part.[121] Mrs Kent had another choice open to her, and she adjusted her position accordingly when the ambulance operator promised that an ambulance was on its way. In that regard, *Kent v Griffiths* is a good example of what the Irish Commission has called 'detrimental reliance' on the part of a victim—where that victim changes his position for the worse, based upon the intervention of the good Samaritan. The author agrees with the Commission's observation that some type of detrimental reliance 'is *more likely* to give rise to a duty of care, as the Good Samaritan's intervention has caused the stranger to be in a position of greater risk or to sacrifice a potentially more successful alternative option'.[122]

Secondly, the ambulance service was considered to be 'part of the health service ... providing services of the category provided by hospitals'.[123] The grouping of ambulance within the rest of the health care profession (and, by corollary, applying the ratio of *Kent v Griffiths* to all HCPs) is significant. As Williams remarks, the traditional role of ambulance services was perceived as merely a 'transport service whose job was to get casualties to hospital', but with emergency ambulances staffed with at least one fully trained paramedic on board, and becoming an essential part of the emergency clinical care network, then a 'broader reading of *Kent v Griffiths*, namely, that it settles the legally significant principle that there can be an initial duty to go to the assistance of an imperilled stranger, better reflects this expanded role.'[124]

Thirdly, there were no policy reasons for denying a duty of care on the part of the ambulance. There was no issue of 'conflicts of interest' arising—it was not as if the task of responding to the call involved conflicting resource issues (given that no explanation for the delay was provided).[125] Here, the ambulance was responding to a specific request from Mrs Kent, and while there *could* feasibly be some conflict between the interests of one caller and the public at large, this was not such a case.[126] Of course, cases could arise where an ambulance is required to attend a scene of an accident in which a number of people need transporting to hospital, but, said Lord Woolf MR, 'as the numbers involved would be limited, I would not regard this as necessarily leading to a different result. The result would depend on the facts.'[127] The ambulance's duty-to-assist here was to be contrasted to the fire brigade's duty or the police's duty, which are owed to *the public at large* to prevent the spread of fire and to protect the public from criminal activity, respectively—both of which may involve a conflict between the interests of various owners of premises or persons at risk.[128] Moreover, the policy concern of 'distributive justice' which has been posed in academic commentary ('[t]he alarm bells will ring for some, including politicians in the Department of Health, because yet again it could be seen as the courts' potentially diverting precious financial resources from the treatment and care of patients to compensation claims'[129]) was not raised by the Court of Appeal. Instead, the policy notion of 'corrective justice' was applied. Both trial judge,[130] and Lord Woolf MR on appeal,[131] referred to what they considered that 'common humanity' and 'a well-informed member of the public' would consider to be the *right* outcome in a case of this type, which was 'out of the ordinary' and 'unusual in the extreme'.

Fourthly, the Court of Appeal accepted as 'good sense' the general no-duty-to-assist rule in English common law, and confirmed that members of the public are not required by law to act as Good Samaritans.[132] However, the ambulance service was not covered by that general rule, because it 'was under at least a public law duty ... The provision of ambulances is its statutory function. The LAS and its crews are paid out of public moneys to provide their services. It is wholly inappropriate to regard the LAS and its employees as volunteers'.[133] In fact, other cases involving rescuers (the fire brigade: *Capital and Counties*, and the police: *Alexandrou v Oxford*[134]) had shown that a public authority with a role to protect the community, in general, from foreseeable dangers (usually under statutory powers or duties) did **not** bear a legal duty of care to safeguard *individual members of the community* from those dangers. However, this case was different, because it involved 'not a case of general reliance, but specific reliance', and the ambulance was 'dealing with a named individual upon whom the duty becomes focused'.[135]

This reasoning, in combination, means that HCPs who are called upon to render emergency services to a stranger, who agree to assist, and who induce reliance on the victim's part (i.e., where the victim changes his position in some way, expecting the HCP to provide that which he said he would), will owe a duty of care to that stranger to provide emergency assistance and treatment — unless some conflict of resources, or some incapacity, precludes any assistance being provided. On one view, Lord Woolf MR's judgment means that any such conflict/incapacity arising on the facts would preclude a duty-to-assist from being owed to the victim; on another view, a duty-to-assist would be owed, as soon as the request, and undertaking to assist, occurred, but no *breach* of duty would be found, if conflicting demands on resources meant that no immediate assistance could be provided to the victim—either way, the victim's claim would fail in that scenario.

3. An emergency request, and a refusal to assist

It is one thing if a HCP *undertakes to assist* a person in medical need, and ultimately does not do so in sufficient time or manner to avoid the victim's damage, per a *Kent v Griffiths*-type scenario. It is, however, quite another, where a request for assistance is made by a person in medical need, and where there is **no** undertaking by the HCP to provide assistance—rather, the request by the victim is *refused*. Nevertheless, can the HCP be fixed with a duty of care towards that victim, giving rise to potential liability in negligence?

To date, no English authority has been prepared to go that far. However, that is precisely what the New South Wales Court of Appeal held in *Lowns v Woods*[136]—a decision which remains the pivotal nadir in Australia's law of negligence surrounding a HCP's duty to attend a medical emergency. There was no antecedent relationship in that case whatsoever: the victim was a complete stranger to the defendant doctor, the doctor refused a request to attend the victim, and yet was liable in negligence for the injuries thereafter suffered by the victim. The Irish Law Reform Commission is correct when it says that *Lowns v Woods* 'goes further' than *Kent v Griffiths* did.[137] They are most definitely **not** the same type of case.

This Section explores the decision in *Lowns v Woods*, the judicial and academic reaction to it, and whether its outcome and reasoning would be likely to find favour in English law, were a similar case to arise for determination by an English court.

(a) The facts and reasoning in *Lowns v Woods*
The case arose out of a family holiday:

In *Lowns v Woods*, the victim, Patrick Woods (PW), a 11-year-old boy with a history of epilepsy, suffered an epileptic fit one morning in a holiday flat which his family were staying at, whilst his mother was out for a walk. Upon her return, around 8.55 am, Patrick's mother urgently sent her 18-year-old son to fetch an ambulance from the nearby station, and her 14-year-old daughter Joanna was dispatched to 'get a doctor'. The daughter ran to GP Dr Lowns' surgery, about 300 metres away, and told him that her brother was 'having a bad fit', and requested him to come. Dr L declined, and asked for PW to be brought to his surgery. Joanna said, 'he's having a bad fit, we can't bring him down', to which Dr L replied that an ambulance should be called for. Joanna said, 'we need a doctor. We have already got an ambulance', but Dr L declined to attend. (Dr L's case was that this conversation never occurred, but on that point, the evidence of Joanna was preferred by the trial judge.) PW was treated by ambulance officers who arrived at the flat, and was rushed to another surgery, but the fitting could not be brought under control. By the time that the fitting ended in hospital, PW had suffered serious and irreversible brain damage. At trial,[138] it was found that, had Dr L attended to PW at the point of request, he would have treated him by using rectal Valium, and that this would have commenced some 17–20 minutes earlier than it did, and PW would not have suffered brain damage. Badgery-Parker J held that 'the elements of physical proximity, circumstantial proximity and causal proximity ... created such a relationship ... as to attract a duty of care.'[139] **Held:** on appeal (by majority[140]): Dr L had a duty to attend/assist PW in this emergency (PW was awarded damages of approximately A\$3.2M).

The ratio of the case has since been explained[141] in accordance with the traditional framework that applies to novel duty scenarios in negligence. First of all, given what Joanna explained in the conversation, the risk of injury to the victim Patrick Woods was *reasonably foreseeable* if the doctor, once requested, did not attend to treat Patrick Woods.[142] *Proximity* between Dr Lowns and Patrick Woods was established by a combination of factors:

- the request for help was directly made in a professional context, given that the doctor was at his place of practice and ready to begin his day's work when the request was made;[143]
- the doctor was in reasonable physical proximity to the victim (300 metres, 3–4 minutes walk from Patrick Woods' holiday flat);[144]
- there was no impediment (e.g., dealing with another patient), or significant or material inconvenience, which prevented the doctor from responding to the request and treating the victim;[145]
- the request involved no health or safety risk to the doctor, and there was no physical or other reason that he could not travel to and treat the victim (e.g., he was not tired, ill or inebriated);[146] and
- the doctor was fully aware of the need for urgent attention to a serious medical emergency.[147]

Finally, a *policy* reason given by the majority as to why a duty of care *ought* to be imposed upon a doctor, obliging him to treat someone not already a patient who is in urgent need of treatment, was that, by virtue of his training, qualifications and registration, a doctor is permitted by the community to be one of a relatively small group of persons who are 'accorded the privilege of affording medical treatment to those who require it'[148]—so that the *quid pro quo* of that privileged position is the burden of rendering treatment to strangers who request it, in the circumstances outlined above.

Additionally, there was another factor at play in *Lowns v Woods*, in the unusual form of s 27(1)(h) of the Medical Practitioners Act 1938 (NSW), which defined 'misconduct' as follows:[149]

---

s 27(1) Meaning of 'misconduct in a professional respect'
– [includes where medical practitioners]
(h) refuse or fail, without reasonable cause, to attend, within a reasonable time after being requested to do so, upon a person for the purpose of rendering professional services in the capacity of a registered medical practitioner in any case where he has reasonable cause to believe that such person is in need of urgent attention by a registered medical practitioner but shall not be guilty under this paragraph of such conduct if he causes another registered medical practitioner to attend as aforesaid.

Both majority justices in *Lowns v Woods*, Kirby P and Cole JA, and the trial judge Badgery-Parker J, placed a great deal of emphasis upon the effect of this provision. They considered it significant for three reasons:

1. s 27(1)(h) created no remedy in tort, in that it conferred no right to damages if breached—but it did provide evidence of what the public (via its elected Parliamentary officials who passed the legislation), the medical profession (because they agreed to the legislation), and Dr Lowns himself (via a concession at the trial[150]) considered to be an appropriate response, if an emergency request for medical assistance was made.[151] Kirby P put it this way—the section 'goes beyond what is expected, and imposed by the law, in the case of other professions. It goes far beyond what may be expected and demanded of an ordinary citizen. But in the noble profession of medicine, it is the rule which Parliament has expressed; which the organised medical profession has accepted; and which Dr Lowns himself acknowledged and did not contest';[152]
2. as a matter of statutory construction, the sub-section referred to 'person', broader than the word 'patient', confirming that Parliament intended misconduct to occur if a stranger's needs were not attended to upon request (per Badgery-Parker J);[153]
3. s 27(1)(h) represented a 'very clear statement of public policy' as to what is expected of a doctor who was requested to visit an ill person, and mirrored 'public perceptions of what the content of a particular duty should be' (per Badgery-Parker J).[154]

However, *Lowns v Woods* was only a majority decision—the dissenter, Mahoney JA, categorically denied that Dr Lowns was under any duty to attend Patrick Woods, a stranger to himself, and one to whom he had given no undertaking to assist. His Honour's contrary views, which can be summarised in four points, are of interest:[155]

- Parliament had already made some provision for a GP's failing to attend an emergency (disciplinary sanctions could follow for breach of any of the obligations in s 27), but the sub-section did not create a civil action for damages by creating a duty of care to non-patients;
- just because Dr Lowns may have had a 'moral or professional obligation' to attend the victim did not mean that he should be liable in negligence—statutes which regulated professional conduct, and ethical codes of conduct, were useful to define whether a professional committed a *breach* of a duty, but they could not themselves create a positive duty to act towards a stranger. If a doctor was to be held to be under a legal duty to

attend to a person in medical need with whom he had no previous relationship, the effect would be 'blunt', (because '[l]aw, as an instrument of social control, is a blunt instrument'); whereas professional obligations can be qualified by whether *all the circumstances* show that a professional default occurred, and if so, whether that default warrants censure (and, if so, what form). As counter to any suggestion that the public and the profession expected emergencies to be responded to, Mahoney JA's response was that such expectations are met by disciplinary, and not legal, sanctions, and that the reasons for non-attendance are so multifarious in practical life that '[t]he imposition of the obligation by the creation of a tort sanctioned by damages would, in my opinion, be an inappropriate method of dealing with the problem.'[156] In any event, regardless of whether Dr Lowns' had conceded that s 27(1)(h) accurately reflected what he should have done, 'such concession as was made was not a concession of legal liability ... legal liability remained to be determined by the court';

- were a duty to attend to be imposed, where would its limits be set? What time of day or night would the duty to attend upon a stranger arise, would the duty apply 24/7? Would the duty attach, whether the treatment could only occur in surgery, or would it also attach if the doctor could feasibly get to the victim's home? What assistance could paramedics and ambulance officers reasonably be expected to provide, and what could the doctor reasonably expect of the state's publicly-funded emergency services, before the doctor was subject to this duty to attend? What degree of inconvenience is 'expected' of a doctor? What extent of intervention would be sufficient? What impact would the field of practice and specialism of the doctor have upon the duty to attend?

- the quantum of damages in this case ($3.2 million) was 'no small thing' for medical insurers—and to be imposed retrospectively, when no such duty had been legally recognised at the time that Dr Lowns did not respond to the request, showed just how costly such a duty could become for insurers.

The duty-to-attend principle has not been applied in any Australian case since. Subsequently, Australian law reform opinion called it a 'controversial decision'.[157]

(b) Reaction to *Lowns v Woods*

Australian academic commentary regarding *Lowns v Woods* has been mixed, with some supportive of the majority's views, and some fiercely critical of the verdict against Dr Lowns. Table 5.1 summarises the key points arising from the literature.

Thus far, there has been no judicial consideration of *Lowns v Woods* (or even any reference to it) by English courts, so far as the author's searches can ascertain.[158] Nor has there been any case in England quite like it. Clearly, although *Bishara v Sheffield Teaching Hospitals NHS Trust*[159] has some characteristics in common with *Lowns v Woods*, the interim determination of the Court of Appeal to send the matter for trial falls a *long* way short of endorsing a duty of care by a HCP towards one who requests medical assistance, in circumstances where the HCP refuses to do so, and cannot provide an adequate justification for why such assistance was not given.

The English Law Commission has not yet had occasion to consider *Lowns v Woods* either. However, in its recent review of Samaritan law, the Irish Commission appeared to reduce the importance and impact of the decision by noting that the outcome 'was based upon the particular circumstances of the case', and that the decision did **not** create any general duty to assist.[160]

Unsurprisingly, academic commentary on the crucial question—would *Lowns v Woods* be followed in England?—is divided. Some commentators have considered that a similarly-positioned doctor in England *would* be held liable in negligence,[161] while others seem to doubt that proposition

Table 5.1   Some pertinent Australian academic commentary about _Lowns v Woods_[162]

- the fierce Parliamentary debate that accompanied the introduction of s 27(1)(h) rather negated the supposed 'clear policy' which the section, years later, was judicially said to demonstrate;[163]
- the very award of a significant sum of damages in this case, for an omission to assist, 'may seem tolerable only because the defendant was a physician—protected, no doubt, by liability insurance';[164]
- on the other hand (it is said), the effect of damages on limited insurance funds (as Mahoney JA referred to) should not be relevant to the question whether there should be a duty to give emergency treatment;[165]
- a duty to rescue/assist is appropriate to impose upon persons when rescue is the very thing for which some members of society, such as practising doctors in this case, and by extension, lifeguards, firefighters, police and coastguards, are trained;[166]
- _Lowns v Woods_' verdict was compromised by the fact that Kirby P's reliance upon what Dr Lowns believed his ethical obligations to be (had the conversation happened as Joanna Woods said it did, which he denied) should not found a duty of care—'Dr Lowns' musings about his ethical obligations expressed in cross-examination did not relieve Patrick Woods from having to prove that Dr Lowns was under a legal duty to act on them';[167]
- there was insufficient legal proximity between Dr Lowns and Patrick Woods, and this decision was explicable purely on policy grounds—two express (the supposed community expectations reflected in the legislation, and the privileged position of the medical profession), and one unspoken ('there was an unfortunate plaintiff who needed compensation and the court felt he should have it');[168]
- it remains unclear whether the decision is explainable on the basis of the particular legislation to which Dr Lowns was subject or whether, because of the request and geographical proximity between Dr Lowns and victim, the case could have more general application: a common law duty to attend/intervene;[169]
- subsequent to _Lowns v Woods_, the HCA said that, 'as a general rule, professionals such as doctors and social workers owe a duty of care to those for whom and to whom they make their services available',[170] and if Dr Lowns did not 'make himself available', then he ought not to have been liable.[171]

(e.g., in an extra-curial speech, Lord Cullen, then Lord Justice-General of Scotland, called the decision 'remarkable'[172]).

In this author's view, as English law presently stands, the decision would **not** be followed, were a similar fact scenario to come before the English courts, for reasons explored in section (c) below.

(c) Would English law follow _Lowns v Woods_?

The majority's reasoning in _Lowns v Woods_ certainly went where Australian law had not gone before, and the possibility that English law would follow suit is naturally of potential concern to the English medical profession. However, there are four reasons why it is most unlikely that _Lowns v Woods_ would be decided in the same way in England. Dealing with each in turn:

The Terms of Service are distinguishable

First of all, England does not have any equivalent to the statutory provision that proved to be so important in _Lowns v Woods_, whereby the definition of 'misconduct' contained in the Medical Practitioners Act 1938 (NSW) expressly covered non-attendance at an emergency without reasonable cause.

The regulations governing English GP's (but not hospital doctors)—the National Health Service (General Medical Services Contracts) Regulations 2004[173]—stipulate that:

---

reg 15 Essential services

...

(6) A contractor must provide primary medical services required in core hours for the immediately necessary treatment of any person to whom the contractor has been requested to provide treatment owing to an accident or emergency at any place in its practice area.

(7) In paragraph (6), 'emergency' includes any medical emergency whether or not related to services provided under the contract.

(8) A contractor must provide primary medical services required in core hours for the immediately necessary treatment of any person [certain stipulated persons who are not on the contractor's list of patients] who requests such treatment ...

reg 2 Interpretation

...

'patient' means—

... (c) persons to whom the contractor is required to provide immediately necessary treatment under reg 15(6) or (8) respectively.

No sanction is provided in the Regulations themselves for failing to adhere to or comply with them, although disciplinary consequences may follow for non-compliance, nor is the breach of these provisions defined as 'misconduct' as the NSW statute provided. However, if a GP is requested to attend to a stranger's request for urgent medical treatment, and if that stranger is located within the GP's practice area, then conceivably, the failure to respond to any such request may expose a GP to a complaint of misconduct, which may, in turn, constitute an impairment of the GP's fitness to practise.[174]

The GMC's *Good Medical Practice*[175] also places an ethical burden upon all doctors to offer medical assistance in an emergency:

---

para 11:

In an emergency, wherever it arises, you must offer assistance, taking account of your own safety, your competence, and the availability of other options for care.

Breach of this code of conduct may give rise to misconduct charges, and the document itself reminds that 'serious or persistent failure' may put a doctor's registration at risk.[176]

It should be emphasised, however, that breach of the Regulations or Code confers no entitlement on a stranger to damages as of right, nor does any such breach imply that a duty of care towards the stranger existed in the first place. As one leading text states of these documents in combination, '[t]he Terms of Service are not conclusive of the existence or scope of a duty of care at common law.'[177]

On the reasoning of the majority in *Lowns v Woods*, it is arguable that both Regulations and Code provide evidence of what the *public* and the *medical profession*, respectively, consider to be an appropriate response to an emergency—which, in *Lowns v Woods*, assisted to establish a policy reason for finding a duty of care on Dr Lowns' part. The Regulations represent delegated legislation; and the Code represents what the General Medical Council says is 'guidance ... addressed to doctors, but it is also intended to let the public know what they can expect from doctors'.[178] Mahoney JA, of course, dissented on this point, preferring the view that disciplinary sanctions arising from non-attendance were best left to the medical profession itself:

> Any general practitioner will instance patients who call for help needlessly, who seek help at home which could and should be given at the surgery, or whose calls derive from emotional problems rather than actual illness. If professional sanctions are to be imposed, they will ordinarily be imposed in terms which do not impose an absolute obligation and they will be imposed in a way which allows those regulating the profession to assess the circumstances of the case, the qualifications and exceptions to which the general principle is subject, and in the end to do what appears appropriate. That no doubt is why, when failure to attend upon a patient is described as professional misconduct or the like, it is conduct which *may*, not *must*, attract professional sanctions: sanctions are applied only when the circumstances require ... Those concerned with the regulation of professional conduct would see the requirement that a doctor attend a sick person as being, first, a qualified-requirement, and second, as warranting sanctions only if all the circumstances required them.[179]

It is apparent from *Lowns v Woods* that there are two entirely different viewpoints which may be taken about the legal effect of statutory provisions (and professional guidelines) which expect a GP to attend a medical emergency. *Either* they contribute as a policy reason to the creation of a duty of care (and liability in negligence), *or* they serve their purpose by giving rise to potential disciplinary sanctions but nothing more than that. The point remains an undecided one in English medico-legal jurisprudence.[180] The NSW provisions, however, by expressly stipulating that non-attendance was 'misconduct', went somewhat further on their face than do the NHS Regulations and the GMC's *Good Medical Practice*. In this author's view, the reasoning in *Lowns v Woods* on this point would **not** translate to the English setting.

Kent v Griffiths[181] is distinguishable because an express undertaking occurred there

Kent v Griffiths is authority for the proposition that, in an emergency medical scenario, a 'request for assistance + an affirmative undertaking to assist' is sufficient to give rise to a duty of care. The ambulance operator there undertook to provide an ambulance when responding to the 999 call placed by Mrs Kent's GP. However, *absent any undertaking to assist* by some words or by conduct from the HCP—and where no other inducement to the victim to rely upon the HCP is present on the facts—then *Kent v Griffiths* provides **no** support for the proposition that the HCP assumes any responsibility to rescue that other from peril.

Furthermore, the year after *Lowns* was handed down (but without referring to *Lowns*), the English Court of Appeal reiterated in *Capital and Counties plc v Hampshire CC* that '[a]s a general rule, a sufficient relationship of proximity will exist when someone possessed of special skill undertakes to apply that skill for the assistance of another person who relies upon such skill, and there is direct and substantial reliance by the plaintiff on the defendant's skill'[182] (subject to any policy reason as to why to fix a duty would be unfair, unjust and unreasonable). In fact, the *undertaking* 'element of the equation' was precisely what could **not** be proven in *Capital and Counties*. The claimant property owners, whose properties were destroyed by fire when the fire brigade attended and turned off the sprinkler system, argued that there was sufficient proximity between them and the fire brigade because the fire brigade had assumed responsibility to protect their property—but this failed, on the basis that there was no assumption of responsibility on the fire brigade's part towards any *one* property owner, but rather, to the public at large; and merely by taking control of the fire-fighting operations, the fire brigade 'is not to be seen as undertaking a voluntary assumption of responsibility to the owner of the premises on fire'.[183] (In that case, the fire brigade created a *new or different danger* for the claimant property owners by a positive act of misfeasance—turning off the sprinkler system—which is why a duty of care was ultimately created.)

Hence, for a HCP who expressly refuses to assist a victim who requests emergency help, both *Kent v Griffiths* and *Capital and Counties* offer considerable common law protection from liability in negligence—because both emphasise the importance of pointing to some undertaking to assist from the facts, by which to underpin a legal assumption of responsibility on the defendant's part.

Imposing an assumption of responsibility unlikely in the scenario of the non-attending HCP

As Lord Slynn stated in *Phelps v Hillingdon LBC*, the phrase, 'assumption of responsibility' can be misleading because it does not necessarily mean that the defendant 'must knowingly and deliberately accept responsibility ... the test is an objective one', and an assumption of responsibility may be not so much 'assumed as that it is recognised or imposed by law'.[184] In effect, this is probably no different to the usual proximity enquiry under the *Caparo* tri-partite test. Lord Bingham pointed out in *Customs and Excise v Barclays Bank plc* that, '[t]he problem is, as I see it, that the further [the assumption of responsibility] test is removed from the actions and intentions of the actual defendant, and the more notional the assumption of responsibility becomes, the less difference there is between this test and the threefold test.'[185] Hence, the questions of whether the law could impose an assumption of responsibility on a non-attending HCP, and whether there is sufficient proximity between the non-attending HCP and the victim, probably amount to the same thing— and, the answer is very likely to be 'no', under either question.

It must be remembered that a non-attending HCP is being charged with an omission to act—and Lord Scott pointed out in *Mitchell v Glasgow CC* that English law requires some 'additional feature' to transform what would otherwise be a mere omission, a breach at most of a moral obligation, into a breach of a legal duty to take reasonable steps to avoid or lessen the harm which befalls the victim.[186] Finding that 'additional feature' in a *Lowns v Woods*-type scenario would be a difficult task.

For one thing, *physical proximity* between the non-attending HCP and the victim (which, it will be recalled, was a factor in the majority's judgments in *Lowns v Woods*) would not be sufficient to constitute that additional feature. In *Capital and Counties*, it was said, obiter, that 'a doctor who happened to witness a road accident will very likely go to the assistance of anyone injured, but he is not under any legal obligation to do so', and that 'no such duty of care exists, *even though there may be close physical proximity*, simply because one party is a doctor and the other has a medical problem which may be of interest to both.'[187]

Secondly, the mere *vulnerability* of the victim who is in urgent need of medical treatment would not constitute the 'additional feature' either. No duty of care is owed by a coastguard to a person in need of rescue (unless the rescuers positively and directly inflict injury),[188] by a fire brigade towards a person whose property is in danger (unless the fire brigade turns up and makes the situation worse),[189] by the police towards a burgled shopkeeper[190] or towards potential victims of crime,[191] or by a council towards a council tenant in grave and longstanding danger from an abusive and violent co-tenant.[192] In all these cases, the claimants were in vulnerable or disadvantaged positions, and the defendants had the capacity to act, or the control of resources, to avert the danger or harm which the claimants confronted. In all cases, however, no duty of care to avert the victims' personal or property damage was owed. The fact that the ambulance was under a duty to rescue vulnerable Mrs Kent, in *Kent v Griffiths*, was very different, because an undertaking to help had been given by the ambulance (and then actively relied upon, by the husband in not driving his sick wife to the hospital himself). Hence, on the basis of English law, as it stands, the mere vulnerability of a sick person, should a HCP decline to attend and assist, is not sufficient to impose any duty on that HCP to assist.

Thirdly, the '*professional context*' referred to in *Lowns v Woods* is unlikely to cause a court to impose an assumption of responsibility either. The trial judge in *Lowns v Woods* cited this term,[193] to describe the context in which Joanna's request was made of Dr Lowns at his surgery, with his equipment around him, and as he was readying to receive patients and to practise medicine that morning. The purpose of this qualification was, seemingly, to ensure that HCPs such as Dr Lowns were not under a duty-to-assist in a social setting, or while on holidays.[194] Yet, it is an unrigorous qualification upon which to found any requisite proximity, when two counterpoints are equally as valid: first, there are professional contexts in which a duty to rescue/assist has **not** been upheld in English law (as the coastguard, police and fire brigade examples illustrate[195]); and secondly, there will be social settings in which a duty of care *could* be found to exist, if an urgent request is made and if the HCP assumes responsibility for that victim by words or by conduct (as some of the Good Samaritan cases, discussed later in Chapter 6, illustrate).

Hence, imposing an assumption of responsibility upon a non-attending HCP who refuses to attend a medical emergency would seem to be an 'uphill battle', in light of the abovementioned authorities.

The practical limits of any such duty would trouble English courts

The policy reasons underpinning the 'no-duty-to-rescue-someone-in-danger-of-imminent-and-foreseeable-harm' rule have been laid down emphatically by the House of Lords on several occasions, as discussed earlier in this chapter, and were endorsed again as recently as 2009 in *Mitchell v Glasgow CC*.[196]

The practical ramifications of finding in favour of a duty-to-rescue are entirely relevant to the question of whether a duty of care should be found, according to *Mitchell*. The defendant council in that case did not warn one of its tenants, M, that it was holding a meeting with another of its tenants (and M's neighbour), D, about D's violent and abusive behaviour towards M, and about the council's intention to set procedures in place to eject D from the council premises. One of the principal reasons that no duty to warn was imposed on the Council was that, practically speaking, where would its limits feasibly be set for councils to seek to comply with? Would it only apply where threats to kill were made, or to lesser threats? Would it apply in every case where a social landlord had reason to suspect that his tenant may run amok against another tenant?[197] All of this closely reflects the concerns which Mahoney JA (dissenting) had about imposing a duty-to-assist in *Lowns v Woods*. It will be recalled that Mahoney JA asked precisely that question: if a duty were imposed, where are those limits on a HCP to be set?[198]

Furthermore, according to the evidence, Dr Lowns told Joanna Woods that they should 'get an ambulance' to attend to her brother. Given the very rudimentary level of help that has been found to have conferred immunity on intervenors under the so-called 'Good Samaritan statutes' (considered in Chapter 6)—where even just stopping at the scene of an accident to ask whether help was required has been enough to qualify as 'assistance'[199]—some may regard Dr Lowns as having discharged his duty to assist. The scope of a duty to assist, if one were to be legally recognised, could be very difficult to assess.

The uncertainty of the scope of the duty contended for in *Mitchell* was a key factor precluding a duty there, and it is submitted that similar concerns would apply, should any *Lowns v Woods*-type scenario arise for determination in English courts in the future. Of course, plainly the scenarios in *Lowns* and *Mitchell* are not on all fours—in *Lowns*, it was a case of pure omission by a HCP to avert a danger to the victim, whereas in *Mitchell*, the omission was specifically to prevent harm being caused to the victim by the criminal acts of a third party. However, the practical consequences of imposing such a duty, and of defining its limits, are similar in both—and neither seems appropriate to the imposition of a general duty to help another in peril.

In conclusion, and for the four reasons advanced above, it is likely that English common law would not impose a duty of care upon a HCP in Dr Lowns' position, but would leave the sanction for such conduct to the disciplinary arm of the profession. To find any duty of care arising on the HCP's part would require a considerable incremental step to be taken in the English law governing omissions and rescuers.

D   CRIMINAL LIABILITY FOR FAILING TO ASSIST: A SNAPSHOT FROM OTHER JURISDICTIONS

Given the common law's rather pro-defendant stance—with a general tendency to shield those who 'look the other way' in emergencies from liability in negligence—the question arises as to whether medical intervention and assistance towards strangers could be compelled by *penal* sanctions.

There is **no** 'bad Samaritan' legislation in England by which HCPs are compelled to intervene and to assist with an ill or injured victim, failing which criminal liability and punishment will be imposed. Indeed, this type of legislation is rare in common law jurisdictions—although some pockets of it *do* exist. It is of interest and relevance, for any future development of English medical law in this regard, to consider a few of these bad Samaritan criminal provisions from other jurisdictions because, perhaps surprisingly, they have been shown to have some actual or potential application to HCPs.

This section briefly considers the position in three sample jurisdictions: the Northern Territory of Australia; the state of Vermont in the US; and continental Europe (specifically, France and Germany). Each of these jurisdictions has undertaken a more 'stick-like' approach to a person who does not assist in an emergency, and will be considered in turn.

1. The Northern Territory

In 1983, the Northern Territory legislature enacted the following provision as part of its Criminal Code:[200]

---

s 155. Failure to rescue, provide help, &c

Any person who, being able to provide rescue, resuscitation, medical treatment, first aid or succour of any kind to a person urgently in need of it and whose life may be endangered if it is not provided, callously fails to do so is guilty of a crime and is liable to imprisonment for seven years.

There still remains only one case which has turned upon this provision—involving, not a HCP, but a hit-and-run driver.[201] In that decision, however, Kearney J remarked in dicta that '[p]ossible applications of Code s155 are cases involving ... *doctors who fail to make home visits to sick or injured persons* ... [but] the scope of Code s155 is uncertain and broad.'[202] This theoretical application of the general duty-to-rescue to HCPs remains of concern.[203]

Northern Territory's 'crime of omission'[204] has variously been described as 'novel',[205] 'rare',[206] and 'unique in Australian law and to the law of other common law countries'.[207] Its origin is said to have been perhaps rooted in the harsh, remote and unforgiving desert terrain of the Northern Territory, and the distinct possibility of dire consequences for those drivers, walkers, etc, whose need for help are ignored.[208]

More generally, the provision has been critiqued on several bases. For example: the bystander is not excused from the duty to assist, even if to render the assistance would have exposed the bystander to the risk of death or serious injury;[209] the duty cast upon the bystander is not to help just anyone in need, but rather, only someone suffering from 'a potential or actual life-threatening injury',[210] which places a burden upon the bystander to be able to appreciate such a condition;[211] and the broad term, 'succour', used by the drafters is unclear (as is the ambit of the entire provision), but probably does not cover the failure to donate to a charity that is dedicated to reducing starvation, for example![212]

In any event, no attempt has been made to repeat it in other Australian jurisdictions, and its application to HCPs who fail to assist in medical emergencies remains untested.

2. The state of Vermont

Some US states have implemented statutes which compel rescue in defined circumstances, failing which the bystander will be exposed to criminal fines. Known as 'bad Samaritan' statutes,[213] they render it a criminal offence not to assist persons in peril. The state of Vermont's provision, contained in the Duty to Aid the Endangered Act, is one example (and the first to be enacted in the US):[214]

---

§ 519 Emergency medical care

(a) A person who knows that another is exposed to grave physical harm shall, to the extent that the same can be rendered without danger or peril to himself or without interference with important duties owed to others, give reasonable assistance to the exposed person unless that assistance or care is being provided by others.

(b) A person who provides reasonable assistance in compliance with subsection (a) of this section shall not be liable in civil damages unless his acts constitute gross negligence or unless he will receive or expects to receive remuneration. Nothing contained in this subsection shall alter existing law with respect to tort liability of a practitioner of the healing arts for acts committed in the ordinary course of his practice.

(c) A person who willfully violates subsection (a) of this section shall be fined not more than $100.00.

This provision has been applied in the HCP context, in a perhaps surprising, but unsuccessful, fashion:

In *Hardingham v United Counseling Service of Bennington*,[215] United was a private, non-profit organisation which provided counseling and psychiatric treatment to people with mental illness or substance-abuse problems. Mr Hardingham (H) was an employed emergency services counselor, and a known recovering alcoholic. Senior management and medical staff became aware that H was drinking again, but could not persuade H to seek psychological and medical attention. During a visit to H's flat, co-workers found H inebriated, and took away all the alcohol that could be found, but on a subsequent visit to his flat, three co-employees (two of whom were HCPs) again discovered H inebriated and semi-conscious. During this visit, H went to a sink, and drank from a container of windshield wiper fluid (a methanol solution). His co-workers removed the container from H and phoned the police (over H's 'vehement protests'). Two of them then accompanied H to the medical centre emergency room, where one signed an incapacitation order for H, when H refused permission to take a blood test. Next day, tests showed that H had life-threatening concentrations of methyl alcohol in his blood, as a result of a methanol overdose. H sustained severe health problems, including permanent irreversible blindness. H sued the co-workers who had sought to assist him, alleging that they ought to have done more to render aid, that they never informed police or medical staff that he had ingested a bluish liquid that may have been windshield wiper fluid, and that this failure to inform meant that the rescuers did not meet the 'reasonable assistance' threshold stipulated in § 519(a)—rendering them open to criminal liability—and that the failure also constituted 'gross negligence' under § 519(b)—opening up the possibility of a civil action for damages, under Vermont's duty-to-rescue statute **Held:** the rescuers/HCPs eventually defeated the claim on a motion for summary judgment.[216]

Stewart has vehemently criticised[217] the litigation brought by *Hardingham*, and the Vermont statute that facilitated it, on several bases. First, had there not been a statute of this type, it was 'doubtful' that the medical rescuers would have acted any differently towards H (they probably still would have given reasonable assistance to H)—but it was questionable whether the litigation would have been brought, or been so protracted, with the State of Vermont only being saved from a 'full-blown trial due to the summary judgment ruling.' Secondly, although the statute was meant to serve as a shield for rescuers, '*Hardingham* demonstrates how the statute can be used as a weapon to unnecessarily burden the courts and Good Samaritans', because although it 'appears unlikely that there will be a vast increase in criminal prosecutions under duty-to-aid statutes[,] [t]hese proposed laws may, however, spark an increase in civil litigation', with corresponding attempts by the victim to prove gross negligence on the part of the person who did not do enough to meet the 'reasonable assistance' threshold. Thirdly, *Hardingham* was a decision that constituted '[e]vidence of the kind of hornet's nest that can be created when legal duties are thoughtlessly expanded', especially where duty-to-rescue statutes like that of Vermont's allowed for people to be criminally prosecuted and convicted for not providing 'reasonable assistance'.

More generally, the so-called 'bad Samaritan' US state statutes have received a less-than-warm reception from several American commentators.[218] Table 5.2 cites their main concerns.

It is appropriate to round out the brief discussion of 'bad Samaritan' statutes by turning attention from common law to the civil law jurisdictions.

Table 5.2   Academic criticism of the United States' duty-to-rescue/'bad Samaritan' statutes

- such statutes punish 'soullessness' rather than truly culpable acts;
- they invite punishment for 'bad character' rather than for evil acts, and thus go beyond the ordinary way in which the criminal law is used;
- it is difficult to assess *mens rea*, i.e., whether a bystander 'knows' that a victim is at risk of 'grave physical harm' as the Vermont statute requires;
- 'vagueness' is a problem in duty-to-rescue statutes—bystanders who face prosecution must have legal certainty of what acts or omissions are prohibited under the law, but in Vermont's case, for example, the meanings of many elements of the offence are uncertain—a statute that establishes a duty to render assistance should specifically provide for when the duty to assist arises, what degree of personal risk or inconvenience would abrogate the duty, what level of action on the part of the intervenor should be sufficient as a minimum to satisfy the duty, upon whom the duty is cast, and what defences should be available—yet, in each of these, interpretative difficulties have been shown to arise;
- the statutes invite speculation as to why the bystander may not have acted which, in conjunction with the presumption of innocence, renders prosecutions very unlikely to be achieved;
- given the number of bystanders, the costs of investigating and successfully prosecuting bystanders is likely to be prohibitive (and criminal prosecutions under the relevant US statutes are rare in any event);
- the prosecutions, in any event, may respond more to public outrage about a particular incident than upon the meritorious cases;
- how is a bystander going to know for certain whether he will be imperilled in the attempt to rescue the unfortunate victim, as the statutes typically require?
- the state has no business *forcing* someone to go to the aid of somebody else—such statutes encroach upon individual liberties to act, or omit to act, as they choose; and
- the inter-relationship between penal sanctions and civil liability arising from any failure to assist can be vested with uncertainty—is the legislature promoting the view that the common law should recognise a duty to assist, or is the legislature expressing no opinion on that, by enacting such a statute?

3. Continental Europe

Continental Europe has a strong tradition of imposing upon citizens a duty to assist others in peril.[219] As Schiff has noted, '[a]lmost every civil law jurisdiction in Europe, as well as in Latin America, recognizes various types of duties to rescue and related tort actions'.[220]

France has had a longstanding duty to rescue.[221] Within Section III of the French Penal Code (updated 2005[222]), it is provided:

Art. 223–6

Anyone who, being able to prevent by immediate action a felony or a misdemeanour against the bodily integrity of a person, without risk to himself or to third parties, wilfully abstains from doing so, is punished by five years' imprisonment and a fine of €75,000.

The same penalties apply to anyone who wilfully fails to offer assistance to a person in danger which he could himself provide without risk to himself or to third parties, or by initiating rescue operations.

Germany's Criminal Code (as amended 4 July 2009[223]) compels that 'easy rescues' should be undertaken, failing which criminal liability attaches to the bystander:

Section 323c Omission to effect an easy rescue
Whosoever does not render assistance during accidents or a common danger or emergency although it is necessary and can be expected of him under the circumstances, particularly if it is possible without substantial danger to himself and without violation of other important duties shall be liable to imprisonment of not more than one year or a fine.

Studies of the French Penal Code by Tomlinson[224] and by Ashworth and Steiner[225] demonstrate that HCPs have featured, not altogether infrequently, as defendants accused of being 'bad Samaritans'. The latterly-mentioned authors note that this may be explained, in part, because HCPs 'are the first people to be summoned when assistance is necessary.'[226] Scenarios resulting in conviction have included: where a doctor refused to attend to a young sick child who was suffering from encephalitis (inflammation of the brain), because the child was being treated by another doctor;[227] where a doctor refused to make a home visit to attend a boy sick with flu;[228] and where a doctor refused to leave his house at night to attend a knifing victim, upon being told that an ambulance was on its way (the ambulance was, in fact, delayed, and the victim bled to death), but where the doctor had said that he would treat the victim if he could be brought to the surgery.[229]

The criticisms of the French offence provisions by Tomlinson reflect those which have been made of the Northern Territory and American statutes: haphazard use of the offence (or, as Tomlinson describes the French version, 'the statute functions like a loose cannon; prosecutions have occurred in surprising situations never envisioned by most advocates of the duty to rescue'[230]); the vagueness of key words and phrases used by the drafters in the text of the offences, which, in turn, has given rise to serious interpretative difficulties; the fact that prosecutions for a failure to assist/rescue can be publicly-driven (as in the case of the paparazzi who were prosecuted, ultimately unsuccessfully, for failing to assist Princess Diana and her bodyguard at the scene of the Paris car crash); and the difficulties of proving, to a criminal standard, that the bystander confronted a person in grave peril and could have done more to assist that person without exposure to significant inconvenience, pecuniary loss, or personal injury to himself.[231] The inter-relationship between a duty-to-assist/ rescue, and those who are intent upon committing suicide but seek some assistance to do so, has also proven problematical.[232]

4. A 'Bad Samaritan' statute for England?

Recent and relevant law reform consideration of whether it would be apposite to visit criminal liability upon those who decline to intervene or to assist has been negative.

For example, the Irish Commission was asked to examine whether Irish law should be amended to recognise a general duty to intervene, but that request was limited to a consideration of any *civil* liability that should be imposed for a failure to assist.[233] As a result, the prospect of criminal liability was not considered in any detail. However, the Commission did remark that the purpose behind statutory intervention in this area has changed, in that '[i]nstead of *forcing* individuals to intervene on pain of penal sanction, the tendency is now for Good Samaritan statutes to *encourage* intervention by granting immunity from civil liability.'[234] In any event, the Commission labelled all 'bad Samaritan' laws, even those giving rise to civil liability, as 'exceptional',[235] and strongly recommended that no such provision should be implemented into Irish law.[236]

The Law Commission of England and Wales has also reiterated[237] that, in its view, there is no place in English law for any duty-to-assist giving rise to criminal liability. With respect to this example:

> Defendant, who has a telephone, is awoken by a noise coming from his garden. Opening the window, D asks Perpetrator what he is doing. P replies 'go back to bed'. D, although believing that P is about to commit an assault on Victim, goes back to bed. P, encouraged by D's non-intervention, proceeds to assault V.

—the Commission considered that D's callousness should not be punishable by penal sanction:

> In itself, this is not to justify the imposition of criminal liability. In this kind of example, if D could be made criminally liable for his failure to intervene, it would be a case of imposing liability because D was not being a good Samaritan or 'busy body'. That is potentially far too harsh a consequence in cases of non-intervention.[238]

Interestingly, there has been some recent academic discussion as to whether English law *does* require a general 'bad Samaritan' statute—under which someone who fails to aid another whose life is in evident danger would commit a crime—in light of the tragic case of *R v Evans*.[239] A supplier of heroin was found guilty of gross negligence manslaughter, in circumstances where she realised that the heroin addict, her daughter who was living in the same home, had become seriously ill following a heroin injection. Gross negligence manslaughter was made out because the accused did nothing (or too little) to try to save her daughter, who was found dead in bed the next day. Rogers suggests[240] that the law would be more coherent and predictable if bad Samaritan legislation were enacted—albeit that '[s]uch a reform would go beyond the particular problem of looking after drug addicts and would thus undermine our traditional attachment to the act/omission distinction', and that it would be a step regarded by many as 'too revolutionary'.

Indeed, and to conclude, the enactment of criminally-enforceable provisions in England by which to compel rescue appears far-fetched and unnecessary, in light of the following:

- irrespective of what the civil law systems may countenance (and regardless of the rather grand notion expressed by one Quebec judge that legislative compulsion to rescue others merely 'shows the government's increasing awareness that solidarity between individuals belonging to a community is essential to the common well-being'[241]), to impose any penal sanction for failing to rescue would be entirely in conflict with the oft-stated common law principle (upheld on numerous occasions by the House of Lords) that there is no duty-to-rescue cast upon English citizens;
- in any event, any duty-to-assist statute that imposes criminal sanction hardly promotes the English common law's focus upon recovery of damages for injuries suffered by the victims;[242]
- the experience elsewhere demonstrates that 'Bad Samaritan' legislation—even if enacted in England with unsympathetic drug-pushers in mind—could potentially apply to the factually remote situation of the non-assisting HCP. This would be a severely retrograde step, in this author's view;

- there have been too many difficulties associated with both interpreting, and enforcing, such statutes in other jurisdictions, to open that particular 'can of worms' in English law; and
- significant law reform opinion, founded on searching enquiry and wide-ranging societal input, has been negative.

E CAUSATION CONUNDRUMS

Should a common law duty of care to go to the assistance of a stranger be, exceptionally, imposed upon a HCP, then failing to render any assistance will constitute the breach. However, proving the causal link between that breach, and the victim's injury and damage, raises some further potential legal difficulties.

1. How does 'doing nothing' cause the victim's harm?

Where Lord Keith's blind man[243] is observed to walk over the edge of a cliff, and the observer shouts no warning, there are three potential causes of the blind man's death or injury: his own disability, the topography of the land, and the failure to shout the warning. However, the observer did not create the topography or the disability. Similarly, the HCP does not create the medical emergency from which the victim is suffering. Does the HCP's failure to assist in the emergency truly constitute a cause?

Some academic opinion has questioned whether a causal link can be successfully established. The Irish Law Reform Commission remarked, in its study on Samaritan law, that, 'if inaction is incapable of *causing* harm, then it cannot form the basis for a claim in negligence',[244] and that if merely failing to act could give rise to liability, then 'this would be akin to creating a conduct offence under negligence, which would go against the basis of negligence, which seeks to redress those situations in which damage has been caused.'[245] In like terms, Schiff has argued that the essential inability to transpose civil-law-type 'bad Samaritan' statutes into common law jurisdictions centres around causation:

> The causation problem as it relates to duties-to-rescue is significant, for it demonstrates the civil law's willingness to discard the but-for causation theory for a much more inclusive but less rigorous concept of responsibility causation. The adoption of the European approach in common law jurisdictions would require a deep-rooted transformation of the common law sense of causation. As is always the case with bad Samaritans, their 'refraining' is in no sense a causal factor in the harm of the 'victim', but the requirement that the act be a causal factor in the harm is central to common law torts.[246]

As explained in Chapter 2,[247] however, were a positive duty-to-assist to be cast upon a HCP, then there are, arguably, strong grounds for establishing the requisite causal link, by reference to existing English lines of authority, and readers are referred back to that chapter for greater detail. To recap the principal point, English tort law has already created a number of exceptions to the general rule that there is no duty to rescue, and in these exceptional or 'special' cases, the causal link *has* successfully been made out, thereby indicating that pure omissions or non-feasances *can* constitute a 'cause' of harm—based upon the more elliptical method of saying that the defendant 'created the opportunity for harm to occur'. In that regard, although the Irish Commission ultimately concluded that there should be **no** duty introduced to Irish law to intervene or assist a person who is at risk of injury,[248] it said that, if there *were* such a duty, then 'instances involving an affirmative duty to act do not appear to present any particular difficulty in our acceptance of the issue that inaction may, in fact, "cause" harm'.[249] Other academic opinion,[250] and previous English authorities,[251] support this view.

2. Hypothetical scenario: what would the healthcare professional have done?

Furthermore, in a scenario such as that which involved Dr Lowns' non-attendance on Patrick Woods, '[the] court is being asked to consider what might have been'.[252] Again, this causal conundrum—and the common law's counterpunch to it—have been discussed earlier in Chapter 2.[253] To summarise/recap, two cases are of particular relevance on this point.

First, the analysis adopted by the House of Lords in *Bolitho v City and Hackney HA*[254] (which was a failure-to-attend-a-patient case) permits a causal link in the case of an alleged 'failure to act'. According to that authority, the non-patient victim will have to prove that either the HCP (had he attended) would have done something to prevent the victim's harm, or that the HCP (had he attended) would have done nothing to alleviate the victim's peril, and it would have been negligent for him to have done nothing. Either strand of reasoning can establish a good causal link between the non-attendance and the victim's damage.

The other key case is that of *Barnett v Chelsea and Kensington Hospital Management Committee*,[255] considered earlier in this chapter as one of the very few 'Bad Samaritan'-type cases brought against HCPs in English law. In circumstances where the HCP did not attend upon Mr Barnett in the hospital emergency room at all, the court was prepared to hypothesise what the HCP would have done—had Mr Barnett been admitted to the hospital ward, a blood and urine specimen would have been taken, and an antidote to arsenic poisoning administered. However, because that antidote would have been given too late to reverse the disturbance of the enzyme processes which arsenical poisoning causes, causation ultimately failed.

Hence, if a duty to assist a stranger in an emergency were to be part of English law, it is as the Irish Law Commission posited—causal links would likely be found to exist, drawing upon exceptional cases in which omissions have already given rise to liability in other contexts.

F CONCLUSION

It is said that failing to act to assist another is the area of law where 'the distinction between law and morals is nowhere more clearly apparent'.[256]

To reiterate, it is not contended that the incidence of the 'bad Samaritan' HCP will be at all common. However, for the tired, overworked, off-duty, or concerned-about-legal-liability HCP, the general rule operative in English common law—that there is no general duty to assist a victim who requires emergency medical assistance and with whom that HCP has no antecedent professional relationship—provides considerable legal protection from suit.

To such a rule, there are two common law exceptions in English law: the first applies in the case of A&E hospital doctors; and the second applies to all HCPs to whom a request for assistance is made, who provides an undertaking to give it, and where the victim then relies upon that undertaking. Thus far, no equivalent case to *Lowns v Woods* has been litigated in England, and no legislation compelling HCPs to act, failing which criminal penalties will ensue, has been enacted nor contemplated (so far as the author can ascertain). That said, the possible effect of the ECHR upon the no-duty-to-rescue rule remains for judicial determination.

Meanwhile, the '*Potential Liability to Non-Patients and Third Parties: A Synopsis for Healthcare Professionals*' in the Appendix hereto summarises the legal position governing HCPs who decline to assist strangers in medical need.

ENDNOTES

1   Gospel of Luke 10:25–37.
2   See, e.g., the definition of the medical Samaritan provided in: Law Reform Comm of the Victorian Parliament, *The Legal Liability of Health Service Providers* (1997) [2.44]; and Irish LRC, *Civil Liability of Good Samaritans and Volunteers* (CP 47, 2007) (hereafter, '*Irish LRC Consultation Paper*') [1.55].
3   See, e.g.: K Williams, 'Doctors as Good Samaritans: Some Empirical Evidence Concerning Emergency Medical Treatment in Britain' (2003) 30 *J of Law and Society* 258, whose study showed that 78% of doctors surveyed had responded to a medical emergency. Also see: Irish LRC's consultation paper, *ibid*, [3.44] ('The Commission's enquiries indicate that fear of litigation, while present, does not currently deter people from acting as Good Samaritans', citing *Report of Taskforce on Active Citizenship* (2007) 7, 17).
4   e.g.: M Rubin, 'Is there a Doctor in the House?' (2007) 33 *J of Medical Ethics* 158, 159 ('[c]atching germs is not my issue, but other matters do come to mind, and I suspect I am not alone in thinking of them').
5   See, e.g, the observations in: Irish LRC, *Civil Liability of Good Samaritans and Volunteers* (Rep 93, 2009) (hereafter, '*Irish LRC Final Report*') [1.30] ('the potential for civil liability, which ... is likely to be a relatively remote risk ... remains a real worry for some potential volunteers'); Ipp Comm, *Review of the Law of Negligence: Final Report* (2002) [7.21] ('The Panel understands that health-care professionals have long expressed a sense of anxiety' about lawsuits for Samaritan-type activity); Law Reform Comm of the Victorian Parliament, *The Legal Liability of Health Service Providers* (1997) [2.45] ('the Committee has been told that the fear of malpractice suits causes medical practitioners to avoid offering medical attention to people at the scene of an accident or in an emergency').
6   To quote from: *Schacht v R* [1973] 1 OR 221, 30 DLR (3d) 641 (Ont CA) [26].
7   See nn 2 and 5 above. The consultation focussed upon whether statutory immunities should be provided to good Samaritans, but makes several interesting points about Bad Samaritans, and the no-duty-to-rescue rule, too.
8   [1970] AC 1004 (HL) 1060 (Lord Diplock), and approved in: *Smith (or Maloco) v Littlewoods Organisation Ltd* [1987] AC 241 (HL) 261, 271.
9   [1990] 2 AC 1 (HL) 77–78 (Lord Goff) (also known as *F v West Berkshire HA*).
10 [2004] EWHC 1879 (Admin) [84] (Munby J) (emphasis added).
11 [1997] QB 1004 (CA) 1035 (Stuart-Smith LJ). The 'limited circumstances' referred to in this passage were that GP's were obliged, by the then-in-force NHS (General Medical Services) Regulations 1992 (SI 1992/635), Sch 2, para. 4(1)(h), to give treatment that was 'immediately required' to the victim of an accident or emergency in his practice area, and also outside his practice area if he was 'immediately required' and if he agreed to do so. These regulations have been replaced, and the current version is discussed later in the text at pp 177–79.
12 *Irish LRC Final Report* (2009) [2.39], citing: J Fleming, *The Law of Torts* (8th edn, Law Book Co, 1992) 147 ('A doctor may flout his Hippocratic Oath and deny aid to a stranger').
13 *Agnew v Parks*, 172 Cal App 2d 756, 764 (1959), and cited in: *Childs v Weis*, 440 SW 2d 104, 107 (Tex App Ct 1969). In neither case was a non-attending HCP found liable to the victims.
14 [2007] EWCA Civ 353.
15 The facts are taken from the Court of Appeal's judgment; the trial judgment is not available via any electronic database, so far as the author can ascertain.
16 Reference is made, in particular, to two judgments of the Lincoln County Court, dated 30 Jun 2006 and 20 Feb 2006, which decisions in favour of the defendant lead to leave to appeal being granted.

17 [2007] EWCA Civ 353, [9].

18 *ibid*, [14]. The other member of the court, Ward LJ, agreed.

19 [1990] 2 AC 605 (HL).

20 *ibid*, [10].

21 *ibid*, and the quoted extract of the judgment of Smith LJ, who granted leave to appeal, cited in [8].

22 *ibid*, [11], citing: *Stovin v Wise* [1996] AC 923 (HL).

23 According to searches of Westlaw UK; Lexisnexis UK; and the British and Irish Legal Information Institute (Bailii).

24 [2000] OJ No 4863 (Ont SCJ, 21 Dec 2000).

25 *ibid*, [48], [51], [57].

26 *Wagner v Itnl Rwy Co*, 232 NY 176, 180–81 (1921), and cited in, e.g.: *Baker v TE Hopkins & Son Ltd* [1959] 1 WLR 966 (CA) 980 (Willmer LJ); *Frost (White) v Chief Constable of South Yorkshire Police* [1992] 1 AC 310 (HL) 408 (Lord Oliver).

27 A point made, e.g., by: K Williams, 'Medical Samaritans: Is there a Duty to Treat?' (2001) 21 *OJLS* 393, 396–99.

28 See Chapter 2, pp 43–44.

29 *Smith (or Maloco) v Littlewoods Organisation Ltd* [1987] AC 241 (HL) 261 (Lord Goff); *Stovin v Wise* [1996] AC 923 (HL) 943–45 (Lord Hoffmann); *Customs and Excise v Barclays Bank plc* [2006] UKHL 28, [2007] 1 AC 181, [39]; *Mitchell v Glasgow CC* [2009] UKHL 11, [15] (Lord Hope) [39] (Lord Scott); *Gorringe v Calderdale MBC* [2004] 1 WLR 1057 (HL) [17] (Lord Hoffmann).

30 *Gibson (AP) v Orr, Strathclyde Police Chief Constable* [1999] Scot CS 61, Scot SC 420 (OH) 435.

31 *Yuen Kun-Yeu v A-G of Hong Kong* [1988] AC 175 (PC) 192 (Lord Keith), an example recently given endorsement in *Mitchell v Glasgow CC* [2009] UKHL 11, [15] (Lord Hope).

32 *Horsley v MacLaren* (1970), 11 DLR (3d) 277 (CA) [34] (Jessup J). Example also cited to illustrate the no-duty-to-assist rule in: EWLC, *Administrative Redress: Public Bodies and the Citizen* (CP 187, 2008) [3.161].

33 *Home Office v Dorset Yacht Co Ltd* [1970] AC 1004 (HL) 1060 (Lord Diplock).

34 *R v Evans* [2009] EWCA Crim 650, [17] (Lord Judge CJ). This fact situation did occur in the American case of *Handiboe v McCarthy*, 114 Ga App 541, 151 SE 2d 905 (1966).

35 *Mitchell v Glasgow CC* [2008] CSIH 19, 2008 SC 351, [89] (Lord Reed, dissenting), citing: *Yuen Kun-Yeu v A-G of Hong Kong* [1988] AC 175 (PC) 192 (Lord Keith).

36 Per the *Bolam* test of breach: *Bolam v Friern Hospital Management Committee* [1957] 1 WLR 582 (QB).

37 See Chapter 2, pp 27–30 and see, e.g.: *Mitchell* [2009] UKHL 11, [15] (Lord Hope); *Home Office v Dorset Yacht Co Ltd* [1970] AC 1004 (HL) 1037–1038 (Lord Morris); *Smith v Littlewoods Organisation Ltd* [1987] AC 241 (HL) 251 (Lord Griffiths); *Hill v Chief Constable of West Yorkshire* [1989] AC 53 (HL) 60 (Lord Keith).

38 W Norris, 'The Duty of Care to Avoid Personal Injury' [2009] *JPIL* 114, 114–15.

39 Discussed further in, e.g.: *Mitchell* (HL), *ibid*, [76], and earlier: [2008] Scot CS 19 (CSIH) [88].

40 [1996] AC 923 (HL) 945.

41 Note 9 above.

42 [1932] AC 562 (HL) 580 (emphasis added).

43 e.g.: *Mitchell v Glasgow CC* [2008] Scot CS 19 (CSIH) [89]. See too, Lord Cullen, 'From the Celebrated Snail to the Good Samaritan' [Aug 2003] *Advocate* 40, 40; (same), 'The Liability of the Good Samaritan' [1995] *Juridical Rev* 20. Also: *Sutherland SC v Heyman* (1985) 157 CLR 424 (HCA) 478 (Brennan J).

44 [2009] UKHL 11, [39].

45 [1932] AC 562 (HL) 580.

46 e.g.: *Caparo Industries Ltd v Dickman* [1990] 2 AC 605 (HL) 617–18, 633 (Lord Bridge, noting that there is no 'single general principle to provide a practical test which can be applied to every situation to determine whether a duty of care is owed and, if so, what is its scope'; and Lord Oliver, stating that 'it has to be recognised that to search for any single formula which will serve as a general test of liability is to pursue a will-o'-the wisp. The fact is that once one discards, as it is now clear that one must, the

concept of foreseeability of harm as the single exclusive test—even a *prima facie* test—of the existence of the duty of care, the attempt to state some general principle which will determine liability in an infinite variety of circumstances serves not to clarify the law but merely to bedevil its development'). See, also, the discussion in Chapter 2, pp 27–30.

47 *Irish LRC Consultation Paper* (2007) [2.39], citing: J Kortmann, *Altruism in Private Law* (OUP, Oxford, 2005) 10–15.

48 [1996] AC 923 (HL) 943 (Lord Hoffmann).

49 *Modbury Triangle Shopping Centre Pty Ltd v Anzil* [2000] HCA 61, (2000) 205 CLR 254 (HCA) [28] (Gleeson CJ), and cited in *Mitchell v Glasgow CC* [2008] Scot CS 19 (CSIH) [89].

50 *Irish LRC Final Report* (2009) [2.71].

51 J Silver, 'The Duty to Rescue: A Reexamination and Proposal' (1985) 26 *William and Mary L Rev* 423, 430.

52 *ibid*, 430–31 (original emphasis).

53 C McIvor, *Third Party Liability in Tort* (Hart Publishing, Oxford, 2006) 14.

54 *Stovin v Wise* [1996] AC 923 (HL) 943 (Lord Hoffmann).

55 Noted, e.g., by: K Williams, 'Litigation against English NHS Ambulance Services and the Rule in *Kent v Griffiths*' (2007) 15 *Med L Rev* 153, 154.

56 J Silver, 'The Duty to Rescue' (1985) 26 *William and Mary L Rev* 423, 432, further noting, at fn 59, that modern courts are perfectly capable of handling the complexities of trials involving large numbers of defendants.

57 *Stovin v Wise* [1996] AC 923 (HL) 946.

58 *Irish LRC Final Report* (2009) [2.78].

59 *Stovin v Wise* [1996] AC 923 (HL) 944 (Lord Hoffmann).

60 M McInnes, 'Restitution and the Rescue of Life' (1994) 32 *Alberta L Rev* 37, citing, e.g., *Matheson v Smiley* [1932] 2 DLR 787 (Man CA); *Myer v Knights of Pythias*, 178 NW 63, 70 NE 111 (1904); and: G Fridman, *Restitution* (2nd edn, Carswell Thomson, Toronto, 1992) 271; P Maddough and J McCamus, *The Law of Restitution* (Canadian Law Book Inc, Toronto, 1990) 693.

61 K Williams, 'Medical Samaritans: Is There a Duty to Treat?' (2001) 21 *OJLS* 393, 398–99, citing: Lord Goff and G Jones, *The Law of Restitution* (5th edn, Sweet and Maxwell, London, 1998) 474, and *Falcke v Scottish Imperial Ins Co* (1886) 34 Ch D 234 (CA).

62 [2009] QCCQ 5521 (9 Jun 2009).

63 *ibid*, [58]–[60].

64 Air Canada has stated that the decision may be challenged: S Salomon, 'Airlines Must Pay MDs for Non-Emergency Mid-Air Care' (*Canadian Medicine*, 21 Jul 2009) (although decisions of the Small Claims Court cannot be appealed, judicial review may apparently be sought).

65 *Irish LRC Consultation Paper* (2007) [3.42].

66 [1959] 1 WLR 966 (CA).

67 *ibid*, 978 (Ormerod LJ, adopting the words of the trial judge).

68 J Silver, 'The Duty to Rescue: A Reexamination and Proposal' (1985) 26 *William and Mary L Rev* 423, 431.

69 A Ashworth, 'The Scope of Criminal Liability for Omissions' (1989) 105 *LQR* 424, 447–48.

70 *Irish LRC Consultation Paper* (2007) [2.47]–[2.49], citing: E Weinrib, 'The Case for a Duty to Rescue' (1980) 90 *Yale LJ* 247, 248.

71 *Irish LRC Final Report* (2009) [2.89].

72 *ibid*, [2.88].

73 N Duxbury, 'Golden Rule Reasoning: Moral, Judgment, and Law' (2009) 84 *Notre Dame L Rev* 1529, 1581.

74 *Baker v TE Hopkins & Son Ltd* [1959] 1 WLR 966 (CA) 978.

75 Judge Ware, *The Emblem*, 8 F Cas 611, 612–13 (D Maine, 27 Jul 1840), as cited in: P Long, 'The Good Samaritan and Admiralty: A Parable of a Statute Lost at Sea' (2000) 48 *Buffalo L Rev* 591, 609–10.

76 *Irish LRC Consultation Paper* (2007) [2.38].

77 *Irish LRC Final Report* (2009) [2.73].

78   *Lundy v Adamar of New Jersey*, 34 F 3d 1173, 1199–1200 (3rd Cir 1993).

79   J Silver, 'The Duty to Rescue: A Reexamination and Proposal' (1985) 26 *William and Mary L Rev* 423, 434.

80   Noted, e.g., in: *Smith (or Maloco) v Littlewoods Organisation Ltd* [1987] AC 241 (HL) 272–75 (Lord Goff); *Home Office v Dorset Yacht Co Ltd* [1970] AC 1004 (HL) 1060 (Lord Diplock).

81   By virtue of positive duties to protect entrants from dangers posed by the occupier's land, contained in the Occupiers' Liability Act 1957 and Occupiers' Liability Act 1984, respectively.

82   e.g., *Kirkham v Chief Constable of the Greater Manchester Police* [1990] 2 QB 283 (CA). Cf: *Commr of Police for the Metropolis v Reeves* [2000] 1 AC 360 (HL) (prison officer liable for negligently failing to prevent the suicide of an inmate, even if prisoner was mentally competent).

83   e.g., *Haynes v Harwood* [1935] 1 KB 146 (CA).

84   *Goldman v Hargrave* [1967] 1 AC 645 (PC).

85   S Todd, 'The Negligence Liability of Public Authorities: Divergence in the Common Law' (1986) 102 *LQR* 370, 383.

86   These are conveniently summarised in the articles by: M Scordato, 'Understanding the Absence of a Duty to Reasonably Rescue in American Tort Law' (2008) 82 *Tulane L Rev* 1447, 1469–80; and J Silver, 'The Duty to Rescue: A Reexamination and a Proposal' (1985) 26 *William and Mary L Rev* 423, 433–34.

87   E Tomlinson, 'The French Experience with Duty to Rescue: A Dubious Case for Criminal Enforcement' (2000) 20 *New York LJ of Intl and Comp Law* 451, 493–94.

88   *In Re 'Agent Orange' Product Liability Litig*, 597 F Supp 740, 831 (1984).

89   *Lundy v Adamar of New Jersey Inc*, 34 F 3d 1173, 1200 (3rd Cir 1994).

90   *Smith (or Maloco) v Littlewoods Organisation Ltd* [1987] AC 241 (HL) 271 (Lord Goff).

91   Chapter 1, pp 10–11.

92   M Brazier, 'Do No Harm—Do Patients have Responsibilities Too?' (2006) 65 *CLJ* 397, 405–6. See also, for a similar observation: K Williams, 'Medical Samaritans: Is there a Duty to Treat?' (2001) 21 *OJLS* 393, citing, on this point: J Wadham and H Mountfield, *Blackstone's Guide to the Human Rights Act 1998* (Blackstone Press, London, 1999) 65, and J McBride, 'Protecting Life: A Positive Obligation to Help' (1999) 24 *Euro L Rev Human Rights* 43, 54.

93   K Williams, 'Medical Samaritans: Is There a Duty to Treat?' (2001) 21 *OJLS* 393, fn 81.

94   J Wright, *Tort Law and Human Rights* (Hart Publishing, Oxford, 2001) 143.

95   See pp 10–11.

96   N Allen, 'Saving Life and Respecting Death: A Savage Dilemma' (2009) 17 *Medical L Rev* 262, 269–70. The author's example also encompassed, as observers, a law student and a police officer, but these are excluded from discussion for present purposes.

97   Per *Yuen Kun-Yeu v A-G of Hong Kong* [1988] AC 175 (PC) 192, and endorsed in *Mitchell v Glasgow CC* [2009] UKHL 11, [15] (Lord Hope).

98   *Osman v UK* (1998) 29 EHRR 245 (ECtHR).

99   N Allen, 'Saving Life and Respecting Death: A Savage Dilemma' (2009) 17 *Med L Rev* 262, 270.

100 *ibid*.

101 SI 2004/291, which came into force on 1 March 2004, and replaced the National Health Service (General Medical Services) Regulations 1992, SI 1992/635.

102 See Sch 6 to the Regulations, especially Pt 1, 'Provision of Services', and Pt 2, 'Patients'.

103 See further: 'Duties in Contract and Tort', in A Grubb, J Laing and J McHale (eds), *Principles of Medical Law* (3rd edn, OUP, Oxford, 2010) ch 3.

104 *Cassidy v Ministry of Health* [1951] 2 KB 343 (CA) 360 (Denning LJ).

105 *R (on the Application of Burke) v GMC* [2004] EWHC 1879 (Admin) [85].

106 [1969] QB 428.

107 [1969] 1 QB 428, 436.

108 (BC SC, 18 Jul 1991), aff'd: *Egedebo v Bueckert* (1993), 78 BCLR (2d) 63 (CA), leave to appeal ref'd: (1993), 80 BCLR (2d) xxvi (note) (SCC).

109 *ibid* (accessed online, no pp available).

110 E Picard and G Robertson, *Legal Liability of Doctors and Hospitals in Canada* (4th edn, Thomson Carswell, Toronto, 2007) 216–17, and also see discussion at 11, citing *Barnett* and *Egedebo* in support of that proposition.

111 A Grubb *et al* (eds), *Principles of Medical Law* (3rd edn, OUP, Oxford, 2010) [3.45]; and see too: M Jones, *Medical Negligence* (4th edn, Sweet & Maxwell, London, 2008) 139.

112 [1969] 1 QB 428, 436.

113 A sentiment noted by O'Halloran JA in *Fraser v Vancouver General Hosp* (1951), 3 WWR 337 (BCCA), aff'd: [1952] 2 SCR 36 (SCC) (this case concerned the failure to refer X-rays to a radiologist on call, after the victim was admitted, and hence, it is not directly pertinent to the point at issue in the text above).

114 [1969] 1 QB 428, 436.

115 [1997] QB 1004 (CA) 1034.

116 In *Capital and Counties*, the CA held that a fire brigade were not under a common law duty to answer a call for help, or to take care to do so—thereby prompting the ironic comment from one commentator that English law has created the 'extraordinary rule ... that the public rescue services have no duty to rescue anyone: D Howarth, 'Public Authority Non-Liability: Spinning out of Control?' (2004) 63 *CLJ* 546, 547. However, if the fire brigade does indeed turn up, and then by their negligence *create the danger* which causes property damage to the claimant by some positive act of misfeasance, then the fire brigade will be liable. This sentiment, in fact, has been applied to the case of *good* Samaritan HCPs (those who help out, and who make the victim's condition worse), as will be discussed in Chapter 6.

117 [2001] QB 36 (CA). Lord Woolf MR delivered the judgment of the CA.

118 *ibid*, [49] (emphasis added).

119 e.g., K Williams, 'Litigation against English NHS Ambulance Services and the Rule in *Kent v Griffiths*' (2007) 15 *Med L Rev* 153, 159, citing, as support for that view: J. Kortman, *Altruism in Private Law* (OUP, Oxford, 2005) 62. Also: C Witting, 'Duty of Care: An Analytical Approach' (2005) 25 *OJLS* 33, 49–50; and A Grubb, 'Medical Negligence: Liability of Ambulance Service' (2000) 8 *Med L Rev* 349, (accessed online, no pp available) ('It may be that the reliance issue did not go to the existence of the duty of care. Although necessary to succeed in a claim, it was really an aspect of establishing that the defendant's negligence caused the claimant's injuries because they would otherwise have been avoided'); M Jones, *Medical Negligence* (4th edn, Sweet & Maxwell, London, 2008) 142 ('the duty as expressed in *Kent* would seem to apply, even where there is no other means of obtaining the medical assistance that the claimant needs', i.e., without proof of any detrimental reliance).

120 [2001] QB 36 (CA) [9].

121 Note that this was the way in which Mrs Kent's case was framed: noted *ibid*, [14].

122 *Irish LRC Final Report* (2009) [3.29] (emphasis added).

123 [2001] QB 36 (CA) [45].

124 K Williams, 'Litigation against English NHS Ambulance Services and the Rule in *Kent v Griffiths*' (2007) 15 *Med L Rev* 153, 160, citing: *What CHI Has Found In: Ambulance Trusts* (Comm for Health Improvement, 2003) 17.

125 [2001] QB 36 (CA) [27], [47].

126 *ibid*, [45].

127 *ibid*, [46].

128 *Capital and Counties* [1997] QB 1004 (CA) 1036 (Stuart-Smith LJ); *Kent v Griffiths* [2001] QB 36 (CA) [45] (Lord Woolf MR).

129 See, e.g., A Grubb, 'Medical Negligence: Liability of Ambulance Service' (2000) 8 *Med L Rev* 349, (accessed online, no pp available).

130 [1999] Lloyd's Rep Med 424 (QB) 453.

131 [2001] QB 36 (CA) [51]–[52].

132 *ibid*, [19], citing: *Horsley v MacLaren (The Ogopogo)* [1972] SCR 441, (1972), 22 DLR (3d) 545 for this point, although the principle is entrenched in English law by virtue of the authorities discussed in Section B.

133 *ibid*, [18]–[19] (Lord Woolf MR).

134 [1990] EWCA Civ 19, [1993] 4 All ER 328 (CA).

135 [2001] QB 36 (CA) [14], and [9], respectively.

136 [1996] Aust Torts R ¶81-376 (NSWCA).

137 *Irish LRC Consultation Paper* (2007) [2.29].

138 (1995) 36 NSWLR 344 (SC) (Badgery-Parker J).

139 *ibid*, 359.

140 Kirby P and Cole JA, Mahoney JA dissenting.

141 Law Reform Comm of the Victorian Parliament, *The Legal Liability of Health Service Providers* (1997) [2.54].

142 [1996] Aust Torts R ¶81-376 (NSWCA) 63,170 (Cole JA).

143 Point made by the trial judge, Badgery-Parker J (1995) 36 NSWLR 344 (SC) 358, 360, an analysis with which Kirby P expressly agreed on appeal: [1996] Aust Torts R ¶81-376 (NSWCA) 63, 155.

144 *ibid*, 63, 175–76 (Cole JA), and Badgery-Parker J, *ibid*, 359.

145 *ibid*, 63, 176 (Cole JA).

146 Badgery-Parker J (1995) 36 NSWLR 344 (SC) 360.

147 *ibid*, 63, 176 (Cole JA).

148 Another point made by Badgery-Parker J (1995) 36 NSWLR 344 (SC) 358.

149 The provision was inserted by the Medical Practitioners Amendment Act 1963 (NSW), s 4(1). See, now, Medical Practice Act 1992 (NSW), s 36(1)(l). A similar provision also exists in the Medical Practitioners Act 1930 (ACT), s 35(1)(h). However, no other State or Territory in Australia has adopted this provision.

150 While Dr Lowns made that concession under cross-examination, he did not concede that the conversation between Joanna and himself had occurred.

151 [1996] Aust Torts R ¶81-376 (NSWCA), 63,176–77 (Cole JA),

152 *ibid*, 63, 155 (Kirby P).

153 (1995) 36 NSWLR 344 (SC) 359–60, and approved by Kirby P on appeal: *ibid*, 63, 155.

154 *ibid*, 358 and 359, respectively.

155 These reasons appear at: [1996] Aust Tort Rep ¶81-376 (NSWCA) 63, 165–69.

156 [1996] Aust Torts R ¶81-376 (NSWCA) 63, 169.

157 Law Reform Comm of the Victorian Parliament, *The Legal Liability of Health Service Providers* (1997) [2.35].

158 The case does not appear in any judicial decision uploaded in the electronic libraries and databases available via: Westlaw UK; Lexisnexis UK; and the British and Irish Legal Information Institute (Bailii).

159 [2007] EWCA Civ 353.

160 *Irish LRC Final Report* (2009) [2.40]–[2.42].

161 A Grubb, 'Medical Negligence: Duty of Care and Bolam' (1998) 6 *Med L Rev* 120, 123 ('It is suggested that English law would follow suit and recognise a duty of care in a case such as *Lowns v Woods*', also calling Mahoney JA's dissenting arguments, 'overkill by judicial hyperbole'). See too, for support that the ratio of *Lowns v Woods* is, and should be, part of English law: K Williams, 'Litigation Against English NHS Ambulance Services and the Rule in *Kent v Griffiths*' (2007) 15 *Med L Rev* 153, 160; and 'Medical Samaritans: Is there a Duty to Treat?' (2001) 21 *OJLS* 393.

162 See, too: O Melnitchouk, 'Extending Liability for Medical Negligence' (1996) 4 *Tort LJ* 259; L Skene, *Law and Medical Practice: Rights, Duties, Claims and Defences* (2nd edn, Lexisnexis Butterworths, 2004) 217; L Crowley-Smith, 'Duty to Rescue Unveiled: A Need to Indemnify Good Samaritan Health Care' (1997) 4 *JLM* 352; B McDonald and J Swanton, 'Issues in Medical Negligence' (1996) 70 *Aust LJ* 688; P Gerber, 'Is a General Practitioner Legally Bound to Render Assistance to a Stranger?' (1996) 165 *Medical J of Aust* 159; L Haberfield, '*Lowns v Woods* and the Duty to Rescue' (1998) 6 *Tort L Rev* 56.

163 K Day, 'Medical Negligence: The Duty to Attend Emergencies and the Standard of Care: *Lowns v Woods*' (1996) 18 *Sydney L Rev* 386, 389, and fn 36.

164 L Murphy, 'Beneficence, Law and Liberty: The Case of Required Rescue' (2001) 89 *Georgetown LJ* 605, 663.

165 K Williams, 'Medical Samaritans: Is There a Duty to Treat?' (2001) 21 *OJLS* 393, 396.

166 N Gray and J Edelman, 'Developing the Law of Omissions: A Common Law Duty to Rescue?' (1998) 6 *Tort LJ* 240.

167 D Mendelson, 'Dr Lowns and Obligation to Treat: Creative Lawmaking in the New South Wales Court of Appeal' (1997) 3 *Tort L Rev* 242, 246.

168 K Amirthalingam and T Faunce, 'Patching up "Proximity": Problems with the Judicial Creation of a New Medical Duty to Rescue' (1997) 5 *Tort LJ* 27 (quote at 30).

169 A Abadee, 'A Medical Duty to Attend?' (1996) 3 *JLM* 306.

170 *Sullivan v Moody* [2001] HCA 59, (2001) 207 CLR 562, [38].

171 J Tibballs, 'Legal Liabilities for Assistance and Lack of Assistance Rendered by Good Samaritans, Volunteers and their Organisations' (2005) 16 *Ins LJ* 254.

172 'From the Celebrated Snail to the Good Samaritan' [Aug 2003] *Advocate* 40, 44.

173 SI 2004/291, in force 1 Apr 2004, pursuant to the General Medical Services and Personal Medical Services Transitional and Consequential Provisions Order 2004. See too: National Health Service (Personal Medical Services Agreements) Regulations 2004, SI 2004/627, reg 2, 'Interpretation', and the definition of 'contractor's practice area' as 'the area specified in the agreement as the area in which essential services are to be provided'.

174 Pursuant to the Medical Act 1983, c 54, s 35C. See, on this point, e.g.: M Brazier, 'Do No Harm—Do Patients have Responsibilities Too?' (2006) 65 *CLJ* 397, 405 and fn 35; M Brazier and N Cave, *Medicine, Patients and the Law* (4th edn, Penguin Publishing, London, 2007) 156–57; J Herring, *Medical Law and Ethics* (2nd edn, OUP, Oxford, 2008) 95; E Jackson, *Medical Law: Text, Cases and Materials* (OUP, Oxford, 2006) 135; K Williams, 'Litigation Against English NHS Ambulance Services and the Rule in *Kent v Griffiths*' (2007) 15 *Med L Rev* 153, 157; A Grubb, 'Medical Negligence: Duty of Care and *Bolam*' (1998) 6 *Med L Rev* 120, 122–23.

175 *Good Medical Practice* (2006), in effect 13 Nov 2006, and available at: <http://www.gmc-uk.org/guidance /good_medical_practice/GMC_GMP.pdf>.

176 *ibid*, 5.

177 A Grubb *et al* (eds), *Principles of Medical Law* (3rd edn, OUP, Oxford, 2010, forthcoming) [3.37].

178 *Good Medical Practice* (2006) 4.

179 (1996) Aust Torts Rep ¶81-376 (NSWCA) 63,166.

180 Note the comment in: M Jones, *Medical Negligence* (4th edn, Sweet & Maxwell, London, 2008) 144 ('[i]t remains to be seen whether a court could be persuaded that [the GMC guidelines, para 11] of an appropriate professional standard can be translated into a legal obligation sounding in damages for breach').

181 [2001] QB 36 (CA).

182 [1997] QB 1004 (CA) 1034, citing: *Hedley Byrne & Co Ltd v Heller & Partners Ltd* [1964] AC 465 (HL); *Henderson v Merrett Syndicates Ltd* [1995] 2 AC 145 (HL).

183 *ibid*, 1036.

184 [2001] AC 619 (HL) 654. For similar observations that any assumption of responsibility is to be objectively assessed, see, e.g.: *Henderson v Merrett Syndicates Ltd* [1995] 2 AC 145 (HL) 181; *Caparo Industries plc v Dickman* [1990] 2 AC 605 (HL) 637; *Smith v Eric S Bush* [1990] 1 AC 831 (HL) 862.

185 [2006] UKHL 28, [2007] 1 AC 181, [5].

186 [2009] UKHL 11, [2009] 1 AC 874, [40].

187 [1997] QB 1004 (CA) 1035 (emphasis added).

188 *OLL Ltd v Secretary of State for Transport* [1997] 3 All ER 897 (QB).

189 *Capital & Counties plc v Hampshire CC* [1997] QB 1004 (CA).

190 *Alexandrou v Oxford* [1993] 4 All ER 328 (CA).

191 *Hill v Chief Constable of West Yorkshire* [1989] AC 53 (HL); *Smith v Chief Constable of Sussex Police; Van Colle v Chief Constable of the Hertfordshire Police* [2008] UKHL 50.

192 *Mitchell v Glasgow CC* [2009] UKHL 11.

193 (1995) 36 NSWLR 344 (SC) 359 (Badgery-Parker J). It was not cited expressly on appeal, but the two majority justices, Kirby P and Cole JA, expressly approved of the trial judge's reasoning: [1996] Aust Torts Rep ¶81-376 (NSWCA) 63,155 (Kirby P), 63,176 (Cole JA).

194 A point also made in, e.g.: K Day, 'Medical Negligence—The Duty to Attend Emergencies and the Standard of Care' (1996) 18 *Sydney L Rev* 386, 392–93.

195 For an argument that the police, coastguard and fire services should be under a common law duty of professional rescue, but where breach of that duty should, necessarily, be difficult to prove, see, e.g.: K Williams, 'Emergency Services to the Rescue, or Not, Again' [2008] *JPIL* 265; and earlier, by the same author: 'Emergency Services to the Rescue' [2008] *JPIL* 202.

196 [2009] UKHL 11, and the comments variously made at: [15]–[23] (Lord Hope) [39]–[44] (Lord Scott), [56]–[63] (Lord Rodger), [74]–[77] (Baroness Hale), [81]–[84] (Lord Brown).

197 *ibid*, [29] (Lord Hope).

198 Discussed in text accompanying n 155 above.

199 *McDowell v Gillie*, 626 NW2d 666, 672 (ND 2001), interpreting the provisions of ND Cent Code 32-03.1-02 (2001).

200 The Criminal Code of the Northern Territory (NT), scheduled to the Criminal Code Act 1983 (NT) as Sch 1.

201 *Salmon v Chute* (1994) 70 A Crim R 536, [1994] NTSC 21. Ultimately, the driver was not liable, because his failure to stop and assist the victim was due to 'blind panic' rather than 'callous disregard'. See, for comment, e.g.: I Leader-Elliott, 'Good Samaritan Legislation: Appeal against Conviction following Plea of Guilty' (1996) 20 *Criminal LJ* 102.

202 *ibid*, [68] (emphasis added).

203 Note, e.g., the comments by Sarah Bird, a Medico-Legal Claims Manager in that jurisdiction, that the NT legislation 'requires any person to provide assistance to another irrespective of their training':'Good Samaritan' [2008] *Professional Practice* 570, 570.

204 As Kearney J described it in *Salmon v Chute* (1994) 70 A Crim R 536, [1994] NTSC 21, [39].

205 *ibid*, [26].

206 P Williams and G Urbas (Aust Institute of Criminology), 'Heroin Overdoses and Duty of Care' (*Trends and Issues in Crime and Criminal Justice Series*, No 188) 4.

207 Law Reform Comm of the Victorian Parliament, *The Legal Liability of Health Service Providers* (1997) [2.60].

208 L Murphy, 'Beneficence, Law and Liberty: The Case of Required Rescue' (2001) 89 *Georgetown LJ* 605, fn 234.

209 S Yeo, 'Manslaughter Versus Special Homicide Offences: An Australian Perspective' in C Clarkson and S Cunningham (eds), *Criminal Liability for Non-Aggressive Death* (Ashgate Publishing, Aldershot, 2008) ch 10, 227, contrasting the provision to: Canadian LRC, *Recodifying Criminal Law* (Rep 31, 1987), cl 54 Draft Code.

210 As Kearney J remarked in *Salmon v Chute* (1994) 70 A Crim R 536, [1994] NTSC 21, [90]. Oddly, if a victim is doomed to die in any event, such a victim is still a person 'whose life may be endangered': at [90].

211 M Eburn, *Emergency Law* (2nd edn, Federation Press, Sydney, 2005) 57.

212 D Lanham *et al*, *Criminal Laws in Australia* (Federation Press, Sydney, 2006) 171.

213 J Dressler, 'Some Brief Thoughts (Mostly Negative) About "Bad Samaritan" Statutes' (2000) 40 *Santa Clara L Rev* 971, fn 16.

214 Vt Stat Ann title 12, 519(a) (1967), effective 22 Mar 1968, revised 2002. Other, less broad, 'Bad Samaritan' statutes have been enacted in Rhode Island and Minnesota, Wisconsin and Hawaii: *ibid*.

215 164 Vt 158, 667 A 2d 289 (Va Sup Ct 1995).

216 164 Vt 478, 672 A 2d 480 (Va Sup Ct 1995).

217 M Stewart, 'How Making the Failure to Assist Illegal Fails to Assist: An Observation of Expanding Criminal Omission Liability' (1998) 25 *Am J of Criminal Law* 385, 426–27.

218 The criticisms in Table 5.2 are variously drawn from: P Romohr, 'A Right/Duty Perspective on the Legal and Philosophical Foundations of the No-Duty-to-Rescue Rule' (2006) 55 *Duke LJ* 1025, 1028–32; P Lake, 'Recognizing the Importance of Remoteness to the Duty to Rescue' (1997) 46 *De Paul L Rev* 315, 316; J Dressler, 'Some Brief Thoughts (Mostly Negative) About "Bad Samaritan" Statutes' (2000) 40 *Santa Clara L Rev* 971, 981–84; C White, 'No Good Deed Goes Unpunished: The Case for Reform of the Rescue Doctrine' (2002) 97 *Northwestern U L Rev* 507, 512–13; K Ridolfi, 'Law, Ethics and the Good Samaritan: Should there be a Duty to Rescue?' (2000) 40 *Santa Clara L Rev* 957, 959, drawing

interesting hypotheticals from the cannibalism case of *R v Dudley and Stephens* (1884) 14 QBD 273; S Lifshitz, 'Distress Exploitation Contracts in the Shadow of No Duty to Rescue' (2008) 86 *North Carolina L Rev* 315, 353–54; L Murphy, 'Beneficence, Law and Liberty: The Case of Required Rescue' (2001) 89 *Georgetown LJ* 605, 606–7; S Hoffman, 'Statutes Establishing a Duty to Report Crimes or Render Assistance to Strangers: Making Apathy Criminal' (1984) 72 *Kentucky LJ* 827, 852–64.

[219] To cite some discussions of the duty-to-rescue enactments across Europe, from either a singular or comparative perspective, see, e.g.: A Cadoppi, 'Failure to Rescue and the Continental Criminal Law' in M Menlowe and A McCall Smith (eds), *The Duty to Rescue* (Dartmouth, Aldershot, 1993) 93, 100; F Feldbrugge, 'Good and Bad Samaritans: A Comparative Study of Criminal Law Provisions Concerning Failure To Rescue' (1996) 14 *Am J of Comp Law* 630; K DeKuiper, 'Stalking the Good Samaritan: Communists, Capitalists and the Duty to Rescue' [1976] *Utah L Rev* 529; S Levmore, 'Waiting for Rescue: An Essay on the Evolution and Incentive Structure of the Law of Affirmative Obligations' (1986) 72 *Virginia L Rev* 879; M Scordato, 'Understanding the Absence of a Duty to Reasonably Rescue in American Tort Law' (2008) 82 *Tulane L Rev* 1447; P Agulnick and H Rivkin, 'Criminal Liability for Failure to Rescue: A Brief Survey of French and American Law' (1998) 8 *Touro Intl L Rev* 93; *Irish LRC Consultation Paper* (2007) [2.02]–[2.25]; E Weinrib, 'The Case for a Duty to Rescue' (1980) 90 *Yale LJ* 247; M Vranken, 'Duty to Rescue in Civil Law and Common Law: Les Extremes se Touchent?' (1998) 47 *ICLQ LQ* 934; B Markesinis, 'Negligence, Nuisance and Affirmative Duties of Action' (1989) 105 *LQR* 104; J Kortmann, *Altruism in Private Law* (OUP, Oxford, 2005) ch 4.

[220] D Schiff, 'Samaritans: Good, Bad and Ugly: A Comparative Law Analysis' (2005) 11 *Roger Williams U L Rev* 77, 79.

[221] Introduced in occupied France in 1941 by Marshall Petain. For a fascinating discussion of why the law was introduced, and of tragic earlier cases—including that of Blanche Monnier, reclused in her room for over 30 years to the knowledge of people in Poitiers—see: E Tomlinson, 'The French Experience with Duty to Rescue: A Dubious Case for Criminal Enforcement' (2000) 20 *New York LJ of Intl and Comp Law* 451, 470–75.

[222] The text is taken from the translation available at: <http://195.83.177.9/upl/pdf/code_33.pdf>, translation dated 12 Oct 2005. Previously enacted as Art 63(2).

[223] The text is taken from the translation available at: <http://www.iuscomp.org/gla/statutes/StGB.htm>.

[224] E Tomlinson, 'The French Experience with Duty to Rescue: A Dubious Case for Criminal Enforcement' (2000) 20 *New York LJ of Intl and Comp Law* 451.

[225] A Ashworth and E Steiner, 'Criminal Omissions and Public Duties: The French Experience' (1990) 10 *Legal Studies* 153, 159–60.

[226] *ibid*, 159.

[227] Court of Appeal of Bordeaux, 28 Oct 1953, D 1954.13 (noted by Ashworth and Steiner's study, *ibid*, at 159).

[228] TC Charleville, 6 Feb 1952, 1953 JCP II 6987 (noted in Tomlinson's study, at 479).

[229] TC Nancy, 2 Jun 1965, 1965 GP 1 97 (first level trial court); CA Nancy, 27 Oct 1965, 1966 D Jur 30 (second level trial court) (noted in Tomlinson's study, at 488–89).

[230] E Tomlinson, 'The French Experience with Duty to Rescue: A Dubious Case for Criminal Enforcement' (2000) 20 *New York LJ of Intl and Comp Law* 451, 457.

[231] *ibid*, 495–99.

[232] *ibid*, 480–82.

[233] *Irish LRC Final Report* (2009) [2.01].

[234] *ibid*, [4.13].

[235] *Irish LRC Consultation Paper* (2007) [2.11].

[236] *Irish LRC Final Report* (2009) [2.89] (emphasis added), and earlier in the Consultation Paper, *ibid*, [2.52].

[237] *Participating in Crime* (Rep 305, 2007).

[238] *ibid*, [3.41]. The topic was not raised earlier in: EWLC, *Murder, Manslaughter and Infanticide* (Rep 304, 2006).

[239] [2009] EWCA Crim 650.

240 J Rogers, 'Death, Drugs and Duties' [2009] *Archbold News* 6, 8–9. For discussion of a duty-to-rescue in light of *R v Evans*, see too: G Williams, 'Gross Negligence Manslaughter and Duty of Care in "Drugs" Cases' (2009) 9 *Criminal L Rev* 631.

241 The Hon Mr Justice Charles Gonthier, 'Liberty, Equality, Fraternity: The Forgotten Leg of the Trilogy, or Fraternity: The Unspoken Third Pillar of Democracy' (2000) 45 *McGill LJ* 567, [32], referring to s 2 of the Quebec Charter of Human Rights and Freedoms, which compels rescue of anyone whose life is in peril.

242 A point made in, e.g.: K Williams, 'Medical Samaritans: Is there a Duty to Treat?' (2001) 21 *OJLS* 393, 413.

243 Per *Yuen Kun-Yeu v A-G of Hong Kong* [1988] AC 175 (PC) 192, a hypothetical example given in this case.

244 *Irish LRC Consultation Paper* (2007) [2.42]–[2.43] and fn 33, citing both J Kortmann, *Altruism in Private Law* (OUP, Oxford, 2005) 24–27 and E Weinrib, 'The Case for a Duty to Rescue' (1980) 90 *Yale LJ* 247, 249–51.

245 *Irish LRC Final Report* (2009) [2.75].

246 D Schiff, 'Samaritans: Good, Bad and Ugly: A Comparative Law Analysis' (2005) 11 *Roger Williams U L Rev* 77, 140.

247 See Chapter 2, pp 49–53.

248 *Irish LRC Final Report* (2009) [2.82], [2.89].

249 *ibid*, [2.75].

250 J Adler, 'Relying Upon the Reasonableness of Strangers: Some Observations about the Current State of Common Law Affirmative Duties to Aid or Protect Others' [1991] *Wisconsin L Rev* 867, 913 ('Where a special relationship has been recognized, the law has not hesitated to recognize, as "causes" of harm, omissions that did not independently increase the risk to the plaintiff').

251 e.g., *Carmarthenshire CC v Lewis* [1955] AC 549 (HL); and the failed strike-out suit in *Home Office v Dorset Yacht Co Ltd* [1970] AC 1004 (HL) also provides an equivalent scenario. In both cases, the defendant's culpability was failing to control the actions of a third party who caused the harm to the claimants.

252 *Lowns v Woods* [1996] Aust Torts R ¶81-376 (NSWCA) 63,156 (Kirby P).

253 See Chapter 2, pp 49–53.

254 [1998] AC 232 (HL), where Lord Browne-Wilkinson adopted the earlier analysis of Hobhouse LJ in *Joyce v Merton, Sutton and Wandsworth HA* (1995) 7 Med LR 1 (CA) 20.

255 [1969] 1 QB 428.

256 *Brownie Wills v Shrimpton* [1999] PNLR 552 (NZCA, Tipping J) (accessed online, no pp available).

Chapter 6

'Good Samaritan' Liability:
Intervening to Assist Non-Patients

A INTRODUCTION

In contrast to the HCP who declines to assist a 'stranger' in need of urgent medical attention (and who was the subject of analysis in Chapter 5), this chapter considers the true 'medical Samaritan'. This HCP is one who volunteers to help that stranger, in circumstances where an existing HCP–patient relationship does not exist between them, it is an emergency scenario, and the HCP may not possess the medical skills entirely appropriate to the emergency.[1] Nevertheless, the HCP intervenes, and things do not go well—following which the victim (the non-patient) sues, claiming that the medical treatment was negligently-administered. This chapter examines when, and why, an intervening HCP will be liable in negligence.

An analysis of this sort is somewhat hampered by the fact that, with the exception of the United States, very few cases have arisen in which a HCP of any discipline has been sued for attending and rendering medical Samaritan assistance to a victim—and even more strikingly, the author's searches have revealed no cases in which liability has been *successfully* made out against a HCP in these circumstances in England, Canada or Australia to date.

Interestingly, though, other jurisdictions have busily enacted legislation by which to confer legal immunities upon Samaritans who intervene to try to help another. Various legislatures in Canada, Australia and the United States have considered that the Good Samaritan deserves, not only bouquets for intervening in the first place, but the law's *protection*. A rather startling number of statutes have sprouted over the past decade, which seek to provide Good Samaritans in general—and medical Samaritans in particular—with immunities from civil liability, provided that certain preconditions are satisfied.

The issue has been especially topical, 'closer to home', where the Irish Law Reform Commission, in 2007, consulted[2] upon whether negligent Good Samaritans ought to receive an exemption from civil liability, in light of a Private Member's Bill which was debated in the Irish Parliament in December 2005.[3] The Commission ultimately recommended, in 2009, that Good Samaritan legislation *should* be enacted for the protection of those who go to the assistance of others in Ireland.[4]

With this lightly-sketched background in mind, certain legal questions inevitably arise. What protection does the English common law *already* provide for HCPs who act in a Samaritan-type capacity? These principles are discussed in Section B. As will be seen, the modern common law offers considerable protection from civil liability. This seems only fair, given how much protection is provided by the common law for the *non-intervening* HCP too (a no-duty-to-rescue rule, with few exceptions, as Chapter 5 discussed). Hence, some legal symmetry between the intervenor and the non-intervenor is desirable—bearing out the comments of one Canadian judge that the good Samaritan 'deserves the world's accolades because he had no legal duty to act and would not have been civilly liable if he, too, had crossed over to the other side, as did the Levite and the priest.'[5]

However, would the introduction of Good Samaritan legislation in England provide any further protections—any greater *ex ante* certainty—that the common law does not already offer? Is legislation of this sort desirable for the English statute books, so as to provide clarity for the HCP who may be hesitant to 'get involved' in a medical emergency? This conundrum is discussed in Section C. Indeed, whether the so-called 'accolades' for a Samaritan should take the form of proactive legislative immunities has become an important and vexed legal issue for legislatures throughout common law jurisdictions.

In reality, damages payouts for the rescues of strangers that 'go wrong' are far more likely to concern a medical indemnity insurer, given that, nowadays, many HCPs' indemnity policies commonly provide worldwide cover for Good Samaritan acts undertaken by the insured.[6] Several major airlines have also taken out insurance policies indemnifying HCPs who come forward to assist in an 'in-flight' emergency.[7]

Regardless of the wide availability of insurance cover, however, the question of where the burden of the good Samaritan's negligent conduct *should* fall—whether on the HCP (or his insurer), or on the victim (bearing non-compensated injuries)—has become as much of a policy, as a legal, issue.

B JUDGING THE GOOD SAMARITAN AT COMMON LAW

1. Some illustrative medical scenarios

Cases from England and Canada aptly demonstrate the legal principles applicable to the HCP who intervenes to assist another in a medical emergency. Ironically enough, the leading cases concerning Good Samaritan liability in English and Canadian law both concerned St John Ambulance volunteers:

> In *Cattley v St John Ambulance Brigade*,[8] the victim, 15-year-old Sean Cattley (C), had a motorcycling accident at a schoolboy motor scrambling event near Bedford, in northern England. C came off his bike, fell flat on his back, and was injured. He was treated at the scene by the Brigade's officers, and lifted to his feet and taken to hospital. C suffered an incomplete paraplegia, and although he recovered the ability to walk, suffered permanent damage to the spine. As a result, he was left with some serious weakness and physical limitations. C alleged negligent treatment track-side by the Brigade officers. **Held:** the claim in negligence against the officers failed.

> In the British Columbia case of *St Jules v Chen*,[9] baby Matthew St Jules (M) was born at a Health Clinic at Gold River, a small community on Vancouver Island. His twin was born about 3:50 am, and M at about 5:20 am. During that intervening time, M was deprived of oxygen or blood supply to the brain, and was born with significant brain damage, resulting in severe mental and physical disabilities. M sued the community's family physicians for his negligence in handling the birth. In fact, the scenario at Gold River was precarious: it had no doctor practising obstetrics, no hospital, no operating facilities, and no birthing facilities apart from several emergency delivery kits. The Health Centre had an emergency treatment room and basic laboratory and x-ray equipment. **Held:** the claim in negligence against the physicians failed. As the judge said, 'it was notorious knowledge in Gold River that it was not a safe place for a woman to give birth', whereas the nearby Campbell River had an obstetrics department, and it was the preferred place to give birth. The court called the events here 'an unplanned delivery in the unsuitable Gold River health clinic.' M's mother was

not keen to travel to Campbell River at the relevant time, and (the court said), it was because of the mother's 'obduracy in remaining in Gold River [that] she, uninvited by Dr LeHuquet, thrust upon him her perilous quandary. He, in the best tradition of the Hippocratic oath and as a good Samaritan, came to the rescue of her and her unborn children. In a wholly unsuitable facility ... he tried to do the best possible under the circumstances.'[10]

In the Ontario case of *Stevenson v Clearview Riverside Resort*[11] (considered previously in Chapter 5), Mr Stevenson (S) dived off a jetty, in the dark, into a river, which was 12 inches deep in that part. He broke his neck and was rendered a quadriplegic. Three friends at the party observed the tragic events from the jetty. As dealt with in Chapter 5, one observed the rescue but did not enter the water (and no liability was established). The other two friends entered the water when they realised that S was not 'joking'. One turned S over in the water to enable him to breathe, and the other assisted to pull S out of the water. These rescuers may have contributed to S's catastrophic injuries by moving him as they did. Both had rudimentary medical training (a first aid course and a 'dated CPR' course, but neither was a qualified HCP). **Held:** the claims against them both were struck out as disclosing no cause of action.

In the BC case of *Smith v Moscovich*,[12] the victim, a skier, Dr Smith (S, who happened to be a GP), had a skiing accident, and injured his shoulder. A member of the ski resort's emergency medical team was Dr M, a cardiologist, and he attended the scene of the accident to assist. Dr M believed (incorrectly) that S's shoulder was dislocated, and performed a procedure called a Kocher reduction of the shoulder by manipulation, which caused S physical injury. **Held:** Dr M was not negligent.

Notwithstanding the extremely scant case law in England in which good Samaritan HCPs have been sued at all, the fear of being sued generally is one that the English medical profession appears to hold particularly close. Williams' empirical study points to a scenario in which the English medical profession 'has a strong tendency to exaggerate its exposure to the risk of being sued',[13] albeit that 'the actual or predicted Samaritan behaviour of doctors appears to be largely unaffected ... by their fear of potential legal liability'.[14] As discussed in the following sections, however, the legal principles do not bear out this concern.

2. A duty of care owed by the healthcare professional to a stranger

Once a HCP voluntarily intervenes and renders assistance to a person in medical emergency, then a duty of care to avoid or to minimise injury and harm is owed to the victim. It is one of the great ironies of the common law that '[w]hile there is no liability attached to a person who stands by while another is in peril in the absence of a special relationship [the typical Bad Samaritan], a duty of care does attach once a person voluntarily undertakes to rescue another.'[15] The Supreme Court of Canada has remarked that this result gives rise to 'some incongruity';[16] and the great torts scholar Fleming has called it an 'anomaly'[17]—yet the distinction continues to hold good.

In *Cattley*, for example, it was conceded that a duty of care was owed by ambulance volunteers who 'offer first-aid medical help to those they come across who need their assistance and whom they feel they can help' and who attend sporting or other events 'realis[ing] that they are attending an event where they are likely to be called upon to render first-aid, perhaps for very serious injuries'.

The court held that there was 'no doubt' that, in holding themselves out to attend events as they did, the ambulance volunteers owed a duty of care to victims to whom they had to render first-aid.[18]

Such observations have wider application to any HCP who voluntarily intervenes in a roadside emergency, to a call-out in a theatre, and the like.

3. Where is the legal standard of care set for the Good Samaritan?

Rescuing an injured or sick person from ill-effects is infested with conflicting interests. On the one hand, the victim has the right to expect his Samaritan rescuer to act reasonably. On the other hand, a legal standard of care which is set too high may be a definite disincentive to 'getting involved' in the first place.[19] The public policy of encouraging selfless rescue may also be undermined by setting the bar at a point where breach becomes almost inevitable.

Legally-speaking, the so-called 'accolades' to be given to a Samaritan HCP are manifested in a lower (more easily satisfied) standard of care than would ordinarily occur. Hence, although it may be said with some justification that the law 'almost discourages the Good Samaritan' because of the fact that a duty of care is owed to the victim,[20] the law also offers the Good Samaritan considerable protection. At common law, the standard is suppressed in two respects.

(a) The effect of 'battle conditions'

First, with a medical rescue, the standard of care is not that of a hypothetical HCP working in ordinary conditions, but rather, the rescuer will be judged by a lower standard appropriate to a *reasonable* individual faced with an *emergency*.

Indeed, there have been several clear indications that English judges view 'emergency' medical scenarios—in which resources may be stretched (or unavailable), and hasty judgments made—as giving rise to a lower standard of care, thereby making it easier for the rescuer to achieve the 'reasonable standard', and rendering any breach far less likely.

The term, 'battle conditions', was coined by Mustill LJ in *Wilsher v Essex AHA*[21] to describe an emergency medical scenario in which the HCP is forced by circumstances to do too many things at once, or where he must make difficult decisions on the spur of the moment. In such cases, mistakes 'should not lightly be taken as negligence'.[22] In *Kent v Griffiths* too, both trial judge[23] and Court of Appeal[24] emphasised that, in a situation of emergency confronted by ambulances responding to competing calls, the consequent duty will not be set at an unrealistically or unattainably high level, and that, in emergency conditions, a court may be more inclined to find that an 'error of judgment' was made (i.e., a mistake which nevertheless satisfied the reasonable standard of care). The House of Lords too has expressly remarked, in *In re F (Mental Patient: Sterilisation)*, that '[i]n an emergency, a doctor has little time to ponder the choices available. He must act in the best interests of his patient, as he sees them, but he can be more readily forgiven if he errs in his judgment.'[25] While none of these cases dealt with a Good Samaritan HCP who intervened to assist a stranger in need, the principle is clear—while the relevant legal standard remains that of a reasonable HCP, the emergency rescue situation being dealt with is one of the factors, and a persuasive one, to be taken into account when assessing whether the reasonable standard was met by a rescuer.

Cattley's case made the point that, regardless, the conduct of the St John volunteers had still to be reasonable, objectively assessed:

> Anyone confronted with an emergency situation is not to be held to the standard of conduct normally applied to one who is not in that situation. This does not mean that any different standard

is to be applied in the emergency. The conduct required is still that of a reasonable person under the circumstances as they would appear to one who was using proper care, and the emergency is to be considered only as one of the circumstances. An objective standard must still be applied and a person's own judgment or impulse is still not the sole criterion. He may still be found negligent if, notwithstanding the emergency, his acts are found to be unreasonable.[26]

The actions of the St John Ambulance officers met the requisite standard. In fact, the much earlier English authority of *Everett v Griffiths*[27] had also supported the notion that the standard which the HCP had to reach was to be objectively set, whether it was in the context of emergency assistance rendered at the roadside to a stranger, or given to a patient in a hospital setting. Atkin LJ (in obiter dicta) cast the obligation upon a volunteer doctor as being a duty to use a reasonable degree of special care and skill which 'would, in my judgment, apply to a doctor acting gratuitously in a public institution, or in the case of an emergency in a street accident'.

One of realities of 'battle conditions' is the state of equipment which the HCP has at his disposal. A recently-publicised incident involving an Australian doctor is illustrative. Half an hour into an international flight, the call for a doctor to come forward was put over the plane's intercom. The following events were described in one media report in these terms:

> Dr Metledge then spent the next four hours assisting an elderly man with a bowel obstruction, followed by a young woman vomiting explosively and finally a violent young couple believed to be on hallucinogenic drugs. 'What made it all so much worse was the poor state of the medical kit, which only had one pair of sterile gloves, one needle in poor condition, no sharps container and medications not labelled in English' ... A UK specialist on a flight to Africa recently had a similar experience ... Dr Osman A Dar, an endocrinologist from Cambridge, had to make do with a poorly equipped medical kit. Dr Dar offered to help when an elderly man, who did not speak English, experienced severe chest pains. The equipment available was one stethoscope, a sphygmomanometer, chewable antacid tablets, paracetamol and GTN spray. There was no aspirin.[28]

'Battle conditions' also encompass an unhelpful environment. In *Stevenson v Clearview Riverside Resort*, Wilson J referred to the 'agony of the moment' in which the rescuers found themselves—trying to assist a grievously-injured man, in the dark, following a sudden and unexpected event at what had been, up until then, a happy social occasion, and when the rescuers' rudimentary medical training little prepared them for the dangerous events quickly unfolding.[29] In *Smith v Moscovich* too, Gibbs JA described a hospital as 'a vastly different environment compared with the ski hill conditions Dr Moscovich had to contend with.'[30]

(b) No relevant specialism

The second reason that the legal standard of care may be suppressed for a rescuer HCP is that he will not be judged by reference to skills that he never professed to have, but to the skills possessed by the reasonable HCP Samaritan acting in that moment.

Hence, for the medical student who delivers a baby in an emergency or for the dermatologist who assists a heart attack victim in a plane,[31] these rescuers will not be held to the higher standard of care of a consultant obstetrician or cardiologist respectively, precisely because, thrust into emergencies, they never professed to have those skills.

Similarly, in the leading Good Samaritan cases raised in this chapter, the standards of care were not particularly onerous. In *St Jules v Chen*,[32] the GP who delivered the baby at the Health

Clinic at Gold River never held himself out as possessing experienced obstetrical skills—and the standard of care which the British Columbia Supreme Court applied to the GP was that of 'a general practitioner made captive by an emergency', which standard he met, on the evidence. The main point of criticism of his conduct—that he did not try to communicate by telephone with an obstetrician in Campbell River or elsewhere—was held not to fall below the standard of ordinary care expected of him, acting under emergency conditions.[33] In *Cattley* too,[34] the St John Ambulance officers had to meet (and met) the standard of the ordinary skilled first-aider exercising and professing to have that special skill of a first-aider trained in accordance with the First Aid Manual. The two rescuers in *Stevenson* were also held to a standard of care that was not particularly stringent: '[w]ithout specialized medical training with respect to possible neck injuries, it would be predictable that a rescuer's reaction in a potential drowning situation, would be seek to remove that person from the water as quickly as possible, to ensure that they are not choking, vomiting and are able to breathe.'[35]

(c) What does not suppress the standard of care

Notably, the court in *Cattley* refused to countenance setting any lower standard, simply because the defendants were volunteers.[36] As Williams notes, under English common law, it is not correct to say that liability in negligence is to be avoided purely for reasons of altruism.[37]

Hence, to conclude, the standard of care applicable to medical rescues is suppressed in medical rescues—so that either emergency conditions and/or a lack of specialist skill will offer considerable legal protection to the Good Samaritan HCP.

4. How is breach assessed for a Good Samaritan?

Assessing whether the Good Samaritan's act or omission constituted a breach of the duty is, perhaps, the most unsatisfactory part of the common law's treatment of the person who chooses to 'wade in' and assist a victim. There are some contrary indications as to the appropriate test to apply—and crucially, the tests are capable of producing varying results. The three possibilities are shown in Figure 6.1.

Perfection in legal treatment is clearly **not** the legal requirement—but which of those, below it, is the correct test of breach? All of them have been judicially canvassed from time to time. Dealing with each in turn:

(a) The *Bolam* test of breach

In *Cattley*, the English High Court applied the usual *Bolam* test of breach:

> the test to be applied to determine whether negligence has been proved against the first-aider, like Mr Nicholson, or the St John's Ambulance Brigade, is the test set out in *Bolam* ... Mr Nicholson or any other person holding himself out as a first-aider trained in accordance with the [First Aid Manual], would be negligent if he failed to act in accordance with the standards of the ordinary skilled first-aider exercising and professing to have that special skill of a first-aider.[38]

According to the evidence at trial, given by those skilled in first-aiding and by consultants in spinal injuries, the Brigade officers treated the injuries sustained by victim Sean Cattley in accordance with the ordinary skills to be expected of a St John Ambulance first-aider, trained in accordance with the Manual. In the same vein, in the Canadian case of *St Jules*,[39] the GP who delivered the

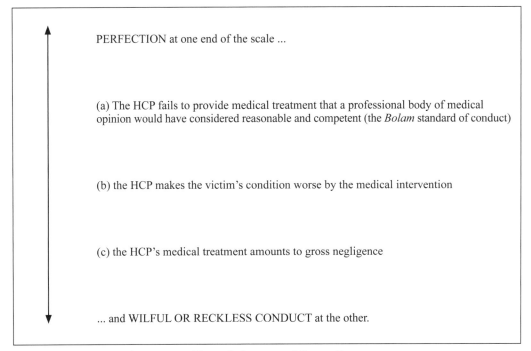

PERFECTION at one end of the scale ...

(a) The HCP fails to provide medical treatment that a professional body of medical opinion would have considered reasonable and competent (the *Bolam* standard of conduct)

(b) the HCP makes the victim's condition worse by the medical intervention

(c) the HCP's medical treatment amounts to gross negligence

... and WILFUL OR RECKLESS CONDUCT at the other.

Figure 6.1   The various tests of breach for a good Samaritan

claimant in an emergency at Gold River's Health Clinic satisfied the *Bolam* test—a view that has been endorsed as the applicable breach test for rescuers by other Canadian case law too.[40]

However, in spite of the *Bolam* test being applied in *Cattley*, English law is not as clear as all this, due to the appellate authorities discussed below.

(b) The 'making it worse' rule
Of all the possible tests by which to gauge whether the Good Samaritan was in breach, the most controversial is that, by his intervention, he must not make the victim's condition worse than it would have been without his intervention. The test, fuzzy though it be, has considerable English judicial support, albeit by way of dicta.

In *Kent v Griffiths*,[41] Lord Woolf MR said that it made 'good sense' that a Samaritan member of the public would not be in breach unless 'his own acts cause damage beyond that which the claimant would have suffered if he had not intervened.'[42] In fact, in that case, given that the ambulance service to which a 999 call had been placed on behalf of a very ill woman undertook three times to provide an ambulance to her, Lord Woolf regarded it as 'wholly inappropriate to regard the LAS and its employees as volunteers', because the ambulance service and its crews were paid out of public moneys.[43] Nevertheless, the comments about what test of breach should apply to good Samaritan intervention reflected earlier statements, also by the Court of Appeal, in *Capital and Counties plc v Hampshire CC*,[44] where it was said about a doctor who happened to witness a road accident: 'if he volunteers assistance, his only duty as a matter of law is not to make the victim's condition worse.'[45] Other English cases support this view: 'in the case of a doctor who goes to the assistance of a stranger injured in an accident[,] he does not, as a rule, undertake the patient–doctor relationship so as to make him liable for lack of care, but only a duty not to make the condition of the victim worse';[46] and 'the act of undertaking to cater for the medical needs of a victim of illness or injury will generally carry with it the duty to exercise reasonable care in addressing those needs [but] this may not be true of the volunteer who offers assistance at the scene of an accident'.[47]

None of these cases concerned good Samaritan intervention by HCP volunteers—and none of them referred to *Cattley*. In turn, *Cattley* did not refer to the 'making it worse' test of breach.

The 'making it worse' test has received strong academic criticism, for several reasons:

- Grubb argues[48] that, by doing the minimal and allowing a victim to die, a Samaritan HCP does not take an *affirmative* step to 'make it worse' (as the phrase seems to contemplate)— yet if the evidence suggests that there was something that the HCP could have done to improve, or prevent a deterioration in, the victim's condition, then that *should* be sufficient to establish a breach;

- Williams admonishes[49] the rule by making the point: 'what exactly does "not making worse" mean in this context: "not worse" than if nobody had stopped to help the victim at all? or "not worse" than if timely and competent treatment had been provided by a Samaritan doctor?'

- Williams further argues[50] that the 'making it worse' rule brings into play issues that are better dealt with under causation. Take, for example, the scenario in *Kent v Griffiths*[51]—the ambulance took almost 40 minutes to turn up after the 999 call was first accepted by the ambulance operator. If the victim, her husband, and her attending GP had realised that such delay would occur, then the victim's husband would have driven her to the hospital himself, but Lord Woolf MR observed that 'if an ambulance service is called and agrees to attend the patient, those caring for the patient normally abandon any attempt to find an alternative means of transport to the hospital'.[52] By its inexcusable delay, the ambulance *did* make the situation worse—but, argues Williams, whether the victim would have acted differently is more relevant to causation than to the question of whether the ambulance *breached* its duty;[53]

- Lord Cullen, writing extra-curially, questions[54] whether the 'making it worse' rule has any 'sound basis in law for so limiting the duty of a doctor' acting as a Samaritan rescuer, given that it appears to directly conflict with Atkin LJ's comments in *Everett v Griffiths*.[55]

In the author's view, to these may be added some further criticisms:

- surely sufficient leeway is given to a Samaritan HCP by the suppression of the standard of care (via the emergency and specialist skill elements, discussed previously), without recourse being needed to such a sympathetic test of breach as 'not making the victim's condition worse';

- in the leading cases considered earlier in this chapter involving good Samaritan HCPs which applied the *Bolam* test of breach, in none of them was liability proven—proving that the *Bolam* test will not necessarily lead to a floodgates of successful claims against Good Samaritans; and

- there is much to be said for Judge Prosser QC's viewpoint, in *Cattley*, that the clarity of the law pertaining to Samaritans is best served by a 'simple' test of standard of care—and that philosophy should be extended to the appropriate test of breach, in this author's view. A common test of breach—the *Bolam* test, as amended by the *Bolitho* 'gloss' (should the professional body of opinion prove to be 'irrational or illogical')—should apply to *all* medical treatment, no matter in what circumstances it is provided. If a different test of breach is to be used, just for Samaritan assistance, then difficult scenarios may arise: Was the doctor really acting as a *volunteer*? Was there an absence of any antecedent relationship? Was it truly an *emergency* Samaritan scenario? Precisely these sorts of disputes have arisen under the Good Samaritan statutes (as will be discussed shortly in Section C), and it behoves the common law to avoid such uncertainties.

(c) The gross negligence test

In *Cattley v St John's Ambulance Brigade*,[56] the ambulance officers argued that the test of negligence which should be applied to them should differ from that which normally applies to HCPs—instead (they argued), their conduct would have to be 'manifestly short of the standard to be expected', so as to amount to gross negligence, before they could be found liable. In other words, a first-aider should only be found negligent 'in exceptional circumstances and not where he has acted conscientiously and in good faith'. This submission was categorically rejected by the court. Judge Prosser QC remarked that 'gross negligence' was not a concept much used in English common law, and that such a test 'would be confusing and ... unnecessary'.[57]

The issue of 'gross negligence' has arisen most frequently in English common law in the (limited) context of awards of exemplary damages. Relevant case law[58] demonstrates that the term can bear one of *three* possible meanings. It can indicate a degree of intent, i.e., wilfully reckless and wanton conduct by the defendant; or, it can point to a very large departure from the ordinary standard of care, some act or omission that truly plumbs the depths of incompetence; or, it can indicate the severity of the victim's injury, by showing a high magnitude of damage resulting from the negligent act.

Interestingly, the view that all other defendants should be liable for 'ordinary negligence', but that Good Samaritans should only be liable for 'gross negligence', is a commonly-invoked provision in 'Good Samaritan' statutes which have been enacted in other jurisdictions, as the discussion in Section C will address. In that context too, the term, 'gross negligence', has given rise to real interpretative difficulties.

In any event, under English common law, Samaritans' conduct is **not** to be assessed against a gross negligence test: there is no judicial support for that proposition.

5. Conclusion

To summarise this section, two factors—emergency conditions and a standard that does not attribute to the HCP any skills that he did not profess to have—have limited the standard of care owed by medical Samaritans. Furthermore, the tests of breach that apply to a good Samaritan—whether that be the 'making it worse' rule, or the *Bolam* test of breach—are difficult to make out.

These common law principles reflect a judicial concern 'not to discourage benevolence and altruism',[59] and to promote the 'social policy concern [of] selfless rescue'.[60] In combination, they tend to render a HCP an unlikely defendant when delivering Samaritanesque help. The less-than-encouraging prospects of a successful legal action (per 'the traditional benevolence shown by the law under the normal rules of negligence to those who take affirmative action in an emergency'[61]) no doubt explains, in part, why the instances of any actions being instituted against Good Samaritans are rare. There are, no doubt, other possible reasons too—a reluctance of victims to 'bite the hand that helped them'; the fact that Samaritan help is a small fraction of all the medical treatment rendered;[62] a reluctance to become involved in litigation; the difficulties in proving medical negligence in *any* context; and settlement of cases prior to trial.[63]

Against this backdrop, it is perhaps surprising, then, that the Canadian provincial and Australian state legislatures have been so active in implementing Good Samaritan legislation (to add to the extensive good Samaritan legislation existing in the United States). More recently still, the Irish Law Reform Commission has recommended similar legislation for Samaritans in that jurisdiction.[64]

Attention will now turn to this Good Samaritan legislation. Samples of legislation will be used to illustrate how they have operated to date, and to assess whether these types of statutes have anything to offer the would-be Samaritan HCP in England.

C   GOOD SAMARITAN LEGISLATION: ANY LESSONS FOR ENGLAND?

Bad Samaritan statutes impose a duty, whereas Good Samaritan statutes are said to appeal to the conscience, and, at the same time, encourage rescue efforts with the fear of litigation removed. As one US District Court has observed:

> Generally, the Good Samaritan laws are meant to shield persons who render help from liability for wrongdoing born out of their attempted assistance ... These laws encourage our citizens to provide assistance to those in need. A classic example is a doctor driving by the scene of a car accident. Without the shield of the Good Samaritan law, the doctor may drive by the accident scene, instead of stopping to provide help.[65]

It is of interest, first of all, to review some key law reform opinion, as to whether or not such statutes are desirable additions to the legislative landscape.

1. The desirability of Good Samaritan legislation: law reform opinion

Interestingly, law reform opinion has been quite divided. Relevant reform bodies in Ireland[66] and Victoria[67] favoured the enactment of protective legislation for rescuers, for reasons that reflect the US District Court's concerns:

- the Victorian Parliamentary Committee said that it 'would hopefully provide the incentive for health service providers to give assistance in emergency situations without fear of litigation',[68] which would be to the general public's advantage;
- the Committee proposed that the practical effect of such legislation would be to educate the medical profession as to the law, and to 'dispel some myths' among members of the profession about what, precisely, their obligations and their exposure to liability amounted to;[69] and
- the Irish Commission noted that, even though most Samaritans save lives, and most often their acts lead to 'profound thanks' from the victims, there was, at least, the potential for a claim of liability in the event of a botched rescue, and for that unusual possibility, good Samaritan legislation was 'worth the candle'.[70]

On the other hand, the Ipp Committee, in its review of the Australian law of negligence,[71] and some 30 years earlier, the Manitoba[72] and the Ontario[73] Law Reform Commissions, had all categorically considered such legislation to be unnecessary, inappropriate, and fraught with difficulties:

- the Ipp Committee noted that there was no relevant Australian case against a good Samaritan up to the time of its Report,[74] which rendered the effort to debate and enact legislation rather otiose;
- the common law already offered sufficient protections to the good Samaritan[75]—so that to introduce legislation conferring immunity in *extra* circumstances would 'tip the scales of personal responsibility too heavily in favour of intervenors and against the interests of those requiring assistance';[76]
- the Ipp Committee remarked upon the lack of any real insurance-related problems in the area;[77] and
- the Manitoba Law Reform Commission concluded that the drafting of elements of such legislation would be fraught with problems, and noted (similarly to the Ipp Committee) that prior to the enactment of the Good Samaritan statutes in Canada, there had not been a single reported decision involving a suit successfully brought against a rescuer.[78]

2. The legislative position in Australia, Canada and the United States

In spite of its preceding Law Reform Commission's opinion on the issue, Manitoba enacted good Samaritan legislation,[79] as have most of the Canadian provinces, but not in exactly the same terms.[80] Australia's state legislatures also, by and large, ignored the Ipp Committee's recommendations that no further protection was required for rescuers over and above that already provided by the common law, and all states and territories have now enacted good Samaritan statutes.[81]

Of the legislation, Canadian and Australian academic commentators have been less-than-enthused. Various bases of criticism are summarised in Table 6.1.

There has been extensive good Samaritan legislation enacted in the United States[82] (although their wording varies significantly from state to state) which, in general, immunises from civil damages any person acting negligently who, in good faith, rendered emergency aid to a victim at the scene of an emergency. In addition, HCPs providing good Samaritan care in certain specifically-defined circumstances may also be protected.[83]

All of the abovementioned good Samaritan legislation has a socially-responsible sentiment—but without any *blanket* protection being provided for a Samaritan. It is a 'qualified exemption'[84] only. Immunity from liability is only achieved where the good Samaritan rescuer satisfies a number of threshold tests. A typical one, common among the statutes, is that the good Samaritan must have acted without expectation of remuneration. Notably, all statutes require a measure of responsible behaviour from the good Samaritan, whether it be acting 'in good faith', 'honestly', 'without gross negligence', or 'not recklessly' (although these terms are rarely, if ever, statutorily defined). A good Samaritan's liability is merely excused in *most* circumstances, i.e., where the Samaritan has been negligent in the ordinary sense.[85]

Otherwise, the pre-conditions vary. Some of the relevant statutes cover only HCPs, and some have a wider coverage than that. The statutes apply where 'emergency assistance' (or similar phrase) had to be provided—but whether that covers both medical treatment and medical *advice* is not always treated consistently. Under some statutes, the protection conferred is removed altogether by instances of statutorily-defined misbehaviour on the part of the Samaritan, such as intoxication, whilst other statutes are silent on the issue.

The employment status of an individual HCP is not treated consistently among the statutes either. Some provide protection for the HCP for his negligent 'good Samaritan' acts, but render his *employer* vicariously liable for the sins of its employee; whereas other statutes also protect the

Table 6.1   Canadian and Australian academic criticism of their respective good Samaritan legislation

---

- there was no 'pressing need' for the legislation at all, given the paucity of case law;[86]
- there was no evidence that the existence of such statutes elsewhere had encouraged more rescues;[87]
- it was arguable that legislation that provided immunity for all injuries caused (whether by negligence or by gross negligence) could, in effect, grant rescuers a licence to act unreasonably and inefficiently, which would be a socially undesirable consequence.[88]
- legislation excusing good Samaritan liability has 'exacerbated the existing divide between negligence and moral blameworthiness', as there will be 'no liability in many instances of culpable wrongdoing';[89]
- intensive medical lobbying produced the legislation,[90] which, ironically, has not necessarily allayed the concerns of HCPs, with refusals to offer assistance *still* attracting media attention;[91]
- to introduce good Samaritan legislation, on top of already-existing Acts that provided various limitations of liability to rescuers (e.g. ambulance officers, coastguard and lifesavers) causes a morass of uncertainty and confusion in a very sensitive area: '[m]ost, if not all, of the emergency services that are established by an Act of Parliament have the benefit of some clause designed to limit liability, and none of them is the same. The fact that Parliament has passed legislation designed to cover "civil liability" whilst leaving so many other Acts still in place, with special and different rules for various members of different organisations and professions, suggests an *ad hoc* approach to legislative reform';[92]
- the statutes, although reasonable consistent, differ slightly from one jurisdiction to another, causing unwanted complexities and uncertainties;[93]
- as a further irony, if the legislation was meant to protect HCPs in the position of Dr Lowns in *Lowns v Woods*,[94] the GP who did not attend a seriously-fitting Patrick Woods, and who was ultimately held liable at common law for failing to do so, that scenario would not be covered by the relevant New South Wales legislation—Dr Lowns would not have received any immunity from liability under these provisions, had they been enacted at the time—because the statutory protection is predicated upon a doctor who 'comes to the assistance' of the victim. Dr Lowns, however, did not attend.[95]

---

vicariously-liable employer. Location can also be very significant. Some statutes may require the HCP to have provided the assistance at a hospital or medical centre only, whilst other statutes may again be silent, thereby presumably covering all areas in which Samaritan assistance is rendered.

By way of illustration only, three separate provisions are reproduced below, for reference and comparison. First, ***Ontario's*** Good Samaritan Act 2001 provides (extract only):

---

s 1 Definition

In this Act,

'health care professional' means a member of a College of a health profession set out in Schedule 1 to the Regulated Health Professions Act, 1991.

s 2 Protection from liability; Persons covered; Reimbursement of expenses

(1) Despite the rules of common law, a person described in subsection (2) who voluntarily and without reasonable expectation of compensation or reward provides the services described in that subsection is not liable for damages that result from the person's negligence in acting or failing to act while providing the services, unless it is established that the damages were caused by the gross negligence of the person.

(2) Subsection (1) applies to,

    (a) a health care professional who provides emergency health care services or first aid assistance to a person who is ill, injured or unconscious as a result of an accident or other emergency, if the health care professional does not provide the services or assistance at a hospital or other place having appropriate health care facilities and equipment for that purpose; and

    (b) an individual, other than a health care professional described in clause (a), who provides emergency first aid assistance to a person who is ill, injured or unconscious as a result of an accident or other emergency, if the individual provides the assistance at the immediate scene of the accident or emergency.

(3) Reasonable reimbursement that a person receives for expenses that the person reasonably incurs in providing the services described in subsection (2) shall be deemed not to be compensation or reward for the purpose of subsection (1).

The New South Wales' good Samaritan provisions, contained in the Civil Liability Act 2002, are reproduced below—

---

s 56 Who is a good samaritan

For the purposes of this Part, a 'good samaritan' is a person who, in good faith and without expectation of payment or other reward, comes to the assistance of a person who is apparently injured or at risk of being injured.

s 57 Protection of good samaritans

(1) A good samaritan does not incur any personal civil liability in respect of any act or omission done or made by the good samaritan in an emergency when assisting a person who is apparently injured or at risk of being injured.

(2) This section does not affect the vicarious liability of any other person for the acts or omissions of the good samaritan.

---

s 58 Exclusion from protection

(1) The protection from personal liability conferred by this Part does not apply if it is the good samaritan's intentional or negligent act or omission that caused the injury or risk of injury in respect of which the good samaritan first comes to the assistance of the person.

(2) The protection from personal liability conferred by this Part in respect of an act or omission does not apply if:

    (a) the ability of the good samaritan to exercise reasonable care and skill was significantly impaired by reason of the good samaritan being under the influence of alcohol or a drug voluntarily consumed (whether or not it was consumed for medication), and

    (b) the good samaritan failed to exercise reasonable care and skill in connection with the act or omission.

(3) This Part does not confer protection from personal liability on a person in respect of any act or omission done or made while the person is impersonating a health care or emergency services worker or a police officer or is otherwise falsely representing that the person has skills or expertise in connection with the rendering of emergency assistance.

Thirdly, as an example of a US statute, *Minnesota's* relevant legislation (Civil Liability Limitations Good Samaritans) states:

---

§ 604A.01 (2002), subd 2. General immunity from liability

(a) A person who, without compensation or the expectation of compensation, renders emergency care, advice, or assistance at the scene of an emergency or during transit to a location where professional medical care can be rendered, is not liable for any civil damages as a result of acts or omissions by that person in rendering the emergency care, advice, or assistance, unless the person acts in a willful and wanton or reckless manner in providing the care, advice, or assistance. This subdivision does not apply to a person rendering emergency care, advice, or assistance during the course of regular employment, and receiving compensation or expecting to receive compensation for rendering the care, advice, or assistance.

Finally, it is of interest to compare the provisions which the most recent law reform opinion on the issue considered to be desirable and feasible. The *Irish Commission* drafted a Civil Liability (Good Samaritans and Volunteers) Bill 2009 in these terms:

---

s 2 Definitions

In this Act, unless the context otherwise requires—

'assistance, advice or care' includes administering first-aid and, or alternatively, using an automated external defibrillator;

'damage' includes death of or personal injury to any person;

'gross negligence' means—

    (a) the individual was, by ordinary standards, negligent;

    (b) the negligence caused the injury at issue;

    (c) the negligence was of a very high degree;

    (d) the negligence involved a high degree of risk or likelihood of substantial personal injury to others, and

    (e) the individual was capable of appreciating the risk or meeting the expected standard at the time of the alleged gross negligence;

'personal injury' includes any injury or illness;

...
s 3 Civil liability of good samaritans
(1) A good samaritan shall not be held liable in any civil proceedings for damage caused to another person in the circumstances referred to in subsection (2), unless the damage is caused by the gross negligence of the good samaritan.
(2) The circumstances are that the good samaritan provides assistance, advice or care to another person who has been injured in an accident or in an emergency or other circumstance of serious or imminent danger.
(3) in this section and Act, a 'good samaritan' is an individual who provides assistance, advice or care in the circumstances referred to in subsection (2) without any expectation of payment or other financial reward.

Notwithstanding the best of intentions, the very terminology of the statutes can give rise to drafting and interpretative difficulties. The definition and scope of what constitutes a Samaritan, and Samaritan activity, contain numerous 'loop-holes', by which protection can be lost, and by which the Samaritan can then be exposed to an action for ordinary negligence. The purpose of the following section is to consider some factual scenarios and legal issues that have arisen in American, Australian, and Canadian case law to date, involving HCPs who have acted as good Samaritans, and the interpretative difficulties which they have raised under their respective statutes.

3. Drafting and interpretation problems under 'Good Samaritan' statutes

While the case law in Australia and Canada under their respective 'Good Samaritan' statutes has been relatively sparse, there have been a large number of cases arising under the equivalent US statutes, many of which have involved HCPs. Those which are discussed below are merely chosen for illustrative purposes, without any attempt herein to undertake a comprehensive case-wide or jurisdiction-wide analysis of the relevant American law on the topic.[96] The overriding impression gained from considering American 'Good Samaritan' jurisprudence is that many aspects of, and phrases used in, the Commonwealth 'Good Samaritan' legislation remain to be tested by inventive claimants, for whom medical intervention did not prevent injury.

There are ten particular areas where considerable room for legal argument (and, hence, the need for careful drafting choices) exists. Dealing with each in turn (and specifically in the context of a defendant HCP who has intervened to assist in a medical emergency, and who has then sought the protection of a 'Good Samaritan' statute):

(a) Bad faith/gross negligence
'Good Samaritan' statutes are usually drafted so as to excuse ordinary negligence on a HCP's part, but leave that party exposed to civil liability for worse degrees of culpability—i.e., for 'gross negligence', 'bad faith', wilful negligence', and the like. Typically, use of these phrases has caused interpretative difficulties.

Regarding the use of '*gross negligence*': as mentioned previously,[97] the phrase can bear one of at least three possible meanings: conduct on the defendant's part that amounts to wilful intent; or conduct that manifests a huge degree of incompetence; or conduct that causes a high magnitude of damage to the victim. The term, where it appears, is usually not statutorily defined. Such silence applies under BC's good Samaritan statute[98]—and the issue as to what the phrase meant fell to be considered in what is still the only case which has been brought, to date, against HCPs under any of the Canadian 'Good Samaritan' statutes:

> In *Fraser v Kelowna Motorcycle Club*,[99] the victim, 10-year-old Gregory Fraser (GF), was a competitor in a 250 cc race at a junior motorcycle race at Kelowna, British Columbia, despite the fact that the minimum age for entry was 13. GF and his parents had driven all night from Washington state to compete in the race, with GF sitting on his mother's lap for the drive; GF had never raced 250 cc bikes previously; and he had never ridden at this particular track. Whilst leading the race, he looked back over his shoulder, failed to negotiate a corner whilst doing so, was thrown from his bike following impact with a dirt shoulder, and sustained serious permanent brain damage. Immediately following the accident, GF was attended by St John Ambulance personnel, who cleared his airways and administered oxygen. GF thereafter sued, *inter alia*, the St John Ambulance and its attendants, alleging that their negligent treatment resulted in his hypoxic brain damage. The St John Ambulance argued that GF suffered diffused brain damage as a result of the actual impact, and not from their treatment, and that in any event, the attendants were immune from liability under BC's Good Samaritan Act 1996. **Held:** Gregory failed in his claim for compensation; the Act provided immunity.

Other BC authorities had already considered that 'gross negligence' had a 'plain meaning'— '[i]n the absence of any clear legislative intent to define the concept of gross negligence, it should be given its plain meaning as it has developed under the common law'.[100] However, there was BC precedent that referred to two possible interpretations. On the one hand, the term could mean 'if there is not conscious wrongdoing, there is a very marked departure from the standards by which responsible and competent people ... habitually govern themselves'.[101] On the other hand, it could mean negligence leading to a high magnitude of injury, so that 'if more than ordinary care is not taken, a mishap is likely to occur in which loss of life, serious injury or grave damage is almost inevitable.'[102] In the end, the *Fraser* court did not resolve the issue of which of these interpretations applied under BC's statute. Whichever applied, neither was proven against the St John Ambulance officers in their treatment of Gregory Fraser.[103]

The term is also used in Maryland's Good Samaritan Act[104]—and in *McCoy v Hatmaker*,[105] it was held to mean conduct that constituted a high threshold of wrongdoing: 'mere recklessness is not enough; there must be reckless disregard for human life.'[106] In this case, a rescuer tried (unsuccessfully) to revive a motorist who had suffered cardiac arrest, and the court noted that the victim's estate 'cannot point to any facts that show [the rescuer] made a deliberate choice not to give McCoy a chance to survive, and, at the end of the day, it is deliberateness that lies at the core of the [gross negligence] standard of willfulness and wantonness.'[107] This, of course, is a different meaning of 'gross negligence' from that used in *Fraser*.

Interestingly, in its Draft Civil Liability (Good Samaritan and Volunteers) Bill 2009, the Irish Law Reform Commission chose to define 'gross negligence', by reference to *both* the degree of incompetence ('a very high degree') and the risk of a high level of personal injury ('substantial personal injury') to the victim.[108] One or the other is not sufficient, under the 'gross negligence' definition; both limbs would have to be satisfied by the victim, to successfully sue the Good Samaritan in litigation.

It may be recalled[109] that the defendant ambulance attempted, in *Cattley v St John Ambulance Brigade*,[110] to convince the English High Court that a medical Samaritan should be liable for 'gross negligence' under the common law in this jurisdiction, but for nothing other than that. The submission was rebuffed by the court on the basis that to introduce such a concept into English common law, in this context, would be 'confusing'. Experience elsewhere clearly demonstrates the truth of that statement!

Re the phrases, '*bad faith*' or '*good faith*': some Samaritan statutes (such as New South Wales' Civil Liability Act, reproduced previously) require the rescuer to act in 'good faith', or conversely, require an absence of 'bad faith'. Again, a variety of meanings has been attributed to these terms. The issue arose for consideration, in the context of a HCP rescuer, under New Jersey's Good Samaritan Act:[111]

> In *Lundy v Adamar of New Jersey*,[112] the victim, Mr Lundy (L), 66 years old and with a history of coronary artery disease, was gambling at a blackjack table at TropWorld Casino when he suffered a heart attack and fell to the ground unconscious. He was assisted by three other patrons, and then by an on-duty nurse from the casino's medical station, Nurse Slusher (S). During some of this period, L had no pulse, was not breathing, and had to be given CPR. S was urgently summoned from the medical station, and brought with her an ambu-bag, oxygen, and an airway, but not the intubation kit, because she was not qualified to use it. While he survived the heart attack, L was left with permanent disabilities, and claimed that TropWorld (via its employee S) owed him a duty to provide him with medical care, which it breached by the non-use of the intubation kit, and that Trop World/S lost any immunity which might otherwise have been conferred by New Jersey's good Samaritan law. **Held:** Mr Lundy's claim failed.

In fact, Mr Lundy did not assert that there was bad faith on the part of his rescuer, Nurse Slusher (the case was decided in TropWorld's favour on another point). On the subject of 'bad faith', though, the US Court of Appeals (Third Circuit) reiterated that there was no bad faith on the nurse's part not to fetch the intubation kit so that one of the other bystanders (who happened to be a pulmonary specialist) could use it.[113] The Court accepted that she was unqualified to use the intubation kit, and made a 'a good faith effort to revive Lundy and to maintain his respiration and pulse pending the arrival of the emergency medical technicians'.[114] These comments appear to test the rescuer's conduct from an objective point of view—there was no great departure from the ordinary standard of care that would have been sufficient to warrant a finding of bad faith here.

Conversely, to act in 'good faith' has been said[115] to require that the rescuer acted in 'that state of mind denoting honesty of purpose, freedom from intention to defraud, and, generally speaking, means being faithful to one's duty or obligation' (held the Californian Court of Appeal, when construing a statute that was intended to protect 'hospital rescue teams' from liability).

The Irish Commission did not favour use of a 'bad faith' test whatsoever,[116] preferring academic views[117] that the phrase generally meant a very culpable standard of behaviour judged on an objective basis, and hence, added nothing to the phrase, 'gross negligence'.

Re the phrase, '*wilful negligence*': Texas's Good Samaritan statute[118] prefers the phraseology that the rescuer is not liable, unless his acts are 'wilfully or wantonly negligent.' (It will be recalled that Minnesota's good Samaritan provisions, reproduced previously, refer to 'wilful *and* wanton'). As recently as 2009, the District Court for the Southern District of Texas had to outline just what the Texas statute meant, in a case arising out of alleged negligence committed in a hospital emergency room in the treatment of a serious bacterial infection. The following passage as to what the disjunctive phrase 'wilfully or wantonly negligent' means seems, with the greatest respect, somewhat unclear:

> wilful or wanton requires one or the other. 'Wilful' means deliberate, intentional. 'Wanton' means merciless, inhumane, without check or limitation. As modifiers of 'negligence', the difference

between 'wilful or wanton' and 'wilful and wanton' is difficult to discern. Negligence could not be 'wilful' without being 'wanton'. The difference between 'or' and 'and' does not make the latter standard so vague that it is really no rule at all ... It is clear that the wilful and wanton negligence standard of §74.153 requires, at a minimum, the same level of proof as gross negligence. Mathematical precision indicating where, if at all, 'wilful and wanton negligence' falls along the spectrum between gross negligence and malice is not required.[119]

The District Court was (optimistically?) confident that courts and juries had sufficient guidance to assist their determination of whether a good Samaritan warranted immunity under Texas's provision.

Hence, were English law reformers to look at the possibility of introducing some Good Samaritan legislation, they would need to carefully consider what level of incompetence would attract statutory protection, what level would lose statutory protection, and how to define those levels—and it seems strongly preferable that the definition occur in the legislation itself.

(b) No expectation of fee or reward

Generally speaking, a HCP acting in a Samaritan capacity must have provided the medical assistance without fee or compensatory reward, in order to receive the protection of the statutes. Otherwise, if the Samaritan acted with financial gain in mind, then he will be culpable for ordinary negligence, and there will be no need for the victim to prove gross negligence (or whatever level of culpability the particular statute requires). A few points of contention about this requirement have arisen under the relevant Acts.

First, if a HCP is paid his expenses, that has not lost him the protection of the Good Samaritan statute. In *Fraser's* case, the British Columbia Supreme Court held that the volunteer St John's Ambulance officers fell squarely within the terms of that jurisdiction's Good Samaritan Act, being exactly the type of medical rescuers 'envisaged in the Act and singled out for protection'.[120] Further, remarked the court, they were hardly employed staff when they were acting as volunteers at the race track, receiving no remuneration whatsoever.[121] Gregory Fraser had argued that the ambulance attendants were 'employed' with a duty to provide such services in their capacity as trackside ambulance officers, and that they recovered expenses for their services which (it was argued) constituted receiving compensation. This argument failed. The decision thereby signifies a wide construction to be given to what was intended by way of voluntarily-rendered assistance under BC's Good Samaritan Act—expenses do not count.

By contrast, it has been suggested that all professional rescuers who are dispatched to assist as part of a disaster relief effort (such as ambulance and fire crews) will lie outside the protection of the Australian good Samaritan statutes, because all such emergency personnel are undertaking the relief effort with the expectation of being paid a salary.[122] On the thorny issue of in-flight medical emergencies, one Australian commentator has pointed out that no statutory protection is available if a HCP is 'the paid medical escort on an aeromedical evacuation'.[123] American commentators also note that the same position would exist under most good Samaritan state statutes in that jurisdiction, if HCPs were to respond to a call to volunteer their services during a health pandemic, but were paid for those services.[124]

Secondly, the Samaritan may not expect compensation from the victim whom he assists—but he may well expect compensation from *some other source* (say, an employer or agency), for the medical services that he rendered to the victim. If the treating HCP does not expect a fee or reward from *the victim*, is he still a good Samaritan (entitled to an immunity for his ordinary negligence), even though he did indeed obtain *some* economic gain from rendering the service?

This issue potentially arose in *Lundy's* case,[125] although the case did not ultimately turn on the point, and hence there is no judicial comment upon it. Nurse Slusher was employed by TropWorld[126] for the purposes of providing nursing assistance for the casino's patrons as and when required. She surely did so in the expectation of compensation or reward—not from the victim himself, Mr Lundy, but from her employer, because the services to Mr Lundy were provided in the course of her employment at the casino. In the end, the court did not need to decide this issue because Nurse Slusher successfully defended the suit on other grounds (the limited pre-existing duty owed to Mr Lundy as casino patron was discharged). But should someone in Nurse Slusher's position be protected by the provisions of a good Samaritan statute, simply because, in rendering the emergency assistance, she did not expect any reward from Mr Lundy? If her income from the employer *could* be taken into account, then the victim has a much easier task. In that case, the rescuer has acted in expectation of compensation, and the victim only has to prove negligence according to the ordinary standard of reasonable care, rather than having to prove gross negligence (or some other high level of culpability), on the rescuer's part.

This question of whether a Samaritan HCP acted without expectation of remuneration, when his fee was coming from someone other than the victim, has arisen directly for consideration under Illinois' Good Samaritan Act:[127]

> In *Henslee v Provena Hospitals*,[128] the victim, Mrs Johnson (J), suffered an anaphylactic reaction to Chinese food she had eaten, which contained peanuts. She had trouble breathing, her husband drove her to a nearby medical Care Centre, and Dr Drubka (D), a doctor at reception, rushed out to the car to attend to a now-unconscious J. Dr D concluded that J had an emergency medical condition, ran back into the Care Center and returned to the car with an ambu-bag, oral airway, endotracheal tube, and laryngoscope. He treated J in the front seat of the car until police and paramedics arrived. Dr D's evidence was that his treatment of J would have been no different, had she been taken *into* the Care Centre's premises. J arrived in the ambulance at hospital about half an hour later, clinically dead, and having suffered irreversible brain damage. She died prior to trial due to complications. Dr D claimed the protection of the Good Samaritan statute. In this case, Dr D was employed and compensated by Midwest Emergency Associates (MEA). MEA had a contract with the hospital that ran the Care Centre, to provide doctors for both the hospital emergency room and the Care Centre. **Held:** Given that Dr D was paid an hourly fee for his services by MEA, the Good Samaritan Act did not apply to protect him from a claim in negligence.

Mrs Johnson's estate claimed that the statute afforded Dr Drubka no protection because, even though he did not bill Mrs Johnson directly, he worked in anticipation of earning remuneration from MEA for his work at the Centre. In fact, the doctor did not directly bill *any* patient whom he saw at the Centre, but was paid a daily fee for his attendance by MEA. The Illinois statute required a Good Samaritan to 'provide emergency care without fee'. Hence, did this mean that a HCP did not charge a 'fee' if he did not bill the victim directly for the emergency services? Or was the HCP's receipt of economic benefit from MEA by working at the centre a 'fee' for the purposes of the statute? After reviewing relevant authorities, the District Court, unsurprisingly, concluded that the term 'without fee' was ambiguous. It held, however, that the statute should be interpreted according to the legislative intent (which was to establish 'numerous protections for the generous and compassionate acts of its citizens who volunteer their time and talents to help others'), and that the HCP here was *not* a 'volunteer' as the legislature intended.[129] Hence, statutory protection was unavailable.

A third conundrum is that, if the good Samaritan statute only depends upon the HCP's not being paid *by the victim*, surely it is within the HCP's power, then, to decline to render a bill to the victim, and so 'buy' protection under the good Samaritan statute? In other words, money foregone equals legislative protection. In *Henslee v Provena Hospitals*, the District Court accepted (obiter) that, if the HCP himself did not render a bill to the victim, and if, additionally, the hospital never billed the individual for his services, then that was sufficient to shield the HCP from any liability.[130] In either case, the HCP would act 'without fee'. However unfair that may appear to be, the Court said that the language of the statute was so clear and unambiguous that it 'cannot look beyond the plain and ordinary meaning of those words'.[131]

With such conundrums arising in American jurisprudence, the Commonwealth statutes (and the Irish Draft Bill) could arguably have benefitted from tighter drafting in this respect.

(c) Can a corporation be a good Samaritan?

What if a victim alleges that a corporation or entity should have had systems in place to ensure that appropriate emergency medical assistance was rendered to that victim? A tragic American case in which a college student died during lacrosse practice highlights this point of interest in good Samaritan statutes:

> In *Kleinknecht v Gettysburg College*,[132] the victim, college student Drew Kleinknecht (K), 21, died of cardiac arrest during a practice session of the intercollegiate lacrosse team. In an application for summary judgment,[133] it had been held that the College itself had no duty to anticipate and guard against the chance of a fatal arrhythmia in a young and healthy athlete, and thus the College did not negligently breach any duty that it might owe directly to K. **Held:** the finding was reversed on appeal, with a majority holding that 'the College had a duty to provide prompt and adequate emergency medical services to Drew, one of its intercollegiate athletes, while he was engaged in a school-sponsored athletic activity for which he had been recruited'. The matter was sent back for trial on the question of breach.

For present purposes, the court had to consider the legal position as to whether the *college* itself could claim immunity under Pennsylvania's Good Samaritan law,[134] or whether the protection afforded to 'persons' meant that the Act could not apply to corporations. The court noted[135] that Pennsylvania statute defined the term 'person' as including corporations, partnerships, and associations, unless the statutory context indicated otherwise. It was 'unlikely', however, that the Pennsylvania legislature intended that corporations could achieve immunity as good Samaritans, given that the acts of rescue and lending assistance 'can only be taken by a natural person. Therefore, ... we predict that the Supreme Court of Pennsylvania will not hold that a corporation is entitled to immunity under the Pennsylvania Good Samaritan law.'[136]

Interestingly, the Irish Law Reform Commission assumed that its review of Irish good Samaritan law was not intended to cover legal persons, but only individuals who had rendered Samaritan assistance;[137] and that view was carried forth to its Final Report, whereby a 'good Samaritan' and a 'volunteer' are both defined to mean 'an individual'[138]—a view that would be consistent with *Kleinknecht*.

The issue of vicarious liability on the part of a good Samaritan's employer is also significant, although many good Samaritan statutes are silent about it. Pennsylvania's good Samaritan statute fell into this category, but in *Kleinknecht's* case, the Court of Appeals for the Third Circuit remarked[139] that the College was potentially vicariously liable for any acts or omissions of the employees who sought to assist Mr Kleinknecht when he collapsed at lacrosse practice, before the ambulance was able to arrive, even if those employees ended up obtaining immunity from civil liability themselves under the good Samaritan statute. Any vicarious liability was not dependent on the employee's immunity status under the statute; the College could be liable, regardless.

Notably, New South Wales' statute has specifically anticipated this legal dilemma,[140] by expressly preserving the vicarious liability of the good Samaritan's employer.

Hence, under both *Kleinknecht's* judicial interpretation and New South Wales' legislative direction, if an employed HCP rendered Samaritan assistance and was *ordinarily* negligent in doing so, then the good Samaritan statute would immunise the HCP himself (provided that he was not acting in expectation of financial reward), but would leave his employer open to vicarious liability for that ordinary negligence.

As *Lundy v Adamar of New Jersey* suggested,[141] however, if the employee is rendering assistance to the victim in his capacity as an employee, in the course of his employment (and especially if it is done at premises owned and controlled by the employer), it will have been done with the expectation of reward. In that scenario, the good Samaritan protection will not apply to protect the employee either.

(d) Rendering 'assistance'

Undoubtedly medical Samaritans will find this aspect of the typical good Samaritan definition, 'rendering assistance', the easiest to satisfy—although, even on this point, controversy is capable of arising.

First, can *advice* constitute the type of assistance that attracts good Samaritan statutory immunity? Suppose that, to modify the scenario in *Stevenson v Clearview Riverside Resort*[142] (in which Mr Stevenson dived into 12 inches of water and broke his neck), a HCP bystander did not enter the water to turn him over nor assist him from the water, but gave instructions from the jetty as to what was to be done. Is that 'assistance'? The Minnesota legislature saw fit to include reference to 'advice' as comprising medical care that can attract immunity. In the absence of that type of legislative foresight, the matter is not entirely free from doubt. The Irish Commission observed[143] that it wished to cover the widest types of activity possible, so as to encourage the 'broad concept of "active citizenship"', and to that end, referred to 'assistance, advice or care' in its Draft Bill.[144]

Secondly, is *attempting* to render emergency medical care to a victim sufficient to attract good Samaritan immunity, and, if so, what does that term cover?

> In *Gomes v Hameed*,[145] Dr H responded to a 'code blue' in a hospital, to assist a young pregnant woman, Georgette Gomes (G), who had stopped breathing shortly after the premature delivery of her twins. On the doctor's own evidence,[146] he did not act personally during the emergency, but merely observed other HCPs' treatment of the emergency. G was left with severe brain injuries, and contended that because Dr H did not render any care, he could not invoke statutory immunity under Oklahoma's good Samaritan statute.[147] **Held:** Dr H derived good Samaritan immunity under Oklahoma's statute.

The Supreme Court of Oklahoma considered that the Samaritan statute covered the doctor, because whether he administered an alleged overdose of magnesium sulfate to control the patient's contractions himself (which had been alleged on one version of the evidence), or whether he merely responded to the emergency call and found himself an observer of multiple doctors and nurses who were in the room already assisting the patient, his conduct 'qualifie[d] as rendering or attempting to render care, thus invoking the statute's protection from claims of negligence.'[148]

Thirdly, how *minimal* can assistance be, in order to attract statutory immunity for the Good Samaritan? Some cases have sought to answer this question, but have not concerned HCPs *per se*. For example: a Samaritan came across an injured girl and agreed to drive her from the scene of the snow-mobile accident to the medical centre, but the car was hit by a tractor-trailer and the victim was killed—in driving the victim to the centre, the driver was acting as a Samaritan, was rendering assistance, and was protected.[149] Merely stopping at the scene of an accident to ask whether help was required was enough to qualify as 'assistance' and to provide immunity to the would-be Samaritans against any suit in negligence in another case.[150] Turning on safety lights at the scene of an emergency has also qualified as 'assistance'.[151]

Fourthly, does statutory immunity protection under Good Samaritan statutes cover *all care* rendered to the victim—or only medical care? A recent Californian case had to consider this very point, in the context of the California Health and Safety Code, § 1799.102, which reads:

> No person who in good faith, and not for compensation, renders emergency care at the scene of an emergency shall be liable for any civil damages resulting from any act or omission. The scene of an emergency shall not include emergency departments and other places where medical care is usually offered.

> In *Van Horn v Watson*,[152] a group of friends had been smoking marijuana and drinking, and thereafter drove home in two vehicles. One vehicle crashed, and one of the passengers travelling in the other vehicle, Miss Torti (T), pulled her friend, Miss Van Horn (V), out of the crashed vehicle. V alleged that this rescue effort caused her permanent paralysis. The two parties offered entirely different constructions of the provision above. T argued that she was entitled to immunity as a good Samaritan, because the provision broadly applied to both non-medical and medical care rendered at the scene of any emergency, and she provided non-medical care by removing V from the smoking vehicle. V, on the other hand, argued that the provision only applied to the rendering of emergency *medical* care at the scene of a medical emergency, which pulling her from the vehicle did not constitute. **Held:** T did not obtain the benefit of Good Samaritan protection.

The Californian Supreme Court observed that the provision 'is certainly susceptible of Torti's plain language interpretation'. However, it preferred a construction that served the intent of the legislature rather than a literal construction, and the legislative intent apparent in this statute was to encourage citizens and bodies to undertake acts of emergency *medical* care.[153]

(e) Assistance rendered at a hospital/medical centre

One of the most controversial aspects of good Samaritan immunity has been *where* the emergency care may occur, and still qualify for Samaritan protection from ordinary negligence liability. Extraordinarily, in some US jurisdictions, Samaritan protection may occur in a fully-staffed and fully-equipped hospital.

In *Henslee's* case[154] (the chinese food reaction case), the US District Court noted a strange consequence that had ensued from the Illinois Good Samaritan statute with which it was concerned:

> Surprisingly, despite the legislature's original intent to protect volunteer doctors who happened by the scene of an automobile accident and chose to render aid, the Good Samaritan Act has never been applied in such a situation. Instead, Illinois courts have primarily used the Good Samaritan Act to immunize doctors in the context of an emergency situation arising within a hospital.[155]

Indeed, the court noted that, up until the time of its judgment, there was still no reported case in Illinois of a HCP being sued for malpractice after stopping to render aid in an emergency situation arising *outside* of a hospital setting.[156]

By contrast, in *Velazquez v Jiminez*,[157] the Supreme Court of New Jersey held that New Jersey's Good Samaritan statute[158] did **not** extend to emergencies in hospitals, because 'the fundamental problem facing a Good Samaritan on the street (the ability to do little more than render first aid under less than optimal circumstances) is not present'.[159] Rather, the goal underlying good Samaritan legislation had to be that of 'encouraging the rendering of medical care to those who need it but otherwise might not receive it (ordinarily roadside accident victims), by persons who come upon such victims by chance, without the accoutrements provided in a medical facility, including expertise, assistance, sanitation or equipment.'[160]

> In *Velazquez v Jiminez*, Mrs Velazquez's son was born with severe disabilities and brain damage caused by oxygen deprivation during delivery, and died when only three years old. The parents settled with all their health care providers (including the obstetrician whose negligence was the primary cause of the baby's injuries), but sued another obstetrician who was not in a pre-existing doctor–patient relationship with Mrs Velazquez, but who sought to assist when she learned of the emergency on the day in question. **Held:** New Jersey's Good Samaritan Act did not operate to immunise the obstetrician from liability, and while it made no reference to emergencies arising *in a hospital setting*, the Act was not intended to apply in that scenario.

A similar interpretative difficulty could **not** emerge in Ontario, for example, as the statute specifically provides that, in order to obtain protection from liability, the rescuer must not 'provide the services or assistance at a hospital or other place having appropriate health care facilities and equipment for that purpose'.[161] In that regard, the Ontario statute appears to have the car accident-type scenario firmly in mind. Hence, on the facts of *Henslee's* case, no protection would be afforded to the doctor under Ontario's statute, because the care was given at a medical centre (even though the victim Mrs Johnson never made it through the door of the Care Centre, but was treated for anaphylactic shock in the carpark). By contrast, the assistance rendered by Nurse Slusher at the casino blackjack tables in *Lundy's* case and the assistance given by the student trainer to Drew Kleinknecht on an athletics field in *Kleinknecht's* case, were provided at places other than a hospital or medical centre, and hence, these rescuers would presumably satisfy this particular pre-requisite for obtaining protection under Ontario's statute (had any of these cases arisen for decision under that particular enactment).

(f) Emergency medical care

Most medical Samaritans *will* be acting in a scene of emergency and unexpectedness—yet, even under this typical requirement for Good Samaritan statutory protection, debates can arise.

For example, in *Swenson v Waseca Mutual Insurance Co*,[162] the issue was a live one because the Samaritan driver who was transporting an injured girl had proposed to take a quick detour via her home on the way to the medical centre. The Minnesota Court of Appeals noted that the statutory draftsman had not defined 'emergency', but that this event *did* constitute an emergency (and despite the intent to detour), given that the victim was in considerable pain and needed immediate medical assistance for her injuries.[163]

Occasionally the issue has been equally as relevant for HCP Samaritans. Three issues have arisen, in particular.

First, what if the victim's condition is not *critical*—does the medical assistance then constitute emergency care? The following case arose out of the aftermath of a Georgia tornado:

> In *Willingham v Hudson*,[164] a GP was contacted at home by the Grady General Hospital in the early hours of the morning to request his assistance to deal with the influx of patients at the hospital, following a February 2000 tornado. The GP was not the on-call physician nor the emergency response back-up physician on that date, but he (and other local doctors) arrived at the hospital and began treating tornado victims. Mrs Willingham (W) was brought to the hospital suffering from a lengthy and deep laceration to her thigh, which was open to the bone and exposed the femoral artery; a laceration to her right foot; and lacerations to her earlobe, and the GP treated her. Several days after her discharge, a 'foul smelling purulent drainage' was coming from her right foot wound, and she could not move her toes. She was ultimately diagnosed as having a necrotising infection of the right foot, and her right leg had to be amputated. W sued the GP for negligent treatment on the day of her admission. **Held:** the GP was entitled to the protection of the Good Samaritan statute.

An issue for the court was whether the HCP rendered '*emergency* care at the scene of an accident or emergency', as required by the statute.[165] The tornado victim argued that, when she was treated, the bleeding from the deep cut and lacerations was under control, and her vital signs were healthy, which took the HCP outside of the scope of Good Samaritan protection. In other words, it was not an emergency. In fact, the term, 'emergency care', is not defined in the Georgia statute (nor is the equivalent term defined in the Ontario or New South Wales statutes). Nevertheless, the court held that this *was* an emergency. The tornado had resulted in a greater-than-usual influx of patients which created an abnormal situation; the HCP's assistance had been urgently requested; the scene of an emergency could extend to a hospital location;[166] an emergency could exist wherever 'the performance of necessary personal services during an unforeseen circumstance calls for immediate action';[167] and this did not require the victim to be in a critical or life-threatening condition. Here, the thigh cut was an exposed and dirty wound which presented a high likelihood of infection; and an emergency doctor told the HCP that the wound would need to be further explored and irrigated under anaesthesia. Mrs Willingham's treatment, as a whole, constituted '*emergency* care'.[168]

Secondly, does it matter if the HCP is *summoned* to render assistance—can that still constitute an emergency? The issue arose recently in a 2009 New Jersey case:

> In *Leang v Jersey City Board of Education*,[169] the victim, Ms Leang (L), a teacher, was heard to say that 'I'm so stressed out that I can kill 22 people.' The school authorities became alarmed, and summoned the Jersey City Medical Center Mobile Crisis Unit and its Emergency Medical Technicians to transport L to hospital, where she underwent physical and psychiatric evaluations. L sued, *inter alia*, the medical personnel, who claimed that they were entitled to an immunity under New Jersey's Good Samaritan Act.[170] **Held:** the statutory immunity had no application where HCPs were summoned to assist with an emergency (but *another* type of statutory immunity applied).

The Supreme Court of New Jersey held that, while the statute did not define 'accident' or 'emergency', 'the statement that accompanied the bill that became the Good Samaritan Act makes it plain that the statute's intent was to apply to events such as *roadside accidents and like emergencies* ... [These] medical defendants did not come upon plaintiff "by chance" but instead came upon her when responding to a call for their assistance.'[171]

Thirdly, what if the HCP is *at the scene*, poised to act if need be—can an unfolding drama that requires the HCP's intervention constitute an emergency? For example, Foster explains the uncertainty which good Samaritan legislation may pose for those who are placed in supervision of students on a school trip, where they are trained to act in the case of, say, anaphylactic shock:

> it may be asked whether the administration of emergency medication qualifies as 'emergency medical services or aid' within the meaning of the [British Columbia] statute. After all, teachers are forewarned of the identity of the potential victim, the specific nature of the 'emergency' with which they may be confronted, and the specific act (the administration of a specified medication in a specified manner) which must be performed to respond appropriately and will or should have been instructed (where instruction is necessary) in the performance of that act. Indeed, from the perspective of school personnel, the only unknown is whether it will ever be necessary to administer the medication to the pupil while he or she is under their control and supervision. Thus, whether this element of uncertainty warrants treating the administration of emergency medication as 'emergency medical services or aid' remains to be seen.[172]

Interestingly, the Irish Commission preferred the term, 'emergency', to that of 'accident'—because it was a wider term that could cover situations detached from the scene of the accident (such as the transportation of the victim), and because it also covered situations which were not arising from accidents at all, yet implied that 'assistance which is provided in the heat of battle is protected.'[173]

(g) Level of injury

What (if any) minimum level of victim's injury attracts Good Samaritan protection? Of the three statutory provisions reproduced earlier, Ontario's is the widest, pertaining to a victim who is 'ill, injured or unconscious'. Although the New South Wales statute does not refer to 'illness' *per se*, presumably those who were ill on the international flights, referred to in the media report previously mentioned,[174] would qualify as victims and would thus enable the attending doctors to claim good Samaritan immunity. The Irish Commission noted that there is no minimum threshold of gravity for the injury suffered by the victim stipulated in most good Samaritan statutes,[175] and proposed none in their Final Bill.

(h) A 'voluntary' act (the problem of a pre-existing duty to rescue/assist)

Of the Good Samaritan statutory provisions reproduced at the beginning of this section, only one—Ontario's—requires the Samaritan rescuer to act 'voluntarily'. What does that word mean in this context, legally-speaking?

As McInnes describes,[176] it has given rise to two different interpretations in Canada. The Yukon legislature apparently took it to mean that the rescuer acted *willingly*[177]—and yet, McInnes asks, what rescuer would intervene unwillingly and unwittingly? To construe the word, 'voluntarily', to mean 'willingly', seems otiose. Further, McInnes argues that 'voluntarily' probably means, in this context, that the rescuer was *not under a pre-existing duty to intervene* (because of some special relationship, already recognised at common law, as giving rise to a duty to intervene to assist another[178]). If there was a pre-existing duty on the rescuer's part to assist, then the rescuer is not a good Samaritan, and the good Samaritan legislation should not apply, on this viewpoint.

It will be recalled that, in *Lundy v Adamar of New Jersey*,[179] the court had to consider whether a pre-existing duty to assist casino patron Mr Lundy was already owed by Nurse Slusher. It was, and for this reason, New Jersey's Good Samaritan Act did not apply (nevertheless, Nurse Slusher met the standard of care expected of her under her common law duty, and the claim failed).

However, what if the legislature does **not** require that the rescuer acts 'voluntarily'? McInnes poses the question whether rescuers could then come within the scope of the good Samaritan legislation, even if they were already obliged to provide assistance.[180] This obligation could feasibly arise via a pre-existing duty in tort, or under a contract of employment, or where the rescuer is under a statutory duty to rescue.

The Irish Draft Bill raises this conundrum on its face, because it omits any reference to a good Samaritan acting 'voluntarily'—yet, the Irish Commission was clearly alive to the issue when it commented that '[a]s the purpose of the proposed legislation is to encourage people who are not otherwise obliged to act, the Commission considers that it need not and should not apply to persons who already have a legal obligation to act.'[181] But without specifying that a good Samaritan must act voluntarily, it is open to argument that a rescuer who is under a pre-existing duty to help others could still feasibly fall within the good Samaritan definition of 'providing assistance, advice or care to another person who has been injured in an accident or in an emergency or other circumstance of serious or imminent danger'.[182]

(i) The effect of inebriation on the part of the rescuer, etc.

When drafting good Samaritan legislation, it is, of course, possible to provide for the Samaritan to lose his immunity by reason of his own behaviour.

As Eburn notes,[183] the Australian state legislatures did not, however, act consistently when drafting these limitations. For example, intoxication removes the immunity in every jurisdiction, except Victoria—but why, one may ask, should intoxicated rescuers receive the benefit of any immunity? As another exclusion of protection—in New South Wales, the Samaritan legislation specifically provides that the rescuer cannot rely upon the immunity if he causes the injury in the first place,[184] whereas, in Victoria, the good Samaritan **can** rely on the statute if he was the one to create the emergency.[185]

These issues are perhaps unlikely to arise in the case of a HCP who is acting as a Samaritan in a medical emergency—but, more generally, they are matters to which English law-makers may wish to have express regard, should any similar legislation ever be contemplated for this jurisdiction.

(j) The type of healthcare professional protected

The class of persons protected by good Samaritan statutes differs enormously across the relevant statutes. For example, while the New South Wales legislation covers anyone who comes to the assistance of another,[186] the position just north of the border, in Queensland, is not nearly as generous. In that state, only doctors and nurses are protected as good Samaritans,[187] as well as those members of listed entities that 'provide services to enhance public safety'.[188] The same disparate treatment of who is protected is evident in Canada, with only physicians and surgeons protected from civil liability for their good Samaritan acts under Prince Edward Island's legislation.[189]

McInnes criticises good Samaritan legislation which adopts a narrow band of protected persons, remarking that:

> while it is true that Good Samaritan laws of general applicability invite rescue from those who may lack proper medical training, it is also likely that in most cases, relief does not presuppose expertise. When a doctor is not present, a victim will usually be better served by assistance from a lay-person than by no assistance at all. Given the foregoing, one may wonder if the special status enjoyed by doctors in Prince Edward Island is not simply a product of the political power wielded by that group.[190]

The Irish Law Reform Commission, too, preferred a 'more inclusive approach' to the question of who should be a protected person. Its primary reason for drafting its Bill to encompass *any* individual who 'provides assistance, advice or care to another person' was that a narrow definition of who or what may comprise a good Samaritan 'would be incompatible with the concept of "active citizenship"'.[191]

D CONCLUSION

Some cautionary tales can be gleaned from this chapter's analysis of good Samaritan intervention.

In those jurisdictions where good Samaritan statutes have been enacted, numerous potential 'loop-holes' exist for claimant victims who allege that the Samaritan assistance provided by HCPs was negligently provided. Whether HCPs do indeed obtain the protection from civil suit which good Samaritan statutes ostensibly provide is very much dependent upon the wording of the relevant statute, and how the court chooses to interpret the key phraseology (if the Parliamentary draftsmen have left the phrases statutorily undefined). For example, the key benefit derived from good Samaritan statutes is that a HCP will only be liable for gross negligence and not ordinary negligence. However, the precise meaning to be attributed to that phrase would need to be clearly explained and understood, preferably by legislative articulation, given the several meanings which it can bear in other contexts in English law.

Relevant Australian and Canadian Good Samaritan legislation is largely untested to date, but the interpretative difficulties that have accompanied various US Good Samaritan statutes indicate just how carefully such enactments must be drafted, to provide the 'clarity' that is supposedly missing from the common law itself. There has also been the suggestion that such legislation does not abate the anxieties of the medical profession in any event—which is little wonder, given the interpretative difficulties discussed in this chapter. Given the ten interpretation difficulties canvassed in Section C, it is difficult not to agree with Zaramski's opinion that American Good Samaritan statutes are 'dangerously ambiguous', and that whatever motivation such statutes may have had to encourage Samaritan rescue activity, they have certainly encouraged activity of the *legal* kind.[192]

The fact remains, however, that there has been no successful civil liability established against a medical Samaritan in England to date under the common law—primarily due to the lower standard of care, and the *Bolam* and/or 'making it worse' tests of breach, all of which favour a HCP defendant. The common law already provides significant protections to HCPs who act in a Good Samaritan capacity. Additional statutory 'comfort blankets', over and above that which the common law already provides, would appear to be an unwanted obfuscation. There is, perhaps, also much to be said for the proposition, stated succinctly by one American commentator, that '[n]egligent samaritans are not good, and "good" samaritans don't need legislative immunity'.[193]

On the basis of the analysis contained in this chapter, this author remains unconvinced that English law requires Good Samaritan legislation, and suggestibly, it would create as many difficulties as it purported to solve.

Meanwhile, the principles pertaining to what the common law expects of medical Samaritans who intervene to help another may provide some guidance, and these are outlined in '*Potential Liability to Non-Patients and Third Parties: A Synopsis for Healthcare Professionals*', contained in the Appendix.

ENDNOTES

1 The features noted, e.g., in: the Explanatory Memorandum to the Wrongs and Other Acts (Public Liability Insurance Reform) Bill 2002 (Vic), cl 9; and Irish LRC, *Civil Liability of Good Samaritans and Volunteers* (CP 47, 2007) ('*Irish LRC Consultation Paper*') [1.55].

2 *Irish LRC Consultation Paper* (2007).

3 The Good Samaritan Bill 2005. The Commission noted (*ibid*, 2) that the Bill did not proceed past the Second Stage, but the Attorney-General nevertheless requested that it consider all aspects of good Samaritan law.

4 *Civil Liability of Good Samaritans and Volunteers* (Rep 93, May 2009) ('*Irish LRC Final Report*') [4.55]. No legislative implementation has occurred at the time of writing.

5 *Hall v Hebert* (1993), 101 DLR (4th) 129, [1993] 2 SCR 159 (SCC) (Sopinka J, dissenting) [138]. Also: *Brodie v Singleton SC* [2000] HCA Trans 508 (S44/1999, McHugh J) ('The good Samaritan was not acting pursuant to any duty of care and the Levite was not in breach of any common law duty of care when he passed by on the other side').

6 A point made, e.g., by: M Jones, *Medical Negligence* (4th edn, Sweet & Maxwell, London, 2008) 141, fn 336.

7 See discussion of these issues in, e.g.: S Bird, 'Good Samaritans' [2008] *Professional Practice* 570, 570. Some medical indemnity policies do not, however, cover doctors for *non-emergency* treatment rendered as a good Samaritan—a natural cause of further concern to doctors, as discussed in: S Salomon, 'Airlines Must Pay MD's for Non-Emergency Mid-Air Care' (*Canadian Medicine*, 21 Jul 2009),discussing medical treatment rendered by a Canadian doctor on an international flight, available at: <http://www. canadianmedicinenews.com/2009/07/airlines-must-pay-mds-for-non-emergency.html>.

8 QB, 25 Nov 1988, Judge Prosser QC. For case comment, see: G Griffiths, 'The Standard of Care Expected of a First Aid Volunteer' (1990) 53 *MLR* 255.

9 [1990] BCJ No 23 (SC).

10 *ibid* (accessed online, no pp available).

11 [2000] OJ No 4863 (SCJ, 21 Dec 2000).

12 (1989), 40 BCLR (2d) 49 (SC).

13 K Williams, 'Legislating in the Echo Chamber?' (2005) 155 *NLJ* 1938, 1938; and by the same author: 'Medical Samaritans: Is there a Duty to Treat?' (2001) 21 *OJLS* 393, 405–6.

14 K Williams, 'Doctors as Samaritans: Some Empirical Evidence Concerning Emergency Medical Treatment in Britain' (2003) 30 *J of Law and Society* 258, 280.

15 Noted in: *Stevenson v Clearview Riverside Resort* [2000] OJ No 4863 (SCJ, 21 Dec 2000) [57] (Wilson J).

16 *Horsley v MacLaren* [1972] SCR 441, (1972), 22 DLR (3d) 545, [47] (Ritchie J).

17 J Fleming, *The Law of Torts* (9th edn, LBC Information Services, Sydney, 1998) 163.

18 QB, Judge Prosser QC, 25 Nov 1988 (accessed online, no pp available).

19 Points made in: *Stevenson v Clearview Riverside Resort* [2000] OJ No 4863 (SCJ, 21 Dec 2000) [63]–[65].

20 M Brazier, *Medicine, Patients and the Law* (new edn, Penguin Books, London, 1992) 118.

21 [1987] QB 730 (CA) 749.

22 *ibid* (dicta only—no 'battle conditions' were present during the treatment of a premature baby in this case).

23 [1999] Lloyd's Rep Med 424 (QB, Turner J).

24 [1998] EWCA Civ 1941, (1998) 47 BMLR 125, 134 (Kennedy LJ); and later: *Kent v Griffiths* [2000] EWCA Civ 25, [2001] QB 36, [46] (Lord Woolf MR). Breach was proven in this case, because no satisfactory explanation was provided for the delay in the ambulance attending at the home of an ill woman). See, too, the observation in: K Williams, 'Litigation Against English NHS Ambulance Services and the Rule in *Kent v Griffiths*' (2007) 15 *Med L Rev* 153, 173, that '[t]he fact that ambulances will

commonly be responding to what is believed to be an emergency must inevitably weigh heavily with a court when breach questions come to be considered.'

25   [1990] 2 AC 1 (HL) 17 (Lord Donaldson).

26   QB, Judge Prosser QC, 25 Nov 1988 (accessed online, no pp available).

27   [1920] 3 KB 163 (CA) 213.

28   J Kron, 'Flying into Trouble' (*Australian Doctor*, 15 Apr 2008), available at: <http://www.australiandoctor. com.au/news/1e/0c055c1e.asp>.

29   [2000] OJ No 4863 (SCJ, 21 Dec 2000) [66].

30   (1989), 40 BCLR (2d) 49 (SC) [23].

31   Ipp Comm, *Review of the Law of Negligence: Final Report* (2002) [7.23].

32   BCSC, 9 Jan 1990.

33   Citing: *Challand v Bell* (1959), 27 WWR 182 (Alta SC) 188. See too: *Stevenson v Clearview Riverside Resort* [2000] OJ No 4863 (SCJ, 21 Dec 2000) [65].

34   QB, 25 Nov 1988, Judge Prosser QC.

35   [2000] OJ No 4863 (SCJ, 21 Dec 2000) [66].

36   Judge Prosser QC, 25 Nov 1988 [no pp available].

37   K Williams, 'Legislating in the Echo Chamber?' (2005) 155 *NLJ* 1938, 1938.

38   QB, 25 Nov 1988.

39   [1990] BCJ No 23 (SC) (the professional body of medical opinion 'falls far short of proving Dr LeHuquet to have been guilty of failing to act with ordinary care, indeed, if anything the preponderance of the evidence is to the contrary').

40   *Nelson v Victoria (County)* (1987), 81 NSR (2d) 334 (NS SC (Trial Div)) [26]–[27]. The court noted that this option was followed by the Nova Scotia legislature of the time: Volunteer Services Act, SNS 1977, c 20, ss 2, 4. In fact, the fire brigade which arrived too late to save a vacant house was not liable in ordinary negligence, and hence, there was no need for the fire brigade to seek recourse to the statute for protection.

41   [2000] QB 36 (CA).

42   *ibid*, [18]. The court cited, for this point, *Horsley v MacLaren (The Ogopogo)* [1972] SCR 441 (SCC) 452 (guest on cruiser fell overboard; attempts to rescue him alive failed; action in negligence against cruiser operator failed; no breach; '[w]hatever may be said in criticism of MacLaren's conduct, his efforts at rescue cannot be said to have worsened Matthews' condition': per Schroeder J).

43   *ibid*, [19].

44   [1997] QB 1004 (CA).

45   *ibid*, 1035 (the other members of the CA agreed).

46   *Powell v Boldaz* [1998] Lloyd's Rep Med 116, (1998) 39 BMLR 35 (CA) 45 (the other members of the CA agreed).

47   *Watson v British Boxing Board of Control Ltd* [2001] QB 1134 (CA) [57].

48   A Grubb, 'Medical Negligence: Duty of Care and *Bolam*' (1998) 6 *Med L Rev* 120, 125. On this point, see, too: I Kennedy and A Grubb, *Medical Law* (3rd edn, Butterworths, London, 2000) 297–98.

49   K Williams, 'Medical Samaritans: Is there a Duty to Treat?' (2001) 21 *OJLS* 393, 394.

50   K Williams, 'Litigation against English NHS Ambulance Services and the Rule in *Kent v Griffiths*' (2007) 15 *Med L Rev* 153, fn 34; and also, see *ibid*, fn 57.

51   [2001] QB 36 (CA).

52   *ibid*, [9].

53   Whether the victim would have acted differently is also relevant to whether the victim *relied* upon the HCP's intervention, which is crucial to establishing a duty of care owed by the HCP to the victim. For further discussion, see Chapter 5, pp 171–73.

54   'From the Celebrated Snail to the Good Samaritan' [Aug 2003] *Advocate* 40, 45.

55   [1920] 3 KB 163 (CA) 213.

56   QB, Judge Prosser QC, 25 Nov 1988.

57   *ibid*, (accessed online, no pp available).

58 See, e.g. the discussion of 'gross negligence' meanings in a variety of Commonwealth courts, and in the context of alleged medical negligence: *A v Bottrill* [2002] UKPC 44, [2003] 1 AC 449, on appeal from: *Bottrill v A* [2001] 3 NZLR 622 (CA); *McLaren Transport Ltd v Somerville* [1996] 3 NZLR 424 (HC); *Midalco Pty Ltd v Rabenalt* [1989] VR 461 (VSC); *Dybongco-Rimando Estate v Jackiewicz* (Ont SCJ, 4 Feb 2002).

59 As noted in, e.g.: *McLoughlin v O'Brian* [1981] QB 599 (CA) 611 (Stephenson LJ). An appeal was allowed: [1983] 1 AC 410 (HL), but this point was not criticised.

60 *Stevenson v Clearview Riverside Resort* (Ont SCJ, 21 Dec 2000) [65].

61 E Picard and G Robertson, *Legal Liability of Doctors and Hospitals in Canada* (4th edn, Thomson Carswell, Toronto, 2007) 219.

62 Williams' important empirical study demonstrated that 78% of respondent doctors had acted as medical Samaritans, but that the incidents of such activities were still relatively rare, when compared to general medical practice: K Williams, 'Are Doctors Good Samaritans?' (2004) 71 *Medico-Legal J* 165.

63 See, on this point: *Irish LRC Consultation Paper* (2007) [3.44]; M McInnes, 'Good Samaritan Statutes: A Summary and Analysis' (1992) *U British Columbia L Rev* 239, [9]–[10].

64 See n 4 above.

65 *Sabree v Williams*, 2008 US Dist Lexis 49659, at 46 (DNJ, 30 Jun 2008).

66 *Irish LRC Final Report* (2009).

67 Law Reform Comm of the Victorian Parliament, *The Legal Liability of Health Service Providers* (1997).

68 *ibid*, [2.65].

69 *ibid*, [2.65].

70 *Irish LRC Final Report* (2009) [3.101]–[3.107].

71 *Review of the Law of Negligence: Final Report* (2002).

72 *The Advisability of a Good Samaritan Law* (Rep 11, 1973).

73 OLRC, *Fourth Annual Report* (1970) 13; OLRC, *Fifth Annual Report* (1971) 13, as noted in: M McInnes, 'Good Samaritan Statutes: A Summary and Analysis' (1992) *U British Columbia L Rev* 239, [6] and fn 21.

74 *Review of the Law of Negligence: Final Report* (2002) [7.21]. Nor has there been a case since.

75 *ibid*, [7.22]–[7.23].

76 *ibid*, [7.24].

77 *ibid*, [7.21].

78 *The Advisability of a Good Samaritan Law* (Rep 11, 1973) 9–10.

79 Manitoba's Good Samaritan Protection Act 2006, CCSM c G65.

80 Ontario's Good Samaritan Act, SO 2001, c 2; British Columbia's Good Samaritan Act, RSBC 1996, c 172; Prince Edward Island's Medical Act RSPEI 1988, c M-5, s 50; Nova Scotia's Volunteer Services Act, RSNS 1989, c 497, s 3; Saskatchewan's Emergency Medical Aid Act, RSS 1978, c E-8; Newfoundland and Labrador's Emergency Medical Aid Act, RSNL 1990, c E-9; Alberta's Emergency Medical Aid Act, RSA 2000, c E-7; Yukon's Emergency Medical Aid Act, RSY 2002, c 70; New Brunswick's Medical Act, SNB 1981, c 87, s 68; Northwest Territories and Nunavat's Emergency Medical Aid Act, RSNWT 1988, c E-4. In Quebec: Civil Code of Quebec, art 1471.

81 Wrongs Act 1958 (Vic), s 31B; Personal Injuries (Liabilities and Damages) Act 2003 (NT), s 8; Civil Liability Act 2002 (WA), ss 5AB–5AE; Civil Law (Wrongs) Act 2002 (ACT), s 5; Civil Liability Act 2002 (NSW), ss 56–58; Civil Liability Act 1936 (SA), s 74; Law Reform Act 1995 (Qld), ss 15–16; Civil Liability (Amendment) Act 2008 (Tas), inserting into the Civil Liability Act 2002, ss 35A–35C. In fact, Queensland already had good Samaritan legislation in effect prior to the Ipp Committee's Report: Voluntary Aid in Emergency Act 1973 (Qld), s 3 (now defunct).

82 Nowlin notes that: 'The first Good Samaritan statute was passed in 1959 in California. Since then, all states have enacted some form of Good Samaritan legislation', listing these statutes in fn 47: C Nowlin, 'Don't Just Stand There, Help Me!: Broadening The Effect of Minnesota's Good Samaritan Immunity Through *Swenson v Waseca Mutual Insurance Co*' (2004) 30 *William Mitchell L Rev* 1001, 1007. See, also: S Pegalis, *The American Law of Medical Malpractice*, vol 2 (3rd edn, Thomson West, Eagan Minnesota, 2005) [7.13] ('There currently exists a Good Samaritan statute in all 50 states, the District of Columbia,

and the Virgin Islands. Originally enacted by the California legislature in 1959, the statutes are intended to protect the Good Samaritan from tort liability').

83   See, e.g.: Business and Professional Code (California), §2396 (conveys immunity from liability arising from rendering emergency care for complications after prior care by another).

84   A term used, e.g., in the Explanatory Memorandum of the Civil Liability Amendment Bill 2003 (WA), Part 1D.

85   For judicial insights into the connectivity between gross negligence, recklessness, and ordinary negligence, in the context of a workplace health and safety incident, see, e.g.: *R v General Scrap Iron & Metals Ltd* [2003] ABQB 22, (2003), 11 Alta LR (4th) 213, [66]–[75].

86   E Picard and G Robertson, *Legal Liability of Doctors and Hospitals in Canada* (4th edn, Thomson Carswell, Toronto, 2007) 218–19; M McInnes, 'Good Samaritan Statutes' (1992) 26 *UBC L Rev* 239, [7].

87   Picard and Robertson, *ibid*; M McInnes, *ibid*, [39].

88   M McInnes, 'The Economic Analysis of Rescue Laws' (1992) 21 *Manitoba LJ* 237, [63].

89   J Goudkamp, 'The Spurious Relationship between Moral Blameworthiness and Liability for Negligence' (2004) 28 *Melbourne U L Rev* 343, 373.

90   H Luntz, 'A View from Abroad' [2007] *U of Melbourne Law School Research Series* 2, [no pp] (accessed via: <www.austlii.edu.au>). See too: J Tibballs, 'Legal Liabilities for Assistance and Lack of Assistance Rendered by Good Samaritans, Volunteers and their Organisations' (2005) 16 *Ins LJ* 254.

91   L Skene and H Luntz, 'Effects of Tort Law Reform on Medical Liability' (2005) 79 *Aust LJ* 345, 347, citing at fn 19: 'Hospital refuses to help accident victim' (*Sydney Morning Herald*, 25 Sep 2004). See also: D Watson, 'Beyond the Call of Duty' (*Australian Doctor*, 22 Apr 2004).

92   M Eburn, 'Protecting Volunteers?' (2003) 18(4) *Aust J of Emergency Management* 7, 11.

93   M Eburn, *Emergency Law* (2nd edn, Federation Press, Sydney, 2005) 46; J Gulam and J Devereux, 'A Brief Primer on Good Samaritan Law for Health Care Professionals' (2007) 31 *Aust Health Rev* 478.

94   [1996] Aust Torts Rep ¶81-376 (NSWCA). See Chapter 5 for detailed discussion, pp 173–82 above.

95   H Luntz, 'The Australian Picture' (2004) 35 *Victoria U of Wellington L Rev* 40, fn 60.

96   For useful discussion of relevant American statutes, and for further academic analysis of several of the points discussed in this section, see, e.g.: C Nowlin, 'Don't Just Stand There, Help Me!: Broadening The Effect of Minnesota's Good Samaritan Immunity Through *Swenson v Waseca Mutual Insurance Co*' (2004) 30 *William Mitchell L Rev* 1001; J Pardun, 'Good Samaritan Law: A Global Perspective' (1998) 20 *Loyola of Los Angeles Intl and Comp LJ* 591; M Scordato, 'Understanding the Absence of a Duty to Reasonably Rescue in American Tort Law' (2008) 82 *Tulane L Rev* 1447; B Sullivan, 'Some Thoughts on the Constitutionality of Good Samaritan Statutes' (1982) 8 *Am J of Law and Medicine* 27; L Murphy, 'Beneficence, Law and Liberty: The Case of Required Rescue' (2001) 89 *Georgetown LJ* 605; J Hodge *et al*, 'The Legal Framework for Meeting Surge Capacity Through the Use of Volunteer HCPs During Public Health Emergencies and other Disasters' (2005) 22 *J of Contemporary Health Law and Policy* 5; H Dagan, 'In Defence of the Good Samaritan' (1999) 97 *Michigan L Rev* 1152.

97   See p 209 above.

98   Nor was it defined under the predecessor statute: Good Samaritan Act, RSBC 1979, c 155.

99   (1988), 9 ACWS (3d) 56 (BCSC). See further: S Wexler, 'Case Comment' (1994) 52 *Advocate* 251.

100   *Doern v Phillips Estate* (1994), 2 BCLR (3d) 349 (SC), 51 ACWS (3d) 1368, [92]. The court was considering the term as it appeared in s 21(3) of the Police Act, SBC 1988, c 53.

101   Specifically: *Walker v Coates* [1968] SCR 599 (SCC) 601, citing the earlier statement of Duff CJC in: *McCulloch v Murray* [1942] SCR 141 (SCC) 145.

102   *Doern v Phillips Estate* (1994), 2 BCLR (3d) 349 (SC), 51 ACWS (3d) 1368, [93], citing: *Ogilvie v Donkin* [1949] 1 WWR 439 (BCCA) 441.

103   (1988), 9 ACWS (3d) 56 (BCSC) [17].

104   Md Code (1973, 1998 Repl Vol), §5-603(a) & (b), which provides: '(a) A person described in subsection (b) of this section is not civilly liable for any act or omission in giving any assistance or medical care, if:
       (1) The act or omission is not one of gross negligence;
       (2) The assistance or medical care is provided without fee or other compensation; and

(3) The assistance or medical care is provided:
    (i) At the scene of an emergency;
    (ii) In transit to a medical facility; or
    (iii) Through communications with personnel providing emergency assistance.

[105] 135 Md App 693, 763 A 2d 1233 (Ct App Md 2000).

[106] *ibid*, 706, citing: *Tatum v Gigliotti*, 80 Md App 559, 568, A 2d 354 (1989).

[107] *ibid*, 708.

[108] *Irish LRC Final Report* (2009) [4.81].

[109] See p 209.

[110] QB, 25 Nov 1988, Judge Prosser QC.

[111] §2A:62A-1 NJ provides that any person 'who in good faith renders emergency aid at the scene of an ... emergency to the victim ... shall not be liable for any civil damages as a result of acts or omissions by such person in rendering the emergency care.'

[112] 34 F 3d 1173 (3rd Cir 1993).

[113] *ibid*, 1180–81.

[114] *ibid*, fn 10.

[115] *Lowry v Henry Mayo Newhall Memorial Hosp*, 185 Cal App 3d 188, 195–96 (Cal CA, 1986), construing the phrase, 'good faith', as used in: s 1317 of the California Health and Safety Code.

[116] *Irish LRC Final Report* (2009) [4.76].

[117] In particular: E Loh, 'Legal Risks of Volunteer Firefighters—How Real are They?' (2008) 23 *Aust J of Emergency Management* 47; and M Henry, 'Statutory Immunities: When is Good Faith Honest Ineptitude?' (2000) 15 *Aust J of Emergency Management* 10.

[118] Texas Civil Practice and Remedies Code, §74.152.

[119] *Guzman v Memorial Hermann Hosp Sys*, 2009 US Dist Lexis 23445, at 37–39 (SD Tex).

[120] (1988), 9 ACWS (3d) 56 (BCSC) [17].

[121] *ibid*, [13].

[122] M Eburn, *Emergency Law* (2nd edn, Federation Press, Sydney, 2005) 48.

[123] As quoted in: 'Legal Clouds Gather when the Worst Happens' (*West Australian*, 4 Jun 2008, 4).

[124] S Hoffman, 'Responders' Responsibility: Liability and Immunity in Public Health Emergencies' (2008) 96 *Georgetown LJ* 1913, 1917; C Coleman, 'Beyond the Call of Duty: Compelling Health Care Professionals to Work During an Influenza Pandemic' (2008) 94 *Iowa L Rev* 1, 44.

[125] 34 F 3d 1173 (3rd Cir 1993).

[126] That will be assumed for present purposes. There was some debate as to whether the nurse was arguably an employee of an independent contractor of Trop World.

[127] 745 Ill Comp Stat 49/25, which provides: 'Any person licensed under the Medical Practice Act of 1987 or any person licensed to practice the treatment of human ailments in any other state or territory of the United States who, in good faith, provides emergency care without fee to a person, shall not, as a result of his or her acts or omissions, except willful or wanton misconduct on the part of the person, in providing the care, be liable for civil damages.'

[128] 373 F Supp 2d 802 (ND Ill 2005).

[129] *ibid*, 807–15.

[130] *ibid*, 810, citing, on this point: *Rivera v Arana*, 322 Ill App 3d 641, 749 NE 2d 434, 440 (Ill App Ct 2001); *Johnson v Matviuw*, 176 Ill App 3d 907, 531 NE 2d 970, 972 (Ill App Ct 1989); *Villamil v Benages*, 257 Ill App 3d 81, 628 NE 2d 568 (Ill App Ct 1993).

[131] *ibid*, 809.

[132] 989 F 2d 1360 (3rd Cir 1993).

[133] *Kleinknecht v Gettysburg College*, 786 F Supp 449 (MD Pa 1992).

[134] 42 Pa Cons Stat Ann §8332(a), (b)(2) (1982), which provided, in part: '(a) General rule. Any person who renders emergency care, first aid or rescue at the scene of an emergency ... shall not be liable to such person for any civil damages as a result of any acts or omissions in rendering the emergency care, first aid or rescue ... except any acts or omissions intentionally designed to harm or any grossly negligent acts or omissions which result in harm to the person receiving the emergency care, first aid, or rescue.'

[135] 989 F 2d 1360, 1374–75 (3ʳᵈ Cir 1993).

[136] *ibid.*

[137] *Irish LRC Consultation Paper* (2007) [1.13].

[138] *Irish LRC Final Report* (2009), cll 3(3) and 4(3) of the Draft Bill.

[139] 989 F 2d 1360, 1375 (3ʳᵈ Cir 1993), citing also: *Muntan v City of Monongahela*, 406 A 2d 811, 813–14 (Pa Commw Ct 1979); *Wicks v Milzoco Builders Inc*, 360 A 2d 250, 253 (Pa Commw Ct 1976).

[140] Civil Liability Act 2002 (NSW), s 57(2).

[141] 34 F 3d 1173 (3ʳᵈ Cir 1993) (the claim failed for other reasons unrelated to this point).

[142] [2000] OJ No 4863 (SCJ, 21 Dec 2000).

[143] *Irish LRC Final Report* (2009) [4.64]–[4.66].

[144] Section 2, reproduced at p 215 above.

[145] 184 P 3d 479 (Okla SC, 22 Jan 2008).

[146] The doctor's deposition, reproduced in fn 6 of the judgment, read: 'I was just there to see if my help would be needed.' 'Okay. Did you ever do anything in the code, yourself?' 'My help was never needed.' 'So you were an observer?' 'I was an observer'.

[147] 76 Oklahoma Stat §5(a)(1) provides: 'Where no prior contractual relationship exists, any person licensed to practice any method of treatment of human ailments, disease, pain, injury, deformity, mental or physical condition ... who, under emergency circumstances that suggest the giving of aid is the only alternative to probable death or serious bodily injury, in good faith, voluntarily and without compensation, renders or attempts to render emergency care to an injured person or any person who is in need of immediate medical aid, wherever required, shall not be liable for damages as a result of any acts or omissions except for committing gross negligence or willful or wanton wrongs in rendering the emergency care.'

[148] 184 P 3d 479, 485 (Okla SC, 22 Jan 2008).

[149] *Swenson v Waseca Mutual Ins Co*, 653 NW2d 794 (Minn Ct App 2002), interpreting the provisions of Minn Stat 604A.01 (2002).

[150] *McDowell v Gillie*, 626 NW2d 666, 672 (ND 2001), interpreting the provisions of ND Cent Code 32-03.1-02 (2001).

[151] *Flynn v US*, 902 F 2d 1524 (10th Cir 1990). These, and several other decisions exploring the meaning of terms such as 'assistance', are discussed in C Nowlin, 'Don't Just Stand There, Help Me!: Broadening The Effect of Minnesota's Good Samaritan Immunity Through *Swenson v Waseca Mutual Insurance Co*' (2004) 30 *William Mitchell L Rev* 1001.

[152] 45 Cal 4ᵗʰ 322 (Cal SC, 18 Dec 2008).

[153] *ibid*, 327–31.

[154] *Henslee v Provena Hosp*, 373 F Supp 2d 802 (ND Ill 2005).

[155] *ibid*, 808, and citing also, for the general trends in American Good Samaritan Statutes to allow the acts to apply to doctors in hospitals: SR Reuter, 'Physicians as Good Samaritans: Should They Receive Immunity for their Negligence when Responding to Hospital Emergencies?' (1999) 20 *J of Legal Medicine* 157.

[156] *ibid*, fn 7, citing: *Blanchard v Murray*, 771 NE 2d 1122, 1129 (Ill App Ct 2002).

[157] 172 NJ 240, 798 A 2d 51 (2002).

[158] NJ Stat § 2A:62A-1.

[159] 172 NJ 240, 259–60, 798 A 2d 51 (2002).

[160] *ibid*, 250.

[161] Good Samaritan Act 2001, s 2(2)(a).

[162] 653 NW2d 794 (Minn Ct App 2002).

[163] *ibid*, 800. Discussed, e.g., by C Nowlin, 'Don't Just Stand There, Help Me!: Broadening The Effect of Minnesota's Good Samaritan Immunity Through *Swenson v Waseca Mutual Insurance Co*' (2004) 30 *William Mitchell L Rev* 1001, 1017–18.

[164] 274 Ga App 200, 617 SE 2d 192 (Ga App 2005).

[165] Good Samaritan Statute, OCGA § 51-1-29, which provided: 'Any person, including any person licensed to practice medicine and surgery ... who in good faith renders emergency care at the scene of an accident or emergency to the victim or victims thereof without making any charge therefor shall not be liable for any civil damages as a result of any act or omission by such person in rendering emergency care or as a

result of any act or failure to act to provide or arrange for further medical treatment or care for the injured person.'

166 274 Ga App 200, 203 (Ga App 2005), citing also, on this point, e.g.: *Clayton v Kelly*, 183 Ga App 45, 357 SE 2d 865 (1987), and *McIntyre v Ramirez*, 109 SW 3d 741 (Tex Sup Ct 2003).

167 *ibid*, 204, citing, e.g: *Anderson v Little & Davenport Funeral Home*, 242 Ga 751, 753 (1978).

168 *ibid*, 205.

169 198 NJ 557, 969 A 2d 1097 (NJ SC, 16 Apr 2009).

170 NJSA 2A:62A-1 provides that certain licensed practitioners of healing arts and emergency or first aid volunteers 'who in good faith render ... emergency care at the scene of an accident or emergency ... or while transporting' the victim for care 'shall not be liable for any civil damages as a result of [their] acts or omissions'.

171 *ibid*, 592–93 (emphasis added).

172 W Foster, 'Medication of Pupils: Teachers' Duties' (1995–96) 7 *Education LJ* 45, 59.

173 *Irish LRC Final Report* (2009) [4.68]–[4.69].

174 See p 205.

175 *Irish LRC Consultation Paper* (2007) [1.29].

176 M McInnes, 'Good Samaritan Statutes: A Summary and Analysis' (1992) 26 *U British Columbia L Rev* 239, [35].

177 Debates and Proceedings of the Yukon Legislative Assembly, 7th Session, 23rd Legislature (1976) 31, cited by McInnes, *ibid*, fn 110.

178 Say, a landowner towards an adjoining landowner whose property is threatened by fire, or a gaoler and prisoner.

179 34 F 3d 1173 (3rd Cir 1993).

180 M McInnes, 'Good Samaritan Statutes' (1992) *U British Columbia L Rev* 239, [36].

181 *Irish LRC Final Report* (2009) [4.78].

182 Draft Bill, cll 3(2) and (3), read together. There is no discussion of this point by the Commission, when considering 'parallel' common law duties and their proposed statutory regime, in *ibid*, [4.88].

183 M Eburn, *Emergency Law* (2nd edn, Federation Press, Sydney, 2005) 46; and by the same author: 'Protecting Volunteers?' (2003) 18 *Aust J of Emergency Management* 7, 8.

184 Civil Liability Act 2002 (NSW) s 58. Reproduced at p 214 above.

185 Wrongs Act 1958 (Vic), s 31B(3).

186 Civil Liability Act 2002 (NSW) s 56. Reproduced at p 213 above.

187 Law Reform Act 1995 (Qld) s 16.

188 Civil Liability Act 2003 (Qld) s 23. These entities include, e.g., St John Ambulance Australia Ltd, the Surf Life Saving Queensland and the State Emergency Service.

189 Medical Act, RSPEI 1988, c M-5, s 50.

190 M McInnes, 'Good Samaritan Statutes: A Summary and Analysis' (1992) 26 *U British Columbia L Rev* 239, [23].

191 *Irish LRC Final Report* (2009) [4.60].

192 M Zaremski, 'The "Good Samaritan" Goes to Court: Does the Law Protect Him?' (1979) 1 *J of Legal Medicine* 30, as cited in: S Pegalis, *The American Law of Medical Malpractice*, vol 2 (3rd edn, Thomson West, Eagan Minnesota, 2005) 161.

193 S Pegalis, *ibid*, 162.

PART III
Actual or Potential Negligence Liability for Non-Physical Injuries to Non-Patients

Chapter 7

Pure Economic Loss Claims by Third Parties Associated with the Patient

A INTRODUCTION

This chapter concerns various scenarios in which the patient is subjected to medical mistreatment, mis-diagnosis or erroneous advice from the HCP, and as a result of this negligence visited upon the patient, a third party (or institution) bears financial loss, damage or injury as a result. The third party may be completely unknown to the HCP. This chapter considers whether, and if so in what circumstances, the third party (i.e., the non-patient) may recover damages for that pure economic injury[1] from the HCP (or his insurer).

In a broader context, there have been a relatively small number of cases in which liability has been imposed on *professionals in general* (in our case, the defendant, D) for economic loss suffered by third parties (people other than the professional's client). For example, a statement may have been prepared by a financial expert (say, a bank) at the request of X, for the express purpose of the advice being communicated to Y, who then relied upon the accuracy of the statement and suffered economic loss when the advice turned out to be incorrect.[2] There is also the small group of cases in which D (say, a solicitor, or an insurance company) undertook to perform work for its client X, which entailed conferring a financial benefit on third party Y, but where, due to D's negligence, the benefit to Y never passed. In such cases, the duty to X is concurrent with a duty owed to third party Y, to enable Y to recover for an unexpected loss of benefit.[3] There are also cases in which D, who made a statement to X about Y, did so with a lack of reasonable care, thereby causing Y financial harm.[4] Yet another narrow category of case shows that third party Y, who is not the immediate object of D's negligence (X was), has recovered *directly* against D for the economically-injurious effect of that negligence upon him.[5] In each of these scenarios, Y was a third party, and recovered for his pure economic loss which was caused by D's negligence towards X.

However, the circumstances in which a third party may sue *a negligent HCP* in respect of economic losses have been less-than-clear, for a number of reasons. In some cases considered in this chapter, the courts have *assumed* that a duty of care was owed to the third party, without detailed (or any) analysis as to why that might have been so. In other instances, the relevant proximity factors that may have precluded a duty of care have been only discursively discussed, and public policy has rated from all-important to barely-mentioned. The novelty and importance of third party actions against HCPs for economic loss or damage has been frequently commented upon—with Huband JA noting what an 'unusual' case *Freeman v Sutter*[6] was (a failed abortion case in which the mother's partner sued the relevant HCP), and with Laws LJ remarking, in *Whitehead v Searle*,[7] that the question of the father's potential third party claim against the HCP in that case (a wrongful birth claim) raised a 'large question' in an area of the law that was 'still developing'. Moreover, some of the third-party-against-professional-defendant examples referenced in the previous paragraph are quite removed from cases which have been brought by third parties against HCPs, and as such, they can lack any real analogous effect.[8]

All of this must be considered against a backdrop in which the common law typically places less importance upon the recovery of pure economic loss than physical injury. As recently and succinctly stated (in another context altogether, but the comment is equally applicable to HCP liability), '[t]he courts have traditionally observed some caution and conservatism in economic loss cases. Attempts to open the floodgates ... have ultimately been rejected. An incremental approach is favoured'.[9]

Section B outlines four potential scenarios that have given rise to pure economic losses suffered by third parties as a result of negligent medical treatment of patients—the wrongful conception cases; the wrongful birth cases; the cases in which a third party has claimed the costs of caring for a patient; and the cases in which a third party has foregone financial assets or income as a result of the HCP's alleged negligence towards the patient.

Section C then examines the way in which a duty of care has been constructed (or demolished) in such cases. As is usual in third party claims, reasonable foreseeability of financial injury on the part of the third party is not, usually, the legal difficulty. Establishing the requisite proximity, and finding that a duty of care on the HCP's part is a fair, just, and reasonable result, are typically more problematical. Section D concludes.

B THE POTENTIAL SCENARIOS

1. The failed sterilisation/failed abortion cases

(a) Relevant cases

The category of cases commonly known as the 'wrongful conception' cases—whereby the parents seek monetary compensation for the physical and/or financial consequences of the birth of an 'unwanted child' which has come about due to a negligently-performed sterilisation operation upon either parent—can give rise to third party claims against the relevant HCP for pure economic loss. The medical negligence can occur because either the HCP failed to take reasonable care when performing the operation, or failed to advise the parents to use other contraceptive methods for a period thereafter.

Failed abortion cases throw up the same issues. Where both parents wish to abort the child, and this is negligently-performed, as a result of which a child is born, the child's biological father may sue the HCP who performed the abortion, even though the father was not the HCP's patient and had never consulted, nor met with, the HCP.

The Scottish case of *McFarlane v Tayside Health Board*[10] sets the bounds of what damages can be recovered in a wrongful conception action, in English common law. The parents are unable to recover the costs of raising and maintaining a healthy child, conceived and born following a failed sterilisation, on the basis that it is not fair, just or reasonable to impose liability for these economic losses on the negligent HCP—in notable contrast to the Australian position, where such claims are allowed (per the majority verdict in *Cattanach v Melchior*[11]—a decision which some Australian state jurisdictions have since reversed by statute[12]). The financial losses which *are* recoverable are the mother's general damages for the pain, suffering and inconvenience of pregnancy and childbirth, and (by majority) the special damages for extra medical expenses, clothing and loss of earnings associated with the pregnancy and birth.[13] Lord Millett artistically explained this last-mentioned head as follows:

A baby may come trailing clouds of glory, but it brings nothing else into the world. Today he requires an astonishing amount of equipment, not merely the layette but push-chair, car seat, carry cot, high chair and so on. The expense of acquiring these is considerable ... If Mr and Mrs McFarlane disposed of them in the belief that they would have no more children the cost of replacing them should be recoverable as a direct and foreseeable consequence of the information they were given being wrong.[14]

What the damages should be in a case where an *unhealthy* child is born as the result of a failed sterilisation operation was a question left open in *McFarlane* for later decision. Subsequently, in *Parkinson v St James's and Seacroft University NHS Trust*,[15] a disabled child was born subsequent to a failed sterilisation operation. *McFarlane* was distinguished; the Court of Appeal held that, in respect of a *disabled* child, the measure of damages obtainable from the negligent HCP could include the costs of providing for the child's special needs and care relating to his disability—all the extra expenses associated with bringing up a child with congenital disabilities. However, the *ordinary* costs of bringing up and caring for the child, which would have been incurred had the child been healthy, were not recoverable, in accordance with *McFarlane*. Brooke LJ called upon the principles of distributive justice: 'I believe that ordinary people would consider that it would be fair for the law to make an award in such a case, provided that it is limited to extra expenses associated with the child's disability';[16] while Hale LJ remarked that '[t]he difference between a normal and disabled child is primarily in the *extra* care that they need, although this may bring with it *extra* expenditure. It is right therefore that the parent who bears those *extra* burdens should have a claim.'[17]

In addition, it appears that, whether the child is healthy or disabled, a so-called 'conventional sum' will be available to the parents, as 'victims of a legal wrong', for the loss of their right to limit the size of their family (per *Rees v Darlington Memorial Hospital NHS Trust*[18]).

A critique of the reasoning underpinning *McFarlane*, *Parkinson* and *Rees* is beyond the scope of this book.[19] Instead, the capacity for *the non-patient* (i.e., the one who was not operated on) to bring a wrongful conception action against the HCP is the focus of discussion.

(b) Joint and solo claims

Claims by the sterilised patient only. Sometimes, in wrongful conception cases, only the parent who underwent the sterilisation operation has brought the action for wrongful conception. This may have been a tactical litigation decision because all the damages were the patient's; or it may have been necessary because, say, the father had deliberately withdrawn from any involvement in the child's upbringing. Where only the sterilised patient has been the claimant, the status of *the other parent*, as a *non-patient* of the HCP, has not arisen, and inevitably, there has been no discussion of whether the HCP owed a duty to that other parent.[20]

In other failed sterilisation cases, the patient has instituted a failure-to-warn-of-the-risks-of-failure claim, which was the patient's alone, and again, whether the HCP owed any duty to the other parent, as non-patient, did not arise on the facts.[21]

Claims by both parents jointly. In yet other cases in which one or other of the parents has undergone a failed, negligently-performed, sterilisation, both parents have brought the action and recovered damages in a joint claim.[22] *McFarlane* was one such decision:

> In *McFarlane v Tayside Health Board*,[23] the patient, Mr McFarlane (M), the father of four children, had a vasectomy operation. By agreement with his wife (the non-patient for our purposes), they

did not wish to have a larger family. Following negligent advice from the defendant surgeon that M was now infertile, the couple ceased using other contraceptive measures, and Mrs McFarlane then fell pregnant, giving birth to a healthy baby girl, Catherine. **Held:** the issue of whether a duty of care was owed to Mrs McFarlane, as a non-patient, was not discussed. Rather, the House of Lords explicitly observed[24] that the claims for 'financial loss as a consequence of the birth of the said child' was brought by both parents jointly. Clearly the damages for the pain, suffering and inconvenience of pregnancy and childbirth were Mrs McFarlane's alone, and she was entitled, by majority verdict,[25] to recover these.

There was no discussion in any of the Lordships' judgments as to whether, and why, the surgeon owed Mrs McFarlane a duty of care—this appears to have been presumed. Since the decision, it has been said that, just because the surgeon's letter informing him that the vasectomy was successful was addressed to Mr McFarlane alone, did not mean that there was no duty to Mrs McFarlane.[26]

Similarly, in the leading Australian decision in *Cattanach v Melchior*, Gleeson CJ remarked that the parents' claim 'was a joint claim, and joint damages were awarded',[27] while Kirby J described the claim as one 'in common for consequential loss'.[28] Subsequently, the New South Wales Supreme Court remarked, in *McDonald v Sydney South West Area Health Service*, that the *McFarlane* decision 'does not assist on the issue of whether the duty of care of the doctor extends to the partner of his patient'[29] (and nor did *Cattanach*).

The question as to whether a HCP, whose medical treatment of his own patient was negligent, owes any duty of care to the patient's sexual partner for the economic consequences of a failed sterilisation or abortion, becomes important in those scenarios where the parents are not able nor willing to bring their claim jointly—for example, because they are separated, or because the injury is to one parent only. That leaves the 'other parent' who was not the patient, and upon whom the sterilisation operation was not performed, with a rather uncertain legal status. Are they owed a separate duty of care by the HCP?

Claims by the non-patient/third party parent. There is some English obiter support for the proposition that the biological parent of the child born of a failed sterilisation, but who was not the sterilised parent, can claim damages for economic injury from the HCP who performed the botched sterilisation operation:

> In *Parkinson v St James and Seacroft University Hospital NHS Trust*,[30] the patient, Mrs Parkinson (P), underwent a sterilisation operation, which was performed negligently by the defendant surgeon. A child was subsequently conceived, and Mrs P was warned during the pregnancy that the child might be born with a disability. P declined to have her pregnancy terminated. Thereafter, P's marriage broke down, and her husband (the non-patient) left the family home three months before she gave birth to baby Scott (her fifth child). The baby was severely disabled. There was no claim for damages by the father against the surgeon. **Held:** the issue of the father's legal status did not arise on the facts of the case.

As an obiter comment in her judgment, Hale LJ said that the proximity between HCP (surgeon) and his patient's sexual partner in such cases was 'quite close', and that where any claim was made by a father 'who not only has, but meets, his parental responsibility to care for the child', then her 'tentative view' was that the father should have a potential claim against the HCP too.[31]

Some interesting case law has arisen elsewhere, in which biological fathers have sought damages for economic losses arising from unwanted births, following some negligent conduct by

HCPs regarding the contraceptive advice/treatment given to their female partners. Their results are something of a 'mixed bag':

In the British Columbia case of *Kovacvich v Ortho Pharmaceutical (Canada) Ltd*,[32] the patient, Ms Ferguson (F), was in a relationship with Mr Kovacvich (K, the non-patient), in which neither party wished a pregnancy to occur. F's GP admitted that he provided F with a three-month supply of sample packages of the 28-day birth control pill, but had intended to provide the 21-day pill. A pregnancy subsequently occurred. The GP was held to be 70% liable, and F 30% contributorily negligent (for failing to reconcile the 28-day pill packet with the discussion of the 21-day pill that had occurred at their consultation). K, who had separated from F shortly afterwards, was ordered to pay maintenance for the child; and he sued the GP to recover the economic costs of fathering that child. **Held:** the GP owed no duty of care to K; the matter came before the court for a ruling on the question, '[w]hether or not a medical doctor prescribing birth control pills to a woman owes any duty of care to a putative father', but the court held that, on these facts, no duty was owed, because 'it would not in my view be reasonable to infer that the doctor knew or should have known that reliance was being placed on his skill and judgment by [K].'

In the Manitoba case of *Freeman v Sutter*,[33] following a relationship between Mr Freeman (F) and a woman, a child was conceived. The mother of the child requested an abortion, which was negligently performed by HCP#1, and another doctor, HCP#2, negligently failed to diagnose the continuing pregnancy. As a result, a healthy child was born. F, as the child's biological father, sued the two HCPs in negligence. He had not been the HCPs' patient, nor had he consulted with them. F claimed general damages, plus indemnity for any future maintenance he might have to pay for the child. **Held:** the claim was struck out as disclosing no cause of action on F's part; no duty of care was owed by the HCPs to F as the biological father.

In the New South Wales decision of *McDonald v Sydney South West Area Health Service*,[34] the patient, Ms Foster (F), underwent a sterilisation operation, but it was negligently performed by the defendant surgeon. A healthy child was subsequently conceived. F's claim in negligence against the surgeon settled. The biological father of the child, Mr McDonald (M), commenced proceedings, claiming the costs of raising the baby boy (which Mrs McDonald had not claimed). The issue was a live one—whether the father, M, was owed a separate duty by the HCP. **Held:** an independent and severable duty of care was owed to M, on the basis that 'as an existing partner' of the mother, the relationship between surgeon and Mr McDonald as father was 'so close or special that a duty of care does arise'.[35]

Given that neither *Cattanach* nor *McFarlane* answered the question of whether the duty of care of a HCP extends to the partner of his patient, the decision in *McDonald* broke new ground. As will be revisited in Section C, the precise scope of the duty was that the HCP owed the biological father a duty 'to ensure that his partner, Ms Foster, was properly treated so that she or the plaintiff did not suffer the financial burden of raising an additional child'.[36]

All of the cases discussed thus far concern whether a duty of care could be owed by a HCP towards a parental non-patient who was the patient's *current* sexual partner at the time that the alleged medical negligence occurred. What, though, of the patient's *future* partners—can a duty of care be owed to that category of persons?

(c) Failed sterilisation and future sexual partners

Perhaps a sterilisation operation was negligently performed on a patient, and years later, the patient conceives a child with a partner who, at the time of the sterilisation operation, was not known to the patient, much less to the HCP. Under English law, the surgeon will **not** be in a sufficiently proximate relationship with the third party/future sexual partner, and the third party will be unable to recover any costs associated with the birth (the child-rearing costs would not be recoverable in any event, since *McFarlane*).

> In *Goodwill v British Pregnancy Advisory Service*,[37] the patient, Mr MacKinlay (M) underwent a vasectomy operation, and was thereafter advised by the BPAS (a charity which arranged and provided for sterilisation operations including vasectomies and associated counselling services) of 'permanent sterility'. The operation spontaneously reversed, without warning of this having been given to M by BPAS. Ms Goodwill (G) subsequently entered into a relationship with M, and in reliance upon what M told her about his prior vasectomy, G ceased to use other contraceptive measures. G conceived a child, three years after the operation on M had been performed, and sued, as non-patient, for the expenses associated with her daughter's birth, and for the costs of raising. **Held:** No duty of care was owed to G by BPAS. The contention was called 'manifestly unsustainable'.[38]

(d) Failed sterilisation and siblings

Suppose that, as a result of a negligently-performed sterilisation operation, a child is born, and that child's siblings allege that the unplanned child deprived them of a portion of the care, love, training, and financial support, which they would otherwise have received from their parents. Such a claim has been brought, unsuccessfully, as a non-patient claim in the United States:

> In *Cox v Stretton*,[39] the patient, Richard Cox (C) underwent a vasectomy, which was negligently-performed by the defendant surgeon. The other children of Mr Cox sued the surgeon, alleging that they had suffered and would suffer financial and other losses as a result of the negligently-performed operation. **Held:** the children's claim failed.

Rather than focus upon the duty of care question, the Supreme Court of New York held that the non-patient claimants had not suffered any recognisable damage which the law of tort could compensate. Thus far, there has been no equivalent claim in English law, so far as the author's searches can ascertain.

(e) Summary

In summary, then: although there is no English authority directly on point, there is support for the contention that, in respect of an *existing* sexual partner of a patient who has suffered negligent contraceptive treatment or advice, a duty of care *will* be owed by the HCP to that non-patient. For policy reasons, there will not be any liability attaching to the HCP for the costs of raising a child who was conceived and born subsequently to the failed sterilisation (except to the extent that the child is disabled, and the costs associated specifically with the child's disability can be recovered). However, in respect of future sexual partners of the patient, or siblings of the unplanned child, no English authorities support the imposition of any duty of care on the HCP's part to avoid pure financial losses on the part of those non-patients.

2. Wrongful birth scenarios

(a) Relevant cases

The 'wrongful birth' type of claim arises where a HCP negligently fails to diagnose or detect a condition in a foetus (e.g., Down's Syndrome, spina bifida, disabilities arising from the mother's exposure to rubella during pregnancy) which, had it been pointed out to the mother, would have resulted in the mother's choosing to abort the foetus. The allegation of negligence is that, because of the mis-diagnosis, the mother was deprived of the opportunity to lawfully terminate the pregnancy.

The disabled child does not have a cause of action against the negligent HCP—that is a 'wrongful life' claim, and such a claim is disallowed, both under English common law[40] and, since 22 July 1976, by statute.[41] Wrongful birth can only be a parental claim, not the child's. Both wrongful birth and wrongful life claims (were the latter allowed) are predicated on the basis that, but for the HCP's negligence, the child would have been lawfully aborted.[42]

According to *Rand v East Dorset HA*,[43] a claim for wrongful birth entitles the claimant parent/s to recover the extra costs of caring for and raising the disabled child (over and above the costs that would have been involved if the child had been born healthy, which are non-recoverable under *McFarlane*). One of the reasons that a wrongful life claim is deemed to be so repugnant is that it requires the court to assess the damages by undertaking a comparison between the life of a disabled child, and the non-existence of that life altogether (but for the negligence, the child's argument is that it would not have been born at all, as it would have been aborted). However, in wrongful birth claims brought by the parents, the court will undertake, instead, a comparison between a healthy child and a disabled child. Furthermore, according to *Rand*, the mother will have a claim for damages for pain and suffering relating to the pregnancy and birth, because these will have occurred as a direct result of her desire to have another non-disabled child (to 'prove to herself and to others that she could have a normal child'); the mother can also recover damages for shock and distress upon discovering the birth of a disabled child; and both parents will be entitled to recover damages for the additional stress and strain resulting from the care of a disabled child, as compared with a healthy child.[44]

Given that wrongful birth scenarios are associated with a mis-diagnosis of the disabled foetus, the mother is the patient in these scenarios. It has been judicially pointed out that the status of the non-patient parent (the father) in wrongful birth claims has sometimes been glossed over. According to Laws LJ in *Whitehead v Searle*, '[i]n some of the wrongful birth cases, it seems to have been assumed, without argument, that the father as well as the mother may claim. The possibility is certainly not ruled out in the learning. It is clear, as I think both counsel accepted, that the law on the topic is still developing.'[45]

(b) Joint and solo claims

Claims only by the mother. Where the mother (as patient) has sued, alone, for the damages brought about by the mis-diagnosis, the husband's position has not been judicially addressed,[46] so far as the author's searches can ascertain.

Claims by the father, jointly with the mother. In some other cases, the father, as non-patient, has sued jointly with the mother, in respect of the negligent failure to provide advice that would have resulted in the termination of the pregnancy, but with no judicial discussion as to the status of the father in the law suit.[47]

In a couple of these joint claims, the father recovered some damages in his own right—but without any detailed discussion of why the HCP owed the father a duty of care:

In *Rand v East Dorset HA*,[48] Mrs and Mrs Rand were the parents of K, a child born with Down's Syndrome. They sued the health authority for negligence arising from the fact that, while Mrs R was pregnant with K, the defendant doctors employed by the health authority had omitted to inform her of the results of a routine scan which indicated that Mrs R was likely to give birth to a child suffering from the condition. Had Mrs R been informed of the results of the scan, she would have elected to abort K. The health authority conceded negligence, but disputed the amount and heads of damages to which Mr and Mrs Rand were entitled. **Held:** Mr and Mrs R recovered £118,746 for the wrongful birth claim. Mr R recovered general damages of £5,000 separately, as compensation to reflect 'the true nature of the wrong done to the Rands, who have been deeply affected in their private lives by having to devote more time to the care and upbringing of K than the care and upbringing of a healthy child would have involved.'[49]

In *McLelland v Greater Glasgow Health Board*,[50] Mrs McLelland gave birth to a son, Gary, who suffered from Down's Syndrome. Both parents sued, alleging that staff at the Glasgow Royal Maternity Hospital negligently failed to carry out an amniocentesis test and failed to diagnose Gary's condition, and advise the parents of it, at the appropriate stage of pregnancy, and that if this had been done, and the results advised to Mrs M, she would have had the pregnancy terminated. Negligence was admitted, and the only issue was quantum of damages. Some of the heads of damage were claimed by Mrs M alone (a claim for solatium and for lost wages), some were claimed by the parents jointly (the past and future care and maintenance of Gary), and most significantly for present purposes, Mr M brought a claim for solatium in his own right. **Held:** Mr M was awarded £5,000 for his claim for solatium. Any detailed discussion as to the basis in law upon which this should be awarded was precluded by the fact that the Health Board had *admitted liability to both parents* at trial. In these circumstances, Lord Prosser remarked:

The question of whether an award of solatium should be made will often depend on whether there was any duty of care. In the present case, that is not the question. The defenders have admitted liability. That being so, the Lord Ordinary took as the appropriate starting point the fact that the defenders had admitted that they owed a duty of care to both pursuers, and had acted in breach of that duty: they were therefore liable in damages for any loss, injury and damage suffered by the pursuers or either of them as a result ... In presenting the reclaiming motion, counsel for the defenders acknowledged that this was not a case where one was considering whether there was a duty of care, which had been breached. That had been conceded. His contentions were at times hard to reconcile with that concession: they came close to a submission that in principle the father in a case such as this would never have a claim for solatium.[51]

Hence, these respective English and Scottish decisions do not provide much assistance upon the question of whether, and why, the HCP should owe a duty of care to the father, in a wrongful birth scenario.

Claims by the father alone. As with the wrongful conception cases, the issue of whether the father, as a non-patient, is owed a duty of care by the relevant HCP falls into much sharper relief where the biological father is bringing a sole independent claim. The question has recently arisen in English law (albeit in unusual circumstances), in a wrongful birth case, regarding financial burdens which were the father's alone to bear:

In *Whitehead v Searle*,[52] David McLeish was born to his mother, Paula McLeish (Ms M), in 1986. David was born suffering from spina bifida. Mr Whitehead (Mr W), the biological father of David, left Ms M not long after the birth. Ms M commenced a wrongful birth claim against the health authority in negligence for failing to detect spina bifida in her unborn child at a time when she could have elected to terminate the pregnancy. In 1995, before the action had been set down for trial, Ms M committed suicide. Mr W thereafter took care of David. On legal advice, Ms W's action was settled for £20,000. Mr W then sued Ms M's legal representatives for professional negligence, for failing to bring the mother's action against the health authority to a successful outcome *before* the date of her death, as a result of which the quantum of damages recoverable from the health authority were much reduced. This part of the claim succeeded. Mr W also brought a personal claim for damages, to compensate him for the cost of David's care, on the basis that Ms M's legal representatives had failed to advise and to prosecute a claim *on his behalf* against the health authority. This part of the claim failed. However, the question arose as to whether Ms M's treating doctors *could* owe Mr W a duty of care at all. **Held:** Rix LJ held that it was arguable that, in some cases, a father will have a sole cause of action for damages for wrongful birth: there was a 'potentially difficult but realistically arguable claim by Mr W in his own right, once he had shouldered parental responsibility, for the extra costs of David's care over and above those costs which would have been involved in a normal birth.'[53] The other two members of the Court did not decide the issue.

As Rix LJ pointed out, a solo wrongful birth claim by the father should also be feasible, if a mother (who would, herself, have had such a claim) died in childbirth, leaving all the care costs to be borne by the father of the disabled child.[54] Whatever the precise circumstances, his Lordship would not rule out the possibility of the father having a successful action in negligence—which would amount to a duty of care being owed by the HCP to the father as a non-patient. Notably, Rix LJ did not point to any particular proximity factors, as between a father and the HCP who missed the signs of spina bifida. Hale LJ did not do so either, in the context of a wrongful conception claim in *Parkinson v St James and Seacroft University Hospital NHS Trust*, merely remarking that 'if there is a sufficient relationship of proximity between the tortfeasor and the father ... then the father too should have a claim.'[55]

Section C will undertake the task of eliciting the proximity factors between HCP and father that could certainly warrant a duty of care being found as between HCP and the parental non-patient.

3. The costs of caring for a negligently-treated patient

Where a patient is injured as a result of the HCP's medical negligence, it may fall to a third party (or institution) to expend money or forego income, in order to care for that patient. Can that third party sue the negligent HCP? Suits of this sort have been attempted, both in England and elsewhere, as the following sample shows:

In *Islington LBC v University College London Hosp NHS Trust*,[56] the patient, Mrs J, was advised by her cardiac surgeon's secretary that she should not recommence taking Warfarin, an anticoagulant medication, after her operation for a mitral valve replacement was postponed. Ten days later, Mrs J suffered a serious and disabling stroke. Thereafter, she required institutional care, funded by her local authority, Islington LBC. Islington LBC was under a statutory duty to provide care accommodation for Mrs J. It could charge the patient for such accommodation, unless (as was the case with Mrs J) the accommodated person was unable to pay, due to lack of personal resources. Mrs J remained in that care from 1998 until 2003. In 2003, the NHS Trust reached a settlement with Mrs J for the payment to her of substantial damages in respect of its negligence (as part of the structured settlement, Mrs J was able to live with her daughter in a newly-purchased house suitable for her needs; but those damages could not (because of relevant legislation governing the NHS) include any compensation for the cost of care which she had received from Islington LBC free of charge. Hence, Islington LBC bore the cost of Mrs J's care during that five-year period, and it sued the NHS Trust directly, alleging that the NHS Trust owed a duty not to treat/fail to treat Mrs J in such a way that she would foreseeably suffer injury, which would cause financial loss to Islington LBC, in providing the care that it was obliged to provide to Mrs J. **Held:** no duty of care was owed by the NHS Trust to Islington LBC. The economic injury to the Council was reasonably foreseeable, but there was not a sufficient degree of proximity between the parties to base a duty of care and it was not fair, just and reasonable to impose such a duty on the NHS Trust.

In the Canadian case of *Brown v University of Alberta Hospital*,[57] the patient, baby Nadine (N), had been seriously abused by her father. When N was brought to the hospital by her father following one incident, she displayed symptoms of 'shaken baby syndrome', but the radiologist failed to report his suspicions, noting that the CT scan was abnormal but 'not of clinical significance'. Thereafter the abuse continued, such that N's brain was almost destroyed by massive subdural haematomata which left her severely and permanently disabled. N's mother (the non-patient in this case) sued the doctors who had failed to diagnose and report the abuse upon presentation of N in A&E, for the economic and other damages suffered because she had to care for the gravely disabled child. **Held:** the decision only dealt with limitation issues relevant to the mother's claim. However, the Alberta Court of Queen's Bench held that, while the mother was not in a patient–doctor relationship, a duty was owed by the radiologist to N's mother, separately. 'Because it was foreseeable that a breach of the duty of care by physicians and/or nurses might cause injuries to the infant plaintiff which would result in expenditures by the parents, there was a duty of care owed to baby Nadine's parents'.[58]

As one Canadian commentator has noted[59] in respect of *Brown*, the abuser is often insolvent, and the non-reporting doctor (or his insurer) presents a much 'deeper pocket' against which to seek to recover substantial damages in tort, hence the significance of this case.

In the Australian case of *McCann v Buck*,[60] the patient, Catherine McCann (CM), 30, suffered from cancer, and was (incorrectly) informed by the defendant, a specialist oncologist, that experimental treatment offered in the US for her type of cancer was unavailable in Australia. Her parents (the non-patients) funded their daughter's trip to the US in order to obtain the treatment, by taking out a bank loan over their house in order to meet the expenses. The treatment was to no avail, and CM died from the disease. The parents sued CM's oncologist, alleging that, had he made enquiry of domestic hospitals, then he would not have made the statement, the parents would not have incurred the financial expenses which they did, and that it was negligent of him not to make further enquiries. **Held:** a duty of care was owed by HCP to the parents; it was reasonably foreseeable that failing to take care in providing advice would cause the parents financial loss, and there was a separate relationship between CM's oncologist and her parents (however, no breach was found, since the oncologist did not know about the locally-conducted clinical trial, and could not be expected to have known about it).[61]

4. Where third parties incur other financial losses brought about by a patient's negligent treatment

Other, more unusual, scenarios of a third party claim arising out of pure economic loss have been attempted:

> In the English case of *West Bromwich Albion Football Club Ltd v El-Safty*,[62] the patient, professional footballer Michael Appleton (A), was signed by premiership football club, WBA, on a 3.5 year contract, in January 2001. In November 2001, A suffered a serious injury to his right posterior cruciate ligament in training, and in accordance the terms of his contract of employment with WBA, he was treated by a physiotherapist employed by WBA, who on-referred A to surgeon Dr E. A reconstruction of A's knee was unsuccessful, and A was forced to retire from professional football. It was admitted that Dr E's advice to A to undergo reconstructive surgery was negligent, and that, had conservative treatment been adopted, A would have made a recovery within four months, and would have returned to professional football. A recovered damages against the surgeon.[63] WBA suffered an economic loss, because A's value had considerably diminished on the transfer market, and WBA was put to the cost of replacing him. The club sued the surgeon to recover that loss ('potentially several million pounds'[64]). Invoices for the consultation and treatment were prepared by Dr E's wife, and were addressed to WBA. Dr E had treated over 30 players for WBA. To whatever extent the surgeon's fees were not covered by the players' health insurance, the balance was paid for by the club. **Held:** Dr E did not owe WBA a duty of care, hence, no action for negligence could succeed.
>
> In the Australian case of *AAA v BBB*,[65] the female patient, Mrs AAA, attended a counsellor for marriage counselling. An affair developed between counsellor and Mrs AAA, which brought about the breakdown of AAA's marriage. The former husband (AAA, the non-patient, and described as a 'high net worth individual') sued the counsellor, alleging that he suffered financial losses and emotional distress as a result of the collapse of his marriage. **Held**: the counsellor HCP did not owe the husband any duty of care to avoid the economic losses and other damage incurred by the husband.

The basket of cases considered above, of course, truly highlights the fact that attempts to push the boundaries of HCP liability in innovative ways are ever-present—and, not unexpectedly, the likely outcomes are far from predictable. A legal analysis of these decisions will be undertaken in the following Section.

C CONSTRUCTING (AND DECONSTRUCTING) A DUTY OF CARE IN PURE ECONOMIC LOSS SCENARIOS

As will be recalled from Chapter 2,[66] claims for pure economic loss are analysed by means of three broad approaches: (1) the test of foreseeability, proximity and public policy, per the *Caparo* test; (2) the test of assumption of responsibility and reliance; and (3) the incremental test.[67] However, these are, ultimately, approaches of high abstraction—the facts and circumstances of each third party claim have to be examined closely, to determine whether a duty of care should be owed by the HCP to that third party. Courts tend to pay close regard to the *Caparo* test—in particular, whether the requisite legal proximity exists between HCP and third party, and whether policy reasons should militate against any duty of care being found.[68]

It is worth noting, at the outset, that while a duty of care *can* be owed by HCPs to third parties to avoid economic injury in some circumstances, the judicial reasoning underpinning why a duty is, or is not, owed, can be quite varied. Clearly courts are feeling their way. Take the case of *Islington LBC v University College London Hospital NHS Trust*[69] as an example—the case in which Mrs J was told to discontinue taking Warfarin, she suffered a stroke, and thereafter, for five years, the Islington Council was put to the cost of caring for Mrs J. The Council could not recover its economic costs from the NHS Trust. The judicial reasoning, however, differed considerably. The trial judge had held that the economic injury to the Council was not reasonably foreseeable (because the NHS Trust was not to know that Mrs J was a person of insufficient resources to pay for the residential care herself). He was overruled on appeal (having applied the wrong test of foreseeability, said the Court of Appeal). The trial judge also held that there was insufficient proximity between the NHS Trust and the Council. Two members of the Court of Appeal agreed with him, but Buxton LJ dissented, considering that if the economic injury was foreseeable, 'then it is difficult to see how the relationship between [the parties] fails for lack of proximity'.[70] All judicial members who heard the case, however, considered that the economic injury should not be recoverable, for reasons of public policy. Hence, it is clear that judges will perceive the role of each element of the *Caparo* test somewhat differently, and that they are on a 'journey of exploration' in these novel cases.

1. Reasonable foreseeability of economic injury or harm

It has been relatively uncontentious that the economic injuries suffered by the third parties, in the cases outlined in Section B, were reasonably foreseeable to the relevant HCPs, as a consequence of the medical mis-treatment of patients.

As mentioned above, the point was somewhat at issue in *Islington LBC*, because of the fact that the trial judge's finding on this was overturned on appeal. At first instance, it was held that the Council's economic injury (the costs of caring for patient Mrs J) was not reasonably foreseeable, because the NHS Trust neither knew, nor could they reasonably know, that Mrs J was a person of insufficient resources to pay for the residential care herself. That, however, was the wrong test to have applied:

> [the NHS Trust], which must inevitably have worked closely with local authorities in arranging post-hospital care, must be taken to have known that the range of patients whom it treated would have a range of care requirements and financial needs. Care by a local authority in a case in which it could not recover the cost of the care cannot be seen as so unusual as to fall outside that range ... It is not necessary that a particular claimant local authority should be identifiable as *the* local authority that will necessarily provide the care.[71]

Hence, it was not necessary that the NHS Trust should have foreseen that this particular patient, Mrs J, would require care at the expense of this particular Council. It was enough that some patients with disabling strokes would fall into the class of persons for whom the Council would become liable to pay the costs of care. Ouseley LJ clarified: '[t]he precise level of knowledge which a tortfeasor hospital may have of the patient's means or residence will not usually alter the foreseeability of that loss.'[72]

In the failed sterilisation case of *Freeman v Sutter*, the potential economic impact upon the biological father of an unplanned child could well be foreseen by the HCPs, held the court—'[b]ut there must be some pragmatic limitations on those who may sue an alleged tortfeasor'.[73]

Those 'pragmatic limitations' have been provided by proximity and policy, which have proven far more difficult to surmount for non-patients claiming for their economic injuries.

2. The requisite proximity between healthcare professional and third party

Of the 'proximity basket' outlined in Table 2.1,[74] several factors have tended to weigh *against* sufficient proximity between HCP and third party in pure economic loss cases—and where a duty *has* been found, the proximity factors were very specifically in favour of the third party.

Ability to control the patient or take other precautions

Rarely will a HCP be in a position to exercise control over the patient's actions, sufficient to guard the third party against the economic harm that befell him—and although the HCP's ability to take precautions to prevent the harm to the third party will also be relevant to the proximity enquiry, warnings or other counter-measures to prevent economic loss have not usually been practicable, or even possible, in such scenarios.

For example, the psychologist who offered marriage counselling services in *AAA v BBB* could hardly be said to be in a position of control (said the Western Australian Supreme Court), when he had no reason to believe that either his patient (the wife) or the third party (the husband) would act upon his diagnosis or recommendations concerning the marriage; nor was any warning to the husband reasonably feasible, given the affair.[75] Note also, in *Goodwill v British Pregnancy Advisory Service* (the case of the reversed vasectomy), the inability of the defendant surgeon to warn his patient's future sexual partners of the possibility of spontaneous reversal, or to ensure that his patient would pass on any information about that possibility.[76] In *Freeman v Sutter* too (the case of the failed abortion), the Manitoba Court of Appeal distanced the HCP from the non-patient father, when it said: '[i]t is not alleged that he had any discussion with the mother as to her intended treatment, or that he was privy to her instructions to her physicians.'[77] In that event, it was impossible to conceive of how the GP could have sought to protect the non-patient father. No duty of care was found in any of these cases—and the inability of the defendant HCPs to control the actions or the decisions of the patient contributed significantly to that outcome.

By contrast, if the HCP was in a position to give the third party a suitable warning about the risk of economic injury arising from the patient's treatment, that is likely to be highly significant to the impositon of a duty of care in the third party's favour. For example, the surgeon had the ability to warn Mr McDonald about the risks of a sterilisation operation failing, as an existing sexual partner of the female patient, in *McDonald v Sydney South West Area Health Service*, given that both parents attended the pre-operative consultation.[78] A duty of care towards Mr McDonald, as the non-patient and biological father, was upheld, partly on this basis.

Temporal proximity

A considerable time-lag between the alleged wrongdoing of the HCP, and the economic harm caused to the non-patient, may certainly discourage the finding of a sufficient nexus between them.

In *Goodwill v British Pregnancy Advisory Service*, where the non-patient was a sexual partner who formed a relationship with the patient well after the sterilisation operation was negligently performed, there was a lack of temporal proximity. She was—

no nearer the doctor adviser than one who some three and half years after the operation commenced a sexual relationship with his patient ... a doctor is entitled to scorn the suggestion that he owes a duty of care to such a band so uncertain in nature and extent and over such an indefinite future span.[79]

The same point was made, as a hypothetical statement, in *Islington LBC v University College London Hospital NHS Trust*, i.e., if the costs of caring for a negligently-treated patient arose 'a substantial time after the negligent treatment', then both proximity, and foreseeability of harm to the carer, could be difficult to establish (said Buxton LJ[80]).

Knowledge of the identity, or of the existence, of the non-patient

Whether the HCP knew of the identity—or, if not that, of the existence, of the non-patient who suffered the economic injury, as a *specific person* in the patient's background—will be highly relevant to the proximity enquiry. Figure 7.1 outlines the spectrum of relevant cases on this point:

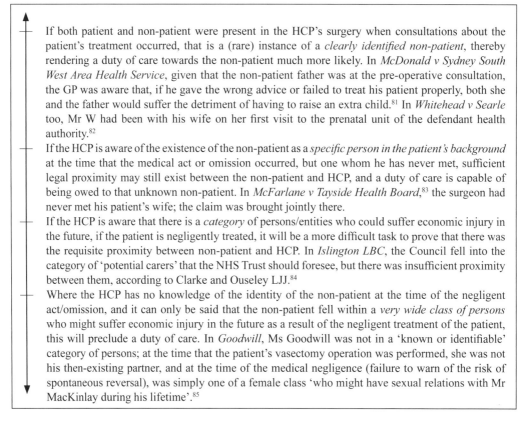

If both patient and non-patient were present in the HCP's surgery when consultations about the patient's treatment occurred, that is a (rare) instance of a *clearly identified non-patient*, thereby rendering a duty of care towards the non-patient much more likely. In *McDonald v Sydney South West Area Health Service*, given that the non-patient father was at the pre-operative consultation, the GP was aware that, if he gave the wrong advice or failed to treat his patient properly, both she and the father would suffer the detriment of having to raise an extra child.[81] In *Whitehead v Searle* too, Mr W had been with his wife on her first visit to the prenatal unit of the defendant health authority.[82]

If the HCP is aware of the existence of the non-patient as a *specific person in the patient's background* at the time that the medical act or omission occurred, but one whom he has never met, sufficient legal proximity may still exist between the non-patient and HCP, and a duty of care is capable of being owed to that unknown non-patient. In *McFarlane v Tayside Health Board*,[83] the surgeon had never met his patient's wife; the claim was brought jointly there.

If the HCP is aware that there is a *category* of persons/entities who could suffer economic injury in the future, if the patient is negligently treated, it will be a more difficult task to prove that there was the requisite proximity between non-patient and HCP. In *Islington LBC*, the Council fell into the category of 'potential carers' that the NHS Trust should foresee, but there was insufficient proximity between them, according to Clarke and Ouseley LJJ.[84]

Where the HCP has no knowledge of the identity of the non-patient at the time of the negligent act/omission, and it can only be said that the non-patient fell within a *very wide class of persons* who might suffer economic injury in the future as a result of the negligent treatment of the patient, this will preclude a duty of care. In *Goodwill*, Ms Goodwill was not in a 'known or identifiable' category of persons; at the time that the patient's vasectomy operation was performed, she was not his then-existing partner, and at the time of the medical negligence (failure to warn of the risk of spontaneous reversal), was simply one of a female class 'who might have sexual relations with Mr MacKinlay during his lifetime'.[85]

Figure 7.1   Knowledge of identity or existence of the third party/non-patient in cases of economic loss

Of course, the scenarios towards the bottom end of the spectrum—involving classes of potential third party claimants whose identities and existence are unknown to the defendant HCP, and who may suffer some economic injury well after the negligent act or omission of the HCP—are of most concern to medical insurers. In that regard, though, and insofar as economic loss claims arising from medical negligence are concerned, the law is holding a firm line of 'thus far, and no further'. *Goodwill* has shown that a non-patient falling within the sub-class of 'future sexual partners of the patient' is not sufficiently distinguishable from the public at large, and no duty would be owed to that non-patient. In fact, the submission was made in *Goodwill* that, with societal changes, the class of whom Mrs Goodwill was a member was perfectly foreseeable (even if her identity was not known to the surgeon at the time of the vasectomy operation), and that it would be an incremental step to extend a duty of care to Mrs Goodwill.[86] This, however, was rejected—principally for policy reasons, given the prospect of the surgeon being potentially liable to an indeterminate class. In that regard, Davies has called the claim in *Goodwill* a 'rather exotic attempt to develop the duty of care owed to third parties'.[87]

Furthermore, *Islington* has demonstrated that, even if a third party is within a foreseeable category of parties who could suffer economic loss if the patient is mistreated, that *of itself* does not establish proximity of relationship between HCP and third party, at least according to the majority view. As Tettenborn notes,[88] this may seem to be an unfair result—'that, on a lay view of what was just and right, the cost of picking up the pieces should rest with the hospital, whose fault it was, and not with Islington Council'—but the device of proximity is an effective bulwark against third party claims which do not exhibit sufficient factors to establish the 'close and direct relations' that English law demands.

Finally, it must be emphasised that the mere fact that the HCP knew precisely who the third party was is **not** conclusive, in proving that the requisite proximity between them automatically existed—as the decision in *West Bromwich Albion Football Club Ltd v El-Safty*[89] demonstrates. There was only one third party there, the football club, which had referred players to the orthopaedic surgeon over 30 times previously. Still, no duty of care was owed by the HCP to the club (for other reasons discussed shortly).

Reliance on the HCP, or lack thereof

A lack of any reliance by the non-patient upon the skill and judgment of the HCP will tend to negate a duty of care. This has proven to be the downfall of the non-patient in a number of the cases considered in this chapter.

In *Kovacvich v Ortho Pharmaceutical (Canada) Ltd*, where the GP negligently prescribed the wrong birth control pill to his female patient, and the biological father of a subsequently-conceived child thereafter sued to recover the costs of raising the child, no duty was owed to the father:

> The [father] neither sought information from Dr Henshaw nor did Dr Henshaw know of his existence. It would not in my view be reasonable to infer that the doctor knew or should have known that reliance was being placed on his skill and judgment by the plaintiff.[90]

Similarly, in *Goodwill's* case (the failed vasectomy case), the English Court of Appeal was equally dismissive that any reliance sufficient to base a duty could be found. It was not reasonable for Ms Goodwill to act upon any information that her partner, the patient, might have passed on about the vasectomy procedure ('receiving [the surgeon's] advice at second hand'[91])—she should (said the court) have made independent enquiry about contraceptive measures. By contrast, in *McDonald v Sydney South West Area Health Service*, Mr McDonald was present at the consultation with his partner and with the defendant HCP, where sterilisation methods were discussed, and he was entitled to rely upon the HCP, since the HCP would have known that Mr McDonald was there, either as the father of the unborn child or as the partner of Ms Foster.[92]

Moreover, it appears that the third party will have to rely upon the HCP to avoid causing that non-patient, specifically, *financial loss*—it will not be sufficient to simply allege that the non-patient relied upon the HCP to ensure that the patient was medically treated in a sound manner. Such a distinction appears to be highly artificial, for treating the patient competently would have avoided the financial loss which the third party ended up sustaining, and hence, surely the third party was vitally interested in both. Nevertheless, this was the reasoning applied in *West Bromwich Albion Football Club Ltd v El-Safty*:

> This case is quite unlike the typical case where an adviser knows that his advice will be relied on by third parties with relevant financial interests. The immediate interest here is medical, not financial. WBA is interested, but principally as a good employer not as an investor in player contracts, and it appears on the scene, in the person of [its in-house employed senior physiotherapist] Mr Worth, in the form of a referring HCP, and not in a managerial or business context ... The dominant relationship is that of the doctor and his patient, and the dominant context is that of Mr Appleton's health, not his employer's financial security.[93]

The mere fact that WBA appealed at all, and the millions of pounds which the club was claiming in this law suit, are perhaps indicative of the fact that WBA was extremely interested in its investment in Michael Appleton! Surely wishing to protect its investment can sit coincidentally, and properly, alongside its concern for the player's medical welfare, and that the club relied upon the surgeon in both respects. However, the purpose for which WBA was relying upon the HCP was not the *right* purpose, in the Court of Appeal's view.

According to Rix LJ, '[i]f WBA had wanted El-Safty's advice for the purposes of its own interests, it could have made that plain to him.'[94] As commentators Griffiths and Whale rightly note, this case highlighted that, as between sporting clubs, HCPs and the sportspersons who represent the high-value patients, '[w]ell-worn and perhaps practical arrangements will no longer suffice. How many other sports clubs are relying upon ... the provision of indirect advice [from HCP to third party club], without realising the potential risk to their balance sheets?'[95] The lack of reliance upon the surgeon for *its own economic interests* was fatal to WBA's claim.

Payment to HCP by third party not conclusive

Just because the HCP was paid by the third party for the medical services rendered to the patient does not automatically fix the HCP with a duty or care, nor establish proximity between the parties, in and of itself.

It may be recalled, in *Customs and Excise v Barclays Bank plc* (a case involving, not alleged medical negligence, but banking negligence), Lord Bingham said that the 'paradigm situation' in which a defendant can be said to have assumed legal responsibility for what he does to the claimant is where the parties are in some relationship 'having all the indicia of contract, save consideration'.[96]

That situation was present in *West Bromwich Albion Football Club Ltd v El-Safty*[97]—because the club had a longstanding practice of sending its injured players to the defendant surgeon; the in-house senior physiotherapist employed by the club accompanied the player to the medical appointments and considered the medical advice together with the player; and the surgeon always looked to WBA for payment of his fees, to whatever extent that the club's players' policy with a private health insurer did not do so. Hence, the arrangement between this HCP and the club *was* something that was, arguably, 'closely akin to contract'.[98] Nevertheless, not only did the Court of Appeal consider that there was an absence of the requisite proximity (for reasons discussed above), but it also considered that it was not fair, just or reasonable to impose a duty on the surgeon (as will be canvassed in Section 3 below).

3. Relevant policy factors

The primary policy consideration, in cases where a third party is suing a HCP for pure economic loss, is that of conflicts of interests, actual or potential. As Rix LJ observed in *WBA v El-Safty*, this factor remains of great relevance in all third party cases.[99] Other policy factors, however, have also figured prominently in the economic loss cases outlined in Section B.

Indeed, the matrix of policy factors may be a complex one in suits of this type. In the case of *Islington LBC v University College London Hospital NHS Trust*, where the local authority was the entity which had to bear the costs of Mrs J's care rather than the NHS Trust whose employee had issued negligent advice to Mrs J, Buxton LJ candidly admitted that it 'seems all of fair, just and reasonable that [the NHS Trust] rather than Islington should bear the cost of Mrs J's care.'[100] Yet, the NHS Trust did not do so, for policy reasons. In fact, had Mrs J been able to afford to pay for the costs of residential care herself, then that would have been a component of the damages which she recovered from the NHS Trust. But she could not, and hence, the loss fell on the Council. Furthermore, had Mrs J been cared for *privately*, then she could have recovered those carer's costs from the NHS Trust, as part of the damages amount, with those damages being held in trust for the carer (under the principle of *Hunt v Severs*[101]). Hence, it was something of an accident of coincidence ('adding insult to injury', as Tettenborn puts it[102]) that the Council was left to bear the costs of Mrs J's care, rather than the culpable NHS Trust having to do so. Yet, *still* public policy dictated *against* Islington being able to recover those costs, as a third party.

It is also an inescapable reality, under English common law, that pure economic loss, that arises out of a personal injury or property damage to some other party, is difficult to recover. Buxton LJ commented on this in *Islington*:

> That has been recognised since as long ago as *Cattle v Stockton Waterworks* (1875) LR 10 QB 453 as an area into which the law will not easily enter ... This diffidence is in truth only a particular example of the inability of a party to build on a wrong to someone else.[103]

In *McCann v Buck* too, reference was made by the trial judge[104] to the fact that the parents' claim for the expenses of experimental treatment for their daughter's (allegedly mis-treated) cancer were financial only. However, ultimately, the specialist oncologist treating their daughter was held to owe them a duty to avoid their economic damage on appeal (overturning the trial judge on this point, although no breach was found).[105]

With these caveats in mind, it is now appropriate to deal with the particular policy reasons that have arisen in non-patients suits against HCPs, where pure economic loss has been claimed:

Conflicts of interest

If to impose a duty upon the HCP to avoid causing a non-patient economic injury would place the non-patient's interests above those of his patient, then a conflict of interest will arise, and a duty will be precluded.

A perfect example of this was the marriage counselling case of *AAA v BBB*.[106] To hold that the counsellor owed a duty of care to the wronged husband would have placed that party in a position of conflict:

> the duty owed to his patient cannot readily be regarded as coincidental with duties owed to the [non-patient husband] ... the doctor might properly have felt obliged to express views about the [husband's] conduct in the marriage as described to him by the patient that were likely to have an adverse effect upon the continuance of the marriage.[107]

In other words, the duty to wife, as patient, was not to 'save the marriage', but to provide counselling to that wife; any duties to non-patient husband and patient wife would **not** have been coincidental.[108]

A somewhat less obvious example of this problem occurred in *West Bromwich Albion Football Club Ltd v El-Safty*. One of the reasons as to why the surgeon did not owe the football club a duty of care was that his concern 'is or ought to be, not only primarily, but exclusively, with his patient's well-being, and not with the Club's financial circumstances'.[109] It is somewhat difficult to understand, however, just how these interests could be at variance—is it suggested that the treatment of the player would be compromised by, say, a short-term gain to the club in getting him back out onto the field? This scenario would surely be very unlikely—whatever was in the best interests of the player, medically-speaking, would surely be in the best economic interests of the football club too, given their keenness to protect their investment in the player. Other academic commentary has also suggested that aligned, rather than conflicted, interests, were perhaps more likely on these facts.[110]

The prospect of liability to an indeterminate (or large) class

The size of the potential class whose members may suffer economic injury arising from the act of medical negligence towards a patient, can give rise to the prospect of liability to an indeterminate (or large) class. This will often convince a court to dismiss a duty of care to avoid the economic injury complained of by the non-patient. The fact that a HCP owes no duty to the future sexual partners of his patient, per *Goodwill* (where the class was described as an 'indeterminately large class of females') has already been mentioned[111] (although Jones questions the description of Mrs Goodwill's class as large and indeterminate, given that the class was likely to comprise the first sexual partner of the patient's *to become pregnant*—after that event, the patient would presumably be aware that he was not, in fact, sterile[112]).

There is also the prospect of how other non-patients could align themselves with a particular third party, should a duty of care be upheld in the instant case (i.e., the 'precedential effect' of the decision). This was a factor applied in *Islington LBC v University College London Hospital NHS Trust*,[113] to deny that the NHS Trust owed any duty of care to the Council. If Islington succeeded, then so could many others who were in the 'same boat' of outlaying costs for patient care, where the patients had been medically-harmed. Rather than attribute this to policy, however, Ouseley LJ dealt with this issue as one of proximity.[114] In any event, the result was the same. Too many other third parties could fall within a similar basket, if Islington were to succeed—they could include, say, voluntary carers who presently had no direct cause of action against a tortfeasor under English law,[115] businesses deprived of the services of a negligently-treated patient or of a negligently-injured road user,[116] and education authorities, obliged to provide gratuitous services to a child who had special educational needs because of a medical mis-diagnosis.[117]

Notably, it did not assist the football club, in *West Bromwich Albion Football Club Ltd v El-Safty*,[118] to argue that it, WBA, was the *only* third party in question. If Mr El-Safty were held to owe a duty of care to West Bromwich Albion, then the precedent would be set, whereby, generally speaking, doctors could owe a duty to *their patients' employers*, as well as to their patients. O'Sullivan observes that the 'floodgates' problem was not necessarily present in the case itself here—but it could certainly have manifested if the surgeon had been found liable.[119]

The prospect of an indeterminate (or large) quantum of liability

The prospect of exposing a HCP to the risk of an indeterminate (or large) quantum of liability is also a factor that plays heavily upon the minds of courts in these scenarios. Claims for pure economic loss can be, even if not uncertain, at least very large.

In that respect, it did not assist the Islington Council to argue that the NHS Trust's liability towards it was defined and circumscribed (computed by the precise costs of care which the Council had expended on Mrs J's care over the five-year period of her residential care). Public policy reasons still denied any liability on the NHS Trust's part. In both *Islington* and *WBA v El-Safty*, the amounts of damages were significant (WBA were claiming 'millions of pounds in damages',[120] while the costs to the Islington Council to care for Mrs J until she returned to her daughter's care was calculated to be £81,211[121]). The trial judge in *WBA v El-Safty*, Royce J, also posed the question as to where the limits of a HCP's liability in negligence would be drawn, if this football club were to succeed:

> Should a consultant for example advising a Rooney or a Beckham or a Flintoff have a potential tortious liability to their club/county or England for negligent treatment—a liability running to many millions of pounds? What about negligent treatment of a resident conductor of an orchestra or a leading player in a rock band or the managing director of a major company? The consultant would probably know each patient was a valuable asset ... one only has to pose these questions to conclude that it would not be fair, just and equitable for there to be liability in such cases.[122]

As Dugdale notes, the decisions in both of these cases involved large amounts of money, and 'threatened to expose service providers to large numbers of new claims. Both decisions will be greeted with relief by those funding compensation paid in medical cases.'[123]

A matter for Parliament

Occasionally, where third party suits are concerned, courts have resiled from holding in the third party's favour, preferring to adopt the view that, if the third party is to be permitted to recover, then it is a matter for Parliament, not for the courts, to decide

This was a crucial factor in *Islington LBC v University College London Hospital NHS Trust*,[124] where it was two public authorities at loggerheads—and the Court of Appeal was unwilling to use the law of negligence to shift the loss away from where it presently lay, i.e., on the local authority who bore the cost of caring for the negligently-mistreated patient. It is worth setting out Buxton LJ's concerns in full:

> although I have referred in general terms to [the NHS Trust] and Islington as both being public authorities, they are public authorities of rather different sorts and with conspicuously different sources of funding. While the court would not pretend to detailed understanding of the differences, it can at least take notice that [Trust] is part of the 'national' health service, in principle subject to control by national government and financed out of national taxation; whereas Islington is at least in theory controlled and financed by those who pay the community charge in that borough; however much it may be that a high proportion of its income in fact comes from national government, and its freedom of action is, as in the present case, controlled by the national government acting through Parliament. As between these different authorities, it may be the case that the obligation that rests on Islington in relation to impecunious persons in need of care has arisen by statutory accident; and it is very doubtful whether it has arisen in pursuit of any desire to aid the tortfeasor. But the sorting out of the present position, accidental or not, would seem to be essentially a matter for Parliament, or at least for political decision, rather than for a court deciding a particular case.[125]

Buxton LJ made the further point that Parliament had conferred *on the NHS* the right to recover the costs of hospital care spent on the victims of negligence from negligent parties[126]—but that was undertaken only after a great deal of law reform and Parliamentary consideration.[127] Some similar exercise would be necessary in order to permit *local authority* recovery against tortfeasors.

It is worth noting that academic commentary has been somewhat critical of this policy factor. Spencer makes the point that, if Parliament is inclined to look after the NHS and allow it the right, as a third party, to recover its costs from tortfeasors who injured a victim, then there was 'no intelligible reason why local authorities should not be able to do the same', and that the whole area probably warranted another Parliamentary scrutiny.[128] The authors of a leading English Torts commentary also state that the judicial deference shown in *Islington* was perhaps overstated: '[t]here are enough previous examples of judicial innovation in areas raising complex questions of policy to suggest that deference to Parliament can easily be overcome in cases seen by the judges as appropriate for this purpose.'[129]

Where the burden for the third party's loss should 'naturally lie'

Pragmatically speaking, the law of negligence is about allocating, and shifting, losses around various parties—and this is particularly of interest in tri-partite scenarios. If the third party/non-patient suffers a financial injury as a result of a HCP's negligence, then there are three options: either the third party bears it himself out of his own pocket; or the third party's insurer bears the loss, if the loss is one that is insurable and insured against; or the HCP's indemnity insurer must pay for the loss. If a court considers that insurance for such liabilities 'naturally lie' with the third party (regardless of whether or not the third party actually *held* that policy of insurance) and not with the HCP, then that may be a policy reason for holding that it would not be fair, just or reasonable to impose a duty of care on the HCP.

This was a key factor in *West Bromwich Albion Football Club Ltd v El-Safty*. Where the medical mistreatment of employees (such as football player Mr Appleton) caused the employer (the football club, WBA) financial loss, then the Court of Appeal considered that insurance against that financial loss 'naturally lies with their employers'.[130] It was not reasonable to expect the HCP to insure against additional loss of an economic kind, suffered by someone *other than his patient*.

This controversial reasoning has received influential academic support. Dugdale agrees with the basic tenet that it was not for the HCP to insure against the risk of some third party football club suffering economic injury if the HCP's patient (and the club's star player) was medically mistreated: 'it is likely that the club or company will turn out to be the most efficient insurer: it knows the value of its asset. As the World Cup injury to Michael Owen revealed, club and country do insure against injury to star assets.'[131] Jones adds that it was 'debatable' whether insurance cover *would* be available for HCPs to protect them against the risk of economic injury to employers of their patients; and even though 'medical negligence actions can involve the risk of high value claims (brain damaged baby cases are, perhaps, the most common; and permanent disabling injury to a high earner would be another example), ... it is doubtful that they would stretch to the tens of millions of pounds that some Premiership footballers are reputedly worth in the modern, highly inflated, transfer market.'[132] Jones also points out that the football market itself generates such inflated figures of players' value, and it was arguably unfair for medical indemnity insurers to bear that loss.[133]

However, the mere fact that West Bromwich Albion *could* have insured against the loss of their player simply means that the insurer of the disablement policy would presumably seek to claim against the HCP's insurer under the right of subrogation—in which case it becomes a 'battle of the insurers'. In that sense, the 'insurance argument' in *WBA v El-Safty* is capable of challenge on a number of fronts. First of all, the practical effect of the Court of Appeal's decision is that the player's employer should pay for (or 'internalise') the consequences of medically-caused negligence to its asset (whether by the employer's own means, or by taking out the relevant insurance). However, the very purpose of the law of negligence is to determine **which** of the two insurers who are often standing behind the litigation should bear the burden—in this case, the employer's insurer, which will be seeking to shift legal responsibility for the damage to another insurer rather than bear the loss itself, or the HCP's professional indemnity insurer, which will be seeking to avoid any negligence decision against its insured whose medical conduct damaged the employee. Insurers are in the business of measuring risk and estimating exposure, should the risk manifest because of the conduct of the insured. As Lord Hobhouse pointed out (in an entirely different context), just because insurance is available to the claimant does not remove the function of the law of tort, which is to allocate responsibilities among insured parties.[134] Furthermore, Stapleton has observed that basing liability upon observations about the relative insurance positions of claimant and defendant is 'dangerous. They are not only indeterminate criteria but can mislead us into suppressing any corrective justice or deterrence goals we may have for tort liability'.[135] Thirdly, in another context of an unusual suit in the medico-legal field—that of a boxer against the British Boxing Board of Control for failure to ensure that an injured boxer would receive timely medical assistance ringside, if brain injury occurred in the ring[136]—it was baldly stated by Lord Phillips MR (with whom the other members of the Court of Appeal agreed) that '[c]onsiderations of insurance are not relevant'.[137]

Hence, it is apparent that 'where the insurance liability should naturally lie' was one of the more debatable policy reasons advanced in *WBA v El-Safty* (although the decision was supportable for other reasons considered in this Section).

Whether the decision exposes a lacuna in the law

If there is no lacuna in the law—no gap in compensation—that requires filling by imposing liability upon the HCP towards a non-patient, then the courts will not fill it. By corollary, if there is a lacuna or gap, then finding a duty of care in favour of the non-patient *may* be 'fair, just and reasonable'.

Whilst the lacuna argument has been put on behalf of non-patients who have suffered financial loss in this field of negligence, it has proven relatively unsuccessful in recent English jurisprudence.

For example, in *Islington*, merely because the Council could not recover its costs of caring for Mrs J did not imply that there was a gap in compensation that required filling—indeed, to the contrary, where Parliament has already intervened in the general area, any gap was seen to be deliberate, or at least, not one for the courts to fill. The trial judge agreed ('the inability of the Local Authority to recover care costs in cases such as this is the result of a statutory scheme which has been thoroughly reviewed in the decisions of Courts ... Parliament has imposed liability on tortfeasors under the Road Traffic Acts and recently far more broadly under the Health and Social Care (Community Health and Standards) Act 2003. If intervention is needed Parliament can decide to be involved'), and this was upheld by the Court of Appeal.[138]

The point was also raised in the wrongful birth claim in *Whitehead v Searle*.[139] This was the case in which the non-patient father sued a law firm for failing to advise him that the defendant HCPs (who failed to detect that his unborn child had spina bifida at time when his wife could have chosen to terminate her pregnancy) may owe him a duty of care to avoid causing him economic injury. His wife committed suicide after David's birth, and as biological father, the claimant brought a personal claim against the law firm, for damages, to compensate him for the cost of David's care, on the basis that the legal representatives had failed to advise and to prosecute a claim on his behalf against the health authority. But did he have such a claim? It will be recalled that Rix LJ considered that the father did have a 'difficult but realistically arguable claim ... in his own right, once he had shouldered parental responsibility, for the extra costs of David's care over and above those costs which would have been involved in a normal birth'.[140] Moreover, even though David did not have a lawful 'wrongful life' claim ('wholly understandably', said Rix LJ), it could still be fair, just and reasonable for the father's undertaking of the care of the child, in the absence of a deceased mother, to form the basis of a claim against the health authority. Moreover (and recalling the first policy factor considered in this section), '[i]t is not as though [the father's] claim and David's interests are in conflict.'[141]

Where a duty of care on the HCP's part would lead to inconsistencies in the law

It may not be fair, just or reasonable to impose a duty of care upon a HCP towards a third party which suffered economic injury, by reason of the HCP's negligence, where any such duty could give rise to inconsistencies and illogicalities in the law. Particularly in novel areas, courts will be unwilling to 'unpick' or undermine jurisprudence that has been laid down as accepted authority for many years.

For example, if a private voluntary carer cannot sue a tortfeasor *directly* for expenses and other losses incurred while caring for a person injured by the tortfeasor's negligence (per the 1994 decision *Hunt v Severs*), then it would be inconsistent to allow a local authority to sue the tortfeasor directly, as the Council was seeking to do in Islington. As Buxton LJ observed, damages recovered for a private carer are 'achieved by the construction of a notional liability of the injured party, and notional payment in respect of that liability by the injured party to the carer; rather than by the imposition of direct liability between the tortfeasor and the carer'.[142] His Lordship admitted that a carer's eventual recovery of damages under the *Hunt v Severs* principle was 'artificial', and that it would probably be 'far easier' to allow the carer to sue the negligent party directly—but that is not how the principle has been constructed.[143] Clarke LJ also noted that, according to the principle in

Hunt v Severs, 'the tortfeasor does not owe a duty of care to a carer'.[144] All of this rendered a direct duty of care from a negligent health trust to a publicly-funded carer very unlikely.

Where the HCP is unable to disclaim liability

Finally, where a HCP is providing medical advice to a patient, then the HCP may seek to disclaim liability (to the extent that the law allows), charge a fee for his professional services, and explain the risks associated with the services. Conversely, the *inability* of the HCP to disclaim liability, etc, and where no contract between the HCP and third party was contemplated, may count against a duty of care being owed to the third party.

This point was relevant in *WBA Football Club Ltd v El-Safty*, where Rix LJ held that if WBA had wanted Mr El-Safty's advice for the purposes of its own interests, it could have made that clear to him, and then: '[h]e would then have been put in a position where he could choose to charge for that advice and the risks involved in giving it, and/or of disclaiming liability.'[145] The fact that he had no opportunity to do that was one reason why it was not fair, just or reasonable to impose a duty of care upon him, in WBA's favour.

D CONCLUSION

Whether or not third parties ought to be able to recover their economic losses, in the event that a HCP mis-treats or mis-diagnoses or ill-advises a patient, is a matter upon which reasonable opinion will differ. For example, academic commentary has variously described the outcome in *WBA v El-Safty* as 'a welcome precedent',[146] or 'controversial'.[147]

Notably, the majority of third party suits against HCPs for economic injury sustained by reason of a physical injury to the patient have failed. In most, the economic injury was held to be foreseeable, but the degree of proximity necessary to base a duty of care was absent, or it was not fair, just or reasonable to impose a duty. Hence, the duty to provide the patient with reasonably competent medical care was not accompanied by a concurrent duty of care not to cause financial loss to a third party.

Insofar as the incremental test is concerned, non-patient suits against HCPs for economic injury have been dealt a serious blow by the twin failures in *Islington* and *WBA v El-Safty*. In the latter, Rix LJ specifically noted that '[a]s for incremental liability, no direct precedent apparently exists ... Indeed, the single authority cited which comes closest to the present facts [*Islington*] is unfavourable to WBA and places on [WBA] the burden of stressing matters to distinguish it',[148] which could not be done. Unless the facts of the non-patient's suit are closely analogous to one of the few successful cases in this field (e.g., the non-patient in a wrongful conception case), these sorts of suits for economic injury suffered by third parties appear to have become extremely problematical in the medico-legal field.

This chapter has concentrated upon the duty of care conundrums associated with a non-patient's claim for economic injury. It has drawn out the difficulties with establishing proximity (based upon, say, the HCP's knowledge of the financially-injured non-patient, and temporal proximity between act/omission and damage) and the policy difficulties in such claims. It is also worth noting that, in some of the non-patient scenarios canvassed in this chapter, considerable difficulties in proving the *causal link* between the HCP's breach and the non-patient's damage may arise. For example, suppose that a father *were* able to bring a wrongful birth action against a health authority, in his capacity as a non-patient, for a HCP's failure to diagnose a defect in his unborn child. Whether the father can bring such a claim is not entirely settled in English law, as the members of the Court of Appeal in *Whitehead v Searle* did not resolve the issue. But even if the claim were allowed, causation may be difficult, because the father's claim would depend upon his proving that, had the mother known of the foetus's defect, she would have chosen to undergo a termination.[149]

Meanwhile, based upon the case analyses referenced in this chapter, a guideline has been prepared which highlights the potential for non-patient claims for economic injury, arising out of medical services provided to patients, may be useful. It is the aim of the *'Potential Liability to Non-Patients and Third Parties: A Synopsis for Healthcare Professionals'* in the Appendix to clarify for HCPs those matters which will govern a court's analysis of whether a duty should be imposed upon a HCP to avoid pure economic loss to a non-patient by reason of the HCP's negligence.

ENDNOTES

[1] The term connotes that the financial damage resulting to the third party is not consequent upon, nor ancillary to, any personal injury or property damage on the part of that third party.

[2] e.g., *Hedley Byrne & Co Ltd v Heller & Partners Ltd* [1964] AC 465 (HL); *Smith v Eric S Bush, Harris v Wyre Forest DC* [1990] 1 AC 831 (HL); *Law Society v KPMG Peat Marwick* [2000] 4 All ER 540 (CA); *Punjab National Bank v de Boinville* [1992] 1 Lloyd's Rep 7 (CA); *Henderson v Merrett Syndicates Ltd* [1995] 2 AC 145 (HL). Cf: *Caparo Industries plc v Dickman* [1990] 2 AC 605 (HL); *James McNaughten Papers Group Ltd v Hicks Anderson & Co* [1991] 2 QB 113 (CA).

[3] e.g., *White v Jones* [1995] 2 AC 207 (HL); *Gorham v British Telecommunications plc* [2000] 1 WLR 2129 (CA); *Dean v Allin & Watts* [2001] EWCA Civ 758.

[4] e.g., *Spring v Guardian Ass plc* [1995] 2 AC 296 (HL).

[5] e.g., *Kirkham v Boughey* [1958] 2 QB 238; *Walker v Mullen* (QBD, *The Times*, 19 Jan 1984).

[6] [1996] 4 WWR 748, (1996), 110 Man R (2d) 23 (CA) [2].

[7] [2008] EWCA Civ 285, [2009] 1 WLR 549 (CA) [47].

[8] Noted by Buxton LJ in: *Islington LBC v University College London Hospital NHS Trust* [2005] EWCA Civ 596, [28]–[30].

[9] *Galliford Try Infrastructure Ltd v Mott MacDonald Ltd* [2008] EWHC 1570 (TCC) [190].

[10] [2000] 2 AC 59 (HL).

[11] [2003] HCA 38, (2003) 215 CLR 1.

[12] See, e.g.: Civil Liability Act 2002 (NSW), s 71 ('In any proceedings involving a claim for the birth of a child to which this Part applies, the court cannot award damages for economic loss for: (a) the costs associated with rearing or maintaining the child that the claimant has incurred or will incur in the future, or (b) any loss of earnings by the claimant while the claimant rears or maintains the child').

[13] All members of the House of Lords, except for Lord Clyde, allowed this part of the claim.

[14] [2000] 2 AC 59 (HL) 114–15.

[15] [2002] QB 266 (CA).

[16] *ibid*, [50].

[17] *ibid*, [94] (original emphasis).

[18] [2003] UKHL 52, [2004] 1 AC 309, [8] (Lord Bingham). For critique, see, e.g.: M Jones, *Medical Negligence* (4th edn, Sweet & Maxwell, London, 2008) 112–14.

[19] See, e.g., for a selection of relevant commentary: L Hoyano, 'Misconceptions about Wrongful Conception' (2002) 65 *MLR* 883; P Cane, 'The Doctor, the Stork and the Court: A Modern Morality Play' (2004) 120 *LQR* 23, and 'Another Failed Sterilisation' (2004) 120 *LQR* 189; T Weir, 'The Unwanted Child' (2000) 59 *CLJ* 238; N Priaulx, 'Damages for the Unwanted Child: Time for a Rethink' (2005) 73 *Medico-Legal J* 152; Jones (2008), *ibid*, 96–118. The policy reasons denying recovery for the costs of raising are the same for both sterilised patient and third party, and hence, discussion of these falls outside the scope of this book.

20 e.g.: *Udale v Bloomsbury AHA* [1983] 1 WLR 1098 (QB); *Rees v Darlington Memorial Hosp NHS Trust* [2003] UKHL 32, [2004] 1 AC 309 (HL) [23], [79]; *Emeh v Kensington and Chelsea and Westminster AHA* [1985] QB 1012 (CA); *R v Bro Taf HA* [2002] Lloyd's Rep Med 182 (QB); *Groom v Selby* [2001] EWCA Civ 1522, (2002) 64 BMLR 47 (CA); *Greenfield v Irwin* [2001] EWCA Civ 113, [2001] 1 WLR 1279 (CA).

21 As occurred, e.g., in: *Gold v Haringey HA* [1988] QB 481 (CA) (the mother's claim failed).

22 As occurred, e.g., in: *Thake v Maurice* [1986] QB 644 (CA).

23 [2000] 2 AC 59 (HL), on appeal from the Scottish Inner House of the Court of Session.

24 *ibid*, 98 (Lord Clyde) 107 (Lord Millett).

25 Lord Millett dissented, *ibid*, 114.

26 *Islington LBC v University College London Hosp NHS Trust* [2004] EWHC 1754 (QB), [37].

27 [2003] HCA 38, (2003) 215 CLR 1, [151].

28 *ibid*, [9].

29 [2005] NSWSC 924, [64].

30 [2001] EWCA Civ 530, [2002] QB 266.

31 *ibid*, [93].

32 (1995), 57 ACWS (3d) 119 (BCSC) [34]. For further discussion of the case, see, e.g.: E Picard and G Robertson, *Legal Liability of Doctors and Hospitals in Canada* (4th edn, Thomson Carswell, Toronto, 2007) 223.

33 [1996] 4 WWR 748, (1996), 110 Man R (2d) 23.

34 [2005] NSWSC 924.

35 *ibid*, [69].

36 *ibid*, [69].

37 (1006) 31 BMLR 83 (CA). For case comment, see: M Davies, 'Reliance on Medical Advice by Third Parties: The Limits of Goodwill' (1996) 12 *PN* 54; B Mahendra, 'A Snip Makes a Statement' (1996) 146 *NLJ* 407.

38 *ibid*, 91.

39 77 Misc 2d 155, 352 NYS 2d 834 (Sup Ct 1974).

40 *McKay v Essex AHA* [1982] QB 1166 (CA).

41 Congenital Disabilities (Civil Liability) Act 1976, c 28, s 1.

42 The terminology in this area tends to be very confusing, but this chapter follows the 'classification of claims' outlined in: A Stewart, 'Damages for the Birth of a Child' (1995) 40 *J of Law and Society* 298, and cited with approval in *Anderson v Forth Valley Health Board* (1998) 44 BMLR 109, 1998 SLT 588 (CSOH) 592.

43 (2000) 56 BMLR 39 (QB, Newman J).

44 See discussion at *ibid*, 43, 58, 68.

45 *Whitehead v Searle* [2008] EWCA Civ 285, [2009] 1 WLR 25 (CA) [50].

46 e.g.: *Hardman v Amin* [2000] Lloyd's Rep Med 498 (QB) (husband closely involved in care of disabled son; mother exposed to rubella during pregnancy; transcript indicates husband was not a claimant in the litigation).

47 Both parents recovered damages jointly in their wrongful birth suits in, e.g.: *Salih v Enfield HA* [1991] 3 All ER 400 (CA) (child born with congenital rubella syndrome); *Anderson v Forth Valley Health Board* 1998 SLT 588, (1997) 44 BMLR 108 (CSOH) (two sons born with muscular dystrophy; genetic testing and counselling would have revealed that mother was a carrier and that her foetus was male; condition is due to X-linked recessive gene which affects males only).

48 (2000) 56 BMLR 39 (QB).

49 *ibid*, 69.

50 2001 SLT 446 (SCIH).

51 *ibid*, [7].

52 [2008] EWCA Civ 285, [2009] 1 WLR 549 (CA) [50] (also known as *Whitehead v Hibbert Pownall & Newton (a firm)*).

53 *ibid*, [67].

54 *ibid*, [63].

55 [2002] QB 266 (CA) [93].

56 [2005] EWCA Civ 596, [2006] LGR 50.

57 (1997), 145 DLR (4th) 63 (Alta QB).

58 *ibid*, [21], [166].

59 N Bala, 'Tort Remedies and the Family Law Practitioner' (1998) 16 *Canadian Family LQ* 423, [no pp].

60 [2001] WASCA 78, overturning the earlier trial decision in which it had been held that there was no special relationship nor any separate assumption of responsibility by the oncologist towards the parental non-patients, and hence, no duty of care was owed to them: [2000] WADC 81.

61 *ibid*, [160].

62 [2006] EWCA Civ 1299, [2007] PIQR P7 (CA), affirming: [2005] EWHC 2866, [2006] PNLR 18 (QB).

63 See: *Appleton v El-Safty* [2007] EWHC 631 (QB). Mr Appleton recovered £1.5M in damages in his personal action against the surgeon.

64 [2005] EWHC 2866 (QB) [33].

65 [2005] WASC 139. For an unusual and somewhat analogous case, in which a HCP mis-diagnosed a patient as having syphilis, and that patient (the wife) became suspicious and upset that her husband had engaged in extra-marital sexual activities, leading to the break-down of the marriage, and following which the husband (non-patient) sued the doctor for his emotional distress and other damages flowing from the marriage break-down, see: *Molien v Kaiser Foundation Hosp*, 27 Cal 3d 916, 616 P 2d 813 (Cal 1980) (claim upheld).

66 Chapter 2, pp 27–28.

67 *Caparo Industries plc v Dickman* [1990] 2 AC 605 (HL) 617–18 (Lord Bridge).

68 As emphasised, e.g., in: *Islington LBC v University College London Hosp NHS Trust* [2005] EWCA Civ 596, [7], citing: *Spring v Guardian Ass plc* [1995] 2 AC 296 (HL).

69 [2005] EWCA Civ 596, [6].

70 *ibid*, [22].

71 *ibid*, [17] and [24] (Buxton LJ) (original emphasis), and also [48] (Ouseley LJ) ('It does not matter ... that a doctor or UCH as an institution might not have been able to foresee which of those carers would be involved').

72 *ibid*, [48].

73 [1996] 4 WWR 748, (1996), 110 Man R (2d) 23 (CA) [13].

74 See Chapter 2, pp 31–32.

75 [2005] WASC 139, [79].

76 See, on this point: (1996) 31 BMLR 83 (CA) 90–91 (Peter Gibson LJ); and C Witting, 'Duty of Care: An Analytical Approach' (2005) 25 *OJLS* 33, 49.

77 [1996] 4 WWR 748, (1996), 110 Man R (2d) 23 (CA) [11].

78 [2005] NSWSC 924, [65].

79 (1996) 31 BMLR 83 (CA) 92 (Thorpe LJ).

80 [2005] EWCA Civ 596, [24].

81 [2005] NSWSC 924, [65].

82 [2008] EWCA Civ 285, [2009] 1 WLR 549, [64] (Rix LJ).

83 [2000] 2 AC 59 (HL).

84 [2005] EWCA Civ 596. Buxton LJ considered that Islington's claim failed for policy reasons, under the third limb of *Caparo*.

85 (1006) 31 BMLR 83 (CA) 91.

86 (1996) 31 BMLR 83 (CA) 88.

87 M Davies, *Textbook on Medical Law* (2nd edn, OUP, Oxford, 2008) 66.

88 A Tettenborn, 'Free Care: Who Foots the Bill?' (2005) 155 *NLJ* 1050, 1050.

89 [2007] PIQR P7 (CA).

90 (1995), 57 ACWS (3d) 119 (BCSC) [32], [35].

91 (1996) 31 BMLR 83 (CA) 92 (Thorpe LJ).

92 [2005] NSWSC 924, [32], [65].

93   [2007] PIQR P7 (CA) [59], [60].
94   *ibid*, [63].
95   R Griffiths and S Whale, 'Uneasy Bedfellows?' (2006) 156 *NLJ* 1821, 1821.
96   [2006] UKHL 28, [2007] 1 AC 181, [4].
97   [2006] EWCA Civ 1299, [2007] PIQR P7 (CA).
98   As WBA's counsel put it in *ibid*, [53].
99   e.g., the fact that there was no conflict of interest was a key factor in supporting a duty of care in the third party pensions case of *Gorham v British Telecommunications plc* [2000] 1 WLR 2129 (CA), which Rix LJ distinguished in *WBA v El-Safty* on the basis that, in *Gorham*, there was a 'fundamental community of interest between a pensions' investor and his dependants': [2006] EWCA Civ 1299, [2007] PIQR P7 (CA) [59].
100 [2005] EWCA Civ 596, [33].
101 [1994] 2 AC 350 (HL) 358.
102 A Tettenborn, 'Free Care: Who Foots the Bill?' (2005) 155 *NLJ* 1050, 1050.
103 *Islington LBC v University College London Hospital NHS Trust* [2005] EWCA Civ 596, [7], citing: *Bourhill v Young* [1943] AC 92 (Lord Wright).
104 [2000] WADC 81, [134]–[135].
105 *McCann v Buck* [2001] WASCA 78.
106 [2005] WASC 139.
107 *ibid*, [78].
108 *ibid*, [85].
109 [2007] PIQR P7 (CA) [59].
110 See: J O'Sullivan, 'Negligent Medical Advice and Financial Loss: "Sick as a Parrot?"' (2007) 66 *CLJ* 14, 16.
111 *Goodwill v British Pregnancy Advisory Service* (1996) 31 BMLR 83 (CA) 92 (Thorpe LJ), 91 (Peter Gibson LJ).
112 See: M Jones, *Medical Negligence* (4th edn, Sweet & Maxwell, London, 2008) 175.
113 [2005] EWCA Civ 596.
114 *ibid*, [50].
115 By virtue of *Hunt v Severs* [1994] 2 AC 350 (HL).
116 Both examples provided in *Islington* [2005] EWCA Civ 596, [50] (Ouseley LJ).
117 *ibid*, [37] (Buxton LJ).
118 [2006] EWCA Civ 1299, [2007] PIQR P7.
119 J O'Sullivan, 'Negligent Medical Advice and Financial Loss: "Sick as a Parrot?"' (2007) 66 *CLJ* 14, 15.
120 [2005] EWCA Civ 596, [4].
121 Noted in [5] of the trial judgment, and cited, *ibid*, [2].
122 [2005] EWHC 2866, [2006] PNLR 18 (QB) [64]–[65].
123 T Dugdale, 'No Medical Duty to Third Parties' (2006) 22 *PN* 193, 193.
124 [2005] EWCA Civ 596.
125 *ibid*, [38], and see, too, [37].
126 Pursuant to the Health and Social Care (Community Health and Standards) Act 2003, Pt 3, and enforced by the Compensation Recovery Unit. Along similar lines, the NHS can recover the cost of car accident victims' NHS medical care from negligent motorists, pursuant to the Road Traffic (NHS Charges) Act 1999.
127 [2005] EWCA Civ 596, [41].
128 J Spencer, 'Liability for Purely Economic Loss Again: "Small Earthquake in Chile, Not Many Dead?"' (2006) 65 *CLJ* 13, 15.
129 S Deakin, A Johnston and B Markesinis, *Markesinis and Deakin's Tort Law* (6th edn, OUP, Oxford, 2008) 198.
130 [2007] PIQR P7 (CA) [63] (Rix LJ), [84] (Mummery LJ).
131 T Dugdale, 'No Medical Duty to Third Parties' (2006) 22 *PN* 193, 196.
132 M Jones, 'Doctors' Duties to Third Parties' (2007) 23 *PN* 36, 41.

133 *ibid*, 41.

134 See: *Transco plc v Stockport MBC* [2003] UKHL 61, [2004] 2 AC 1, [60].

135 J Stapleton, 'Tort, Insurance and Ideology' (1995) 58 *MLR* 820, 843. Also: M Jones, *Medical Negligence* (4ᵗʰ edn, Sweet & Maxwell, London, 2008) 178.

136 *Watson v British Boxing Board of Control Ltd* [2001] QB 1134 (CA).

137 *ibid*, 1163. It had been submitted for the Board that a duty of care should not be imposed upon the Board because it was a non-profit-making organisation and did not carry insurance, but the CA disagreed.

138 [2005] EWCA Civ 596, [40] (Buxton LJ), and with trial judge quoted in [35].

139 [2008] EWCA Civ 285, [2009] 1 WLR 549 (CA).

140 *ibid*, [67].

141 *ibid*, [67].

142 *Islington LBC v University College London Hospital NHS Trust* [2005] EWCA Civ 596, [31].

143 *ibid*, [40].

144 *ibid*, [45].

145 [2006] EWCA Civ 1299, [2007] PIQR P7, [63].

146 S Lindsay, 'Clinical Negligence: Duty of Care in Contract and Tort' [2006] *JPIL* C62, C64, commenting upon the trial judge's decision (the appeal upheld Royce J's decision denying a duty of care).

147 J O'Sullivan, 'Negligent Medical Advice and Financial Loss: "Sick as a Parrot?"' (2007) 66 *CLJ* 14, 15.

148 [2007] PIQR P7 (CA) [61]–[62].

149 As pointed out in: [2008] EWCA Civ 285, [2009] 1 WLR 549, [51].

Chapter 8

Pure Psychiatric Injury Claims by Third Parties Associated with the Patient

A INTRODUCTION

It is one of the great disappointments of Tort law—for HCPs, for patients, and for all other potential claimants—that the topic of negligently-inflicted pure psychiatric illness[1] is afflicted with so many vagaries and complexities.

In *Tredget and Tredget v Bexley HA*, the court described the law, in somewhat of an understatement, as 'by no means straightforward'.[2] In that case, a baby boy was resuscitated after a terrible birth that was described as 'chaos' and 'pandemonium', and died within 48 hours from his injuries. Both his parents brought an action for psychiatric illnesses that developed as a result of the scenario, in which they were successful. His Hon Judge White said: '[a]t times, the arguments must have seemed to the parents as they listened, to have an air of unreality, but unsatisfactory as the legal frame-work has ... been shown to be, the court can only act within its constraints.'[3] Soberingly, even the House of Lords has admitted that, on this topic, 'the search for principle has been called off'.[4]

Of course, one medically-related incident that has graphic or tragic consequences for a patient has the potential for numerous claims—whereby close relatives, friends, even strangers, may seek to bring claims against a HCP for pure psychiatric illness arising from what they saw. Their identities are often not known to the HCP, and hence, this is an area rife with claims by parties who are true 'strangers' to the HCP–patient relationship. Sensible limits need to be imposed, because of the number and type of potential claimants[5]—and even more so when they may be disturbed or shocked, either 'from a distance', or well after the medical event.

As opposed to some other topics covered in this book where the potential claims by non-patients against HCPs may become a burgeoning feature of future English litigation, negligently-inflicted pure psychiatric illness claims brought by non-patients in the medical context certainly belongs to the 'here and now'. Hence, this type of lawsuit presents interesting and topical concerns for HCPs and their insurers.

Section B sets the context by making a few preliminary points about pure psychiatric claims in general, and by discussing the threshold requirement of a genuine psychiatric disorder, in order to trigger a potential claim in negligence. Section C then outlines the scenarios which, by reference to decided English cases, can give rise to allegations of pure psychiatric illness arising out of medical negligence. The Section also outlines the possible legal avenues which a psychiatrically-injured non-patient may argue against a HCP: that he was a so-called 'primary victim'; that he was a 'secondary victim'; or that he was neither a primary nor a secondary victim, but should nevertheless recover under some other basis altogether. Section D then analyses the many legal conundrums which have arisen for the 'primary victim' of negligently-inflicted psychiatric illness in the medical context, while Section E concentrates upon the secondary victim.[6] Section F considers other routes to potential recovery for psychiatrically-injured claimants. Section G concludes.

Where appropriate, references are made in these Sections to key law reform criticisms of the legal rules governing recovery in this area, drawn from the studies conducted by the English Law Commission in 1998,[7] the Australian Ipp Committee in 2003,[8] and the Scottish Law Commission in 2004.[9] Regard will also be had, as and where appropriate, to leading decisions from other Commonwealth jurisdictions (particularly to the points of contrast between Commonwealth jurisprudence and the English legal position), in order to enhance the legal analysis of these Sections.

It is worth recalling the cautionary statement of Staughton LJ in *Sion v Hampstead HA*, one of the leading English medical cases dealing with pure psychiatric illness:

> The common law has to choose a frontier, between those whose claims succeed and those who fail. Even the resources of insurance companies are finite, although some jurists are slow to accept that. Nor is it in the public interest that every misfortune in this life, even if caused by the negligence of another, should lead to litigation and damages.[10]

Despite the truisms in this passage, it is fair to say that, in medical negligence, the psychiatrically-injured claimants who fall one side of the 'frontier' or the other have not necessarily been treated with consistency or with cogency. Indeed, the special rules governing the establishment of a duty of care towards these types of injured claimants are among the most-criticised of any area of tort law. Apart from the previously-mentioned law commission studies,[11] academic commentators,[12] House of Lords members,[13] and foreign judiciary,[14] have all contributed their pithy critiques and unhappy sentiments upon the subject.

B SETTING THE CONTEXT

1. Some preliminary points

First of all, non-patients will face considerable problems in seeking to establish a *duty of care* on the HCP's part to avoid their pure psychiatric injury—and, hence, this chapter will concentrate upon that first limb of the negligence action, for that is where the vast majority of the legal controversy lies. Occasionally, however, other aspects of the negligence action can also be in issue.

For example, no breach of the duty was made out in *AB v Tameside and Glossop HA*,[15] where a HCP formerly involved in obstetric treatment had tested HIV-positive, the defendant Health Authority had to inform women who had been treated by that HCP of the very slight risk of HIV infection, and letters were sent advising women of the availability of 'further advice, counselling and possibly a test.' A duty to take care when conveying accurate, but distressing, news was *conceded* by the Health Authority.[16] However, it ultimately succeeded in defending the claim, on the basis that breaking the news to the women in the way that it did was not negligently done.[17]

Causation, too, can present real difficulties for non-patients alleging psychiatric illness arising out of the treatment of a patient. The non-patient will be required to establish that the actual (or perceived[18]) harm which befell the patient was caused by the HCP's acts or omissions; and further, that it was the shock of appreciating the patient's actual or perceived injury or danger that caused the non-patient's psychiatric injury. In *Toth v Jarman*,[19] where a father alleged that a GP's failure to administer glucose intravenously to his son, Wilfred, who was suffering from a hypoglycaemic fit, was negligent (the young boy died a week later, having never regained consciousness), no causal link could be established between this breach, and Wilfred's death. The trial judge was not satisfied that, had the GP given Wilfred an injection as he should have done when called to the house, it would have saved Wilfred's life, because, by that stage, Wilfred had already suffered irreversible brain damage. It has been judicially commented that 'the causative burden is not easy to discharge' in such cases.[20]

Secondly, it is important to note that, while this chapter focuses upon non-patients' claims against HCPs for the recovery of damages for negligently-caused psychiatric illness, occasionally *the patient himself* may bring such a claim. This occurs where the patient (by reason of what he alleges to have been mistreatment or mis-diagnosis by the HCP), may be exposed to physical damage but suffers none that could be sued for—but suffers psychiatric damage instead. In reality, this type of claimant will be fairly rare, for most patients who complain of some medical negligence are likely to have been *physically* harmed in some way, and hence, a claim for *pure* psychiatric illness will not lie. Mothers who have given birth in difficult circumstances, and who suffer psychiatric injury from witnessing the effects of the birth upon their newborn, probably fall within this 'primary victim' category of patient, because they were exposed to the risk of physical harm during the course of birth.[21] In addition, a few further examples of this unusual category of claim, arising in English medico-legal jurisprudence, are worth a brief mention:

In *Bancroft v Harrogate HA*,[22] the patient, Ms Bancroft (B), was treated for cervical cancer in 1983, and suffered from intermittent vaginal bleeding for four years thereafter, during which the defendant gynaecologist recommended conservative treatment. Finally, in 1987, B was advised to undergo a hysterectomy, from which she made a good recovery. B then sued her gynaecologist, alleging that the operation should have been performed earlier, and that the delay had caused her to suffer personality change, loss of self-esteem and depression. **Held:** B could not recover, for she did not suffer from a 'recognised psychiatric illness'.

In *RK (on behalf of AK and MK) v Oldham NHS Trust*,[23] the patient, baby MK, suffered a spiral fracture of her leg when two months old. MK was taken to A&E and was seen by a consultant paediatrician, who diagnosed the injury as an 'inflicted' and 'non-accidental' injury. As a result, MK was removed from her parents' home and discharged into the care of her aunt. During this period, MK's aunt picked her up from a couch, and MK suffered bilateral femoral fractures. Further biochemical and metabolic tests on blood and urine (which had not been carried out when the previous injury was suffered) then caused experts in paediatric bone disease to diagnose that MK's history and injuries were consistent with the congenital disorder *osteogenesis imperfecta* (brittle bone disease). MK was returned to her parents' care, after a separation of eight months. MK sued the paediatrician for psychiatric damage sustained as a result of relationship disruption between her parents and herself. No psychological injury for MK had been diagnosed—but the question was whether the court should recognise the difficulties in identifying potential harm in young children who may not be able to vocalise their feelings; or that an abnormal period of development of 'the attachment dynamic' between parents/child could amount to an injury recognisable by law? **Held** (at trial[24]): MK had no valid claim at law—she had suffered no physical harm nor any recognisable psychiatric disorder (said the psychological experts), and this was not an area 'in which the court should infer that there has been an injury where experts in the field do not.'[25]

In *Younger v Dorset and Somerset Strategic HA*,[26] the patient, Mrs Younger (Y), had been incorrectly diagnosed with coeliac disease,[27] as a result of which she was ordered to undertake a gluten-free diet. She was subsequently retested, and the diagnostic error was corrected. Y alleged that she had suffered some psychological harm from the gluten-free diet. **Held:** the claim failed; there could be no recovery at law for Y's psychological injury, being less than a recognised psychiatric illness.

Hence, and coincidentally, each of these claims came unstuck on the threshold requirement of proving some recognised psychiatric disorder (discussed shortly in Section 2).

Thirdly, it is highly unlikely that any non-patients could ever feasibly bring a claim against a HCP for the intentional infliction of emotional distress, per the rule in *Wilkinson v Downton*.[28] According to this rule, a defendant will be liable if he tells the claimant information, knowing it to be untrue, so that, believing it, the claimant suffers psychiatric illness, where it can be shown that the defendant has 'wilfully done an action calculated to cause physical harm to the plaintiff ... which in fact caused physical harm to her'.[29] However unlikely that scenario may be, it has been litigated, at a preliminary stage, in American case law:

> In *Humer v Bayer*,[30] the parents of a child sued a HCP who had been treating their sick child, alleging that the HCP had told the parents that the child had a possible cancer, when in fact he knew that the child was suffering from only a mildly infected appendix. The HCP sought to strike out the action. **Held:** the action would not be struck out. If believed, these facts did constitute an independent cause of action on behalf of the parents, as non-patients, for intentional infliction of emotional distress.

Closer to home, a non-patient's claim based upon the rule in *Wilkinson v Downton* was rejected by the English Court of Appeal in *Powell v Boldaz*[31]—and, consistent with the outcome in that case, it is almost inconceivable that the requisite intent on a HCP's part to cause injury would be proven.

Finally, the particular scenario in which parents are wrongfully accused of child abuse, and bring actions against negligent psychologists and other HCPs, and against the NHS Trusts who employed them, for the psychiatric injuries resulting from enforced separation from their children, is discussed in Chapter 10. The policy issues associated with these types of parental claims for psychiatric injury are extremely complex (and judicially divisive), and warrant separate analysis.

2. A genuine or recognised psychiatric illness

In order to succeed in a claim for pure psychiatric illness, the non-patient must establish that he suffered a 'recognised' (or, as some prefer, 'recognisable'[32]) psychiatric illness. The requirement has a distinguished pedigree in English law,[33] and is accepted to be the legal position in other Commonwealth jurisdictions too[34] (subject to some notable objection considered further below).

To determine this threshold, English courts traditionally have regard to what the Court of Appeal has referred to as the 'considerable degree of international agreement on the classification of mental disorders and their diagnostic criteria',[35] *viz*, the American Diagnostic and Statistical Manual of Mental Disorders, DSM-IV (1994),[36] and the International Statistical Classification of Mental and Behavioural Disorders, ICD-10 (1992).[37]

This means that human emotions of grief, distress, discomfort, apprehension, annoyance, worry, sorrow, fear, anxiety, deprivation, irritation, horror, or despondency, are not compensable at law, when brought as pure psychiatric illness claims—or, as one court put it, '[e]motional responses to unpleasant experiences of even the most serious type do not found a claim for damages'.[38] Some emotional difficulties with physical consequences (say, fear, with vomiting and sweating) are not sufficient either, because the harm falls short of a recognisable psychiatric condition, and the physical manifestations are only consequential.[39] In that regard, having to prove a genuine psychiatric disorder operates as a 'powerful control mechanism'[40] for all claimants.

As noted earlier, Mrs Bancroft, baby MK, and Mrs Younger, were all unable to surmount the hurdle; and additionally, some non-patients who have witnessed medical negligence to loved ones have also failed on the basis that they suffered no recognised psychiatric illness that the law would accept.[41] In *Ward v Leeds Teaching Hospitals NHS Trust*, for example, the accepted psychiatric evidence was that the claimant mother had suffered 'a severe and prolonged bereavement reaction', which was described by the court in terms that cast doubt on whether it was a recognised psychiatric illness worthy of compensation.[42] On the other hand, in *Tredget and Tredget v Bexley HA* (the case of the birth which was conducted amid chaos and pandemonium in the delivery theatre, and where the baby boy died of his injuries when two days old), both parents were able to recover for what the psychiatric evidence described as 'pathological unresolved mourning'.[43] This was, in the eyes of the law, seemingly more worthy of compensation than the 'bereavement reaction' of Mrs Ward. Much will depend upon the psychiatric evidence, and the delineations between compensable and non-compensable injuries can appear, at least to the lay-person, to be very fine indeed.[44]

Permitting recovery for pure psychiatric injury *at all* has been viewed with some suspicion— primarily for four reasons, as the High Court of Australia explained:

> (i) psychiatric harm is less objectively observable than physical injury and is therefore more likely to be trivial or fabricated and is more captive to shifting medical theories and conflicting expert evidence, (ii) litigation in respect of purely psychiatric harm is likely to operate as an unconscious disincentive to rehabilitation, (iii) permitting full recovery for purely psychiatric harm risks indeterminate liability and greatly increases the class of persons who may recover, and (iv) ... liability for purely psychiatric harm may impose an unreasonable or disproportionate burden on defendants ('[i]t would be an entirely unreasonable burden on all human activity if the defendant who has endangered one person were to be compelled to pay for the lacerated feelings of every other person disturbed by reason of it, including every bystander shocked at an accident, and every distant relative of the person injured, as well as all his friends').[45]

Other judges have frankly admitted that 'psychiatric injury is difficult to prove or disprove'; that 'the line between physical and mental or emotional injury in a particular case may be obscure'; that proof of a recognised psychiatric injury 'depends so greatly upon the credibility of the claimants and their expert witnesses whose advocacy is often impossible to refute', and that '[i]n these kinds of cases there must necessarily be a healthy measure of judicial scepticism if there is to be a fair adjudication'.[46]

The reasoning goes, however, that insistence upon proof of a recognised psychiatric illness limits the scope for abusive or vexatious claims: 'many of these concerns recede if full force is given to the distinction between emotional distress and a recognisable psychiatric illness.'[47]

Nevertheless, there have been many critics of the law's reliance on the official psychiatric classification systems, DSM and ICD, by which to prove the threshold requirement of a 'genuine psychiatric illness'. These criticisms have come from numerous quarters:

- some English judiciary has said that the diagnostic classifications are of 'only marginal help' when psychiatrists 'use different language and terminology to describe the same mental disorder, illness or injury', and that if a psychiatrist's evidence convinces that the claimant has suffered 'either an acute or a chronic genuine mental condition, it matters not what label is put on the condition';[48]

- according to some expert psychiatric opinion, the classifications 'were designed for research and clinical purposes, not legal use. Conceptual issues thus arise if the classifications are used in the law; their inbuilt checks and balances should not be ignored—though they often are';[49]

- academically, it has been remarked that the legal weight to be given to the classifications is problematical, when courts are prepared to accept a diagnosis of pathological grief disorder, and yet the condition has yet to be accepted in either classification[50] (and given the controversy that accompanied the certification of post-traumatic stress disorder[51]);

- law reform opinion has also been uneasy about close adherence to the diagnostic classifications, with the Ipp Committee pointing out[52] that DSM-IV itself warns against its use in legal contexts, and that it was developed as a tool for clinical, not legal, purposes;

- some judiciary in other jurisdictions have expressly preferred the view that even mental sorrow and distress suffered by grieving relatives ought to be compensable, provided that the 'mental suffering is of the order, *or approaching the order*, of a psychiatric illness and therefore plainly outside the range of ordinary human experience' (a minority view of the New Zealand case of *J&P Van Soest v Residual Health Management Unit*[53]). This view has been supported in some judgments elsewhere.[54] The majority in *Van Soest* did not agree, however, on the basis that it was difficult to say what degree of suffering would fall outside 'ordinary human experience', rendering the test unworkable.[55] Furthermore, the floodgates fear reasserted: '[i]t does not seem in the best interests of society either to throw the courts open to everyone caused *distress* by the negligent injuring of a loved one'.[56]

Clearly, then, there is some level of unease about the delineation between degrees of compensable psychiatric damage, and the utility of the diagnostic classification systems in the courtroom. Nevertheless, the threshold requirement of a recognisable psychiatric illness continues to hold good in English law.

C   ILLUSTRATIVE SCENARIOS OF NON-PATIENT CLAIMS FOR PURE PSYCHIATRIC INJURY

In a wide variety of scenarios, parties who have stood outside the HCP–patient relationship (i.e., strangers to that relationship) have sued the HCP for pure psychiatric injury arising from the treatment of a patient. A tri-partite relationship inevitably arises in such scenarios, per Figure 8.1.

The HCP undoubtedly owes a duty of care to avoid injury to the patient; but is a duty also owed to the non-patient, to avoid or minimise the risk of his suffering from psychiatric injury? It may be useful to categorise and summarise the facts and verdicts of relevant English cases, as a prelude to their analysis in later Sections.

First, there have been those relatives/bystanders who have seen the results of alleged or actual medical negligence in the hospital where it occurred, i.e., the non-patient was in the near vicinity of the patient's injury or death, and suffered a psychiatric injury.

In *Ward v Leeds Teaching Hospitals NHS Trust*,[57] the patient, Katherine, entered hospital to have her wisdom teeth removed, but failed to regain consciousness after the operation, and died two days later. The NHS Trust admitted negligence in respect of the medical treatment. Mrs Ward (W) was Katherine's mother, and brought an action in negligence, claiming that she saw her daughter

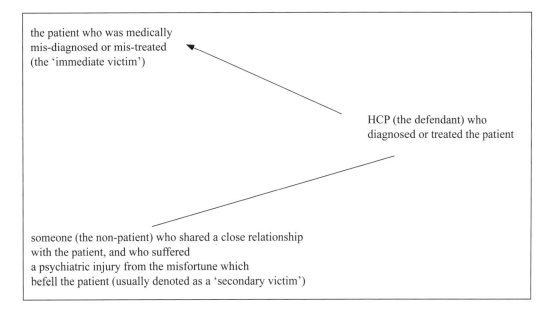

Figure 8.1 Pure psychiatric illness claims arising from medical negligence

at the hospital prior to the death, and also saw the body in the mortuary afterwards, resulting in post-traumatic-stress-disorder. **Held:** W could not recover for her psychiatric injury.

In *Sion v Hampstead HA*,[58] the patient, Lionel Sion, 23, was injured in a motorcycle accident and was taken to the defendant's hospital. The hospital staff failed to diagnose substantial and continuing bleeding from his left kidney, which resulted in the son falling into a coma from which he never recovered. He died 14 days after admittance. Mr Sion Snr (S) maintained a bedside vigil throughout this time, witnessing his son's deterioration and eventual death. S sued for psychiatric injury incurred because of the alleged negligence of the hospital in caring for his son. **Held:** no recovery for psychiatric injury permitted; action struck out.

In *Tredget and Tredget v Bexley HA*,[59] a son (the patient) was born to Mrs T, amid chaos and pandemonium in the delivery theatre. The baby boy was delivered in a distressed condition (severely asphyxiated), and required immediate resuscitation. Mr T was present in the room, and was requested by medical staff to encourage his wife in her efforts in delivery. The baby died of his injuries when two days old. The parents sued for pathological grief reaction caused by the death of their child. **Held:** both parents recovered for their psychiatric injuries (£32,500 for Mr T, and £17,500 for Mrs T).

In *North Glamorgan NHS Trust v Walters*,[60] the patient, Elliot (E), 10 months, developed acute hepatitis which doctors at the hospital did not correctly diagnose or treat. E suffered a seizure in front of his mother Ms Walters (W), in the hospital room in which both were being accommodated. W was initially told that E had suffered no long-term damage from the seizure. E lost the opportunity to undergo a liver transplant because of the mis-diagnosis. E was transferred to another hospital, where W was told that E had been severely brain-damaged, would never recognise her, and would have practically no quality of life. W agreed to turn off the life support machine, 36 hours after the initial seizure, and thereafter sued for pathological grief reaction. **Held:** W recovered £20,000 for her psychiatric injury.

In *Farrell v Merton, Sutton and Wandsworth HA*,[61] Mrs Farrell (F) entered hospital to give birth to her son Karol (K). Due to the admitted negligence of the defendants, K was born with severe and irreversible brain damage (F was under anaesthetic during the course of the birth itself). F sued for psychiatric injury, allegedly due to the shock of learning of K's condition, and long-term depression and anxiety. F was not allowed by the hospital staff to see K until he was one day old, nor was she told about the grievous nature of his brain injuries in that 24-hour period. Instead, she was shown a photograph of K lying on a mattress shortly after he was born, and was told that he 'had had a hard time with the Caesarian'. **Held:** F recovered £75,000 for psychiatric injury.

Next, there have been cases in which the relatives/bystanders were told bad news—along the lines that a loved one had died or was seriously injured as a result of medical negligence—and then went to the hospital to view the loved one's condition or body.

In *Taylor v Somerset HA*,[62] the patient, Mrs Taylor's husband, was not diagnosed and treated for heart disease, negligently. Many months later, Mr T suffered a heart attack at work and died. Mrs T, the non-patient, was told he was ill at hospital, she visited the hospital 20 minutes later, and was shortly thereafter told of his death. She could not believe the fact of her husband's death, and needed to view his body as 'proof'. She sued the defendant HA for shock and distress. **Held:** no recovery for psychiatric injury was permitted.

In *Tan v East London and City HA*,[63] Mrs Tan attended the defendant's hospital to give birth by Caesarean section. Due to negligent treatment, the baby girl died *in utero* before the operation, and was stillborn by Caesarean section four hours later. Mr T, the non-patient, was told of the death over the phone by the hospital staff about 20 minutes after it occurred, and travelled straight to the hospital, where he was present during the operation. He held his dead baby daughter after delivery and at times during the night, and watched her placed in a metal box the following day. He later suffered severe depression, contributing to his loss of employment. **Held:** Mr T could not recover for his psychiatric injury.

Then there are the cases where the relatives/bystanders witnessed the results of alleged or actual medical negligence, at some time and place remote from where the medical treatment actually occurred.

In *Froggatt v Chesterfield and North Derbyshire Royal Hosp NHS Trust*,[64] the patient, Mrs Froggatt, 28, underwent a mastectomy following a mis-diagnosis that she was suffering from cancer. Three weeks after the operation, Mrs F was informed of the mis-diagnosis. Her husband Mr F brought an action for psychiatric injury suffered when he saw his wife undressed for the first time following the operation (at least 12 days after the operation); and her son brought an action for psychiatric injury suffered when he overheard a phone conversation in which he heard his mother telling a friend that she had been diagnosed with cancer. **Held:** Mr F recovered £5,000 for his psychiatric injury; Mrs F's son recovered £1,000 for his psychiatric injury.

In *Hall v Gwent Healthcare NHS Trust*,[65] the patient, Andrew Hall, was mentally disturbed, and under the care of a local health authority for treatment of mental illness, and for whose family certain care orders were in place. Mr H was the target of a cruel hoax played on him by his work colleagues, and it mentally destabilised him. Mr H heard 'voices' commanding him to kill his 12-year-old daughter Emma, which he acted upon one night in the family home. Mrs H, the non-patient, was in the house at the time of the fatal attack, and took the knife from her husband following the fatal stabbing, but she was not herself at risk of physical injury, nor had she unwittingly contributed to her daughter's peril (quite the opposite, she had ensured that no knives were kept in the family home, but her husband purloined one from his sister's house during a brief visit there). Mrs H suffered from psychiatric illness as a result of the terrible event. **Held:** the claim was struck out, as having no basis in law.

In *Palmer v Tees HA*[66] (the facts of which were considered previously in Chapter 3), Mrs Palmer's daughter Rosie (R) was killed by a psychotically disturbed man, Armstrong (A), who was under the care of psychiatrists employed by the defendant HA (and to whom he had admitted that he had sexual feelings towards children before his release into community care). R was killed almost a year after A's release; A lived in the next street to R and her mother. Mrs P, as non-patient, suffered depression, following the rape, murder and mutilation of her daughter. **Held:** Mrs P's claim for severe post-traumatic stress disorder and pathological grief reaction failed.

Cases have also occurred where the relatives/bystanders were informed of bad news, ostensibly that medical negligence had brought about the death or injury of a patient—but that news turned out to be mistaken and incorrect.

In *Farrell v Avon HA*,[67] Mr Farrell (F), the non–patient, excitedly attended a hospital operated by the defendant HA to see his newborn son Jordan (J), born of a brief relationship with J's mother (F and the mother were not a couple at the time of J's birth). Upon arriving, he was told that the baby had died, and he was given a corpse to cradle. Twenty minutes later, he was then told that baby J was alive, and was shown J, where he stayed for five minutes before going out to the carpark where he was sick. F sued the defendant for the negligent communication of such news, and claimed that, as a result, he had incurred post-traumatic stress disorder and alcohol and drug dependency. F never maintained any father/son relationship with J, and indeed, never saw J after that day in hospital. F was diagnosed as having a pre-existing psychological problem which rendered him more at risk than others of developing post-traumatic-stress disorder, according to the psychiatric evidence. **Held:** F was permitted to recover £10,000 for psychiatric injury.

In *Allin v City and Hackney HA*,[68] Mrs Allin gave birth to a baby, but was told that the baby had died. Mrs A discovered about six hours later that the baby was alive. The defendant HA claimed that no such misstatement was made. Mrs A sued for post-traumatic-stress disorder as a result of hearing the inaccurate information, and for the failure to refer her for psychological treatment afterwards. **Held:** Mrs A recovered £10,000 for psychiatric injury.

Finally, there are the miscellaneous cases in which the relatives/bystanders suffered pure psychiatric injury, but in circumstances that do not fit well into any of the previously-mentioned scenarios, because of their oddity:

In *Powell v Boladz*,[69] the patient, Robert Powell (R), 10, died of Addison's disease,[70] which went undiagnosed and untreated by the defendant doctors. The doctors admitted that the mis-diagnosis was negligent. The parents' claim against the relevant HA settled. Thereafter, Mr and Mrs P (the non-patients) brought a complaint against R's GP, and allegedly learnt during these proceedings that different documents (a clinical summary sheet and letter from the hospital consultant paediatrician to R's GP) had been substituted which pertained to R's death (which allegations were strongly denied). The parents claimed that the alleged 'cover up' caused them psychiatric injury. (The parents were patients on the GP's register, but in respect of this particular incident, R was the only patient.[71]) In particular, Mr P claimed that he suffered psychiatric injury as a result of learning of the removal and substitution of documents (that 'my head exploded'), whereas Mrs P's claim for psychiatric injury (which had commenced from the very original time of R's death) was an exacerbation to her condition caused by the events of the alleged substitution. **Held:** no recovery for Mr or Mrs P's psychiatric injuries was permitted, as they were owed no duty of care by the defendants HCPs.

In *AB v Leeds Teaching Hosp NHS Trust*,[72] three mothers, Mrs Shorter, Mrs Carpenter and Mrs Harris, claimed damages for psychiatric injury from the defendant NHS Trust, arising from the fact that they learnt that their children's organs (brains, hearts, lungs) had been removed post-mortem, retained and then disposed of without their knowledge and consent. This practice of retaining organs for histopathological examinations had developed in several hospitals in England, where babies and very young children died from natural and unexplained causes, and where the organs were retained for the purposes of eliciting information, especially as medical knowledge advanced, which could identify to assist and prevent such deaths in the future. When the news about the organ retention came to light, group litigation was instituted on behalf of some parents who alleged psychiatric illnesses.[73] The three test claimants argued that the defendant HCPs had breached their duty of care by not explaining to the parents that the organs would be removed during the post-mortem examinations, and possibly retained. **Held:** H and C could not recover for their psychiatric illnesses; S recovered £2,750 in damages for her psychiatric injury.

Those round out the categories in English law whereby pure psychiatric injuries on the part of non-patients have allegedly arisen from instances of medical negligence practised upon the patient. As will be seen in later Sections, the legal principles governing these claims are difficult, policy-driven, and often lack consistent application.

Claimants in pure psychiatric illness suits usually divide into a primary or secondary victim classification. In *Alcock v Chief Constable of South Yorkshire Police*, the distinction was defined by Lord Oliver as being between one (the primary victim) 'who was *involved, either mediately or immediately, as a participant*', as opposed to the secondary victim 'who was no more than a passive and unwilling witness of injury caused to others.'[74] Each type of victim has special rules to satisfy, in order to prove that the defendant owed him a duty to avoid the risk of psychiatric injury occurring. It is easier to establish the rules for primary victim status than for secondary victim status. Legally-speaking, a primary victim 'is always in a much stronger position',[75] and hence, non-patients will prefer to get themselves within that classification if they can legally manage to do so. However, as will be evident, although primary victims have several advantages over their secondary victim counterparts, neither type of claimant enjoys an easy time of proving that a duty of care was owed.

Furthermore, the law is rendered rather 'messy' by the fact that no bright-line division between the two categories has been maintained, especially in the field of medical negligence. Some of this must inevitably be traced back to the phrase, 'mediately or immediately as a participant'—because, as Hobhouse LJ remarked in the workplace accident case of *Young v Charles Church (Southern) Ltd*, the phrase 'potentially includes some of those who might be regarded as "secondary victims". (Indeed, this implication arises from the use of the word "mediately".'[76]) Just to add to the confusion, some claimants have succeeded against the HCP by disregarding the primary/secondary victim classification altogether. These issues will be explored in the following Sections.

D CLAIMS BY NON-PATIENTS AS PRIMARY VICTIMS AGAINST HEALTHCARE PROFESSIONALS

There are actually **two** avenues by which such a non-patient can seek to establish primary victim status in English law: *either* by proving that he was somehow a 'participant' in the events unfolding around the patient; *or* that there was no other primary victim of the medical negligence, in which case *he* must be the primary victim. A third potential avenue—by relying upon the tri-partite test for novel duty of care scenarios set out in *Caparo Industries plc v Dickman*,[77] without recourse to the primary/secondary victim classification—has **not** been used in claims against HCPs by psychiatrically-injured non-patients as yet.[78]

1. Proving that the non-patient was a 'participant'

After *Alcock* (per Lord Oliver) defined a primary victim as a 'participant' in 1992, the definition underwent several refinements over the years. In *Page v Smith* (1996, re a traffic accident), a primary victim was someone 'directly involved in the accident, and well within the range of foreseeable physical injury.'[79] In *White v Chief Constable of South Yorkshire Police* (1999, re the Hillsborough disaster), it was taken to mean a person who was objectively exposed to danger and a risk of physical injury, or reasonably believed that he was so exposed.[80] In *W v Essex CC*[81] (2001, re foster care arrangements), a primary victim was expanded to potentially include those who also believed that they were the unwitting cause of another's injury or death. In *The Pleural Plaques Litigation*[82] (2007, re employer liability), the primary victim was expressed in *Page v Smith*-type terms, and *W v Essex* was not referred to. The House of Lords' inconsistency in its definition of the primary victim has rendered this (as the author has stated elsewhere) 'one of the messiest nooks of torts jurisprudence ... [where] [a]ll too frequently the courts have chosen to sacrifice doctrinal clarity to help unfortunate claimants.'[83]

Of the abovementioned versions, the non-patient relative is never going to be able to prove that he was, himself, in the zone of physical danger as a result of the HCP's negligent act/omission towards the patient—nor is that relative going to claim on the basis of some guilt-ridden complex about bringing about the patient's downfall. However, a tragedy may unfold in a hospital (or elsewhere) that places that non-patient squarely in the midst of the events—events that can be attributed to the HCP's actual or alleged negligence. Attempts to argue that psychiatrically-damaged non-patients were primary victims on that basis, however, have failed to date. This outcome is particularly illustrated by the cases of the three mothers—Ms Walters,[84] Ms Hall,[85] and Ms Palmer[86]—all of whom brought claims for pure psychiatric illness arising out of the death of their children, all of whom were closely exposed to and involved with the events surrounding the children's deaths, and all of whom lost their primary victim claims.

The only one of this trio to recover at all was Mrs Walters (£20,000 for pathological grief reaction)—but she only succeeded as a *secondary* victim. At trial, it was argued that Mrs Walters' close proximity to Elliot throughout the final 36 hours of his life, culminating in her turning off his life support machine, qualified her as an 'unwilling participant' in the medical negligence that brought about Elliot's death. This submission, however, was rejected, on the basis that she was not within the range of foreseeable physical injury herself, nor did she play any causative role in her son's death.[87] The Court of Appeal briefly agreed that Mrs Walters could not constitute a primary victim,[88] and the appeal was only conducted on the question of whether she could satisfy secondary victim status. In *Hall v Gwent Healthcare NHS Trust*, on a strike-out application, the court was satisfied that Ms Hall could not satisfy the definition of a primary victim, even though she was in the house at the time that her husband, gripped by insanity, murdered her daughter, and she took the knife from him after the attack; she could only be a secondary victim at best.[89] Similarly, in *Palmer v Tees HA*, Ms Palmer failed to prove primary victim status for precisely the same reasons as Ms Hall and Ms Walters after her, with Stuart-Smith LJ declaring that '[a]lthough at one stage [counsel] suggested that the claimant was a primary victim, he did not seriously argue the point; in my judgment, she clearly was not'.[90]

The issue is not, however, without controversy. Some commentators (such as Lyons[91]) accept that Mrs Walters was 'plainly' a secondary victim, whereas others (such as Peart[92]) disagree, arguing that Mrs Walters was arguably a primary victim on the definitions applicable to that category. In this author's view, and in light of the considerable narrowing of the definition of primary victim, it was appropriate to deny Mrs Walters primary victim status, for precisely the reasons to which the trial judge had regard, which reasons are consistent with post-*Alcock* House of Lords' jurisprudence on the issue. Primary victims, seemingly, are no longer 'participants'—they need something more than that to qualify.

2. Elevating an apparent secondary victim to primary victim status

The second way in which a non-patient may seek primary victim status is by arguing (by reference to Figure 8.1) that there is no *immediate victim* of the HCP's medical mis-treatment or mis-diagnosis. While the HCP may have been culpable in some way in the incident giving rise to the non-patient's psychiatric injury, there is no *harmed* immediate victim. Legally speaking, how should the non-patient be legally treated then—as a secondary victim for whom there is no immediate victim, or as a primary victim, because there is no immediate victim to whom he could be a secondary victim? Controversially, it is the second of these options which has been adopted in the key medical cases to date.

In *AB v Leeds Teaching Hospital NHS Trust*[93] (the case arising out of the practice of harvesting deceased children's brains, hearts, and lungs without their parents' knowledge and consent), the three test claimants were all classified as primary victims.[94] The principal reason was that their children were not immediate victims to whom a duty could have been owed by the HCPs, because no duty is owed post-mortem. If there was no immediate victim in respect of whom the parents could be secondary victims, then they must be primary victims, said Gage J: 'in my view, there is force in the argument that the children were not primary victims. Neither the clinicians nor the pathologists could possibly have owed any duty of care to them after their death. In my opinion, it follows that if the claimants are victims at all they must be primary victims.'[95] However, the facts—that these parents were not participants in the post-mortem activities, were not guilt-ridden claimants in the *W v Essex* sense in that they did not cause or contribute to the decision to harvest the organs, and were not in the range of foreseeable physical harm themselves—raise the question of how they could possibly have been considered to be primary victims on *any* basis? They do not satisfy any of the House of Lords' definitions of 'primary victim'. If they were so classified, it could only be on the basis that they were 'participants' in a wide sense—yet, as discussed in the previous section, that wide view has been discredited elsewhere in medical negligence claims.

Another example of this conundrum is found in *Farrell v Avon HA*[96]—the extraordinary case in which Mr Farrell (F) excitedly attended hospital to see his newborn son Jordan (J), was inaccurately told that J had died during birth and was given a baby's corpse to hold, who then suffered the trauma of being told that the corpse was not J, and who sustained post-traumatic stress disorder and subsequent alcohol and drug dependency. F was permitted to recover £10,000 for psychiatric injury. One of the most interesting legal aspects of this case (and there were many), was whether F was a primary or a secondary victim. It was an important issue because, arguably, F could not have satisfied the various secondary victim pre-requisites for recovery. It was fortunate, then, that he was decreed to be a primary victim. Again, the basis for this conclusion was that there was no other primary victim—fortunately, J was born a healthy baby, and so 'the only victim of the incident was the claimant himself'.[97] Clearly, though, F did not fit the classic modern definition of primary victim, for he himself was never in the zone of physical danger, nor was he the guilt-ravaged *W v Essex*-type claimant.[98]

The author has argued elsewhere[99] that, instead of elevating these claimants to primary victim status, Mr Farrell and the parents in *AB v Leeds* ought to have been treated as secondary victims, with no immediate victim existing. This would enable the primary victim definitions couched by the House of Lords to be applied consistently and meaningfully, rather than departing from those definitions in sympathetic cases, and simply because of the coincidental matter that the immediate victims did not happen to be the subject of any medical negligence which harmed them. Given the easier task which primary victims face in establishing a duty of care (explored in Section 3), a bright-line division between the categories is, surely, all the more important to maintain.

Furthermore, to hold that these claimants, F and the parents, must have been primary victims, suffers from a further and significant legal difficulty. It suggests that any duty to a secondary victim must be *derivative* (i.e., that it can only be established if there was some proven negligence towards the immediate victim). However, this is incorrect. Any duty owed by the HCP to a secondary victim is **not** derivative from, or dependent upon, a finding that the HCP was negligent towards the patient/immediate victim. Legally-speaking, it is possible for a HCP to be found to have been negligent towards a secondary victim without the immediate victim/patient having any cause of action at all, or suffering any harm whatsoever. The English Law Commission reiterated the point that a duty could conceivably be owed to the secondary victim, even if no negligence could be made out by the immediate victim due to a waiver or other defence.[100] The Ipp Committee also reiterated that any duty owed to the secondary victim who can establish the necessary pre-requisites is separate and distinct.[101] Moreover, in *Alcock v Chief Constable of South Yorkshire Police*, Lord Oliver remarked that:

> There may, indeed, be no primary 'victim' in fact. It is, for instance, readily conceivable that a parent may suffer injury, whether physical or psychiatric, as a result of witnessing a negligent act which places his or her child in extreme jeopardy but from which, in the event, the child escapes unharmed. I doubt very much, for instance, whether *King v Phillips* [1953] 1 QB 429, where a mother's claim for damages for shock caused by witnessing a near accident to her child was rejected, would be decided in the same way today in the light of later authorities.[102]

Lord Oliver also gave the example of where a mother saw an empty lorry running downhill towards her, and around a bend past which her children had just disappeared. She would be able to recover for psychiatric illness against the driver who had negligently left the lorry unattended, even if her children had not suffered any injury at all.[103] All these parents could be secondary victims (said Lord Oliver), even though there was no primary *victim*. Although some courts since have suggested[104] that any duty to the secondary victim is derivative, this assertion clearly goes against this House of Lords' dicta. The better view is that the duty to the secondary victim is entirely independent of any duty of care owed to/negligence toward/harm suffered by, the immediate victim. To elevate bystanders to primary victim status because no other person was 'physically involved in the incident as a potential victim'[105] appears to be inconsistent with both precedent and logic.

To summarise the foregoing section—where a non-patient has suffered psychiatric injury as a result of a medical mishap to a patient, then he may attempt to prove primary victim status by alleging that, first, he was a 'participant' in the medical drama in a broadly-construed sense, and secondly, that he should be treated as a primary victim in the absence of any immediate victim. Non-patients have had more success in the latter category than in the former (for reasons that appear to be legally dubious), but even so, few non-patients, as strangers to the HCP–patient relationship, have succeeded as primary victims at all. Most have resorted to pleading secondary victim status—but often with a lack of success.

3. Proving a duty of care, as a primary victim in medical negligence scenarios

For non-patients who assert that they are primary victims, the requirements of a duty of care can conveniently be divided into five issues:

(a) The test of foreseeability of psychiatric injury
The non-patient will have to prove that it was foreseeable that he would suffer a *psychiatric* injury by reason of the HCP's acts or omissions towards the patient. Had the non-patient been in the zone of physical danger himself but suffered merely psychiatric injury instead, then it would be sufficient, under the principle of *Page v Smith*,[106] if it was only foreseeable that *physical* injury would result to him from the HCP's negligence—but bystanders to medical mishaps are not in that category, and hence, that wider and more advantageous test of reasonable foreseeability will not apply to them.[107]

Very occasionally, non-patients will *not* be able to prove that psychiatric injury was a reasonably foreseeable consequence of the medical wrongdoing. In *AB v Leeds Teaching Hospital NHS Trust*,[108] for example, two out of the three claimant mothers failed to satisfy Gage J that it was reasonably foreseeable that they would suffer psychiatric injuries when they discovered that their dead children's organs had been retained, given that they were described by the judge as 'robust' and 'well-adjusted, practical and sensible' women, for whom anger and distress may have been foreseeable, but psychiatric injury was most certainly not.[109] The third test claimant[110] was only able to recover because she was emotionally vulnerable and, fortunately for her legal claim, the normal fortitude rule does not apply to primary victims (one of the advantages of primary victim status, as discussed below[111]).

(b) The role of proximity
For a non-patient who is not deemed to be a 'participant' in the medical events as they unfold, and who is a stranger to the HCP–patient relationship, establishing a legal proximity between the

HCP and himself is likely to be problematical. Clearly, the non-patient's mere physical proximity to tragic medical events brought about by medical negligence is not sufficient for primary victim status (as exemplified by *North Glamorgan NHS Trust v Walters*[112]). Some significant lapse of time between the HCP's wrongdoing and the events leading to the onset of psychiatric harm may preclude primary victim status too (as illustrated in *Palmer v Tees HA*[113]).

In fact, for the non-patients concerned, the requisite proximity in both of the 'elevated primary victim' cases was proven on a very fact-specific basis. In *AB v Leeds Teaching Hospital NHS Trust*, Gage J held that sufficient proximity existed between the paediatricians treating the children who ended up dying of natural causes, and the parents whose consent to organ retention was not obtained, on the narrow and fact-specific basis that there existed a form of doctor–patient relationship between them when the consents to the post-mortems were obtained. Gage J said that 'the evidence of the doctors and the experts show that doctors can owe a duty of care to a mother after a death of her baby on a doctor–patient basis. In the case of a child born alive but dying shortly afterwards the paediatrician would inevitably have a duty to advise the mother about future pregnancies'; and in that event:

> taking consent for a post-mortem was not just an administrative matter bringing a doctor into contact with a mother. It was ... part of the continuing duty of care owed by the clinicians to the mother following the death of a child. In the circumstances, in my judgment, the necessary test of proximity between the claimants and clinicians is established.[114]

Once that doctor–patient relationship was established, then the duty of care extended to alerting the parents to the fact that organs might be retained.[115]

In *Farrell v Avon HA*, Judge Bursell QC considered that Mr Farrell was 'physically involved in the incident itself'—given the unusual events involving his 'dead' baby son and being given a newborn corpse to hold until the error was realised—and on that basis, sufficient legal proximity was established.[116]

(c) No requirement that the non-patient is of 'normal fortitude'

A significant advantage of primary victim status is that a claimant can recover for his psychiatric illness, even if it was sustained because he lacked the mental fortitude or 'natural phlegm' of an ordinary person.[117] By contrast, secondary victims must prove that the defendant should have reasonably foreseen psychiatric injury to *a person of normal fortitude*, before they can recover.[118]

Hence, it was not fatal to Mrs Shorter's claim in *AB v Leeds Teaching Hospital NHS Trust* that she was an 'emotionally fragile person' who was in a very distressed state following the birth of her daughter and then her death at a very early stage. Gage J concluded that 'the reasonable consultant obstetrician would have reasonably foreseen that this event would result in some psychiatric injury in Mrs Shorter'.[119] Possibly, Mr Farrell's claim may also have benefited from his primary victim status. According to the psychiatric evidence given in that trial (which the court accepted),[120] 'the claimant was probably always going to react badly to death',[121] given his previous psychological history, treatment of heroin addiction with a methadone programme, and alcohol dependence. Hence, he was more at risk of developing post-traumatic-stress disorder than the general population. Even if it were possible to argue that a father of normal fortitude is likely to have withstood the shock of what was undeniably a terrible incident without suffering psychiatric illness, as a primary victim, the HCPs had to take Mr Farrell exactly as they found him.

Interestingly, in their recent law reform considerations of pure psychiatric illness, the Scottish Law Commission, the Ipp Committee, and the Law Commission of England and Wales all favoured that the common law be changed on this point. They preferred the view that, wherever a claimant sued for pure psychiatric harm, then the defendant should not be liable if the claimant suffered that harm *merely because he was abnormally vulnerable*; rather, the defendant should be entitled to assume that those whom he is dealing with are ordinarily robust—unless the defendant knew (or ought to have known) that *the particular claimant* was abnormally susceptible to psychiatric harm. In other words, if the non-patient only suffers mental injury because he was an 'egg-shell skull' personality (and unless the HCP knew that), the mental injury to the non-patient was not reasonably foreseeable.

The Scottish Commission[122] noted that, by treating mentally-injured victims under a rule whereby the defendant cannot assume that the claimant is a person of normal fortitude, the rule is asymmetrical with that governing recovery for *physical* injury. In physical injury cases, the 'egg shell skull rule' only applies *after* liability is made out—until then, the defendant is entitled to assume that the claimant is a person of normal physical robustness, and the test of foreseeability of harm is based upon that assumption. Once the egg-shell claimant proves that physical harm, even for a person of normal physical vulnerability, was foreseeable, then as a matter of quantum, the defendant must take the claimant as he finds him and compensate him for *all* his losses. In psychiatric injury cases, however, the defendant cannot assume that the claimant is ordinarily robust. The Commission disparaged this anomaly, which presently favours primary victims, as 'stalk[ing] the current law' on recovery for pure psychiatric illness.[123] It concluded that the common law should be changed so that a defendant could assume ordinary mental robustness on the part of all primary or secondary victim claimants.[124] The Ipp Committee agreed,[125] and pointed out that a defendant can assume that a *secondary* victim is a person of normal mental fortitude. Hence, if a secondary victim has an abnormal susceptibility to mental harm, his claim will fail, because that harm would not be reasonably foreseeable. The Ipp Committee lent its weight to the proposition that, to bring about more symmetry in the law, the normal fortitude rule should be applied to *all* claimants seeking damages for pure psychiatric harm. The English Law Commission described the normal fortitude rule as a 'deceptively difficult issue',[126] calling it a 'blunt and arbitrary control device',[127] and citing Lord Ackner's remark in *Page v Smith* that 'normal fortitude', in any event, was an 'imprecise phrase'.[128] The Commission concluded that, 'in deciding whether psychiatric illness was reasonably foreseeable (and analogously to reasonable foreseeability in physical injury cases), one can take into account the robustness of the population at large to psychiatric illness'.[129] In other words, primary victims should have no advantages over secondary victims or over physically-injured claimants.

In any event, as the law presently stands, the fact that he cannot be assumed to be a person of ordinary mental fortitude, and that his psychiatric injury will be foreseeable even if he is mentally vulnerable, gives a primary victim a great advantage.

(d) Any requirement of shock?

It remains unclear, under English common law, whether the non-patient's psychiatric illness must have been induced by a 'shock', where he claims as a primary victim. This term means, in the legal sense (according to *Alcock*), 'a sudden assault on the nervous system',[130] 'the sudden appreciation of a horrifying event, which violently agitates the mind, [as opposed to] the accumulation over a period in time of more gradual assaults on the nervous system',[131] and 'a sudden and unexpected shock to the nervous system'.[132]

Certainly, for secondary victims, their psychiatric injury must have been shock-induced[133]—but in the employment context, both Scottish[134] and English[135] case law has doubted whether shock is a requirement for primary victims (earlier English case law, in the non-medical context, casts doubt on the requirement[136]). The English Commission noted, in its 1998 report, that whether shock applies to primary victims at all was an open question,[137] while the Scottish Commission accepted that it was not a pre-requisite for some so-called primary victims, such as work stress claims.[138] In any event, the shock requirement was heavily criticised by both Commissions, insofar as it has been applied to secondary victims. As will be seen in our discussion of secondary victims later in the chapter,[139] 'shock' has been judicially-stretched to cater for some claimants in a most artificial manner, and there is a strong argument that the requirement to prove a 'shock' should be abandoned for *any* claimant who suffers pure psychiatric illness.[140]

On the facts of *Farrell* and *AB v Leeds*, the parental claimants undoubtedly suffered a shock at learning the news of what had happened to their children—but as it stands, whether a non-patient must prove a 'shock' to the nervous system by reason of what happens in a medical event is still a moot point.

(e) Public policy considerations

There are two ways in which floodgates concerns may manifest in mental injury claims. First, if a claimant succeeds as a primary victim, so too may many others, in related scenarios. That concern has arisen, where a series of *patients* sued their HCPs for the adverse results of a clinical trial in England[141]—but it has not yet manifested in any case where a non-patient has brought a primary victim claim. The second potential floodgates scenario applies to *secondary* victims who witness an incident—because there may be *numerous* such bystanders. Consideration of this point will be deferred to later in the chapter, when secondary victims are discussed.

In summary, where non-patients are attempting to prove that they were 'primary victims' of a medical mishap because of a HCP's act or omission, the non-patients must prove that they suffered a recognisable psychiatric illness; that their psychiatric injury was foreseeable as a result of the HCP's acts or omissions; that there was a sufficient legal proximity between HCP and non-patient; and that no policy reasons should preclude their recovery of damages for mental injury. On the present state of the law, non-patients who are asserting primary victim status do not need to prove that the psychiatric injury would have been suffered by one of normal fortitude, and they probably do not have to prove injury by shock either.

E CLAIMS BY NON-PATIENTS AS SECONDARY VICTIMS AGAINST HEALTHCARE PROFESSIONALS

To reiterate, by contrast to the primary victim who is a 'participant', a secondary victim is 'in the position of a spectator',[142] someone who was a 'passive and unwilling witness of injury caused to others'.[143] Non-patients to medical negligence mishaps are, naturally, far more likely to fall within this classification. However, the path for a non-patient to establish that the HCP owed him a duty of care to avoid his psychiatric injury, as a secondary victim, is littered with difficulties— certainly sufficient to cast secondary victim classification as an 'exceptional' path to the recovery of damages.[144]

Before the 'control mechanisms' governing secondary victim recovery are discussed, an intriguing legal question needs to be addressed.

1. Can a non-patient be both 'primary' and 'secondary' victim?

With respect to the primary-versus-secondary-victim classification, the House of Lords has appeared to vacillate as to whether a claimant has to be either/or, or whether he can be both. In *Alcock*,[145] Lord Oliver described primary victims, and 'on the other hand', secondary victims. In *White*,[146] Lord Steyn described primary victims and then stated that 'all other victims, who suffer pure psychiatric harm, are secondary victims'. Paradoxically, however, in *Page v Smith*,[147] Lord Lloyd rationalised some earlier cases as examples of where the claimant was 'both primary and secondary victim of the same accident'. In *W v Essex CC*[148] too, Lord Slynn allowed the parental claimants to take both primary and secondary victim claims to trial. As the author has critiqued elsewhere,[149] the lack of a clear-cut distinction between the two categories has been both confusing (given that different rules apply to each category), and 'symptomatic of the courts' inability to produce a stable definition of the primary victim'.

The medical case of *Farrell v Merton, Sutton and Wandsworth HA*[150] well-illustrates this lack of a clear demarcation. This was the case in which Mrs Farrell's son, Karol, was born with severe and irreversible brain damage, due to the admitted negligence of the HCPs who managed the birth, and Mrs Farrell suffered the shock of learning of Karol's condition, and longterm depression and anxiety. She ultimately recovered £75,000 for psychiatric injury. However, the court made no bold statement as to what type of victim Mrs Farell happened to be, but hedged its bets. It was prepared to find that Mrs Farrell was either a primary victim, directly involved in the events (the trauma of the birth), or a secondary victim who witnessed the aftermath of the medically-caused injury suffered by Karol.[151] As Hilson notes,[152] whether this was a *pure* psychiatric illness case at all is debatable, given that Mrs Farrell also made a claim for pain and suffering associated with the birth, as well as for post-operative care, but in any event, the case raised and dealt with the claim as if it were governed by pure psychiatric illness rules.

Another negligence-tainted birth (in which the baby died of his injuries when two days old), the case of *Tredget and Tredget v Bexley HA*,[153] demonstrated the same uncertainty. Both parents recovered for their psychiatric injuries. The judgment of Judge White is not entirely conclusive as to whether the parents were primary or secondary victims. At one point, the parents were described as 'directly involved in and with the event of the delivery', and they were 'each principals rather than passive witnesses';[154] whereas earlier in the judgment,[155] the legal requirements for the parents to fulfill were described in secondary victim-type terms.

Hence, and quite unsatisfactorily for the clarity of the law, it is apparent that non-patients can be both primary and secondary victims. Probably the mothers in these two cases could be considered primary victims on the basis that they were themselves in a zone of physical danger during the births; but Mr Tredget could only have been a primary victim on the basis that he was a participant in the events unfolding around him, where physical injury occurred to a loved one from the HCP's medical negligence. While this 'participant theory' certainly accords with the wide *Alcock* primary victim definition, it is totally at odds, for example, with *North Glamorgan NHS Trust v Walters*.

2. Proving a duty of care, as a secondary victim in medical negligence scenarios

Amongst other pre-requisites for establishing a duty of care on the HCP's part, secondary victims have to satisfy the legal loopholes known as the '*Alcock* control mechanisms' (named in recognition of that Hillsborough case,[156] although their origin was earlier[157]). These are noted colloquially (at least in academic literature[158]) as 'dearness, nearness and hearness'. Each provides a considerable safeguard against unrestricted liability. The context in which they were confirmed in *Alcock* is significant, as McIvor explains:

> To understand the motivation behind the formulation of the '*Alcock* control mechanisms', it is crucial to bear in mind the factual context of the claims brought in that case. *Alcock* concerned a huge disaster scenario involving thousands of people and hence a large number of potential secondary victims. While this of course does not justify the arbitrary and unprincipled nature of the rules that were then formulated by the House of Lords, it does at least help to explain why the Law Lords felt that it was necessary to place limits on the number of claims making it through ... [this] serves to highlight the unpredictability of secondary victim claims, in the sense that they could be brought by any number of people who just happened to be in the vicinity of the accident at the time. Unlike physical impact force which, in accordance with the laws of physics, can only travel so far before it dissipates, the remit of psychological trauma is potentially limitless.[159]

Medical negligence scenarios inevitably tend to be somewhat different—typically a few HCPs, one patient who suffers medical mistreatment of one type or another, and a limited number of non-patients (usually relatives) who suffer psychiatric illness. Notwithstanding, however, the *Alcock* control mechanisms have posed significant barriers to non-patients' recovery as secondary victims.

(a) Reasonable foreseeability of psychiatric harm

For a non-patient suing a HCP for psychiatric harm incurred as a result of some medical negligence towards a patient, '[f]oreseeability of psychiatric injury remains a crucial ingredient, when the plaintiff is the secondary victim'.[160]

Proving this criterion has not been a particular problem for most secondary victim relatives.[161] For example, in *Tredget*,[162] the court was satisfied that psychiatric harm on the part of the parents was reasonably foreseeable, because the psychiatric evidence suggested that neonatal death is apparently more difficult to bear, where birth and death are wrapped up in the same moment.

One notable exception occurred in *Powell v Boldaz*[163] (the case in which Mr and Mrs Powell's son died of undiagnosed Addison's disease, and where the Powells brought a disciplinary complaint against Robert's GP). Neither parent recovered for psychiatric injuries. It was not reasonably foreseeable (said the court) that a parent in Mr Powell's position would suffer psychiatric injury because of the mere substitution of a document written on A5 paper for one with the same contents written on A4, or that a substituted clinical summary sheet could invoke in the parents such a reaction, especially when it was 'far from clear that the substitution ... made any material difference to the medical history'.[164] Neither was it foreseeable that Mrs Powell's condition would be exacerbated by the events surrounding the substitution. Hence, if the secondary victim's psychiatric illness is considered to be extreme and idiosyncratic, then the risk of its developing is not one which the law of negligence will require a reasonable HCP to avoid, and no duty to avoid it will be owed by the HCP to the secondary victim. The failure of any close relative's case due to the test of foreseeability—however surprising it may be—does bear out the sentiment that '[some] limitation exists in the concept of reasonable foreseeability itself [to] ... provide a safeguard against unrestricted liability'.[165]

However, the rest of the criteria, necessary for a non-patient to establish a duty of care on the HCP's part, 'work harder', legally-speaking, to limit the number of claims by relatives in medical negligence scenarios.

(b) Relationship proximity: close tie of love and affection

In *Alcock*, Lord Keith stated that close ties between the secondary victim and the immediate victim (see Figure 8.1) were essential for the secondary victim's recovery. Whether based upon family relationships or close friendships, this sort of 'relational proximity'[166] is crucial, because it is 'the existence of such ties which leads to mental disturbance when the loved one suffers a catastrophe'.[167] In some types of relationship, close ties may be presumed (according to *White*, spouses, parents, and children could fall into the presumed category), but otherwise, must be established by evidence.[168]

Non-patients who witness the medically-induced physical injury caused by HCPs to their spouses, children, siblings, or parents, will comfortably satisfy this criterion. In the 2000 case of *Farrell v Merton, Sutton and Wandsworth HA*,[169] for example, the fact that baby Karol was 'only hours old' did not diminish the close emotional tie which existed between Mrs Farrell, as secondary victim, and her child as immediate victim.

Perhaps an example of where this factor *could* have mattered (had the non-patient been classified as a secondary victim) was in the 2001 case of *Farrell v Avon HA*[170]—notably, Mr Farrell never maintained any father/son relationship with his son Jordan, and indeed, never saw him after that day in hospital. Mr Farrell was permitted to recover £10,000 for psychiatric injury—but, it will be recalled, he was treated as an 'elevated primary victim', and so this *Alcock* control mechanism did not apply to him. In *Page v Smith*, Lord Lloyd stated that: 'In claims by secondary victims, it may be legitimate to use hindsight in order to be able to apply the test of reasonable foreseeability at all'.[171] Mr Farrell's lack of close ties with his son surely would have rendered that test very difficult to satisfy, *ex post facto*. Judicial,[172] law reform,[173] and academic[174] opinions all suggest that the preferable view ought to be that the degree of closeness between secondary victim and immediate victim be analysed in hindsight. However, in *Farrell*, Judge Bursell QC seemed to suggest that the HCP defendants could *not* point to the lack of relationship if that came to their notice *after* the negligence had occurred: 'the defendants' foreseeability of risk [of psychiatric harm] must be on the basis of an ordinary paternal relationship with the unborn child.'[175] This comment was dicta, of course, as Mr Farrell was assessed as a primary, not as a secondary, victim.

Before leaving this criterion, it is worth noting that the law's insistence that the secondary victim prove a close tie of love and affection with the immediate victim has drawn significant law reform criticism. The Ipp Committee thought that it could be abandoned altogether, because '[s]uch evaluative concepts are undesirable ... they necessitate the forensic examination and assessment of the nature and quality of intimate human relationships in a way that may bring the law into disrepute'[176] (or, in less fancy language, it can be distasteful to require secondary victims to 'prove the love' in the witness box). The Committee considered that, if other restrictions on the duty of care were properly applied, then it should not be necessary to resort to the further control mechanism of a close relationship.[177] Obversely, the Scottish[178] and English[179] Commissions both considered this requirement to be central to secondary victim claims, but were keen to articulate (in their Draft Bills) a wider list of relationships than had been judicially sanctioned. The Scottish particularly favoured the use of the term, 'close relationship', as something slightly wider than the term, 'close tie of love and affection', in order to give those with feelings of 'personal responsibility' (say, a nanny towards a child) or loyalty (say, employees or neighbours towards each other) a clear opportunity to prove that sufficient ties existed to warrant recovery as secondary victims.[180] Interestingly, though, and in a different context, when the Criminal Injuries Compensation Scheme was implemented in 1996,[181] the drafters opted to persevere with the requirement of a 'close tie' for secondary victims under that Act, because, as Miers remarked, 'this test was thought to be more sensitive in its application than simple categories of relationships'.[182] In any event, the draft Bills of the Scottish and English Commissions have never been enacted.[183]

(c) Spatial and temporal proximity

Simply put, a non-patient, as secondary victim, 'must have been present at the accident or its immediate aftermath'.[184] Or, as Lord Oliver described in *Alcock*:

> the plaintiff in each [successful earlier] case was either personally present at the scene of the accident or was in the more or less immediate vicinity and witnessed the aftermath shortly afterwards; ... there was not only an element of physical proximity to the event but a close temporal connection between the event and the plaintiff's perception of it.[185]

The aftermath period appears somewhat arbitrary.[186] In the non-medical context: two hours after the negligence/injury was within the period in *McLoughlin v O'Brian* (car accident) (although right 'on the margin of what the process of logical progression would allow'[187]), whereas eight to nine hours after the negligence/injury event was outside it in *Alcock* (Hillsborough accident).[188] Two hours and 10 minutes was within it in *Galli-Atkinson v Seghal*[189] (car accident), whereas three hours was too long in *Hevican v Ruane*[190] (another car accident). Indeed, in the foster child case of *W v Essex CC*, Lord Slynn appeared to suggest that, for secondary victims, the 'immediate aftermath' could entail learning of events at least four weeks after they started, under a 'flexible' interpretation![191]

Although the House of Lords has said that medical mishaps can give rise to a duty of care owed by HCP/hospital towards one who 'suffer[ed] nervous shock through seeing or hearing the event or its immediate aftermath',[192] in fact, physical proximity to the event of medical negligence can be quite difficult to make out.[193] Obviously, non-patient relatives will often be physically or temporally remote from that event—the medical treatment or misdiagnosis will have occurred behind closed doors, in operating theatres or recovery rooms, or in doctors' surgeries. Often, all the non-patient witnesses is the effects of the negligence upon the immediate victim afterwards, in the hospital ward, or later at home. The aftermath of the medical wrongdoing may be immediately apparent, or it may take hours, days, even weeks, to manifest—all the while removing the non-patient's mental illness from the point at which the medical negligence actually occurred.

The corollary of medical negligence not neatly fitting the *Alcock* pattern is a great inconsistency in the manner in which claims for pure psychiatric illness are legally treated in medical negligence. Indeed, English courts have compromised (softened) the spatial and temporal proximity requirement in two important respects.

First of all, if the time and distance between the non-patient's perception of the effects of medical negligence, and the medical negligence itself, were brought about, in part, by the HCP's *own actions*, then the aftermath doctrine will be more sympathetically construed in favour of that non-patient. For example, in *Farrell v Merton, Sutton and Wandsworth HA*[194] (the case in which newborn baby Karol was removed for a day from his mother, who was then told that he 'had had a hard time with the Caesarian' and shown a photograph of Karol on a mattress), Mrs Farrell recovered £75,000 as a secondary victim, because what she witnessed and which caused her shock was within the 'immediate aftermath' of the trauma of the birth. This was particularly so, given that the delay was brought about by the conduct of the hospital itself in removing the baby for that first day: 'the unusual delay of just over a day between the claimant giving birth and first seeing her son was wholly attributable to the defendant, who had chosen not to take her to the hospital to which her baby had been sent and not to tell her of the injury and difficulties which had occurred.'[195] Her lack of immediate knowledge and perception of Karol's condition was solely due to the hospital staff's conduct.

Secondly, witnessing the *effects* of the medical negligence *may* be considered to have been within the aftermath doctrine. In *Froggatt v Chesterfield and North Derbyshire Royal Hospital NHS Trust*[196] (the case in which Mrs Froggatt underwent an unnecessary mastectomy following a cancer mis-diagnosis), her husband, who recovered damages for his shock at her post-operative appearance, suffered that shock some 12 days after the operation. Forbes J held,[197] though, that there was a 'closeness in time' between the mis-diagnosis and the husband's shock (although the term, 'aftermath doctrine' was, surprisingly, not referred to at all in the judgment). Some medical negligence cases elsewhere (e.g., *Pang Koi Fa v Lim Djoe Phing* in Singapore[198] and *Lew v Mt Saint Joseph Hospital Society* in Canada[199]) also indicate that, provided that the relative was closely proximate to the effects of the medical negligence (say, by viewing the critically-ill patient in intensive care), a sufficient legal proximity will be arguable. Nevertheless, as English law stands, it must be doubtful whether *Froggatt* was correctly decided. Plenty of secondary victims have witnessed the 'effects' of medical negligence, and that has simply not been sufficient to base recovery for pure psychiatric illness (e.g., of the basket of cases considered previously: Mrs Palmer, Mrs Hall, Mr Tan, and Mr Sion all failed). Other academic commentators have similarly doubted the cogency of the decision—as Allen remarks, both the father's and son's recoveries for pure psychiatric illness 'stretches the boundaries of the "immediate aftermath" way beyond anything that the House of Lords has found to be acceptable',[200] while Jackson observes this case to be the 'one of the most strikingly "claimant friendly" judgments in recent years'.[201]

However, in the absence of either of these two factors, the requisite spatial and temporal proximity has notably proven the downfall of some English non-patient claims in the medical scenario. For example, in *Taylor v Somerset HA*,[202] Mrs Taylor, who visited her husband's body in hospital 20 minutes after he had died there, failed proximity, because the news of her husband's death was not within the 'immediate aftermath' of the original medical negligence of failing to diagnose and treat his heart condition—it was far too removed in time.[203] With such a short aftermath period being denied in this case, it is no surprise, then, that Mrs Palmer too[204] was never within the aftermath doctrine in respect of the negligence of the psychiatrist who released Armstrong into the community, despite his confessions beforehand of his evil intentions towards young children. Rosie Palmer's murder, almost a year after Armstrong's release, was far too removed in time from the alleged medical negligence. Mr Tan, too, was not within the aftermath of the negligently-caused death of his baby daughter *in utero*—his presence at the operation to remove the foetus, and watching over her for the following day until her burial, was not sufficient.[205]

Unsurprisingly, law reform opinion has been highly critical of the vagaries of the aftermath doctrine as a control mechanism, for reasons of inconsistency and lack of necessity. Both the Scottish and English Commissions recommended that the requirement of spatial and temporal proximity be abolished.[206] In particular, the Scottish Commission remarked[207] that the 'immediate aftermath' requirement was a blunt instrument which discriminated against those who were simply too far away from the scene or the hospital to make it in time to obtain compensation for psychiatric injuries. Also, what constituted the 'immediate aftermath' varied—20 minutes, a few hours, a couple of days, had been differently treated amongst the cases. The English Commission observed[208] that, in addition to the unsatisfactory tensions between decided cases as to what constituted a compensable aftermath, the most important factor to both ring-fence the number of potential secondary victims, and to explain the aetiology of psychiatric injury, was whether a close tie of love and affection existed, and not the fact of how proximate to the event was the secondary victim.[209]

To date, however, the restriction remains firmly part of English law, and is one that non-patients may have considerable difficulty in overcoming, unless judicial sympathies are particularly apparent.

(d) Direct perception of events

The non-patient's psychiatric injury 'must have been caused by direct perception of the accident or its immediate aftermath and not by hearing about it from somebody else.'[210]

Hence, in *Tredget and Tredget v Bexley HA*,[211] the 'chaos' and 'pandemonium' of the birth process in the delivery theatre, and continuing throughout the following 48 hours of the child's life in intensive care until his death, undoubtedly assisted a finding of direct perception. Whatever was happening to the baby happened 'in full sight' of Mr Tredget, who was encouraged by hospital staff to encourage his wife in her efforts in delivery; and Mrs Tredget, whilst sedated and suffering from exhaustion and not fully conscious of what was happening around her, had sufficient senses and instinct during the course of labour and birth to know that something was terribly wrong.[212] Direct perception (and recovery) was made out for both claimants.

However, again, several medical cases demonstrate how difficult it can be for a non-patient to prove this element, where much of what happens to the patient occurs out of sight. They may be sitting in waiting rooms, whilst the medical activity itself is occurring behind the closed doors of an operating theatre.[213]

For example, receiving bad news from the hospital by phone renders this element extremely difficult to satisfy. In *Tan v East London and City HA*,[214] where Mr Tan was told of the death of his daughter via a phone call from the hospital, he was simply not able to directly perceive of the negligence that occurred, even though he was intimately involved in the events thereafter (present during the operation to remove the dead baby girl; watching over her during the night; assisting to place her in a coffin the following day). All this was insufficient. In fact, in those claims where information about medical negligence has been conveyed in writing, by phone or by other media, after the event, the only occasions upon which non-patients—the recipients of the bad news—have succeeded in establishing any duty of care was where such a duty was conceded,[215] or where the non-patient brought the action in negligent misstatement,[216] or where the non-patient avoided secondary victim classification altogether but was one to whom the HCP assumed a duty of care to avoid psychiatric injury.[217]

As a twist on the facts, where a non-patient receives bad news about medical negligence and its consequences for a loved one, and then witnesses the patient's dead body, that is not generally sufficient for direct perception to be satisfied either. Mrs Taylor's failed claim against the Somerset HA[218] demonstrates the problem—viewing her husband's body 'as proof' was not sufficient, because the law cannot (said the court) compensate for shock brought about by communication of the news by the doctor as third party.[219] Nor was the communication to Mrs Palmer that they had found Rosie's mutilated body, and her observance of that body a few days later, sufficient to constitute 'direct perception' in *Palmer v Tees HA*.[220] By contrast, communication of bad news, plus the sight of the 'dead' body of his baby son, grounded recovery for Mr Farrell in *Farrell v Avon HA*[221]—but Mr Farrell, was a *primary* victim, and that allowed him to tiptoe around this common law rule governing secondary victim recovery which Mrs Taylor, Mr Tan and Mrs Palmer were unable to surmount.

Moreover, earnest efforts by the hospital and HCPs to minimise the trauma of the events surrounding a patient's extremely grave situation may also reduce the non-patient's 'direct perception' of events. For example, in *Ward v Leeds Teaching Hospitals NHS Trust*[222] (the wisdom teeth case), the mother Mrs Ward failed, in part, because:

the nurses and medical staff were careful to keep the claimant informed of the gravity of Katherine's condition without alarming her unduly or exposing her to any sights or sounds which might cause her distress. Even the viewing of Katherine's body at the mortuary, assuming for these purposes it was sufficiently proximate in time, did not take place without the claimant's nephew first taking the trouble to view the body to ensure that nothing untoward would be seen.[223]

The court concluded that 'the overwhelming factor in the claimant's psychiatric illness was the fact of the death of her cherished daughter rather than the events at the hospital.'[224]

The one 'bright light' for non-patients under this criterion is where the allegation of medical negligence was a mis-diagnosis. The secondary victim case law shows a more marked degree of sympathy for non-patients in that context—something of an 'extended direct perception' requirement. The decision in *Froggatt v Chesterfield and North Derbyshire Royal Hospital NHS Trust*[225] (the unnecessary mastectomy case) signifies that a direct perception, by sight or by ear, of the *consequences* of that mis-diagnosis for a loved one, can adequately satisfy this pre-requisite. The son's claim was particularly interesting in that regard: '[i]n Dane's case, the sudden appreciation came as a result of overhearing his mother's telephone conversation and his immediate belief, based on the negligent advice that had been given to his mother and that she felt obliged to repeat to him, that she had cancer and was likely to die. He was completely unprepared for such a shock and, as a result, he suffered a moderate Post Traumatic Stress Disorder that affected his every day life at home and at school'.[226] The mis-diagnosis of Elliot's hepatitis in *North Glamorgan NHS Trust v Walters* also arguably fell within this rule of 'extended direct perception', whereby Ms Walters as secondary victim was witnessing with her own unaided sense, not the medical acts or omissions per se, but the *effects* of that upon her son, the immediate victim. Being told incorrect diagnoses of Elliot's condition, and then realising the awful truth as events were unfolding in, and between, the hospitals, was sufficient for direct perception.[227]

Just as with the previous control mechanism, the requirement of 'direct perception' has drawn plenty of law reform criticism. The Scottish Commission was critical of the ungenerous attitude which the law took towards those who were told of the death of a loved one but who were too distraught, or coincidentally too far away, to directly perceive of the negligence or of its immediate aftermath.[228] It recommended that the rule be abolished. Similarly, the Ipp Committee[229] regarded the requirement of direct perception as giving rise to distinctions which were arbitrary and artificial. The English Commission[230] further noted that the secondary victim's proximity to the event or its aftermath was not always a relevant factor in determining how the secondary victim would react to it—calling to mind the medical testimony given in *Ravenscroft v Rederiaktiebolaget Transatlantic*[231] that there is no diagnostic or medical difference in the anxiety status of a person who has witnessed an accident, or a person who was present at the aftermath, and of a person who simply is told about the accident by another person.

Nevertheless, as the law stands presently, the 'direct perception' criterion remains another difficult one for non-patients to surmount.

(e) Non-patient of 'normal fortitude'

Where the non-patient is a secondary victim (as opposed to a primary victim), a HCP is not liable for a psychiatric injury that the non-patient suffers merely because he is a person abnormally susceptible to psychiatric illness. In other words, if the non-patient is especially vulnerable to psychiatric injury, then he will have to prove that a person of ordinary fortitude, or 'customary phlegm', would have suffered in the same way, in order to recover damages.[232] It is important to appreciate that the rule does *not* require the non-patient *himself* to be a person of normal fortitude. As the Ipp Committee noted, 'being a person of normal fortitude is not a precondition of being owed a duty of care' as a secondary victim.[233] However, once the non-patient satisfies the normal fortitude rule, then an emotionally fragile non-patient can recover for the *full extent* of his psychiatric injury (as a manifestation of the so-called 'egg shell skull rule').[234]

The normal fortitude rule appears to emanate from the early (non-medical) case of *Bourhill (or Hay) v Young*,[235] in which a pregnant lady heard a vehicular crash in which a motorcyclist was killed, saw the scene afterwards (but not the accident itself), and the bloodstains on the road from where the motorcyclist had come to rest. She suffered a psychiatric illness from what she had seen and heard, and also gave birth to a stillborn child. However, she failed in her compensation claim, and the following statement explained, in part, the reasons for that decision:

> The driver of a car or vehicle, even though careless, is entitled to assume that the ordinary frequenter of the streets has sufficient fortitude to endure such incidents as may from time to time be expected to occur in them, including the noise of a collision and the sight of injury to others, and is not considered negligent to one who does not possess the customary phlegm.[236]

Of course, the rule does not apply to primary victims (and, hence, the fact that Mr Farrell, the non-patient in *Farrell v Avon HA*,[237] had a pre-existing psychological history which rendered him more at risk than others of developing post-traumatic-stress disorder, was legally irrelevant— although being given a baby's corpse to hold in the mistaken belief that it was his own son was perhaps the type of exceptionally catastrophic event that was likely to cause psychiatric injury even in people of ordinary fortitude[238]).

Parental claimants who have lost children as a result of medical negligence have fared variously under this rule. In *Powell v Boldaz* (the case concerning the substitution of one page for another), the normal fortitude rule was an insurmountable barrier for both non-patient parents. Mrs Powell had an innate pre-disposition to develop an anxiety disorder,[239] while Mr Powell was 'still grieving' about son Robert's death at the time when the substitution occurred.[240] It seemed likely that normally robust claimants would have withstood news of the alleged substitution without succumbing to psychiatric illness; or, in other words, it was unlikely that the same injury would have been sustained by persons of normal fortitude. On the other hand, Mr and Mrs Tredget recovered damages for their 'pathological unresolved mourning', following the death of their son Callum at two days old, despite the fact that the medical opinion put forward was that each parent 'had a prior susceptibility towards an aggravated reaction to Callum's birth and death. There had been the prior loss or termination of pregnancies.'[241] The two results appear to be arbitrarily different, and the cogency of the verdict in *Tredget* has been academically doubted in this respect.[242]

The Scottish Law Commission was particularly dismissive of the normal fortitude rule which applies to secondary victims. The Commission made the point that 'there is a wide range of susceptibility to mental harm among the general population. Thus, ordinary fortitude is difficult to assess.'[243] It called the rule 'a legal construct which is difficult to evaluate'.[244]

The normal fortitude rule still, however, remains a firmly-established control mechanism for secondary victims in English (and Scottish) law.

(f) Shock

If claiming against a HCP for negligently-inflicted pure psychiatric illness, as a secondary victim, the non-patient must establish that his illness was induced by 'shock'—a concept which, it will be recalled, was described in *Alcock*, in 1992, as 'a sudden assault on the nervous system'.[245] This was the first occasion in English law in which 'shock' emerged as an independent criterion for liability governing secondary victim recovery.[246] In other words, 'stress, strain, grief or sorrow or from gradual or retrospective realisation of events' are not sufficient.[247]

Several non-patients have had difficulty in proving shock in medical scenarios—especially if they also failed the 'direct perception' requirement. For example, the terrible news about his daughter's death had already been communicated to Mr Tan, and his visit to the hospital was made in the full knowledge that the baby had died.[248] He did not (said the court) suffer a shock in the legal sense. Similarly, there was doubt about whether Mrs Ward had suffered a sudden shock with the death of her daughter Katherine after the wisdom teeth operation—'[a]n event outside the range of human experience, sadly, does not ... encompass the death of a loved one in hospital unless also accompanied by circumstances which were wholly exceptional in some way so as to shock or horrify'.[249] Both of these claimants had also failed the direct perception requirement. In *Sion v Hampstead HA*, Mr Sion, whose son suffered a mis-diagnosis of a bleeding kidney, and who died 14 days afterwards, having slipped into a coma, also failed to establish shock.[250] When a week of hospitalisation had elapsed, Mr Sion realised that it was almost certain that his son would not survive, and when death came, 'he was not surprised and felt that in a way he had been preparing himself for this to happen.'[251] Such a description did not satisfy the requirement of shock.

Thus, both *Ward* and *Sion* support the proposition that dawning realisations and gradual appreciations of the fate to befall the patient—typical of medical negligence scenarios rather than calamitous disasters—are not conducive to proving a secondary victim claim for the non-patient.[252] Without an assault on the senses, the non-patient is vulnerable to the finding that the injury should be borne without compensation. However, the element is imbued with a measure of real inconsistency, in two particular respects.

A series of assaults. First, some courts have held the shock requirement to constitute a *series of events and assaults* which, although separate, can comprise one shocking event. This interpretation, where it applies, enables the medical scenario to play out over several hours—and, clearly, what one judge may consider to be a 'dawning realisation' of the fate to befall a patient may comprise a sudden and violent agitation of the mind to another. In *North Glamorgan NHS Trust v Walters*[253] (where baby Elliot's acute hepatitis was not diagnosed, and where he suffered seizures which lead to eventual severe brain damage and death 36 hours later), it will be recalled that Ms Walters sued for pathological grief reaction, and recovered £20,000 for this psychiatric injury. She did so as a secondary victim, and succeeded in proving one shocking event and a 'seamless tale':

> an inexorable progression from the moment when the fit occurred as a result of the failure of the hospital properly to diagnose and then to treat the baby, the fit causing the brain damage which shortly thereafter made termination of this child's life inevitable and the dreadful climax when the child died in her arms. It is a seamless tale with an obvious beginning and an equally obvious end. It was played out over a period of 36 hours, which for her both at the time and as subsequently recollected was undoubtedly one drawn-out experience ... [and] ... the assault on [Ms Walters'] nervous system had begun and she reeled under successive blows as each was delivered.[254]

In *Tredget* too (regarding the birth which was 'pandemonium'), the parents recovered damages for psychiatric illnesses because their full appreciation of their newborn's condition 'only came with time', and it was—

> unrealistic to separate out and isolate the delivery as an event, from the other sequence of happenings from the onset of labour to Callum's death two days later, as a whole ... although lasting for over 48 hours from the onset of labour to the death, this effectively was one event.[255]

The author has criticised the lack of consistency displayed by the decision in *Walters* elsewhere,[256] and some other academic commentary since has not been particularly kind to it either.[257] Of course, Mrs Ward and Mr Sion would no doubt argue that their experiences in hospital were equally as seamless, with an initial expectation that their children were ill but would recover, but then a realisation that their lives were ending. Furthermore, the psychiatric evidence given in *Walters* suggested that it was the *longer* duration of events surrounding Elliot's death, rather than his sudden death, which resulted in Ms Walters' shock: 'the psychiatric impact is more severe than if the child had died suddenly, as it was compounded by uncertainties over the diagnosis and re-admission to various hospitals.'[258] Surely the protracted experiences of Mr Sion and Mrs Ward were just as capable of producing that type of shock? The inconsistencies in outcome are obvious, despite Ward LJ's assertion in *Walters* that *Sion* was 'a very different case'.[259] The Scottish Law Commission's semantic discussion[260] of how the cases differ—that *Walters* demonstrates that the 'sudden realisation of danger within a continuing process' is compensable whereas *Sion's* 'continuing process [of realisation]' is not—only serves to emphasise the difficulties inherent in the reasoning of the two decisions. Horne remarks that the rigour of *Sion* 'appears to have given way [in *Walters*] to a more pragmatic interpretation of what can constitute the necessary event' giving rise to shock.[261] Regarding *Tredget* too, Puxon observes[262] that the parents' condition of 'pathological unresolved mourning', and the events in that case, would appear to have had more in common with a gradual realisation of Callum's impending death than with a sudden assault of their nervous systems or sudden appreciation of a horrifying event.

In that respect, the law may well have moved on to embrace what Lord Ackner envisaged in *Alcock*—that shock 'has yet to include psychiatric illness caused by the accumulation over a period of time of more gradual assaults on the nervous system'.[263] That position, it seems, *has* been reached in English law, and an explicit acknowledgment of that fact should have been made in *Walters*. Instead, Ward LJ considered that the verdict for Mrs Walters had not achieved any change in the law;[264] Clarke LJ said that, *if* a finding in favour of Ms Walters did mean that an incremental step in the law needed to be taken, 'I for my part would take that step on the facts of this case';[265] and Sir Anthony Evans agreed with both judgments. *Walters* has received judicial endorsement in lower courts,[266] and the House of Lords has since described the *Walters/Tredget* decisions as a 'distinct line of authority'[267] in the field of pure psychiatric illness and secondary victim recovery. From the foregoing, it may fairly be deduced that the law on this point of 'drawn-out shock' is, overall, most unsatisfactory.

Of course, it is all very well to concede that a shocking event is not 'restricted by *Alcock* ... to a frozen moment in time.'[268] At the same time, a series of events of a 'seamless nature', as found to have occurred in *Walters*, is a concept that has its limits too. The same challenge of defining boundaries arises, for example, in the non-medical context—a wife's suicide, some six months after a negligently-caused car accident, induced in her claimant husband a pathological grief reaction, but did not induce a 'shock' of the type that would be required to recover as secondary victim.[269] In the medical context, the Hong Kong case of *Wong Fung Sze v Tuen Mun Hospital*[270] demonstrates that a four-month period from May 2001 (when the patient's cancer was missed in a negligent mis-diagnosis) until September, when the patient died from untreatable cancer of the brain, skull and upper neck, could not give rise to shock on the part of the patient's wife. Principally, while the District Court admitted that *Walters* showed a 'very realistic approach' to medical negligence cases, it considered that it was too big a step to say that a 36-hour horrifying event and a four month-long series of events could be equated.[271] However, in the Singaporean case of *Pang Koi Fa v Lim Djoe Phing*,[272] a mother who watched her daughter's gradual deterioration after negligently-performed surgery over a three-month period, until the daughter's inevitable death, was allowed to recover. According to Amarjeet JC, the elements of suddenness may not have been present, but this was an unusual case whereby 'psychiatric illness assaults the nervous system, builds up and manifests itself over some short period of time', and which constituted 'an incremental and analogous extension of existing cases'.[273] Whatever flexibility the *Walters* approach may provide for non-patient claims against HCPs, limits have to be drawn, and, of course, the concept of a 'seamless tale' will inevitably comprise a somewhat arbitrary judgment.

Viewing bodies. The second marked inconsistency with the shock requirement, in the context of non-patient claims against HCPs in medical negligence, has been the shock that comes from viewing a patient's body, in order to fully comprehend the consequences of the medical negligence.

It will be recalled that, in *Taylor v Somerset HA*,[274] Mrs Taylor failed because the purpose of the mortuary visit was only to 'settle her disbelief', and it was not 'shocking' in the sense that the body 'bore no marks or signs to her of the sort that would have conjured up for her the circumstances of his fatal attack.'[275] However, contrast the husband's recovery of £5,000 for psychiatric damage in *Froggatt v Chesterfield and North Derbyshire Royal Hospital NHS Trust*.[276] Mr Froggatt knew that his wife had undergone a (needless, as it turned out) mastectomy. Yet, the court was willing to hold that, 'when he saw [his wife] undressed for the first time after the mastectomy, he was quite unprepared for what he saw and he was profoundly and lastingly shocked by it.'[277] Mrs Taylor witnessed her dead husband; Mr Froggatt witnessed his disfigured wife; and yet only the latter could recover at law.

Hence, to summarise: in non-patient suits against HCPs, the requirement for a 'sudden shock' has tended to be applied either strictly or in a distinctly watered-down version, with little consistency demonstrated in the case law. The concept is artificial, for something that 'violently agitates the mind' may occur over a fairly lengthy period. Indeed, the protracted nature of a patient's decline may be the very reason that the non-patient sustained 'shock' in the medical scenario.[278] It also leads to factual lotteries, for if the non-patient happens to have been told something that raises his hopes but those hopes prove false (as in *Walters*), it may be easier to prove the requisite shock. Moreover, in *Walters*, the Court of Appeal was invited to take a 'small incremental step ... to replace the shock requirement and substitute a requirement that the psychiatric illness need only be caused by directly witnessing or experiencing some trauma.'[279] Ultimately, this step was not taken—but Mrs Walters succeeded by proving a 'series of assaults' on her nervous system equating to shock. Moreover, as Chico notes, there is now a considerable body of psychiatric evidence that 'the shock requirement is not supported by psychiatric opinion about how mental illness is caused';[280] and notably, psychiatric reports in such litigation have queried or omitted the term of 'nervous shock' altogether.[281] Yet the House of Lords continues to insist upon the shock requirement.[282] All of this constitutes a confused legal position.

The Scottish Commission recommended the abolition of the shock requirement for three reasons: (a) it represented an outdated mode of medical and judicial understanding as to how mental injury was incurred; (b) some forms of psychiatric injury for which shock is a precursor to diagnosis, such as post-traumatic stress disorder, are inherently more compensable, in comparison to a mental illness such as depression, for which shock is not necessarily a precursor; and (c) shock has not been applied to other so-called primary victims such as those who claim work-related stress damages.[283] The English Commission provided several further reasons for its similar recommendation that the secondary victim should not have to prove that his psychiatric injury was induced by shock.[284] The requirement of a sudden assault, etc., failed to take account of the cases in which the full extent of the injury to the immediate victim only becomes apparent over a period of time. The fixing of any cut-off point for 'suddenness' was always essentially arbitrary, and as a control mechanism, it was blunt and crude. It also excluded those worn down by a lifetime of caring for the immediate victim, whom society may feel *most* worthy of compensation. Furthermore, to retain the shock requirement inevitably emphasised the requirement of proximity of time and space, itself a problematical control mechanism. Many of these points have already been made throughout the chapter.

For non-patients seeking to recover against HCPs for negligently-inflicted pure psychiatric illness, the shock requirement remains the most unsatisfactory control mechanism of them all.

(g) Public policy considerations

The following comments by Hayne J perhaps best describe the sorts of concerns which can arise, if bystanders to an incident are permitted to recover for pure psychiatric injuries:

> The common law has long shown a marked reluctance to allow damages for psychiatric as distinct from physical injury ... Floodgates arguments have been advanced. More recently, these floodgates arguments are based in what are asserted to be the possible consequences of wide media dissemination of tragic events, often dissemination by broadcasting those events as they are occurring. Television broadcasts of the destruction of the World Trade Center buildings in New York on 11 September 2001 provide an obvious example of an horrific event broadcast to an immense audience as it was happening ... [but] floodgates arguments can be understood as being based in fears about the capacity of the courts to distinguish between cases of real and feigned injury. It may be suggested that references to indeterminate liability, and to imposing unreasonable burdens on defendants, serve only to mask fears of the kind described. If concerns about indeterminate liability or the burden on defendants are not based in those fears, it is said, or at least implied, that there is no reason to distinguish between a negligently caused event leading to widespread physical injury (such as a release of poisonous fumes from a factory) and a negligently caused event which leads to numerous cases of psychiatric injury. Especially is that so when it is recognised that the line between physical and psychiatric injury may not be clear and bright.[285]

Thus far, this factor has not dissuaded non-patients from recovering pure psychiatric illness damages in medical negligence cases, although the prospect of such a finding remains ever-present, if a number of relatives were to be affected by one medical incident.

Insofar as secondary victims are concerned, the policy factor, 'distributive justice', has also figured in the non-medical context. This factor requires judges to determine whether they reasonably believe that ordinary people in the community ('commuters on the Underground'[286]) would consider it to be just and fair to compensate the particular claimant, in light of what those people would consider to be a just and fair distribution of financial burdens and losses among members of a society. It was applied in *White v Chief Constable of South Yorkshire*[287] to disallow the psychiatric illness claims by the police officers who performed rescue and other services during and following the Hillsborough stadium disaster (when the relatives had received nothing in the *Alcock* litigation seven years earlier), but has been much-criticised as a policy factor (note, for example, Witting's comment that '[p]olicy decisions based upon distributive concerns are inherently contentious and contestable ... The range of distributive goals that might be pursued is as diverse as the political spectrum. There is no "right" answer to the dilemmas of distributive justice. For every argument in favour of policy X, there is an argument against policy X (and in favour of policy Y).'[288]

In the context of the non-patient claims considered throughout this chapter, distributive justice has not been explicitly articulated as a reason for the outcomes—and, it is suggested, it would be a difficult policy factor to apply consistently and credibly in any event. The sense of which relative is 'deserving' of compensation, and which is not, is problematical. For example, once a mis-diagnosis occurs, the consequences of that may be wide-ranging—Elliot's fit occurred before Mrs Walters' eyes because she happened to be in the same hospital room as he was; whereas Mr Taylor died at work of his undiagnosed heart condition, and so Mrs Taylor lost her claim, and Mr Sion, who maintained a vigil beside his dying son's bedside in hospital for two weeks (following a bleeding kidney mis-diagnosis) failed in his claim too. Some courts have clearly applied the *Alcock* control mechanisms more 'mechanistically' than have others.

To summarise this Section: non-patients who seek secondary victim status in medical negligence scenarios have a number of hurdles to overcome, if they are to prove that a negligent HCP owed them a duty to avoid or minimise their psychiatric injury. They must prove that their injury was a recognisable psychiatric illness; that psychiatric injury of some kind was reasonably foreseeable; that they shared a tie of love and affection with the patient; that they were present at the medical accident or its immediate aftermath; that their psychiatric injury was caused by the direct perception of the accident or its immediate aftermath; that a person of normal fortitude would likely have suffered psychiatric injury in the same way as they did; and that their psychiatric injury was induced by shock. To reiterate the author's view, expressed elsewhere:

> queries and concerns have been raised about how secondary claimants should be permitted recovery when their loved ones are the victims of medical malpractice ... Both psychiatrically-damaged claimants, and negligent defendants (and their insurers), deserve a better, more certain, definition of the legal parameters of liability for secondary victims than presently exists.[289]

F NON-PATIENT CLAIMS FOR PSYCHIATRIC INJURY, VIA OTHER AVENUES

It was suggested by Gage J in the organ-retention case of *AB v Leeds Teaching Hospital NHS Trust*[290] that those claiming for pure psychiatric injury must be placed in either primary or secondary victim categories—and the majority of English cases have made an earnest attempt to adhere to this viewpoint. However, it is clear that a claimant can also recover such damages without actually establishing primary or secondary victim status at all. This imbues the area with even further uncertainty.

Medically-related scenarios have demonstrated that there are **two** circumstances in which claimants have sought to entirely avoid having to satisfy the primary or secondary victim pre-requisites: by reliance upon the tri-partite *Caparo*[291] test for establishing a duty of care in novel scenarios; and via the principles of negligent misstatement.

1. Recovery under *Caparo* principles

Occasionally, for claimants who have suffered pure psychiatric illness, courts have found in their favour on the basis of: foreseeability of injury (in this case, psychiatric injury, the type of damage being claimed for), proximity between HCP and claimant, and no public policy reason precluding the recovery of damages for psychiatric injury. In such cases, instead of categorising the claimant as a 'primary victim' or as a 'secondary victim', the courts have followed the mandate of Lord Oliver in *Alcock*, that—

description[s] [of primary victim and secondary victim] must not be permitted to obscure the absolute essentiality of establishing a duty owed by the defendant directly to him—a duty which depends not only upon the reasonable foreseeability of damage of the type which has in fact occurred to the particular plaintiff but also upon the proximity or directness of the relationship between the plaintiff and the defendant.[292]

The *Caparo*-type of claimant has featured, in the non-medical context, in claims against the Home Office,[293] a utilities supplier,[294] a firm of solicitors for alleged professional negligence,[295] and the police.[296] In the medical context, this approach was also adopted by Morland J in the fear-of-the-future case of *Creutzfeldt-Jakob Disease litigation; Group B Plaintiffs v Medical Research Council*.[297] The claimants were treated for signs of stunted growth with injections of human growth hormone (HGH) under clinical trial, and much later suffered psychiatric injuries after realising that this type of HGH was capable of infecting injectees with Creutzfeldt-Jakob disease, a brain-wasting and untreatable condition that the court said consigned its sufferers to unimaginable suffering and certain death. They recovered for their psychiatric injuries—but given that they comprised fear-of-the-future claims, the principles governing their recovery are more appropriately dealt with in Chapter 9.

However, these cases are unusual. The vast majority of cases—and certainly those which feature relatives and medical negligence—revert to *Alcock*, and not to *Caparo*. As Stanton rightly notes, *Alcock* has created 'the basic reference point' for pure psychiatric illness recovery, and the relevant law is a specialised area that has been developed in accordance with that decision.[298] Nevertheless, for those commentators who prefer the complete abolition of the primary/secondary victim classification, such as Mullany, the *CJD Litigation* was significant as:

> may be the beginning of a new British order ... Recovery was allowed without reference to the debate concerning the legal significance of the way in which the claimants became aware of the risk to which they had been negligently exposed and the relevance of physical and temporal proximity. By implication, this orthodox focus was recognised as simply inappropriate and irrelevant in the particular circumstances. Indecorous distinctions must be eliminated from all species of psychiatric injury claim.[299]

Similarly, McIvor welcomes a departure:

> in continuing the movement away from the primary/secondary victim distinction, and thereby limiting the remit of the *Alcock* control mechanisms, it helps to free the law in this area from the shackles of its ignoble past and thereby paves the way for the formulation of a more rational and coherent set of duty principles.[300]

There has been no sign of that 'freeing the shackles', where non-patients have brought secondary victim claims in medical negligence, however.

2. Negligent misstatement

The second scenario in which the primary and secondary victim classification has been departed from, in suits by non-patients against HCPs, concerns inaccurate medical advice which gave rise to psychiatric illness.

In *Allin v City and Hackney HA*[301] (where Mrs Allin was told that her newborn had died, but was then told six hours later that he was alive), Mrs Allin was not classified as either primary or secondary victim. Instead, she recovered £18,500 on the basis of the principles governing negligent misstatement.[302]

Hence, in these respects, the directive in *AB v Leeds* has clearly not been adhered to in all English medical cases.

G CONCLUSION

Where non-patients (usually relatives of the patient) seek to recover for pure psychiatric injuries sustained as a result of some medical mistreatment of the patient, the law suffers something of a confused melt-down.

The distinction between primary and secondary victim appears reasonably clear in theory, but in practice, is riddled with inconsistencies. The House of Lords has changed its definitions of each category over the years, especially since the dichotomy was outlined in *Alcock*. As a result, lower courts, unsurprisingly, often find it difficult to decide which of the two categories the claimant most adequately fits, so declare that the claimant could be both—or, at the other end of the spectrum, fail to engage with the primary/secondary victim classification at all. Some claimants who appear to be secondary victims are 'elevated' to primary victim status because there is no immediate 'victim' damaged by the defendant's conduct. All of this has left the law in a state which is both uncertain and difficult to apply.

Non-patients have rarely established that they were primary victims; but the potential for secondary victim claims against negligent HCPs is very real. In *Walters*, the defendant NHS Trust had argued that the drain on medical insurers was 'sufficiently alarming' without encouraging secondary victim claims. The Court of Appeal replied that if the law needed to be changed to preclude that possibility, then 'Parliament must do it'[303] (a call that has been repeated by the House of Lords too[304]).

Proving the existence of a duty of care is the *principal* battleground for non-patients alleging pure psychiatric illness and for HCPs—and unless Parliament introduces appropriate legislation to imbue the area with greater clarity (and restrictiveness), that position is unlikely to change in England. The Department for Constitutional Affairs indicated, in 2007, that it rejected the English Law Commission's recommendation of 1998 to legislate in this area: 'the Government considers it preferable to allow the courts to continue to develop the law in this area'.[305] Both the English and Scottish attempts to clarify the law have, so far, fallen upon deaf legislative ears, and that is unlikely to change either.

In *Walters*, Clarke LJ said that 'I do not think that those mechanisms [the *Alcock* control mechanisms] should be applied too rigidly or mechanistically'.[306] Yet, many of the array of unsuccessful non-patients discussed in this chapter, including Mrs Ward, Mrs Taylor, Mrs Palmer, Mrs Hall, Mr Tan, and Mr Sion, would no doubt say that this was exactly why they lost their secondary victim claims.

With this complexity as a backdrop, the guideline contained in the Appendix, '*Potential Liability to Non-Patients and Third Parties: A Synopsis for Healthcare Professionals*', has been drawn up to seek to assist HCPs to determine how, and when, a duty of care to avoid a non-patient's pure psychiatric illness may arise.

ENDNOTES

1   i.e., one that is not consequential upon physical injury to the claimant. The term, 'nervous shock', once so common in this field of negligence law, will not be used, given the disfavour with which it is now viewed. As Sir Thomas Bingham once noted, the label 'is not only misleading and inaccurate but, with its echoes of frail Victorian heroines, tends to disguise the very serious damage which is, in many cases, under discussion': 'Foreword' in N Mullany and P Handford, *Tort Liability for Psychiatric Damage* (Law Book Co, Sydney, 1993) vii.

2   [1994] 5 Med LR 178 (Central London CC).

3   *ibid*, 179. See too: *Taylorson v Shieldness Produce Ltd* [1994] PIQR P329 (CA) 336 ('[t]o these Plaintiffs, their family and friends, the distinctions and principles which this Court is required to apply must seem to be as unconvincing as they are surprising. The rejection of their claim will no doubt add grievance to their anger ... That, I fear, cannot be helped by the law and must be endured': per Ralph Gibson LJ).

4   *Frost (White) v Chief Constable of South Yorkshire Police* (hereafter '*White*') [1999] 2 AC 455 (HL) 511 (Lord Hoffmann).

5   Oft-reiterated by the House of Lords, e.g.: *McLoughlin v O'Brian* [1983] 1 AC 410, 421–22 (Lord Wilberforce) ('because "shock" in its nature is capable of affecting so wide a range of people, [there is] a real need for the law to place some limitation upon the extent of admissible claims'); *White*, *ibid*, 493–94; *Page v Smith* [1996] AC 155, 197; *JD v East Berkshire Community Health NHS Trust* [2005] 2 AC 373, [133] (Lord Brown).

6   Section E draws upon, and updates, the author's previous commentary, 'Medical Negligence, Secondary Victims and Psychiatric Illness: Family Tragedies and Legal Headaches' in R Probert (ed), *Family Life and the Law* (Ashgate Publishing, Aldershot, 2007) ch 5.

7   *Liability for Psychiatric Illness* (Rep 249, 1998) (the '*English Report*').

8   *Review of the Law of Negligence: Final Report* (2002) (the '*Ipp Report*') ch 9, 'Mental Harm'.

9   *Damages for Psychiatric Injury* (Rep 196, 2004) (the '*Scottish Report*').

10   [1994] 5 Med LR 170 (CA) 173.

11   See too: British Columbia LRC, *Pecuniary Loss and the Family Compensation Act* (WP 69, 1992).

12   From a vast array, the following are just a sample: P Case, 'Secondary Iatrogenic Harm: Claims for Psychiatric Damage Following a Death Caused by Medical Error' (2004) 67 *MLR* 561; P Handford, 'Psychiatric Injury Resulting from Medical Negligence' (2002) 10 *Tort L Rev* 38; C Hilson, 'Liability for Psychiatric Injury: Primary and Secondary Victims Revisited' (2002) 18 *PN* 167; J Moore, 'Negligently-Caused Psychiatric Injury: A Way Forward?' (1995) 10 *Liverpool L Rev* 153; D Butler, 'An Assessment of Competing Policy Considerations in Cases of Psychiatric Injury Resulting from Negligence' (2002) 10 *Torts LJ* 13; D Nolan, 'Psychiatric Injury at the Crossroads' [2004] *JPIL* 1; H Teff, 'Liability for Negligently Inflicted Psychiatric Harm: Justifications and Boundaries' (1998) 56 *CLJ* 91, and by the same author: 'Liability for Psychiatric Illness after Hillsborough' (1992) 12 *OJLS* 441; N Mullany, 'English Psychiatric Injury Law: Chronically Depressing' (1999) 115 *LQR* 30; S Allen, 'Post-Traumatic Stress Disorder: The Claims of Primary and Secondary Victims' [2000] *JPIL* 108; M Jones, *Medical Negligence* (4th edn, Sweet & Maxwell, London, 2008) 178–219; I Kennedy and A Grubb, *Medical Law* (3rd edn, Butterworths, London, 2000) 392–406.

13   e.g.: *White* [1992] 2 AC 455 (HL) 511 (Lord Hoffmann) ('the search for principle has been called off'), 500 (Lord Steyn) (the law 'represents a patchwork quilt of distinctions which are difficult to justify', and 'is [neither] coherent [n]or morally defensible'); *Alcock v Chief Constable of South Yorkshire Police* ('*Alcock*') [1992] 1 AC 310 (HL) 417 (Lord Oliver) (the law 'is not wholly logical').

14   e.g.: *Williams v The Minister for Aboriginal Land Rights Act 1983 and The State of NSW* [2000] NSWCA 255 (Heydon JA) [166] ('In a period when the profession of psychiatry has increased greatly, though perhaps not as fast as the number of persons claiming to suffer from psychiatric illness, the English authorities, for example, have moved into an unsatisfactory condition').

15   [1997] 8 Med LR 91 (CA).

16   *ibid*, 82, 92.

17   *ibid*, 94 (Brooke LJ), 101 (Kennedy LJ) (Nourse LJ agreeing). The trial judge had earlier permitted recovery.

18   It is possible that, in rare cases, the patient was not actually harmed by the HCP's error, and yet the non-patient sustained psychiatric injury, a topic that will be discussed further in Section C, p 273.

19   [2006] EWCA Civ 1028 (otherwise, Mr Toth would have recovered as a secondary victim: at [3]).

20   *Pang Koi Fa v Lim Djoe Phing* [1993] 3 SLR 317 (Sing HC).

21   e.g.: *Kralj v McGrath* [1986] 1 All ER 54 (QB); *Farrell v Merton, Sutton and Wandsworth HA* (2001) 57 BMLR 158 (QB).

22   [1997] 8 Med LR 398 (QB).

23   [2003] Lloyd's Rep Med 1 (QB).

24   This aspect of the litigation was never appealed (whereas the parents' claims *were* appealed). MK's claim is discussed briefly in that appeal at: *JD v East Berkshire Community Health NHS Trust; RK and MAK v Dewsbury Healthcare NHS Trust; RK and AK v Oldham NHS Trust* [2005] UKHL 23, [2005] 2 AC 373, [19].

25   [2003] Lloyd's Rep Med 1 (QB) [20].

26   [2006] Lloyd's Rep Med 489 (Southampton CC).

27   An affliction where the small intestine fails to digest and absorb food: *Oxford Concise Colour Medical Dictionary* (4th edn, OUP, Oxford, 2007) 149.

28   [1897] 2 QB 57.

29   The expression used by Wright J in *Wilkinson v Downton*, *ibid*, 58. In this passage, 'physical harm' includes within its realm psychiatric harm, and distress falling short of a recognised psychiatric illness: J Murphy, *Street on Torts* (12th edn, OUP, Oxford, 2007) 244.

30   178 NJ Super 310, 428 A 2d 966 (1981).

31   (1997) 39 BMLR 35 (CA) 46–48 ('the facts do not begin to establish the necessary degree of foresight for imputed intent' on the part of the defendant HCPs).

32   *J&P Van Soest v Residual Health Management Unit* [1999] NZCA 206, [2000] 1 NZLR 179, [66], adopting the EWLC's preference for this phrase, to take account of *future* developments in psychiatric medicine: *English Report*, [2.3]. In the *Scottish Report*, the SLC favoured the term, 'a medically recognised mental disorder': [3.7], [3.9].

33   Established by several HL authorities, e.g.: *McLoughlin v O'Brian* [1983] 1 AC 410 (HL) 431; *Alcock* [1992] 1 AC 310 (HL) 416; *Page v Smith* [1996] AC 155 (HL); *White* [1999] 2 AC 455 (HL) 469; *R v Ireland* [1998] AC 147 (HL) 156; *Wainwright v Home Office* [2003] UKHL 53, [2004] 2AC 406, [45]–[47] (Lord Hoffmann) [62] (Lord Scott).. See, too: *Hinz v Berry* [1970] 2 QB 40 (CA) 42–43; *Hicks v Chief Constable of South Yorkshire Police* [1992] 1 All ER 690 (CA) 693.

34   In Australia, e.g.: *Tame v New South Wales; Annetts v Australian Stations Pty Ltd* [2002] HCA 35, (2002) 211 CLR 317, [7]; *Jaensch v Coffey* (1984) 155 CLR 549 (HCA) 587; *Mount Isa Mines v Pusey* (1970) 125 CLR 383 (HCA) 394, and in the medical context: *Masri v Marinko* [1998] NSWSC 467 (accessed online, no pp available); *Tori v Greater Murray Health Service* [2002] NSWSC 186, [25]; *Hunter Area Health Service v Marchlewski* [2000] NSWCA 294, [115], [120]. In Singapore, e.g.: *Pang Koi Fa v Lim Djoe Phing* [1993] 3 SLR 317 (HC) 319, 333–34; *Ngiam Kong Seng v Lim Chiew Hock* [2008] SGCA 23, with this point discussed in: TK Leng, 'Duty of Care for Psychiatric Harm: Back to *Anns*' (2008) 24 *PN* 154, 159. In Canada, e.g.: *Devji v District of Burnaby* [1999] BCCA 599, [2]–[3], [47]. In Ireland, e.g.: *Fletcher v Commr of Public Works* [2003] IESC 13, [105]. In New Zealand, e.g.: *A-G v Gilbert* [2002] NZCA 55, [81]; *J&P Soest v Residual Health Management Unit* [1999] NZCA 206, [65], [76].

35   *Sutherland v Hatton* [2002] EWCA Civ 76, [5] (Hale LJ).

36   (4th edn, American Psychiatric Assn, published 1994, text revision published in 2000), available in full-text at: <http://www.psychiatryonline.com/resourceTOC.aspx?resourceID=1>.

37   (10th revision, World Health Organisation), available in full-text at: <http://www.who.int/classifications/icd/en/bluebook.pdf>. The first draft of ICD-11 is expected in 2010.

38   *RK v Oldham NHS Trust* [2003] Lloyd's Rep Med 1 (QB) [20]. And earlier: *Behrens v Bertram Mill Circus* [1957] 2 QB 1 (CA) 28 (Devlin LJ).

[39]   e.g.: *Reilly v Merseyside HA* (1994) 23 BMLR 26 (CA) 29, 30 (a trapped-in-a-lift case; 'here there was no recognisable psychiatric injury, but only normal emotion in the face of a most unpleasant experience').

[40]   *Creutzfeldt-Jakob Disease Litigation; Group B Plaintiffs v Medical Research Council* [2000] Lloyd's Rep Med 161 (QB) 163 (Morland J).

[41]   e.g.: *McKenzie v Lichter* [2005] VSC 61, [12] ('compensation is not payable in the present case because of the grief and upset flowing from the death ... for many months'); [43]. In *BT v Oei* [1999] NSWSC 1082, AT's estate brought a claim for pure psychiatric injury, for the depression he felt upon learning that he had passed on the HIV virus to his partner (his partner BT succeeded in her claim, for reasons explored in Chapter 4), but AT failed because his 'sorrow and distress' did not qualify as psychiatric injury: [188]. In Canada, e.g., the question was left to the jury in: *Brown v Taylor* [2003] BCSC 408, [8], [14].

[42]   [2004] EWHC 2106, [2004] Lloyd's Rep Med 530 (QB) [22].

[43]   [1994] 5 Med LR 178 (Central London CC) 181.

[44]   See, too: *Scottish Report*, [2.3] ('drawing the line between a recognised psychiatric injury and mere stress or anxiety may not be easy').

[45]   *Tame v New South Wales* [2002] HCA 35, (2002) 211 CLR 317, [192] (Kirby and Gummow JJ), listing the reasons by reference to, e.g., *White* [1998] UKHL 45, [1999] 2 AC 455 (HL) 493–94. Internal quote from *Prosser and Keeton on the Law of Torts* (5th edn, 1984) 366.

[46]   *Devji v District of Burnaby* [1999] BCCA 599, [3], [47] (McEachern CJ).

[47]   *Tame v New South Wales* [2002] HCA 35, (2002) 211 CLR 317, [193].

[48]   *Creutzfeldt-Jakob Disease Litigation, Andrews v Secretary of State for Health (Damages Assessments)* (1998) 54 BMLR 111 (QB) 113.

[49]   D Gill, 'Proving and Disproving Psychiatric Injury' (2008) 76 *Medico-Legal J* 143, 154.

[50]   P Case, 'Secondary Iatrogenic Harm: Claims for Psychiatric Damage following a Death caused by Medical Error' (2004) 67 *MLR* 561, 569.

[51]   D Nolan, 'Psychiatric Injury at the Crossroads' [2004] *JPIL* 1, 20. Barrett notes that '[i]t was not until 1980 that post-traumatic stress disorder was included as a psychiatric diagnostic category (in the American Diagnostic and Statistical Manual of Mental Disorders, DSM-III': B Barrett, 'Psychiatric Stress—An Unacceptable Cost to Employers' [2008] *J of Business Law* 64, fn 3.

[52]   *Ipp Report*, [9.6], and see recommendation 33 (suggesting that some guidelines for psychiatric illnesses, which the law would compensate, should be developed by a panel of experts for use in litigious contexts).

[53]   [1999] NZCA 206, [2000] 1 NZLR 179, [83] (Thomas J).

[54]   e.g.: *Rhodes v Canadian National Rwy* (1990) 75 DLR (4th) 248 (BCCA) 289 (Southin JA), cited in: *Van Soest, ibid*, [57]; *Coates v Government Ins Office of NSW* (1995) 36 NSWLR 1 (CA) 12 (Kirby P), cited in: *Van Soest*, [54], [102]. Some Canadian case law has also permitted recovery for mental distress falling short of a diagnosis of psychiatric illness: *Mason v Westside Cemeteries Ltd* (1996), 29 CCLT (2d) 125; 135 DLR (4th) 361 (Ont Gen Div); *Vanek v Great Atlantic & Pacific Co of Canada* (1997), 39 OTC 54 (Ont Gen Div), both cited with apparent approval in: *Anderson v Wilson* (1998), 37 OR (3d) 235 (Div Ct).

[55]   *Van Soest, ibid*, [76] (Gault, Henry, Keith and Blanchard JJ).

[56]   *ibid*, [69] (emphasis added).

[57]   [2004] EWHC 2106, [2004] Lloyd's Rep Med 530.

[58]   [1994] 5 Med LR 170 (CA).

[59]   [1994] 5 Med LR 178 (Central London CC).

[60]   [2002] EWCA Civ 1792, [2003] Lloyd's Rep Med 49.

[61]   (2001) 57 BMLR 158 (QB).

[62]   [1993] 4 Med LR 34 (QB).

[63]   [1999] Lloyd's Rep Med 389 (Chelmsford CC).

[64]   [2002] All ER (D) 218 (QB, Forbes J, 13 Dec 2002).

[65]   [2004] EWHC 2748 (QB). Mrs Hall also failed to establish a cause of action against those who perpetrated the hoax, and an appeal against this was dismissed: [2005] EWCA Civ 919.

[66]   [1999] EWCA Civ 1533, [2000] PNLR 87.

67   [2001] Lloyd's Rep Med 458 (QB).

68   [1996] 7 Med LR 167 (Mayor's and City of London Court).

69   (1997) 39 BMLR 35 (CA). The case is also reported as *Powell v Boldaz*.

70   A hormonal/adrenaline imbalance due to progressive deterioriation of the adrenal cortex: *ibid*, 40, and *Oxford Concise Colour Medical Dictionary* (4th edn, OUP, Oxford, 2007) 9.

71   *ibid*, 44–45.

72   [2004] EWHC 644, [2005] QB 506. For equivalent litigation arising in Scotland, brought by parents who were advised by letter that organs of their children had been retained, see: *Stevens v Yorkhill NHS Trust* [2006] CSOH 143, (2006) 95 BMLR 1.

73   Known as The Nationwide Organ Retention Group Litigation. See GLO No 9, dated 16 Jun 2001, details of which are available at: <http://www.hmcourts-service.gov.uk/cms/150_551.htm>.

74   [1992] 2 AC 310 (HL) 407, and paraphrased in *North Glamorgan NHS Trust v Walters* [2002] EWCA Civ 1792, [12].

75   As noted recently: A Gore, 'Psychiatric Injury' [2009] *JPIL* C39, C42. See too: M Jones, *Medical Negligence* (4th edn, Sweet & Maxwell, London, 2008) 186.

76   (1997) 39 BMLR 146 (CA) 158. The *Oxford Dictionary of English* (2nd edn, revised, OUP, Oxford, 2006) 1091, defines 'mediately' as 'connected indirectly through another person or thing; involving an intermediate agency'.

77   [1990] 2 AC 605 (HL) 618 (Lord Bridge).

78   Although it has succeeded in a fear-of-the-future claim: *Creutzfeldt-Jakob Disease Litigation; Group B Plaintiffs v Medical Research Council* [2000] Lloyd's Rep Med 161 (QB), as discussed in Chapter 9.

79   [1996] AC 155 (HL) 184 (Lord Lloyd) (emphasis added).

80   [1999] 2 AC 455 (HL) 499 (Lord Steyn). Also see 469 (Lord Goff), 496 (Lord Steyn), 589 (Lord Hoffmann).

81   [2001] 2 AC 592 (HL) 601 (Lord Slynn, with whom the other members agreed).

82   *Johnston v NEI Intl Combustion Ltd; Rothwell v Chemical and Insulating Co Ltd; Topping v Benchtown Ltd (the Pleural Plaques Litig)* [2007] UKHL 39 (a conjoined appeal from: *Grieves v FT Everard & Sons Ltd* [2006] EWCA Civ 27).

83   R Mulheron, 'The "Primary Victim" in Psychiatric Illness Claims: Reworking the "Patchwork Quilt"' (2008) 19 *King's LJ* 81, 82. This article traces the changing primary victim definition in English law.

84   *North Glamorgan NHS Trust v Walters* [2002] EWCA Civ 1792, [2003] Lloyd's Rep Med 49.

85   *Hall v Gwent Healthcare NHS Trust* [2004] EWHC 2748 (QB).

86   *Palmer v Tees HA* [1999] EWCA Civ 1533, (1998) 39 BMLR 35.

87   *Walters v North Glamorgan NHS Trust* [2002] EWHC 321 (QB), [2003] PIQR 2, [21]–[22].

88   [2002] EWCA Civ 1792, [12].

89   [2004] EWHC 2748 (QB) [16]–[17].

90   [1999] EWCA Civ 1533, [35].

91   M Lyons, 'Psychiatric Harm: Death of a Child' [2003] *JPIL* 23, 24–25.

92   G Peart, 'Psychiatric Injury Claims' [2003] *JPIL* 25, 31. On a separate note, employees have sought to be regarded as 'participants' in accidents at work that brought about the death or injury of workmates, even though they were not in danger themselves nor did they satisfy the various requirements of a secondary victim: *Young v Charles Church (Southern) Ltd* (1997) 39 BMLR 146 (CA), allowing recovery, and overruling: *Young v Charles Church (Southern) Ltd* (1997) 33 BMLR 101 (QB). See too: *Gregg v Ashbrae Ltd* [2006] NICA 17, disallowing recovery, and overruling: *Gregg v Ashbrae Ltd* [2005] NIQB 37. For thoughtful discussion of workplace claims for pure psychiatric illness, see, e.g.: N Tomkins, 'Psychiatric Injury: Extra Routes to Recovery?' [2006] *JPIL* 251; F Leverick, 'Counting the Ways of Becoming a Primary Victim' [2007] *Edinburgh L Rev* 258; B Barrett, 'Psychiatric Stress—An Unacceptable Cost to Employers' [2008] *J of Business Law* 64.

93   [2004] EWHC 644, [2005] QB 506.

94   However, only one test claimant recovered damages (£2,750); the other two failed for reasons to be discussed in Section 3.

95   *ibid*, [199].

⁹⁶ [2001] Lloyd's Rep Med 458 (QB).

⁹⁷ *ibid*, 466, and also: 'How can there be a secondary victim if there is no other person who was physically involved in the incident as a potential victim?' (at 471).

⁹⁸ A point also noted in: C McIvor, 'Liability for Psychiatric Harm' (2007) 23 *PN* 249, 254.

⁹⁹ 'The "Primary Victim" in Psychiatric Illness Claims: Reworking the "Patchwork Quilt"' (2008) 19 *King's LJ* 81, 93–94.

¹⁰⁰ *English Report* (1998) [2.22]–[2.24].

¹⁰¹ *Ipp Report* (2002) [9.31].

¹⁰² [1992] 1 AC 310 (HL) 412.

¹⁰³ Modifying the facts of: *Hambrook v Stokes Bros* [1925] 1 KB 141 (CA).

¹⁰⁴ *Farrell v Merton, Sutton and Wandsworth HA* (2000) 57 BMLR 158 (QB) 161; *Hall v Gwent Healthcare NHS Trust* [2004] EWHC2748 (QB) [16]. In the employment context: *Storey v Charles Church Developments plc* (1995) 73 Con LR 1 (QB) 19.

¹⁰⁵ As Judge Bursell QC put it in: *Farrell v Avon HA* [2001] Lloyd's Rep Med 458 (QB) 471.

¹⁰⁶ [1996] AC 155 (HL).

¹⁰⁷ The principle in *Page v Smith* thus runs counter to the *Wagon Mound* principle (per *Overseas Tankship (UK) Ltd v Morts Dock and Engineering Co Ltd, The Wagon Mound (No 1)* [1961] AC 388 (PC) 426), which states that the damage suffered must have been of a reasonably foreseeable type. The *Page v Smith*-type claimant is an exception to that principle, because he recovers for *psychiatric* injury when it was *physical* injury that was foreseeable, given that he was in the zone of physical danger. For the other types of claimant who sue for pure psychiatric injury, they must prove foreseeability of psychiatric injury, and if that claim is proven, will recover for precisely that type of injury, thus complying with the *Wagon Mound* principle. For this reason, some have been very critical of *Page v Smith*. e.g., *Scottish Report*, [1.10], [3.32].

¹⁰⁸ [2004] EWHC 644 (QB), [2005] QB 506.

¹⁰⁹ *ibid*, [252]–[253] (Mrs Harris) and [279] (Mrs Carpenter).

¹¹⁰ *ibid*, [268] (Mrs Shorter).

¹¹¹ See pp 279–81.

¹¹² [2002] EWCA Civ 1792, [2003] Lloyd's Rep Med 49.

¹¹³ [1999] EWCA Civ 1533, [2000] PNLR 87.

¹¹⁴ [2004] EWHC 644, [2005] QB 506, [200]–[203].

¹¹⁵ *ibid*, [206].

¹¹⁶ [2001] Lloyd's Rep Med 458 (QB) 458.

¹¹⁷ *Page v Smith* [1996] AC 155 (HL) 189, 197; *AB v Leeds Teaching Hosp NHS Trust* [2004] EWHC 644, [190]; *McLoughlin v O'Brian* [1983] 1 AC 410 (HL) 429; *Bourhill v Young* [1943] AC 92 (HL) 110, 117.

¹¹⁸ *Greatorex v Greatorex* [2000] 1 WLR 1970 (QB) 1985.

¹¹⁹ [2004] EWHC 644, [2005] QB 506, [268].

¹²⁰ [2001] Lloyd's Rep Med 458 (QB).

¹²¹ *ibid*, 464.

¹²² *Scottish Report*, [2.16].

¹²³ *ibid*, [3.19].

¹²⁴ *ibid*, [2.20].

¹²⁵ *Ipp Report*, [9.16] and [9.19].

¹²⁶ *English Report*, [5.21].

¹²⁷ *ibid*, [5.26].

¹²⁸ *ibid*, citing: *Page v Smith* [1996] AC 155 (HL) 170.

¹²⁹ *ibid*, [5.26].

¹³⁰ *Alcock v Chief Constable of Yorkshire Police* [1992] 2 AC 310 (HL) 396–98 (Lord Keith).

¹³¹ *ibid*, 401 (Lord Ackner).

¹³² *ibid*, 416–17 (Lord Oliver).

¹³³ As discussed at pp 289–93.

134 *Cross v Highlands & Islands Enterprise* 2001 SLT 1060 (OH) [61].

135 *Alexander v Midland Bank plc* [1999] IRLR 723 (CA) [50].

136 *Chadwick v British Railways Board* [1967] 1 WLR 912 (QB), in which the claimant rescued victims of the Lewisham rail disaster throughout the night; his estate recovered for the psychiatric injury which he suffered.

137 *English Report*, [2.62].

138 *Scottish Report*, [2.5].

139 See pp 289–93.

140 R Mulheron, 'The "Primary Victim" in Psychiatric Illness Claims: Reworking the "Patchwork Quilt"' (2008) 19 *King's LJ* 81,109–110.

141 e.g., floodgates concerns were explicitly referred to in: *The Creuztfeldt-Jakob Disease Litigation; Group B Plaintiffs v Medical Research Council* (1997) 41 BMLR 157 (QB) 160–61.

142 *Page v Smith* [1996] AC 155 (HL) 184 (Lord Lloyd).

143 *Alcock v Chief Constable of South Yorkshire Police* [1992] 1 AC 310 (HL) 407 (Lord Oliver).

144 *Lawrence v Pembrokeshire CC* [2006] EWHC 1029, [133].

145 [1992] 1 AC 310 (HL) 407–8.

146 [1999] 2 AC 455 (HL) 496–9.

147 [1996] AC 155 (HL) 190.

148 [2001] 2 AC 592 (HL).

149 'The "Primary Victim" in Psychiatric Illness Claims: Reworking the "Patchwork Quilt"' (2008) 19 *King's LJ* 81, 87.

150 (2001) 57 BMLR 158 (QB). For a remarkably similar Canadian case in which a mother who gave birth to a severely brain-damaged twin due to medical negligence was also classified as a potential primary *and* secondary victim, see: *Dawe v BC Children's Hospital* [2003] BCSC 443, [30].

151 *ibid*, 164.

152 C Hilson, 'Liability for Psychiatric Injury: Primary and Secondary Victims Revisited' (2002) 18 *PN* 167, 170.

153 [1994] 5 Med LR 178 (Central London CC).

154 *ibid*, 183.

155 *ibid*, 182 (referring to 'five shorthand tests which the parties in *Sion v Hampstead HA* agreed').

156 *Alcock v Chief Constable of South Yorkshire Police* [1992] 2 AC 310 (HL).

157 *McLoughlin v O'Brian* [1983] 1 AC 410 (HL) 421–23 (Lord Wilberforce).

158 See, e.g., C Thomas, 'Satisfying the Hearness Test' (2003) 153 *NLJ* 953, and see too, the reference to American commentary's use of the terms in: *White* [1996] EWHC Admin 173 (CA) [70].

159 C McIvor, 'Liability for Psychiatric Harm: *Butchart v Home Office*' (2007) 23 *PN* 249, 251–52. See too: O Segal and J Williams, 'Psychiatric Injury, Policy and the House of Lords' [1999] *JPIL* 102, 108 ('Although the court in *Alcock* in a sense goes through the motions of applying the previous case law it is clear that they were dominated by the prospect, if the plaintiffs succeeded, of the courts facing a large volume of claims').

160 *Page v Smith* [1996] AC 155 (HL) 184 (Lord Lloyd).

161 Easily established, e.g., in: *North Glamorgan NHS Trust v Walters* [2002] EWCA Civ 1792, [12]; *Sion v Hampstead HA* (1994) 5 Med LR 170 (QB) 176.

162 [1994] 5 Med LR 178 (Central London CC) 183.

163 [1998] Lloyd's Rep Med 116 (CA).

164 *ibid*, 124, and 122, respectively.

165 *J&P Van Soest v Residual Health Management Unit* [1999] NZCA 206, [2000] 1 NZLR 179, [93] (Thomas J).

166 The label used, e.g., in: *Devji v District of Barnaby* [1999] BCCA 599, [38]; *Van Soest, ibid*, [72]; *A-G v Gilbert* [2002] NZCA 55, [2002] 2 NZLR 342, [78].

167 *Alcock v Chief Constable of South Yorkshire Police* [1992] 1 AC 310 (HL) 397, 411.

168 *White v Chief Constable of South Yorkshire Police* [1999] 2 AC 455 (HL) 502 (Lord Hoffmann). Work colleagues fall into the non-presumed category, e.g.: *Gregg v Ashbrae Ltd* [2006] NICA 17.

169 (2000) 57 BMLR 158 (QB) 163.
170 [2001] Lloyd's Rep Med 458 (QB).
171 [1996] AC 155 (HL) 197, and subsequently cited and applied in: *AB v Leeds Teaching Hospital NHS Trust* [2004] EWHC 644 (QB), [199].
172 *Alcock* [1992] 1 AC 310 (CA) (Nolan LJ) 384–85 ('[t]he identification of the particular individuals who come within that category [of close tie of love and affection] ... could only be carried out *ex post facto*'), an observation cited with approval on appeal (at 404).
173 *English Report*, [6.34], recommendation 15, and cl 1(3)(b) of the Draft Negligence (Psychiatric Illness) Bill.
174 e.g.: P Case, 'Curiouser and Curiouser: Psychiatric Damage Caused by Negligent Misinformation' (2002) 18 *PN* 248, 250.
175 [2001] Lloyd's Rep Med 458 (QB) 472.
176 *Ipp Report*, [9.25]. See, too, comment by Stapleton that the 'close tie' requirement leads to distasteful exercises in 'proving (and disproving) the love': J Stapleton, 'In Restraint of Tort' in P Birks (ed), *The Frontiers of Liability* (OUP, Oxford, 1994) vol II, 94–96.
177 *ibid*, [9.26].
178 *Scottish Report*, [3.54]–[3.55], and cl 5 of the Reparation for Mental Harm (Scotland) Bill.
179 *English Report*, [6.10], [6.26]–[6.33], and cl 3 of the Negligence (Psychiatric Illness) Bill.
180 *Scottish Report*, [3.54].
181 By virtue of: Criminal Injuries Compensation Act 1995, s 1 (in force 1 Apr 1996).
182 D Miers, 'Rebuilding Lives: Operational and Policy Issues in the Compensation of Victims of Violent and Terrorist Crimes' [2006] *Criminal L Rev* 695, 701, fn 24.
183 See, respectively: <http://www.scotlawcom.gov.uk/html/impleg.php>; and <http://www.lawcom.gov.uk/docs/implementation_list_master_120509.pdf>.
184 *White v Chief Constable of South Yorkshire Police* [1999] 2 AC 455 (HL) 502 (Lord Hoffmann), 477 (Lord Goff). Earlier: *Alcock v Chief Constable of South Yorkshire Police* [1992] 1 AC 310 (HL) 402, 404 (Lord Ackner), 411 (Lord Oliver), 422 (Lord Jauncey); *Page v Smith* [1996] AC 155 (HL) 189 (Lord Lloyd).
185 [1992] AC 310 (HL) 411.
186 See, e.g., S Allen, 'Personal Injury Update' (2003) 102 *LSG* 34, 34, who cites cases noted in the text above.
187 [1983] 1 AC 410 (HL) 419 (Lord Wilberforce).
188 [1992] 1 AC 310 (HL).
189 [2003] EWCA Civ 679.
190 [1991] 3 All ER 65 (QB).
191 [2001] 2 AC 592 (HL) 601.
192 *JD v East Berkshire Community Health NHS Trust* [2005] UKHL 23, [10].
193 As noted, e.g., in: P Case, 'Secondary Iatrogenic Harm: Claims for Psychiatric Damage Following a Death Caused by Medical Error' (2004) 67 *MLR* 561, 562 ('The relative is unlikely to witness at first hand the sudden shocking event currently required by English law as, unlike the typical accident environment, the hospital is a highly controlled space where the family's view of tragedy is often occluded by the intervention of hospital personnel').
194 (2001) 57 BMLR 158 (QB).
195 *ibid*, 164.
196 [2002] All ER (D) 218 (QB, Forbes J, 13 Dec 2002).
197 *ibid*, [78]–[80].
198 [1993] 3 SLR 317 (HC) (mother recovered damages for psychiatric injury; at her daughter's bedside following pituitary gland operation; brought daughter back to hospital as her condition deteriorated; and at the bedside when her daughter died; sufficient proximity to enable recovery).
199 [1997] BCSC 2588 (husband saw wife in intensive care after anaesthesia accident during routine operation, resulting in irreversible and fatal brain damage; strike-out application failed; arguably, husband fell within

immediate aftermath), leave to appeal denied: [1997] BCJ No 2461. See, too: *Dawe v BC Children's Hospital* [2003] BCSC 443.

200 S Allen, 'Personal Injury Law' (2003) *LSG* 34, 34.

201 E Jackson, *Medical Law: Text, Cases and Materials* (OUP, Oxford, 2006) 115. See too: P Case, 'Secondary Iatrogenic Harm' (2004) 67 *MLR* 561, 574 (the case 'indicates a very generous application of the *Alcock* requirements').

202 [1993] 4 Med LR 34 (QB).

203 *ibid*, 37. The court quoted (at *ibid*, 35) Lord Wilberforce's statement in *McLoughlin v O'Brian* [1983] 1 AC 410 (HL) 422 ('It is, after all, the fact and consequence of the defendant's negligence that must be proved to have caused the "nervous shock"').

204 *Palmer v Tees HA* [1999] EWCA Civ 1533, (1998) 39 BMLR 35. Similarly, *Maulolo v Hutt Valley Health Corp Ltd* [2002] NZAR 375 (HC, Wellington) (woman killed by psychotic partner almost a year after he was negligently released from psychiatric facility; relatives failed to recover for pure psychiatric illness).

205 *Tan v East London and City HA* [1999] Lloyd's Rep Med 389 (Chelmsford CC).

206 In Australia, the High Court has abolished direct spatial and temporal proximity as independent requirements for secondary victim recovery: *Tame v New South Wales; Annetts v Australian Stations Pty Ltd* [2002] HCA 35, (2002) 211 CLR 317, and discussed, e.g., in: J Dietrich, 'Nervous Shock' (2003) 11 *Torts LJ* 11.

207 *Scottish Report*, [2.23].

208 *English Report*, [6.11]–[6.16].

209 *ibid*, [6.10], citing: *Jaensch v Coffey* (1984) 155 CLR 549 (HCA) 600.

210 *White v Chief Constable of South Yorkshire Police* [1999] 2 AC 455 (HL) 502 (Lord Hoffmann). Earlier: *Alcock v Chief Constable of South Yorkshire Police* [1992] 2 AC 310 (HL) 398 (Lord Keith) 405 (Lord Ackner) 411 (Lord Oliver); *McLoughlin v O'Brian* [1983] 1 AC 410 (HL) 422–23 (Lord Wilberforce).

211 [1994] 5 Med LR 178 (Central London CC).

212 *ibid*, 183.

213 See, e.g., M Jones, *Medical Negligence* (4th edn, Sweet & Maxwell, London, 2008) 197, fn 585, citing: *Hobbs v Bexley HA* (1992) (case settled).

214 [1999] Lloyd's Rep Med 389 (Chelmsford CC).

215 *AB v Tameside and Glossop HA* [1997] 8 Med LR 91 (CA).

216 *Allin v City and Hackney HA* [1996] 7 Med LR 167 (Mayor's and City of London Court).

217 *Creutzfeldt-Jakob Disease Litigation; Group B Plaintiffs v Medical Research Council* (1997) 41 BMLR 157 (QB); *Farrell v Avon HA* [2001] Lloyd's Rep Med 458 (QB).

218 [1993] 4 Med LR 34 (QB).

219 *ibid*, 37.

220 [1999] EWCA Civ 1533.

221 [2001] Lloyd's Rep Med 458 (QB).

222 [2004] EWHC 2106, [2004] Lloyd's Rep Med 530.

223 *ibid*, 535.

224 *ibid*, 535.

225 [2002] All ER (D) 218 (QB, Forbes J, 13 Dec 2002).

226 *ibid*, [80].

227 [2002] EWCA Civ 1792, [35], [40] (Ward LJ). Also discussed in: R Mulheron, 'Secondary Victim Psychiatric Illness Claims' (2003) 14 *King's College LJ* 213, 215–16.

228 *Scottish Report*, [2.23]–[2.24]. Even so, if a person who was told bad news sought recovery as a secondary victim, that claimant would still be subject to whether the psychiatric injury was reasonably foreseeable: [3.59, example (h)].

229 *Ipp Report*, [9.24]. This requirement has been abolished under Australian law: *Tame v New South Wales; Annetts v Australian Stations Pty Ltd* [2002] HCA 35, (2002) 211 CLR 317. See, for discussion, e.g.: J Dietrich, 'Nervous Shock' (2003) 11 *Torts LJ* 11; P Bates *et al*, *Australian Health and Medical Law Reporter* (CCH Australia Ltd, Sydney, 1991–, looseleaf) ¶16-675.

230 *English Report*, [6.10]–[6.16].

231 [1991] 3 All ER 73 (CA) 79 (Ward LJ).

232 *Page v Smith* [1996] AC 155 (HL) 189; *AB v Leeds Teaching Hospital NHS Trust* [2004] EWHC 644, [190].

233 *Ipp Report*, [9.13].

234 As explained in more detail in, e.g.: D Butler, 'Voyages in Uncertain Seas with Dated Maps: Recent Developments in Liability for Psychiatric Injury in Australia' (2001) 9 *Torts LJ* 1, 17.

235 1942 SC (HL) 78, [1943] AC 92 (HL).

236 *ibid*, 98 (SC), 117 (AC) (Lord Porter, read by Lord Wright). For similar comments about the 'usual fortitude of our citizens' which the law can expect, see, e.g.: *Devji v District of Burnaby* [1999] BCCA 599, [69].

237 [2001] Lloyd's Rep Med 458 (QB).

238 As suggested at *ibid*, 462. Had he been deemed to be a secondary victim, Mr Farrell may have failed the 'close tie of love and affection' criterion, however, as discussed previously at pp 284–85.

239 [1998] Lloyd's Rep Med 116 (QB) 123.

240 *ibid*, 124.

241 *Tredget and Tredget v Bexley HA* (1994) 5 Med LR 178 (London CC) 181.

242 M Puxon, 'Comment' to the *Tredget* decision, *ibid*, 184.

243 *Scottish Report*, [2.20].

244 *ibid*, [1.5].

245 [1992] 2 AC 310 (HL) 396–98 (Lord Keith). See discussion at pp 280–81.

246 See: N Mullany, 'Personal Perception of Trauma and Sudden Shock–South Africa Simplifies Matters' (2000) 116 *LQR* 29, 33 ('Prior to *Alcock*, the requirement of "sudden shock" had not received express judicial ratification in England ... Their Lordships' suggestion that the requirement was implicit in all previous cases is questionable. Although its pedigree is cloudy, the "sudden shock" rule has wreaked havoc'). Also critiqued in: H Teff, 'The Requirement of "Sudden Shock" in Liability for Negligently Inflicted Psychiatric Damage' (1996) 4 *Tort L Rev* 44.

247 *Sion v Hampstead HA* (1994) 5 Med LR 170 (CA) 173 (Staughton LJ).

248 [1999] Lloyd's Rep Med 389 (Chelmsford CC).

249 [2004] EWHC 2106, [2004] Lloyd's Rep Med 530 (QB) 535.

250 [1994] 5 Med LR 170 (QB 176. Also: *Taylorson v Shieldness Produce Ltd* [1994] PIQR P329 (CA) (death of two boys arising from motor vehicle accident; parents' claim for pure psychiatric illness by reason of shock as part of the immediate aftermath of the accident failed; son died after three days).

251 *ibid*, 174, citing from the claimant's medical report.

252 A point also made by Amarjeet JC in *Pang Koi Fa v Lim Djoe Phing* [1993] 3 SLR 317 (HC).

253 [2002] EWCA Civ 1792, [2003] Lloyd's Rep Med 49.

254 *ibid*, [34] and [40] (Ward LJ).

255 *Tredget and Tredget v Bexley HA* (1994) 5 Med LR 178 (Central London CC) 183–84.

256 'Secondary Victim Psychiatric Illness Claims' (2003) 14 *King's College LJ* 213; and 'Medical Negligence, Secondary Victims and Psychiatric Illness: Family Tragedies and Legal Headaches' in R Probert (ed), *Family Life and the Law* (Ashgate Publishing, Aldershot, 2007) 70–74.

257 e.g.: V Chico, 'Saviour Siblings: Trauma and Tort Law' (2006) 14 *Med L Rev* 180, 211–12 ('there is now conflicting authority, adding to the arbitrary nature of the sudden shock requirement ... the requirement that the claimant's illness be caused in such a manner is illogical and unfair and should be overruled'); J Laing, 'Clinical Negligence: Secondary Victims and Recovery for Nervous Shock' (2003) 11 *Med L Rev* 121, 124 ('it is a matter of debate to what extent this does not represent a small extension of liability ... Perhaps the most worrying aspect is that the decision could lead to restrictive practices towards family members being present in hospitals, in particular, to the detriment of parents and relatives of seriously ill patients being given limited access or excluded from Intensive Care Units'); M Lyons, 'Psychiatric Injury: Death of a Child' [2003] *JPIL* 23, 25 (the decision 'is perhaps a generous interpretation of some of those control mechanisms'); S Webber, 'Case in Focus: Psychiatric Injury of a Secondary Victim' (2003) 9 *Clinical Risk* 157.

258 [2002] EWCA Civ 1792, [10].

259 *ibid*, [29].

260 *Scottish Report*, [2.4].

261 M Horne, 'Commentary' [2004] Lloyd's Rep Med 536.

262 M Puxon, 'Comment' (1994) 5 Med LR 184, and a similar observation at: (1994) 5 Med LR 177.

263 [1992] 2 AC 310 (HL) 400.

264 [2002] EWCA Civ 1792, [43].

265 *ibid*, [51].

266 *Galli-Atkinson v Seghal* [2003] EWCA Civ 697, [25] ('an event itself may be made up of a number of components; this was accepted by this court in *Walters*'); *Toth v Jarman* [2006] EWCA Civ 1028, [3].

267 *JD v East Berkshire Community Health NHS Trust* [2005] UKHL 23, [2005] 2 AC 373, [107] (Lord Rodger).

268 To adopt the phrase in: *Galli-Atkinson v Seghal* [2003] EWCA Civ 697, [25] (Latham CJ).

269 *White v Lidl UK GmbH* (QB, 21 Apr 2005, Hallett J).

270 [2004] HKDC 154 (leave to appeal denied, Judge To, 11 Oct 2004).

271 *ibid*, [25]–[29].

272 [1993] 3 SLR 317 (HC).

273 *ibid*, 333–34.

274 [1993] 4 Med LR 34 (QB).

275 *ibid*, 37–38.

276 [2002] All ER (D) 218.

277 *ibid*, [79].

278 This was the psychiatric evidence in: *North Glamorgan NHS Trust v Walters* [2002] EWCA Civ 1792, [10].

279 *ibid*, [19(iv)].

280 V Chico, 'Saviour Siblings: Trauma and Tort Law' (2006) 14 *Med L Rev* 180, 211.

281 See, e.g., the discussion of *Brady v West Middlesex University Hosp NHS Trust* (issued in June 2001, and settled), by D Brahams, 'Nervous Shock: New Developments in the Context of Clinical Negligence Claims' (2002) 70 *Medico-legal J* 53 (accessed online, no pp available) (the psychiatrist 'examined Mr Brady and provided a supportive psychiatric report which did not use the term "nervous shock"'). Also: V Chico, *ibid*, citing the expert medical report given in *White v Chief Constable of South Yorkshire Police* which stated: 'In fiction, and perhaps in a layman's view of shock as a psychological event, the individual experiences a grossly untoward event or situation with one or more sensory modalities but almost always vision, and is instantaneously "shocked" or traumatised. In practice this almost never occurs'.

282 *JD v East Berkshire Community Health NHS Trust* [2005] UKHL 23, [107]–[108].

283 *Scottish Report*, [2.4]–[2.5].

284 *English Report*, [5.29], and expressly abolished in: Draft Negligence (Psychiatric Illness) Bill, cl 5(2).

285 *Tame v New South Wales, Annetts v Australian Stations Pty Ltd* [2002] HCA 35, (2002) 211 CLR 317, [243]–[244].

286 *McFarlane v Tayside Health Board* [2000] 2 AC 59 (HL) 82 (Lord Steyn).

287 [1999] 2 AC 455 (HL) 510.

288 C Witting, 'Duty of Care: An Analytical Approach' (2005) 25 *OJLS* 33, 40. Also: D Horwarth, 'Many Duties of Care—Or A Duty of Care? Notes from the Underground' (2006) 26 *OJLS* 449, 456; V Chico, 'Saviour Siblings: Trauma and Tort Law' (2006) 14 *Med L Rev* 180, 183; O Segal and J Williams, 'Psychiatric Injury, Policy and the House of Lords' [1999] *JPIL* 102, 112.

289 'Medical Negligence, Secondary Victims and Psychiatric Illness: Family Tragedies and Legal Headaches' in R Probert (ed), *Family Life and the Law* (Ashgate Publishing, Aldershot, 2007) 76.

290 [2004] EWHC 644 (QB), [2005] QB 506, [197].

291 *Caparo Industries plc v Dickman* [1990] 2 AC 605 (HL) 618.

292 *Alcock v Chief Constable of South Yorkshire Police* [1992] 1 AC 310 (HL) 411.

293 *Butchart v Home Office* [2006] EWCA Civ 239, [2006] 1 WLR 1155 (CA) (strike-out application by the defendant ultimately failed).

294 *Attia v British Gas plc* [1988] QB 304 (CA) (strike-out application by the defendant failed on appeal).

295 *McLoughlin v Jones* [2001] EWCA Civ 1743, [2002] QB 1312 (held, as a preliminary issue, that his solicitors owed him a duty of care to avoid causing claimant client psychiatric injury).

296 *Swinney v Chief Constable of Northumbria Police* [1997] QB 464 (CA); *Leach v Chief Constable of Gloucestershire Constabulary* [1999] 1 WLR 1421 (CA).

297 [2000] Lloyd's Rep Med 161 (QB).

298 K Stanton, 'Professional Negligence: Duty of Care Methodology in the Twenty-first Century' (2006) 22 *PN* 134, 145. See too: N Tomkins, 'Psychiatric Injury—Extra Routes to Recovery?' [2006] *JPIL* 251, 251 ('The decisions of their Lordships in those cases [*Alcock* and *Frost*] shaped the law as it is today').

299 N Mullany, 'English Psychiatric Injury Law—Chronically Depressing' (1999) 115 *LQR* 30, 36.

300 C McIvor, 'Liability for Psychiatric Harm: *Butchart v Home Office*' [2007] *PN* 249, 250.

301 [1996] 7 Med LR 167 (Mayor's and City of London Court). Also: *AB v Tameside and Glossop HA* [1997] 8 Med LR 91 (CA).

302 See, further:: N Mullany, 'Liability for Careless Communication of Traumatic Information' (1998) 114 *LQR* 380.

303 *North Glamorgan NHS Trust v Walters* [2002] EWCA Civ 1792, [44] (Ward LJ).

304 *White v Chief Constable of South Yorkshire Police* [1999] 2 AC 455 (HL) 500, 504; *Johnston v NEI International Combustion Ltd (the Pleural Plaques Litigation)* [2007] UKHL 39, [54].

305 DCA, *The Law on Damages* (CP 9, 4 May 2007) ch 3, [97].

306 [2002] EWCA Civ 1792, [48].

Chapter 9
'Fear-of-the-Future' Claims by Non-Patients

A INTRODUCTION

'Fear-of-the-future' claims arise where the claimant becomes anxious that he will develop or contract an illness or disease in the future, as a result of the defendant's negligence, and he seeks damages to compensate for the mental harm of having to live with the prospect, however small, that the worst might happen.[1]

This type of claim can typically arise, say, in cases of environmental pollution[2] or from wrongful exposures to harmful substances in the workplace[3]—where that 'substance', to which the claimant has been exposed, can be either some toxic agent (e.g., asbestos, Agent Orange, fibre-glass) or some disease-causing micro-organism (e.g., the HIV or Hepatitis C viruses), any of which may lead to future serious illness or death.[4] The same problem potentially arises in the medical scenario—when *either patients or non-patients* are exposed to the risk of infection or disease due to negligently-performed medical procedures or diagnoses.[5]

The 'fear' component of this chapter's title is rather crucial to the legal analysis which follows. As discussed previously in Chapter 8,[6] English law sets, as a pre-condition for recovery in any claim for mental injury that is not ancillary to physical injury, that the fear must result in a *recognisable psychiatric injury*. Unsurprisingly, given how tough that threshold is to meet, claimants have variously sought to bring their cases for genuinely-borne anxiety and emotional distress falling short of that threshold—but with zero success in English litigation to date.

Of course, in the medical context, fear-of-the-future claims arise more frequently for patients who were the direct recipients of medical services. Some interesting examples from North America have included where: numerous patients received transplants of tissue/bone from an ear bank and were then informed that the ear bank had maintained incomplete and inadequate records about whether donors had been properly screened for HIV, and Hepatitis B and C;[7] a patient was pricked by a syringe that was left in the linens on her hospital bed;[8] patients were treated by a HCP who was ill with Hepatitis B[9] or HIV;[10] and several patients were informed of the possibility that use of unsterilised instruments[11] or inadequate infection control procedures[12] had exposed them to serious infections.

For the purposes of this chapter, however, it will be the *non-patients*, who have been exposed to the risk of infection or disease due to a HCP's negligence, that will be considered. They may have been exposed to patients who themselves were disease-carriers, or they may have been directly exposed to sub-standard medical hygiene practices in or around a medical facility, for example. They have not developed any disease or illness yet, but they fear that they will.

Just to clarify, of course, some third parties actually *do* contract an infectious disease from a patient. Sub-standard infection control, or a negligently-missed diagnosis of the patient's illness, may have exposed the non-patient (say, a hospital visitor) to the risk, which risk *actually manifests*. The scenario of non-patients who actually do contract disease from patients raises different legal issues, and is discussed in Chapter 4.

Section B considers examples of non-patient claims against HCPs which have arisen in the Commonwealth and in America, concerning fear-of-the-future-type claims. Attention then turns, in Section C, to the preliminary issue which bedevils this area—proving that 'fear-of-the-future' claimants suffered a legally-recognisable injury at all. Of course, many of those exposed to disease will be anxious, fearful and angry, but on a strict view, these human emotions are not grounds for compensable damage under English law. A recognisable psychiatric injury is mandated. The reasons for the English position, in the *specific context of fear-of-the-future claims*, will be explored in this Section—together with discussion of the two avenues by which fear-of-the-future claimants have sought to circumvent that strict approach, albeit with mixed success. Section D considers how English law determines whether a negligent HCP owes a non-patient a duty of care to avoid fear-of-the-future psychiatric injury. The area constitutes a peculiar nook of pure psychiatric illness law, and it has been rightly noted that fear-of-the-future claims require courts 'to consider the boundaries of "nervous shock" more carefully'.[13] Section E briefly considers the American jurisprudence arising from fear-of-the-future claims, indicating the different analysis that has been adopted in that jurisdiction—as a counterpoint to the English legal treatment. Section F concludes.

Fear-of-the-future claims have been judicially noted by one Australian court to be 'a developing area of the law of [medical] negligence',[14] and in the leading Canadian medical case of this type, the Ontario Court of Appeal noted 'the uncertain state of the law'.[15] The area is not without its controversy in England either, given that (in the context of exposure by employees to asbestos in their workplaces), the House of Lords denied a fear-of-the-future claim by all test claimants,[16] in a judgment that will have ramifications for the likelihood of success for fear-of-the-future claims in other contexts too. Given the evolving and difficult nature of these claims, it is rather surprising, then, that they have not garnered further attention in key law reform studies in recent times. In its study of negligently-inflicted pure psychiatric illness, the English Law Commission gave one footnote over to the area.[17] Although the quantity of English litigation remains relatively minuscule at the present time (as it was then, in 1998), the principles surrounding recovery are sufficiently murky, and the scenarios giving rise to fear-of-the-future claims in medical negligence, especially, are sufficiently plentiful, to have arguably warranted a more detailed treatment. Similarly, in its consideration of possible reform of Australian negligence law,[18] the Ipp Committee, while studying mental harm, ignored fear-of-the-future claims altogether. The Scottish Law Commission also declined to mention such claims in either its Discussion Paper[19] or Final Report[20] on negligently-inflicted psychiatric illness.

As this chapter will demonstrate, the legal principles governing recovery for fear-of-the-future claims are challenging. Moreover, they are not altogether consistent with other areas of recovery for pure psychiatric illness. The reality is that, although fear-of-the-future claims *are* permissible in English law, the law suffers from a real lack of clarity, in both proving some recognisable damage/injury, and in proving the basis for a duty of care to avoid such injury.

B FEAR-OF-THE-FUTURE CLAIMS IN MEDICAL SCENARIOS

1. The English position

The leading fear-of-the-future case in England concerned a clinical trial, from which some participants developed a fear of contracting the dreadful brain-wasting Creutzfeldt-Jakob disease (CJD).[21] Strictly speaking, the clinical trial participants were not patients, but were nevertheless treated as being in a relationship something 'akin to that of doctor and patient, one of close proximity'.[22]

In *Creutzfeldt-Jakob Disease Litigation, Group B Plaintiffs v Medical Research Council*,[23] a group of children, whose growth was stunted as a result of a deficiency in the secretion of growth hormone in their pituitaries, were treated under a therapeutic programme between 1959–85, with doses of Hartree Human Growth Hormone ('Hartree HGH') extracted from the pituitaries of human cadavers. By 1 July 1977, the MRC, who authorised and oversighted the programme, were aware of the risk that injections of Hartree HGH could lead to the development of CJD, and were found to be in breach in not suspending the programme, after that date, for *new* patients (other than hypoglycaemia sufferers), although there was no breach for failing to recommend suspension of the therapeutic programme for *ongoing* recipients of HGH as from 1 July 1977.[24] In this group litigation, Group A Patients were either the representatives of victims who had died or individuals for whom CJD had already been diagnosed; and the Group B Patients were those who had not been diagnosed with CJD, but who were informed, in 1992, that they were at risk of developing CJD. Some sustained psychiatric illnesses as a result. **Held:** Group B patients were permitted to recover damages.

This decision has been academically noted[25] to be one that must be considered with some circumspection, as a first instance decision on a preliminary issue. Somewhat surprisingly, however, the case remains, more than a decade later, the only judicial decision on fear-of-the-future claims in English medical law. For that reason alone, it warrants close attention. That is not to say that there is no potential for medico-legal litigation of this type—to the contrary, Jones has noted, for example, that in 2008, the English Healthcare Commission reported on a number of incidents in which patients had been exposed to radiation unnecessarily, or to levels of radiation that were excessive.[26] However, fear-of-the-future claims have been a very much under-litigated scenario on the English medical landscape.

The other leading fear-of-the-future case in England, the *Pleural Plaques Litigation*,[27] was employment-related. Various employees had been negligently exposed by their employers to asbestos dust in the workplace. Each claimant had developed pleural plaques, which amounts to a fibrous thickening of localised areas of the pleura, the membrane covering the lung. Although the cause of the plaques is medically debatable, it is believed that asbestos fibres on the pleura cause a prolonged low-grade inflammatory response, leading in turn to the laying down of fibrous tissue on the pleura, causing the thickening. These asbestos fibres, once in the lungs, cannot be removed. The claimants alleged that developing pleural plaques meant that they were at risk of developing long-term asbestos-related diseases (such as asbestosis or mesothelioma), and that they had suffered anxiety at that prospect (although only one of the claimants, Mr Grieves, had suffered a genuine psychiatric illness, namely, depression). *All* test claimants failed, by majority, in the Court of Appeal[28] and then, unanimously in the House of Lords. The reasons for their failure, by analogy, have significant impact upon the likely direction of fear-of-the-future claims in medical negligence as well, and will be canvassed in Section C. As a matter of interest, exposure of employees to asbestos risk, and to blood contaminated by Hepatitis B and C and HIV in the prison workplace, have also arisen in Ireland[29] and in Scotland,[30] respectively.

2. Relevant case law from elsewhere

In contrast to the dearth of case law in England, there has been a very significant body of medical malpractice case law in the United States giving rise to fear-of-the-future claims (by patients, as well as by hospital employees, visitors, and others).

The impact of the US jurisprudence in this area of English law is light, but not entirely absent. In the *CJD litigation*, Morland J commented that '[i]n my judgment, American cases are not particularly helpful. The culture of American personal injury litigation is very different from ours and thus public policy considerations.'[31] However, in the asbestos litigation brought by Mr Grieves and others, the Court of Appeal referred to American authority[32] to support its decision that a claimant who is negligently exposed to the risk of asbestos-induced cancer was not in the 'zone of danger'.[33] Hence, although there has not been any notable inclination on the part of English judges to follow the particular analysis of fear-of-the-future claims adopted in the United States, some of the cases and ideas from that jurisdiction are instructive.

By way of a few noteworthy American examples of non-patient fear-of-the-future cases:

In *Carroll v Sisters of Saint Francis Health Services*,[34] the non-patient, Mrs Carroll (C), was visiting her terminally ill sister in a hospital intensive care unit in Memphis, Tennessee. After applying lotion to her sister's skin, C washed her hands in a nearby wash basin and then tried unsuccessfully to extract a paper towel from a container located on the wall to the right of the wash basin. C lifted the top of the container and reached inside, where three of her fingers were pricked by sharp objects. C spoke to a nurse on duty, who told her that the container was not a paper towel holder, but was a receptacle for 'contaminated needles'. C became fearful of contracting AIDS from the punctures, and was tested for HIV. These were negative. C was retested on five occasions over a three-year period since the incident, and all were negative. C sued the hospital, alleging negligence in placing the needles container, which resembled a paper towel dispenser, closer to the wash basin than the actual paper towel dispenser, and for failing to attach warning labels to the needles container. C claimed 'great anxiety, fear and emotional distress that she may contract AIDS'. **Held:** the claim failed.

In *Johnson v West Virginia University Hospitals*,[35] the non-patient, Mr Johnson (J), a hospital security guard employed by university police, was called to restrain an unruly patient. When the patient's bed fell over and the HCPs needed help in restraining the patient, J attempted to assist. As he was lifting the patient back onto the bed, the patient bit J on J's forearm, having bitten himself first to draw blood into his mouth. J claimed that, at that point, he negligently had not been told by any HCP at the hospital that the patient was infected with AIDS, although the HCPs dealing with the patient knew this (he was told afterwards, when he was washing out the wound). Although J tested negative for AIDS thereafter, he alleged emotional damage as a result of the fear of developing the disease. **Held:** the claim succeeded.

In *Williamson v Waldman*,[36] the non-patient, Ms Williamson (W), a cleaner, was emptying a rubbish bin in a dental surgery, when she was pricked with a lancet. The lancet should have been disposed of in a sharps container, but it had been negligently put in the common rubbish bin instead. W became alarmed over the potential of contracting AIDS, and was tested several times, all of which were negative. W received medical advice that her chances of having contracted HIV from the finger prick were 'slim or remote'. Nevertheless, W sued the HCPs who operated the surgery, alleging that their disposal practices had negligently caused her anxiety and emotional distress. **Held:** the claim succeeded (at least for the relevant 'window of anxiety').

In *Madrid v Lincoln County Medical Center*,[37] the non-patient, Ms Madrid (M), was transporting medical samples from the Medical Center to laboratories in Albuquerque. During the trip, one of the sample containers leaked, and M was splashed with bloody fluid. At the time, M had unhealed paper cuts on her hands which came in contact with the bloody fluid. M feared that she may have contracted AIDS, by contact with blood or other bodily fluids through these unhealed cuts. She was tested for HIV several times over a six-month to one-year period, although the sample blood did not test positive for HIV, and nor did M. **Held:** the claim could possibly succeed; so matter sent to trial.

In *Funeral Services by Gregory Inc v Bluefield Community Hospital*,[38] the non-patient, Mr Gregory (G), a mortician, unknowingly embalmed the corpse of an AIDS victim, 'John Doe'. The only medical history about JD reported by the defendant hospital concerned his pneumonia and use of antibiotics. On the day of JD's funeral, G learned that JD had AIDS at the time of his death. Although G wore protective clothing, including gloves, during the embalming, which entailed direct physical contact with the blood, tissue, and other body fluids of the corpse, G claimed that after learning that the corpse was an AIDS victim, he and his wife lived in fear of AIDS. G claimed damages for emotional distress stemming from that fear. **Held:** the claim failed.

The reasons for these different outcomes essentially turns upon the actual-exposure-versus-potential-exposure requirement in US jurisprudence, and will be considered in Section E.

Finally, it is of legal interest to consider developments in Canada and Australia, where the legal approach to pure psychiatric illness claims follows a broadly similar (but certainly not identical) path to England's. Due, in no small part, to the sophisticated class actions legislation in place in the Canadian provinces,[39] Canadian case law has thrown up a very interesting cluster of medically-rooted fear-of-the-future cases. Typically, in these types of class actions, there may be a variety of sub-classes—infected patients, persons who contracted disease from infected patients (cross-infected claimants), and the non-infected claimants who are either patients or true non-patients (e.g., hospital visitors) who are waiting to see whether they develop the disease. Hence, these cases tend to generate a real variety of legal issues. Several of them have turned upon the first certification requirement in class actions litigation, *viz*, whether 'the pleadings disclose a cause of action', for which the threshold is not high—in fact, it has been termed 'extremely low'.[40] Hence, some of these fear-of-the-future claims in Canada have not proceeded to full trial, but have been considered in the preliminary certification or strike-out context, and must be considered in that light. Although Canadian fear-of-the-future cases have arisen in other scenarios too,[41] it is the medical negligence context that provides real interest. The leading Canadian non-patient fear-of-the-future claim arose out of undiagnosed TB (the class of cross-infected claimants has been previously considered in Chapter 4):

In *Healey v Lakeridge Health Corp*,[42] patient AB was admitted to a Toronto hospital very ill. AB's illness went undiagnosed for some period of time, until TB was revealed by tests. Shortly thereafter, AB died. The health authorities issued a news release, notifying that, as a precaution, they would notify all individuals who may have been in contact with AB (visitors to the hospital, as well as other patients) to determine the extent of their exposure and whether they required TB testing. Almost 3,000 individuals were contacted. In the end, 164 tested positive to TB but none had developed the active (as distinct from a latent) form of the disease. Over 2,500 uninfected persons (mainly hospital visitors) formed a sub-class, claiming damages for the psychological trauma of being told of the possibility of infection, and the resultant uncertainty as to whether they were infected with TB until they received negative test results. This sub-class alleged that the defendant hospital and treating respirologist, failed to exercise reasonable care in their diagnosis and treatment of AB's tuberculosis. **Held:** a potential cause of action existed; class action was permitted to proceed.[43]

As a final point of interest, Australia has also seen some unfortunate CJD litigation involving participants in a medical treatment programme:

> In *APQ v Commonwealth Serum Laboratories*,[44] the claimant was treated as a patient, between 1980–85, with human pituitary gonadotrophins ('HPG'), manufactured from human pituitary glands, as part of a fertility treatment programme. It emerged that the risk of developing CJD arose from the HPG used in the treatment. **Held:** the patient's claim survived a strike-out application.[45]

In any English legal treatment of the subject, a particular difficulty is the issue of whether any *damage* can be established, negligence only being actionable on proof of damage[46] (and something more than *de minimis* damages at that[47]). Australian[48] and Canadian[49] decisions have also noted that fear-of-the-future litigation is an area in which courts have been asked to express a view upon whether a cause of action exists *at all*. The question of a recognisable injury is addressed in the following section.

C PROVING A LEGALLY-RECOGNISABLE INJURY

When a person is fearing the worst, and living with the knowledge that, through medical negligence of some type, he may be struck down with a serious disease in the future, anxieties may well develop, even if that risk of future disease is ever so remote.

In the *Pleural Plaques* employment litigation, there was only a 5% risk of developing mesothelioma, and a 1% risk of developing asbestosis.[50] The litigation shows, however, that for some claimants, worries about the future can constitute a significant blight on their lives—even more so, than for some who *have suffered* negligently-caused physical injuries. In that litigation, Mr Grieves was the only test claimant to be able to point to a recognisable psychiatric injury—for his co-claimants, it became a 'scrap' as to whether they had suffered any legally-recognised 'damage' at all. They lost that argument.

The crucial point is that, under English law, a 'freestanding claim' for damages for *mere anxiety* arising from exposure to the risk of contracting a disease—without being attached to any physical injury on the claimant's part—constitutes a claim for *pure* mental harm. For that sort of claim, any disorder that falls short of a genuine psychiatric disorder is not permitted at law. Hence, the question arises—should a fear-of-the-future claimant be required to prove a genuine psychiatric illness (as discussed in Section 1 below), or should some lesser serious psychological trauma suffice for fear-of-the-future claims (as canvassed in Section 2)? Clearly, the arguments on this question are not all one-sided. Furthermore, judges in other jurisdictions have increasingly become concerned about precluding anxiety-based claims for those claimants who are fearful of developing a future disease or illness.

1. Why a 'genuine psychiatric illness' should be mandatory for fear-of-the-future claimants

In the *CJD Litigation*, Morland J categorically stated: '[i]t is not enough that distress and upset has been caused by becoming aware of the risk. Natural ordinary persistent worry and concern about the risk does not suffice.'[51]

In fact, three key reasons have been postulated by courts who have dealt with fear-of-the-future claims, both in England and elsewhere, to support the traditional view that pure psychiatric claims of any type **must** be based on nothing less than a genuine psychiatric illness.

First, the requirement of a genuine psychiatric illness ring-fences the potential number of fear-of-the-future claimants. It acts as a 'powerful control mechanism'[52] (as Morland J put it). As such, the reason why anxiety cannot be treated as a free-standing head of damage has variously been judicially described as 'one of policy',[53] and as promoting 'some degree of discipline in the application of this type of claim'.[54]

Hence, in the Australian decision of *APQ v Commonwealth Serum Laboratories Ltd*,[55] where the operator of the fertility programme argued that the case against it was flawed because 'mere worry or fear about the contraction of a disease is not sufficient to sustain the plaintiff's cause of action', Harper J disagreed: 'her allegations [are] about severe stress syndrome, severe psychiatric reaction, depression and shock'.

Secondly, there is the prospect that allowing recovery for mere anxiety could actually *create* that type of 'psychological injury'. Morland J put this reasoning forward early on in the *CJD Litigation*:

> Every man and woman will receive bad news about himself or herself ... It is the inevitable experience of life. Naturally, such bad news will cause grief, stress, worry, concern, unhappiness, a feeling of being depressed. Such reactions are normal. Their severity will vary from person to person. Every man and woman is expected to face such situations with such fortitude as he or she can muster. In my judgment, it would be an unhealthy society that thought it was entitled to monetary compensation in such situations. Indeed, the existence of the belief to such entitlement might well create the psychological injury which otherwise would not have occurred.[56]

Thirdly, there is the problem of defining what, precisely, is 'anxiety', and quantifying the damages for it. On the question of a possible duty to take reasonable care not to cause anxiety by exposing employees to asbestos, the Court of Appeal majority in *Pleural Plaques* remarked:

> The difficulty of proving anxiety, of determining the moment at which a cause of action arises, and of quantifying damages in respect of both past and future anxiety may be reason enough for not permitting free-standing claims for this form of prejudice.[57]

On the quantification point, the majority concluded that, if damages for mere anxiety were to be awarded, there would be a 'too much or too little' dilemma arising:

> An award of damages in such a case could only be computed on the basis of the chance of contracting the disease. The passage of time is bound to demonstrate that the award was unjust. If the Claimant contracts the disease, the award that he has received will be inadequate compensation. If he does not, it will become apparent that he has received a windfall award at the expense of the Defendant.[58]

However, the majority went on to note that this 'unsatisfactory state of affairs' is equally true where the claimant suffers from some physical injury, and obtains as part of his 'pain and suffering' damages an amount to compensate him for the risk of subsequent disease (which may or may not develop).[59] Hence, it must be acknowledged that this particular 'policy justification' for refusing free-standing anxiety-based damages is not a particularly strong one.

In addition to these reasons, English courts have set out a number of reasons for requiring a pure psychiatric illness in *any* context in which physical damage has not been suffered, which reasons have been fully considered in Chapter 8.[60]

2. Falling short: the options

Given two legal propositions—that anxiety, fear, worry and/or similar human emotion, falling short of a genuine psychiatric illness, is not legally compensable, *and* that the risk of something bad happening in the future, by way of disease or illness developing, is not an 'injury' that is compensable on its own either[61]—what avenues does a non-patient have, to press his claim for damages?

There are two possible options. First, the non-patient may seek to prove an anxiety-based claim is a *consequential* component of a physical injury claim (so as to make the claim for the risk of contracting a future disease parasitic upon that physical injury claim, which is permitted). Or secondly, the non-patient may argue that, notwithstanding the arguments summarised in Section 1 above, anxiety *should* provide a proper base for pure psychiatric illness claims in the specific context of fear-of-the-future claims.

There is support for both positions away from England's shores, but neither appears to have any present prospects of success in English courts. Dealing with each, and drawing particularly upon judicial discussion in *medical negligence* cases to date:

(a) A consequential fear-of-the-future claim

If a HCP's act or omission causes some physical injury to a claimant, and this also has created the risk that the claimant will suffer *further* physical damage in the future (say, some disease or illness), then general damages will be increased to reflect the chance of that physical injury manifesting in the future. The cause of action is complete upon proof of the *immediate* physical damage, and then damages are recoverable for any anxiety associated with the knowledge that a disease could later develop. In *Pleural Plaques*, this point was articulated by the House of Lords ('if he has a cause of action, his damage must include the risks that other serious conditions might eventuate'[62]), by the majority in the Court of Appeal ('no claim can be made in respect of the chance of contracting a future disease if this is not consequent upon some physical injury'[63]) and by the dissenter in the Court of Appeal ('the risk of serious disease and the concomitant anxiety are not in themselves enough to found a cause of action. To found the cause of action, there must be damage which includes personal injury'[64]).

Hence, if there is some physical injury to the non-patient, then the fear of developing a future disease would be attached to, or *consequential* upon, physical injury, and anxiety would simply be one of the components of the 'pain and suffering' or 'loss of amenity' assessment.[65] Essentially, anxiety-based damages become a form of 'parasitic damages' upon the 'host claim' for physical injury.[66] Of course, this avenue conveniently circumvents the legal requirement for the claimant to prove a recognisable psychiatric illness.

Again, the English legal position described above is policy-based—proof of some physical damage acts as a boundary rope around the possible number of anxiety-based claims.[67] The consequence of this is that those claimants 'fortunate' enough to have suffered some physical injury can recover for anxiety-based damages (falling well short of a recognisable psychiatric illness), whereas those claimants who suffer no physical injury cannot recover anything for debilitating anxieties about developing a future illness, unless they can prove a genuine psychiatric illness and thereby bring a free-standing claim for pure psychiatric illness—however arbitrary or unfair that dividing line might appear.[68]

Unsurprisingly, then, for a non-patient whose mental injury falls short of a genuine psychiatric injury, it will be to that non-patient's advantage, in a fear-of-the-future claim, to assert that he *did* suffer some form of physical injury or harm, in addition to his fear of developing the disease. At least four 'physical harms' have variously been alleged, in relevant cases from England and elsewhere—but with very mixed success.

Some physiological change to the human body

If a HCP's act or omission means that the non-patient suffers some physiological change in the non-patient's body, then that change could herald disease in the future (even if there is no statistical probability that disease will develop if the physiological change has occurred). Furthermore, as a 'bottom line', the non-patient was not born with that condition—it has resulted from the exposure.

This was one of the most important aspects of the English pleural plaques litigation. All claimants other than Mr Grieves (for only Mr Grieves had been diagnosed with depression) argued that the very presence of pleural plaques in their lung linings constituted a physiological change to their bodies which amounted to physical damage, to which their anxiety could 'tag' (and they had a line of authority which appeared to support that very proposition with respect to pleural plaques[69]). However, this submission was rejected unanimously by the House of Lords[70] (and by the Court of Appeal below, by majority[71]). They had not suffered physical injury of any type, their anxiety was therefore a free-standing claim, and hence, they could not recover because they had suffered no legally-recognisable injury which English law would compensate. The view that no damage was sustained by these employees, merely because of a physiological change in the body, has received weighty support, with the leading English commentary on damages concluding that the House of Lords' decision was 'rightly held, departing from two decades of first instance decisions'.[72] The opposing points of view that emerged during the *Pleural Plaques* appellate litigation are shown in Table 9.1.

It follows that, for non-patients too, the possibility of physical injury *damage* being proven by some sub-cellular or physiological change to the human body is likely doomed to fail in English law, in light of *Pleural Plaques*.

Interestingly, some American courts have anticipated that physical change to a body's cellular or molecular systems, as a result of exposure to a specific toxin, *could be* sufficient to constitute damage under the so-called 'physical manifestation rule'.[73] That rule reflects the same principle as in English law—it requires the claimant to prove that the defendant's negligence caused the claimant to suffer 'accompanying physical injury, illness, or other physical consequences'. For example, in *Potter v Firestone Inc*,[74] an impairment of a claimant's immune system arising from cellular damage was argued to be damage, but the issue was not ultimately decided; in *Brafford v Susquehanna Corporation*,[75] evidence of chromosomal damage ('present, permanent, and irreparable genetic and chromosomal damage as a result of their exposure to the radiation emitted from the mill tailings') was held to raise a question of fact as to whether it could be a 'a definite, present physical injury'; and in *Werlein v US*,[76] the court accepted that it was a matter for trial as to whether the claimant who had been exposed to contaminated air and drinking water had suffered an actual physical injury 'in the form of chromosomal breakage, and damage to the cardiovascular and immunal systems'. In this last-mentioned case, the District Court of Minnesota remarked that 'the human body is a complex organism',[77] and, by implication, it was a similarly-complex

Table 9.1   The pleural plaques debate

Why the plaques did **not** constitute damage (majority of CA, unanimously in the HL):	Why the plaques did constitute damage (Smith LJ, CA):
• fibre penetration + the risk that the asbestos fibres could give rise to disease + anxiety generated about this risk did not, in combination, equal injury (rendering the 'aggregation theory' of damage of nil effect: 'nought plus nought plus nought equals nought'[78]); • a *de minimis* threshold of damage is required, and something that is symptomless, having no adverse effect on any bodily function, and having no effect on appearance, does not surmount that threshold; • pleural plaques do not increase susceptibility to other asbestos-related diseases, or shorten life expectancy, so 'damage' could not be constructed on that basis either; • a mere physiological change in the body is not sufficient to constitute damage in English law; • damage is an abstract concept of being worse off, physically or economically, it does not simply mean a physical change; • policy reasons dictated *against* holding this to be damage—to find that the plaques were 'damage' would encourage litigation by employees against employers, litigation is stressful for claimants, this type of litigation may be driven by claims managers, and the costs of the litigation will far exceed the damages recovered;[79] • some claimants may accept final awards, and therefore preclude themselves from ever claiming for future asbestos-related diseases.	• symptoms could result from large amounts of plaques (coughing, breathlessness), but it is not the symptoms which are the injury, it is the plaques themselves —symptoms merely show how serious the injury is; • pleural plaques are no different from a skin lesion or scar on the outside skin of the body—both hidden plaques and lesions amount to a 'tissue change' and, as such, constitute an injury to the body; • pleural plaques should be treated as a disease because they were capable of progression.

question as to what constituted an 'injury' to it. It must be said, though, that other US courts have strongly resisted the notion that physiological change can be equated to damage.[80]

Academically, US commentators such as d'Entremont[81] have questioned whether a physiological change in the body (such as sub-cellular damage) *should* constitute damage, in an era when low doses of chemicals found in common products (e.g., cosmetics, perfumes, and even in the resins that line food cans), which are presently considered safe, may in fact pose significant dangers to human health in the future, and when scientific investigative techniques are becoming more capable of greater accuracy. However, d'Entremont argues:

Assuming that [fear-of-the-future] claims could be established based solely on evidence of subcellular damage, it is easy to imagine widespread use of screening programs to seek out as many potential plaintiffs as possible, regardless of the relative merits of such claims. Such a scenario could easily overwhelm the justice system with less than meritorious suits. In addition, it risks unnecessarily eroding the assets of culpable manufacturers and other parties by forcing them to defend claims brought by individuals who suffer no present impairment, thereby potentially diminishing the assets available to compensate the most aggrieved or seriously injured parties. Given these considerations, at this point the potential of toxicogenomics to breathe new life into most fear of cancer claims appears limited.[82]

Similarly to this assessment, the *Pleural Plaques* litigation appears to preclude any argument, by non-patients against HCPs, that anxiety-based damages could be consequential upon some physiological injury.

Physical disturbance from an injection

Can physical harm be based on an immunisation injection given to a non-patient, *after* the exposure, in order to reduce the prospects of the disease developing in the future?

In *Fakhri v Alfalfa's Canada Inc*[83] (a non-medical case, concerning distribution of food contaminated with the Hepatitis A virus), it was suggested by the British Columbia Court of Appeal that the very fact that some of the claimants underwent an immunisation serum injection within two weeks of consuming the contaminated food, to seek to prevent Hepatitis A from developing, constituted a 'physical disturbance' that could attract damages of itself, without the need to prove a genuine psychiatric disorder. The court did not need to decide the issue, however.

Physical symptoms from the exposure

It has been suggested by some US jurisprudence[84] that, where the claimant suffers from physical symptoms (e.g., headaches, nausea, insomnia) that flow naturally and proximately from exposure to a toxic agent, then that could constitute the necessary physical injury upon which anxiety-based damages could be 'tagged'.

Cantley, however, has called this a requirement that there be a 'physical manifestation' of injury, and criticises it as both distorting the physical injury requirement and for encouraging 'exaggerated pleading' of the claimant's anxiety symptoms.[85]

Mere ingestion of substances

Finally, can the mere ingestion of substances into the human body constitute damage, even if no physiological change can be pointed to by the non-patient as constituting the damage, to which anxiety-based damages can be tagged?

In *Ring v Canada (A G)*,[86] which concerned exposure to herbicides on the part of those who resided on a military base, and where fears of future lymphomas (cancers of the lymph nodes) was claimed, the Canadian government argued that the claimants who had not been diagnosed with a lymphoma had failed to establish a cause of action because they were seeking a remedy without having first established an injury. However, the court held that there *was* a compensable physical harm at issue here—'[t]he injury the Plaintiffs say they have suffered is the absorption of toxic chemicals, which may cause lymphomas in the future.'[87]

Some US case law[88] also supports the notion that inhalation, ingestion or absorption of hazardous chemicals is, of itself, sufficient to satisfy the requirement that the claimant suffered some physical injury or illness, and that, 'although the effects of the exposures may be undetectable for long periods of time, the plaintiffs have suffered a present physical effect as a result.'[89] Where this argument has been successful, courts have turned a deaf ear to a defendant's pleas that the claimant did not present proper proof of physical manifestation since there was no medical evidence that chemical particles affected any internal organ. The mere ingestion of the toxic agent was sufficient.

Summary

As things stand, English authority does not support that any of these four 'things' can constitute physical damage upon which a claim for anxiety-based damages could be grafted. Indeed, *Pleural Plaques* positively rejects the first-mentioned—mere physiological change which is symptomless—as constituting 'injury'.

Hence, if a HCP causes a non-patient physical injury, then that claimant's general damages will include compensation for 'pain and suffering', and this may include damages to compensate for the anxiety of developing a future disease or for the fear of dying prematurely from contracting a disease in the future. However, in most fear-of-the-future cases, an already-incurred physical damage is impossible to point to, which rules out a free-standing claim for damages for mere anxiety—or does it?

(b) Should anxiety about the future be sufficient?

It is apparent that a more relaxed view about anxiety-based damages has been mooted by Canadian jurisprudence—to the extent that the leading Canadian commentator on the law of damages notes that cautious increments in extending liability in Canadian law appear to be in the wind:

> The law of torts has been understandably reluctant to establish a cause of action for negligent injury to feelings and mental distress standing alone but it seems to be moving in the direction of enlarging liability.[90]

Given this development, the question arises—insofar as fear-of-the-future claims are concerned, *should* the anxiety and fear of developing a future disease be a free-standing basis for damage, in and of itself, in English law too? Should the English legal position on this point be amended from its present high threshold of requiring a genuine psychiatric illness? It is of interest to note that four arguments have been judicially put forward by Canadian judges[91] as to why stand-alone anxiety-based damages should be compensable.

First, it has been suggested that a lesser standard of illness simply warrants a lesser sum of damages. In the Canadian case of *Vanek v Great Atlantic & Pacific Co of Canada*,[92] a 'chronic anxiety' about the prospect of a family member developing long-term consequences from ingesting a toxic substance from a drink container, which fell short of a psychiatric illness, was compensable at trial. The Ontario General Division described this reasoning from an earlier case[93] as having 'unassailable logic and good sense':[94]

> It is difficult to rationalize awarding damages for physical scratches and bruises of a minor nature but refusing damages for deep emotional distress which falls short of a psychiatric condition. Trivial physical injury attracts trivial damages. It would seem logical to deal with trivial emotional injury on the same basis, rather than by denying the claim altogether.[95]

However, when the decision was appealed, the Ontario Court of Appeal ultimately held that it was not reasonably foreseeable that the Vaneks would suffer any psychiatric damage, and specifically refused to deal with the psychiatric illness-versus- mere-anxiety point.[96]

Secondly, it is arguable that mere emotional distress is even more foreseeable, and hence, worthy of compensation. In *Mason v Westside Cemeteries Ltd*, Ontario judge Molloy J noted:

> I cannot see any reason to deny compensation for the emotional pain of a person who, although suffering, does not degenerate emotionally to the point of actual psychiatric illness. Surely emotional distress is a more foreseeable result from a negligent act than is a psychiatric illness.[97]

However, insofar as English law is concerned, this clearly does not take the matter very far, because even should a type of harm be *very* foreseeable, the control mechanisms of proximity and public policy will prove crucial, according to Lord Bridge's test in *Caparo Industries plc v Dickman*.[98]

Thirdly, the point has been made by one Alberta case[99] that to allow free-standing recovery for mental anguish, falling short of a psychiatric illness, would provide symmetry between negligent and deliberate acts, because deliberate infliction of mental distress (per the rule in *Wilkinson v Downton*[100]) can base a cause of action (in English law, however, it is likely that intentionally causing mere *distress* is not sufficient under this rule, and that proof of some recognised psychiatric illness is required[101]). More significantly for English purposes, though, Waddams makes the point[102] that, since compensation for mental distress that flows from breach of contract is permitted by English courts,[103] then it would provide symmetry to the law if tortiously-caused mental distress were also to be actionable.

Finally, it has been suggested that a lower-level type of harm works, provided that it is circumscribed by a suitable ring-fence—which the requirement of an *actual exposure* to the toxic agent provides. In *Morris v Johnson Controls Ltd*,[104] a Manitoban exposure-to-asbestos-in-the-workplace case, Master Harrison allowed the case to proceed to trial, noting that the claimants had been exposed to air-borne asbestos dust over a two-week period, so that there had been actual exposure to a dangerous product, and hence, their fears of future illness were objectively reasonable. In that regard, the Master referred to some American jurisprudence which applies an 'actual exposure + objectively-reasonable fears' requirement to limit the number of possible claims. That Canadian courts should adopt the more fluid American approach, over that of their more restrictive English counterparts, has received approval from one commentator:

> it is not uncommon in the 'fear of future illness' cases for Canadian courts to refer to the American jurisprudence. This may be explained by the fact that in many of these cases the need to prove a recognizable psychiatric illness is perceived as an unduly severe burden on deserving plaintiffs. The American approach which emphasizes the nature of the exposure and the reasonableness of the fear and de-emphasizes the seriousness of the harm is attractive.[105]

This US approach to fear-of-the-future litigation is considered more fully in Section E.

(c) Conclusion

Notwithstanding the position that has been adopted or argued for in the Canadian decisions mentioned above—that anxiety arising from the fear of developing some dreaded disease, is or should be sufficient—clearly, it is not the case in England.

House of Lords authority has consistently established that a genuine psychiatric illness is a mandatory precondition for *all* pure psychiatric illness claims, and the Lords showed no inclination in *Pleural Plaques* to create an exception within the context of fear-of-the-future claims (hence, Mr Grieves, who suffered from depression, was the only test claimant able to take his claim forward). Law reform also supports that position in England: when the English Law Commission examined the area of psychiatric illness in 1998, it accepted that the law is willing to compensate for recognisable psychiatric illnesses but not for lesser reactions such as grief or distress,[106] and its draft legislation clearly was predicated upon that assumption too.[107]

Hence, assuming that a non-patient can prove that his worry about developing a disease in the future amounts to a genuine psychiatric illness (as could all the CJD claimants, and Mr Grieves), the next conundrum is whether a HCP owed the non-patient a duty to prevent that type of harm.

D PROVING THE DUTY IN ENGLISH LAW

1. Denying fear-of-the-future claimants primary victim status

As discussed in Chapter 8,[108] recovery for free-standing psychiatric injury depends, in the main, upon whether the claimant is a primary or a secondary victim.

Clearly, fear-of-the-future claimants cannot be secondary victims. However, nor do they look much like the car accident victim Mr Page either, as being in the zone of immediate physical danger from the HCP's acts or omissions but who suffer from psychiatric injury instead.[109] (It will be recalled that the principle in *Page v Smith* allows that type of primary victim to recover for psychiatric illness, even if it was not foreseeable in all the circumstances.)

English law has been quite emphatic—fear-of-the-future claimants are **not** primary victims under the principle of *Page v Smith*. It has been decreed that the principle in *Page v Smith* cannot properly be extended, so as to render a defendant who negligently exposes a claimant to the risk of contracting a disease, liable for free-standing psychiatric injury caused by the fear of contracting the disease.[110] The reasons given in the *CJD Litigation*[111] and in *Pleural Plaques*[112] for this conclusion are summarised in Table 9.2.

Nevertheless, despite their lack of primary victim status, fear-of-the-future claimants have been able to recover for pure psychiatric injury, under a separate route—under the ordinary *Caparo* test for establishing a duty of care for novel scenarios. Morland J permitted this in the CJD Litigation, and even in *Pleural Plaques*, where Mr Grieves, the sufferer of a depressive illness, lost his fear-of-the-future claim, both House of Lords and Court of Appeal considered that the ordinary principles of negligence offered, theoretically at least, an 'alternative route'[113] to possible recovery for these particular claimants.

These cases aptly demonstrate that there are certain claimants who do not fit comfortably within the primary-versus-secondary-victim dichotomy, but whom the law considers to have deserving claims for compensable psychiatric illness (work-related stress claims is another category which has stepped outside the primary-secondary victim dichotomy, to assume a niche of its own[114]). Indeed, it is difficult not to conclude that Morland J was striving to garner some path to recovery for the CJD claimants before him who lived with the prospect, however small, of a horrendous death from an untreatable illness.[115]

Table 9.2   **Why fear-of-the-future claimants are *not* primary victims**

- in *Page v Smith*, all physical danger had passed by the time that the psychiatric illness (chronic fatigue syndrome) manifested, whereas for the CJD claimants, they feared contracting a ghastly terminal disease in the future, the physical danger for them was very much in the future—hence, this was 'so far removed' from the factual situation of *Page v Smith* (*Pleural Plaques*, HL; *CJD Litigation*);
- in *Page v Smith*, the defendant's negligent driving which exposed the other driver to the risk of physical injury, and the onset of the latter's psychiatric injury, were simultaneous or contemporaneous, whereas in the *CJD Litigation*, the two events—receiving the injections and the onset of the psychiatric illness—could be years apart, separated by receiving the news that was the actual cause of the psychiatric injury to the CJD claimants (*Pleural Plaques*, HL; *CJD Litigation*);
- in *Page v Smith*, the claimant was involved in a traumatic event (the car accident), a participant in what was happening around him, which induced in him a sudden shock and triggered the psychiatric illness; whereas the actual act of injecting Hartree HGH was not traumatic in the *Page v Smith* sense, nor was it the precise trigger for psychiatric illness—rather, the traumatic event for the CJD claimants was learning afterwards of the news of the possibility of contracting CJD, so that the shock was quite removed from the negligent act itself (*Pleural Plaques*, HL; *CJD Litigation*);
- certain American authority[116] has doubted whether a claimant who was negligently exposed to the risk of asbestos-induced cancer could be treated as being in the 'zone of danger' (*Pleural Plaques*, CA);[117]
- in English law,[118] recovery for psychiatric illness in tort is based upon the 'thus far and no further' strategy of judicial law-making; so that if fear-of-the-future claimants were to be treated as primary victims to whom a duty was owed to prevent psychiatric injury, it was up to Parliament to develop the law in that regard (*Pleural Plaques*, CA);
- the HGH recipients were not primary victims for policy reasons—if they were so categorised, then so too could many other persons who had been exposed to dangerous substances—primary victims could possibly include those who had consumed contaminated food or water, or lived near radiation-emitting premises, having 'ramifications [that] would be incalculable'—insurance could be difficult to obtain by manufacturers and service providers who supplied a huge range of products to the market which could possibly cause disease in the future—also, warnings about the dangers posed by a product or processed food could be precluded for fear that, among those who had already used the product or eaten the food, some might bring a claim as a primary victim for psychiatric injury triggered by the warning (*CJD Litigation*).

---

2. Recovery under the *Caparo* test

Under the *Caparo* test, in order to establish that a duty of care was owed to the non-patient by the HCP to avoid the psychiatric injury caused by worrying about developing a disease in the future, the non-patient would need to prove (1) the non-patient's *psychiatric* injury was a reasonably foreseeable consequence of the HCP's breach of duty; (2) the non-patient and the HCP were in a sufficiently proximate relationship; and (3) no public policy reasons precluded the HCP from owing the non-patient a duty to prevent the psychiatric injury.[119]

In fact, the primary victim (*Page v Smith*) route would have three advantages over the *Caparo* route, for fear-of-the-future claimants. First, it is not fatal to a primary victim's claim if his psychiatric injury is so unlikely as to be unforeseeable, because a reasonable foreseeability of *physical* injury is sufficient—it does not matter if his psychiatric injury was unforeseeable. *Caparo*-type claimants do not enjoy the fruits of that flexible test. Secondly, primary victims do not have to be persons of ordinary fortitude—a duty can be owed towards them even if they are abnormally susceptible to psychiatric injury (and, in that sense, a defendant must 'take a primary victim as he finds him'—so that even those who are particularly susceptible to psychiatric illness, as Mr Page was because of a 'recrudescence' of a pre-existing condition, ME, can recover under the *Page v Smith* principle).[120] By contrast, in *all* other cases of pure psychiatric illness recovery, including for *Caparo*-type claimants, the claimant must prove that it was reasonably foreseeable that the event which actually happened would cause psychiatric illness to a person of reasonable fortitude.[121] Thirdly, a primary victim's proof that he was in the zone of danger also couches the relationship between defendant and psychiatrically-injured claimant as being one of sufficient proximity (i.e., proximity is, essentially, *presumed*, because of the zone of danger in which the claimant was placed by the defendant's negligence), whereas *Caparo*-type claimants must prove proximity via relational and other proximity means.

In fact, the *Caparo*-type elements were dealt with in contrasting fashions in *Pleural Plaques* and the *CJD Litigation*.

(a) Reasonable foreseeability of psychiatric harm

Psychiatric injury on the part of the HGH recipients was readily foreseeable in the *CJD Litigation*. Factors that contributed to this finding were: the particularly gruesome prospect that confronted the recipients of Hartree HGH,[122] the fact that some recipients had died from CJD (rendering the prospect, whilst unlikely, a reality),[123] and the fact that media reports of the issue tended to sensationalise and distort the facts in a way that was likely to have a depressing and distressing impact upon the recipients.[124]

Furthermore, the normal fortitude rule was met in the *CJD Litigation*. Morland J held that the operators of the clinical trial should have reasonably foreseen that, if deaths occurred from CJD caused by contaminated Hartree HGH, some of the recipients, *including some of normal phlegm and ordinary fortitude*, might well suffer psychiatric injury on becoming aware of the risk to them. Then, any recipient, regardless of 'whether of normal phlegm and ordinary fortitude or having a vulnerable personality, who can prove that his psychiatric illness was caused by his becoming aware of the risk of CJD to him and that he has suffered a genuine psychiatric illness, can recover compensation.'[125] As mentioned in Chapter 8,[126] if the reasonable fortitude rule can be met, then even individuals of vulnerable nervous disposition can recover—the rule does not mean that *only* persons of reasonable fortitude can recover.

By contrast, Mr Grieves failed to prove the test of foreseeability in his fear-of-the-future claim. His depression was not a reasonably foreseeable consequence of his employer's breach of duty in failing to protect its employees against asbestos dust.[127] According to the medical evidence, Mr Grieves presented as a most unusual patient—his clinical depression was a complication which apparently arose because he had long-feared developing an asbestos-related disease, ever since he had learnt about the dangers of exposure some decades previously. One medical expert, who had assessed a cohort of about 80 men with asbestos exposure, called his case, 'relatively unique'.[128] It could not be proven that employees of normal fortitude would have suffered genuine psychiatric injury if they were in Mr Grieves' position of learning that, as a result of developing pleural plaques, their exposure to asbestos carried with it a risk of developing mesothelioma, lung cancer or other serious disorder.[129]

Hence, a non-patient can recover compensation for a genuine psychiatric illness, caused as a result of living with the anxiety that a serious illness could manifest in the future as a result of being exposed to a disease-causing agent by some medical negligence of a HCP, where a non-patient of reasonable fortitude could foreseeably have reacted in that way. Having proven that, then it matters not that the particular non-patient may have been an obsessive or neurotic type who was predisposed to suffering psychiatric illness through the worry and fear of the worst to come—at that point, the HCP must take his non-patient as he finds him.

(b) Proximity between healthcare professional and non-patient

The *CJD Litigation* was an unusual case, whereby the recipients of the HGH had a relationship with their treating HCPs that was 'akin to that of doctor and patient, one of close proximity'. As children at the time of the therapeutic trial, they were vulnerably-placed, they were labouring under disability ('the purpose of the treatment was to improve the child's prospects in adulthood—both physically and, significantly, psychologically—of coping with life. The children were handicapped by dwarfism'), the HCPs were undertaking highly skilled and specialist medical services, all the claimants were identifiable to the defendants, and the defendants were monopolistic providers of the medical services and of the information given to the claimants, which, in turn, enhanced the claimants' vulnerability.[130] By 1 July 1977, information had been received by the Department of Health which indicated that it was unsafe to continue with the clinical trials, which was communicated to key Committees with an advice to immediately withdraw HGH supplies for clinical use, but this was not done.

On the other hand, non-patients who are *unknown* to the HCPs, when the medical act or omission occurs which exposes the non-patient to the risk of future illness or disease, may find proof of proximity between themselves and the HCPs somewhat more difficult. The issue was a prominent one in *Healey v Lakeridge Health Corp*,[131] for the uninfected class who had been exposed to TB by their contact with patient AB, and who were advised by a public health authority or hospital that they may have contracted TB and should be tested.[132] Although Cullity J did not need to form any concluded view on the issue,[133] his Honour pointed to some potential proximity factors. First, the uninfected class were those who were in close physical proximity to AB—because that very physical proximity identified those individuals who were particularly exposed to the risk of harm.[134] Secondly, the regional health department was statutorily required[135] to inform the public health authorities of AB's infection in a timely manner, and in turn, it was necessary that all persons who were exposed to TB by their contact with AB had to be contacted by a public health authority or by the hospital with advice about their potential exposure. The intervention of governmental or regulatory authorities as a consequence of a hospital's breach of a duty regarding a patient, and the defined class of uninfected individuals who had to be contacted in this way, assisted in establishing proximity between the hospital/HCPs and those non-patients affected by such intervention.[136]

Of course, in fear-of-the-future claims, the non-patients' psychiatric injuries are **not** triggered by the actual medically-negligent act (the missed TB diagnosis, the ear tissue transplant, the injection of human growth hormone, etc.). That act is merely 'a potent causative fact in the development of psychiatric injury'.[137] It is *learning of the risk* of developing a future disease—at some point after the medical negligence—that triggers the psychiatric illness. The English legal position is that, provided that the claims are brought within the relevant limitation periods for negligently-inflicted damage,[138] the interval between breach and psychiatric injury does not preclude temporal proximity. In the *CJD Litigation*, Morland J expressly dealt with this point:

> I can see no logical reason why foreseeability of, or responsibility for, shock and psychiatric injury should be limited to an area of time contemporaneous or almost contemporaneous with the negligent physical event, i.e., the injection of Hartree HGH. If the psychiatric injury was reasonably foreseeable, it should be untrammelled by spatial physical or temporal limits ... I do not consider that a delay between the shock of the news of the first cases of CJD and the onset of the psychiatric injury should defeat a plaintiff's claim. A psychiatric injury can be readily induced by

an accumulative awareness or drip-feed of information over a prolonged period of time, although the court will scrutinise rigorously a claim so based.[139]

That passage has been cited with approval since.[140] Whether *Caparo*-type claimants have to prove that their psychiatric injury was triggered by 'shock' at all is doubtful[141]—but even so, the shock does not need to be contemporaneous with the medical negligence, at least under the *Caparo* route to recovery.

(c) Public policy considerations

In the context of medical wrongdoing that exposes a class of *patients* to worries about developing future illness, the potential for 'floodgates' of claims is not a concern, but for a class of *non-patients*, it could be. Any problem of this type was dismissed in the *CJD Litigation*, because the pool of claimants was quite specific—those whose treatment began after 1 July 1977, who received Hartree HGH, and who could prove a genuine psychiatric illness: '[o]nly a very small number of these could qualify for compensation. They would probably be numbering tens rather than hundreds.'[142] In *Healey*—regarding the potentially wide class of hospital visitors—the court similarly dealt with any floodgates problem in a robust and pro-claimant way:

> I do not think liability should be considered to be objectionably indeterminate simply because, in theory, any member of the public could have come in contact with AB. The possibility that any member of the public could be on a highway at a particular time is not considered to be inconsistent with duties of care owed to such persons by the drivers of motor vehicles ... Here, the members of the two groups are limited to those who were exposed to TB by their contact with AB, and advised by a public health authority, or by the defendants, that they may have contracted TB.[143]

Cullity J made the point that *extensive* liability does not equate to *indeterminate* liability.[144]

In the leading fear-of-the-future English cases, there is no doubt that policy reasons have figured prominently—in different ways. In the *CJD Litigation*, given what the risk entailed—'not merely the risk of lethal disease, but of a disease which would cause the victim ghastly suffering, not capable of treatment or amelioration',[145] and involving recipients who were disadvantaged children at the time of the treatment—it was a sympathetic case. As Hilson argues,[146] the 'dread factor' too was a likely motivation for the decision. By contrast, in *Pleural Plaques*, the policy reasons which suggested that a free-standing claim for *anxiety-based* damages should **not** be permitted have already been mentioned in Table 9.2. One of these was that a positive result for the employees could possibly encourage employment-linked litigation in the employment context, where claims managers have a considerable influence. In that regard, the 'real' policy reason behind the decision, as a whole, may be as Steele has stated: 'the law's own variation of fear for the future: a largely untested concern over the quantum of liability for asbestos-related diseases.'[147] This is particularly borne out by the Association of British Insurers who noted, when the Court of Appeal litigation was resolved in the employers' favour, that 'their members are delighted with an outcome which could prevent 100,000 court cases, thereby saving the industry £1–£1.4 billion (US$1.79–2.5 bn)'.[148]

3. The case for rethinking fear-of-the-future claims

Bearing in mind the aforementioned discussion in Sections 1 and 2, and for the sake of logical consistency and coherent development in this messy area of law, should fear-of-the-future claimants who wish to proceed against HCPs for some negligent act/omission that creates a risk of future disease or illness, be treated as *primary* victims, rather than as 'special' *Caparo*-type victims who fall outside the traditional primary/secondary victim classification? Arguably, yes—such non-patients should be analysed as primary victims, for four reasons:

(a) The zone-of-danger test

First of all, it is difficult to conceive of how the HGH recipients were **not** individuals in the zone of physical danger created by the medical defendants in the *CJD Litigation*, and how they were not participants, just as much as Mr Page was in his car accident, by virtue of their very exposure to the toxic agent. They met the 'threshold requirement' posed by Lord Steyn in *Frost* that they had, on an objective assessment, been exposed to danger and a risk of physical injury, or reasonably believed that they were so exposed.[149] Moreover, the similarities between Mr Page (who was treated as a primary victim in the zone of danger) and Mr Grieves (who was not so treated, in *Pleural Plaques*) are odd. Both were exposed to danger of physical injury (the car accident and the exposure to asbestos dust, respectively); both suffered extreme reactions to those dangers; both were idiosyncratic claimants, given Mr Page's previous suffering of the psychiatric illness ME, and given Mr Grieves' long-term obsession about asbestos-related diseases; both were exposed to physical danger in the most commonplace of environments where accidents occur on a daily basis (on the roads and in the workplace); and neither suffered a physical injury, but some recognisable psychiatric illness instead. Yet, one recovered over £130,000 in damages, and the other recovered nothing. The opposite ways in which the law treated their claims invites criticism, especially when the legal distinctions drawn between what is a *Page v Smith*-type scenario, and what is not, are blurred at best.

Other academic commentators, such as Wheat,[150] Lee[151] and Jones,[152] all share the view that the CJD recipients fell within the classic primary victim definition—notwithstanding that Morland J did not describe them as such. Similarly, for the non-patient who was in the vicinity of a sick patient (such as in *Healey*), the claimant is still 'directly involved' in the incident, and within the 'zone of danger' around that sick patient.

(b) The timing point

Timing is everything, according to English jurisprudence on why fear-of-the-future claimants are not primary victims. Lord Hope said, in *Pleural Plaques*:

> The category of primary victim should be confined to persons who suffer psychiatric injury caused by fear or distress resulting from involvement in an accident caused by the defendant's negligence or its immediate aftermath. A person like Mr Grieves who suffers psychiatric injury because of something that he may experience in the future as a result of the defendant's past negligence is in an entirely different category. The immediacy that is characteristic of the situation that applies to primary victims as contemplated in *Page v Smith* is lacking in his case.[153]

However, what does 'immediacy' mean? Would the CJD claimants really have teetered into primary victim status, if they had learnt, the same afternoon as receiving the injections, that they could develop an incurable brain-wasting disease in the future? Would it have made a difference if the clinician had shown the HGH recipient a newsflash bulletin, warning of the dangers presented by hormone injections of this sort, at the appointment itself, or in the following days? Again, as with so many areas of the law governing recovery for pure psychiatric illness, the area is bedevilled by distinctions that seem to lack a principled basis.

Furthermore, immediacy was lacking in *W v Essex CC*[154] too, yet the House of Lords permitted the claimant parents there to proceed as potential primary victims. The parents learnt of the shocking news that all four of their children had been sexually abused by a foster child well after the negligent act of the Council in placing that child with them. It invites inconsistency in the law to allow one type of claimant to proceed as primary victim and yet to deny that status to others, where for both, the negligent act and the development of psychiatric injury lacked contemporaneity.

Finally, on the matter of timing, there is an inherent unfairness that emerges in the English case law. Mr Page may have feared physical injury in the car accident, and he was in the 'zone-of-danger' for the instant that it took the collision to happen, but the physical injury was *never* going to happen after that instant. The event was over. Yet he attracted primary victim status, and all the legal advantages that go with it. On the other hand, the 'zone of danger' time period went on and on for the *CJD* and *Grieves* litigants, the risk could manifest as a deadly physical disease at any point in their futures. Yet they were not accorded primary victim status. Jones emphasises this point well: 'if anything, Mr Grieves' claim on the law's benevolence is stronger than Mr Page's, since not only did the foreseeable physical injury in Mr Page's case not occur, it is known (with hindsight, of course) that it never can occur, whereas it is still possible that Mr Grieves' physical injury will materialise.'[155]

If a zone of danger test is to be used to define primary victim status, then surely that zone should be permitted to continue for as long as a risk of future disease *could* manifest.

(c) Extending the *Page v Smith* principle to other scenarios

Of course, whilst the fact scenarios—car accident and medical treatment—differ enormously, *Page v Smith* has been applied equally, in order to accord claimants primary victim status, to traumatic events such as carrying out police surveillance on criminal activity,[156] being shot at in a war zone,[157] and entering a burning building.[158]

Any argument that *Page v Smith* was distinguishable from, or inapplicable to, fear-of-the-future litigation because the two courts were dealing with different factual situations particularly fails to impress when one considers the case of *McLoughlin v Jones*[159]—a case which, like fear-of-the-future claims, involved no physical accident or immediate danger either. In *McLoughlin*, the claimant sued his solicitors in negligence for failing to conduct his trial for grievous bodily harm and robbery with due competence.[160] After three months' imprisonment, the claimant was acquitted, and he sued for the psychiatric injury (depression) caused by his wrongful imprisonment. As a preliminary issue, he was treated as a primary victim—'the same sort of primary victim as the claimant in *Page v Smith*'.[161] Thus, to equate Mr Page's risk of broken bones to Mr McLoughin's wrongful imprisonment clearly extends *Page v Smith* far beyond its original context.

(d) The role of policy

In the *CJD Litigation*, there were a large number of policy reasons canvassed by Morland J as to why the HGH recipients could not be deemed to be primary victims (these have been canvassed in Table 9.2). To these, however, two counterpoints may be made.

First, in *Pleural Plaques*, Lord Hoffmann rather doubted Morland J's concern that psychiatric injury caused by the apprehension of illness related to exposure to asbestos, radiation, or contaminated food would become actionable at the behest of primary victims—'[w]hether such liability would have the disastrous consequences for society which the judge predicted may be debatable'.[162] Nevertheless, Lord Hoffmann continued, fear-of-the-future claims 'would involve an extension of the [*Page v Smith*] principle to cases which I do not think were contemplated by the House.'[163] However, and as a second counterpoint, in *McLoughlin v Jones* (the wrongful imprisonment case in which a significant extension to the car accident scenario was canvassed by the Court of Appeal), it was noted that policy considerations are just as important to negligently-inflicted psychiatric illness claims as they are to pure economic claims.[164] Hence, there is no reason why a fear-of-the-future claimant should not be designated to be a primary victim—but then, that policy reasons could preclude a duty of care from being owed, on the particular facts and circumstances before the court.

In summary then, a cleaner and more logical resolution to fear-of-the-future claimants, in this author's opinion, would have been to explicitly acknowledge that fear-of-the-future claimants *may be* primary victims, and that they should **not** be treated as a 'special' *Caparo*-type case of claimant. In addition, in such cases, the role of policy should remain paramount in determining the question of duty, i.e., whether it is fair, just and reasonable for the fear-of-the-future claimant to be owed a duty of care in all the circumstances. The primary-versus-secondary-victim classification is seemingly too well-entrenched now, in English law, to be abandoned. Hence, if the law of pure psychiatric illness (including that governing fear-of-the-future claimants) is to be clarified, then the delineation of who is a primary victim must be vastly improved.

E SOME AMERICAN INSIGHTS ABOUT FEAR-OF-THE-FUTURE LITIGATION

In stark contrast to the position in England, fear-of-the-future litigation in the US is voluminous. In fact, it has been variously described as 'coming to the forefront of American tort law',[165] as 'a developing body of law',[166] and as an area of jurisprudence where '[a]lthough recovery varies by jurisdiction, progression toward wider recovery persists'.[167]

It has even been suggested[168] that the financial and critical success of certain books and films (e.g., *China Syndrome*, *Outbreak*, *Silkwood*, *A Civil Action*, and *Erin Brockovich*), and the perceived public concerns about exposure to toxins which these examples of popular culture played up, saw (at that time) a corresponding willingness of American courts to relax the 'physical manifestation' rule and to permit greater recovery for anxiety caused by toxic exposures.

The legal analysis of fear-of-the-future claims in US jurisprudence follows a far different course from that of England's. Where a claimant seeks compensation for negligent infliction of emotional distress, then by virtue of the physical impact rule, a claimant is required to show that he sustained a distinct physical injury before being allowed to recover for emotional or mental injuries—which term can cover 'great anxiety, fear and emotional distress' that a disease may be contracted in the future, leading to a loss of enjoyment of life,[169] or for 'damages for mental anguish' that entails some 'assault upon the mind, personality or nervous system of the plaintiff which is medically cognizable and which requires or necessitates treatment by the medical profession'.[170] That is, a lower threshold than a 'recognised psychiatric injury', as that is interpreted in English law, is sufficient.[171]

As alluded to earlier in the chapter,[172] some US courts have circumvented the physical injury requirement by couching the 'injury' as constituting the mere ingestion of substances, for example. Hence, in *Carroll v Sisters of Saint Francis Health Services Inc*, the Supreme Court of Tennessee explained as follows:

> Under the older law, a plaintiff was required to show that he or she had sustained a distinct physical injury before being allowed to recover for emotional or mental injuries. The physical injury requirement served to objectify the inquiry; it assured that the plaintiff's allegations of emotional injury were grounded in an independently verifiable event. Although the degree of physical injury

required to substantiate the plaintiff's emotional damages claim was not always consistent, and was sometimes quite negligible, the requirement nevertheless remained central to this area of negligence law. It is certainly true that the physical injury requirement has been gradually weakened so that a minimal physical injury will now suffice. This shift in the law, however, does not signal an abandonment of the objectivizing function served by the physical injury requirement, but is rather a product of the realization that the physical injury requirement no longer properly serves that function in many modern actions for emotional damages. Many actions for emotional damages brought today are radically different from the cases which gave rise to the requirement in that they involve an exposure to an extremely dangerous agent—such as asbestos, dioxin, or HIV—which may have serious adverse health consequences at some point far into the future. Given this fact, this Court has realized that in some situations, whether the plaintiff has incurred a literal physical injury has little to do with whether the emotional damages complained of are reasonable.[173]

Thereafter, in fear-of-the-future claims based upon the negligent infliction of emotional distress, two stages of analysis typically[174] are used to limit the number of claims: proof of exposure, and proof that the claimant's fear or anxiety was objectively reasonable. Although the following does not purport to be a comprehensive treatment of the US fear-of-the-future jurisprudence,[175] these legal techniques for ring-fencing anxiety-based damages claims offer some interesting points for English law, should a lesser type of damage ever be countenanced for fear-of-the-future claims.

1. Exposure to the disease-causing agent

(a) The options: actual or possible exposure

The biggest legal dilemma under this requirement is whether the claimant must prove that he suffered an *actual* exposure to the toxic agent, or whether it is sufficient that he fears that he was *possibly* exposed to the agent through a medically-sound channel of transmission (which does not require proof of actual exposure to the agent). Under the former, stricter, view, anything less than proof of actual exposure means that the claim for emotional distress will be denied. The more lenient view (which holds sway in a minority of US jurisdictions[176]) holds that a possible exposure to the agent is sufficient.

This distinction means that if, say, a surgeon performs invasive surgery on two patients after the surgeon is diagnosed with AIDS, but with no evidence that any blood or other bodily fluids from the surgeon entered the patients and mixed with their blood and bodily fluids, then actual exposure cannot be proven. In that case, a claim based upon *possible exposure*, if allowed, may succeed.[177] On the other hand, if a HIV-positive doctor is accidentally cut during an operation and his blood mixes with the patient's blood, then actual exposure to the HIV virus will be proven.[178]

In the context of alleged medical negligence, some US cases have required proof of some actual exposure,[179] but there are a number of authorities which have preferred the possible exposure approach.[180]

In three of the *non-patient* fear-of-the-future cases canvassed earlier in Section B, the actual exposure test was applied. In *Carroll*,[181] the hospital visitor who thought that a sharps container was a paper towel dispenser could not prove that the needle which pricked her fingers was contaminated with HIV, and thus failed to prove actual exposure. In *Gregory* too,[182] the case of the mortician who embalmed the AIDS-infected corpse, there was no evidence of actual exposure, given the protective steps that Mr Gregory always took when undertaking embalmings. The Supreme Court of Appeals of West Virginia held that 'if a suit for damages is based solely upon the plaintiff's fear of contracting AIDS, but there is no evidence of an actual exposure to the virus, the fear is unreasonable, and this Court will not recognize a legally compensable injury.'[183] By contrast, in *Johnson*,[184] where the security guard was bitten by an AIDS-infected patient, actual exposure was proven, because the patient was HIV-infected, and the patient had bitten himself just before biting the officer, so that there was blood in the patient's mouth at the time of the bite.

On the other hand, two of the cases involving non-patients, highlighted in Section B, demonstrate the 'possible exposure' requirement. In *Williamson* (the case of the cleaner who was cut by the lancet in the dental surgery), the New Jersey Supreme Court allowed recovery, even though there was no evidence that the cleaner had suffered actual exposure to the HIV virus from the lancet—'it cannot validly be said, as a matter of law, in light of common knowledge, that a person who receives a puncture wound from medical waste reacts unreasonably in suffering serious psychic injury from contemplating the possibility of developing AIDS ... following a series of negative test results'.[185] The damages recoverable, however, were limited from the time of possible exposure, until it was no longer reasonable to apprehend a bad outcome, following a series of negative tests. In *Madrid* too, concerning the spilt container of bodily fluids that came in contact with the driver's paper cuts, the court held that actual proof of HIV exposure via a medically-sound channel of transmission was not required.[186]

(b) The arguments for and against

Whether fear-of-the-future claims should be ring-fenced by proof of actual exposure is a question upon which the arguments are finely balanced. Several reasons have been advanced by US courts (and commentators) as to why actual exposure to a disease-causing agent *should* be necessary.[187] These are summarised in Table 9.3 (where C = the claimant):

Table 9.3   Why actual exposure should be required

• fear-of-the-future claims are intended to allow C to recover, where he is worried about whether he will contract the disease in the future. They should not be permitted to also cover scenarios where C is worried about whether he was actually exposed to the disease-causing agent by HCP's act or omission in the first place;
• actual exposure limits the number of potential claimants, and acts as a useful control mechanism for such claims;
• proof of some actual exposure is an objective standard, and helps to give fear-of-the-future claims stability, consistency, and predictability;
• to allow 'possible exposure' to base a claim could actually compound the public's fear of exposure to the HIV virus, for example, by encouraging such claims, and by giving them a credibility; and could also open up the prospect that damages could be based on the public's 'imagined possibilities';
• a requirement of actual exposure is reflective of scientific fact—the statistical probability of contracting most diseases (e.g., HIV from a single needle stick exposure to contaminated blood) is very small;
• an actual exposure requirement prevents C from recovering damages for fear of contracting a disease, where that fear is actually based on a lack of information or awareness, or on inaccurate information, regarding the transmission of the disease. A fear-of-the-future claim should be based upon exposure to disease, and not upon C's own ignorance about that disease.

However, the arguments are by no means one-sided, and the 'possible-exposure-should-be-enough' camp has cogent support too, as summarised in Table 9.4:

Table 9.4   Why possible exposure should be sufficient

- the essential question in fear-of-the-future claims must be whether C's fear of developing a disease was reasonable or not—and whether there has been actual exposure is *one* consideration towards that assessment, rather than a compulsory requirement. Ultimately, C's fear must be supported by sufficient indicia of genuineness and reasonableness;
- C sometimes cannot prove an actual exposure (and this may be entirely due to the HCP's conduct, because the HCP has discarded the needle so that it cannot be tested, for example). In the circumstances of an 'information gap' that is not C's fault, requiring a blanket proof of actual exposure would prejudice that C unduly;
- the potential for a 'floodgates' of claims is limited by the requirement that C's damages should be restricted to the 'window of anxiety' that occurs between the potential exposure and the later knowledge of negative test results;
- to permit the softer 'possible exposure' threshold may encourage HCPs to take the necessary steps to improve medical practices and to promote public health, by instituting better safety precautions to prevent the medical wrongdoing in the first place;
- severe emotional stress can result from a needle-stick injury, regardless of whether or not C can prove that the needle actually contained HIV-tainted blood, because it is medically impossible to rule out HIV infection for 6–12 months from stick injury. The fear during that window should be compensable;
- what amounts to an 'actual exposure' is not always consistently applied by the courts, insofar that the 'channel of communication' to C's body is not always clear-cut, yet 'actual exposure' can be made out. A more consistent approach is that C must have reasonably feared a substantial, medically-verifiable possibility of contracting the disease.

As noted earlier, however, it is the tougher 'actual exposure' requirement which has garnered most support in US states.

Clearly, the arguments have been persuasively put on each side. However, in this author's view, the 'actual exposure' requirement has much to recommend it, if such a doctrine were to be considered for the purposes of English law, for three reasons. First, the objective standard which it represents is most attractive, in a field of negligence law that is (and, rightly or wrongly, always will be) rife with suspicion. Secondly, the requirement of 'actual exposure' effectively 'ring-fences' the number of claims that may be brought, and to that end, achieves a balance between claimant redress and insurers' concerns about 'compensation culture-driven' law. Thirdly, to insist upon 'actual exposure' acknowledges that not every psychiatrically-injured 'worrier' will be compensated—but that admission is in perfect symmetry with *physically*-damaged claimants too, for whom the rules of remoteness of damage ensure that physical harm which flowed from the defendant's act or omission but which was unforeseeable, will go uncompensated. The requirement of 'actual exposure' and the rules governing remoteness of damage have, as a similar policy objective, an intent to curtail the number of claimants who may seek recovery via the tort of negligence.

2. Proving that the anxiety was objectively reasonable

The second ring-fence around fear-of-the-future cases in American law is that the claimant's 'fear is reasonable and causally related to the defendant's negligence.'[188] As one early case stated, if the circumstances showed that the claimant's fears were objectively reasonable, then that provided a 'guarantee of genuineness',[189] while later courts have described the need for the fears to have 'a rational basis'.[190]

What characterises an objectively-reasonable fear, as opposed to a spurious and vexatious concern which the law has no business in remedying? Relevant factors emerging from US case law have included (but are not necessarily limited to) the following:

- where actual exposure to the disease-causing agent is required, and the claimant proves it, then that may establish a *prima facie* case, so that the claimant's fear is manifestly reasonable; conversely, where actual exposure is required and the claimant cannot prove it, then any fear of contracting a disease in the future is, 'as a matter of law, unreasonable';[191]
- some courts have required corroboration, by reliable medical or scientific opinion, that future development of the disease as a result of exposure was likely *on the balance of probabilities*,[192] in order to prove that the fear was objectively reasonable. This is a standard which commentator Cantley has called 'an almost insurmountable threshold for recovery in fear of cancer cases'[193] and which Greenstein has described as a 'strict' and 'stringent' approach that is entirely policy-driven (e.g., to prevent exposing HCPs to a source of potential liability which would drive up insurance costs).[194] Other courts have been less strict, not requiring a balance of probabilities assessment, but only that there be a reasonable connection between the claimant's emotional distress and the prediction of a future disease: 'the central focus of a court's inquiry in such a case is not on the underlying odds that the future disease will in fact materialize.'[195] In fact, very low probabilities of disease developing have still lead to successful recovery of damages in some cases.[196] If the probability is fairly low, then on one view, that should impact upon the amount of compensation—for example, one Texas court held that it was enough if the claimant's mental anguish 'arises from fear of diseases that are a substantial concern, but not medically probable. The fact that the evidence does not establish a reasonable medical probability that Dartez will develop either disease is relevant to the ... reasonableness of the anguish he feels and the amount of compensation to which he is entitled.'[197] The concept of 'reasonableness', under these latter decisions, is not equivalent to probability or certainty, but will depend upon a court being satisfied of the genuineness of the claim;[198]
- the fact that the claimant was informed by a reliable source (e.g., his doctor) that his exposure to the toxic agent had heightened his risk of developing a deadly disease, has been a pointer to a reasonable fear;[199]
- a strong line of expert medical opinion and/or empirical evidence establishing a causal link between the toxic agent and the disease (e.g. between the prevention-of-miscarriage drug diethylstilbestrol (DES) and cancer), supports the contention that the fear was a reasonable one;[200] and
- the fact that the connection between toxic agent and disease had entered widely into the public consciousness, via educational lectures to students or sporting clubs, radio advice from life insurance companies, or newspaper daily articles by doctors, can also point to a genuine and reasonable fear.[201]

Hence, the abovementioned jurisprudence is of some interest for English law-makers and HCPs, if English law were to adopt the proposition that some emotional distress or trauma falling short of a genuine psychiatric illness were a compensable injury in fear-of-the-future medical cases. Clearly, techniques could be developed by which the law could impose certain 'control devices' as the *quid pro quo* for allowing a less serious type of mental harm, in order to maintain HCPs' liability within reasonable limits.

F CONCLUSION

The possibility that a HCP could be liable to a non-patient for the *mere prospect* of physical illness or disease, due to exposure to a toxic agent that came about because of a HCP's negligent act or omission, undoubtedly causes alarm for the medical profession and for liability insurers. Academic commentary has referred to the 'incalculable consequences', should fear-of-the-future claims be widely accepted by the courts.[202]

To permit this sort of claim has significant policy ramifications too. For example, there may be distributive justice concerns, i.e., by allowing damages for emotional distress claims, that could substantially reduce the pool of money available to compensate victims who are *actually* infected by disease as a result of medical treatment or who are suffering some more cognisable injury from negligent medical treatment.

On the other hand, several academic commentators have mooted a greater development of fear-of-the-future claims. Mullany has posited the view that '[i]ndividuals have the legal right to expect both phsyical and psychiatric tranquillity. Both are essential to complete human existence. Violation of either must be actionable without the need to negotiate indefensible obstacles to relief.'[203] Osborne has pointed out that litigation could be expected to increase, with advances in scientific knowledge which can link products, chemicals and compounds to illness, and the emergence of serious contagious viral illnesses such as HIV and SARS.[204] Hilson has suggested that a more generous legal framework for recovery in fear-of-disease cases should be embraced, given that any lack of physical injury leaves claimants arguing their cases on the basis of stand-alone psychiatric injury, with all of its inherent legal difficulties.[205]

However, two bulwarks posed by English law suggest that fear-of-the-future claims are not likely to feature in the medical negligence landscape any time soon. First, the refusal in *Pleural Plaques* to expand the meaning of physical injury so as to include physiological changes to the body which are symptomless is significant. This decision meant that anxiety-based claims (as opposed to claims for a genuine psychiatric illness) could not be framed as a 'parasitic claim'. Hence, this discourages future attempts to point to some chromosomal breakage, sub-cellular change, physical manifestation of anxiety, ingestion of toxic substances, or other types of 'injury' which have occasionally been countenanced elsewhere. Secondly, in light of both *Pleural Plaques* and the *CJD Litigation*, English courts will clearly lean towards the use of *all three limbs* of the *Caparo* test—with the attendant propensity to deny fear-of-the-future claims, if the claimants are not patients or 'akin to patients'. As *Pleural Plaques* demonstrated, even proving foreseeability of psychiatric harm can be challenging.

The '*Potential Liability to Non-Patients and Third Parties: A Synopsis for Healthcare Professionals*', contained in the Appendix, outlines the relevant principles in this controversial area of negligence law.

ENDNOTES

[1] There may also be an attempt to claim the costs of ongoing medical monitoring and testing. These damages cover 'the cost of future periodic medical examinations that are designed to detect and treat at an early date a disease caused by toxic exposure ... However, litigants may not recover for preventative

care and periodic check-ups that one should prudently undertake anyway': C Depel, '"Fear of Cancer" Claims in California' (1995) 3 *Intl Ins L Rev* 30, 31. This is a common claim in the US jurisdiction, and it has emerged in Canada too, e.g.: *Ring v Canada (A-G)* [2007] NLTD 146 (SC App) [102] ('the availability of a remedy of medical surveillance and testing, a pure economic loss claim, is novel in Canada, although recognized by American courts'). However, the possibility of an economic claim, within the NHS-funded medical service, is not considered further herein.

2   e.g.: M Lee, 'Civil Liability of the Nuclear Industry' (2000) 12 *J of Environmental Law* 317; and by the same author: 'Pollution and Personal Injury: Problems and Prospects' (2001) 3 *Environmental L Rev* 15.

3   e.g.: *Johnston v NEI International Combustion Ltd* [2007] UKHL 39, [2008] 1 AC 281 (HL); *Pratt v The Scottish Ministers* 2009 SLT 429 (CSOH).

4   P Osborne, 'Manitoba Cases since the Turn of the Century' (2005) 31 *Manitoba LJ* 25, [39].

5   For excellent academic treatment of this area, see, e.g.: N Mullany, 'Fear for the Future: Liability for Infliction of Psychiatric Disorder' in Mullany (ed), *Torts in the Nineties* (LBC Information Services, Sydney, 1997) ch 5; and by the same author: 'Compensation for Fear and Worry-Induced Psychiatric Illness: The Australian Position' (1997) 4 *Psychiatry, Psychology and Law* 147. Also: J O'Sullivan, 'Liability for Fear of the Onset of Future Medical Conditions' (1999) 15 *PN* 96.

6   See pp 268–70.

7   *Birrell v Providence Health Care Society* [2009] BCCA 109, (2009), 89 BCLR (4th) 205 (only preliminary points of law such as statute of limitations and procedural matters reported to date).

8   *Babich v Waukesha Memorial Hospital*, 1996 Wisc App LEXIS 994 (30 Jul 1996) (claim failed). Being pricked with syringes is a common cause of fear-of-the-future claims, both in the medical context, e.g.: *Burk v Sage Products Inc*, 747 F Supp 285 (ED Pa 1990) (claim failed), and in public places, such as in taxis, e.g.: *Fitzgerald v Tin* [2003] BCSC 151, (2003), 11 BCLR (4th) 375 (claim succeeded); *Garner v Blue & White Taxi Co-operative Ltd* (Ont Gen Div, 31 Aug 1995) (claim succeeded).

9   e.g.: *Anderson v Wilson* (1999), 44 OR (3d) 673, 175 DLR (4th) 409 (Ont CA), leave to appeal refused: (2000), 185 DLR (4th) vii (note) (patients underwent ECG tests at defendants' clinic; over 18,000 patients informed by public health authorities that there could be a link between an outbreak of Hepatitis B and tests, because of infected technician who performed tests, and that they should be tested; at least 75 patients contracted disease, some violently; sub-class of patients, who received the notification letter and showed no symptoms after testing, brought claim for compensation for fear of serious infection and anxiety during waiting period; the class action permitted to proceed; arguable cause of action for the uninfected patients).

10   e.g.: *Faya v Almaraz*, 620 A 2d 327 (Md 1993) (A performed invasive surgery on two women, knowing, at the time of both surgeries, that he was HIV-positive, and prior to second operation, diagnosed with AIDS; after reading about A's death from local newspaper, patients underwent blood tests for the AIDS virus (negative); but both women succeeded in fear-of-the-future claims from potential exposure to HIV).

11   e.g.: *Rideout v Health Labrador Corp* [2005] NLTD 116, 12 CPC (6th) 91 (SC) (medical instruments used at gynecological clinic were, allegedly, not properly sterilised; over 300 patients were sent letters to undergo medical testing for Hepatitis B and C, HIV, Chlamydia, and Gonorrhea; class action certified, on basis that arguable cause of action existed for patients).

12   e.g.: *Rose v Pettle* (2004), 43 CPC (5th) 183 (Ont SCJ) (patients receiving course of acupuncture treatments contracted skin infection Mycobacterium abscessus, and alleged that treatments administered without use of disposable needles; class action certified, as disclosing a potential cause of action).

13   *Morris v Johnson Controls Ltd* [2002] MBQB 313, (2002), 169 Man R (2d) 183 (Master) [30] (an employment case, in which employees at a Canadian Forces Base were exposed to asbestos during its removal).

14   *APQ v Commonwealth Serum Laboratories Ltd* (Vic SC, Harper J, 2 Feb 1995) (accessed online, no pp available).

15   *Anderson v Wilson* (1999), 44 OR (3d) 673, 175 DLR (4th) 409 (Ont CA) [18].

[16] *Johnston v NEI International Combustion Ltd (the Pleural Plaques Litigation)* [2007] UKHL 39, [2008] 1 AC 281 (HL), affirming: *Grieves v FT Everard & Sons* [2006] EWCA Civ 27.

[17] EWLC, *Liability for Psychiatric Illness* (Rep 249, 1998) 29, fn 134. A deficiency in the report also pointed out by: N Mullany and P Handford, 'Moving the Boundary Stone by Statute: The Law Commission on Psychiatric Illness' (1999) 22 *U of New South Wales LJ* 350, (accessed online, no pp available).

[18] Ipp Comm, *Review of the Law of Negligence: Final Report* (2002) ch 9, 'Mental Harm'.

[19] *Damages for Psychiatric Injury* (DP 120, 2002).

[20] *Damages for Psychiatric Injury* (Rep 196, 2004).

[21] Described as: 'a progressive disease of middle life, with dementia, peripheral muscular wasting and degeneration of the pyramidal and extrapyramidal systems, giving spasticity and tremors and other involuntary movements', and: 'the suffering undergone by its victims is agonising and the anguish and distress of those who love and care for them are painful and intense. This ghastly disease attacks the central nervous system. It is progressive and invariably fatal': *The Creutzfeldt-Jakob Disease Litigation, Newman v Secretary of State for Health* (2000) 54 BMLR 85 (CA) 86.

[22] *The CJD Litigation; Group B Plaintiffs v Medical Research Council* (1997) 41 BMLR 157 (QB) 164.

[23] *ibid.* For comment, see, e.g.: R Owen, 'The Human Growth Hormone Creutzfeldt-Jakob Disease Litigation' (1998) 65 *Medico-Legal J* 47.

[24] *The CJD Litigation, Plaintiffs v United Kingdom Medical Research Council* (1996) 54 BMLR 8 (QB).

[25] M Mildred, 'The Human Growth Hormone (Creutzfeldt-Jakob Disease) Litigation' (1998) *JPIL* 251, 267.

[26] M Jones, 'Liability for Fear of Future Disease?' (2008) 24 *PN* 13, fn 3, citing: Healthcare Comm, *Ionising Radiation (Medical Exposure) Regulations 2000, A report on regulation activity from 1 November 2006 to 31 December 2007* (Mar 2008), citing errors such as: x-raying the wrong patient, operator error, x-raying the wrong part of the body, and unnecessarily-repeated procedures.

[27] *Johnston v NEI International Combustion Ltd; Rothwell v Chemical and Insulating Co Ltd; Topping v Benchtown Ltd* [2007] UKHL 39, [2008] 1 AC 281 (HL).

[28] *Grieves v FT Everard & Sons* [2006] EWCA Civ 27. Earlier, the trial judge had found in favour of the claimants: [2005] EWHC 88 (QB).

[29] *Fletcher v Commr of Public Works in Ireland* [2003] 1 IR 465 (SC Ire) (damages for nervous anxiety denied). See, for discussion, e.g.: J Blennerhassett, 'Toxic Torts and the Irish Courts—What Fear for the Future?' (2006) 1 *Quarterly Rev of Tort Law* 27.

[30] *Pratt v The Scottish Ministers* 2009 SLT 429 (CSOH) [2], [7] (prison officer intervened to break up fight between prisoners, and ingested quantity of blood from a prisoner known to be an injecting drug user; officer tested for infectious diseases; found it hard to cope waiting for test results over three to six month window; developed depression, retired due to ill-health; claim permitted to proceed; recognisable psychiatric injury had occurred).

[31] (1997) 41 BMLR 157 (QB) 161.

[32] *Norfolk & Rwy Co v Freeman Ayers*, 538 US 135, 146 (2003); *Metro North Commuter Rail Co v Buckley*, 521 US 424, 138 L Ed 2d 560 (1997).

[33] [2006] EWCA Civ 27, [88]–[89].

[34] 868 SW 2d 585 (SC Tenn, 1993).

[35] 186 W Va 648, 413 SE 2d 889 (W Va 1991).

[36] 150 NJ 232, 696 A 2d 14 (NJ 1997). Discussed in, e.g.: J Greenstein, 'New Jersey's Continuing Expansion of Tort Liability: *Williamson v Waldman* and the Fear of AIDS Cause of Action' (1999) 30 *Rutgers LJ* 489.

[37] 122 NM 269, 923 P 2d 1154 (NM 1996). Discussed in, e.g.: E Knapp, 'Turning Blood into Whine: "Fear of AIDS" as a Cognizable Cause of Action in New Mexico' (1998) 28 *New Mexico L Rev* 165.

[38] 186 W Va 424, 413 SE 2d 79 (W Va 1991).

[39] See, for further discussion, R Mulheron, *The Class Action in Common Law Legal Systems: A Comparative Perspective* (Hart Publishing, Oxford, 2004) ch 1.

[40] *Millard v North George Capital Management Ltd* (2000), 47 CPC (4th) 365 (Ont SCJ) [37].

41 e.g.: regarding safety of food: *Fakhri v Alfalfa's Canada Inc* [2004] BCCA 549, 34 BCLR (4th) 201 (BC CA) (class action certified); *Vanek v Great Atlantic & Pacific Co of Canada* (1997), 39 OTC 54 (Ont Gen Div) (claimant recovered damages). Re test spraying of herbicides at military base: *Ring v Canada (A-G)* [2007] NLTD 146 (SC) (class action certified; arguable cause of action existed). Against taxi companies, as in n 8 above. Against employers: *Morris v Johnson Controls Ltd* [2002] MBQB 313, 169 Man R (2d) 183 (strike-out failed, claim permitted to proceed).

42 (2006), 38 CPC (6th) 145 (Ont SCJ).

43 *ibid*, [84].

44 (Vic CA, 28 Apr 1995), refusing leave to appeal from: (SC Vic, 2 Feb 1995).

45 No further reference to the matter appears in either reported or unreported case law.

46 Reiterated in: *Grieves v FT Everard & Sons (Pleural Plaques Litig)* [2006] EWCA Civ 27, [19], citing: *Fairchild v Glenhaven Funeral Services* [2003] 1 AC 32 (HL) [8].

47 On the basis of: *Cartledge v E Jopling & Sons Ltd* [1963] AC 758 (HL) 773–74 (Lord Evershed) ('it cannot ... be in doubt ... that the cause of action from such a wrong accrues when the damage—that is, real damage as distinct from purely minimal damage—is suffered'). See further, on this point: C Hilson, 'Let's Get Physical: Civil Liability and the Perception of Risk' (2009) 21 *J of Environmental Law* 33, 47.

48 *APQ v CSL Ltd* (Vic CA, 28 Apr 1995).

49 *Morris v Johnson Controls Ltd* [2002] MBQB 313, 169 Man R (2d) 183 [24].

50 *Pleural Plaques* [2007] UKHL 39, [2008] 1 AC 281, [80] (Lord Rodger).

51 *The CJD Litigation, Andrews v Secretary of State for Health (Damages Assessments)* (1998) 54 BMLR 111 (QB) 113.

52 *The CJD Litigation; Group B Plaintiffs v Medical Research Council* (1997) 41 BMLR 157 (QB) 162.

53 *Pleural Plaques* [2006] EWCA Civ 27, [26].

54 *P (MN) v Whitecourt General Hospital* [2004] ABQB 761, (2004), 42 Alta LR (4th) 150, [387]. Interestingly, this case was selected by Hoaken as: 'The Five Most Noteworthy [Canadian] Medical Malpractice Cases of 2004' (Health Law and Medical Malpractice: A National Forum, Metro Toronto Convention Centre, 3 Feb 2005), but principally for the *causal* difficulties which the case exhibited.

55 (Vic SC, Harper J, 2 Feb 1995) (accessed online, no pp available).

56 *The Creutzfeldt-Jakob Disease Litigation* (1996) 54 BMLR 79 (QB) 80.

57 [2006] EWCA Civ 27, [2006] ICR 1458, [63].

58 *ibid*, [62].

59 *ibid*.

60 See Chapter 8, pp 281, 293–94.

61 *Pleural Plaques* [2007] UKHL 39, [67] (Lord Scott), [88] (Lord Rodger), citing: *Gregg v Scott* [2005] UKHL 2, [2005] 2 AC 176 (HL), *Law Society v Sephton & Co* [2006] 2 AC 543 (HL), and *Brown v North British Steel Foundry Ltd* 1968 SC 51 (OH) 68.

62 *Pleural Plaques* [2007] UKHL 39, [2008] 1 AC 281, [22] (Lord Hoffmann). See also: [66]–[67] (Lord Scott).

63 *Pleural Plaques* [2006] EWCA Civ 27, [24] (Lord Phillips CJ and Longmore LJ).

64 *ibid*, [111], and [134] (Smith LJ).

65 Note, though, that the leading English commentary on damages, *McGregor on Damages* (18th edn, Sweet & Maxwell, London, 2009) when discussing the circumstances in which mere mental distress can be recovered (at para [3.011]), does not refer to a single instance of this type of claim having been made. After discussion of *Pleural Plaques* in which the mental anxiety over future disease was not recoverable because the pleural plaques were not physical injury, the learned author continues: 'However, once liability has been established, then in certain torts compensation for injury to feelings may be included in the damages', and thereafter gives a number of examples, but none concerning compensation for fear-of-the-future mental distress.

66 A phrase adopted from: C Depel, '"Fear of Cancer" Claims in California' (1995) 3 *Intl Ins L Rev* 30, 30.

67 *Pleural Plaques* [2006] EWCA Civ 27, [24], [66].

68   A point made by Smith LJ, *ibid*, [143].
69   i.e., damage had been made out in previous pleural plaques cases: *Church v MOD* (1984) 134 NLJ 623 (QB); *Sykes v MOD* (1984) 134 NLJ 783 (QB); *Patterson v MOD* [1987] CLY 1194, all referred to in *Pleural Plaques* [2007] UKHL 39, [3]–[6] (Lord Hope), [43], [47]–[50] (Lord Hope).
70   *Pleural Plaques* [2007] UKHL 39, see particularly: [2], [7], [10]–[22] (Lord Hoffmann), [38]–[49] (Lord Hope), [67]–[73] (Lord Scott), [88]–[91] (Lord Rodger), [103] (Lord Mance).
71   [2006] EWCA Civ 27, [18]–[26]. Smith LJ dissented: [116]–[118].
72   H McGregor, *McGregor on Damages* (18th edn, Sweet & Maxwell, London, 2009) [35.007].
73   As espoused, e.g., in: *St Louis, Iron Mountain & Southern Rwy Co v Buckner*, 115 SW 923 (Ark 1909); *Driscoll v Gaffey*, 92 NE 1010, 1011 (Mass 1896); *Payton v Abbott Laboratories*, 437 NE 2d 171, 176 (Mass 1982); *Moresi v State Dept of Wildlife & Fisheries*, 567 So 2d 1081, 1095 (La 1990).
74   6 Cal 4th 965 (Cal 1993).
75   586 F Supp 14, 17 (D Colo 1984).
76   746 F Supp 887, 901 (D Minn 1990).
77   *ibid*, 906.
78   [2007] UKHL 39, [2008] 1 AC 281 (HL) [73] (Lord Scott).
79   See *Pleural Plaques* [2006] EWCA Civ 27, [67], although, on appeal, Lord Hope was less-than-enthused about these policy reasons: *ibid*, [50], and Lord Hoffmann regarded 'some of these as rather speculative': at [17].
80   See, e.g., the discussion by J d'Entremont, 'Fear Factor: The Future of Cancerphobia and Fear of Future Disease Claims in the Toxicogenomic Age' (2006) 52 *Loyola L Rev* 807,823–29, citing: *Caputo v Boston Edison Co*, 1990 WL 98694 (D Mass, 9 July 1990), aff'd: 924 F 2d 11 (1st Cir 1991); *In re Rezulin Products Liability Litig*, 361 F Supp 2d 268 (SDNY 2005); *Parker v Brush Wellman Inc*, 377 F Supp 2d 1290 (ND Ga 2005); *Rainer v Union Carbide Corp*, 402 F 3d 608 (6th Cir 2005), cert denied: 126 S Ct 562 (2005).
81   d'Entremont, *ibid*, 807, citing also: J Childs, 'Toxicogenomics: New Chapter in Causation and Exposure in Toxic Tort Litigation' (2002) 69 *Defense Counsel J* 441, 445; G Marchant, 'Genetics and Toxic Torts' (2001) 31 *Seton Hall L Rev* 949, 976, and by the same author: 'Genetic Data in Toxic Tort Litigation' (2006) 14 *J of Law and Policy* 7, 29.
82   d'Entremont, *ibid*, 833, quote at 834–35.
83   [2004] BCCA 549, 34 BCLR (4th) 201, [16] (this was an appeal against a class actions certification order; Donald JA, speaking for the CA, said: 'I do not presume to decide these matters, I simply raise them to indicate that it is by no means certain that the [patients] will be put to individual proof of psychiatric illness').
84   e.g., *Molien v Kaiser Foundation Hospital*, 167 Cal Rptr 831, 838 (1980).
85   S Cantley, 'Every Dogma Has its Day: Cancerphobia Precedent in Aids Cases' (2001) 40 *Brandeis LJ* 535, 541, 544.
86   [2007] NLTD 146 (SC).
87   *ibid*, [103].
88   *Laxton v Orkin Exterminating Co Inc*, 639 SW 2d 431, 434 (Tenn 1982) (upholding the trial court's finding that '[i]f [the claimants] ingested any amount of the toxic substance, it is the judgment of the Court that that is at least a technical physical injury'); *Plummer v US*, 580 F 2d 72, 76 (3rd Cir 1978) ('the effects of a concededly minute tubercle bacillus are potentially no less lethal than, for example, the impact of an automobile'); *Hughes v Johns-Manville Corp*, 7 Phila C Rptr 620, 637 (1982) ('under the impact rule, medically demonstrable inhalation and retention of asbestos particles might be of a sufficient physical impact to permit recovery in this Commonwealth for the attendant emotional distress').
89   *Merry v Westinghouse Electricity Corp*, 684 F Supp 847, 852 (MD Pa 1988).
90   S Waddams, *The Law of Damages* (looseleaf edn, Canada Law Book, Aurora Ontario, 2006) [updates available to 18 Oct 2009] [3.1250], citing, among other authorities: *Anderson v Wilson* (1999), 175 DLR (4th) 409 (CA).

91 Although such views are by no means restricted to Canadian judges, as noted in, e.g.: N Mullany and P Handford, *Tort Liability for Psychiatric Damage* (Law Book Co, Sydney, 1993) 45–51; and see too: *J&P Van Soest v Residual Health Management Unit* [1999] NZCA 206, [2000] 1 NZLR 179, [83] (Thomas J); and the several earlier authorities which are cited by: N Mullany, 'Fear for the Future: Liability for Infliction of Psychiatric Disorder' in Mullany (ed), *Torts in the Nineties* (LBC Information Services, Sydney, 1997) ch 5, fn 54.

92 (1997), 39 OTC 54 (Ont Gen Div).

93 *Mason v Westside Cemeteries Ltd* (1996), 135 DLR (4th) 361 (Ont Gen Div).

94 *Vanek* (1997), 39 OTC 54 (Ont Gen Div) [8].

95 *Mason v Westside Cemeteries Ltd* (1996), 135 DLR (4th) 361 (Ont Gen Div) [54] (Molloy J), cited in *Vanek, ibid.*

96 *Vanek v Great Atlantic & Pacific Co of Canada* (1999), 48 OR (3d) 228 (Ont CA) [65]–[66] (MacPherson JA).

97 *Mason v Westside Cemeteries Ltd* (1996), 135 DLR (4th) 361 (Ont Gen Div) [54], cited in, e.g.: *Vanek* (1997), 39 OTC 54 (Ont Gen Div) [8].

98 [1990] 2 AC 605 (HL) 617–18.

99 *P (MN) v Whitecourt General Hospital* [2004] ABQB 2, 25 Alta LR (4th) 21, fn 50, citing: S Waddams, *The Law of Damages* (looseleaf edn, Canada Law Book, Aurora Ontario, 2006) [3.1250].

100 [1897] 2 QB 57.

101 Suggested by: *Wainwright v Home Office* [2004] 2 AC 406 (HL) 426 (Lord Hoffmann). On this point, see discussion in, e.g.: S Deakin *et al*, *Markesinis and Deakin's Tort Law* (6th edn, OUP, Oxford, 2008) 471–73; W Rogers, *Winfield and Jolowicz on Tort* (17th edn, Sweet & Maxwell, London, 2006) 127.

102 Waddams, *ibid*, [3.1250], and [3.1330]–[3.1350]. See too, e.g.: N Mullany and P Handford, *Tort Liability for Psychiatric Damage* (Law Book Co, Sydney, 1993) 51–56.

103 e.g.: *Jarvis v Swan Tours Ltd* [1973] QB 233 (CA); *Jackson v Horizon Holidays* [1975] 1 WLR 1468 (CA).

104 *Morris v Johnson Controls Ltd* [2002] MBQB 313, (2002), 169 Man R (2d) 183.

105 P Osborne, 'Manitoba Tort Cases Since the Turn of the Century' (2005) 31 *Manitoba LJ* 25, [47].

106 EWLC, *Liability for Psychiatric Illness* (Rep 249, 1998) [5.3], [5.5]–[5.6].

107 Several references are made in the Negligence (Psychiatric Illness) Bill to 'recognisable psychiatric illness'.

108 See Chapter 8, pp 274–75, 294–95.

109 *Page v Smith* [1996] AC 155 (HL).

110 As described in *Pleural Plaques* [2006] EWCA Civ 27, [90], aff'd: [2007] UKHL 39.

111 *CJD Litigation; Group B Plaintiffs v Medical Research Council* (1997) 41 BMLR 157 (QB) 163–64.

112 [2007] UKHL 39, and see, especially, the distinction drawn by Lord Hope (at [52]–[56]), by Lord Hoffmann (at [31]–[33]), by Lord Scott (at [76]–[77]), by Lord Rodger (at [94]–[96]), and by Lord Mance (at [104]).

113 The term used in: *Pleural Plaques* [2006] EWCA Civ 27, [92].

114 e.g.: *Barber v Somerset CC* [2004] UKHL 13, [2004] 2 All ER 385, and earlier: [2002] EWCA Civ 76; *Melville v Home Office* [2005] EWCA Civ 6.

115 As Jones notes, Morland J 'refused to apply the primary/secondary categorisation, but, in effect, treated the claimants in *CJD* as *sui generis*, possibly motivated by the horrendous nature of the death suffered by the victims of CJD': M Jones, 'Liability for Fear of Future Disease?' (2008) 24 *PN* 13, 21.

116 *Norfolk & Rwy Co v Freeman Ayers*, 538 US 135, 146 (2003); *Metro North Commuter Rail Co v Buckley*, 521 US 424, 138 L Ed 2d 560 (1997).

117 [2006] EWCA Civ 27, [88]–[89].

118 *White (Frost) v Chief Constable of South Yorkshire Police* [1992] AC 455 (HL) 500 (Lord Steyn).

119 The *Caparo*-type avenue to recovery is discussed in further detail by the author in: 'The "Primary Victim" in Psychiatric Illness Claims: Reworking the "Patchwork Quilt"' (2008) 19 *Kings LJ* 81, 99–106.

120 See Chapter 8, pp 279–80, and see also: *McLoughlin v Jones* [2001] EWCA Civ 1743, [2002] QB 1312, [56] (for true primary victims, 'the question of what might be foreseen in a person of ordinary phlegm does not arise').

121 See, e.g., discussion of this point in *Pleural Plaques* [2007] UKHL 39, [30] (Lord Hoffmann).

122 *The CJD Litigation; Group B Plaintiffs v Medical Research Council* (1997) 41 BMLR 157 (QB) 169.

123 *ibid*, 168–69.

124 *ibid*, 166.

125 *ibid*.

126 See pp 288–89.

127 [2007] UKHL 39, [2008] 1 AC 281 (HL) [25]–[26] (Lord Hoffmann), [54]–[58] (Lord Hope), [75] (Lord Scott), [99]–[100] (Lord Rodger).

128 Noted, *ibid*, [57]. See, earlier, for similar observations: *Pleural Plaques* [2006] EWCA Civ 27, [76].

129 *ibid* (HL) [27] (Lord Hoffmann).

130 *The CJD Litigation; Group B Plaintiffs v Medical Research Council* (1997) 41 BMLR 157 (QB) 164–66.

131 (2006), 38 CPC (6th) 145 (Ont SCJ), especially the discussion at [33]–[71].

132 The terms in which the sub-class was described in *ibid*, [18].

133 This was merely a certification motion in which all that had to be proven was that a potential cause of action was evident on the face of the pleadings.

134 (2006), 38 CPC (6th) 145 (Ont SCJ) [35]–[36]. See, though, [72], where no concluded decision was formed on the proximity point.

135 By virtue of Health Protection and Promotion Act, RSO 1990, c H 7, s 26.

136 *ibid*, [68].

137 *The CJD Litigation; Group B Plaintiffs v Medical Research Council* (1997) 41 BMLR 157 (QB) 163.

138 See discussion, in the context of fear-of-the-future claims, in, e.g.: *Pleural Plaques* [2006] EWCA Civ 27, [128] (Smith LJ). Also: *Birrell v Providence Health Care Society* [2007] BCSC 668.

139 (1997) 41 BMLR 157 (QB) 169.

140 *Fletcher v Commr of Public Works in Ireland* [2003] IESC 13, [2003] 1 IR 465, [125]–[126]; *Pleural Plaques* [2006] EWCA Civ 27, [95].

141 As discussed, by reference to other sources and viewpoints, in: R Mulheron 'The "Primary Victim" in Psychiatric Illness Claims: Reworking the "Patchwork Quilt"' (2008) 19 *Kings LJ* 81, 109–110.

142 (1997) 41 BMLR 157 (QB) 164.

143 (2006), 38 CPC (6th) 145 (Ont SCJ) [75].

144 *ibid*.

145 (1997) 41 BMLR 157 (QB) 164.

146 C Hilson, 'Let's Get Physical: Civil Liability and the Perception of Risk' (2009) 21 *J of Environmental Law* 33.

147 J Steele, 'Pleural Plaques in the House of Lords: The Implications for *Page v Smith*' (2008) 67 *CLJ* 28, 28.

148 'Asbestos Condition not Compensable: UK Court', *Reuters* (26 Jan 2006).

149 *White (Frost) v Chief Constable of South Yorkshire Police* [1999] 2 AC 455 (HL) 496.

150 K Wheat, 'Proximity and Nervous Shock' (2003) 32 *Common Law World Rev* 313 (accessed online, no pp available).

151 M Lee, 'Pollution and Personal Injury: Problems and Prospects' (2001) 3 *Environmental L Rev* 15, 25.

152 M Jones, 'Liability for Fear of Future Disease?' (2008) 24 *PN* 13, 21.

153 [2007] UKHL 39, [2008] 1 AC 281, [54].

154 [2001] 2 AC 592 (HL).

155 M Jones, 'Liability for Fear of Future Disease?' (2008) 24 *PN* 13, 24. See too, by the same author: *Medical Negligence* (4th edn, Sweet & Maxwell, London, 2008) 205–210.

156 *Donachie v Chief Constable of The Greater Manchester Police* [2004] EWCA Civ 405.

157 *Bici v MOD* [2004] EWHC 786 (QB).

158 *Cullin v London Fire and Civil Defence Authority* (QB, 31 Mar 1999).

159 [2001] EWCA Civ 1743, [2002] QB 1312.

160 The allegation of lack of due care ultimately failed at trial, and this finding of no breach was upheld on appeal: *McLoughlin v Jones* [2006] All ER (D) 51 (CA).

161 [2001] EWCA Civ 1743, [2002] QB 1312, [56]–[57].

162 [2007] UKHL 39, [2008] 1 AC 281, [34].

163 *ibid.*

164 [2002] 2 WLR 1279 (CA) 1288 (Brooke LJ), and cited on this point in: *AB v Leeds Teaching Hospital NHS Trust* [2004] EWHC 644 (QB) [182].

165 M Donovan, 'Is the Injury Requirement Obsolete in a Claim for Fear of Future Consequences?' (1994) 41 *UCLA L Rev* 1337, 1340.

166 S Cantley, 'Every Dogma Has its Day: Cancerphobia Precedent in Aids Cases' (2001) 40 *Brandeis LJ* 535, 556.

167 A Santee, 'More than Just Bad Blood: Reasonably Assessing Fear of Aids Claims' (2001) *Villanova L Rev* 207, 221.

168 J d'Entremont, 'Fear Factor: The Future of Cancerphobia and Fear of Future Disease Claims in the Toxicogenomic Age' (2006) 52 *Loyola L Rev* 807, 814–16.

169 *Carroll v Sisters of Saint Francis Health Services Inc*, 868 SW 2d 585, 587 (SC Tenn 1993).

170 *Sears, Roebuck & Company v Devers*, 405 So 2d 898, 902 (Miss 1981) (being 'very upset' is not sufficient)

171 For an interesting trace of the development in US law of this lower threshold of emotional damages, falling short of a recognised psychiatric injury, by reference to decisions such as *Rodrigues v Hawaii*, (1970), 472 P 2d 509 (Haw), and *Molien v Kaiser Foundation Hosp*, 167 Cal Rptr 831, 27 Cal 3d 916, 616 P 2d 813 (Cal 1980), see, e.g.: N Mullany and P Handford, *Tort Liability for Psychiatric Damage* (Law Book Co, Sydney, 1993) 48–50.

172 See pp 319–20, and n 88 above.

173 868 SW 2d 585, 593–94 (SC Tenn 1993).

174 There may be variations, e.g., requiring actual exposure to a disease-causing agent plus a balance of probabilities proof that the disease will develop, as in: *Kerins v Hartley*, 33 Cal Rptr 2d 172 (App 1994), as discussed in: S Cantley, 'Every Dogma Has its Day: Cancerphobia Precedent in Aids Cases' (2001) 40 *Brandeis LJ* 535, 547–48.

175 For excellent treatments, see e.g.: N Mullany, 'Fear for the Future: Liability for Infliction of Psychiatric Disorder' in Mullany (ed), *Torts in the Nineties* (LBC Information Services, Sydney, 1997) ch 5, 144–66, in addition to the academic commentaries noted in n 187 below.

176 According to Knapp, 'Turning Blood into Whine: "Fear of AIDS" as a Cognizable Cause of Action in New Mexico' (1998) 28 *New Mexico L Rev* 165, fn 4, and Cantley, *ibid*, fn 4, New Mexico, New Jersey, Louisiana, and Maryland, are the only jurisdictions in which the *highest* courts explicitly permit recovery in the absence of actual exposure.

177 *Faya v Almaraz*, 620 A 2d 327 (Md 1993) (A performed invasive surgery on Sonja Faya and Perry Mahoney Rossi, respectively; at the time of both surgeries, A knew he was HIV-positive, and prior to Rossi's operation, had been diagnosed with AIDS; after reading about A's death from local newspaper, F and R underwent blood tests for HIV; tests negative, but women alleged they were potentially exposed to HIV and feared contracting AIDS; claims succeeded).

178 As in, e.g.: *Wolgemuth v Milton S Hershey Medical Center*, No 2694-S-1991 slip op (Ct of CP, Dauphin County Pa 30 Jan 1992), as cited in: L Camillo, 'Adding Fuel to the Fire: Realistic Fears or Unrealistic Damages in AIDS Phobia Suits?' (1994) 35 *Texas L Rev* 331 (HIV-positive doctor attended at operation, and was accidentally cut by other surgeon, causing him to bleed into patient; patient's fear of AIDS resulting from an actual exposure to the doctor's blood objectively reasonable; claim succeeded).

179 e.g.: *Burk v Sage Products Inc*, 747 F Supp 285 (ED Pa 1990); *Doe v Doe*, 519 NYS 2d 595 (Sup 1987); *Brzoska v Olson*, 668 A 2d 1355 (Del 1995); *KAC v Benson*, 527 NW 2d 553 (Minn 1995); *Ordway v County of Suffolk*, 583 NYS 2d 1014 (Sup Ct 1992); *Doe v Surgicare of Joliet Inc*, 643 NE 2d 1200 (Ill App Ct 1994); *Vallery v Southern Baptist Hosp*, 630 So 2d 861 (La Ct App 1993); *Barrett v Danbury Hosp*, 232 Conn 242, 654 A 2d 748 (Conn 1995); *Russaw v Martin*, 472 SE 2d 508 (Ga 1996); *Falcon*

v Our Lady of the Lake Hosp Inc, 729 So 2d 1169 (La Ct App 1999); *Majca v Beekil*, 701 NE 2d 1084 (Ill 1998); *Fosby v Albany Memorial Hosp*, 675 NYS 2d 231 (NY App Div 1998); *Roes v FHP Inc*, 985 P 2d 661 (Haw 1999); *Bain v Wells*, 936 SW 2d 618, 620 (Tenn 1997).

[180] e.g.: *Kerins v Hartley*, 33 Cal Rptr 2d 172 (Ct App 1994); *De Milio v Schrager*, 666 A 2d 627 (NJ S Ct 1995); *Hartwig v Oregon Trail Eye Clinic*, 580 NW 2d 86 (Neb 1998); *Madrid v Lincoln County Med Ctr*, 923 P 2d 1154 (NM 1996); *Williamson v Waldman*, 150 NJ 232, 696 A 2d 14 (1997); *Howard v Alexandria Hosp*, 429 SE 2d 22 (Va 1993); *Bordelon v St Frances Cabrini Hosp*, 640 So 2d 476 (La App 1994); *Doe v Noe*, 690 NE 2d 1012 (Ill 1997).

[181] *Carroll v Sisters of Saint Francis Health Service*, 868 SW 2d 585, 594 (Tenn 1993).

[182] *Funeral Services by Gregory Inc v Bluefield Community Hosp*, 413 SE 2d 79 (W Va 1991).

[183] *ibid*, 84.

[184] *Johnson v West Virginia Univ Hosp*, 413 SE 2d 889, 894 (WVa 1991).

[185] *Williamson v Waldman*, 696 A 2d 14, 23 (NJ 1997). See also: *Castro v New York Life Ins Co,* 588 NYS 2d 695, 697 (Sup Ct 1991) (cleaning worker stuck with hypodermic needle improperly discarded in ordinary waste container; able to recover for emotional distress and fear of AIDS, on the basis that '[i]f a claim can be tied to a distinct event which could cause a reasonable person to develop a fear of contracting a disease like AIDS, there is a guarantee of genuineness of the claim,' without proving actual exposure).

[186] *Madrid v Lincoln County Medical Center*, 923 P 2d 1154, 1163 (NM 1996).

[187] These reasons are derived from a reading of the cases in nn 34–8 above, and are canvassed extensively in academic commentary, e.g.: E Knapp, 'Turning Blood into Whine: "Fear of AIDS" as a Cognizable Cause of Action in New Mexico' (1998) 28 New *Mexico L Rev 165;* A Santee, 'More than Just Bad Blood: Reasonably Assessing Fear of Aids Claims' (2001) *Villanova L Rev* 207; M Donovan, 'Is the Injury Requirement Obsolete in a Claim for Fear of Future Consequences?' (1994) 41 *UCLA L Rev* 1337; J Trachtenberg, 'Living in Fear: Recovering Negligent Infliction of Emotional Distress Damages Based on the Fear of Contracting AIDS' (1999) 2 *DePaul J of Health Care Law* 529; J Greenstein, 'New Jersey's Continuing Expansion of Tort Liability: *Williamson v Waldman* and the Fear of AIDS' (1999) 30 *Rutgers LJ* 489; T Watkins, 'Fear of AIDS Claim Requires Showing of Actual Exposure Unless Defendant Destroys Evidence of Exposure Creating a Rebuttable Presumption Against Defendant' (2000) 69 *Mississippi LJ* 1243.

[188] *Hagerty v L&L Marine Services Inc*, 788 F 2d 315, 318 (5th Cir 1986).

[189] *Ferrara v Galluchio*, 152 NE 2d 249, 252 (NY 1958). This is typically described as the seminal fear-of-the-future case in US jurisprudence, although, as Cantley notes, recovery for fear of cancer has been allowed since as early as 1912, citing: *Alley v Charlotte Pipe & Foundry Co*, 74 SE 885, 886 (NC 1912): S Cantley, 'Every Dogma Has its Day: Cancerphobia Precedent in Aids Cases' (2001) 40 *Brandeis LJ* 535, 539.

[190] *Dangler v Town of Whitestown*, 672 NYS 2d 188, 190 (NY App Div 1998), citing: *Wolff v A-One Oil*, 627 NYS 2d 788, 789 (NY App Div 1995).

[191] As in: *Drury v Baptist Memorial Hosp System*, 933 SW 2d 668, 675 (Texas 1996); *Russaw v Martin*, 472 SE 2d 508, 512 (Ga 1996).

[192] *Potter v Firestone Tire & Rubber Co*, 863 P 2d 795, 816 (Cal 1993); *Gideon v Johns-Mansville Sales Corp*, 761 F 2d 1129, 1137–38 (5th Cir 1985).

[193] S Cantley, 'Every Dogma Has its Day: Cancerphobia Precedent in Aids Cases' (2001) 40 *Brandeis LJ* 535, 544.

[194] J Greenstein, 'New Jersey's Continuing Expansion of Tort Liability: *Williamson v Waldman* and the Fear of AIDS Cause of Action' (1999) 30 *Rutgers LJ* 489, 496.

[195] *Sterling v Velsicol Chemical Corp*, 855 F 2d 1188, 1206 (WD Tenn 1986).

[196] *Heider v Employers Mutual Liability Ins Co of Wisconsin*, 231 So 2d 438, 441–42 (La 1970) (emotional distress arising from 2–5% risk of becoming epileptic compensable); *Clark v US*, 660 F Supp 1164, 1175 (WD Wash 1987) (fear reasonable, even where higher than one in a million chance of contracting future disease).

[197] *Dartez v Fibreboard Corp*, 765 F 2d 456, 468 (5th Cir 1985).

[198] T Kiely, *Modern Tort Liability: Recovery in the '90s* (John Wiley & Sons, New York, 1990) 420.

[199] *ibid*, 468.

[200] *Wetherill v Uni of Chicago*, 565 F Supp. 1553, 1560 (ED Ill, 1983). Also evident, e.g., in: *Ferrara v Galluchio*, 152 NE 2d 249, 252–53 (NY 1958).

[201] *Ferrara v Galluchio*, *ibid*, 252.

[202] A Graf, 'The Contaminated Blood Scandal in France: Are Insurers still the "Prime Suspects"?' (1997) 5 *Intl Ins L Rev* 67, 70.

[203] N Mullany, 'Fear for the Future: Liability for Infliction of Psychiatric Disorder' in N Mullany (ed), *Torts in the Nineties* (LBC Information Services, Sydney, 1997) 172.

[204] P Osborne, 'Manitoba Tort Cases Since the Turn of the Century' (2005) 31 *Manitoba LJ* 25, [39].

[205] C Hilson, 'Let's Get Physical: Civil Liability and the Perception of Risk' (2009) 21 *J of Environmental Law* 33, 34.

Chapter 10
Wrongfully-Accused Third Parties in Neglect or Abuse Cases

A   INTRODUCTION

This chapter focuses upon investigations of alleged child abuse and other mistreatment which are undertaken by HCPs of all descriptions (e.g., psychiatrists, social workers, GP's, psychologists, family therapists, and the like). The child is perhaps best described as a 'limited patient'[1]—he has been examined/interviewed by HCPs who have been engaged to do so by health authorities or local authorities, pursuant to a statutory framework for child protection. If, as a result of a negligently-conducted investigation, an assessment of abuse or neglect is made and the HCPs conclude (incorrectly) that the wrongdoing against the child was perpetrated by a parent or other guardian, this can lead to tragic and unfortunate circumstances—for the wrongfully-accused, as well as for the child—often predicated upon an enforced separation of the parties.

In these circumstances, both child and the accused may suffer from a legally-recognisable damage—whether it be some psychiatric illness as a result of the separation, or some economic loss which would not have occurred, but for the wrongful accusation. In a worst-case scenario, wrongful accusations may lead to the permanent break-up of a family. For example, in the recent case of *Webster v Norfolk CC*,[2] three of the claimant's four children were adopted on the recommendation of experts who mistakenly considered that the children's nutritional deficiencies and fractures were non-accidental and non-natural, and the adoption orders could not, ultimately, be reversed.

Traditionally, in a suit in negligence against the mistaken HCP, the duty of care which the HCP owed *to an examinee child* was a very limited one indeed—a duty 'simply to take care in the course of the examination not to make the patient's condition worse'[3] or 'not to damage the applicant in the course of the examination'[4] (called, hereafter, the 'traditional duty'). Hence, if the child examinee was physically harmed, in circumstances where he would not have been, had reasonable competence been shown by the HCP, then negligence would lie. However, following a somewhat tortuous and controversial path, in which the House of Lords has vacillated on the question in recent years, English law now provides that a child examinee is owed a much wider duty than simply the minimalist traditional duty. This legal reworking is described in Section B.

It is important to preface discussion of the parental claims—the *true focus* of this chapter, given the non-patient status which the wrongfully-accused holds—with a brief consideration of the child's claim, in order to fully appreciate how the parental claim has **not** 'enjoyed' the same judicial munificence to date in English law. By a series of innovative arguments, this category of non-patients has been a determined one, seeking to 'push the boundaries', and remove the immunity from liability, which the leading House of Lords' decision of *JD v East Berkshire Community Health NHS Trust*[5] has come to represent. However, successes have been very much in short supply—and the bulwark of *East Berkshire* has important ramifications for wrongfully-accused parents, and for HCPs and their insurers. The judicial attitude towards this type of non-patient claim is considered in Section C.

The wrongfully-accused's claim has also garnered significant attention in the European Court of Human Rights, in light of the European Convention on Human Rights (ECHR), and to the extent that this jurisprudence has impacted upon the common law negligence claims of the wrongfully-accused, this is examined in Section D.

Where HCPs investigate alleged abuse or neglect cases involving children who are seemingly at risk, they are doing so in the interests of the community as a whole; and if the investigation is done negligently and if the child and/or parent suffers a legally-recognisable damage, the reasons for or against any liability in negligence are, essentially, matters of legal and public policy. Traditionally, for the wrongfully-accused, at least, English law has viewed that individual's damage as 'sacrificial', or as a 'necessary price to be paid', to uphold the wider community interest of ensuring the safety of children.[6]

B   THE CHILD CLAIMANT

At the outset, it must be reiterated that the infliction of some legally-recognised damage is a pre-requisite to proving the tort of negligence. Some child claimants, who have been removed from their parents because of erroneous allegations of abuse made against those parents by HCPs, have not suffered any such injury (sometimes by virtue of their extreme youth,[7] or perhaps because of the relatively short period of removal[8]), and hence, no action by the child has been possible for that reason.

Assuming that recognisable damage *can* be proven, the much more difficult legal issue has been whether the HCP owes that child claimant a duty of care to avoid the latter's (psychiatric, etc.) injury. In the early days, no such duty was owed. As the law stands now, however, the HCP can owe the child examinee a wide duty to avoid *all foreseeable injury* arising out of negligently-conducted child abuse investigations.

1. The early days

In *X (Minors) v Bedfordshire CC; M (A Minor) v Newham LBC; E (A Minor) v Dorset CC,*[9] a series of cases went to the House of Lords, on what was termed 'a question of great importance and difficulty' common to each case: 'may a child maintain an action for damages (whether for breach of statutory duty or common law negligence) against a local authority [or health authority] for steps taken or not taken in relation to the child by that authority as the responsible social services authority?'[10]

The particular case of relevance to the issues in this Section was child M's action in *Newham*. Unlike in *Bedfordshire*,[11] the defendants in the *Newham* case included a HCP—the psychiatrist who interviewed the child at the centre of the abuse investigation—and the action against the HCP was one for direct negligence (for which Newham LBC was sued vicariously). Hence, the liability of the HCP for direct wrongdoing was squarely at issue. This was the first time that the House had been asked to assess the legal relationship between a child the subject of alleged abuse, and investigating HCPs. Sir Thomas Bingham MR noted that there 'was not, on any showing, a typical doctor-patient relationship' on the facts.[12]

In *M (A Minor) v Newham LBC*, KM, a young girl, was put on the child protection register, after a social worker had concerns that M was being sexually abused. KM was interviewed by the

defendant HCPs (social worker and psychiatrist). At the end of the questioning, KM's mother, TP, was told that KM had been sexually abused, and that XY (the mother's current partner) was the abuser. When TP privately asked KM, after the interview, whether XY had abused her, M shook her head and said 'no'. TP relayed this to both HCPs, but she was not believed (her information was perceived as an attempt to protect her partner, and to persuade KM to retract the allegation which the HCPs understood her to have made). On the basis that the mother would be unable to protect KM against further abuse by XY, KM was removed, made a ward of the court, and placed with foster parents. Upon herself viewing the taped interview about a year later, TP realised that KM had not identified XY as the abuser (the person identified was, in fact, a cousin who had previously lived at the house and who had the same first name as TP's partner). KM was reunited with her mother TP. They were separated for almost a year. Both KM and TP alleged that this separation had caused them psychiatric harm. They each sued the HCPs in negligence for breach of a direct duty of care which the HCPs allegedly owed to them both, and also sued the local authority (employer of the social worker) and the health authority (employer of the psychiatrist) for vicarious liability.[13]
Held (by majority): both claims, mother's and child's, failed.

The main allegations by mother and child against the psychiatrist and social worker were that they failed to investigate the facts and make enquiries with proper care and thoroughness, and failed to conduct KM's interview and to discuss their conclusions with TP, with reasonable professional skill—and that, as a result of the enforced separation, both KM and TP suffered a genuine psychiatric disorder, *viz*, anxiety neurosis.

To clarify, it is the claimant child's and parent's negligence suits against *the individual HCPs* (and the vicarious liability of the HCPs' employer which that would entail, if successful), rather than any negligence suit against the HCP's public authority employer directly (and the complexities which a claim against a public authority which is operating within a statutory framework entails[14]), that the following discussion particularly focuses upon. Consistently with the rest of the book, the aim of this chapter is to elucidate whether, and if so when, *a HCP may be taken to have owed a duty of care to a non-patient*—in this case, to the wrongfully-accused parent in child protection investigations. This duty, in turn, depends upon proof of an assumption of responsibility on the HCP's part towards that particular claimant, and upon complex policy issues that determine whether such a duty would be 'fair, just and reasonable' in all the circumstances. In that regard, the question of whether the HCP's employer was vicariously-liable for the HCP's wrongdoing is, as McIvor notes, a 'much narrower and more tightly constrained' question than that concerning his employer's liability for direct negligence.[15]

(a) The no-duty viewpoint

KM failed in her action against the psychiatrist and the social worker, both at Court of Appeal (by majority, Lord Bingham dissenting)[16] and, again, in the House of Lords (unanimously). The claim was struck out as disclosing no cause of action in negligence. The traditional duty was upheld—and, clearly, KM had suffered no physical harm during the interview. The extent of the HCPs' duties were no wider than that, and no duty could be cast on them to avoid the injuries to KM which resulted from a year's enforced separation from her mother. There were, essentially, two reasons for that outcome.

First of all, the HCPs had not assumed the requisite legal responsibility to take care of KM's welfare—the HCPs' duties, and the assumption of a wide responsibility to take due care in the performance of the investigations, were owed to *the HCPs' employers*:

The social workers and the psychiatrists were retained by the local authority to advise the local authority, not [KM and her mother TP]. The subject matter of the advice and activities of the professionals is the child. Moreover the tendering of any advice will, in many cases, involve interviewing and, in the case of doctors, examining the child. But the fact that the carrying out of the retainer involves contact with and relationship with the child cannot alter the extent of the duty owed by the professionals under the retainer from the local authority. The Court of Appeal drew a correct analogy with the doctor instructed by an insurance company to examine an applicant for life insurance. The doctor does not, by examining the applicant, come under any general duty of medical care to the applicant. He is under a duty not to damage the applicant in the course of the examination: but beyond that his duties are owed to the insurance company and not to the applicant ... in the present cases [*Newham* and *Bedfordshire*] the social workers and the psychiatrist did not, by accepting the instructions of the local authority, assume any general professional duty of care to the plaintiff children. The professionals were employed or retained to advise the local authority in relation to the well being of the plaintiffs but not to advise or treat the plaintiffs.[17]

Secondly, that the traditional duty of care on the HCP's part, not to cause physical harm to the child, could not be extended to cover a duty to avoid psychiatric injury caused to KM from the separation, was directly attributable to policy.[18] It was neither just nor reasonable to impose that wider duty on the HCPs, for the reasons canvassed in Table 10.1.

It has been said that 'very potent counter considerations' are required to override the policy that wrongs should be remedied.[19] *Newham's* scenario was deemed to be such a case, and appeared to constitute a fairly effective bulwark against any future prospects of success for children in their suits against HCPs, at least in a negligence action (the children in both *Bedfordshire* and in *Newham* had more success in their claims that their Convention rights had been violated, considered shortly[20]).

However, these policy factors were certainly not all tending the one way, as the dissenting judgment of Sir Thomas Bingham MR in *Newham* (CA) clearly demonstrated.

(b) The pro-duty viewpoint

In *Newham* (CA), Sir Thomas Bingham MR would have found a wider duty of care than simply not to damage the M, the child examinee, during the interview. It is worth summarising these contrary views of the Master of the Rolls (in Table 10.2), as to why a duty not to cause psychiatric damage *should* have been imposed on the HCPs—because, in fact, these policy reasons have ultimately come to define the *current* legal position between the examining HCP and the child examinee.[21]

Undoubtedly, the no-duty-to-child rule formulated by the House of Lords in *Newham* appeared to have an artificial ring to it. After all, as Jones points out, the reasoning did not sit well with other professional negligence contexts:

The fact that it might be 'difficult' for a court to disentangle strands of responsibility for negligence is hardly a basis for concluding that there should be no duty of care (as a glance at the law reports involving claims against professionals in complex commercial transactions would demonstrate); nor is the fact that professionals have to make difficult (or 'delicate') judgments—that is, something that 'goes with the territory' of being a professional and the consequences of error can be just as serious in other contexts (a misdiagnosis by a doctor, for example, can cause serious harm or death) ... in any event, when translated into the conduct of individuals, what possible 'defensive' strategy could a social worker or healthcare professional adopt? ... The only 'defensive strategy' likely to

Table 10.1   The policy reasons for no duty to a child examinee in *Newham* (HL)

- the statutory system set up for the protection of children at risk from abuse or neglect was inter-disciplinary, involving the participation of police, educational bodies, HCPs, local authorities, etc, and it required discussions, recommendations and decisions of a joint nature. To hold that, out of all of these parties, only the HCPs were subject to a duty of care, would be manifestly unfair. But equally, to extend the duty to all would lead to huge problems of contribution among all these parties;
- dealing with children at risk is very complex and delicate. HCPs have to consider the physical health of the child, the desirability of not disrupting the family unit, the harm potentially caused by wrongfully leaving the child *in situ* versus the harm potentially caused by removing the child wrongfully, the dangers of acting too soon or not soon enough—working all the while with parents who are, themselves, often in need of help. Introducing a legal duty of care into this fragile mix was fraught;
- imposing a duty of care on HCPs would lead to 'defensive medicine'—HCPs would be likely to adopt a more cautious and time-consuming approach (i.e., not acting until 'concrete facts' were known about abuse or neglect, possibly too late to prevent injury to the child). All child abuse investigations would be prejudiced by the increased workload per case; and defending this litigation would divert money and human resources away from the performance of important social services;
- where the HCPs recommended that the child be removed from the home, and the parents naturally wished to keep the child with them, conflicts, deep feelings and hostility were likely. All of this could result in fertile litigation, unless the law deemed such litigation to be impossible;
- it was not as if the wronged child had no other remedy. Complaints procedures, and references to local authorities' Ombudsmen schemes, were possible. And even if compensation might not be possible under these avenues, that would not justify imposing a tortious duty of care;
- the law must proceed incrementally, and by analogy with decided cases. The purpose of the statutory social welfare scheme was to protect the weak (children). Under similar scenarios of victims of crime versus police, investors versus regulators of financial markets, etc, the law had not imposed a common law duty of care on the 'protector' (police, regulators). Hence, no close legal analogies could be found;
- in the case of very young children, given the suspension of their limitation periods until majority, their suits could be brought at any time up to age 21. The prospect of 'sleeper actions' for long-ago grievances would place the legal system under an intolerable and uncertain burden.

Table 10.2   Policy reasons in *Newham* (CA, Bingham MR, dissenting) in favour of a duty to a child examinee

- it was just and reasonable for a duty of care to be imposed on the examining HCP, because only very serious acts/omissions would justify a breach of that duty. Few claims would succeed, so there was no prospect of opening the 'floodgates';
- no greater defensive measures would be taken by the HCP if he knew that he owed a duty to the child examinee, other than a knowledge that he should be sound in the performance of his professional duty;
- just because a policeman, financial regulator, or teacher may not be liable to third parties is hardly relevant; each new case—including those involving HCPs—must be judged on its particular facts;
- the limitation point was not cogent. It was Parliament's view that children should be able to prosecute for civil wrongs done to them, up to 21 years of age. If that was to be disallowed on 'policy grounds', by precluding any duty of care being owed by HCPs, then courts would be substituting their own policy for Parliament's;
- the *first* claim on policy is that wrongs should be remedied—and no strong policy grounds went against that, in the context of negligently-conducted investigations of alleged child abuse or neglect;
- no other redress for *compensation* was possible for the child examinee against the HCPs, except for the action brought in negligence in this case.

succeed in this situation is for the professional to exercise reasonable care in reaching a judgment as to the appropriate course of action to take.[22]

Moreover, there was no prospect of conflict of interests—rather, the interests of the child and the local authority were surely aligned in this scenario. As Jones again remarks:

> the child's interests were essentially the *only* interests at stake in [*Newham*], and therefore, it was distinctly odd that a doctor could be said to owe a duty to exercise reasonable care in advising the local authority, but not to the child, when the very purpose of the duty owed to the local authority was to enable it to act in the best interests of the child ... It remains something of a mystery why, in *M (A Minor) v Newham*, their Lordships considered that there was such a conflict between the duty owed by the psychiatrist to the local authority and a potential duty of care owed to the child. It could not be in the interests of either the child or the local authority that the authority should act upon negligent advice (whether the careless advice is to the effect that the child has been abused or that it has not been abused). There is simply no conflict between these duties.[23]

In any event, the law did not stop at *Newham* (HL)'s position for very long. For a child who was examined/interviewed by a HCP, with no harm occurring to the child's person during the examination, but who suffered (usually psychiatric) injury when the HCP's diagnosis of child abuse turned out to be wrong, two decisions turned around the rather hopeless scenario which *Newham's* case had decreed.

2. Key interim developments

(a) The *Phelps* and *Barrett* shifts in view

In 2000, and some five years after *Newham*, the House of Lords, in *Phelps v Hillingdon LBC*,[24] had to consider the position of a child again—on this occasion, one who was examined by an educational psychologist who was employed by the local education authority. Hence, the scenario involved alleged educational, rather than medical, negligence. Again, as with *Newham's* case, the defendants were operating within a statutory framework, whereby the local education authority was under a duty to make an assessment of the special educational needs of any child, and where the education authority had to seek educational, medical and psychological advice (the last-mentioned being provided by an educational psychologist).[25]

> In *Phelps*, Pamela Phelps (P), 11, had learning difficulties, but the educational psychologist, M, reported that she could find no specific weaknesses with P. However, towards the end of her school education, P was discovered to be dyslexic. P claimed against the psychologist (and her employer, for vicarious liability), alleging that, via this negligent diagnosis, P had suffered economic loss, given the employment opportunities that were denied to her. **Held**: P's action against M (and vicariously, her employer) was upheld (with general damages of £12,500); a duty of care was owed.

The Court of Appeal[26] had earlier followed the *Newham* lead and held that M was employed by the local education authority to give it advice in respect of children suffering from learning difficulties, and that M assumed no responsibility towards child P. However, the House of Lords disagreed.

With respect to the HCP's personal liability to child P for the alleged medical misdiagnosis, Lord Slynn (with whom all other members agreed) set down two initial propositions. First, any duty of care which the psychologist might owe to child P did not depend upon the existence of any contractual relationship between them (or the lack of it, in this case). Secondly, there was 'no justification' for a blanket immunity to be conferred upon HCPs who were acting in the capacity of education officers performing the functions of a local education authority with respect to children with special educational needs.[27]

Thereafter, Lord Slynn expressly referred, and adhered closely, to the classic tri-partite *Caparo* test,[28] in order to determine whether a common law duty of care was owed by the HCP to the child. Lord Slynn was satisfied that reasonable foreseeability of damage was proven in the instant case ('persons exercising a particular skill or profession may owe a duty of care in the performance to people who, it can be foreseen, will be injured if due skill and care are not exercised, and if injury or damage can be shown to have been caused by the lack of care'—and an educational psychologist was such a person).[29] Furthermore, duties of care owed by the psychologist to both the local authority and to the child examinee could feasibly co-exist:

> The fact that the educational psychologist owes a duty to the authority to exercise skill and care in the performance of his contract of employment does not mean that no duty of care can be, or is, owed to the child.[30]

There was also, according to Lord Slynn, a requisite proximity between psychologist and child in respect of the child's educational needs, which was based upon an assumption of responsibility that was *imposed*, rather than *assumed*, by the HCP towards that child:

> where an educational psychologist is specifically called in to advise in relation to the assessment and future provision for a specific child, and it is clear that the parents acting for the child and the teachers will follow that advice, *prima facie* a duty of care [in favour of the child] arises ... It is not so much that responsibility is assumed as that it is recognised or imposed by the law.[31]

Furthermore, no public policy reasons dictated against a wide duty of care being imposed on the educational psychologist. In particular, the appeals review procedure did not give 'sufficient redress' for the wrong alleged here; the imposition of a wider duty of care was unlikely to lead to defensive practices; and to impose a duty on the psychologist would still only require the attaining of reasonable, not unreasonably high, standards of practice from educational defendants.[32] This policy reasoning is very reminiscent of Bingham MR's dissent in *Newham*. In that regard, and as Booth and Squires point out, the particular importance of *Phelps* was that it did not seek to distinguish the facts of *Newham/Bedfordshire*, but rather, it 'questioned the underlying validity of the policy arguments relied upon' in that latter case.[33]

Finally, the type of damage which the educational psychologist had a duty to avoid or to minimise, on child P's part, was to be widely-construed:

> the result of a failure by an educational psychologist to take care may be that the child suffers emotional or psychological harm, perhaps even physical harm ... [damage for the purpose of an action in negligence] can [include] a failure to diagnose a congenital condition and to take appropriate action as a result of which failure a child's level of achievement is reduced, which leads to loss of employment and wages.[34]

Hence, while an examining HCP in this scenario *always did* owe a traditional duty not to physically harm the examinee, *Phelps* went further than that, imposing a duty of care on the psychologist to avoid acts or omissions that would cause *all* foreseeable damage to the claimant examinee (where, of course, that damage was causally linked to those acts or omissions). Moreover, some of the policy reasons relied upon by the House of Lords in *Newham/Bedfordshire* to preclude a duty on the HCP's part towards the examinee child were significantly undermined in *Phelps*. Accordingly, if the psychologist failed to diagnose dyslexia, as a result of which the child's education was seriously prejudiced, the psychologist could be directly liable in negligence to the child, for which the local authority could be vicariously liable.

In the second important decision, that of *Barrett v Enfield LBC* (delivered in 1999[35]), the House of Lords showed a marked willingness to limit *Newham* to its facts, to distinguish it as necessary, and to permit a claimant to sue social workers in negligence, albeit in a different scenario.

> In *Barrett v Enfield LBC*, Keith Barrett (B), the claimant, was only 10 months old when he was admitted to hospital suffering from injuries inflicted by his mother. Thereafter, he was placed under the care of Enfield LBC, from then until he was 17 years old. During this time, B endured almost ten different foster home care arrangements, had sporadic contact with his mother which did not go well, was separated from his half-sister, and suffered various physical and psychiatric disorders. B alleged that the social workers employed by Enfield LBC, and the local authority itself, were under a duty to act in *loco parentis*, and to provide him with the standard of care which could be expected of a reasonable parent, including a duty to provide a home and education, to take reasonable steps to protect him from physical, emotional, psychiatric or psychological injury, and to promote his development. **Held:** B's claim would not be struck out; it disclosed a potential cause of action against the social workers and local authority.

The factual situation in *Barrett*, while involving HCPs working in the child protection field, was significantly different from that in *Newham/Bedfordshire*, because the latter held that no duty could be imposed by HCPs who were *investigating* whether or not to take a child into care, with all the difficult aspects which that involved. In *Barrett*, on the other hand, the child was *already* taken into care, and in that case, it was plausible that acts or omissions on the part of the relevant social workers during the period of care orders could ground a claim in negligence.[36] Nevertheless, again, some of the policy arguments put forward in *Newham* were dismissed as being of little significance in *Barrett*, with Lord Slynn rejecting the 'defensive practice' policy reason, for example, as being 'normally a factor of little, if any, weight'.[37]

As a result of *Barrett* and *Phelps*, the judicial mood shifted. In the 2000 case of *S v Gloucestershire CC*, for example, the Court of Appeal remarked upon two points. Firstly, the 'child abuse cases' which might be brought against HCPs and local or health authorities were **not** bound to fail as a class—and that there was no question of any 'blanket immunity' operating, in such cases, in the defendants' favour. Secondly, decisions made by social workers in investigations/examinations concerning child welfare were indeed capable of being held to have been negligent, 'by analogy with decisions of other professional people.'[38] Academic commentary has variously observed that, in combination, *Barrett* and *Phelps* marked 'a more expansive view of the liability of public authorities',[39] heralded a welcome move to adopt a more case-specific approach to the duty of care question,[40] 'evinced the Law Lords' renewed faith in the objectives of negligence law',[41] constituted a 'reaction against the over-restrictive environment hitherto applying to negligence claims in the child protection area',[42] and signalled the willingness of the House of Lords to meet the challenge of ensuring that English negligence law was rendered compatible with Convention rights.[43]

To add to the turnaround of judicial mood, the Privy Council also considered the issue in 2003, in relation to an appeal from the New Zealand Court of Appeal, concerning the child protection statutory framework operative in that jurisdiction:

> In *B v A-G (New Zealand)*,[44] a social worker had made a complaint under the Children and Young Persons Act (New Zealand) 1974, to the effect that B, the father of two daughters aged seven and five, had sexually abused his younger daughter. That Act imposed on the Director General of Social Welfare the duty of inquiry, where he knew or had reason to suspect that any child or young person was suffering or likely to suffer from ill-treatment. B and his daughters claimed damages in respect of the allegedly negligent way in which the complaint had been investigated by the clinical psychologist and the social worker involved. **Held:** the Privy Council refused to strike out the claim in negligence brought by the daughters against the HCPs involved (but B's claim was struck out).

The Privy Council held that a duty of care *was* owed to any child in respect of whom the statutory duty to arrange for a prompt inquiry existed; and that '[t]here can be nothing surprising in holding that a psychologist owes to a child whom she is examining a duty to exercise due professional skill and care.'[45] Accordingly, the statutory framework within which the social welfare department, and its employed HCPs, acted was consistent with the imposition of a common law duty of care.

In light of all these developments, the *Newham* decision, and the policy reasons underpinning it, were becoming somewhat marginalised and restricted—an impression only heightened by events in Strasbourg.

(b) Some interim successes in Strasbourg

Post-*Newham/Bedfordshire*, some of the failed claimants who were meeting a rockface in English negligence law were prepared to test whether the relevant defendants had violated any Convention rights which would provide a right of reparation to those claimants under s 7 of the Human Rights Act 1998.

Indeed, in both of the conjoined appeals in *Newham/Bedfordshire*, the European Court of Human Rights ruled, in both cases, that the respective defendants had breached the claimants' Convention rights. In the case of the mistreated and neglected children who were the subject of the decision in *X v Bedfordshire* itself, the children were eventually successful (in *Z v UK*[46]) in establishing that the Council had acted in contravention of art 3 of the ECHR (the right to freedom from torture or inhuman or degrading treatment or punishment) and art 13 (the right to an effective remedy), and were awarded, in combination, £320,000 in damages. The level of horrific abuse had reached the threshold of inhuman and degrading treatment required under art 3, and was reflected in the size of the award.

In the other case of more relevance to this chapter (because the defendants included a psychiatrist who was sued directly in negligence, and a health authority which was sued vicariously), that of *M v Newham*, both mother (TP) and daughter (KM) established a violation of art 8 of the ECHR, in the case of *TP and KM v UK*.[47] This violation occurred, not because a decision to remove M from the mother's care and home had been made based on suspicions of sexual abuse being suffered by M, but because of the failure to immediately disclose to the mother the matters relied on (particularly the video interview with M) as showing that the child could not be returned safely to her care. Had the video been *promptly* shown to the mother, she would have realised who was identified by M, and it would have avoided the period of separation which followed, and which was said to have caused psychiatric disorders to both mother and child.[48]

The scene was set, then, for a potentially seismic change of view in English law, regarding whether a HCP owed a duty of care to avoid causing injury to a child examinee, which duty went well beyond the traditional duty not to physically damage the child during any physical examination. The case which provided the characters for that scene emerged in the Court of Appeal decision of *JD v East Berkshire Community Health NHS Trust; RK and MAK v Dewsbury Healthcare NHS Trust; RK and AK v Oldham NHS Trust.*[49]

3. The *East Berkshire* (CA) decision

This was a series of three conjoint appeals, in which various mistaken allegations of child abuse and mistreatment had been made. In two of the cases (*Oldham*[50] and *Dewsbury*[51]), both the child and the parental claimant/s brought actions in negligence for alleged psychiatric harm that they each suffered because of the separation that they endured (in the third, *East Berkshire* itself, the child did not sue—the claim in negligence was brought *only* by the mother, JD). In each of these actions, one or more NHS Trusts were sued as defendants (vicariously, for the alleged wrongdoing of paediatricians who were involved in the diagnostic process[52]), and a local authority was also sued in *Dewsbury*.[53]

The childs' claims are the subject of consideration in this Section. On that score, MK's action against Oldham NHS Trust failed, because no recognisable psychiatric damage could be proven to have occurred to a child so young.[54] More significantly, the claim in negligence by the child RK, in the case of *RK and MAK v Dewsbury Healthcare NHS Trust,*[55] was permitted to proceed.[56] In doing so, the Court of Appeal took the most unusual step of **not** following the House of Lords' precedent in *Newham*. Of course, in *Newham*, all that the House of Lords had been prepared to cast upon the investigative HCPs was the traditional duty not to physically harm the child examinee during the course of an abuse or neglect investigation—and RK was not physically harmed during the investigations at which she was the centre. However, the Court of Appeal allowed RK's claim to go forth, on the basis that HCPs who were employed by a health authority might be in such a relationship with the child (who was the subject of negligent investigations and mis-diagnoses of abuse) as to owe a *wider* common law duty of care to that child, breach of which would render the health authority vicariously liable (the claim against the local authority was permitted to proceed too[57]).

The Court of Appeal unanimously concluded that the law had moved on since the days of *Newham/Bedfordshire*:

> In so far as the position of a child is concerned, we have reached the firm conclusion that the decision in *X (Minors) v Bedfordshire County Council* cannot survive the Human Rights Act. Where child abuse is suspected the interests of the child are paramount. Given the obligation of the local authority to respect a child's Convention rights, the recognition of a duty of care to the child on the part of those involved should not have a significantly adverse effect on the manner in which they perform their duties. In the context of suspected child abuse, breach of a duty of care in negligence will frequently also amount to a violation of Article 3 or Article 8. The difference, of course, is that those asserting that wrongful acts or omissions occurred before October 2000 will have no claim under the Human Rights Act. This cannot, however, constitute a valid reason of policy for preserving a limitation of the common law duty of care which is not otherwise justified. On the contrary, the absence of an alternative remedy for children who were victims of abuse before October 2000 militates in favour of the recognition of a common law duty of care once the

public policy reasons against this have lost their force. It follows that it will no longer be legitimate to rule that, as a matter of law, no common law duty of care is owed to a child in relation to the investigation of suspected child abuse and the initiation and pursuit of care proceedings. It is possible that there will be factual situations where it is not fair, just or reasonable to impose a duty of care, but each case will fall to be determined on its individual facts.[58]

(A HRA claim was not available to the child victim against the Dewsbury Healthcare NHS Trust, because the harm in question had occurred prior to 2 October 2000.) In the end, the Dewsbury Trust did not dispute the Court of Appeal's decision to allow RK's action in negligence to proceed against it. When the trio of cases went on appeal to the House of Lords, that appeal concerned whether any duty of care could, as a matter of law, be owed by investigative HCPs to a *wrongfully-accused parent*.

Despite some doubts as to what the House of Lords would actually do in the appeal, in the face of the Court of Appeal's departure from *Newham* (HL),[59] the House did not criticise the 'bold'[60] approach taken by the lower appellate court in allowing child RK's claim to proceed. To the contrary, it was accepted by the House, unanimously, that the policy reasons that underpinned *Newham/Bedfordshire* were, by and large, eroded. Lord Bingham remarked that 'it could not now be plausibly argued that the common law duty of care may not be owed by a publicly-employed healthcare professional to a child with whom the professional is dealing.'[61] Lord Rodger concurred, and expressed the duty owed by the examining HCP to a child examinee, such as RK, in the widest of terms: '[t]he duty to the children is simply to exercise reasonable care and skill in diagnosing and treating any condition from which they may be suffering.'[62] In essence, and over a relatively short period, the decisions in *Phelps, Barrett, B v A-G of New Zealand*, and *S v Gloucestershire CC*, had collectively undermined the cogency of reasoning in *Newham/Bedfordshire*.

That the Court of Appeal in *East Berkshire* (or, more specifically, in the *Dewsbury* action that formed part thereof) departed from previous House of Lords' precedent in *Newham*, rendered it (in academic opinion) a 'truly remarkable',[63] 'brave',[64] 'radical',[65] 'very bold',[66] and 'historic'[67] judicial landmark for the child examinee. Unsurprisingly, perhaps, given the contentious split of opinion evident in *Newham/Bedfordshire* itself, the change of view has also drawn critical academic commentary.[68] Nevertheless, two points are worth making. First, it has been judicially emphasised, since *East Berkshire*, that for the Court of Appeal to depart from House of Lords' precedent in seeking to take account of Strasbourg jurisprudence concerning the Convention,[69] and to be 'forgiven for such *lese majeste*',[70] could only happen where the 'facts were of extreme character'[71] and in 'wholly exceptional circumstances'.[72] Secondly, even in light of the House of Lords' change of view in *East Berkshire/Dewsbury*, a court will still have to ask whether there is anything *about the circumstances in the particular case before it* that would mean that a duty on the HCP's part, in favour of a child, would not be fair, just and reasonable.[73]

Thus, to conclude—the modern position for a child examinee is that an investigative/examining HCP potentially owes a wide duty of care to that child, to avoid causing him *all foreseeable harm* (physical, psychiatric or economic) that may arise out of, and be caused by, a negligently-performed examination. The scope of that duty is 'light years' from the traditional duty toward the child that was cast by *Newham/Bedfordshire*. The law in this area has moved on, as Lord Rodger has said, 'remarkably swiftly'.[74]

It has **not** moved on nearly as swiftly, however, for the wrongfully-accused parental claimant— indeed, 'stagnant' would be a better description. Having set the context of the child's claim, the focus must now turn to the *true non-patient* in these scenarios.

C THE WRONGFULLY-ACCUSED CLAIMANT

It will be recalled that, in *Newham* (1995), the mother's claim in negligence against the psychiatrist and social worker was struck out as disclosing no cause of action—unanimously by Court of Appeal *and* House of Lords.

However, the parental claim was not the main question in *Newham*, it was a mere secondary issue.[75] Besides, in the interim between *Newham* and *East Berkshire* (CA, 2003[76]), the child's claim had been viewed sufficiently sympathetically to warrant a change in the law. Moreover, in *L and P v Reading BC*,[77] heard in 2001, the Court of Appeal had refused to strike out a negligence claim brought by a wrongfully-accused *father* against a social worker (and a police officer), on the grounds that (1) there was an 'arguable case' that there was a relationship of proximity between the social worker (and police officer) and *both* the child *and the father*, based upon a legal assumption of responsibility and a 'special relationship' between them, and (2) then-recent authorities[78] suggested that extreme care had to be taken in striking out claims in what was an evolving area of the law, and that it would be inappropriate to hold that it was not fair, just and reasonable to impose a duty of care in favour of the father, on the basis of assumed facts in the pleadings.[79]

In light of all this, could parental claimants persuade the House of Lords to consider a change in their favour too? That was the precise question which went to the House in April 2005, in *East Berkshire*—and the parents failed in that mission.

1. The *East Berkshire* (HL) decision

In the three conjoint appeals in *East Berkshire*,[80] each claimant parent was falsely and negligently accused of abusing or harming his or her child. Each sued to recover in negligence against various paediatricians (and in one case, a social worker) who, in discharging professional functions concerning child welfare, made the unfounded and negligent statements. It was assumed that each parent had suffered some recognisable psychiatric injury, and that this was a foreseeable result of the mis-diagnoses and incorrect allegations made.

> In *RK and AK v Oldham NHS Trust*, RK was the father of baby MK. When MK was two months old and was being lifted from a lounge settee, she screamed with pain, and was taken to hospital. Hospital notes incorrectly recorded that MK had been 'yanked up' from the couch. The defendant paediatrician diagnosed MK as having an 'inflicted injury', a spiral fracture of the femur, and did not investigate further the possibility of a diagnosis of osteogenesis imperfecta ('brittle bones'). The police and social services were informed, the welfare authority obtained an interim care order, MK was discharged from hospital into the care of an aunt—and thereafter sustained further similar fractures while in her aunt's care. Further tests were carried out, and the revised medical opinion was that of brittle bone disease. After eight months of separation, MK was returned to the care of her parents. Both parents (RK and wife AK) suffered psychiatric injury, and sued the paediatrician directly in negligence, and his employer health authority vicariously.[81]

> In *JD v East Berkshire Community Health NHS Trust*, JD was a registered children's nurse, and mother of son M. M had suffered from severe (medically-investigated) allergic reactions all his life. When M was five, he was diagnosed by the defendant paediatrician as suffering from Munchausen's Syndrome by Proxy.[82] It was concluded that M's condition had been fabricated by his mother JD. JD herself was unaware of this opinion. M was put on the 'At Risk' register.

Some time later, when M was an in-patient at Great Ormond Street hospital, JD happened to see a handwritten minute, which contained the allegation that she was fabricating M's condition and harming him. She arranged to see a psychiatrist, who found nothing wrong with her. When M was eventually confirmed to have severe allergic problems, M was removed from the 'At Risk' register. JD alleged that she suffered psychiatric injury as a result of the misdiagnosis of M's condition, and that she had not returned to nursing since the negligent misdiagnosis was made, thereby suffering economic loss. (Mother and child were not separated in this case.)

In *RK and MAK v Dewsbury Healthcare NHS Trust*, RK suffered from Schamberg's disease (a progressive pigmented purpuric dermatitis or capillaritis), which manifested by purple patches on the skin. Her father MAK took RK to her GP with bruising on the legs, but the marks disappeared after treatment and no diagnosis of Schamberg's disease was made. Subsequently, when RK was nine, her swimming teacher expressed concern about marks on the insides of her legs, and the defendant paediatrician diagnosed that the marks did not appear to be the result of skin disease, but were suggestive of abuse. RK's mother was told that RK had been sexually abused, and, as a result, her father and elder brother were told that they should not sleep at home when RK was released from hospital. In the hospital that evening, in front of other ward patients and visitors, MAK was told that he was not allowed to see RK. Finally a correct diagnosis was made of RK's condition, and it was accepted by the Dewsbury Healthcare NHS Trust by letter that there was no question of abuse having occurred. MAK sued the paediatrician in negligence, claiming that he had suffered psychiatric injury and financial loss resulting from the mis-diagnosis and subsequent events.[83]

The precise question (as a preliminary issue) was whether the HCPs owed a common law duty of care to each parent which, in turn, would render their NHS Trust employers vicariously liable. The House of Lords answered this, by majority, 'no' (but with a strong dissenting judgment by Lord Bingham). Hence, as a result, where HCPs accept instructions from a relevant authority, court or other 'employer', to examine and report upon a child, an examining HCP does not assume any general professional duty of care to the parents.

Interestingly, proximity between HCPs and parents was made out. In all three cases, the parental claimants specifically *sought out* medical help for their children, and as Lord Bingham said, '[i]f one thinks in terms of proximity, it is hard to think of a relationship very much more proximate than that between parent and doctor when the parent, concerned about the medical condition of a child, takes the child to see the doctor and seeks the doctor's help'.[84] Rather, the cases were argued, and decided/analysed upon, the third limb of the *Caparo* tri-partite test, *viz*, policy, but with a caveat: '[t]he focus of debate is on whether it is fair, just and reasonable to impose a duty of care on health care and child protection professionals involved in cases such as these. But it is acknowledged ... — and in my view rightly—that this question cannot be divorced from consideration of proximity.'[85]

While the House of Lords' majority was prepared to accept *East Berkshire/Dewsbury* (CA)'s reformulation of a wider duty *to the child*, based upon policy grounds, it would **not** entertain any action being available to the aggrieved parents against an allegedly negligent HCP. The Privy Council had earlier come to the same view, in relation to the father's claim, in the previously-mentioned decision of *B v A-G of New Zealand*.[86] Moreover, in *East Berkshire*, the *Reading* (CA, 2001) decision was referred to by Lord Nicholls[87] as being one case where a wrongfully-accused parent's claim *had* survived a strike-out claim, but it was explained away on the basis that the question had been 'left open' in that case.

Hence, the highest legal protection that will be afforded to parents suspected of abusing or mistreating their children is that the defendants must act in good faith:

[Those investigating child abuse] must not act recklessly, that is, without caring whether the allegation of abuse is well founded or not. Acting recklessly is not acting in good faith [and] In principle the appropriate level of protection for a parent suspected of abusing his child is that clinical and other investigations must be conducted in good faith. This affords suspected parents a similar level of protection to that afforded generally to persons suspected of committing crimes.[88]

Several policy reasons were judicially cited[89] in *East Berkshire* for this bulwark against the claims of wrongfully-accused parents, and they are summarised in Table 10.3 below. Indeed, given that these policy reasons reflect, to some degree, the earlier reasons given in *Newham/Bedfordshire* as to why a HCP owed no duty to a *child examinee*, it is true to say, as Case points out, that 'much of the *X v Bedfordshire* judgment remains good law with regard to the *accused claimant*'.[90]

Table 10.3   *East Berkshire* (HL, majority) policy reasons against a duty to wrongfully-accused parents

> - the relationship between the HCP and the parent will frequently be one of irreconcilable conflict, 'poles apart'. The HCP's duty to act in the best interests of the child (i.e., to remove him and to report the suspicion of abuse) might mean acting in a way adverse to the personal interests of the parent (to keep the child within the home, for any suspicion not to be reported, and to give the parent the presumption of innocence). At the time of the investigation, the HCP does not know whether there has been abuse by the parent or not, which means that, at that point, the interests of child and parents are diametrically opposed. Then, '[i]t will always be in the parents' interests that the child should not be removed. Thus the child's interests are in potential conflict with the interests of the parents';
> - there is a serious risk that vexatious claims, or even seriously-grounded claims with the aim of restoring the parent's reputation, could be brought years after the HCP's decisions concerning the child;
> - if the HCP did owe a duty to the parents, then those responsible for the protection of a child against criminal conduct would owe suspected perpetrators a duty of care to prevent foreseeable harm to them;
> - HCPs already have sufficient burdens here—having to consider the short term and long-term welfare of the child; making decisions on limited information; deciding what to tell family members. It would be wrong to add to them by having potential claims by aggrieved parents in the back of the mind;
> - child abuse and mistreatment is a serious social problem ('appallingly prevalent in our society'), and HCPs play a vital part in combating the risk and in protecting the vulnerable from such harm. It is best attacked by relieving HCPs of the fear of legal proceedings brought by parents arising out of their investigations. Uncompensated innocent parents pay the price, but that is a necessary price;
> - the potential for indeterminate liability in these cases is real, with potential suits from anyone suspected of being abuser (other relatives, school-teachers, babysitters, neighbours, total strangers);
> - suppose that a HCP negligently allows a child to die, and the parent suffers a recognisable psychiatric injury. Unless that parent can prove that he is a 'secondary victim' within the strict control mechanisms, he cannot recover—and there the child is lost forever. There is even less reason to permit a parent to recover for psychiatric injury when *temporarily* separated from his child in this case;
> - it is no answer to say, 'impose a duty, but excuse the HCP if he has met the reasonable standard of care'. Imposing any duty to the parent would be an 'insidious' influence on the HCP's conduct (not consciously though, as HCPs are 'surely made of sterner stuff' than that); and to allow that route would be to expose a HCP to the risk of costly and vexing litigation in trying to prove no breach;
> - shared information between parent and HCPs, and involving parents in the decision-making process, is an ideal and should be done as fully as is compatible with the child's best interests. But it is quite a step from this to saying that the HCPs personally owe a suspected parent a duty sounding in damages.

Notably, Lord Bingham dissented in *East Berkshire* (HL), and would have allowed the parents' claims to proceed to trial. It will be recalled that his Lordship was the dissenter in *Newham* (CA) too, prior to his elevation to the House of Lords, re the *child's* claim—and that dissenting viewpoint eventually prevailed, such that a duty of care by the examining HCP to the child has come to be recognised. Hence, this arguably vests Lord Bingham's dissent in *East Berkshire* (HL) with 'particular importance'.[91] Lord Bingham noted that it was not as if parents had *never* had the ability to bring a suit against HCPs and other professionals who were engaged in child protection, and against the local authority which employed them—in other contexts, actions by parents against childcare professionals and against the employer authority *had* been permitted to proceed, on the basis that there was a proven, or arguable, duty of care owed to the parents.[92] His Lordship's views, as to why it was 'fair, just and reasonable' to impose a duty of care in favour of the particular parental claimant who was wrongfully-accused of abusing or mistreating their children, are summarised in Table 10.4:[93]

Table 10.4   *East Berkshire* (Lord Bingham, dissenting) policy reasons in favour of a duty to wrongfully-accused parents

- if the argument (per *Bedfordshire*) that to impose a duty of care on HCPs would 'cut across' the whole statutory and inter-disciplinary system for protecting children at risk, and raise almost impossible problems of ascertaining and allocating responsibility, does not apply to preclude a child's suit any longer, then it is hard to see why it should preclude a claim by the parent;
- the work of HCPs in dealing with children at risk (and with their parents) is 'extraordinarily delicate' and a 'fraught and difficult situation', but that, of itself, should not preclude a duty of care from being owed to the parents—besides, 'the professional is not required to be right, but only to be reasonably skilful and careful', so that 'the breach stage would protect [HCP's] who made reasonable mistakes';
- it is not cogent to say that to impose a duty of care on HCPs towards parents would be to foster a more cautious and defensive approach, because they are hardly likely to be encouraged to overlook signs of abuse which they should recognise, just because a duty is capable of being owed (and individuals are rarely personally liable in any event);
- in any event, imposing a duty of care 'could help to instil a due sense of professional responsibility', while to say that it would have an 'insidious effect' on the mind of a potential defendant 'is to undermine the foundation of the law of professional negligence' (i.e. sound professional performance is the HCP's best defence to an action in negligence);
- there is no undue risk of conflict between HCP and parent. For one thing, domestic authority, ministerial guidance and Strasbourg authority all encourage and envisage a co-operative partnership between HCPs and parents in the child's interests. For another, the scope of the duty owed to the parents is a duty not to cause harm to a parent by failing to exercise reasonable and proper care in the making of a diagnosis of child abuse. That is essentially the same duty as the HCPs already owe to the child. If the parent *is* the abuser, then in reality, there is no conflict, because the duty to parent would not be breached;
- to cast a duty upon HCPs towards parents would mean a 'small, analogical, incremental development' of the law, given the new-found duty of care to the child arising out of the same scenarios;
- it is in the lawful interests of a parent that a skilful and careful diagnosis of the medical condition of their child be made. If the parent is the abuser, then an undetected abuser will never be heard to complain that the duty was breached; and an innocent parent should have the same rights to recover for the consequences of an incorrect allegation as the child has;
- even if to impose a duty of care in favour of the parents would make recruiting and retaining skilled HCPs (paediatricians, etc) to work in the child protection field more difficult, it is not for the courts to 'calibrate duties of care so as to regulate shortages in the professional labour market'.

Lord Bingham's dissenting views have been mirrored in strident academic criticisms of the *East Berkshire* majority verdict. For example:

- Jones has argued, '[h]ow can a professional fulfil a duty to protect the interests of the child by simultaneously negligently causing psychiatric harm to the parent? It cannot possibly be in the interests of children to have their parents traumatised, and pushed over the edge into mental illness, by negligent allegations of abuse';[94]
- Burns has called the *East Berkshire* rule 'mightily worrying' and of 'tremendous concern' because of its undermining of the family unit;[95]
- Williams discounts the majority's concern about defensive practices being adopted by the HCP, both because *East Berkshire* (CA) had already held that the threat of litigation will 'henceforth be present, whether the anticipated litigation is founded on the Human Rights Act or on the common law duty of care',[96] and because 'numerous inquiries ... show that the common causes of child protection failures are overstretched resources, poor information-sharing, and inadequate training, supervision and co-ordination, rather than litigation-induced staff timidity';[97]
- Hoyano and Keenan note that the majority were clearly split on what effect the policy reason of 'defensive practices' should have upon the question of duty—with Lord Nicholls chiding that HCPs should be 'made of sterner stuff' than to be swayed in their behaviour by the spectre of a duty being owed to parent/s as suspected abuser/s, whereas Lord Brown was prepared to accept that to cast a duty on the HCPs *would* have some such effect—'suddenly tending to the suppression of doubts and instincts which, in the child's interests, should rather be encouraged';[98]
- Stanton explains the majority's verdict in *East Berkshire* as being another example of 'resolving leading cases simply in terms of what it deems to be the best result';[99] and
- Case concludes that the policy reasons against a duty which were articulated by the *East Berkshire* majority were 'precarious', and that a better solution would have been to adopt Lord Clyde's viewpoint in *Phelps*, i.e. to hold that a duty of care was owed by defendant professional to parent, but to reiterate that to prove that the defendant's conduct fell below the *Bolam* standard of professional care would be a difficult task (recognising that, in such difficult areas as child abuse allegations, plenty of room should be left for 'differences of view on the propriety of one course of action over another'). In fact, a number of different viewpoints about the child's care arrangements could meet the requisite standard.[100]

Other commentators, however, support all (or aspects) of the majority's reasoning. For example, in their leading study of public authority liability in negligence, Booth and Squire remark that the policy reason of 'defensive practices' is one that carries crucial significance in the child protection context, because 'wariness [on the HCP's part] might not be in the best interests of the child, and no duty of care ought therefore to be imposed which might encourage it'.[101] McIvor agrees—because if the HCPs hesitate and delay, the 'greatest potential victim ... will always be the vulnerable child'.[102]

The deep division within the House of Lords in *East Berkshire* was also reflected in their application of the so-called 'incremental test'.[103] As far as Lord Bingham (dissenting) was concerned, recognition that a duty of care could be owed to a wrongfully-accused parent was a 'small, analogical and incremental development' in the law, given that it was now accepted that a duty may be owed to a child.[104] On the other hand, Lords Nicholls and Rodger, of the majority, regarded whatever the law said about the child's claim as giving 'no guidance on how "wrongly suspected parent" cases should be decided',[105] and that it 'by no means follows that [HCPs] owed any similar duty of care to the parents.'[106] Plainly, then, what is an incremental step to one judge is a 'long jump' to others!

Undoubtedly senior English judges have regularly expressed 'sympathy for the wronged parent',[107] with one recently describing the scenario before him as 'the most terrible experience that a father can face, being falsely accused of sexually assaulting his three year old daughter'.[108] However, the House of Lords has treated the dilemma with a large dollop of pragmatism—when public policy favours limiting litigation against those who are acting in the interests of the wider community, then there is 'always a price to be paid by individuals' for that policy.[109] In this case, those individuals are wrongfully-accused parents, whose damage goes uncompensated—and, consistently with that notion, *East Berkshire* has been fatal to such claimants since.[110] Very recently, the House of Lords reiterated the bulwark against parental claims in the strongest of terms:

> [in *Newham/Bedfordshire*] this House held that no duty of care was owed either to the child or to the mother. Subsequent cases ... have placed a question mark against the conclusion that no duty of care was owed to the child, but the authority of the *Newham* case for the proposition that no duty of care was owed *to the mother* remains unshaken. The social worker's, and the council's, statutory duty had been owed to the child. That duty provided no basis for the imposition on the authority of a duty of care owed to the mother.[111]

As a final brief note, England is not alone in its protective attitude towards HCPs who 'get it wrong' in child abuse investigations and accuse a party incorrectly.[112] A number of Commonwealth cases (in Australia,[113] Canada,[114] Scotland,[115] and New Zealand[116]) have held or suggested, for policy reasons reminiscent of *East Berkshire*, that a HCP involved in child abuse or neglect investigations owes **no** duty of care to that wrongfully-accused. US jurisprudence on the topic has been decidedly mixed[117]—some parents who have been wrongly accused of harming their own children (and some of these in circumstances where a psychotherapist negligently implanted recovered memories of childhood abuse in a patient) have established a duty of care in their favour,[118] whereas others have failed to do so.[119] The various policy reasons invoked by these US courts, on each side of the scales, closely reflect the dichotomy of views expressed by *East Berkshire's* majority versus Lord Bingham (dissenting).[120] Some jurisdictions have adopted the legislative route (illustrated in Canada, for example[121]), of precluding any liability on the part of a HCP who acts in good faith when making an inaccurate accusation of child abuse against a party, and which causes that party loss and damage.

2. Some applications of the rule in *East Berkshire* (HL)

The inability of wrongfully-accused parents to successfully state a cause of action against those involved in child abuse or mistreatment investigations was cemented by the *East Berkshire* decision, and since then, some extension and clarifications of the principle have emerged, which are of importance to putative HCPs:

First, mere operational decisions are also covered by the principle. Specifically, *East Berkshire* precluded a HCP from owing a duty of care to a parent in the conduct of investigations of child abuse or child mistreatment—so that where the defendant's decision is an *evaluative* one, based upon policy considerations, no duty of care is owed to that parent. However, what if the act or omission by the HCP is not an evaluative decision (e.g., whether or not to put a child on the protection register), but merely an operational decision (e.g., how to interview the child)? Notably, an attempt to distinguish *East Berkshire* on this score[122] has failed:

> In *L (a minor) and B v Reading BC*,[123] a father, B, was wrongly accused of abusing his three-year-old daughter L, after the child's mother made allegations of sexual abuse against the father. The child was interviewed twice by a social worker and a police officer; the second interview was video-recorded. On the basis of these interviews, the social worker and police officer formed the view that the father had abused L. The father was arrested, and although he was later released without charge, the social worker stated at a child protection case conference that L had said things that indicated that some sexual activity had occurred. B was denied contact with L throughout this period. However, after a 26-day trial, the judge found that the father had not sexually abused L in any way, and was highly critical of the statements made by the social worker and police officer about the interview with L, and of their professional conduct as a whole. Eventually L went to live with her father B. B claimed damages for loss of employment and for depression suffered as a result of the wrongful accusations. He accused the social worker and police officer of negligent operational activities/decisions, arguing that L had been removed from the family home on the basis of an error-prone interview; L's responses and demeanour had not been not recorded; and the outcome of the interview was relayed without the benefit of contemporaneous notes. **Held:** B's claim failed. No duty of care was owed to him by the defendants.

The claimant father had argued the errors committed around the interview process constituted merely operational decisions and functions, and did not involve the type of conflicts of duty and finely-balanced evaluative judgments discussed in *East Berkshire*. However, the distinction did not hold sway. *East Berkshire* held that a duty of care was not owed to parents in respect of *any aspect* of an investigation into the abuse of children. The father's argument was unworkable, said Keith J:

> Its effect would be to impose a duty of care on social workers to the parents of children who were the subjects of investigation of abuse in respect of some aspects of the investigation and not others. The interviewing of a child, and the relaying of the contents of that interview, are just as much part of the investigation as the evaluation of that and other material to decide whether intervention was necessary ... a duty of care cannot exist for some purposes in the course of an investigation into child abuse and cease to exist for other purposes because of a shift in the factual matrix. It either exists for all purposes in the investigation or for none.[124]

As has been academically pointed out,[125] the borderline between evaluative and operational decisions is notoriously difficult to pinpoint, and hence, Keith J's judgment undoubtedly avoids the prospect of satellite litigation in this most sensitive of areas.

Secondly, the *East Berkshire* rule covers social workers, as well as doctors and HCPs generally. In *East Berkshire*, no difference in principle was held to be applicable between doctors and social workers—neither owed the parents a duty of care, when involved in child care investigation and protection. This was reaffirmed in *Lawrence v Pembrokeshire CC*, where Auld LJ said that 'there is logically, and from a public policy point of view, no difference for this purpose between doctors and social workers—and the majority of the House of Lords in *East Berkshire* made no such distinction. It is immaterial that social workers, not doctors, place children on the Child Protection Register or take them into care, since child protection work requires social service departments to work closely with the police, doctors, community health workers, the education service and others.'[126]

Thirdly, the *East Berkshire* rule covers the *whole* investigative process. In *AD v Bury MBC*,[127] it was argued that the ratio of *East Berkshire* was that no duty of care towards wrongfully-accused parents arose because of the inevitable conflict of interest which existed between parent and child during the *initial* period of the investigation, but that the majority would have entertained the imposition of a duty of care to parents *after* an interim care order had been made. This argument was rejected: the freedom from liability in negligence which HCPs and others involved in child care and protection enjoy 'lasts throughout the investigatory process; and where (as here) care proceedings are instituted, the investigatory process itself lasts until such time as a final care order is made, or the proceedings are discharged'.[128]

Fourthly, the *East Berkshire* rule applies to allegations of direct (systemic) negligence too which lead to incorrect accusations being made against the parents. The principle, precluding a duty to the parental claimant, strictly arose in circumstances where the alleged wrongdoer was a doctor, social worker, or other HCP, and where the NHS Trust (or possibly, the local authority) was sued *vicariously* as employer of that wrongdoer. There was no duty of care owed by the employee HCPs in *East Berkshire*, and obviously, no vicarious liability either. Those were the strict facts and findings of *East Berkshire*.

However, what if the NHS Trust or other employer were to be sued directly for *systemic* breach? What if the parental claim is framed along the lines that, had the NHS Trust had a reasonably competent system in place (for training its employees, and in making sure that they were aware of the local and national guidance relating to the investigation of child abuse allegations, say), then the doctor or social worker would have acted differently, that inadequate training was the cause of the mistake, and that, in turn, caused the separation from the child and the parent's psychiatric damage? *East Berkshire* did not deal with that scenario. However, it has been clarified since that *East Berkshire* precludes a parental claim against an NHS Trust based on a direct duty, just as effectively as it bars a claim based upon an allegation of vicarious liability for the wrongdoing of an employed doctor. The Court of Appeal stated, in *L (a minor) and B v Reading BC*, that—

> there is nothing in the report of [*East Berkshire*] which suggests that Lord Nicholls or the other members of the majority intended to confine their statements of principle to cases in which the basis of the Defendant's liability is vicarious responsibility for the breach of duty on the part of a doctor or social worker. On the contrary, the approach of the majority seems to us to apply both to cases of vicarious liability and to cases of what may be called a direct liability [of an NHS Trust or local authority involved in abuse investigations].[129]

As Douglas notes, the *Reading* (CA) decision confirms that English law maintains that, even where it is the entity which is being sued directly for systemic negligence, a 'conflict of interest is likely to arise if employed professionals are required to weigh the interests of the parents—as potential abusers—of a child alongside those of the child whom they are examining.'[130]

Finally, the *East Berkshire* principle applies to front-line and back-room professionals. In *Lawrence v Pembrokeshire CC*,[131] the Court of Appeal confirmed that the principle applies, to preclude any duty of care to wrongfully-accused parents, whether the HCP, social worker, etc., had face-to-face and proximate contact with the parents, or were engaged in enquiries or decision-making without any personal contact with the parent at all. The physical proximity between professional and parent did not impact upon the duty question.

In summary: English authorities are adamant: in child abuse/neglect cases, and for policy reasons, no duty is owed by a HCP (or employer NHS Trust) to a wrongfully-accused parental or similarly-positioned claimant. As noted at the outset of this Section, the law has not moved as 'swiftly' for the parental claimant as it has for the child examinee.

D THE IMPACT OF THE ECHR ON THE WRONGFULLY-ACCUSED'S LEGAL POSITION

For any events occurring after 2 October 2000, ss 7 and 8 of the Human Rights Act 1998 (HRA) enables a claimant ('victim') to recover reparation. To claim such reparation, breach of a Convention article must be proved. Two bases—the right of access to the court under art 6,[132] and the right to respect for family life under art 8[133]—have been particularly in issue, in suits brought by wrongfully-accused parents under the HRA, and are discussed briefly below.

1. The *East Berkshire* rule and art 6

According to an obiter statement by the House of Lords in *Seal v Chief Constable of South Wales Police*,[134] the rule in *East Berkshire* that precludes a duty of care from being owed towards a wrongfully-accused parent does not constitute a denial for that parent of access to the courts, in violation of art 6 of the ECHR. It is merely an example of 'the price to be paid for the established principle (and the assurance it provides) protecting various classes of prospective defendants against claims in negligence.'[135] It was said that the *East Berkshire* principle does not engage art 6 in any way.

In fact, this view is entirely consistent with the earlier holding of the European Court of Human Rights in *TP and KM v UK*.[136] This litigation involved the same parties who had been unsuccessful in the *Newham* case before the House of Lords (the case which was part of the *Bedfordshire* conjoint appeals, in which the defendants thought that child KM was being abused by her mother's partner, whereas the abuser was, in fact, a relative). When they took their grievances to Strasbourg, both mother (TP) and daughter (KM) claimed that, in light of the combined findings in *Newham/ Bedfordshire*,[137] the fact that no duty of care was owed to them 'deprived them of access to court as it was effectively an exclusionary rule, or immunity from liability, which prevented their claims being decided on the facts.'[138] However, the European Court of Human Rights concluded that there was no denial of access to the court, and hence, no violation of art 6.[139] The court pointed to various matters, including that: TP and KM were not precluded from bringing their claims before the domestic courts (to the contrary, legal aid funding was used to appeal the case to the House of Lords); there was no 'blanket exclusionary rule' at play here, because 'the House of Lords found, applying ordinary principles of negligence law, that the local authority could not be held vicariously liable for any alleged negligence of the doctor and social worker', and in so doing, the merits of the claim, according to the principles of negligence, were fully ventilated; and although the House of Lords' strike-out of KM and TP's actions ended the case, without the factual matters being determined on the evidence, this was permissible—

> if as a matter of law, there was no basis for the claim, the hearing of evidence would have been an expensive and time-consuming process which would not have provided the applicants with any remedy at its conclusion. There is no reason to consider the striking out procedure which

rules on the existence of sustainable causes of action as *per se* offending the principle of access to court.[140]

Art 6 related to the overall fairness of the hearing, and that fairness was present, regardless of the fact that, ultimately, no duty of care was owed to TP and KM under the *Bedfordshire/Newham* ruling.

2. Recovery by the wrongfully-accused under art 8

The *East Berkshire* rule is, on the surface, rather dismissive of family life. Rupture of familial relationships, to the point of permanent disrepair, can result from negligent investigations of child abuse or mistreatment which 'point the finger' at parents. The crucial question for those parents, under art 8(2), has been whether the child's removal or separation from the family was 'necessary in a democratic society'—if so, then no violation of art 8 will be proven. Case conveniently summarises[141] the crucial points arising from Strasbourg jurisprudence on this point:[142]

- a public authority's decision-making, in cases in which child abuse is suspected, will inevitably involve *some* interference with family life;
- removal or separation may need to occur 'to protect the child in an emergency, in which case it will not always be practicable to afford the parent the opportunity to be involved in the decision-making process, as to do so may put the child at further risk';
- once the emergency is over, though, and the child's safety is assured, 'then the state is under a duty to ensure that a careful assessment is made of the options for caring for the child', and at that point, more considered assessment is required (a 'stricter scrutiny', as it was termed in *TP and KM v UK*[143]), especially of 'any steps which may curtail parental rights of access';
- the state's procedural obligations 'include legal representation for the parents where court proceedings are employed to determine a child's future caring arrangements; not pursuing draconian steps, such as adoption, without thorough consideration of less severe options; and involving parents in decision-making, including an opportunity to respond to the evidence against them upon which the allegations of wrongful treatment are founded'; and
- 'taking a child into care is to be regarded as a temporary measure, to be discontinued as soon as possible.'

Notwithstanding some academic opinion which envisaged that any parental action for redress under the HRA, for a contravention of art 8, would be 'exceedingly unlikely'[144] after *East Berkshire*, there has been the odd success under art 8 for the wrongfully-accused parent. The successful suit by mother TP in *Newham* has already been mentioned (*TP and KM v UK*[145]). It was not the removal of M, but the failure of process after the video interview was conducted, which constituted the violation of TP's art 8 rights.[146] A violation of art 8 was made out in *Venema v Netherlands*[147] too. Again, this was not because an 11-month-old child was removed for five months from his mother as a result of a negligent diagnosis of the mother as suffering from Munchausen Syndrome by Proxy, but because the parents had not been sufficiently involved in the decision-making process and had not been able to put forward their point of view before the court order was made.[148]

However, a claim under the HRA for an alleged violation of art 8 failed, for example, in *RK and AK v UK*.[149] This litigation involved the same parties as in the *Oldham* 'brittle bone' litigation, which formed part of the *East Berkshire* appeal cases.[150] The European Court of Human Rights pointed out that, just because health and other professionals made errors in judgment about potential abuse situations did not render their conduct incompatible with the requirements of art 8: '[t]he authorities, medical and social, have duties to protect children and cannot be held liable every time their genuine and reasonably held concerns are proved retrospectively to have been misguided.'[151] In this case, there had been pertinent and sufficient reasons for the authorities to have taken protective measures, which had been proportionate in the circumstances to the aim of protecting baby MK. In particular, the claims by AK and RK (mother and father, respectively, of baby MK)—

> very much amount to criticising the way in which the professionals, medical and legal, were prepared to suspect the worst on the information available to them and failed immediately to perceive their innocence or give them the benefit of any doubt. Nonetheless, it must also be noted that, while an interim care order was issued with a view to protecting MK, steps were also taken to place the baby within her extended family and in close proximity to the [parents'] own home so that they could easily and frequently visit. And crucially, as soon as a further fracture occurred outwith the [parents'] care, further tests were quickly pursued and within weeks MK was returned home.[152]

In light of this decision, it has been noted by Bailey-Harris that, '[t]he availability of redress [for the parents] under the Human Rights Act in respect of alleged negligence by child care professionals after 2 October 2000 may be more theoretical than real'.[153] Along the same lines, Ruck and Holt have observed that, 'for parents who come to the attention of the authorities in relation to the care of their children, one has to question whether the HRA is a meaningful mechanism for parents who seek to challenge social services' or doctors' decisions', especially where a HRA action does not compensate those parents for their full tortious pecuniary losses, but only for breach of their human rights—'[t]his situation will only be met ... by a direct duty owed to the parents.'[154]

3. Does the common law need to change in light of art 8?

As a separate question—can the *East Berkshire* rule survive art 8's requirement of respect for family life, or should the common law be amended, in the light of art 8, in order to recognise that a duty of care toward the wrongfully-accused parent *does* exist?

(a) The *East Berkshire* (HL) obiter dicta

The events giving rise to the conjoint appeal in *East Berkshire* occurred before the HRA came into force (the events predated October 2000), so the parental claimants could not seek damages for any possible breach of a Convention right. Nevertheless, members of the House gave explicit consideration to the issue of whether art 8 should countenance *against* the common law's hardline attitude towards the wrongfully-accused parent. On this question, the House had rather mixed views.

Some of the majority judgments made reference to the abovementioned cases in which art 8 violations *had* been successfully pleaded by wrongfully-accused parents, but did not consider that these developments compelled English tort law to recognise a duty of care by HCPs and other professionals towards those parents.[155] As remarked upon in a later case,[156] there was no detailed discussion by the majority of how art 8 could or should contribute to the development of the common law on this point, aside from 'some peripheral mention' (as opposed to the duty of care to the child, the development/emergence of which the invocation of art 8 had *certainly* contributed to). Lord Rodger, on the other hand, seemed to leave the question open—'I should wish to reserve my opinion as to whether, in such a case, it would be appropriate to modify the common law of negligence rather than to found any action on the provisions ... of the Human Rights Act 1998'.[157]

At the other end of the spectrum, Lord Bingham (dissenting) cited the sympathetic-to-parents Strasbourg authority of *TP* and *Venema*, and preferred the view that domestic law *should* recognise a duty of care owed by investigating professional to wrongfully-accused parent:

> the question does arise whether the law of tort should evolve, analogically and incrementally, so as to fashion appropriate remedies to contemporary problems or whether it should remain essentially static, making only such changes as are forced upon it, leaving difficult, and, in human terms, very important problems to be swept up by the Convention. I prefer evolution.[158]

In a different context, art 8 has **not** required the creation, in English law, of a general law of invasion of privacy—that submission was specifically rejected in *Wainwright v Home Office*;[159] and in *Watkins v Home Office*,[160] Lord Rodger also considered that the common law of England did not require a bold re-writing to map all rights of redress that a claimant may have under the Convention:

> The Convention rights form part of our law and provide a rough equivalent of a written code of constitutional rights, albeit not one tailor-made for this country. In general, at least, where the matter is not already covered by the common law but falls within the scope of a Convention right, a Claimant can be expected to invoke his remedy under the Human Rights Act rather than to seek to fashion a new common law right.[161]

It was not until 2007, however, that the question as to whether the *East Berkshire* principle needed modifying, for the English common law to comply with art 8, arose for direct judicial consideration.

(b) The *Lawrence v Pembrokeshire* ratio

The English Court of Appeal has unanimously held that the principle in *East Berkshire*, barring a claim by the wrongfully-accused parent in negligence, *did* survive the implementation of art 8 into domestic law.

> In *Lawrence v Pembrokeshire CC*,[162] Mrs Lawrence (L) sued the Pembrokeshire CC for the conduct of their child protection team, and for failing to follow due procedures. The Lawrence family had come to the notice of the Council's child protection team in 1999; eventually, after sporadic investigations, in April 2002 the Council had placed L's children on the Child Protection Register, because it was thought that they were at risk of physical and/or emotional harm from L or their father. However, they were then removed from the register in June 2003. L complained to the Ombudsman about maladministration by the Council, and in December 2004, the Ombudsman upheld these complaints. L was paid £5,000 by the Council in compensation. L sued the Council, alleging negligence *and* a violation of her right to respect for family life under art 8, because of the conduct of social workers employed by the council towards her and her children in placing the children's names on the Child Protection Register. L alleged that this conduct caused her psychiatric injury. **Held:** the claims, both in negligence and under art 8, were struck out.[163]

East Berkshire governed this claim: a duty of care was not owed by investigating professionals, or by public authorities who employed them, to parents suspected of child abuse. L claimed that, for events post-dating October 2000, the policy reasoning in *East Berkshire*—that a professional ought not to have in the back of his mind the prospect of being exposed to a suit by an aggrieved parent—surely no longer held true. After that date, the potential for an art 8 claim by the parent was something that any professional had to be mindful of (albeit that the suit would have to be brought against the public authority, and not against the individual concerned). In any event, it was an odd situation (went the argument), if a child could sue in negligence and under art 8, and possibly under art 3 if the abuse was sufficiently inhumane, and yet, a wrongfully-accused parent could only sue under art 8, and not in negligence. These, essentially, were the arguments of Mrs Lawrence.

However, the Court of Appeal held that the *East Berkshire* common law principle was compatible with art 8, for four principal reasons:[164]

- To recognise a duty of care towards the wrongfully-accused parent 'would conflict with the more pressing duty to the child to protect him from the risk of parental abuse when suspected', and nothing about the advent of art 8, or the ability of the parents to bring a claim under s 7 of the HRA for violation of art 8, had changed that conflict—that reasoning remained as true now as it did when *East Berkshire* was decided in 2005;
- The 'whole point' of the rule in *East Berkshire* was to forestall possible harm to a child, 'by robust and timely intervention', when a local authority suspected parental abuse of children in the context of their family life. Strasbourg jurisprudence had 'indicated a plain acceptance in principle that interference with family life in this context', to preserve the interests of safety and welfare of children when parents were suspected of abusing them, 'may be regarded, as being in pursuance of a legitimate aim, proportionate and necessary in a democratic society' under art 8(2). Hence, the common law rule was compatible with art 8 and did not need amending;
- Art 8 was **not** concerned with the parental claim for a duty of care, but with 'a threshold of interference by a public authority with family life'—so that, where a parent brought a claim under art 8, it required the public body, which was accused of interfering with family life, to justify its conduct. If this were to be translated into a common law duty of care, it would require the public authority to prove, given its concern for the child's welfare, that it was not in such breach of duty, a reversal in the burden of proof which would result in a 'plain distortion' of the common law action in negligence. It was not necessary, or correct, for English common law to be developed in that way;
- The advent of art 8 to domestic law, 'bringing with it a discrete right to children and parents of respect for their family life, did not undermine or weaken the primacy of the need to protect children from abuse, or the risk of abuse, from their parents.' The *East Berkshire* rule was consistent with the protection of family life, and with art 8.

Notwithstanding this robustly-put view, various arguments have been posed, by academic commentators, as to why cognisance should have been given to Lord Rodger's dicta—that the *East Berkshire* rule may need looking at again in light of the Convention rights now enjoyed by parents.

Some of these academic views support Mrs Lawrence's argument that the policy reasoning underpinning *East Berkshire*, for denying a wrongfully accused parent's claim in negligence, should no longer hold good. For example, Palser has pointed out that the likelihood of any wrongfully-accused parent bringing a successful claim for art 8 infringement is 'remote'[165]—but given that they clearly can, then '[i]t is clear from *TP* and *Venema* that a conflict of interests does not preclude the engagement of an Art 8 claim by a parent, so it should equally not preclude a claim at common law', and that 'if child protection workers' minds are affected by the imposition of Article 8 liability, the conflicts argument can no longer be a bar to negligence liability.'[166] Jones agrees that, given that such professionals may be liable to parents for breach of the parents' Convention rights, it will be a 'particularly well-informed doctor who is able to balance these competing duties with equanimity, even if she is relieved of the burden of weighing the possible effects of a common law duty owed to the parents.'[167]

Other academic opinion points to the 'time and money' limitations of bringing any action under art 8. For example, Douglas remarks that, absent any ability to claim in negligence, remedies for wrongfully-accused parents will remain very 'limited', with paltry compensation available via Ombudsmen's schemes (it will be recalled that Mrs Lawrence only recovered £5,000 by virtue of that route) or with the prospect of lower damages under the HRA.[168] Wright points to the much shorter limitation period[169] and lower awards of damages generally-speaking, which may make litigation under the HRA seemingly less attractive for claimants.[170] Booth and Squires lament that, '[f]rom a common law perspective, the approach taken by the European Court to damages can appear somewhat obscure', with the damages awards seemingly 'impressionistic, ... intended to reflect its view of the gravity of the harm done to the claimant rather than applying clearly articulated principles.'[171]

A third group of academic criticisms point to other disadvantages of a HRA action for breach of the positive obligation arising under art 8. Some of these have been noted previously.[172] Additionally, Jones notes that the *East Berkshire* approach is fundamentally flawed—'[b]y denying the existence of a duty of care, the common law of negligence never gets to the stage of looking at the manner in which the professionals undertook their responsibilities', even in situations where some of the wrongful accusation scenarios that make their way to the courtroom 'demonstrate a terrible history of incompetence, bordering at times on bad faith'.[173] Hoyano and Keenan posit that 'a negligence tort action is a far more refined instrument to yield nuanced principles for determining the parameters and quantum of liability than the HRA can afford. The concept of a standard of care set by negligence law ... draws a much sharper line as to what good professional practice requires in particular circumstances than can the Articles of the European Convention.'[174] McIvor further points to the difficulties which parental claimants have in proving any breach of the positive obligation arising under art 8, especially given the effect of art 8(2)—so that, given the circumstances in which it is permissible to interfere with the right to private life, and given the wide margin of discretion which States enjoy in determining what steps are necessary to comply with the Convention in this context, 'it is likely that third party actions against public authority defendants will continue to be founded on the law of negligence.'[175]

A fourth academic criticism is that this nook of negligence law, involving wrongfully-accused parents, aptly demonstrates the divide between what a victim may seek to achieve in reparation under s 7 of the HRA for breach of the Convention right to private life, and what a claimant can look to achieve under the common law. To say that the rights of suit are not co-extensive is to put the matter too highly; for the parental claimant, they lack any coincidence at all. (Jenny) Steele notes that, contrary to the view that was generally held at the time of the Convention's implementation (that tort law was 'sure to adapt and expand in order to protect Convention rights more fully'), the reality has been quite the opposite, '[an] emerging separation of tort from HRA actions';[176] while Anthony observes that *East Berkshire* clearly illustrates that '[e]xpectations that the common law and the European Convention might develop in tandem ... have proven misplaced.'[177] It should be noted, however, that there are those who *support* that divide, with (Iain) Steele remarking that—

There is no a priori reason why every 'HRA' claim should have a common law cousin. Indeed, Parliament's intention in creating a free-standing cause of action under section 7 of the HRA would arguably be frustrated by invariably allowing claimants to fashion a parallel common law claim and thereby access tort law's more generous limitation periods and measure of damages. The [*East Berkshire*] approach of re-evaluating policy arguments in light of the new 'HRA' liability, and extending common law liability only if those arguments no longer hold weight, is to be preferred.[178]

The fact remains, however, that the rule in *East Berkshire*, while immunising HCPs (and others involved in child abuse investigation and prosecution) from parental claims brought in negligence, stands in stark contrast with the common law's preparedness to shift position and to accommodate the claims of *child* claimants. Of all the non-patient categories of claimant considered in this book, the wrongfully-accused parent is perhaps the least likely claimant to pose any great threat to medical insurance funds in the future. The reasons for that are almost entirely policy-driven.

E   CONCLUSION

Wrongfully-accused parents/guardians are not owed any duty of care by public authorities, or by individuals employed by them, when investigating and or taking steps to protect children whom they consider to be at risk of parental abuse.

When it is all boiled down to the basic question—'in diagnosing the child's condition in a case of possible abuse, is the position of the child *so different* from that of the parent that a duty may sensibly be owed to the one but not to the other?'[179]—the *East Berkshire* (HL) majority answered this, 'yes', and the dissenter, Lord Bingham, answered it, 'no'.

The parental lack of success again calls to mind the dictum of Lord Rodger: 'the world is full of harm for which the law furnishes no remedy.'[180] Or, as one judge has rather bluntly put it, '[n]or does an action lie against medical practitioners and social workers for failing to use reasonable care in assessing the risk that you sexually abused children, even though your reputation may be ruined by their conclusion'.[181] It is upon the parent or other wrongfully accused that the law of negligence deems that the loss should lie, when wrongful accusations of abuse are made by HCPs.

In fact, the wrongfully-accused parent may have little opportunities for redress at all—even if a HRA claim were made out for breach of art 8, the limitation period is only one year, and the damages awarded by the European Court of Human Rights are generally lower. Reliance on other tortious causes of action is also likely to prove a barren course for the unfortunate parent, for as Lord Nicholls emphasised in *East Berkshire*, malicious falsehood will only attract a remedy if a false statement is made maliciously, misfeasance in public office requires some proof of bad faith or recklessness, and malicious prosecution (assuming that the parent is prosecuted) requires proof of malice too[182]—none of which is likely on the facts of well-intentioned, but incompetently-handled, investigations of child abuse.

Meanwhile, the '*Potential Liability to Non-Patients and Third Parties: A Synopsis for Healthcare Professionals*' guideline in the Appendix outlines the reasons as to why English law has furnished a HCP with considerable protection against a suit in negligence, where a parent has been wrongfully and negligently accused of child abuse or mistreatment by that HCP.

ENDNOTES

1   Other types of limited patients, e.g., examinees for the purposes of insurance applications/renewals, or for prospective or continuing employment, or for police, forensic or legal purposes, are beyond the scope of this book, but are considered further in, e.g.: R Mulheron, 'Medical Examinations for Insurance, Employment and Litigation: An Evolving Liability of Healthcare Professionals towards Examinee and Client' [forthcoming, 2010]. Also: A Grubb, 'Doctors Engaged by Third Parties: Duties to Take Care' (1997) 5 *Med L Rev* 348, 350.

2   [2009] EWCA Civ 59, which scenario Wall LJ described, at [3], as 'a disaster' for the parents—'[t]he only mitigation, from their point of view, is the local authority's belated recognition that they are fit and able to care for Brandon [their fourth child]'.

3   *Re N* [1999] Lloyd's Rep Med 257 (CA) 260 (Stuart-Smith LJ).

4   *X (Minors) v Bedfordshire CC* [1995] 2 AC 633 (HL) 753 (Lord Browne-Wilkinson). Whether the traditional duty applies in other contexts, such as examinations for insurance, employment or forensic purposes, has become increasingly controversial, as discussed by the author elsewhere: 'Medical Examinations for Insurance, Employment and Litigation: An Evolving Liability of the Health Professionals towards Examinee and Client' [forthcoming, 2010], by reference to, e.g., *Re N* [1999] Lloyd's Rep Med 257 (CA); *Kapfunde v Abbey National plc* [1998] EWCA Civ 535, (1998) 45 BMLR 176 (CA); *Baker v Kaye* (1996) 39 BMLR 12 (QBD), and contrary decisions emerging from other jurisdictions which take issue with the English common law's 'traditional duty' towards a limited patient.

5   [2005] UKHL 23, [2005] 2 AC 373 (HL).

6   Given the book's emphasis on negligence, the chapter excludes from consideration the topic of witness immunity, which, where it applies, excludes liability on the part of HCPs who are involved in judicial proceedings relating to child abuse and who misidentify the abuser. For discussion of this issue, see, e.g.: L Hoyano and C Keenan, *Child Abuse: Law and Policy Across Boundaries* (OUP, Oxford, 2007) 372–73; M Jones, *Medical Negligence* (4th edn, Sweet and Maxwell, London, 2009) 135–39.

7   *RK and AK v Oldham NHS Trust* [2005] UKHL 23, [2005] 2 AC 373 (child MK suffered from brittle bone disease) where, at trial, [2003] Lloyd's Rep Med 1 (QB) [21], [34], Simon J concluded that the child had not suffered a recognisable psychiatric injury as a result of his temporary removal from the family home.

8   *AD v Bury MBC* [2006] EWCA Civ 1, [2006] 1 WLR 917, [93] (baby OH suffered from brittle bone disease and was removed from the family home for four months; medical evidence, accepted at trial, suggested he had suffered only transient harm as a result of that removal).

9   [1995] 2 AC 633 (HL). The case actually concerned five appeals—in addition to those noted in the text, it included: *Christmas v Hampshire CC*; and *Keating v Bromley LBC*. These two cases, together with *Dorset*, concerned claims of negligence against education authorities (directly and vicariously) in respect of their specific statutory duties towards children with special educational needs. The employees accused of negligence included educational psychologists, head teacher, and doctor. The principles governing these claims vary considerably from those applicable to child protection investigations and the wrongfully-accused parental non-patient, for as Lord Browne-Wilkinson noted (at 763–64), '[t]he position of the psychologists in the education cases is quite different from that of the doctor and social worker in the child abuse cases. There is no potential conflict of duty between the professional's duties to the plaintiff and his duty to the educational authority. Nor is there any obvious conflict between the professional being under a duty of care to the plaintiff and the discharge by the authority of its statutory duties. If, at trial, it emerges that there are such conflicts, then the trial judge may have to limit or exclude any duty of care owed by the professional to the plaintiff. But at this stage no obvious conflict has been demonstrated'. Given the lack of a true non-patient in the educational negligence-type of case, and the different policy reasons governing the duty of care owed by the HCP toward the child in any event, these educational cases will not be considered further in this chapter.

10   *ibid*, 651 (Sir Thomas Bingham MR, CA).

11   The case of *X (Minors) v Bedfordshire CC* itself involved litigation against a local authority, not against HCPs or health authority. Five children had been victims of the most appalling maltreatment and neglect, which had been brought to the notice of the Council, but on which, for several years, the Council officers had failed to act. It was held that the children had no remedy against the Council in negligence.

12   [1995] 2 AC 633 (HL) 660.

13   No direct negligence claim was brought against health authority or local authority in *M v Newham* (*ibid*, 748). Instead, as Lord Browne-Wilkinson noted, at ibid, 751–52, the case was put on the basis that the HCPs, social worker and psychiatrist, each owed a personal duty to the child and to the mother, to exercise reasonable professional skills in the conduct of the interview with the child and to make proper inquiries; that the HCPs were each personally in breach of this duty; and that their employers (the Council and the health authority, respectively) were vicariously liable for that breach.

14   *viz*, whether the performance of a statutory duty can give rise to a common law duty of care so as to found an action in negligence; whether it is alleged that the public authority owes a duty of care in the manner in which it exercises a statutory discretion or whether the duty of care is alleged to arise from the manner in which the statutory duty has been implemented in practice; what decisions of the public authority are considered to be non-justiciable, because they concern matters of social policy or resource allocation. These issues are discussed in detail in, e.g.: C Booth and D Squires, *The Negligence Liability of Public Authorities* (OUP, Oxford, 2006) ch 8; L Hoyano and C Keenan, *Child Abuse: Law and Policy Across Boundaries* (OUP, Oxford, 2007) 319–39.

15   C McIvor, *Third Party Liability in Tort* (Hart Publishing, Oxford, 2006) 110–11.

16   Staughton and Peter Gibson LJJ formed the majority. Notably, Sir Thomas Bingham MR, dissenting, whilst countenancing that a duty was owed to M, seriously doubted whether any breach would be made out in trial.

17   [1995] 2 AC 633 (HL) 752–53 (emphasis added) (Lord Browne-Wilkinson), with whom Lords Jauncey, Lane, Nolan and Ackner agreed. Lord Nolan concurred on these policy reasons for denying a duty of care, but held that there was sufficient proximity between HCPs and examinee child for a duty to be owed.

18   See, for discussion of these policy reasons, *ibid*, 749–51. Lord Browne-Wilkinson said that these policy reasons, as to why a local authority did not owe any direct duty of care to the children, 'apply with at least equal force' to the individual psychiatrist and social worker defendants: at 754.

19   *ibid* (Sir Thomas Bingham MR, CA) 663, point (7), and the sentiment (but not the result) affirmed in the same case in the HL (Lord Browne-Wilkinson), *ibid*, 749. Reiterated in: *Smith v Chief Constable of Sussex Police; Van Colle v Chief Constable of Hertfordshire* [2008] UKHL 50, [2009] 1 AC 225, [56] (Lord Bingham).

20   *TP and KM v UK* (2001) 34 EHRR 42 (ECtHR) [30], [80]–[83], [115]–[117].

21   See [1995] 2 AC 633 (CA) 662–64, for discussion of these policy reasons.

22   M Jones, 'Child Abuse: When the Professionals Get it Wrong' (2006) 14 *Med L Rev* 264, 265.

23   M Jones, *Medical Negligence* (4th edn, Sweet & Maxwell, London, 2008) 126, 127–28 (original emphasis).

24   [2001] 2 AC 619 (HL).

25   As discussed in *ibid*, 666 (Lord Nicholls), citing: Education (Special Educational Needs) Regulations 1994 (SS 1994/1047), reg 6.

26   [1999] 1 WLR 500 (CA), 46 BMLR 100 (CA).

27   [2001] 2 AC 619 (HL) 653.

28   *Caparo Industries plc v Dickman* [1990] 2 AC 605 (HL) 617–18.

29   [2001] 2 AC 619 (HL) 652–53.

30   *ibid*, 654.

31   *ibid*, 654.

32   *ibid*, 653–55. See also, Lord Clyde's discussion of policy factors at 672.

33   C Booth and D Squires, *The Negligence Liability of Public Authorities* (OUP, Oxford, 2006) [8.19].

34   *ibid*, 654.

35 [1999] UKHL 25, [2001] 2 AC 550 (17 Jun 1999). The *Barrett* decision was also notable for the fact that Lord Browne-Wilkinson explained why the European Court of Human Rights had misunderstood the effect of the role of policy in precluding a duty of care, in *Osman v UK* (1998) 5 EHRR 293 (ECtHR). His Lordship noted (at 559–60) that '[i]n English law the decision as to whether it is fair, just and reasonable to impose a liability in negligence on a particular class of would-be defendants depends on weighing in the balance the total detriment to the public interest in all cases from holding such class liable in negligence as against the total loss to all would-be plaintiffs if they are not to have a cause of action in respect of the loss they have individually suffered', and that a decision to preclude a duty, based upon policy considerations, is not a 'blanket immunity' of the type that would invoke a contravention of art 6 of the ECHR, as the *Osman* court had held. It was ultimately accepted by the Strasbourg court, in *Z v UK* (2001) 34 EHRR 97 (ECtHR) 119–20, that the striking-out procedure was 'an important feature of English civil procedure, performing the function of securing speedy and effective justice, *inter alia* by allowing it to be decided promptly which issues need full investigation and trial and disposing summarily of the others. By means of this procedure, it can be determined at an early stage, with minimum cost to the parties, whether the facts as pleaded reveal a claim existing in law'. Hence, no violation of art 6 was involved in the use of the striking-out procedure.

36 *ibid*, 568–69 (Lord Slynn).

37 *ibid*, 568, citing Evans LJ's judgment in the CA.

38 [2001] Fam 313 (CA) 338. On the same note, a child's action survived strike-out in, e.g.: *W v Essex CC* [2001] 2 AC 592 (HL); *L (a minor) v Reading BC* [2001] EWCA Civ 346, [2001] 1 WLR 1575.

39 V Chico, 'Saviour Siblings: Trauma and Tort Law' (2006) 14 *Med L Rev* 180, (accessed online, no pp available).

40 P Cane, 'Tort Law as Regulation' (2002) 31 *Common Law World Rev* 305 (accessed online, no pp available).

41 L Hoyano and C Keenan, *Child Abuse: Law and Policy Across Boundaries* (OUP, Oxford, 2007) 334.

42 R Bailey-Harris and M Harris, 'Local Authorities and Child Protection—The Mosaic of Accountability' [2002] *CFLQ* 117, 125.

43 R Mullender, 'Torts, Human Rights, and Common Law Culture' (2003) 23 *OJLS* 301, 307—although this author questions whether that earlier expansive view of the liability of public authorities can be squared with the recent decision of the House of Lords to disallow the claim in negligence in: *Mitchell v Glasgow CC* [2009] UKHL 11, [2009] 1 AC 874: R Mullender, 'Negligence, Human Rights, and Public Bodies' (2009) 125 *LQR* 384. Readers are referred to Chapter 3, for a critique of what *Mitchell* means for non-patient suits, in the context of a 'dangerous patient'.

44 [2003] UKPC 61, [2003] 4 All ER 833 (Lord Nicholls delivered the judgment of the court).

45 *ibid*, [29].

46 (2001) 34 EHRR 97, [2001] 2 FLR 612 (ECtHR). For detailed commentary, see, e.g.: J Miles, 'Human Rights and Child Protection' [2001] *CFLQ* 431; R Bailey-Harris and M Harris, 'Local Authorities and Child Protection—The Mosaic of Accountability' [2002] *CFLQ* 117.

47 (2001) 34 EHRR 42, [2001] 2 FLR 549 (ECtHR), also critiqued by the commentaries noted *ibid*. They were each awarded £10,000.

48 *ibid*, [30], [80]–[83], [115]–[117]. A violation of art 13 (no right of remedy) was made out too, because the claimants, TP and KM, had no avenues for compensation from the Ombudsman or from any other complaints regime.

49 [2003] EWCA Civ 1151, [2004] QB 558.

50 In *RK and AK v Oldham NHS Trust*, RK was the father of MK, and AK was the child's mother. Both RK and his wife AK were claimants in the case against Oldham NHS Trust. The child, MK, was an original claimant, but no longer pressed her claim by the time of the appeal.

51 In *RK and MAK v Dewsbury Healthcare NHS Trust*, RK was the child, and MAK was her father. Both claimants brought actions in negligence.

52 The facts of the three cases are considered in Section C1, where the position of the wrongfully-accused is considered in further detail.

53 The Kirklees MBC was sued, together with the Dewsbury Healthcare NHS Trust, by MAK and RK.

54 It had been a preliminary issue in this litigation as to whether the child in this case, MK, had suffered any injury for which the law recognised a remedy. Simon J concluded that the medical evidence did not support a finding of psychiatric injury, and this finding was not appealed against, as noted in the CA decision: [2004] QB 558 (CA) [121] and in the HL decision: [2005] UKHL 23, [2005] 2 AC 373, [19].

55 *RK and MAK v Dewsbury Healthcare NHS Trust* [2005] UKHL 23, [2005] 2 AC 373 (child suffered from Schamberg's disease).

56 This was determined by way of a preliminary issue.

57 More recently, see, e.g.: *NXS v Camden LBC* [2009] 3 FCR 157 (QBD), which held that, since *East Berkshire* (CA), it has been 'well established that a local authority which carries out investigations into suspected child abuse owes a duty of care to a child who is potentially at risk ... [including] a duty to take reasonable steps to avoid or prevent her from suffering personal injury'. However, a local authority does not owe a duty to protect its tenants, who have learning difficulties and are child-like in their mental capacities and understandings, to protect them from the criminal acts of others: *X v Hounslow LBC* [2009] EWCA Civ 286, [2009] 3 FCR 266.

58 *JD v East Berkshire Community Health NHS Trust; RK and MAK v Dewsbury Healthcare NHS Trust; RK and AK v Oldham NHS Trust* [2003] EWCA Civ 1151, [2004] QB 558, [83]–[84] (Lord Phillips MR delivered the court's judgment, Hale and Latham LJJ concurring).

59 See, e.g., the comments in: *Leeds CC v Price* [2005] EWCA Civ 289, [33] ('Departing from the House of Lords decision ... has attracted some academic criticism. It remains to see whether this will be echoed by the House itself': Lord Phillips MR), citing: J Wright, '"Immunity" No More: Child Abuse Cases and Public Authority Liability in Negligence after *JD v East Berkshire Community Health NHS Trust*' (2004) 20 *PN* 58.

60 *JD v East Berkshire Community Health NHS Trust* [2005] UKHL 23, [2005] 2 AC 373, [21] (Lord Bingham). The remainder of the HL judges did not specifically comment upon the CA's failure to follow precedent or upon the CA's reluctance to leave any overturn of *Newham/Bedfordshire* (HL) to the HL itself. The oddity of this approach has been academically questioned, e.g.: J Wright, 'Immunity No More: Child Abuse Cases and Public Authority Liability in Negligence' (2004) 20 *PN* 58.

61 *ibid*, [30].

62 *ibid*, [110]. See, too: [124] (Lord Brown).

63 M Jones, 'Child Abuse: When the Professionals Get it Wrong' (2006) 14 *Med L Rev* 264, 269.

64 M Mildred, 'Personal Injury, Psychiatric Harm, Parents, Children' (2004) 1 *JPIL* C9, C12.

65 M Jones, 'Child Protection and Duties to Third Parties' (2007) 23 *PN* 118, 118.

66 C McIvor, *Third Party Liability in Tort* (Hart Publishing, Oxford, 2006) 100.

67 J Steele, *Tort Law: Text, Cases and Materials* (OUP, Oxford, 2007) 418.

68 See, e.g.: C McIvor, 'Police Immunity and the Legacy of *Hill v Chief Constable of West Yorkshire*' (2005) 21 *PN* 201, 206.

69 As domestic courts are mandated to do, pursuant to s 2 of the Human Rights Act 1998.

70 *R (on the application of Purdy) v DPP* [2009] EWCA Civ 92, (2009) 106 BMLR 170, [53].

71 *Kay v Lambeth LBC, Leeds CC v Price* [2006] UKHL 10, [2006] 2 AC 465, [45] (Lord Bingham). These exceptional circumstances were noted to include matters such as: the *Bedfordshire* case was heard in 1995, well before the HRA came into force; none of the *Bedfordshire* opinions referenced the Convention; and the children recovered large amounts of reparation for violation of art 3 when they took their claim to the ECtHR, per *Z v UK* (2001) 34 EHRR 97, [2001] 2 FLR 612.

72 *R (on the application of RJM (FC)) v Secretary of State for Work and Pensions* [2008] UKHL 63, [2008] 3 WLR 1023, [64] (Lord Neuberger).

73 e.g.: *Pierce v Doncaster MBC* [2007] EWHC 2968, (2007) 100 BMLR 76 (QB) [22] (duty owed by local authority, where it returned the claimant to the care of abusive and neglectful parents).

74 *JD v East Berkshire Community Health NHS Trust* [2005] UKHL 23, [2005] 2 AC 373, [82]. See too, Lord Bingham, [3] ('the law in this area has evolved very markedly over the last decade. What appeared to be hard-edged rules precluding the possibility of any claim by parent or child have been eroded or restricted'). For a comprehensive tracing of how quickly this public authority liability landscape has

changed in English law, see: C Booth and D Squires, *The Negligence Liability of Public Authorities* (OUP, Oxford, 2006) [8.07]–[8.26].

75 *ibid*, [30] (Lord Bingham) ('in *M v Newham*, the parent's claims were a very secondary issue … [and] In the House, the parent's entitlement was not separately addressed').

76 [2003] EWCA Civ 1151, [2004] QB 558 (CA).

77 [2001] EWCA Civ 346, [2001] 1 WLR 1575 (CA).

78 *Osman v UK* [1999] 1 FLR 193 (ECtHR); *Barrett v Enfield LBC* [1999] UKHL 25, [2001] 2 AC 550.

79 [2001] EWCA Civ 346, [2001] 1 WLR 1575 (CA) 1587.

80 *JD v East Berkshire Community Health NHS Trust; RK and MAK v Dewsbury Healthcare NHS Trust; RK and AK v Oldham NHS Trust* [2005] UKHL 23, [2005] 2 AC 373.

81 It will be recalled that child MK sued at the beginning too, but was held at first instance not to have suffered a recognisable psychiatric injury, which was not the subject of any appeal: see n 7 above.

82 This is a condition in which a person inflicts harm upon another, such as a child, to garner medical attention: *Oxford Concise Colour Medical Dictionary* (4th edn, OUP, Oxford, 2007) 466.

83 It will be recalled that child RK also sued, and her action was permitted to proceed (see Section B), which decision was not the subject of appeal at HL level.

84 *ibid*, [47].

85 *ibid*, [20] (Lord Bingham).

86 [2003] UKPC 61 (Lord Nicholls, who delivered the judgment of the Board, was in the majority in *East Berkshire*) (social worker believed, incorrectly, that father was abusing child; PC allowed child's claim to proceed, but affirmed that father's claim should be struck out).

87 [2005] UKHL 23, [2005] 2 AC 373, [83].

88 Respectively, [74] and [90] (Lord Nicholls). Also [138] (Lord Brown), and for a similarly-unsympathetic attitude towards suspects of crime in their attempted suits against police, see, e.g.: *Brooks v Metropolitan Police Commr* [2005] UKHL 24, [2005] 1 WLR 1495, [38] (Lord Rodger).

89 These are drawn, especially, from the following passages: *East Berkshire, ibid*, [78], [85]–[88] (Lord Nicholls), [100], [110]–[117] (Lord Rodger), [125]–[133], [137]–[138] (Lord Brown), citing: *Sullivan v Moody* [2001] HCA 59, (2001) 207 CLR 562. Lord Steyn agreed with these majority opinions: at [96]. See also: *East Berkshire* [2004] QB 558 (CA) [86] (Lord Phillips MR); and *B v A-G (NZ)* [2003] UKPC 61, [30] (Lord Nicholls). For a convenient summary of the judgments, see, e.g.: *Jain v Trent Strategic HA* [2007] EWCA Civ 1186, [53]–[58] aff'd: [2009] UKHL 4, [2009] AC 853 (the case concerned a different point, *viz*, cancellation of the registration of nursing home operators, resulting in the closure of a care home and the relocation of its residents, and economic loss to the operators, but the reasoning in *East Berkshire* was extensively considered).

90 P Case, 'The Accused Strikes Back: The Negligence Action and Erroneous Allegations of Child Abuse' (2005) 21 *PN* 214, 215.

91 J Steele, *Tort Law: Text, Cases and Materials* (OUP, Oxford, 2007) 420.

92 Citing: *W v Essex CC* [2001] 2 AC 592 (HL) (foster child abused parents' own four children; arguable that local authority owed a duty of care to the foster parents); *A and B v Essex CC* [2003] EWCA Civ 1848, [2004] 1 WLR 1881 (local authority owed adoptive parents a duty of care in relation to information provided to those parents about the placed child, who turned out to be aggressive and with a history of aggression towards family members); *Lambert v Cardiff CC* [2007] EWHC 869, [2007] 3 FCR 148 (QB) (child made allegations of sexual abuse against her foster father who, with the foster mother, suffered psychiatric harm as a result; local authority conceded that they owed the prospective foster parents a duty of care). For a more recent illustration of where it was arguable that a local authority owed a parent a duty of care, where her children were sexually abused by a neighbour's child and where the local authority did not allegedly take appropriate steps to intervene to stop the abuse, see: *Merthyr Tydfil County BC v C* [2010] EWHC 62 (QB).

93 [2005] UKHL 23, [2005] 2 AC 373, [31]–[36].

94 M Jones, 'Child Abuse: When the Professionals Get it Wrong' (2006) 14 *Med L Rev* 264, 274, and 275 ('[i]t is difficult to come away from [*East Berkshire* (HL)] without the feeling that their Lordships were concerned to protect the professionals involved in making difficult decisions').

95   S Burns, 'Rights versus Duty' (2007) 157 *NLJ* 1002, 1003.

96   [2003] EWCA Civ 1151, [2004] QB 558, [82].

97   K Williams, 'Abusing Parents and Children' (2005) 21 *PN* 196, 200, citing: *Every Child Matters* (2003) Cm 5860. Rather, Williams attributes the *East Berkshire* decision partly to 'the deference traditionally shown by courts to medical decision-making': at 201.

98   L Hoyano and C Keenan, *Child Abuse: Law and Policy Across Boundaries* (OUP, Oxford, 2007) 407, with Lord Brown's comment at: [2005] UKHL 23, [2005] 2 AC 373, [137].

99   K Stanton, 'Professional Negligence: Duty of Care Methodology in the Twenty-first Century' (2006) 22 *PN* 134, 136.

100 P Case, 'The Accused Strikes Back: The Negligence Action and Erroneous Allegations of Child Abuse' (2005) 21 *PN* 214, 221.

101 C Booth and D Squires, *The Negligence Liability of Public Authorities* (OUP, Oxford, 2006) [4.79].

102 C McIvor, *Third Party Liability in Tort* (Hart Publishing, Oxford, 2006) 113.

103 As noted in: *Caparo Industries plc v Dickman* [1990] 2 AC 605 (HL) 618 (Lord Bridge). See Chapter 2, pp 28, 32–33, 38.

104 [2005] UKHL 23, [2005] 2 AC 373, [36].

105 *ibid*, [83].

106 *ibid*, [106].

107 *AD v Bury MBC* [2006] EWCA Civ 1, [32] (Wall LJ) ('I therefore share the sympathy ... for any parent wrongly accused of injuring their child'); *East Berkshire*, *ibid*, [52] ('every parent's nightmare': Lord Nicholls), [97] ('one could only sympathise with anyone in that plight': Lord Rodger), [138] ('readily acknowledging the legitimate grievances' of the parents concerned: Lord Brown); *Hinds v Liverpool CC* [2009] 1 FCR 475 (QB) [67] ('I can understand Mr Hinds' predicament at having lost contact permanently with RH and RQ and contact with RM and can only sympathise').

108 *R v Reading BC* [2009] EWHC 998 (QB).

109 *Van Colle v Chief Constable of Hertfordshire* [2008] UKHL 50, [2009] 1 AC 225, [139] (Lord Brown).

110 e.g.: *AD v Bury MBC* [2006] EWCA Civ 1; *L (a minor) v Reading BC* [2006] EWHC 2443 (QB); *Lawrence v Pembrokeshire CC* [2007] EWCA Civ 446, [2007] 2 FCR 329; *Hinds v Liverpool CC* [2009] 1 FCR 475 (QB).

111 *Trent Strategic HA v Jain* [2009] UKHL 4, (2009) 106 BMLR 88, [25] (Lord Scott) (emphasis added).

112 See, generally: L Hoyano and C Keenan, *Child Abuse: Law and Policy Across Boundaries* (OUP, Oxford, 2007) 319–46, 406–11.

113 *Sullivan v Moody* [2001] HCA 59, (2001) 207 CLR 562; *Hillman v Black* (1996) 67 SASR 490 (SC). See, too: P Bates *et al*, *Aust Health and Medical Law Reporter* (CCH Aust Ltd, Sydney, 1991–, looseleaf) ¶16-675.

114 e.g.: *D(B) v Children's Aid Society of Halton (Region)* (2007), 284 DLR (4th) 682, [2007] SCR 83, citing, at [55]: *G(I) v Rusch* (1999), 179 DLR (4th) 336 (BCSC [In Chambers]), and *S(P) v B (SK)* [1997] OJ No 4089(Ont Gen Div). Cf, e.g.: *B(D), B(R) and B(M) v Children's Aid Society of Durham Region* (1996), 136 DLR (4th) 297 (Ont CA).

115 *Fairlie v Perth and Kinross Healthcare NHS Trust* 2004 SLT 1200 (OH). For recent discussion of the Scottish legal position, see: A Inglis, 'Personal Injury Claims for Child Protection Failures' [2009] SLT 173.

116 *B v A-G (New Zealand)* [2003] UKPC 61, [2003] 4 All ER 833.

117 See, e.g.: A Garton, 'Reconciling the Incongruous Demands of Therapist–Patient Confidentiality and Falsely-Accused Third Parties' (2007) 37 *Cumberland L Rev* 77; L Silverman, 'A Therapist's Duty of Care: Does it Extend to Non-Patients Charged with Child Sexual Abuse?' (2001) *Pennsylvania Bar Assn Quarterly* 18; J Berger, 'False Memory Syndrome and Therapist Liability to Third Parties for Emotional Distress Injuries Arising from Recovered Memory Therapy: A General Prohibition on Liability and a Limited Liability Exception' (2000) 73 *Temple L Rev* 795.

118 e.g., *Sawyer v Midelfort*, 595 NW 2d 423 (Wis 1999); *Hungerford v Jones*, 722 A 2d 478 (NH 1998); *Montoya v Bebensee*, 761 P 2d 285 (Colo Ct App 1988); *Caryl S v Child and Adolescent Treatment Services Inc*, 614 NYS 2d 661 (App Div 1994).

119 e.g., *Althaus v Cohen*, 756 A2d 1166 (Pa 2000); *Bird v WCW*, 868 SW 2d 767 (Tex 1994); *Doe v McKay*, 183 Ill 2d 272, 700 NE2d 1018 (Ill 1998); *Trear v Sills*, 82 Cal Rptr 2d 281 (Ct App 1999); *PT v Richard Hall Cmty Mental Health Care Ctr*, 837 A 2d 436 (NJ Super Ct Law Div 2002).

120 As the policy reasons and reasoning invoked in US cases closely parallel those evident in England, no new perspectives are to be derived from US jurisprudence, and thus, in contrast to other chapters, the US jurisprudence does not warrant detailed treatment in this chapter.

121 e.g., Family Services Act, SNB 1980, c F-2.2, s 3(3); Child, Family and Community Service Act, RSBC 1996, c 46, s 101. See, for further discussion/examples: L Hoyano and C Keenan, *Child Abuse: Law and Policy Across Boundaries* (OUP, Oxford, 2007) 418–21. These authors suggest (at 421) that a similar approach should be adopted in England, by amendment to the Children Act 1989 to confer a qualified immunity from liability in negligence upon all those charged with investigatory responsibilities in connection with child protection.

122 In *AD v Bury MBC* [2006] EWCA Civ 1, [16], the court called attempts to distinguish *East Berkshire* the product of 'ingenuity and skill', but the argument that the parents should be owed a duty nevertheless failed.

123 [2006] EWHC 2449 (QB). Subsequent proceedings reported at: [2006] EWHC 3206 (QB) (a further High Court proceeding), and then appellate proceedings: [2007] EWCA Civ 1313, [2008] 1 FLR 797 (CA). About ten years into the litigation, L discontinued her proceedings.

124 [2006] EWHC 2449 (QB) [28] (Keith J).

125 E Palser, 'Shutting the Door on Negligence Liability' [2009] *CFLQ* 384, (accessed online, no pp available).

126 [2007] EWCA Civ 446, [2007] 2 FCR 329, [22].

127 [2006] EWCA Civ 1, [2006] 1 WLR 917.

128 *ibid*, [22].

129 *L (a minor) and B v Reading BC* [2007] EWCA Civ 1313, [2008] 1 FLR 797, [33], overturning the decision, [2006] EWHC 3206 (QB), in which Keith J refused to strike out the father's claim because it was sufficiently arguable that the Council owed the father a 'direct' duty of care. It will be recalled that the father had already failed to establish that he was owed a duty of care by the social worker on the basis of an operational-versus-policy distinction: [2006] EWHC 2449 (QB). Instead of seeking permission to appeal from that, the father sought leave to amend his claim to allege breach of a direct duty of care. Keith J permitted the amendments, considering that if a duty were owed, it would not conflict with the duty owed to the child, and hence, would not fall within the reasoning applied in *East Berkshire* (HL). The CA overturned that decision.

130 G Douglas, 'Case Reports, Local Authority and Negligence' [2008] *Fam LJ* 314, 'Comment section'.

131 [2007] EWCA Civ 446, [2007] 2 FCR 329, [23] (Auld LJ).

132 Art 6(1) provides: 'In the determination of his civil rights and obligations or of any criminal charge against him, everyone is entitled to a fair and public hearing within a reasonable time by an independent and impartial tribunal established by law'.

133 Art 8 provides: '(1) Everyone has the right to respect for his private and family life, his home and his correspondence. (2) There shall be no interference by a public authority with the exercise of this right except such as in accordance with the law and is necessary in a democratic society in the interests of national security, public safety or the economic well-being of the country, for the prevention of disorder or crime, for the protection of health or morals, or for the protection of the rights and freedoms of others.'

134 [2007] UKHL 31, (2007) 97 BMLR 172.

135 *ibid*, [75] (Lord Brown).

136 [2001] 2 FLR 549 (ECtHR).

137 [1995] 2 AC 633 (HL).

138 As stated in [2001] 2 FLR 549 (ECtHR) [99].

139 *ibid*, [103].

140 *ibid*, [100]–[103], and departing from its views in *Osman v UK* (2000) 29 EHRR 245 (ECtHR) on that point.

141 P Case, 'The Accused Strikes Back: The Negligence Action and Erroneous Allegations of Child Abuse' (2005) 21 *PN* 214, 223.

142 Derived from: *TP and KM v UK* (2002) 34 EHRR 42 (ECtHR); *Venema v Netherlands* [2003] 1 FCR 153 (ECtHR); *P, C and S v UK* [2001] 2 FLR 549 (ECtHR).

143 *ibid*, [34].

144 A Samuels, 'Unfounded Suspicion of Child Abuse' (2006) 74 *Medico-Legal J* 35, 36.

145 (2001) 34 EHRR 42 (ECtHR).

146 *ibid*, [30], [80]–[83], [115]–[117].

147 (2002) 39 EHRR 102 (ECtHR).

148 *ibid*, [90].

149 (2009) 48 EHRR 29, [2008] FLR (ECtHR, 30 Sep 2008).

150 It will be recalled that baby MK was wrongfully diagnosed as suffering fractures from non-accidental injuries, where, in fact, she suffered from brittle bone disease: *RK and AK v Oldham NHS Trust* [2005] UKHL 23, [2005] 2 AC 373.

151 (2009) 48 EHRR 29, [2008] FLR (ECtHR) [36].

152 *ibid*, [37]. However, because the events giving rise to the Oldham claim occurred prior to Oct 2000, no remedy under the HRA was possible, and because of the stance adopted towards the parents by the House of Lords in *East Berkshire*, they were unable to avail themselves of any remedy at all, and hence, the parents had a remedy for breach of art 13: *ibid*, [45].

153 R Bailey-Harris, 'Case Reports, Care, Human Rights' [2009] *Fam LJ* 9, 'Comment' section.

154 M Ruck and E Holt, 'Parental Rights Recognised' (2009) 17 *Med L Rev* 282, (accessed online, no pp available).

155 See, *East Berkshire* [2005] UKHL 23, [2005] 2 AC 373, and Lord Nicholls' discussion of *Venema v Netherlands* (2002) 39 EHRR 102 (ECtHR) [83]–[84].

156 *Lawrence v Pembrokeshire CC* [2007] EWCA Civ 446, [2007] 2 FCR 329 (CA) [10], [27].

157 [2005] UKHL 23, [2005] 2 AC 373, [118], citing: *Fairlie v Perth and Kinross Healthcare NHS Trust* 2004 SLT 1200, [2004] ScotCS 174 (OH) [36] (Lord Kingarth).

158 *ibid*, [50]. His Lordship reiterated his view, as a 'lone voice', in: *Watkins v Home Office* [2006] UKHL 17, [26] ('I have myself questioned [in *East Berkshire*] whether development of the law of tort should be stunted, leaving very important problems to be swept up by the European Convention ... in a case where, in my opinion, the application of familiar principles supported recognition of a remedy in tort'). For further recent discussion of the limits that should apply when developing the common law in light of the Convention, see, e.g.: G Anthony, 'Positive Obligations and Policing in the House of Lords' [2009] *Euro Human Rights L Rev* 538.

159 [2003] UKHL 53, [2004] 2 AC 406, [33]–[34] (Lord Hoffmann).

160 [2006] UKHL 17, [2006] 2 AC 395.

161 *ibid*, [64], and cited in: *Smith v Chief Constable of Sussex Police* [2008] EWCA Civ 39, [53]–[55] (Pill LJ).

162 [2007] EWCA Civ 446, [2007] 2 FCR 329.

163 At first instance, the Council relied on the one-year limitation period imposed by s 7(5)(a) of the HRA, which had elapsed before Mrs Lawrence brought the proceedings. It was unnecessary to decide in the appeal whether it was equitable under s 7(5)(b) to extend that period: at [6].

164 See [34]–[55] (Auld LJ), Richards and Scott-Baker LJJ concurring, the latter delivering a short judgment.

165 E Palser, 'Shutting the Door on Negligence Liability' [2009] *CFLQ* 384, (accessed online, no pp available).

166 *ibid*, fn 19. Point also made in, e.g.: K Williams, 'Abusing Parents and Children' (2005) 21 *PN* 196, 200.

167 M Jones, 'Child Abuse: When the Professionals Get it Wrong' (2006) 14 *Med L Rev* 264, 276.

168 G Douglas, 'Case Report, Local Authority, Negligence' [2007] *Fam LJ* 804, 'Comment' section.

169 Only 12 months, pursuant to s 7(5)(a) of the HRA.

170 J Wright, *Tort Law and Human Rights* (Hart Publishing, Oxford, 2001) 44. See too: M Jones, *Medical Negligence* (4th edn, Sweet & Maxwell, London, 2008) 129, fn 281, citing: EWLC, *Damages Under the Human Rights Act 1998* (Rep 266, 2000). Cf: C Booth and D Squires, *The Negligence Liability of Public Authorities* (OUP, Oxford, 2006) [7.109].

171 Booth and Squires, *ibid*, [7.101].

172 See pp 365–66, 369

173 M Jones, 'Child Protection and Duties to Third Parties' (2007) 23 *PN* 118, 121.

174 L Hoyano and C Keenan, *Child Abuse: Law and Policy Across Boundaries* (OUP, Oxford, 2007) 413.

175 C McIvor, *Third Party Liability in Tort* (Hart Publishing, Oxford, 2006) 98.

176 J Steele, 'Damages in Tort and Under the Human Rights Act: Remedial or Functional Separation?' (2008) 67 *CLJ* 606, 606.

177 G Anthony, 'Positive Obligations and Policing in the House of Lords' [2009] *Euro Human Rights L Rev* 538, 540 and fn 14. See too: K Williams, 'Abusing Parents and Children' (2005) 21 *PN* 196, 201 ('it would have been preferable to [develop] domestic negligence law compatibly with European human rights jurisprudence').

178 I Steele, 'Negligence Liability for Failing to Prevent Crime: The Human Rights Dimension' (2008) 67 *CLJ* 239, 241.

179 The question cast by Lord Bingham in *East Berkshire* [2005] UKHL 23, [2005] 2 AC 373, [46].

180 *ibid*, [100], and providing several examples thereof. Notably, an equally penetrating observation to the contrary is provided by Kirby J: 'Facts may present wrongs. Wrongs often cry out for a remedy. To their cry the common law may not be indifferent': *Harriton v Stephens* [2006] HCA 16, (2006) 226 CLR 52, [35].

181 *The Beach Club Port Douglas v Page* [2005] QCA 475, [13] (McPherson JA), citing: *Sullivan v Moody* [2001] HCA 59, (2001) 207 CLR 562, and *East Berkshire*.

182 *East Berkshire* [2005] UKHL 23, [2005] 2 AC 373, [77].

Appendix

Potential Liability to Non-Patients and Third Parties: A Synopsis for Healthcare Professionals

The Synopsis has been drafted for the assistance of healthcare professionals (HCPs), and aims to fulfil two purposes. First, it seeks to highlight the potential for non-patient/third party claims arising out of the acts or omissions of HCPs undertaking medical services. In so doing, the Synopsis is intended to foster among HCPs an awareness that, in addition to the traditional patient as their 'neighbours in law', potentially a non-patient 'neighbour' is no phantom. Secondly, the Synopsis aims, by a series of 'nutshell propositions', to clarify for HCPs and health authorities the matters which will influence or determine a court's analysis of whether the law will consider non-patients to have been owed a duty of care by HCPs to exercise reasonable care and skill so as to avoid or minimise their injuries (personal, economic, or psychiatric).

The scenarios outlined in this Synopsis arise from non-patient and third party claims which either have already been the subject of litigation in England, or which may feasibly become the subject of litigation in English courts in the future, given trends in other related jurisdictions.

In the Synopsis: HCP = Healthcare Professional; and NP = Non-Patient/Third Party.

GENERAL

1. Where a NP with a grievance against a HCP sues in negligence, claiming compensation for physical injury, for psychiatric injury, or for economic injury, that NP must establish the four requirements of the action in negligence, *viz*:

> **(a)** that the HCP owed the NP a duty of care to avoid causing the type of injury of which he complains;
> **(b)** that the HCP breached the duty of care by falling below the standard of reasonable care which the law demands of a HCP who professes to exercise that particular skill or profession;
> **(c)** that the breach by the HCP (be it an act or an omission) caused the particular damage complained of by the NP; and
> **(d)** that the damage complained of by the NP is not too remote (unforeseeable) at law to be recoverable.

In scenarios involving NPs, establishing a duty of care at all—or, alternatively, establishing a duty of care which has, within its scope, a duty to avoid the particular injury complained of—has been the most problematical aspect. Establishing a causal link between the HCP's negligent act or omission and the NP's loss and damage has also been difficult in some scenarios.

2. Generally, a NP will be complaining of a negligent provision of medical services (diagnosis or treatment or advice) by the HCP towards a patient which, in turn, caused the NP loss and damage. More unusually (e.g., in the scenarios where a HCP either fails to attend to a medical emergency at all, or attends an emergency and is sued for making the victim's condition worse), no other parties will be involved, other than the HCP and the NP. Regardless of this differentiation, where a novel scenario giving rise to a pleaded duty of care is being considered (and most claims by NPs fall within the 'novel' category of case), then there are three broadly-stated tests for deciding whether a duty of care exists in particular circumstances. Not all tests will be expressly applied to all cases involving suits by NPs against HCPs. The three tests for establishing whether a HCP owed a duty of care to a NP, to avoid or to mimimise loss or damage to that NP, may be described as follows:

> **(a)** whether the tri-partite (*Caparo*) test has been met, *viz*:
> (i) it was reasonably foreseeable that the NP would suffer the type of injury complained of as a result of the HCP's negligent act or omission;
> (ii) there was sufficient proximity between the HCP and the NP to justify a duty of care being found (which depends upon geographic, temporal, relational and/or causal proximity factors being present, and which depends upon all the particular circumstances of the case); and
> (iii) it must be fair, just and reasonable that a duty of care be imposed upon the HCP in the particular circumstances of the case (i.e., in other words, that there be no legal or public policy factors that should preclude a duty of care from being owed by the HCP towards the NP);
> **(b)** whether there has been an assumption of responsibility by the HCP towards the NP, together with a consequential reliance by the NP upon the HCP's conducting himself with due care and skill;
> **(c)** whether any duty to be imposed or cast upon the HCP towards a NP in the circumstances of the particular case would be 'incremental' (i.e., similar, or closely analogous) to previously-decided cases in which a HCP had been found to have owed a duty of care.
> Of these three tests, the tri-partite test outlined in (a) is the one most frequently applied to scenarios involving HCPs and NPs.

NON-PATIENTS HARMED BY DANGEROUS PATIENTS

3. It may be claimed by a NP that a HCP foresaw, or ought to have reasonably foreseen, that a patient posed a serious threat of danger to that NP, and that the HCP was under a duty of reasonable care to protect that NP from being harmed by the patient. Depending upon all the circumstances, the harm to the NP may be occasioned by some deliberate, or negligent, act by the patient; or the patient's medical condition may merely create an opportunity for harm to occur to the NP. The 'dangers' which the patient manifests may take various forms, *viz*, where the patient was:

> **(a)** mentally-ill or psychotic;
> **(b)** physically-disabled;
> **(c)** the carrier of some contagious or transmissible disease; or
> **(d)** the bearer of a genetic make-up that poses a risk of hereditary disease on the part of a biological relative (the NP).

4. Thus far, there is no *conclusive* precedent in English law, in any of the abovementioned scenarios, that either:

(a) mandates that a HCP is under any duty to directly warn/disclose/take some other proactive step towards the NP directly, so as to reduce or avoid his risk of personal or other injury (a robust form of legal duty); or

(b) requires that a HCP is under a duty of care to the NP to avoid or minimise the risk of his injury, which duty is to be discharged by treating, or otherwise taking specific steps or actions towards, the 'dangerous patient' which would (at least, on the balance of probabilities) protect the NP from harm (a weaker form of legal duty).

5. Relevant cases from other jurisdictions do, however, support the imposition of a duty of care upon the HCP in each of the instances identified in 3 above. It is feasible that a similar duty could be recognised and cast upon HCPs in English law in the future.

6. Of the two options canvassed in 4 above, the weaker form of legal duty is more likely to gain some measure of acceptance in English law, should a duty to the NP be countenanced in the circumstances of harm caused or occasioned by the so-called 'dangerous patient'. A duty of care owed by a HCP towards that NP will only arise, however, if there is the requisite legal proximity between HCP and NP, and if public and legal policy reasons do not dictate against such a duty being cast upon the HCP.

7. The types of proximity factors to which courts have had regard, in the specific context of 'dangerous patients', include (but are not necessarily limited to) the following:

(a) whether the HCP had the ability to exert any degree of control over the actions of the patient, so as to avoid or minimise the risk of the patient's causing harm or death to the NP;

(b) whether the HCP was in a position to warn, or take other protective or proactive steps towards, the NP;

(c) whether the patient was particularly vulnerable because of the acts or omissions of the HCP (e.g., in that the HCP was the *sole* repository of information about the patient, and the NP could not have acquired necessary information about the patient's threat or risk of harm to the NP from any other source);

(d) whether there was a close temporal proximity between the HCP's breach and the harm suffered by the NP;

(e) whether there was a close geographical proximity between the HCP and patient, on the one hand, and the NP, on the other;

(f) whether the HCP knew of the NP's identity, as a result of his dealings with the patient;

(g) whether the NP was one of an identifiable class of persons whose identities would have been reasonably ascertainable to the HCP; or whether, by contrast, the NP was one of the general public at risk from the patient's activities, with no distinguishing characteristic marking out that NP as being particularly at risk;

(h) whether the HCP had the capacity to take some step that would have prevented the patient from having the opportunity to harm the NP, such that the failure to take that 'intervening step' brought about a causal proximity between the HCP's act or omission and the NP's harm.

8. As a matter of public and legal policy, a court may conclude that no duty of care to avoid or minimise the harm suffered by the NP should be imposed upon HCP. These policy factors may include (but are not necessarily limited to) the following:

> **(a)** whether there was any actual or potential irreconcilable conflict between the duty which the HCP owed to the patient, and the duty which the HCP would owe to the NP, were the latter to be owed a separate duty of care by the HCP;
>
> **(b)** whether the duty of confidentiality which the HCP owes to the patient would be compromised by any duty which the HCP may be held to owe to the NP;
>
> **(c)** whether the size of the class at risk from the patient's 'dangerousness' (of whom the NP was one), was so large as to lead to the prospect of indeterminate liability on the HCP's part, were a duty to be imposed upon the HCP in the instant case.

STRANGERS IN NEED OF EMERGENCY MEDICAL ASSISTANCE (PART 1)

9. As a general rule, in circumstances where a person with whom the HCP has no pre-existing HCP–patient relationship (hereafter, 'the Victim NP') is ill, injured, or unconscious as a result of an accident or other emergency, the HCP is under no *legal* duty to respond to the Victim NP's request for medical help, whether made publicly to a crowd of which the HCP is a member, or directed individually to the HCP. No liability in negligence will attach to the HCP if he fails to provide assistance to the Victim NP. A general awareness that urgent medical assistance is required (either from what the HCP witnesses, or because a request is made by or on behalf of the Victim NP to the HCP) does not, of itself, activate a duty of care at law.

10. In emergency scenarios, neither of the following factors—(a) it is foreseeable that injury will result to the Victim NP if the HCP does not render medical assistance; and (b) the HCP is geographically proximate to the Victim NP—is sufficient to give rise to a duty of care at law.

11. However, there are two common law exceptions to the general rule:

> **(a)** if the HCP is a hospital doctor, then that HCP must respond to an emergency when members of the public present themselves in urgent need of medical attention at an A&E or casualty department; and
>
> **(b)** where a Victim NP requests urgent assistance, where the HCP provides an undertaking to give it, and where the Victim NP relies upon that HCP's undertaking (by adjusting his position in some way in the expectation that the HCP will assist), then an assumption of responsibility on the HCP's part, and consequential reliance by the Victim NP, is likely to be found, sufficient to give rise to a duty of care at law.

In these two exceptional scenarios, if—without reasonable explanation and justification—the HCP does not attend the emergency and provide medical assistance, and if that failure to attend/render assistance causes injury to the Victim NP, then the HCP will be liable to the Victim NP in negligence for damages.

12. To date, there is **no** English precedent which expressly holds that a HCP will be exposed to a claim in negligence for damages, in circumstances where that HCP failed to intervene or to go to the assistance of the Victim NP, and where: the HCP was requested to attend an emergency to provide medical services in a 'professional context' (e.g., while the HCP was at his surgery); the HCP was available and was not disabled or incapacitated from meeting the request; the HCP was geographically proximate to the Victim NP; yet the HCP refused to attend.

13. The National Health Service (General Medical Services Contracts) Regulations 2004 and the General Medical Council's *Good Medical Practice* (2006) impose certain professional and ethical obligations on the HCP towards Victim NPs in emergency situations, breach of which may result in disciplinary sanctions (depending upon all the circumstances). However, these instruments do **not**, of themselves, create a legal duty of care to assist or to rescue a Victim NP who is involved in a medical emergency (and, hence no successful action in negligence by the Victim NP automatically follows from such breach).

STRANGERS IN NEED OF EMERGENCY MEDICAL ASSISTANCE (PART 2)

14. A 'good Samaritan' HCP is one who provides medical services:

> **(a)** voluntarily to a Victim NP who is ill, injured or unconscious as a result of an accident or other emergency;
> **(b)** without reasonable expectation of compensation or reward;
> **(c)** which constitute emergency healthcare services or first aid assistance to the Victim NP; and
> **(d)** where the HCP has no pre-existing HCP–patient relationship with the Victim NP.

15. If a 'good Samaritan' HCP elects to intervene and to go to the assistance of a Victim NP, the standard of care which the law expects of that HCP is that of a reasonable healthcare professional in all the circumstances. In this, as in all areas of medical practice, the law does not expect perfection in either conduct or outcome.

16. The legal standard of care which the law expects of the 'good Samaritan' HCP *will* be suppressed by having regard to the following factors, as applicable:

> **(a)** by the emergency or 'battle conditions' in which the HCP had to provide the medical services required to assist the Victim NP (e.g., by the facilities and equipment which were immediately and reasonably available to the HCP when providing the medical services to the Victim NP); and
> **(b)** by reference to the particular skills and specialty that the HCP professes to possess, and to no other.

17. The legal standard of care which the law expects of the 'good Samaritan' HCP is *not* suppressed by either of the following factors:

> **(a)** by the fact that the HCP acted voluntarily and without reward; or
> **(b)** by the fact that the HCP was motivated by altruism and by the best of intentions in seeking to assist the Victim NP.

18. When assessing whether the 'good Samaritan' HCP breached the legal standard of care expected in all the circumstances, the law poses two alternative tests of breach (English legal authorities support each of them, and which of them will apply is not entirely clear on the law to date):

> **(a)** the first test asks whether the HCP made the Victim NP's condition worse—if the HCP made the condition no worse than would have occurred without the HCP's intervention, a breach will not be proven; or
>
> **(b)** the second test asks whether a responsible body of medical opinion would have performed the medical services in the same way, when acting as a good Samaritan HCP—if so, a breach will not be proven.

19. When providing good Samaritan assistance, a HCP is subject to the standards of reasonable care at all times. There is *no* principle in English common law whereby the HCP is only liable for 'gross negligence' (howsoever that term is legally defined—whether by a large departure from the legal standard of reasonable care, or by wilful or reckless intervention, or for injuries that are of large quantum). Rather, the 'good Samaritan' HCP will be liable for *any* departure from the (suppressed) reasonable standard outlined in 15–16 above.

STRANGERS WHO SUFFER PURE ECONOMIC LOSS

20. 'Pure economic injury' occurs where a claimant suffers some financial harm which is not consequential upon either personal or property damage suffered by that claimant. In medical scenarios, this may occur where a patient was medically mis-treated, mis-diagnosed or ill-advised by a HCP, and a person associated with the patient in some way (as a NP), suffers economically as a result.

21. To date, NP claims against HCPs for pure economic loss have arisen in four particular contexts in English law:

> **(a)** where one parent (the patient) has been negligently sterilised by a HCP, the other biological parent (the NP) may suffer economic loss by reason of the conception and birth of a child subsequently. (These types of parental claims arising from negligently-performed sterilisation procedures are typically given the label, 'wrongful conception' cases);
>
> **(b)** where the father of a child (the NP) alleges that a HCP negligently failed to diagnose or detect a condition in a foetus (e.g., Down's Syndrome, spina bifida, disabilities arising from the mother's exposure to rubella during pregnancy) which, had it been pointed out to the mother (the patient), would have resulted in the mother's choosing to abort the foetus, and which negligence deprived the mother of the opportunity to lawfully terminate the pregnancy, then in some such cases, the father may claim his economic loss as a result of the birth of the disabled child. (These types of parental claims arising from medical negligence which deprives a mother of an opportunity to abort a foetus are typically given the label, 'wrongful birth' cases);
>
> **(c)** where an individual or entity (the NP) is put to the expense of caring for, or funding the treatment of, a patient who was negligently-treated by the HCP, that carer/funder may sue the HCP to recover the costs expended in that care/treatment; and

(d) where a third party (e.g., the patient's employer), as NP, suffers economic loss by reason of the lost value of an employee's services because the employee was injured through medical negligence committed by the HCP, then the employer may sue the HCP to recover damages measured by the cost of those services foregone.

22. To date, there is some (inconclusive) judicial support in English law for NP claims falling within categories 21 (a) and (b). However, there has been no judicial support for NP claims within categories 21 (c) and (d) as yet.

23. NPs have typically been able to establish that their various forms of economic injury were reasonably foreseeable on the part of the defendant HCPs.

24. However, in several cases instituted by NPs in this context, there has been decreed to have been a lack of legal proximity between NP and HCP. Factors which have contributed towards this finding include:

(a) an inability to control the actions of the HCP's patient, or to warn the NP of the risk of economic injury;
(b) a lack of temporal proximity between the HCP's negligent act or omission and the NP's economic injury;
(c) a lack of knowledge of the identity or even of the existence of the NP; and
(d) a lack of reasonable reliance by the NP on the judgment and skill of the HCP to avoid causing him economic injury.

25. Moreover, legal and public policy reasons have frequently been applied to preclude a duty of care being owed by a HCP to the NP who has suffered economic injury by reason of the HCP's negligence towards a patient. These include (but are not limited to):

(a) conflicts between the actual duty owed to patient and the duty to the NP contended for;
(b) the prospect of liability to an indeterminate (or large) class of NPs for an indeterminate (or large) amount; and
(c) that it was for the NP to protect himself financially by insuring against that particular financial loss (where relevant insurance was available).

STRANGERS WHO SUFFER PURE PSYCHIATRIC ILLNESS

26. 'Pure psychiatric injury' occurs where a claimant suffers mental harm which is not consequential upon either personal or property damage suffered by that claimant. A HCP cannot be liable for negligently-caused psychiatric injury unless that mental harm comprises a recognisable psychiatric illness. In other words, where a claimant suffers a range of 'normal human reactions' such as grief, anger, sorrow, anxiety, in response to an event of medical negligence, those human reactions do not base a claim for damages.

27. A HCP will potentially owe a duty of care to a NP (usually the relative of a patient who was mis-treated or mis-diagnosed by the HCP) who suffers from some pure psychiatric injury as a result of an event of medical negligence if the NP:

> **(a)** was not directly a participant in the medical services which the HCP provided to the patient, but
> **(b)** was a mere bystander or spectator who witnessed the death, injury or imperilment of that patient brought about by the HCP's mis-treatment or mis-diagnosis of the patient.

In either of these scenarios, the NP will be considered to be a potential 'secondary victim' of the event of medical negligence.

28. Alternatively, a HCP will potentially owe a duty of care to a NP who suffers from some pure psychiatric injury if the court considers that <u>either</u>:

> **(a)** the NP was a 'participant' in the medical mishap, and as such, constituted the 'immediate victim' of the event of medical negligence; <u>or</u>
> **(b)** there was no patient who was an 'immediate victim' of the medical mishap, and the court substitutes the NP for the missing immediate victim.

In either of these scenarios, the NP will be considered to be a potential 'primary victim' of the event of medical negligence.

To date, there have been no examples in English medical law of primary victim NPs who have constituted 'participants' (in the abovementioned category (a)) by being closely-linked or closely proximate to a medical mishap involving a patient. However, there have been examples in English medical law of primary victim NPs who have been substituted for a missing immediate victim, under category (b).

29. Whether the HCP owes a duty of care to the NP, as a primary victim, will depend upon proof of the following legal factors:

> **(a)** it must have been reasonably foreseeable that the primary victim NP would suffer psychiatric injury by reason of the HCP's acts or omissions—as an exception to this rule, if the NP was in a 'zone of physical danger' himself as a result of the HCP's negligent act or omission, then it will be sufficient if some *physical* injury to the NP was reasonably foreseeable, even if psychiatric injury to the NP was so unlikely as to be unforeseeable;
> **(b)** the HCP must have had sufficient physical and temporal proximity with the primary victim NP; and
> **(c)** there must be no public policy reasons which ought to preclude recovery by the primary victim NP for psychiatric injury (e.g., the 'floodgates' concern of too many potential primary victims).

Alert: Under English law, a primary victim NP can recover for his pure psychiatric injury, even if it was sustained because he lacked the mental fortitude or 'natural phlegm' of an ordinary person. It is also likely that the primary victim NP can recover, even if his psychiatric injury was not caused by 'shock' in the legal sense (i.e., even if the NP did not suffer some sudden assault on the nervous system, or a sudden appreciation of a horrifying event).

30. Alternatively, a HCP will potentially owe a duty of care to a secondary victim NP if the law treats that NP as a bystander or spectator to whom a duty of care to avoid pure psychiatric injury was owed. In those circumstances, whether the HCP owes a duty of care to the secondary victim NP will depend upon proof of the following legal factors:

(**a**) it must have been reasonably foreseeable that the secondary victim NP would suffer psychiatric injury by reason of the HCP's acts or omissions (note that, it is **never** sufficient, in the case of secondary victim NPs, to establish that it was reasonably foreseeable that some physical injury would be suffered by reason of the HCP's acts or omissions—it is *psychiatric* injury which must be reasonably foreseeable);

(**b**) the secondary victim NP and the patient harmed by the HCP's acts or omissions must have shared a close tie of love and affection;

(**c**) the secondary victim NP must have been either proximate in time and space to the scene of the medical acts or omissions complained of, or within their immediate aftermath;

(**d**) the secondary victim NP must have directly perceived the medical acts or omissions complained of, or their immediate aftermath, with his own eyes and ears, rather than just hearing about them; and

(**e**) the secondary victim NP's psychiatric injury must have been induced by 'shock' in the legal sense (i.e., the NP *must* have suffered some sudden assault on the nervous system, or a sudden appreciation of a horrifying event).

Alert: A secondary victim NP who is especially vulnerable to psychiatric injury can only recover for that injury if he can prove that a person of ordinary fortitude would have suffered in the same way (albeit that, *if* that threshold is proven, then the NP can recover for the full extent of his psychiatric injury, in the sense that the HCP must 'take his victim as he finds him').

FEAR OF THE FUTURE CLAIMS

31. 'Fear of the future' claims arise in the medical scenario where some event of medical negligence by a HCP—such as using sub-standard hygiene practices, or mis-diagnosing a patient's illness—exposes a NP to some toxic agent which, in turn, exposes the NP to the risk of developing a future disease or illness, but where the NP does not suffer immediate physical injury of any kind. Consistent with any action in negligence, proof of some *legally-recognised damage* on the part of the NP, arising from that exposure, is a pre-requisite to any possible cause of action in negligence arising.

32. In seeking to prove that the NP suffered from some legally-recognised damage as a result of the exposure to a toxic agent arising from the HCP's negligence, the following propositions apply in English law:

(**a**) the *risk* of the NP's developing a future disease/illness is **not** an 'injury' which the law will recognise as giving rise to the right to compensation;

(**b**) anxiety, fear, anger or other normal human emotions on the part of the NP, caused by the concern about developing future disease/illness, are **not**, either singly or cumulatively, an 'injury' which the law will recognise or compensate either;

(c) however, if the NP suffers some recognised psychiatric illness (e.g., clinical depression), that is an 'injury' which the law will recognise as giving rise to the potential right to compensation (if all the elements of the cause of action in negligence are satisfied).

33. In the event that the NP suffers from some recognised psychiatric illness as a result of 'living with the knowledge' that a future disease/illness could manifest, arising from his exposure to a toxic agent, the following propositions apply in English law:

(a) that NP is **not** viewed by English law to be a 'primary victim'—a participant in an event of medical negligence—to whom a duty of care to avoid pure psychiatric illness is owed;

(b) the NP therefore cannot take advantage of the various legal rules that favour primary victims (*viz*, that it is sufficient to prove reasonable foreseeability of either physical or psychiatric injury in any case where the NP was in the 'zone of physical danger' himself; that it does not matter to the NP's prospects of recovery if he is not a person of ordinary fortitude but is, instead, a person abnormally susceptible to psychiatric illness; and that if a NP can prove that he was in the 'zone of physical danger' from the HCP's acts or omissions, then the NP and HCP are sufficiently proximate to support a duty of care);

(c) instead, the NP must seek to establish that the HCP owed him a duty of care to avoid causing him pure psychiatric illness, under the tri-partite test that applies to all novel scenarios, i.e.,

(i) that the occurrence of psychiatric injury was reasonably foreseeable (in a person of normal fortitude) as a result of the exposure to the toxic agent;

(ii) that the HCP and the NP were in a sufficiently proximate relationship, based upon geographic, temporal, relational and/or causal proximity; and

(iii) that no public or legal policy reasons preclude the HCP from owing the NP a duty of care to avoid causing psychiatric injury brought about by a fear of developing a future illness/disease as a result of the NP's exposure to the toxic agent.

THE WRONGFULLY-ACCUSED CLAIMANTS IN CHILD ABUSE AND NEGLECT INVESTIGATIONS

34. Where investigations of alleged child abuse, mistreatment or neglect are undertaken by HCPs (doctors, social workers, psychologists, family therapists, and so on), and wrongful accusations of mistreatment and abuse are made by HCPs against a parent (or other guardian) of the child, both child and the wrongfully-accused may suffer from a legally-recognised damage. This damage may take the form of psychiatric injury to either party arising from an enforced separation, or economic damage to the wrongfully-accused incurred by countering the wrongful accusations via legal proceedings, or by undertaking other efforts to 'clear one's name'. In such scenarios, the child is a limited patient of the HCPs, and the wrongfully-accused is a NP.

35. The previous English legal position (pre-2005) was that, in negligently-conducted child abuse or child neglect investigations in which wrongful accusations of mistreatment and abuse were made by HCPs against a parent (or other guardian) of the child, no duty of care was owed *to the child*, other than a duty not to injure the child during the course of a physical examination. This narrow duty was the traditional duty owed by HCP to examinee child. However, in 2005, the scope of the HCP's duty towards the child changed. Since then, a HCP owes a duty of care to the child to avoid or minimise psychiatric, economic, and physical harm to the child arising from negligently-conducted investigations (i.e., a duty much wider than the traditional duty).

36. However, regarding the position of the wrongfully-accused parent (or other guardian) NP, the HCP owes no duty of care *to that parent or guardian NP*. Hence, any psychiatric, economic or reputational damage which the parent or guardian suffers as a result of separation from the child, or from the consequences of being wrongfully accused, are irrecoverable in negligence. This legal position is directly attributable to numerous reasons of public and legal policy. Essentially, English law favours the position that, for the ultimate good of child protection and child welfare, a HCP ought to be able to investigate allegations of child abuse, mistreatment or neglect, so as to protect a child allegedly at-risk, without the threat of suit being brought by a person who is wrongfully accused of abusing or mistreating that child.

37. The absence of any duty of care owed by the HCP towards the parent or guardian NP applies in a wide variety of circumstances, e.g.: it applies:

> **(a)** whether a health authority is sued vicariously (for the wrongdoing of its employed HCP) or directly for systemic negligence (for failing to adequately train, supervise, etc, the HCP who made the wrongful accusation);
>
> **(b)** whether the HCP who made the wrongful accusation is 'front-line' staff who had direct face-to-face contact with the child, or comprises one of the 'back-room' professionals who had no direct contact with the child at all;
>
> **(c)** whether the HCP made the erroneous accusation as part of an evaluative decision (e.g., whether to remove the child from the family home), or whether the error was an operational mistake (e.g., the way in which an interview is conducted and recorded); and
>
> **(d)** throughout the investigative process, both prior to any care orders being made and after that point.

Bibliography

[of materials cited in the book]

TEXTS AND MONOGRAPHS

Annas G, *The Rights of Patients* (3rd edn, Southern Illinois U Press, Carbondale, 2004)

Areen J *et al*, *Law, Science and Medicine* (University Casebook Series, Foundation Press, Mineola NY, 1984)

Bates P *et al*, *Australian Health and Medical Law Reporter* (looseleaf edn, CCH Australia Ltd, Sydney, 1991–)

Booth C and D Squires, *The Negligence Liability of Public Authorities* (OUP, Oxford, 2006)

Brazier M and N Cave, *Medicine, Patients and the Law* (4th edn, Penguin Publishing, London, 2007)

Campion J and D Dimmer, *Professional Liability in Canada* (looseleaf edn, Carswell Publishing, Ontario, 1994–)

Davies M, *Textbook on Medical Law* (2nd edn, OUP, Oxford, 2008)

Deakin S, A Johnston and B Markesinis, *Markesinis and Deakin's Tort Law* (6th edn, OUP, Oxford, 2008)

Devereux J, *Australian Medical Law* (2nd edn, Cavendish Publishing, Sydney, 2002)

Dugdale A and M Jones (eds), *Clerk and Lindsell on Torts* (19th edn, Sweet & Maxwell, London, 2006)

Eburn M, *Emergency Law* (2nd edn, Federation Press, Sydney, 2005)

Evans D, *The Law, Standards, and Ethics in the Practice of Psychology* (2nd edn, Emond Montgomery Publications Ltd, Toronto, 2004)

Fleming J, *The Law of Torts* (8th edn, Law Book Co, 1992)

——, *The Law of Torts* (9th edn, LBC Information Services, Sydney, 1998)

Freckelton I and K Petersen (eds), *Controversies in Health Law* (Federation Press, Sydney, 1999)

Fridman G, *Restitution* (2nd edn, Carswell Thomson, Toronto, 1992)

Furrow B *et al*, *Health Law: Cases, Materials and Problems* (6th edn, American Casebook Series, Thomson West St Paul MN, 2008)

Gostin L *et al*, *Law, Science and Medicine* (3rd edn, Foundation Press, New York NY, 2005)

Grubb A *et al* (eds), *Principles of Medical Law* (3rd edn, OUP, Oxford, 2010, forthcoming)

Hall M *et al*, *Health Care Law and Ethics* (7th edn, Aspen Publishers Wolsters Kluwer, New York NY, 2007)

Harlow C, *State Liability—Tort Law and Beyond* (OUP, Oxford, 2004)

Healy J, *Medical Negligence: Common Law Perspectives* (Sweet & Maxwell, London, 1999)

Herring J, *Medical Law and Ethics* (2nd edn, OUP, Oxford, 2008)

Hoggett B, *Mental Health Law* (Sweet & Maxwell, London, 1990)

Hoyano L and C Keenan, *Child Abuse: Law and Policy Across Boundaries* (OUP, Oxford, 2007)

Jackson E, *Medical Law: Text, Cases and Materials* (OUP, Oxford, 2006)

Jones G, *The Law of Restitution* (5th edn, Sweet and Maxwell, London, 1998)

Jones M, *Medical Negligence* (4th edn, Sweet & Maxwell, London, 2008)

Kennedy I and A Grubb, *Medical Law* (3rd edn, Butterworths, London, 2000)

Khan M, M Robson and K Swift, *Clinical Negligence* (2nd edn, Cavendish Publishing, London, 2002)

Khoury L, *Uncertain Causation in Medical Law* (Hart Publishing, Oxford, 2006)

Kiely T, *Modern Tort Liability: Recovery in the '90s* (John Wiley & Sons, New York, 1990)

Kortmann J, *Altruism in Private Law* (OUP, Oxford, 2005)

LaFrance A, *Bioethics: Health Care, Human Rights and the Law* (2nd edn, LexisNexis Publishing, Newark NJ, 2009)

Lanham D *et al*, *Criminal Laws in Australia* (Federation Press, Sydney, 2006)

Laurie G, *Genetic Privacy* (CUP, Cambridge, 2002)

Lee J and B Lindahl, *Modern Tort Law: Liability and Litigation* (Medical Malpractice) (looseleaf edn, Thomson West, 2002–)

Lester (Lord, of Herne Hill) and D Pannick (eds), *Human Rights Law and Practice* (2nd edn, Butterworths, London, 2004)

Linden A, L Klar and B Feldthusen, *Canadian Tort Law: Cases, Notes and Materials* (13th edn, Lexisnexis Canada Inc, Toronto, 2009)

Lunney M and K Oliphant, *Tort Law: Text and Materials* (3rd edn, OUP, Oxford, 2007)

McGregor H, *McGregor on Damages* (18th edn, Sweet & Maxwell, London, 2009)

McIlwraith J and B Madden, *Health Care and the Law* (4th edn, Thomson Law Book Co, Sydney, 2006)

McIvor C, *Third Party Liability in Tort* (Hart Publishing, Oxford, 2006)

Madden B and J McIllwraith, *Australian Medical Liability* (Lexisnexis Butterworths, Sydney, 2008)

Maddough P and J McCamus, *The Law of Restitution* (Canadian Law Book Inc, Toronto, 1990)

Markesinis B, *Foreign Law and Comparative Methodology* (Hart Publishing, Oxford, 1997)

Montgomery J, *Health Care Law* (2nd edn, OUP, Oxford, 2003)

Mulheron R, *The Class Action in Common Law Legal Systems: A Comparative Perspective* (Hart Publishing, Oxford, 2004)

Mullany N and P Handford, *Tort Liability for Psychiatric Damage* (LBC Information Services, Sydney, 1993)

Murphy J, *Street on Torts* (12th edn, OUP, Oxford, 2007)

Patterson R, *Harney's Medical Malpractice* (4th edn, Lexis Law Publishing, Charlottesville VA, 1999)

Pegalis S, *The American Law of Medical Malpractice*, vols 1 and 2 (3rd edn, Thomson West, Eagan MN, 2005)

Picard E and G Robertson, *Legal Liability of Doctors and Hospitals in Canada* (4th edn, Thomson Carswell, Toronto, 2007)

Richards E and K Rathbun, *Medical Care Law* (Aspen Publishers, Gaithersburg, Maryland, 1999)

Robertson G, *Mental Disability and the Law in Canada* (2nd edn, Thomson Carswell, Toronto, 1994)

Rogers W, *Winfield and Jolowicz on Tort* (17th edn, Sweet & Maxwell, London, 2006)

Skene L, *Law and Medical Practice: Rights, Duties, Claims and Defences* (2nd edn, Lexisnexis Butterworths, Sydney, 2004)

Stauch M, K Wheat and J Tingle, *Text, Cases and Materials on Medical Law* (5th edn, Routledge Cavendish, London, 2006)

Steele J, *Tort Law: Text, Cases, and Materials* (OUP, Oxford, 2007)

Waddams S, *The Law of Damages* (looseleaf edn, Canada Law Book, Aurora Ontario, 2006–)

Wright J, *Tort Law and Human Rights* (Hart Publishing, Oxford, 2001)

Yeazell S, *From Medieval Group Litigation to the Modern Class Action* (Yale Uni Press, New Haven, 1987)

LAW REFORM COMMISSION PUBLICATIONS

Australian Law Reform Commission, *Protection of Human Genetic Information* (Issues Paper No 26, 2002)

——, *Protection of Human Genetic Information* (DP 66, 2002)

——, *Essentially Yours: The Protection of Human Genetic Information in Australia* (Rep 96, 2003)

British Columbia (Law Reform Commission of), *Pecuniary Loss and the Family Compensation Act* (WP 69, 1992)

Canadian Law Reform Commission, *Recodifying Criminal Law* (Rep 31, 1987)

England and Wales (Law Commission of), *Report on Injuries to Unborn Children* (Rep 60, 1974)

——, *Liability for Psychiatric Illness* (Rep 249, 1998)

——, *Damages under the Human Rights Act 1998* (Rep 266, 2000)

——, *Murder, Manslaughter and Infanticide* (Rep 304, 2006)

——, *Participating in Crime* (Rep 305, 2007)

——, *Administrative Redress: Public Bodies and the Citizen* (CP 187, 2008)

Irish Law Reform Commission, *Civil Liability of Good Samaritans and Volunteers* (CP 47, 2007)

——, *Civil Liability of Good Samaritans and Volunteers* (Rep 93, 2009)

Manitoba Law Reform Commission *The Advisability of a Good Samaritan Law* (Rep 11, 1973)

Ontario Law Reform Commission, *Report on Class Actions* (1982)

——, *Fourth Annual Report* (1970)

——, *Fifth Annual Report* (1971)

Scottish Law Commission, *Damages for Psychiatric Injury* (DP 120, 2002)

——, *Damages for Psychiatric Injury* (Rep 196, 2004)

PUBLICATIONS AND RESEARCH PAPERS FROM BODIES REPRESENTING THE GOVERNMENT, THE PROFESSION, AND INDEPENDENT RESEARCH FOR GOVERNMENT

American Psychiatric Association, *Diagnostic and Statistical Manual of Mental Disorders, DSM-IV* (4th edn, published 1994, with text revision published in 2000)

American Psychiatric Association's *Principles of Medical Ethics with Annotations Especially Applicable to Psychiatry* (revised edn, 2009)

American Society of Human Genetics and the American College of Medical Genetics, 'Points to Consider: Ethical, Legal, and Psychosocial Implications of Genetic Testing in Children and Adolescents' (1995) 57 *American J of Human Genetics* 1233

American Society of Human Genetics, Social Issues Sub-Committee on Familial Disclosure, 'Professional Disclosure of Familial Genetic Information' (1998) 62 *American J of Human Genetics* 474

Australian Institute of Criminology (P Williams and G Urbas), 'Heroin Overdoses and Duty of Care' (*Trends and Issues in Crime and Criminal Justice Series*, No 188)

British Medical Assn, *Human Genetics: Choice and Responsibility* (OUP, Oxford, 1998)

Civil Justice Council of England and Wales, *Reform of Collective Redress in England and Wales: A Perspective of Need* (A Research Paper for the Civil Justice Council of England and Wales, prepared by R Mulheron, Feb 2008)

——, *Improving Access to Justice Through Collective Actions: Developing a More Efficient Procedure for Collective Actions: Final Report* (Dec 2008)

Clinical Genetics Society Working Party on DNA Banking (J Yates *et al*), *Guidelines for DNA Banking* (1989) 26 *J of Medical Genetics* 245

Commission for the Study of Ethical Problems in Medicine and Biomedical and Behavioural Research, Screening and Counseling for Genetic Conditions (US), *A Report on the Ethical, Social and Legal Implications of Genetic Screening, Counseling and Education Programs* (Washington, Feb 1983)

Department of Constitutional Affairs (Eng), *The Law on Damages* (CP 9, May 2007)

Department of Health (Sir Liam Donaldson), *Making Amends: A Consultation Paper Setting Out Proposals for Reforming the Approach to Clinical Negligence in the NHS* (A Report by the Chief Medical Officer, Jun 2003).

Driver and Vehicle Licensing Agency (Eng), *For Medical Practitioners: At a Glance Guide to the Current Medical Standards of Fitness to Drive* (Feb 2008)

Ethox Centre, *Governing Genetic Databases: Collection, Storage and Use* (Uni of Oxford, 2007)

General Medical Council (Eng), *Serious Communicable Diseases* (Oct 1997)

——, *Confidentiality: Protecting and Providing Information* (2004)

——, *Good Medical Practice* (2006) (updated March 2009)

——, Frequently Asked Questions of real-life scenarios (updated, and available online at: <http://www.gmc-uk.org /guidance/current/library/>)

——, *Consent: Patients and Doctors Making Decisions Together* (2008)

——, *Confidentiality* (2009)

——, *Confidentiality: Disclosing Information about Serious Communicable Diseases* (2009)

——, *Confidentiality: Reporting Concerns About Patients to the DVLA or the DVA* (2009)

House of Commons Science and Technology Committee (Shaw Committee) (Eng), *Third Report, Human Genetics: The Science and its Consequences*, Vol 1 (1995)

Human Genetics Commission (Eng), *Inside Information: Balancing the Interests in the Use of Personal Genetic Data* (Dept of Health, London, 2002)

Ipp Committee (the Hon Justice Ipp, Chairman, *et al*) (Aus), *Review of the Law of Negligence: Final Report* (Sep 2002)

Law Reform Committee of the Victorian Parliament (Aus), *The Legal Liability of Health Service Providers* (May 1997)

Ministry of Justice (Eng), *The Government's Response to the Civil Justice Council's Report: 'Improving Access to Justice through Collective Actions'* (July 2009)

Nuffield Council on Bioethics (Eng), *Report of the Committee on the Ethics of Gene Therapy (the Clothier Committee)* (Cm 1788, 1992)

——, *Genetic Screening and Ethical Issues* (Dec 1993)

——, *The Forensic Use of Bioinformation: Ethical Issues* (Sep 2007)

World Health Organisation, *International Statistical Classification of Mental and Behavioural Disorders, ICD-10* (1992, 10th revision)

CONTRIBUTIONS TO EDITED TEXTS/CHAPTERS

Andrews L, 'The Genetic Information Superhighway: Rules of the Road for Contacting Relatives and Recontacting Former Patients' in B Knoppers (ed), *Human DNA: Law and Policy* (Kluwer Law International, The Hague, 1997)

Beaumont P, 'Wrongful Life and Wrongful Birth' in S McLean (ed), *Contemporary Issues in Law, Medicine and Ethics* (Dartmouth, Aldershot, 1996)

Brown I and P Gannon, 'Confidentiality and the Human Genome Project: A Prophecy for Conflict', in S McLean (ed), *Contemporary Issues in Law and Medicine* (Dartmouth, Aldershot, 1996)

Cadoppi A, 'Failure to Rescue and the Continental Criminal Law' in M Menlowe and A McCall Smith (eds), *The Duty to Rescue* (Dartmouth, Aldershot, 1993)

Firestone M, 'Psychiatric Patients and Forensic Psychiatry' in S Sanbar (ed), *Legal Medicine* (7th edn, Am College of Legal Medicine Textbook Committee, Mosby Elsevier, 2007)

Givelber D, 'The *Tarasoff* Controversy: A Summary of Findings from an Empirical Study of Legal, Ethical, and Clinical Issues' in J Beck (ed), *The Potentially Violent Patient and the Tarasoff Decision in Psychiatric Practice* (American Psychiatric Press, Washington, 1985)

Mulheron R, 'Medical Negligence, Secondary Victims and Psychiatric Illness: Family Tragedies and Legal Headaches' in R Probert (ed), *Family Life and the Law* (Ashgate Publishing, Aldershot, 2007)

——, 'Duties in Contract and Tort', in A Grubb, J Laing and J McHale (eds), *Principles of Medical Law* (3rd edn, OUP, Oxford, 2010) (revisions for third edn)

Mullany N, 'Fear for the Future: Liability for Infliction of Psychiatric Disorder' in N Mullany (ed), *Torts in the Nineties* (LBC Information Services, Sydney, 1997)

Rodgers S, 'A Mother's Loss is the Price of Parenthood: The Failure of Tort Law to Recognize Birth as a Compensable Reproductive Injury' in S Rodgers *et al* (eds), *Critical Torts* (Lexisnexis Canada Inc, Toronto, 2009)

Skene L, 'Legal Regulation of Genetic Testing: Balancing Privacy and Family Interests' in A Iltis *et al* (eds), *Legal Perspectives in Bioethics* (Routledge Taylor & Francis Group, New York NY, 2008)

Stapleton J, 'In Restraint of Tort' in P Birks (ed), *The Frontiers of Liability* (OUP, Oxford, 1994) vol II

Sutton A, 'The New Genetics and Traditional Hippocratic Medicine' in P Doherty and A Sutton (eds), *Man Made Man* (Open Air Press, 1998)

Yeo S, 'Manslaughter Versus Special Homicide Offences: An Australian Perspective' in C Clarkson and S Cunningham (eds), *Criminal Liability for Non-Aggressive Death* (Ashgate Publishing, London, 2008)

PERIODICAL ARTICLES

Abadee A, 'The Medical Duty of Confidentiality and Prospective Duty of Disclosure: Can They Co-exist?' (1995) 3 *J of Law and Medicine* 75

——, 'A Medical Duty to Attend?' (1996) 3 *J of Law and Medicine* 306

Adler J, 'Relying Upon the Reasonableness of Strangers: Some Observations about the Current State of Common Law Affirmative Duties to Aid or Protect Others' [1991] *Wisconsin L Rev* 867

Agulnick P and H Rivkin, 'Criminal Liability for Failure to Rescue: A Brief Survey of French and American Law' (1998) 8 *Touro Intl L Rev* 93

Allen N, 'Saving Life and Respecting Death: A Savage Dilemma' (2009) 17 *Med L Rev* 262

Allen S, 'Post Trauma Stress Disorder: The Claims of Primary and Secondary Victims' [2000] *J of Personal Injury Law* 108

Allen S, 'Personal Injury Update' (2003) 102 *Law Society Gazette* 34

Almy T, 'Psychiatric Testimony: Controlling the 'Ultimate Wizardry' in Personal Injury Actions' (1984) 19 *The Forum* 233

Amirthalingam K and T Faunce, 'Patching up "Proximity": Problems with the Judicial Creation of a New Medical Duty to Rescue' (1997) 5 *Tort LJ* 27

Anthony G, 'Positive Obligations and Policing in the House of Lords' [2009] *Euro Human Rights L Rev* 538

Ashworth A, 'The Scope of Criminal Liability for Omissions' (1989) 105 *Law Quarterly Rev* 424

Ashworth A and E Steiner, 'Criminal Omissions and Public Duties: The French Experience' (1990) 10 *Legal Studies* 153

Bailey-Harris R, 'Case Reports, Care, Human Rights' [2009] *Fam LJ* 9

Bailey-Harris R and M Harris, 'Local Authorities and Child Protection—The Mosaic of Accountability' [2002] *Child and Family LQ* 117

Bala N, 'Tort Remedies and the Family Law Practitioner' (1998) 16 *Canadian Family LQ* 423

Barrett B, 'Psychiatric Stress—An Unacceptable Cost to Employers' [2008] *J of Business Law* 64

Bell D and B Bennett, 'Genetic Secrets and the Family' (2001) 9 *Med L Rev* 9

Berger J, 'False Memory Syndrome and Therapist Liability to Third Parties for Emotional Distress Injuries Arising from Recovered Memory Therapy: A General Prohibition on Liability and a Limited Liability Exception' (2000) 73 *Temple L Rev* 795

Beresford N, 'Taxonomy in the Court of Appeal' (2000) 116 *Law Quarterly Rev* 205

Beyleveld D and S Pattinson, 'Horizontal Applicability and Horizontal Effect' (2002) 118 *Law Quarterly Rev* 623

Bird S, 'Good Samaritan' [2008] *Professional Practice* 570

Black M (the Hon), 'Genetics in the Courtroom' (2003) 26 *U of New South Wales LJ* 755

Blennerhassett J, 'Toxic Torts and the Irish Courts—What Fear for the Future?' (2006) 1 *Quarterly Rev of Tort Law* 27

Block N, 'Case Comment' (2001) 1 *International Sports L Rev* 168

Bottis M, 'Comment on a View Favouring Ignorance of Genetic Confidentiality' (2000) 7 *European J of Health Law* 173

Brahams D, 'Nervous Shock: New Developments in the Context of Clinical Negligence Claims' (2002) 70 *Medico-legal J* 53

Brazier M, 'Do No Harm—Do Patients have Responsibilities Too?' (2006) 65 *Cambridge LJ* 397

Brookbanks W, 'Liability for Discharged Psychiatric Patients' [2002] *New Zealand LJ* 199

Burns S, 'Rights versus Duty' (2007) 157 *New LJ* 1002

Butler D, Voyages in Uncertain Seas with Dated Maps: Recent Developments in Liability for Psychiatric Injury in Australia' (2001) 9 *Torts LJ* 1

——, 'An Assessment of Competing Policy Considerations in Cases of Psychiatric Injury Resulting from Negligence' (2002) 10 *Torts LJ* 13

Camillo L, 'Adding Fuel to the Fire: Realistic Fears or Unrealistic Damages in AIDS Phobia Suits?' (1994) 35 *Texas L Rev* 331

Cane P, 'Tort Law as Regulation' (2002) 31 *Common Law World Rev* 305

——, 'The Doctor, the Stork and the Court: A Modern Morality Play' (2004) 120 *Law Quarterly Rev* 23

——, 'Another Failed Sterilisation' (2004) 120 *Law Quarterly Rev* 189

Cantley S, 'Every Dogma Has its Day: Cancerphobia Precedent in Aids Cases' (2001) 40 *Brandeis LJ* 535

Case P, 'Curiouser and Curiouser: Psychiatric Damage Caused by Negligent Misinformation' (2002) 18 *Professional Negligence* 248

——, 'Confidence Matters: The Rise and Fall of Informational Autonomy in Medical Law' (2003) 11 *Med L Rev* 208

——, 'Secondary Iatrogenic Harm: Claims for Psychiatric Damage Following a Death Caused by Medical Error' (2004) 67 *Modern Law Rev* 561

——, 'The Accused Strikes Back: The Negligence Action and Erroneous Allegations of Child Abuse' (2005) 21 *Professional Negligence* 214

Caulfield T, 'Testing Adolescents for the Alzheimer Gene: Tensions in Law and Policy' (1997) 25 *Manitoba LJ* 31

Chafee Z, 'Bills of Peace with Multiple Parties' (1932) 45 *Harvard L Rev* 1297

Chico V, 'Saviour Siblings: Trauma and Tort Law' (2006) 14 *Med L Rev* 180

Childs J, 'Toxicogenomics: New Chapter in Causation and Exposure in Toxic Tort Litigation' (2002) 69 *Defense Counsel J* 441

Clayton E, 'What should the Law Say about Disclosure of Genetic Information to Relatives?' (1998) 1 *J Health Care L and Policy* 373

Cole R, 'Authentic Democracy: Endowing Citizens with a Human Right in their Genetic Information' (2005) 33 *Hofstra L Rev* 1241

Coleman C, 'Beyond the Call of Duty: Compelling Health Care Professionals to Work During an Influenza Pandemic' (2008) 94 *Iowa L Rev* 1

Crowley-Smith L, 'Duty to Rescue Unveiled: A Need to Indemnify Good Samaritan Health Care' (1997) 4 *J of Law and Medicine* 352

Cullen (The Rt Hon Lord), 'From the Celebrated Snail to the Good Samaritan' [Aug 2003] *Advocate* 40

——, 'The Liability of the Good Samaritan' [1995] *Juridical Rev* 20

d'Entremont J, 'Fear Factor: The Future of Cancerphobia and Fear of the Future Claims in the Toxicogenomic Age' (2006) 52 *Loyola L Rev* 807

Dagan H, 'In Defence of the Good Samaritan' (1999) 97 *Michigan L Rev* 1152

Davies M, 'Reliance on Medical Advice by Third Parties: The Limits of Goodwill' (1996) 12 *Professional Negligence* 54

Dawson J, 'Randomised Controlled Trials of Mental Health Legislation' (2002) 10 *Med L Rev* 308

Day K, 'Medical Negligence: The Duty to Attend Emergencies and the Standard of Care: *Lowns v Woods*' (1996) 18 *Sydney L Rev* 386

Deftos L, 'Genomic Torts: The Law of the Future: The Duty of Physicians to Disclose the Presence of a Genetic Disease to the Relatives of Their Patients with the Disease' (1997) 32 *U San Francisco L Rev* 105

DeKuiper K, 'Stalking the Good Samaritan: Communists, Capitalists and the Duty to Rescue' [1976] *Utah L Rev* 529

Depel C, '"Fear of Cancer" Claims in California' (1995) 3 *Intl Insurance L Rev* 30

Devereux J, 'Negligence' (2000) 7 *J of Law and Medicine* 249

——, '*McCann v Buck*' (2001) 8 *J of Law and Medicine* 249

Dietrich J, 'Nervous Shock' (2003) 11 *Torts LJ* 11

Dimopoulos P and M Bagaric, 'The Moral Status of Wrongful Life Claims' (2003) 32 *Common Law World Rev* 35

Dolgin J, 'Biological Evaluations: Blood, Genes, and Family' (2008) 41 *Akron L Rev* 347

——, 'The Evolution of the "Patient": Shifts in Attitudes About Consent, Genetic Information, and Commercialization in Health Care' (2005) 34 *Hofstra L Rev* 137

Donovan M, 'Is the Injury Requirement Obsolete in a Claim for Fear of Future Consequences?' (1994) 41 *UCLA L Rev* 1337

Doran K, 'Medical Confidentiality: The Role of the Doctrine of Confidentiality in the Doctor–Patient Relationship' (1997) 3 *Medico-Legal J of Ireland* 21

Douglas G, 'Case Reports, Local Authority and Negligence' [2008] *Fam LJ* 314; [2007] *FamLJ* 804

Dressler J, 'Some Brief Thoughts (Mostly Negative) About "Bad Samaritan" Statutes' (2000) 40 *Santa Clara L Rev* 971

Dugdale T, 'No Medical Duty to Third Parties' (2006) 22 *Professional Negligence* 193

Duxbury N, 'Golden Rule Reasoning: Moral, Judgment, and Law' (2009) 84 *Notre Dame L Rev* 1529

Dworkin R, 'Getting What We should from Doctors: Rethinking Patient Autonomy and the Doctor-Patient Relationship' (2003) 13 *Health Matrix* 235

Eburn M, 'Protecting Volunteers?' (2003) 18(4) *Aust J of Emergency Management* 7

Edozian L, 'Disclosure of Medical Information when a Patient Presents a Danger to Others: Duty or Discretion?' (2001) 7 *Clinical Risk* 224

Edwards D, 'Duty-to-Warn—Even if it May Be Hearsay? The Implications of a Psychotherapist's Duty-to-Warn a Third Person When Information is Obtained from Someone other than his Patient' (2006) 3 *Indiana Health L Rev* 171

Ellis P, 'Organ Retention Scandals' [2001] *J of Personal Injury Law* 264

Fairgrieve D and P Craig, '*Barrett*, Negligence and Discretionary Powers' [1999] *Public Law* 626

Feldbrugge F, 'Good and Bad Samaritans: A Comparative Study of Criminal Law Provisions Concerning Failure to Rescue' (1996) 14 *Am J of Comp Law* 630

Felthouse A and C Kachigan, 'To Warn and to Control: Two Distinct Legal Obligations or Variations of a Single Duty to Protect?' (2001) 19 *Behavioral Sciences and the Law* 355

Ferris L, 'In the Public Interest: Disclosing Confidential Patient Information for the Health or Safety of Others' (1998) 18 *Health Law Canada* 119

Flanagan W, 'Genetic Data and Medical Confidentiality' (1995) 3 *Health LJ* 269

Florencio P and E Ramanathan, 'Secret Code: The Need for Enhanced Privacy Protections in the United States and Canada to Prevent Employment Discrimination Based on Genetic and Health Information' (2001) 39 *Osgoode Hall LJ* 77

Foster W, 'Medication of Pupils: Teachers' Duties' (1995–96) 7 *Education LJ* 45

Furman R, 'Genetic Test Results and the Duty to Disclose: Can Medical Researchers Control Liability?' (1999) 23 *Seattle U L Rev* 391

Gardiner B, ''Liability for Sporting Injuries' [2008] *J of Personal Injury Law* 16

Garton A, 'Reconciling the Incongruous Demands of Therapist–Patient Confidentiality and Falsely-Accused Third Parties' (2007) 37 *Cumberland L Rev* 77

Gerber P, 'Is a General Practitioner Legally Bound to Render Assistance to a Stranger?' (1996) 165 *Medical J of Australia* 159

Gilbar R, 'Medical Confidentiality Within the Family: The Doctor's Duty Reconsidered' (2004) 18 *Intl J of Law, Policy and the Family* 195

Gill D, 'Proving and Disproving Psychiatric Injury' (2008) 76 *Medico-Legal J* 143

Ginsberg B, 'Therapists Behaving Badly: Why the *Tarasoff* Duty is not Always Economically Efficient' (2007) 43 *Willamette L Rev* 31

Gilbert M, '"Time-Out" for Student Threats? Imposing a Duty to Protect on School Officials' (2002) 49 *UCLA L Rev* 917

Givelber D, '*Tarasoff*: Myth and Reality: An Empirical Study of Private Law in Action' (1984) *Wisconsin L Rev* 443

Gonthier C, 'Liberty, Equality, Fraternity: The Forgotten Leg of the Trilogy, or Fraternity: The Unspoken Third Pillar of Democracy' (2000) 45 *McGill LJ* 567

Gore A, 'Psychiatric Injury' [2009] *J of Personal Injury Law* C39

Goudkamp J, 'The Spurious Relationship between Moral Blameworthiness and Liability for Negligence' (2004) 28 *Melbourne U L Rev* 343

Graf A, 'The Contaminated Blood Scandal in France: Are Insurers still the "Prime Suspects"?' (1997) 5 *Intl Insurance L Rev* 67

Gray N and J Edelman, 'Developing the Law of Omissions: A Common Law Duty to Rescue?' (1998) 6 *Tort LJ* 240

Greenstein J, 'New Jersey's Continuing Expansion of Tort Liability: *Williamson v Waldman* and the Fear of AIDS Cause of Action' (1999) 30 *Rutgers LJ* 489

Griffiths G, 'The Standard of Care Expected of a First Aid Volunteer' (1990) 53 *Modern L Rev* 255

Griffiths R and S Whale, 'Uneasy Bedfellows?' (2006) 156 *New LJ* 1821

Grubb A, 'Doctors Engaged by Third Parties: Duties to Take Care' (1997) 5 *Med L Rev* 348

——, 'Medical Negligence: Duty to Third Party (Dangerous Psychiatric Patient)' (1999) 7 *Med L Rev* 331

——, 'HIV Transmission: Doctor's Liability to Future Partner' (1997) 5 *Med L Rev* 250

——, 'Medical Negligence: Duty of Care and *Bolam*' (1998) 6 *Med L Rev* 120

——, 'Medical Negligence: Liability of Ambulance Service' (2000) 8 *Med L Rev* 349

Gulam J and J Devereux, 'A Brief Primer on Good Samaritan Law for Health Care Professionals' (2007) 31 *Aust Health Rev* 478

de Haan K, 'My Patient's Keeper: Liability of Medical Practitioners for Negligent Injuries to Third Parties' (1986) 2 *Professional Negligence* 86

Haberfield L, '*Lowns v Woods* and the Duty to Rescue' (1998) 6 *Tort L Rev* 56

Handford P, 'Psychiatric Injury Resulting from Medical Negligence' (2002) 10 *Tort L Rev* 38

Harmon A, 'Back from Wonderland: A Linguistic Approach to Duties Arising from Threats of Physical Violence' (2008) 37 *Capital U L Rev* 27

Henry M, 'Statutory Immunities: When is Good Faith Honest Ineptitude?' (2000) 15 *Aust J of Emergency Management* 10

Herdy W, 'Must the Doctor Tell?' (1996) 3 *J of Law and Medicine* 270

Hilson C, 'Liability for Psychiatric Injury: Primary and Secondary Victims Revisited' (2002) 18 *Professional Negligence* 167

——, 'Let's Get Physical: Civil Liability and the Perception of Risk' (2009) 21 *J of Environmental Law* 33

Hirsch D, 'Doctor's Duty of Care to a Patient's Sexual Partner' (1999) 8 *Aust Health Law Bulletin* 53

Hoaken, E, 'The Five Most Noteworthy [Canadian] Medical Malpractice Cases of 2004' (2005) *Health Law and Medical Malpractice* (proceedings published from A National Forum, Metro Toronto Convention Centre, 3 Feb 2005)

Hodge J *et al*, 'The Legal Framework for Meeting Surge Capacity Through the Use of Volunteer Health Professionals During Public Health Emergencies and other Disasters' (2005) 22 *J of Contemporary Health Law and Policy* 5

Hoffman S, 'Statutes Establishing a Duty to Report Crimes or Render Assistance to Strangers: Making Apathy Criminal' (1984) 72 *Kentucky LJ* 827

——, 'Responders' Responsibility: Liability and Immunity in Public Health Emergencies' (2008) 96 *Georgetown LJ* 1913

Hook C *et al*, 'Primer on Medical Genomics Part XIII: Ethical and Regulatory Issues' (2004) 79 Mayo Clinical Procedure 645

Horne M, 'Commentary' [2004] Lloyd's Rep Med 536

Howarth D, 'Public Authority Non-Liability: Spinning out of Control?' (2004) 63 *Cambridge LJ* 546

——, 'Many Duties of Care—Or A Duty of Care? Notes from the Underground' (2006) 26 *Oxford J of Legal Studies* 449

Hoyano L, 'Misconceptions about Wrongful Conception' (2002) 65 *Modern L Rev* 883

Hubbard A, 'The Future of "The Duty of Protect": Scientific and Legal Perspectives on *Tarasoff's* Thirtieth Anniversary: Symposium' (2006) 75 *U of Cincinnati L Rev* 429

Hunt M, 'The "Horizontal Effect" of the Human Rights Act' [1998] *Public Law* 423

Inglis A, 'Personal Injury Claims for Child Protection Failures' [2009] *Scots Law Times* 173

Jones C, 'Tightropes and Tragedies: 25 Years of *Tarasoff*' (2003) 43 *Medicine, Science and the Law* 13

Jones M, 'Child Abuse: When the Professionals Get it Wrong' (2006) 14 *Med L Rev* 264

——, 'Doctors' Duties to Third Parties' (2007) 23 *Professional Negligence* 36

——, 'Child Protection and Duties to Third Parties' (2007) 23 *Professional Negligence* 118

——, 'Liability for Fear of Future Disease?' (2008) 24 *Professional Negligence* 13

Keeling S, 'Duty to Warn of Genetic Harm in Breach of Patient Confidentiality' (2004) 12 *J of Law and Medicine* 235

King M, 'Physician's Duty to Warn a Patient's Offspring of Hereditary Genetic Defects: Balancing the Patient's Right to Confidentiality against the Family Member's Right to Know: Can or Should *Tarasoff* Apply?' (2000) 2 *Quinnipiac Health LJ* 1

Klar L, 'The Role and Fault of Policy in Negligence Law' (1996–97) 35 *Alberta L Rev* 24

Knapp E, 'Turning Blood into Whine: "Fear of AIDS" as a Cognizable Cause of Action in New Mexico' (1998) 28 *New Mexico L Rev* 165

Kovalesky M, 'To Disclose or not to Disclose: Determining the Scope and Exercise of a Physician's Duty to Warn Third Parties of Genetically-Transmissible Conditions' (2008) 76 *U Cincinnati L Rev* 1019

Lake P, 'Revisiting *Tarasoff*' (1994) 58 *Albany L Rev* 97

——, 'Recognizing the Importance of Remoteness and the Duty to Rescue' (1997) 46 *De Paul L Rev* 315

Laing J, 'Clinical Negligence: Secondary Victims and Recovery for Nervous Shock' (2003) 11 Med L Rev 121

Langford A, 'Doctors' Liabilities to Third Parties' (2001) 75 *Law Institute J* 74

Laurie G, 'The Most Personal Information of All: An Appraisal of Genetic Privacy in the Shadow of the Human Genome Project' (1996) 10 *Intl J of Law, Policy and the Family* 74

——, 'Obligations Arising from Genetic Information: Negligence and the Protection of Familial Interests' (1999) 11 *Child and Family LQ* 109

——, *Responses to the 'Whose hands on your genes?' Consultation*, available at: http://www.hgc.gov.uk/Client/Content_wide.asp?ContentId=424

Leader-Elliott I, 'Good Samaritan Legislation: Appeal against Conviction following Plea of Guilty' (1996) 20 *Criminal LJ* 102

Lee M, 'Civil Liability of the Nuclear Industry' (2000) 12 *J of Environmental Law* 317

——, 'Pollution and Personal Injury: Problems and Prospects' (2001) 3 *Environmental L Rev* 15

Leng T, 'Duty of Care for Psychiatric Harm: Back to *Anns*' (2008) 24 *Professional Negligence* 154

Leverick F, 'Counting the Ways of Becoming a Primary Victim' [2007] *Edinburgh L Rev* 258

Levmore S, 'Waiting for Rescue: An Essay on the Evolution and Incentive Structure of the Law of Affirmative Obligations' (1986) 72 *Virginia L Rev* 879

Liddall K and A Hall, 'Beyond Bristol and Alder Hey: The Future Regulation of Human Tissue' (2005) 12 *Med L Rev* 170

Lifshitz S, 'Distress Exploitation Contracts in the Shadow of No Duty to Rescue' (2008) 86 *North Carolina L Rev* 315

Lindsay S, 'Clinical Negligence: Duty of Care in Contract and Tort' [2006] *J of Personal Injury Law* C62

——, 'Wrongful Birth, Clinical Negligence, and Third Party Laboratory' [2006] *J of Personal Injury Law* C191

Loh E, 'Legal Risks of Volunteer Firefighters—How Real are They?' (2008) 23 *Aust J of Emergency Management* 47

Long P, 'The Good Samaritan and Admiralty: A Parable of a Statute Lost at Sea' (2000) 48 *Buffalo L Rev* 591

Luntz H, 'A View from Abroad' [2007] *U of Melbourne Law School Research Series* 2

Lynch M, 'Doctors' Duties and Third Parties' (2000) 7 *J of Law and Medicine* 244

Lyons M, 'Psychiatric Harm: Death of a Child' [2003] *J of Personal Injury Law* 23

——, 'Human Rights, Mental Health, Negligence and Mental Patients' [2009] *J of Personal Injury Law* C1

McAbee G *et al*, 'Physician's Duty to Warn Third Parties About the Risk of Genetic Diseases' (1998) 102 *Pediatrics* 140

McClarren G, 'The Psychiatric Duty to Warn: Walking a Tightrope of Uncertainty' (1987) 56 *U Cincinnati L Rev* 269

McDonald B and J Swanton, 'Issues in Medical Negligence' (1996) 70 *Aust LJ* 688

McGivern B, 'Tortious Liability for (Selected) Genetic Harm: Exploring the Arguments' (2002) 10 *Torts LJ* 41

McHale J, 'Genetic Screening and Testing the Child Patient' [1997] *Child and Family LQ* 33

McInnes M, 'Good Samaritan Statutes: A Summary and Analysis' (1992) *U British Columbia L Rev* 239

——, 'The Economic Analysis of Rescue Laws' (1992) 21 *Manitoba LJ* 237

——, 'Restitution and the Rescue of Life' (1994) 32 *Alberta L Rev* 37

McIvor C, 'Police Immunity and the Legacy of *Hill v Chief Constable of West Yorkshire*' (2005) 21 *Professional Negligence* 201

——, 'Liability for Psychiatric Harm: *Butchart v Home Office*' (2007) 23 *Professional Negligence* 249

——, 'The Positive Duty of the Police to Protect Life' (2008) 24 *Professional Negligence* 27

McSherry B, '*PD v Harvey and Chen*' (2003) 11 *J of Law and Medicine* 18

Madden D, 'Ethical and Legal Issues in Psychiatric Genetics Research' [2004] *Medico-Legal J of Ireland* 38

Mahendra B, 'A Snip Makes a Statement' (1996) 146 *New LJ* 407

——, 'Medical Disclosure and Confidentiality' (2001) 151 *New LJ* 10

Marchant G, 'Genetics and Toxic Torts' (2001) 31 *Seton Hall L Rev* 949

——, 'Genetic Data in Toxic Tort Litigation' (2006) 14 *J of Law and Policy* 7

Markesinis B, 'Negligence, Nuisance and Affirmative Duties of Action' (1989) 105 *Law Quarterly Rev* 104

Markesinis B and J Fedtke, 'Damages for the Negligence of Statutory Bodies: The Empirical and Comparative Dimension to an Unending Debate' [2007] *Public Law* 299

Mason J, 'The Legal Aspects and Implications of Risk Assessment' (2000) 8 *Med L Rev* 69

Mason J and G Laurie, 'Misfeasance in Public Office: An Emerging Medical Law Tort?' (2003) 11 *Med L Rev* 94

Melnitchouk O, 'Extending Liability for Medical Negligence' (1996) 4 *Tort LJ* 259

Mendelson D, 'Dr Lowns and Obligation to Treat: Creative Lawmaking in the New South Wales Court of Appeal' (1997) 3 *Tort L Rev* 242

Merton V, 'Confidentiality and The "Dangerous" Patient: Implications of *Tarasoff* for Psychiatrists and Lawyers' (1982) 31 *Emory LJ* 263

Miers D, 'Liability for Injuries Caused by Violent Patients' [1996] *J of Personal Injury Law* 314

——, 'Rebuilding Lives: Operational and Policy Issues in the Compensation of Victims of Violent and Terrorist Crimes' [2006] *Criminal L Rev* 695

Mildred M, 'The Human Growth Hormone (Creutzfeldt-Jakob Disease) Litigation' (1998) *J of Personal Injury Law* 251

——, 'Personal Injury, Psychiatric Harm, Parents, Children' [2004] *J of Personal Injury Law* C9

Miles J, 'Human Rights and Child Protection' [2001] *Child and Family LQ* 431

Moore J, 'Negligently-Caused Psychiatric Injury: A Way Forward?' (1995) 10 *Liverpool L Rev* 153

Morris A and S Saintier, 'To Be or Not to Be: Is That the Question? Wrongful Life and Misconceptions' (2003) 11 *Med L Rev* 167

Morris F and G Adshead, 'The Liability of Psychiatrists for the Violent Acts of their Patients' (1997) 147 *New LJ* 558

Mossman D, 'Critique of Pure Risk Assessment or, Kant Meets *Tarasoff*' (2006) 75 *U Cincinatti L Rev* 523

Mrozinksi L, 'Monetary Remedies for Administrative Law Errors' (2009) 22 *Canadian J of Administrative Law and Practice* 133

Mulheron R, 'Secondary Victim Psychiatric Illness Claims' (2003) 14 *King's College LJ* 213

——, 'Some Difficulties with Group Litigation Orders—and Why a Class Action is Superior' (2005) 24 *Civil Justice Q* 40

——, 'From Representative Rule to Class Action: Steps rather than Leaps' (2005) 24 *Civil Justice Q* 424

——, 'Justice Enhanced: Framing an Opt-Out Class Action for England' (2007) 70 *Modern L Rev* 550

——, 'Building Blocks and Design Points for an Opt-out Class Action' [2008] *J of Personal Injury Law* 308

——, 'The "Primary Victim" in Psychiatric Illness Claims: Reworking the "Patchwork Quilt"' (2008) 19 *King's LJ* 81

——, 'The Case for an Opt-out Class Action for European Member States: A Legal and Empirical Analysis' (2009) 15 *Columbia J of European Law* 409

Mullany N, 'Compensation for Fear and Worry-Induced Psychiatric Illness: The Australian Position' (1997) 4 *Psychiatry, Psychology and Law* 147

——, 'Liability for Careless Communication of Traumatic Information' (1998) 114 *Law Quarterly Rev* 380

——, 'English Psychiatric Injury Law: Chronically Depressing' (1999) 115 *Law Quarterly Rev* 30

——, 'Personal Perception of Trauma and Sudden Shock–South Africa Simplifies Matters' (2000) 116 *Law Quarterly Rev* 29

Mullany N and P Handford, 'Moving the Boundary Stone by Statute: The Law Commission on Psychiatric Illness' (1999) 22 *U of New South Wales LJ* 350

Mullender R, 'Torts, Human Rights, and Common Law Culture' (2003) 23 *Oxford J of Legal Studies* 301

——, 'Negligence, Human Rights, and Public Bodies' (2009) 125 *Law Quarterly Rev* 384

Murphy L, 'Beneficence, Law and Liberty: The Case of Required Rescue' (2001) 89 *Georgetown LJ* 605

Ngwena C and R Chadwick, 'Genetic Diagnostic Information and the Duty of Confidentiality' [1993] *Medical Law Intl* 73

Nicastro D, 'Case Focus: Physician Liability to Non-Patients' (2007)' (2008) 52 *Boston Bar J* 20

Nolan D, 'Psychiatric Injury at the Crossroads' [2004] *J of Personal Injury Law* 1

Norris W, 'The Duty of Care to Avoid Personal Injury' [2009] *J of Personal Injury Law* 114

Nowlin C, 'Don't Just Stand There, Help Me!: Broadening The Effect of Minnesota's Good Samaritan Immunity Through *Swenson v Waseca Mutual Insurance Co*' (2004) 30 *William Mitchell L Rev* 1001

O'Sullivan J, 'Liability for Fear of the Onset of Future Medical Conditions' (1999) 15 *Professional Negligence* 96

——, 'Negligent Medical Advice and Financial Loss: "Sick as a Parrot?"' (2007) 66 *Cambridge LJ* 14

Offit K *et al*, 'The "Duty to Warn" a Patient's Family Members about Hereditary Disease Risks' (2994) 292 *J of the Am Medical Assn* 1469

Opie H, 'Negligence Liability of Rule-making Bodies in Sport' (2002) 2 *International Sports L Rev* 60

Oppenheim R, 'The "Mosaic" of Tort Law: The Duty of Care Question' [2003] *J of Personal Injury Law* 151

Osborne P, 'Manitoba Cases since the Turn of the Century' (2005) 31 *Manitoba LJ* 25

Owen R, 'The Human Growth Hormone Cruetzfeldt-Jakob Disease Litigation' (1998) 65 *Medico-Legal J* 47

Palser E, 'Shutting the Door on Negligence Liability' [2009] *Child and Family Law Q* 384

Pardun J, 'Good Samaritan Law: A Global Perspective' (1998) 20 *Loyola of Los Angeles Intl and Comp LJ* 591

Parker C, 'Camping Trips and Family Trees: Must Tennessee Physicians Warn their Patients' Relatives of Genetic Risks?' (1998) 65 *Tennessee L Rev* 585

Parkin A, 'Discretion and Resources in Mental Health Provision' (1991) 141 *New LJ* 1453

Pannick D and A Lester, 'The Impact of the Human Rights Act on Private Law: The Knight's Move' (2000) 116 *Law Quarterly Rev* 380

Peart G, 'Psychiatric Injury Claims' [2003] *J of Personal Injury Law* 25

Perlin M, '"You Got No Secrets to Conceal": Considering the Application of the *Tarasoff* Doctrine Abroad' (2006) 75 *U of Cincinnati L Rev* 611

Peterson K, 'Where is the Line to be Drawn? Medical Negligence and Insanity in *Hunter Area Health Service v Presland*' (2006) 28 *Sydney L Rev* 181

Priaulx N, 'Damages for the Unwanted Child: Time for a Rethink' (2005) 73 *Medico-Legal J* 152

Puxon M, 'Comment' to the *Tredget* decision (1994) 5 *Med LR* 184

Quattrocchi M and R Schopp, 'Tarasaurus Rex: A Standard of Care That Could Not Adapt' (2005) 11 *Psychology, Public Policy and Law* 109

Redmond-Cooper R, E Beswick and H Proctor, 'Negligence: Duty of Care: Health Authorities' [1999] *J of Personal Injury Law* 326

Reuter S, 'Physicians as Good Samaritans: Should They Receive Immunity for their Negligence when Responding to Hospital Emergencies?' (1999) 20 *J of Legal Medicine* 157

Ridolfi K, 'Law, Ethics and the Good Samaritan: Should there be a Duty to Rescue?' (2000) 40 *Santa Clara L Rev* 957

Robertson G, 'A View of the Future: Emerging Developments in Health Care Liability' in Visions (2008) *Health LJ (Special Edn)* 11

Romohr P, 'A Right/Duty Perspective on the Legal and Philosophical Foundations of the No-Duty-to-Rescue Rule' (2006) 55 *Duke LJ* 1025

Rubin M, 'Is there a Doctor in the House?' (2007) 33 *J of Medical Ethics* 158

Ruck M and E Holt, 'Parental Rights Recognised' (2009) 17 *Med L Rev* 282

Samanta A *et al*, 'The Role of Clinical Guidelines in Medical Negligence Litigation: A Shift from the *Bolam* Standard?' (2006) 14 *Med L Rev* 32

Samuels A, 'Unfounded Suspicion of Child Abuse' (2006) 74 *Medico-Legal J* 35

Santee A, 'More than Just Bad Blood: Reasonably Assessing Fear of Aids Claims' (2001) *Villanova L Rev* 207

Schiff D, 'Samaritans: Good, Bad and Ugly: A Comparative Law Analysis' (2005) 11 *Roger Williams U L Rev* 77

Scordato M, 'Understanding the Absence of a Duty to Reasonably Rescue in American Tort Law' (2008) 82 *Tulane L Rev* 1447

Segal O and J Williams, 'Psychiatric Injury, Policy and the House of Lords' [1999] *J of Personal Injury Law* 102

Sestito J, 'The Duty to Warn Third Parties and AIDS in Canada' (1996) 16 *Health Law Canada* 83

Sheldrick B, 'Administering Public Safety: Solicitor-client Privilege, Medical Experts and the Adversarial Process: *Smith v Jones*' (2000) 4 *Intl J of Evidence and Proof* 119

Shuman D and M Weiner, 'The Privilege Study: An Empirical Examination of the Psychotherapist–Patient Privilege' (1982) 60 *North Carolina L Rev* 893

Silver J, 'The Duty to Rescue: A Reexamination and Proposal' (1985) 26 *William and Mary L Rev* 423

Silverman L, 'A Therapist's Duty of Care: Does it Extend to Non-Patients Charged with Child Sexual Abuse?' (2001) *Pennsylvania Bar Assn Q* 18

Simon R, 'The Myth of "Imminent" Violence in Psychiatry and the Law' (2006) 75 *U Cincinnati L Rev* 631

Skene L, 'Patients' Rights Or Family Responsibilities?—Two Approaches To Genetic Testing' (1998) 6 *Med L Rev* 1

——, 'Genetic Secrets and the Family: A Response to Bell and Bennett' (2001) 9 *Med L Rev* 162

Skene L and H Luntz, 'Effects of Tort Law Reform on Medical Liability' (2005) 79 *Aust LJ* 345

Slovenko R, 'Surveying the Attacks on Psychiatry in the Legal Process' (1996) 1 *Intl J of Evidence and Proof* 48

Smith D, '*Wenden v Trikha* and Third Party Liability of Doctors and Hospitals: What's Been Happening to *Tarasoff?*' (1995) 4 *Health L Rev* 12

Smith G, '*Ewing and Goldstein* and the Therapist's Duty to Warn in California' (2006) 36 *Golden Gate U L Rev* 293

Spencer J, 'Liability for Purely Economic Loss Again: "Small Earthquake in Chile, Not Many Dead?"'(2006) 65 *Cambridge LJ* 13

Stanton K, 'Professional Negligence: Duty of Care Methodology in the Twenty-first Century' (2006) 22 *Professional Negligence* 134

Stapleton J, 'Tort, Insurance and Ideology' (1995) 58 *Modern L Rev* 820

Steele I, 'Public Law Liability—A Common Law Solution?' (2005) 64 *Cambridge LJ* 543

——, 'Negligence Liability for Failing to Prevent Crime: The Human Rights Dimension' (2008) 67 *Cambridge LJ* 239

Steele J, 'Pleural Plaques in the House of Lords: The Implications for *Page v Smith*' (2008) 67 *Cambridge LJ* 28

——, 'Damages in Tort and Under the Human Rights Act: Remedial or Functional Separation?' (2008) 67 *Cambridge LJ* 606

Stretton D, 'The Birth Torts: Damages for Wrongful Birth and Wrongful Life' (2005) 10 *Deakin LR* 319

Stewart A, 'Damages for the Birth of a Child' (1995) 40 *J of Law and Society* 298

Stewart M, 'How Making the Failure to Assist Illegal Fails to Assist: An Observation of Expanding Criminal Omission Liability' (1998) 25 *Am J of Criminal Law* 385

Sullivan B, 'Some Thoughts on the Constitutionality of Good Samaritan Statutes' (1982) 8 *Am J of Law and Medicine* 27

Suter S, 'Whose Genes Are These Anyway?: Familial Conflicts Over Access to Genetic Information' (1993) 91 *Michigan L Rev* 1854

Teff H, 'Liability for Psychiatric Illness after Hillsborough' (1992) 12 *Oxford J of Legal Studies* 441

——, 'The Requirement of "Sudden Shock" in Liability for Negligently Inflicted Psychiatric Damage' (1996) 4 *Tort L Rev* 44

——, 'Liability for Negligently Inflicted Psychiatric Harm: Justifications and Boundaries' (1998) 56 *Cambridge LJ* 91

Templeman D and V Lok, 'Failed Attempt to Further Stretch a Doctor's Duty to Patient' (2000) 9 *Aust Health Law Bulletin* 11

Tettenborn A, 'Free Care: Who Foots the Bill?' (2005) 155 *New LJ* 1050

Thomas C, 'Satisfying the Hearness Test' (2003) 153 *New LJ* 953

Thomas M, 'Expanded Liability for Psychiatrists: *Tarasoff* Gone Crazy?' [2009] *J of Mental Health Law* 45

Tibballs J, 'Legal Liabilities for Assistance and Lack of Assistance Rendered by Good Samaritans, Volunteers and their Organisations' (2005) 16 *Insurance LJ* 254

Todd S, 'The Negligence Liability of Public Authorities: Divergence in the Common Law' (1986) 102 *Law Quarterly Rev* 370

——, 'Wrongful Conception Wrongful Birth and Wrongful Life' (2005) 27 *Sydney L Rev* 525

Tomkins N, 'Psychiatric Injury: Extra Routes to Recovery?' [2006] *J of Personal Injury Law* 251

Tomlinson E, 'The French Experience with Duty to Rescue: A Dubious Case for Criminal Enforcement' (2000) 20 *New York LJ of Intl and Comp Law* 451

Trachtenberg J, 'Living in Fear: Recovering Negligent Infliction of Emotional Distress Damages Based on the Fear of Contracting AIDS' (1999) 2 *DePaul J of Health Care Law* 529

Truscott D and K Crook, '*Tarasoff* in the Canadian context: *Wenden* and the Duty to Protect' (1993) 38 *Canadian J of Psychiatry* 84

Twerski A, 'The Cleaver, the Violin, and the Scalpel: Duty and the Restatement (Third) of Torts' (2008) 60 *Hastings LJ* 1

Van Exan J, 'The Legal and Ethical Issues Surrounding the Duty to Warn in the Practice of Psychology' [2004] *Windsor Rev of Legal and Social Issues* 123

Vranken M, 'Duty to Rescue in Civil Law and Common Law: Les Extremes se Touchent?' (1998) 47 *Intl and Comp LQ* 934

Wade H, 'Horizons of Horizontality' (2000) 116 *Law Quarterly Rev* 217

Waller T, '*Estates of Morgan v Fairfield Family Counseling Center*: Application of Traditional Tort Law Post-*Tarasoff*' (1997) 31 *Akron L Rev* 321

Watkins T, 'Fear of AIDS Claim Requires Showing of Actual Exposure Unless Defendant Destroys Evidence of Exposure Creating a Rebuttable Presumption Against Defendant' (2000) 69 *Mississippi LJ* 1243

Webber S, 'Case in Focus: Psychiatric Injury of a Secondary Victim' (2003) 9 *Clinical Risk* 157

Weiner W and D Szyndrowski, 'The Class Action from the English Bill of Peace to Federal Rule of Civil Procedure 23: Is There is a Common Thread?' (1987) 8 *Whittier L Rev* 935

Weinrib E, 'The Case for a Duty to Rescue' (1980) 90 *Yale LJ* 247

Weir T, 'The Unwanted Child' (2000) 59 *Cambridge LJ* 238

Wexler S, 'Case Comment' (1994) 52 *Advocate* 251

Wheat K, 'Proximity and Nervous Shock' (2003) 32 *Common Law World Rev* 313

White C, 'No Good Deed Goes Unpunished: The Case for Reform of the Rescue Doctrine' (2002) 97 *Northwestern U L Rev* 507

Williams G, 'Gross Negligence Manslaughter and Duty of Care in "Drugs" Cases' (2009) 9 *Criminal L Rev* 631

Williams K, 'Medical Samaritans: Is there a Duty to Treat?' (2001) 21 *Oxford J of Legal Studies* 393

——, 'Doctors as Good Samaritans: Some Empirical Evidence Concerning Emergency Medical Treatment in Britain' (2003) 30 *J of Law and Society* 258

——, 'Are Doctors Good Samaritans?' (2004) 71 *Medico-Legal J* 165

——, 'Legislating in the Echo Chamber?' (2005) 155 *New LJ* 1938

——, 'Abusing Parents and Children' (2005) 21 *Professional Negligence* 196

——, 'Litigation against English NHS Ambulance Services and the Rule in *Kent v Griffiths*' (2007) 15 *Med L Rev* 153

——, 'Emergency Services to the Rescue' [2008] *J of Personal Injury Law* 202

——, 'Emergency Services to the Rescue, or Not, Again' [2008] *J of Personal Injury Law* 265

Williamson B, 'The Gunslinger to the Ivory Tower Came: Should Universities Have a Duty to Prevent Rampage Killings?' 60 (2008) *Florida L Rev* 895

Witting C, 'Duty of Care: An Analytical Approach' (2005) 25 *Oxford J of Legal Studies* 33

Wolfe S, 'The Scope of a Psychiatrist's Duty to Third Persons: The Protective Privilege Ends Where the Public Peril Begins' (1984) 59 *Notre Dame L Rev* 770

Wright J, '"Immunity" No More: Child Abuse Cases and Public Authority Liability in Negligence after *JD v East Berkshire Community Health NHS Trust*' (2004) 20 *Professional Negligence* 58

Zaremski M, 'The "Good Samaritan" Goes to Court: Does the Law Protect Him?' (1979) 1 *J of Legal Medicine* 30

PRESS ARTICLES

——, 'Hospital refuses to help accident victim' *Sydney Morning Herald* (25 Sep 2004)
——, 'Asbestos Condition not Compensable: UK Court', *Reuters* (26 Jan 2006)
——, 'Legal Clouds Gather when the Worst Happens', *West Australian* (4 Jun 2008)
Kron J, 'Flying into Trouble', *Australian Doctor* (15 Apr 2008)
Rogers J, 'Death, Drugs and Duties', *Archbold News* (2009:6)
Salomon S, 'Airlines Must Pay MD's for Non-Emergency Mid-Air Care', *Canadian Medicine* (21 Jul 2009)
Watson D, 'Beyond the Call of Duty', *Australian Doctor* (22 Apr 2004)

REFERENCE WORKS

Annotation, 'Liability of One Treating Mentally Afflicted Patient for Failing to Warn or Protect Third Persons Threatened by Patient', 83 ALR 3d 1201
Annotation, 'Liability of Physician for Injury to or Death of Third Party Due to Failure to Disclose Driving-Related Impediment', 43 ALR 4th 153
Annotation, 'Liability of Doctor or Other Health Practitioner to Third Party Contracting Contagious Disease from Doctor's Patient', 3 ALR 5th 370
The Holy Bible, Gospel of Luke, 10:25–37
Oxford Dictionary of English (2nd edn, revised, OUP, Oxford, 2006)
Oxford Concise Colour Medical Dictionary (4th edn, OUP, Oxford, 2007)

Index